PURCHASING AND SUPPLY MANAGEMENT

About the Authors

Michiel R. Leenders is the Purchasing Management Association of Canada Professor of Purchasing Management; and Chairman, Operations Management at the Richard Ivey School of Business at the University of Western Ontario. He received a degree in mining engineering from the University of Alberta, an M.B.A. from the University of Western Ontario, and his doctorate from the Harvard Business School. Mike has written a large number of articles in a variety of magazines and journals. His texts have been translated into eight different languages and include: *Value-Driven Purchasing: The Key Steps in the Acquisition Process* (with Anna E. Flynn), published by Irwin Professional Publishing; *Reverse Marketing, The New Buyer-Supplier Relationship* (with David Blenkhorn), published by the Free Press; *Improving Purchasing Effectiveness Through Supplier Development,* published by the Harvard Division of Research; *Learning With Cases, Writing Cases,* and *Teaching With Cases* with James A. Erskine and Louise Mauffette-Leenders, published by the Richard Ivey School of Business. He has also co-authored six editions of *Purchasing and Supply Management,* published by Richard D. Irwin (most recently by McGraw-Hill). Mike has taught and consulted extensively both in Canada and internationally. He was the Educational Advisor to the Purchasing Management Association of Canada from 1961–1994. He received PMAC's Fellowship Award in 1975, the PMAC Chair in 1993, the Financial Post Leaders in Management Education Award in 1997, and is the director of the Ivey Purchasing Managers Index.

Harold E. Fearon is the National Association of Purchasing Management Professor Emeritus and former Chairman, Purchasing, Transportation and Operations Department, Arizona State University. Hal was the Founder of the Center for Advanced Purchasing Studies (CAPS), and its Director for the first nine years. He is now a member of the CAPS Board of Trustees. He is a graduate of Indiana University (B.S. with distinction, and M.B.A.) and Michigan State University (Ph.D. in Business Administration). He is founding editor, and continues to serve as editor emeritus, of *The Journal of Supply Chain Management,* the scholarly quarterly in the purchasing/materials management area, and has published more than 450 articles in business and academic journals. Hal is also co-editor-in-chief of the fifth edition of *The Purchasing Handbook,* published by McGraw-Hill. Hal has authored and co-authored several texts, including *Purchasing Research in American Industry,* published by the American Management Association; five editions of *Fundamentals of Production/Operations Management,* published by West Publishing Company; and five editions of *Purchasing and Supply Management,* published by Richard D. Irwin (most recently by McGraw-Hill). Hal has been active as a lecturer and consultant both in North America and internationally. He received the "President's Award" from the National Association of Purchasing Management in 1991, and the J. Shipman Gold Medal

Award, NAPM's highest honor, in 1992. In 2000 he was presented the Hans Ovelgönne "Purchasing Research" award by the International Federation of Purchasing and Materials Management in recognition of his worldwide contributions to the profession.

Anna E. Flynn, vice president and Institute for Supply Management (formerly NAPM) associate professor, provides subject matter and instructional design expertise to the educational product development team at the ISM and teaches supply management seminars. Anna was senior lecturer and director of the undergraduate program in Supply Chain Management (SCM) at Arizona State University from January 1993–May 2000. She developed corporate relationships with recruiters, acted as the academic and career advisor to undergraduates, and taught *Purchasing and Supply Management* and *Research and Negotiation.* The SCM Program consistently received the highest ratings from students in the College of Business for teaching, as well as academic and career advising, areas for which Anna was directly responsible. For three consecutive years Anna was one of 11 out of 2,000 faculty awarded a Faculty Appreciation Award. Recipients were singled out by graduating seniors as having had the greatest impact on their lives during their time at ASU. Anna is co-author of the NAPM Supply Management Knowledge Series Volume IV, *The Supply Management Leadership Process* (2000); co-author of *Value-Driven Purchasing: Managing the Key Steps in the Acquisition Process* (1995), and has worked on two earlier editions of *Purchasing and Supply Management.* She earned a bachelor's degree in international studies from the University of Notre Dame, an M.B.A. from Arizona State University, and a Ph.D. in learning and instructional technology from Arizona State University.

P. Fraser Johnson is a graduate of the Honors Business Administration Program at the Richard Ivey School of Business at the University of Western Ontario. Following graduation, Fraser worked in the automotive parts industry where he held a number of senior management positions in both finance and operations. He returned to the Richard Ivey School of Business in 1991 where he earned an M.B.A. and a Ph.D., specializing in Operations Management. After receiving his doctorate, Fraser joined the Faculty of Commerce at the University of British Columbia, where he taught supply chain management, logistics, transportation, and operations. He returned to the Richard Ivey School of Business in 1998, where he is currently an assistant professor, teaching operations management, purchasing and supply management, and logistics. Fraser is an active researcher in the area of purchasing and supply management. He is the author of several articles that have been published in a wide variety of magazines and journals, and has also authored a number of teaching cases. In recognition of his ongoing research, Fraser was awarded the National Association of Purchasing Management Senior Research Fellowship in June 1999. Fraser has taught and consulted in both Canada and the United States. He has delivered a number of management seminars and has actively worked with the Purchasing Management Association of Canada in developing material for the PMAC Accreditation Program.

PURCHASING AND SUPPLY MANAGEMENT

Michiel R. Leenders, D.B.A., PMAC Fellow
Purchasing Management Association of Canada
Professor of Purchasing Management and Chairman, Operations Management
Richard Ivey School of Business
The University of Western Ontario

Harold E. Fearon, Ph.D., C.P.M.
The National Association of Purchasing Management Professor Emeritus
and Founder and Director Emeritus
Center for Advanced Purchasing Studies
Arizona State University

Anna E. Flynn, Ph.D., C.P.M.
Vice President
Institute for Supply Management (formerly NAPM)

P. Fraser Johnson, Ph.D.
Assistant Professor, Operations Management
Richard Ivey School of Business
The University of Western Ontario

Twelfth Edition

Boston   Burr Ridge, IL   Dubuque, IA   Madison, WI   New York   San Francisco   St. Louis
Bangkok   Bogotá   Caracas   Kuala Lumpur   Lisbon   London   Madrid   Mexico City
Milan   Montreal   New Delhi   Santiago   Seoul   Singapore   Sydney   Taipei   Toronto

McGraw-Hill Higher Education ⚛

A Division of The **McGraw-Hill** *Companies*

PURCHASING AND SUPPLY MANAGEMENT

Published by McGraw-Hill, an imprint of The McGraw-Hill Companies, Inc. 1221 Avenue of the Americas, New York, NY, 10020. Copyright © 2002, 1997, 1993, 1989, 1985, 1980, 1975, 1970, 1962, 1957, 1952, 1948 by The McGraw-Hill Companies, Inc. All rights reserved. No part of this publication may be reproduced or distributed in any form or by any means, or stored in a database or retrieval system, without the prior written consent of The McGraw-Hill Companies, Inc., including, but not limited to, in any network or other electronic storage or transmission, or broadcast for distance learning.

Some ancillaries, including electronic and print components, may not be available to customers outside the United States.

This book is printed on acid-free paper.
domestic 1 2 3 4 5 6 7 8 9 0 DOC/DOC 0 9 8 7 6 5 4 3 2 1
international   1 2 3 4 5 6 7 8 9 0 DOC/DOC 0 9 8 7 6 5 4 3 2 1

ISBN 0-07-237060-2

Publisher: *John E. Biernat*
Sponsoring Editor: *Marianne C. P. Rutter*
Editorial Assistant: *Tammy Higham*
Marketing Manager: *Lisa Nicks*
Project Manager: *Scott Scheidt*
Senior Production Supervisor: *Michael R. McCormick*
Media Technology Producer: *Melissa Kansa*
Lead Designer: *Matthew Baldwin*
Supplement Producer: *Susan Lombardi*
Cover Design: *Joanne Schloper*
Typeface: *10/12 Century Schoolbook*
Compositor: *Carlisle Communications, Ltd.*
Printer: *R. R. Donnelley & Sons Company*

Library of Congress Cataloging-in-Publication Data

Purchasing and supply management / Michiel R. Leenders ... [et al.]—12th ed.
   p. cm.
  Rev. ed. of: Purchasing and supply management / Michiel R. Leenders, Harold E.
Fearon. 11th ed. c1997.
   Includes bibliographical references and index.
   ISBN 0-07-237060-2
   1. Industrial procurement. 2. Materials management. I. Leenders, Michiel R. II.
Leenders, Michiel R. Purchasing and supply management.

   HD39.5. L43 2001
   658.7'2—dc21   2001045008

INTERNATIONAL EDITION ISBN 0-07-112223-0
Copyright © 2002. Exclusive rights by The McGraw-Hill Companies, Inc. for manufacture and export.

This book cannot be re-exported from the country to which it is sold by McGraw-Hill.

The International edition is not available in North America.
www.mhhe.com

This twelfth edition of this text continues the prime objective of providing the readers with an up-to-date strategic and practical perspective on purchasing and supply management. Great changes have occurred in the supply field since 1933, when Professor Howard T. Lewis authored the first edition under the title *Industrial Purchasing*. At that time no computers existed, and phrases like "supply chain management," "total customer satisfaction," and "total cost of ownership" were unknown. However, the idea that sound procurement was essential to corporate success was already in its infancy.

Since the eleventh edition, the growth of the Internet and web-based supply solutions have provided new challenges for supply executives, while older issues like market shortages and overages, price escalation, and global competition continue. A new chapter on e-commerce and almost 30 new cases have been added to this edition to properly reflect the major challenges faced today by supply practitioners and academics alike. Each chapter reports the latest research findings, as supply chain management has become a hot topic in both the business world and academic circles.

A major change in this edition is the entry of two new co-authors. Anna E. Flynn previously assisted in the last two editions. Her teaching at Arizona State University resulted in many awards, and her research into participative learning effectiveness was particularly appropriate for this case-based text. P. Fraser Johnson, our second addition, brought a strong logistics background coupled with a superb teaching record. The contributions of these two professionals are evident throughout this text; their joining of the team will provide a sound base for future editions.

Many others also have assisted in the contents and the production of this edition. Reviewers who suggested significant potential improvements included: Dan Kraska, Timothy Butler, Philip Evers, and Rajeey Sawhney.

Case contributors in alphabetical order included: Saud Abbasi, Kersi Antia, Mark Applebaum, Nick Bontis, Kathryn Brohman, Clifford J. E. Campbell, Daniel Campbell, Debbie Compeau, Joerg Dietz, Joanne Gansink, Peter A. Goldthorpe, Mobina Hassan, Margot Huddart, Jennifer S. Jones, Basil Kalymon, Robert Kemp, Marshall King, Ari Kobetz, David Koltermann, Kristina Krupka, Winston Kwok, Larry Menor, Chantell Nicholls, Detlev Nitsch, Catherine Paul-Chowdhury, Barbara Pierce, Shawna Porter, Franz Scherz, Zong Tang, Tim Tattersall, Michelle Theobalds, Sarah Tremblay, Mike Wade, Asad Wali, Mary Margaret Weber, Virginia Webster, David Zeng, and Blair R. Zilkey. Professor John Haywood-Farmer was a major contributor to Chapter 5.

We are grateful for Elaine Carson's magnificent assistance in developing a manuscript that could be sent to the publisher in the proper form and format.

Kathleen Little, C.P.M., also provided valuable assistance in indexing the book.

The support of Dean Larry Tapp, Professor Paul Beamish, and our other colleagues at the Richard Ivey School of Business for this text has been most welcome.

The assistance of the Purchasing Management Association of Canada and the Institute for Supply Management (formerly the National Association of Purchasing Management) in developing appropriate case material and supporting the continuous improvement of supply education is also very much appreciated.

The McGraw-Hill editorial staff has done a great job of supporting the educational principles of this book, while balancing economic and artistic considerations.

Michiel R. Leenders
Harold E. Fearon
Anna E. Flynn
P. Fraser Johnson

BRIEF CONTENTS

C O N T E N T S

1 THE CHALLENGE OF PURCHASING AND SUPPLY MANAGEMENT

Key Questions for the Purchasing Decision Maker

SHOULD WE
- Measure how purchasing affects efficiency and effectiveness in our organization?
- Develop an in-house training program?
- Calculate the effect on our organization's ROA at various purchasing savings levels?

HOW CAN WE
- Get top management to recognize the profit-leverage effect of purchasing/supply management?
- Determine appropriate salary levels for our purchasing personnel?
- Show how supply can affect our firm's competitive position?

These are exciting times for those concerned with an effective and efficient purchasing and supply management process. The explosive growth in business-to-business e-commerce is expected by many to revolutionize the transaction process between buyers and sellers. To what extent, and in what way, these expectations are realized will be one of the most interesting developments in business in the early twenty-first century. There is also growing interest at the executive level in the supply management process and greater recognition of the importance of suppliers and the sourcing process on an organization's ability to achieve its strategic goals and objectives. This shift in perceptions may be the result of at least five factors: (1) the need to control unit costs, (2) the need to reduce the total cost of acquisition, (3) the increasing influence that suppliers have on the purchaser's ability to respond to end-customers, particularly as it affects time-related requirements, (4) an increased reliance on fewer suppliers, and (5) a willingness of purchasers to rely on suppliers to design and build entire subassemblies and subsystems.[1]

The traditionally-held view that multiple sourcing increases supply security has been challenged by a trend toward single sourcing. Results from closer supplier relations and cooperation with suppliers on scheduling and quality assurance systems question the wisdom of the traditional arm's-length dealings between purchaser and supplier. Negotiation is receiving increasing emphasis as opposed to competitive bidding, and longer-term contracts are replacing short-term buying techniques. All of these trends are a logical outcome of increased managerial concern with value and increased procurement aggressiveness in developing suppliers to meet specific supply

---

[1]Robert J. Trent and Robert M. Monczka, "Purchasing and Supply Management: Trends and Changes Throughout the 1990s," *International Journal of Purchasing and Materials Management,* Fall 1998, p. 4.

objectives of quality, quantity, delivery, price, service, continuity, and improvement. However, the availability of e-commerce tools appears to bring into question some of these trends from the 1990s. For example, the possibility of conducting a reverse auction—where the buyer selects suppliers to bid online for business—leads to closer inspection of different categories of purchases in an effort to determine where this tool will add value and where it may be inappropriate. Single sourcing in an effort to build seamless relationships with one supplier may add value in some situations, but in others it may be unnecessary, time-consuming, and costly. Online bidding has added a new twist to the age-old question of how many suppliers an organization should use for a given purchase and which one or ones will best serve the needs of the buyer.

Effective purchasing and supply management can contribute significantly to the success of most organizations. This text explores the nature of this contribution and the management requirements for effective and efficient performance. The acquisition of materials, services, and equipment—of the right qualities, in the right quantities, at the right prices, at the right time, and on a continuing basis—long has occupied the attention of many managers in both the public and private sectors. Today, the emphasis is on the total supply management process in the context of organizational goals and management of supply chains rather than on the transactions associated with purchasing. The rapidly changing supply scene, with cycles of abundance and shortages, varying prices, lead times, and availability, provides a continuing challenge to those organizations wishing to obtain a maximum contribution from this area.

From Purchasing to Supply Management

Although interest in the performance of the purchasing/supply function has been a phenomenon primarily of the twentieth century, it was recognized as an independent and important function by many of the nation's railroad organizations well before 1900. The first book devoted specifically to purchasing, *The Handling of Railway Supplies—Their Purchase and Disposition,* published in 1887, was authored by an executive with the Chicago and Northwestern Railway, Marshall M. Kirkman.[2] Growth of interest in and attention to purchasing was rather uneven in the early 1900s, but by 1915 several books on purchasing had appeared and several articles had been published in the trade press, primarily in the engineering journals.[3]

Yet, prior to World War I (1914–1918), most firms regarded the purchasing function primarily as a clerical activity. However, during the time periods

---

[2]Harold E. Fearon, "The Purchasing Function within Nineteenth Century Railroad Organizations," *Journal of Purchasing,* August 1965, pp. 18–30.

[3]Harold E. Fearon, "Historical Evolution of the Purchasing Function," *Journal of Purchasing,* February 1968, pp. 43–59.

Movement from Clerical to Managerial Activity

of World War I and World War II (1939–1945), the success of a firm was not dependent on what it could sell, because the market was almost unlimited. Instead, the ability to obtain from suppliers the raw materials, supplies, and services needed to keep the factories and mines operating was the key determinant of organizational success. Attention was given to the organization, policies, and procedures of the purchasing function, and it emerged as a recognized managerial activity. During the 1950s and 1960s, purchasing continued to gain stature as the techniques for performing the function became more refined and as the number of people trained and competent to make sound purchasing decisions increased. Many companies elevated the chief purchasing officer to top management status, with titles such as vice president of purchasing, director of materials, or vice president of purchasing and supply.

As the decade of the 70s' opened, organizations faced two vexing problems—an international shortage of almost all the basic raw materials needed to support operations, and a rate of price increases far above the norm since the end of World War II. The Middle East oil embargo during the summer of 1973 intensified both the shortages and the price escalation. These developments put the spotlight directly on purchasing departments, for their performance in obtaining needed items from suppliers at realistic prices spelled the difference between success or failure. This emphasized again to top management the crucial role played by purchasing. As the decade of the 1990s unfolded, it became clear that organizations must have an efficient and effective purchasing/supply function if they are to compete

Integration into Corporate Strategy

successfully with both domestic and international firms. Since outlays for purchased materials and services greatly exceed labor and other costs in most organizations, improving the purchasing/supply function can lead to permanent cost control. In the early twenty-first century, the question is to what extent technology applications will change the purchasing and supply management process and function strategically as well as operationally.

Early in the first decade of the twenty-first century, the focus is likely to be on further integration of the purchasing/supply management function with the total business process. Some organizations are changing the name of the function from purchasing to supply management to reflect the transi-

Transition to a Process-Oriented, Strategic Function

tion from a transaction-based, tactical function to a process-oriented, strategic one. The structure, processes, and people in the function are in transition in many organizations. Structurally, commodity teams, product supply groups, and cross-functional teams are more prevalent than in the past. The process itself is less transaction-oriented, depends on the implementation of good information systems along with a carefully thought out e-commerce strategy, and focuses on closer supplier relations with fewer suppliers, while considering sources from around the world.

According to John F. Welch, CEO of General Electric Company, "We're at the beginning of one of the most important revolutions in business." The Internet "will forever change the way business is done. It will change every relationship, between our businesses, between our customers, between our suppliers. Distribution channels will change. Buying practices will change. Everything will be tipped upside down. The slow become fast, the old become young. It's clear we've only just begun this transformation."[4]

The people in the purchasing/supply function often are divided into two categories—the tacticians who need strong computer and information systems skills, and the strategic thinkers who possess strong analytical and planning skills. The extent to which the structure, processes, and people in a specific organization will match these trends varies greatly from organization to organization, and from industry to industry.

Purchasing's Potential Contribution

The purchasing/supply management department has the potential to, and should, play a key role in developing and operationalizing a strategy leading to sharpened efficiency and heightened competitiveness, through actions such as (1) combating inflation by resisting unwarranted price hikes, (2) significantly reducing dollar investment in materials inventory through better planning and supplier selection,[5] (3) raising the quality level of purchased materials and parts inputs, so that the quality and consistency of end product/service outputs can be improved, (4) reducing the materials segment of cost-of-goods-sold, and (5) effecting product and process improvements through encouraging and facilitating early, open communication between buyer and supplier, to the mutual benefit of both parties.[6] This more-open exchange of information, often occurring in the design stage (called ESI—early supplier involvement), should enable the purchasing organization to give its customers better products or services, at lower prices, and faster. The organization can be a more-effective player in the world of time-based competition.[7]

Process and Knowledge Management Emphasized

Figure 1–1 depicts the movement of the supply management function through time as it evolved from the clerical era through the transaction era and into the strategic era. The future will see a gradual shift from predominantly defensive strategies—resulting from the need to change in order to remain competitive—to aggressive strategies, in which firms take an imaginative approach to achieving supply objectives to satisfy short-term *and* long-term organizational goals.[8] The focus on strategy now includes an

[4]David Joachim, "GE's E-Biz Turnaround Proves that Big is Back," *InternetWeek,* June 8, 2000, *www.internetweek.com.*

[5]As one author commented, "The outsourcing trend is only one of the major changes sweeping the auto industry. In an effort to cut inventory and work more closely with its vendors, most carmakers are cutting their supplier headcount." Paul Eisenstein, "Lear Seating Corp., Sitting Pretty with Big 3 in Outsourcing Effort," *Investor's Business Daily,* July 20, 1995, p. A5.

[6]Neal Templin and Jeff Cole, "Working Together: Manufacturers Use Suppliers to Help Them Develop New Products," *The Wall Street Journal,* Dec. 19, 1994, p. 1.

[7]Thomas E. Hendrick, *Purchasing's Contributions to Time-Based Strategies* (Tempe, AZ: Center for Advanced Purchasing Studies, 1994), p. 13.

[8]Michiel R. Leenders and David L. Blenkhorn, *Reverse Marketing: The New Buyer-Supplier Relationship* (New York: The Free Press, 1988), p. 2.

FIGURE 1–1

Evolution of the Purchasing / Materials / Supply Management Function

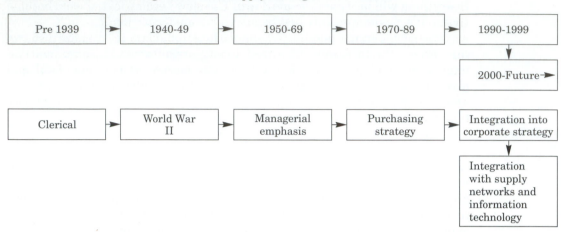

emphasis on process and knowledge management. This text discusses what organizations should do today to remain competitive as well as what strategic, integrated purchasing and supply management will focus on tomorrow.

Growing management interest through necessity and improved insight into the opportunities in the purchasing area has resulted in a variety of or-ganizational concepts. Terms such as *purchasing, procurement, materiel, ma-terials management, logistics, supply management,* and *supply chain man-agement,* are used almost interchangeably. No agreement exists on the definition of each of these terms, and managers in public and private insti-tutions may have identical responsibilities but substantially different titles. The following definitions may be helpful in sorting out the more-common un-derstanding of the various terms.

Purchasing Terminology

In general usage, the term *purchasing* describes the process of buying: learning of the need, locating and selecting a supplier, negotiating price and other pertinent terms, and following up to ensure delivery. *Procurement* is a somewhat broader term and includes purchasing, stores, traffic, receiving, incoming inspection, and salvage.

Materiel has a military or governmental connotation and often includes the same functions as those identified under materials management. The rationale of *materials management* is the integration of related materials functions to provide cost-effective delivery of materials and services to the organization. Although the materials management organization can vary between firms, it can include a number of separate groups, such as mate-rial planning and control, material and purchasing research, purchasing, inbound traffic, incoming quality control, inventory control, production scheduling, receiving, stores, in-plant materials movement, and scrap and

Materials Management Defined

surplus disposal. Other names used for materials management are *integrated logistics* and *supply chain management.* Please note that in this text, the term *purchasing* is used in the same broad strategic and integrative context as materials management. The materials management organization has four basic activities: anticipating material requirements, sourcing and obtaining materials, introducing materials into the organization, and monitoring the status of materials as a current asset. Having a single executive responsible for materials management makes it easier to evaluate and balance trade-offs, such as full truckload rates versus inventory holding costs.

Buyer/Planner Concept

The *buyer/planner concept* evolved from the materials management approach. Traditional materials responsibilities include two job parts: (1) planners, who determine what materials are needed and when, to keep production moving, and (2) buyers, who handle the sourcing and buying. Thus, the planner controls inventory levels, schedules purchased and internally fabricated parts, and expedites to ensure that items are available when and where needed. The buyer selects suppliers, negotiates, and expedites past-due shipments from suppliers. However, due to the overlap of responsibilities, conflicts may arise. For example, the planner may blame purchasing for delays in obtaining the materials needed to fill requisitions, while purchasing may blame inventory control for short lead-time requisitions and forecasts that change too often.

The buyer/planner solution is to combine the planning and purchasing functions into one position, the buyer/planner, who is in charge of a specific line of inventory. This person establishes schedules, issues and analyzes quotations, places orders, monitors supplier performance, and keeps abreast of market trends, supplier capacities, and changes in technology. These procedures are based on the idea that the same person should have the authority and responsibility for *both* the inventory control *and* the purchasing decisions. This is the same approach, on an individual task level, that the materials management concept applies at the organizational level.

Adoption of the materials management concept largely grew out of problems in the airframe industry during World War II. Production of an aircraft requires a large number of individual items, many of which are quite sophisticated and must meet stringent quality standards, purchased from thousands of suppliers located over a wide geographic area. Many of the items are vital to the total functioning of the end product. The objectives of materials management are to solve materials problems from a total company viewpoint (optimize) by *coordinating* performance of the various materials functions, providing a *communications* network, and *controlling* materials flow. As the computer was introduced into organizations, this provided a further reason to adopt materials management, for the materials functions have many common data needs and can share a common database.

Logistics has its origin near the year 1670, when a new staff structure proposed for the French army included the position of "Marechal General des

Logis," who was responsible for supply, transportation, selecting camps, and adjusting marches.[9] Although logistics long has been a military term, its application to nonmilitary management occurred primarily in the 1960s and included "the optimum coordination of the inbound raw material movements, raw material storage, work in process handling, and of the outbound packaging, warehousing of finished products, and movements of finished products to the customer."[10] According to the Council of Logistics Management, logistics is "that part of the supply chain that plans, implements, and controls the efficient, effective flow and storage of goods, services, and related information from the point of origin to the point of consumption in order to meet customers' requirements."[11] This definition includes inbound, outbound, internal and external movements. Logistics is not confined to manufacturing organizations. It is relevant to service and manufacturing organizations, and to both private and public sector firms.

Logistics Management Defined

Traditional organization structures prior to the 1960s had logistics activities scattered throughout the firm. However, the trend has been toward the integration of materials management and physical distribution under one executive to manage overall logistics processes. The major logistics processes are included in Table 1–1:

The attraction of the logistics concept is that it looks at the material flow process as a complete system, from initial need for materials to delivery of finished product or service to the customer. It attempts to provide the communication, coordination, and control needed to avoid the potential conflicts between the physical distribution and the materials management functions.

Purchasing and Logistics

Purchasing influences a number of logistics-related activities, such as how much to buy and inbound transportation. With an increased emphasis on controlling material flows, the purchasing function must be concerned with decisions beyond supplier selection and price. As a result, some companies combine purchasing and logistics into a single organization.

Worldwide Procurement and Logistics at Texas Instruments

Such was the case at Texas Instruments (TI) in 1999. TI had separate warehousing facilities for incoming and outgoing products all over the world. Benchmarking with companies like Wal-Mart revealed better options, including outsourcing, and the plan became to reduce all distribution centers to four: one in Utrecht (the Netherlands), one near Dallas, one in Singapore, and one near Tokyo. The decision was also made to have all centers part of

---

[9]J.D. Little, *The Military Staff, Its History and Development* (Harrisburg, PA: Stackpole Co., 3rd ed., 1961), pp. 48–49.

[10]E.G. Plowman, *Elements of Business Logistics* (Stanford, CA: Stanford Graduate School of Business, 1964).

[11]Council of Logistics Management (CLM), *Definition of Logistics, www.clml.org,* March 2001.

TABLE 1–1   Major Logistics Activities

• customer service	• parts and service support
• demand forecasting/planning	• plant and warehouse site selection
• inventory management	• purchasing
• logistics communications	• return goods handling
• material handling	• reverse logistics
• order processing	• traffic and transportation
• packaging	• warehouse storage

Source: Lambert, D.M; Stock, J.R. and Ellram, L.M., *Fundamentals of Logistics Management* (Burr Ridge, IL: Irwin McGraw-Hill, 1998.)

the worldwide procurement and logistics organization, whereas formerly, some of the regional warehouses had reported to local managers outside the logistics function. The last move in this consolidation occurred in Japan at the end of 1999. TI used to own its own trucks, but it was also decided that this function should be outsourced. Mr. K. Bala, senior vice president at TI, summed up the transformation of TI's logistics activities: "We moved from a situation where inbound and outbound transportation was handled separately from procurement. The warehouses were in local control. We have combined our logistics activities to create one seamless process, with control of our logistics service providers supervised by purchasing."[12]

Although the logistics concept is attractive from a theoretical point of view, encompassing the complete systems approach, two major problems hindered its implementation: first, the ability of a logistics manager to handle a job with this scope, crossing so many traditional lines of organizational authority and responsibility; and second, the state of computer software systems. Advancements in integrated software systems and improvements in computer hardware have made implementation of the systems approach more feasible. Likewise, progressive organizations have focused on training or hiring personnel equipped with the kinds of education, skills, and knowledge to operate in a systems environment. However, the term *logistics* seems to have lost much of its appeal because of its common link to traffic and transportation.

In the past, *supply* often was used in North America by industrial concerns to cover the stores or warehousing function of internally consumed items such as stationery and office supplies. However, today the term is interpreted more along the lines of its use in the United Kingdom and Europe, where *supply* has a broader meaning to include at least purchasing, stores, and receiving. The governmental sector also uses this broader interpretation. In Canada, for example, the Department of Supply and Services is responsible for procurement in the federal government. *Supply management* is

---

[12]Michiel R. Leenders and P. Fraser Johnson, *Major Changes in Supply Chain Responsibilities* (Tempe, AZ: Center for Advanced Purchasing Studies, 2001).

Supply Management Defined

defined in the National Association of Purchasing Management's "Glossary of Key Purchasing and Supply Terms" as: "A systems management concept employed by some organizations, designed to optimize the factors of material costs, quality, and service. This is accomplished by consolidating the following operating activities: purchasing, transportation, warehousing, quality assurance for incoming materials, inventory management, and internal distribution of materials. These activities normally are combined in a single department, similar to the arrangement under a materials management form of organization."[13] This term more accurately depicts efforts to develop better, more responsive suppliers than the term purchasing does.

Supply Chain Management Defined

Supply chain management is a systems approach to managing the entire flow of information, materials, and services from raw materials suppliers through factories and warehouses to the end-customer. The NAPM Glossary defines supply chain management as: "The design and management of seamless, value-added processes across organizational boundaries to meet the real needs of the end customer. The development and integration of people and technological resources are critical to successful supply chain integration."[14]

Supply Networks versus Supply Chains

Even as more organizations adopt the concept, or at least the terminology, of supply chain management, others are questioning the appropriateness of the term given the limitations of the concept of a chain. The term *supply networks* has been suggested by some as a better description of buyer-supplier relationships in progressive supply management organizations. According to Roy Shapiro, Chairman of the Technology and Operations Area at Harvard Business School, who concentrates his research and teaching efforts on technology and operations management, logistics, and supplier management, ". . . [I]n today's world, we're already *beyond* the point where supply chain is the right term because it denotes a linear set of linkages between firms. I'm just waiting for the time when people no longer say 'supply chain' and, instead, only talk about *'supply networks.'* "[15] As early as 1994, Mark Keogh, who at the time was a principal in McKinsey's London office, referred to manufacturers "turning their attention to building *world-class supplier networks.* . . . World-class supplier management also requires continuous improvements in cost, quality, and throughput time. . . . Leading purchasing organizations have the skills to show suppliers how to perform better. One automotive company has ten full-time engineers with deep experience in 'lean manufacturing' techniques who are constantly on the road investigating suppliers' facilities and upgrading their manufacturing practices. World-class purchasing organizations take a deep interest in their

---

[13]National Association of Purchasing Management, *Glossary of Key Terms in Purchasing and Supply Management, www.napm.org,* April 16, 2001.

[14]Ibid.

[15]Roy Shapiro, *Faculty Interview: Moving From Supply Chains to Supply Networks,* Harvard Business School, Executive Education, *www.exed.hbs.edu/faculty/intervw/msc.html,* Nov. 11, 2000.

suppliers' 'manufacturing' processes, even to the point of assessing a supplier's suppliers."[16]

Supply Management versus Supply Chain Management

Supply chain management (SCM) is different from *supply management.* Supply chain management emphasizes all aspects of delivering products to customers, whereas supply management emphasizes only the buyer-supplier relationship. SCM represents a philosophy of doing business that stresses processes and integration. *Supply management* seems to be the term that now is more commonly used to refer to the systems approach when it comes to the purchasing function. This text covers primarily those functions normally included in the purchasing and supply management definitions. The activities usually included in physical distribution management, such as determining finished goods inventory levels, finished goods warehouse locations and levels of inventory, outbound transportation, packaging, and customer repair parts, warranty, and installation service, will receive no special coverage. Our main concern is the inflow of goods and services, rather than the outflow. Even within the materials management area, greater emphasis will be placed on areas such as source selection, buyer-supplier relations, determining the price to be paid, and meeting shifting needs of internal and external customers than on inventory control and transportation.

Purchasing and Supply Management Functions

The use of the concepts of purchasing, procurement, materials management, and supply and supply chain management will vary from organization to organization. It will depend on (1) their stage of development and/or sophistication, (2) the industry in which they operate, and (3) their competitive position. However, the core of all these concepts is the *purchasing* function. Therefore, the term *purchasing* is used in this text as we go through the building blocks of the acquisition process, and *supply* is used as an equivalent term.

The relative importance of the purchasing area compared to the other prime functions of the organization will be a major determinant of the management attention it will receive. How to assess the materials and services needs of a particular organization in context is one of the purposes of this book. Cases are provided to illustrate a variety of situations and to give practice in resolving managerial problems.

Significance of Material Dollars

U.S. manufacturing firms purchased materials totaling $1 trillion, 975 billion, 362 million in 1998, which was about 1.6 times the $1 trillion, 217 billion, 609 million purchased in 1986, and about 2.9 times the amount purchased in 1976. Capital expenditures amounted to $139 billion in 1996, more than 1.8 times the $76 billion in 1986. (See Table 1–2.) The magnitude of

---

[16]Mark Keough, "Buying Your Way to the Top," *Director,* April 1994, p. 75.

these figures emphasizes the importance of performing the purchasing and supply management function in the most effective manner possible.

Purchasing is the largest single dollar control area with which most management must deal. Obviously, the percentage of the sales or income dollar that is paid out to suppliers varies greatly from industry to industry. For example, in a hospital or bank, purchasing dollars as a percentage of operating income will be less than 20 percent, since these industries are labor, rather than material, intensive. But in the manufacturing sector, material dollars typically account for well over half of the sales dollar. According to Dave Nelson, former Vice President of Purchasing at Honda of America, "One of the reasons that Honda recognizes the importance of the purchasing function is due to the fact that 80 percent of the cost of a car is purchased cost. So how goes purchasing is how goes Honda."[17] When an automobile producer sells a new car to a dealer for $18,000, it already has spent more than $10,800 (about 60 percent) to buy the steel, tires, glass, paint, fabric, aluminum, copper, and electronic components necessary to build that car. When a soft drink producer sells $1,000 of packaged beverage to the supermarket, it already has paid to suppliers close to $650 for the sweetener, carbonation, flavoring, bottles, caps, cans and cardboard or plastic containers necessary to make and package the end product.

The Importance of Purchasing at Honda of America

Table 1–2, using data collected by the U.S. Bureau of the Census for their *1998 Annual Survey of Manufactures (ASM),* presents aggregate purchase/sales data for the entire U.S. manufacturing sector, broken down by type of industry. Starting with the 1997 Economic Census—Manufacturing, the Census Bureau used the North American Industry Classification System (NAICS) instead of the Standard Industrial Code to categorize industries. Each establishment surveyed for the ASM was classified into 1 of 473 manufacturing industries. Establishments were included in an industry based on the products they produced. These figures show that in the average manufacturing firm, materials account for 52 percent of the sales dollar; if expenditures for capital equipment are included, this goes up to 56 percent. This is more than 1.35 times the remaining 44 percent available to pay salaries, wages, other operating expenses, taxes, interest, and dividends. And, when compensation (wages, salaries, and fringe benefits) of *all* employees in the manufacturing sector for 1998 is compared to total purchases, it amounts to only about one-third of the purchase percentage.

NAICS Replaces SIC Classification

The Purchase/ Sales Ratio

The total purchase/sales ratio varies dramatically among industries. For example, in NAICS code 312, "Beverage and tobacco product manufacturing," it is only 42 percent, but this industry includes firms that are stemming and redrying tobacco, which are labor intensive activities, firms making cigarettes, cigars, and pipe tobacco, and alcoholic and nonalcoholic beverage manufacturers. On the other hand, in NAICS code 311, "Food manufacturing," it is

---

[17]Cherish Karoway, "The Power of Influence: Do We have It?" *Purchasing Today,* January 1998, p. 32.

TABLE 1–2 Cost of Materials—Value of Industry Shipments Ratios for Manufacturing Firms, 1998

North American Industry Classification System	Industry	Cost of Materials (millions)*	Total Capital Expenditures (millions)†	Total Material and Capital Expenditures (millions)	Value of Industry Shipments (millions)‡	Material/ Sales Ratio	Total Purchase/ Sales Ratio
311	Food	256,345	11,373	267,718	431,820	59	62
312	Beverage and tobacco products	40,721	2,556	43,277	102,982	40	42
313	Textile mills	33,869	2,422	36,291	57,626	59	63
314	Textile product mills	18,056	723	18,779	31,457	57	60
315	Apparel	33,441	1,055	34,496	65,530	51	53
316	Leather and allied products	5,512	137	5,649	10,317	53	55
321	Wood products	57,310	2,763	60,073	92,142	62	66
322	Paper	83,596	8,518	92,114	156,251	54	59
323	Printing and related support activities	40,306	4,761	45,067	101,309	40	44
324	Petroleum and coal products	104,329	5,034	109,363	137,066	76	80
325	Chemical	188,351	21,548	209,899	424,152	44	49
326	Plastics and rubber products	78,575	8,135	86,710	164,041	48	53
327	Nonmetallic mineral products	39,918	4,948	44,866	92,898	43	48
331	Primary metal	97,021	6,616	103,637	166,343	58	62
332	Fabricated metal products	114,449	9,810	124,259	253,342	45	49
333	Machinery	140,248	10,134	150,382	280,857	50	54
334	Computer and electronic products	184,937	21,234	206,171	440,306	42	47
335	Electrical equipment, appliances and components	57,375	4,247	61,622	116,826	49	53
336	Transportation equipment	375,352	20,022	395,374	612,096	61	65
337	Furniture and related products	32,440	1,959	34,399	70,417	46	49
339	Miscellaneous	41,928	3,911	45,839	107,038	39	43

Total

Year	Cost of Materials (millions)*	Capital Expenditures, New (millions)†	Material and Capital Expenditures (millions)	Value of Industry Shipments (millions)‡	Material/ Sales Ratio	Total Purchase Sales Ratio
All Operating Manufacturing Establishments						
1998	2,024,080	151,904	2,175,984	3,914,815	52	56
1997	2,020,476	151,734	2,172,210	3,845,570	53	56
1996	1,975,362	146,467	2,121,829	3,715,428	53	57
1995	1,897,570	134,318	2,031,888	3,594,359	53	57
1994	1,752,735	118,664	1,871,399	3,348,019	52	56
1993	1,647,492	108,628	1,756,120	3,127,620	53	56
1992	1,571,773	110,643	1,682,416	3,004,800	52	56
1991	1,531,221	103,152	1,634,373	2,878,164	53	57
1990	1,574,617	106,462	1,681,079	2,912,228	54	58

Source: Annual Survey of Manufacturers, U.S. Census Bureau, *www.census.gov/www/ma0300.html.*

62 percent. This industry includes firms that transform livestock and agricultural products, whose production process is material intensive and requires a minimum amount of labor cost due to use of highly mechanized/automated manufacturing processes. In NAICS code 324, "Petroleum and coal products," the total purchase to sales ratio is 80 percent. Any function of the firm that accounts for well over half of its receipts certainly deserves a great deal of managerial attention. The total purchase/sales ratio is, therefore, one indicator of the value and role of the purchasing function in companies in a specific industry. If the purchase/sales ratio is high, one would expect that the purchasing function would be of greater importance and more highly valued than in a company in which the ratio was low.

Decision Making in the Purchasing/Supply Management Context

Purchasing Decisions Cover a Wide Range of Areas

One of the challenging aspects of the purchasing function to its practitioners is the variety and nature of the decisions encountered. Should we make or buy? Should we inventory materials and how much? What price shall we pay? Where shall we place this order? What should the order size be? When will we require this material? Which alternative looks best as an approach to this problem? Which transportation mode and carrier should we use? Should we make a long- or a short-term contract? Should we cancel? How do we dispose of surplus material? Who will form the negotiation team and what should its strategy be? How do we protect ourselves for the future? Shall we change operating systems? Should we use reverse auctions? What should our e-commerce strategy be? Should we wait or act now? In view of the trade-offs, what is the best decision? What stance do we take regarding our customers who wish to supply us? Do we standardize? Is systems contracting worthwhile here? Should we use one supplier or multiple suppliers? Decisions like these will have a major impact on the organization and its final customers. What makes the decisions exciting is that they almost always are made in a context of uncertainty.

Decision Tree Model

Advances in management knowledge in recent years have substantially enlarged the number of ways in which supply decisions can be analyzed. The basic supplier selection decision is a classical decision tree model as shown in Figure 1–2. This is a choice between alternatives under uncertainty. In this example, the uncertainty relates to our own demand: We are not sure if it will be high, medium, or low. The outcome is concerned with both price and ability to supply. Does the decision maker wish to trade a higher price against supply assurance under all circumstances? That it is difficult to quantify all consequences reinforces the need for sound judgment in key decisions. It also means that the decision maker's perception of the risk involved may in itself be a key variable. Thus, the opportunity is provided to

FIGURE 1–2

Simplified One-Stage Decision Tree Showing a Supplier Selection Decision

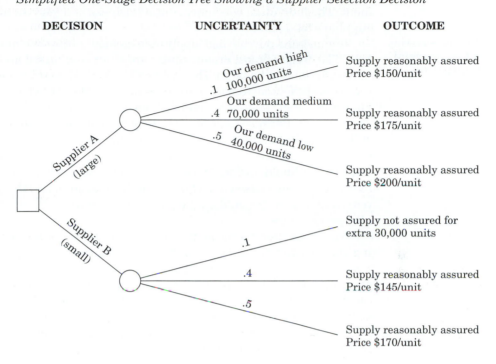

| DECISION | UNCERTAINTY | OUTCOME |

Our demand high
.1 100,000 units
Supply reasonably assured
Price $150/unit

Our demand medium
.4 70,000 units
Supply reasonably assured
Price $175/unit

.5
Our demand low
40,000 units
Supply reasonably assured
Price $200/unit

Supplier A
(large)

Supplier B
(small)

.1
Supply not assured for
extra 30,000 units

.4
Supply reasonably assured
Price $145/unit

.5
Supply reasonably assured
Price $170/unit

blend managerial judgment, gained through experience and training, with the appropriate decision concepts and techniques.

The Differences between Commercial and Consumer Acquisition

Characteristics of Consumer Acquisition

Purchasing is a difficult function to understand because almost everyone is familiar with another version, that of personal buying. For this reason, it is easy for one to presume a familiarity or expertise with the acquisition function. A consumer point of view is characterized by a shopping basket philosophy. It assumes a retail type of marketing operation where there are many suppliers of relatively common items. Every customer buys on a current need basis and also is the final consumer of the product or service acquired. Some price variation may occur from supplier to supplier, depending on what marketing strategy the supplier chooses to follow. The consumer has the freedom to choose the nature and quality of items required and to choose the appropriate supplier. With few exceptions the individual consumer has no power to influence the price, the method of marketing, or the manufacturer chosen by the supplier's management. The individual consumer's total business is a very small portion of the supplier's total sales.

Characteristics of Commercial Acquisition

Commercial purchasing/supply management presents a much different picture. The needs of most organizations are often specialized and the volumes of purchases tend to be large. The number of potential sources may be small, and there may be few customers in the total market. Many buying organizations are larger than their suppliers and may play a multiplicity of roles with respect to their sources. Because large sums of money are involved, suppliers have a large stake in an individual customer and frequently will resort to many kinds of strategies to secure the wanted business. In such an environment, the right to award or withhold business represents real power. Special expertise is required to ensure proper satisfaction of needs on the one hand, and the appropriate systems and procedures on the other, to ensure a continually effective and acceptable performance.

Suppliers spend large sums annually to find ways and means of persuading their customers to buy. Purchasing strength must be pitted against this marketing strength to ensure that the buying organization's needs now and in the future are adequately met. The supply function should be staffed with people who can deal on an equal basis with this marketing force. It is not sufficient in this environment to be only reactionary to outside pressures from suppliers. Foresight and a long-range planning outlook are vital so that future needs can be recognized and met on a planned basis.

Contribution of the Purchasing/Supply Management Function

A Dual Supply Perspective

Operational Contribution of Supply

The contribution of the purchasing/supply function can be described in several ways. First, performance can be viewed in two contexts: operational, which is characterized as *trouble avoidance,* and strategic, which is characterized as *opportunistic* (Figure 1–3).

The trouble avoidance context is the most familiar. Many people inside the organization are inconvenienced to varying degrees when the supply function does not meet with minimum expectations. Improper quality, wrong quantities, and late delivery may make life miserable for the ultimate user of the product or service. This is so basic and apparent that "no complaints" is assumed to be an indicator of good supply performance. The difficulty is that some users never expect anything more and hence may not receive anything more.

The operational side of purchasing/supply is the transactional, day-to-day operations traditionally associated with purchasing. The operational

FIGURE 1–3

Purchasing's Operational and Strategic Contributions

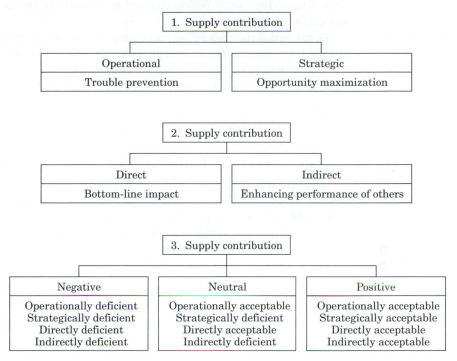

Source: Michiel R. Leenders and Anna E. Flynn. *Value-Driven Purchasing: Managing the Key Steps in the Acquisition Process* (Burr Ridge, IL: Richard D. Irwin, 1995), p. 7.

Strategic Contribution of Supply

side can be streamlined and organized in ways designed to routinize and automate many of the transactions, thus freeing up time for the purchasing manager to focus on the strategic contribution. The strategic side is concerned with the entire process of supply management and its relation and interaction with other functional areas of the organization, the external supply environment, and the needs and wants of the end customer. (Chapter 18 discusses in detail the strategic role.)

The Direct and Indirect Contribution of Supply

The second context is that of purchasing's potential direct or indirect contribution to organizational objectives (see Figure 1–3). Most supply managers believe the potential indirect contribution of supply by enhancing the performance of others is substantially greater than the direct contribution.

The profit-leverage effect and the return-on-assets effect demonstrate the direct contribution purchasing/supply can make to the company's bottom line.

Profit-Leverage Effect. If, through better purchasing, a firm saves $100,000 in the amounts paid to suppliers for needed materials, supplies, and services, that $100,000 savings goes directly to the bottom line (before-tax) account on its profit and loss (P&L) statement. If that same firm sells an additional $100,000 of product, the contribution to profit, assuming a 5 percent before-tax profit margin, would be only $5,000. Purchase dollars are high-powered dollars!

Perhaps an example, using a hypothetical manufacturer, would help:

Gross sales:	$1,000,000
Purchases (assuming purchases account for 50% of the sales dollars)	500,000
Profit (assuming a before-tax profit margin of 5%)	50,000

Now, assume this firm were able to reduce its overall purchase cost by 10 percent through better management of the function. This would be a $50,000 additional contribution to before-tax profits. To increase before-tax profits by $50,000 solely through increased sales would require at least an additional $1,000,000, or a doubling, of sales.

This is not to suggest that it would be easy to reduce overall purchase costs by 10 percent. In a firm that has given major attention to the purchasing function over the years it would be difficult, and perhaps impossible, to do. But, in a firm that has neglected purchasing, it would be a realistic objective. Because of the profit-leverage effect of purchasing, large savings are possible relative to the effort that would be needed to increase sales by the much-larger percentage necessary to generate the same effect on the P&L statement. Since, in many firms, sales already has received much more attention, purchasing may be the last untapped "profit producer."

Purchasing is a Profit Producer

Return-on-Assets Effect. Firms are increasingly more interested in return on assets (ROA) as a measure of performance. Figure 1–4 shows the standard ROA model, using the same ratio of figures as in the previous example, and assuming, realistically, that inventory accounts for 30 percent of total assets. If purchase costs were reduced by 10 percent, that would cause a 10 percent reduction in the inventory asset base. The numbers in the boxes show the initial figures used in arriving at the 10 percent ROA performance. The numbers below each box are the figures resulting from a 10 percent overall purchase price reduction, and the end product is a new ROA of 20.6 percent. This is a highly feasible objective for many firms.

Purchasing Enhances the Performance of Others

The purchasing/supply management function also contributes indirectly by enhancing the performance of other departments or individuals in the organization. For example, better quality may reduce rework, lower warranty costs, increase customer satisfaction, and/or increase the ability to sell more or at a higher price. Involvement of and ideas from suppliers may result in improved design, lower manufacturing costs, and/or a faster idea-to-design-to-product completion-to-customer delivery cycle. Each would improve the or-

FIGURE 1–4

Return-on-Assets Factors

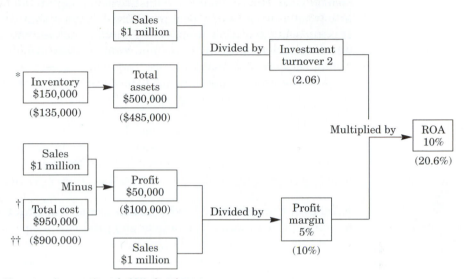

*Inventory is approximately 30% of total assets.
†Purchases account for half of total sales, or $500,000.
††Figures in parentheses assume a 10% reduction in purchase costs.

ganization's competitiveness. Indirect contributions come from purchasing's role as an information source; its effect on efficiency, competitive position, and company image; the management training provided by assignments in the supply area; and its role in developing management strategy and social policy. The benefits of the indirect contribution may outweigh the direct contribution, but measuring the indirect benefits is harder to do since it involves many "soft" or intangible improvements that are difficult to quantify.

Information Source. The contacts of the purchasing function in the marketplace provide a useful source of information for various functions within the organization. Primary examples include information about prices, availability of goods, new sources of supply, new products, and new technology, all of interest to many other parts of the organization. New marketing techniques and distribution systems used by suppliers may be of interest to the marketing group. News about major investments, mergers, acquisition candidates, international political and economic developments, pending bankruptcies, major promotions and appointments, and current and potential customers may be relevant to marketing, finance, research, and top management. Purchasing's unique position vis-á-vis the marketplace should provide a comprehensive listening post.

Effect on Efficiency. The effectiveness with which the purchasing function is performed will show up in other operating results. While the firm's accounting system may not be sophisticated enough to identify poor efficiency as having been caused by poor purchase decisions, that very often is the case. If purchasing selects a supplier who fails to deliver raw materials or parts which measure up to the agreed-on quality standards, this may result in a higher scrap rate or costly rework, requiring excessive direct labor expenditures. If the supplier does not meet the agreed-on delivery schedule, this may require a costly rescheduling of production, decreasing overall production efficiency, or in the worst case it will result in a shutdown of the production line—and fixed costs continue even though there is no output. Many supply departments now refer to user departments as internal customers or clients and focus on improving the efficiency and effectiveness of the function with a goal of providing outstanding internal customer service.

Effect on Competitive Position/Customer Satisfaction. A firm cannot be competitive unless it can deliver end products or services to its customers when they are wanted, of the quality desired, and at a price the customer feels is fair. If purchasing doesn't do its job, the firm will not have the required materials when needed, of the quality needed, and at a price that will keep end-product costs competitive and under control.

Automotive Industry Example of Supply's Indirect Contribution

Some years ago, one of the major automobile producers decided to buy all its auto glass from one firm (a single source). Some months into the supply agreement, it became evident that the forthcoming labor-contract negotiations might result in a deadlock and a long strike. To protect themselves, the auto company built up a 90-day glass stockpile, even though the inventory carrying costs were high and they had problems finding the physical storage facilities for that much glass. They were right: There was a strike in the glass industry, but the union struck only the glass firm supplying that auto producer. The strike lasted 118 days and the auto producer had to shut down its production lines for more than a month.

The auto producer had a large net financial loss that year, since that sales loss dropped them below their break-even point. The president explained to the stockholders that the glass strike cost them the sale of about 100,000 cars (a month's sales). Auto customers evidently were not willing to wait until the strike ended, and they "went across the street" and bought cars made by competitors. The dealer can tell a customer, "Here's the car. Bring it back in a month and we'll put the wheel covers on for you," and make the sale. But it's difficult to convince the customer to take the car now and bring it back later for the windshield! Actually, they probably lost closer to 500,000 future auto sales, because if a customer bought another maker's car, and liked the different make, this person probably went back to the new dealer for future purchases. The supply function potentially can contribute a great deal to the corporate goals of customer satisfaction and continuous improvement.

Effect on Image. The actions of the purchasing department influence directly the public relations and image of a company. If actual and potential suppliers are not treated in a businesslike manner, they will form a poor opinion of the entire organization and will communicate this to other firms. This poor image will adversely affect the purchaser's ability to get new business and to find new and better suppliers. Public confidence can be boosted by evidence of sound policies and fair implementation of them.

Training Ground. The supply area also is an excellent training ground for new managers. The needs of the organization may be quickly grasped. Exposure to the pressure of decision making under uncertainty with potentially serious consequences allows for evaluation of the individual's ability and willingness to take risks and assume responsibility. Contacts with many people at various levels and a variety of functions may assist the individual in charting a career plan and will also be of value as the manager moves up the organization. Many organizations find it useful to include the purchasing area as part of a formal job rotation system for high-potential employees.

Management Strategy and Social Policy. The purchasing/supply management function also can be used as a tool of management strategy and social policy. Does management wish to introduce and stimulate competition? Does it favor geographical representation, minority interest, and environmental and social concerns? For example, are domestic sources preferred? Will resources be spent on assisting minority suppliers? As part of an overall organization strategy, the supply function can contribute a great deal. Assurance of supply of vital materials or services in a time of general shortages can be a major competitive advantage. Similarly, access to a better-quality or a lower-priced product or service may represent a substantial gain. These strategic positions in the marketplace may be gained through active exploration of international and domestic markets, technology, innovative management systems, and the imaginative use of corporate resources in the supply area. Vertical integration and its companion decisions of make or buy (or outsource) are ever-present considerations in the management of materials.

Management Commitment Needed to Realize Potential

The potential contribution to strategy is obvious. Achievement depends on both top executive awareness of this potential and the ability to marshall corporate resources to this end. At the same time, it is the responsibility of those charged with the management of the supply function to seek strategic opportunities in the environment and to draw top executive attention to them. This requires a thorough familiarity with organizational objectives, strategy, and long-term plans, and the ability to influence these in the light of new information. Chapter 18 discusses both the potential purchasing contributions to business strategy *and* the major strategy areas within the purchasing function.

This is a capsule of the potential contributions of the function. It does not just happen, however. In some organizations the supply function is not management's prime concern. Continued lack of management interest and commitment can defeat the objectives of competent supply performance, causing a weak link in the total chain. AT&T's executive vice president for telephone products said, "Purchasing is by far the largest single function at AT&T. Nothing we do is more important."[18] While there are several examples of senior corporate executives who either got their start in purchasing, came up through the purchasing ranks, or have had significant purchasing experience on their way up—for example, Thomas T. Stallkamp, vice chairman and CEO of MSX International, Inc. and former Chrysler president; Raymond C. Stark, Vice President of Six Sigma and Productivity at Honeywell; and G. Richard Wagoner, President of General Motors' North American Operations—the vast majority of senior corporate executives *have* had no direct purchasing/supply management experience. Thus they may view purchasing as still a clerical activity. Yet the experience of many companies has shown that a relatively small amount of time and effort in the supply area will provide a substantial return on investment. This is an opportunity which should be brought to the attention of the key decision makers. One sign of the growing recognition of the importance of the supply function is that in 1997, 32 percent of purchasing professionals reported making strategy presentations to the board of directors versus 18 percent in 1990; and 83 percent reported presenting to the executive committee in 1997 versus just over 50 percent in 1990.[19] An effective supply function can and must be highly responsive to the users' needs in terms of quality, quantity, price, and delivery. It also can contribute to policy objectives as well as the overall public image of the organization. Those in the supply management function cannot accomplish this without assisting and cooperating with, and getting assistance and cooperation from, suppliers, users, and others involved in the total process.

Elevation to Top Executive Status

Progressive managers have recognized these potential contributions of the supply management area and have taken the necessary steps to ensure results. The most important single step in successful organizations has been the elevation to top executive status of the purchasing/supply manager. Although titles are not always consistent with status and value in an organization, they still make a statement within and outside of most organizations. The 1995 CAPS organization study reported that the most common title of the chief purchasing officer was vice president (31 percent) followed by director (30 percent) and manager (18 percent).[20]

The elevation of the chief purchasing officer to executive status, coupled with high-caliber staff and the appropriate authority and responsibility, has

---

[18]Shawn Tully, "Purchasing's New Muscle," *Fortune,* Feb. 20, 1995, p. 75.

[19]Robert J. Trent and Robert M. Monczka, "Purchasing and Supply Management: Trends and Changes Throughout the 1990s," *International Journal of Purchasing and Materials Management,* Fall 1998, pp. 4–5.

[20]Harold E. Fearon and Michiel R. Leenders, *Purchasing's Organizational Roles and Responsibilities* (Tempe, AZ: Center for Advanced Purchasing Studies, 1995), p. 27.

FIGURE 1–5

Characteristics of an Integrated Strategic Procurement and Sourcing Function

Executive leadership
- executive committee support for integration across company and strategic business unit/corporate plans

Strategic positioning—organization
- external/internal customer focus
- matrix management
- high-level positioning—second, third, or fourth levels

Functional leadership
- companywide customer-focused leadership
- establishes integrated visions
- works at results and processes
- drives supply base/supplier management strategies companywide

Functional/SBU horizontal integration
- cross-functional, cross-location teaming
- part of the technology, manufacturing, and SBU planning process

Supply-base strategy
- quality driven
- design standardization
- concurrent engineering
- supply-base optimization
- commercial strategy emerging
- horizontal/vertical supplier strategies

Supplier management
- focused supplier development
- joint performance improvement efforts
- value focused
- total cost improvement
- supplier benchmarking

Measurement
- customer oriented
- total value/cost focused
- benchmarking with best in class

Systems
- global databases
- historical performance data
- strategy
- extensive electronic data interchange (EDI), electronic funds transfer (EFT), computer-assisted design (CAD), and computer-assisted manufacturing (CAM)

resulted in an exciting and fruitful realization of the potential of the supply function in many companies. A 1995 *Fortune* article summarized this by saying that "what used to be a corporate backwater is becoming a fast-track job as purchasers show they can add millions to the bottom line."[21] Figure 1–5 shows the characteristics of an integrated strategic procurement and sourcing function.[22]

Professionalism in Purchasing

Certainly the changes that have occurred over the past several decades have caused top management, in general, to recognize the importance of

---

[21]Tully, p. 75.

[22]Robert M. Monczka and Robert J. Trent, *Purchasing and Sourcing Strategy: Trends and Implications* (Tempe, AZ: Center for Advanced Purchasing Studies, 1995), p. 73.

effective and efficient performance of the purchasing/supply management function. How has this changed the people who perform the purchasing function? How have they grown? While it is not possible to provide any single-number measure of this change, six of the indicators are:

New Assignments. In many organizations, the profession and those persons performing the activity have taken on several new responsibilities. Some of those activities are personnel travel, traffic-transportation, and countertrade-offset planning/execution. Purchasing has assumed an increased role or responsibility in strategic planning, providing economic forecasts/indicators, capital equipment buys, product development, new product evaluation, and cash-flow planning.[23]

Education. Although there are no universal educational requirements for entry-level jobs, most large organizations require a college degree in business administration or management.[24] Several major educational institutions, such as Arizona State University, Bowling Green State University, George Washington University, Miami University, Michigan State University, and Western Michigan University, now offer an undergraduate degree major in Purchasing/Materials/Supply/Supply Chain/Logistics Management as part of the bachelor of science in business administration degree. In addition, many schools offer certificate programs or some courses in purchasing for either full- or part-time students. A number of schools, including Arizona State, Michigan State, and Howard University, also offer a specialization in supply chain management as part of a master of business administration (MBA) degree program.

College Degrees are the Norm

A 2000 survey by *Purchasing* magazine found that 68 percent of respondents had a college degree, and those with a degree "fill the highest-ranking purchasing positions, have the greatest purchasing responsibilities, work for the largest companies, and generally earn the highest average annual compensation." In the 1995 study by the Center for Advanced Purchasing Studies, 96 percent of the chief purchasing officers in the 305 large organizations that supplied data were college graduates. Forty percent held an advanced degree in addition to the bachelor's degree, with 82 percent of these being either an MBA or a management degree. Fifty-eight percent of the bachelor's degree holders majored in business and 19 percent in engineering. As might be expected, more of the chief purchasing officers in the manufacturing sector had engineering degrees (22 percent) than in the service sector (11 percent).[25]

---

[23]Harold E. Fearon, *Purchasing Organizational Relationships* (Tempe, AZ: Center for Advanced Purchasing Studies, 1988), pp. 15–16.

[24]"Purchasing Managers, Buyers and Purchasing Agents," *Occupational Outlook Handbook,* 2000-2001 edition (Washington, D.C.: U.S. Department of Labor, Bulletin 2200), April 8, 2001, *http://stats.bls.gov/oco/ocos023.htm.*

[25]Harold E. Fearon and Michiel R. Leenders, *Purchasing's Organizational Roles,* pp. 30–31.

College Recruitment. Many of the major companies now look to the campus for their input of entry-level personnel into the purchasing/supply management department. This is based on the belief that if persons recruited today will be expected to move into purchasing management responsibilities five years from now, it is essential to start out with the best possible personnel raw material. Their experience has been that this source of entry-level personnel has the highest probability of providing well-rounded, aggressive, successful new hires. Many companies are also looking for more experienced people with a master's degree specializing in supply chain management combined with an undergraduate degree in a different field.

Training Programs. The better-managed firms now provide continuing education/training for their purchasing professionals. This training is organized on a formal, in-house seminar basis in which a given individual may participate in a full-week training session over each of several years, or the firm may use a planned combination of seminars/courses offered by universities, associations, or private training organizations. This purchasing training then is supplemented by various general management courses and seminars.

Salary Levels. While salaries vary widely for purchasing personnel, since duties and responsibilities vary from company to company, some rough indications of compensation levels can be obtained from the annual salary survey done by *Purchasing* magazine. The 2000 salary survey by *Purchasing,* using a survey sample of 3,372 purchasing professionals, found an average salary of $61,300, which was up $3,700 (6.4 percent) from 1999's average of $57,600. The median salary, $53,000, was $3,000 greater than in 1999. This increase occurred at a time when the Consumer Price Index rose only about 3 percent in the 12-month period between the 1999 and 2000 survey. Compensation is rising the fastest at the highest levels of the purchasing profession. Just over half (50.5 percent) reported receiving an annual bonus as part of their total annual compensation, compared to 47 percent in 1998 and only 36 percent in 1988. Overall, the average bonus was 11 percent of base pay, with bonuses for purchasing vice presidents averaging 24.6 percent of base pay, and bonuses for buyers averaging only 6.6 percent.[26]

Average annual compensation for all respondents was $61,300, with college graduates earning on average $67,300 and non-graduates earning $48,500. Executives with MBA degrees have the highest average salary of $90,000. While women respondents to the survey tended to have fewer supervisory responsibilities, be in charge of smaller dollar volumes, have less frequently graduated from college, be younger than the male respondents, and hold senior-level positions less often than the male respondents, average salaries for women continue to lag behind those of men even when the

Average Salaries Rise

---

[26]Kevin R. Fitzgerald, "Purchasing's Value Continues to Rise," *Purchasing Online,* Dec. 16, 1999, *http://www.manufacturing.net/magazine/purchasing*.

**Women's
Salaries Lower
than Men's**

women have comparable experience and responsibilities. According to the survey results, men with a technical degree earned, on average, $70,300 while women with a technical degree earned only $53,800. For men the average salary was higher with a technical degree ($70,300) than a business degree ($67,700), or a liberal arts degree ($65,100). By comparison, women with a technical degree earned, on average, $53,800, while women with a business degree earned, on average, $51,600, and women with a liberal arts degree earned $49,300. Graduate degrees continue to influence compensation, and the average salary for men with an MBA was $93,700 and for women, $71,500.[27]

Professional Associations. As any profession matures, its professional associations emerge as focal points for efforts to advance professional practice and conduct. In the United States, the major professional association is the Institute for Supply Management (ISM), formerly the National Association of Purchasing Management, Inc. (NAPM), founded in 1915 as the National Association of Purchasing Agents.[28] The ISM is an educational and research association with more than 47,000 members, who belong to the ISM through its more than 180 affiliated organizations in the United States.

**ISM
Publications**

In addition to regional and national conferences, ISM sponsors seminars for purchasing people. It publishes a variety of books and monographs and the leading scholarly journal in the field, *International Journal of Purchasing and Supply Management,* which it began in 1965. Since the early 1930s, NAPM has conducted the monthly "NAPM Report on Business," which is one of the best-recognized current barometers of business activity in the manufacturing sector. In 1998, the association initiated the Nonmanufacturing NAPM Report on Business. The survey results normally appear the second business day of each month on the front page of *The Wall Street Journal.* In January 2001, NAPM and Forrester Research initiated the Report on E-Business, which is released every three months. Additionally, NAPM works with colleges and universities to encourage and support the teaching of purchasing and supply management and related subjects and provides financial grants to support doctoral student research.

**Certified
Purchasing
Manager
(C.P.M.)
Designation**

In 1974, the National Association of Purchasing Management initiated the Certified Purchasing Manager (C.P.M.) program, which tests purchasing people. On successful completion of the program, it certifies by award of the C.P.M. designation that the recipient has met the established knowledge, education, and experience standards. Currently, about 32,000 people have earned the C.P.M. designation by passing four written examinations, completing specific education and seminar requirements, and meeting an experience requirement. To retain the C.P.M., evidence of additional education

---

[27]Ibid.

[28]The address of the Institute for Supply Management is 2055 E. Centennial Circle, P.O. Box 22160, Tempe, AZ, 85285-2160, *www.napm.org*.

**Accredited
Purchasing
Practitioner
(A.P.P.)
Designation**

must be provided every five years (recertification). Of the 32,000 people who have earned the C.P.M., it is estimated that about 22,000 now hold a valid C.P.M. In 1995, NAPM established a second professional designation, the Accredited Purchasing Practitioner (A.P.P.) program, for buyers who are primarily involved in the tactical and operational side of purchasing as either the primary, or a secondary, component of the person's job. To date, about 5,300 people have earned the A.P.P. designation. The most recent major innovative professional activity of the National Association of Purchasing Management was to conduct a new job analysis and completely overhaul the C.P.M. and A.P.P. examinations to more accurately reflect what purchasing and supply professionals do on the job.

**Center for
Advanced
Purchasing
Studies**

In 1986, the Center for Advanced Purchasing Studies (CAPS) was established as a national affiliation agreement between NAPM (now ISM) and the College of Business at Arizona State University.[29] The Center has three major goals to be accomplished through its research program: (1) to improve purchasing effectiveness and efficiency, (2) to improve overall purchasing capability, and (3) to increase the competitiveness of U.S. companies in a global economy. CAPS conducts industrywide purchasing benchmarking studies; publishes a quarterly best-practices publication called *Practix;* runs the annual Purchasing Executives' Roundtables in the United States, Europe, and Asia; and conducts and publishes focused purchasing research in areas of interest to industry. Recent innovations to the benchmarking studies include analyzing and applying a methodology to the information gathered in the industrywide studies to identify specific companies within each industry as being best-in-class on various metrics. Finally, CAPS plans to send researchers on visits to the companies that achieve best-in-class designations to study the processes by which they achieve their industry-leading results. Ultimately, CAPS will publish reports on the best practices for each industry. CAPS is also conducting *Project 10X* to help corporations develop purchasing and supply strategies for the new millennium. Designed to create a rolling five-to-ten-year vision of strategies and best practices, this research program is committed to increasing performance by a magnitude of *10 times.* The program will produce a coherent vision across industries, develop future best practices, identify emerging best practices, and develop roadmaps from current practices to future best practices.

**Purchasing
Management
Association of
Canada**

In Canada, the professional association is the Purchasing Management Association of Canada (PMAC), formed in 1919.[30] Its membership of over 8,000 is organized in 10 provincial and territorial institutes from coast to coast. Its primary objective is education, and in addition to sponsoring national conferences, and publishing a magazine, *Progressive Purchaser,* it has

---

[29]The address for the Center for Advanced Purchasing Studies is the Arizona State University Research Park, P.O. Box 22160, Tempe, AZ 85285-2160, *http://capsresearch.org.*

[30]The address of the Purchasing Management Association of Canada is 2 Carlton Street, Suite 1414, Toronto, Ontario, Canada M5B 1J3, *www.pmac.ca.*

designed and offers an accreditation program leading to the C.P.P. (Certified Professional Purchaser) designation. PMAC's accreditation program was started in 1963; some 1,400 purchasing professionals have earned the CPP designation.

Other Professional Purchasing Associations

In addition to ISM and PMAC, there are several other professional purchasing associations, such as the National Institute of Governmental Purchasing (NIGP), National Association of State Purchasing Officials (NASPO), and the American Society for Health Care Materials Management. Several of these associations offer their own certification programs. Most industrialized countries have their own professional purchasing associations, for example, Institute of Purchasing and Supply Management (Australia), Chartered Institute of Purchasing and Supply (Great Britain), Indian Institute of Materials Management, and Japan Materials Management Association. These national associations are loosely organized into the International Federation of Purchasing and Materials Management (IFPMM), which has as its objective the fostering of cooperation, education, and research in purchasing on a worldwide basis among the more than 40 member national associations representing over 200,000 purchasing professionals.[31] Purchasing truly has become an internationally recognized profession.

Challenges Facing Purchasing and Supply Management over the Next Decade

As this chapter has shown, the purchasing/supply function has seen many significant changes in the last half of the twentieth century. Most of these changes have been positive for the function and its recognition as an increasingly important contributor to organizational goals. The individuals performing the purchasing/supply activities have seen their opportunities for professional growth and personal rewards expand as they deal with the challenges of increasing organizational effectiveness. Yet, all is not rosy; there is no shortage of vexing problems. Among the most significant challenges in the beginning of the twenty-first century, which are addressed in the remaining chapters of this text, are these:

Business-to-Business E-Commerce

Achieving Greater Efficiencies Through Technology

One of the most exciting and challenging developments to affect supply management in recent years is the advent of electronic business-to-business (B2B) commerce. New technology tools promise greater efficiencies in purchasing and supply management processes. When fully implemented, these

---

[31]International Federation of Purchasing and Materials Management. Secretariat: Rockhgasse 6 P.O. Box 131, A-1014 Vienna, Austria, Phone ++43 (1) 533 86 38 78 FAX: ++43 (1) 533 86 36 79, secretariat@ifpmm.co.at

tools may enable supply managers to streamline the purchase of lower-value, lower-risk goods and services throughout the supply chain and free up time for more value-adding strategic endeavors. (See Chapter 4.)

Supply Chain Management

Attaining Process Improvements Through Supply Chain Management

Organizations need to achieve continuous process improvement in order to produce their products or services more effectively. This will enable them to give their customers better value. One of the keys to accomplishing this is working with key suppliers to help them provide higher quality; faster and more reliable delivery; innovative design, production, and distribution ideas; and a lower total product or service cost. This kind of supply chain management must be pushed back to first-tier suppliers, who in turn must drive it back to their suppliers. It's a sound concept, but turning idea into reality is not easy. So far, it has received more lip service than accomplishment, except in a few leading-edge companies.

Measurement

Capturing Supply's Contribution Through Better Measurement

For purchasing to be recognized as a major contributor to organizational success, senior management must be able to gauge what results are being achieved. While a great deal of effort has been directed over the past 50 years at improving the methods of evaluating purchasing performance, the currently used measurements are not as specific or convincing as senior management would like. The complexity of purchasing and supply management certainly contributes to the measurement difficulties, but until purchasing measurements become better, and better-accepted, the function will not receive the desired recognition.

Purchase of Nontraditional Goods and Services

Applying Purchasing Expertise to Non-Traditional Purchases

Conventional wisdom suggests that the purchasing department will focus on the traditional purchases of (1) raw materials, (2) special and standard production items, and (3) maintenance, repair, and operating (MRO) supplies. However, the purchasing department, since it understands and can apply the logical, competitive purchasing process, should be in a prime position to get better value in the purchase of many (or all) of the other, nontraditional goods and services an organization buys. These nontraditional purchases include categories as diverse as computer hardware and software, real estate, resale items, advertising, health benefits, consulting, hazardous waste disposal, legal, telephone/communications, training, travel, and workers' compensation insurance. Presently the purchasing department handles only one-fourth of the expenditure for services and low percentages of some goods purchases (for real estate, only 2 percent).[32] Chapter 16 addresses some of the ways the purchasing department can increase its involvement in the purchase of nontraditional goods and services, where the savings potential is great.

Contribution to Corporate Strategy

Increasing Supply's Contribution to Corporate Strategy

A corporate strategic plan (the big picture of where we want to go in the future and how, in broad terms, we will get there) is the key building block for most major corporate initiatives. Considering the magnitude of the purchasing dollars and the influence of purchase results on overall operations (speed, quality, innovation, cost, and continuous process improvement), it would seem that the purchasing department would be directly involved in, and contributing to, corporate strategic planning initiatives. Yet that does not seem to be the case. The purchasing department in large organizations has only a "slight" to "moderate" role/responsibility/involvement in such major corporate activities as corporate mergers/acquisitions/alliances, technology planning, new-product development, capital project/investment planning, and outsourcing.[33] Purchasing is not yet a major player in establishing corporate strategy and has a significant way to go before it is meaningfully involved. The challenge, of course, is how to make this happen.

Recognition by Senior Management

Convincing Senior Management of Supply's Value

People in the purchasing department often express the feeling that "We don't get any respect!" And there is some truth to that old colloquialism. A recent study found that many CEOs/presidents of major corporations do not have a particularly high opinion of what their purchasing department could do or was doing for their firm. Many say it adds high value only to the firm's bottom-line profit and to production/operations.[34] The CEO/president is the individual from whom purchasing really needs respect and support if it is to be positioned to exert the influence needed to produce real results. The challenge is to convince senior management that, if given the opportunity to contribute, results will be forthcoming.

---

[32]Harold E. Fearon and William A. Bales, *Purchasing of Nontraditional Goods and Services* (Tempe, AZ: Center for Advanced Purchasing Studies, 1995), p. 29.

[33]Harold E. Fearon and Michiel R. Leenders, *Purchasing's Organizational Roles,* p. 25.

[34]William A. Bales and Harold E. Fearon, *CEO's/Presidents' Perceptions and Expectations of the Purchasing Function* (Tempe, AZ: Center for Advanced Purchasing Studies, 1993), p. 6.

Questions for Review and Discussion

1. "In the long term, the success of any organization depends on its ability to create and maintain a customer." Do you agree? What does this have to do with purchasing and supply management?
2. Differentiate between purchasing, procurement, materials management, logistics, supply management, and supply chain management.
3. What is the profit-leverage effect of purchasing? Is it the same in all organizations?
4. How does purchasing and supply management affect return on assets (ROA)? In what specific ways could you improve ROA through purchasing/supply management?
5. How has the purchasing function changed over the last several years? What factors have influenced this evolution? How will it change over the next 10 years? What are the various professional associations in purchasing trying to accomplish?
6. In the petroleum and coal products industry, the total purchase/sales ratio is 80 percent, while in the beverage and tobacco products industry it is only 42 percent. Explain what these numbers mean. Of what significance is this number for a purchasing manager in a company in each of these industries?
7. "Purchasing is not profit making; instead, it is profit taking since it spends organizational resources." Do you agree?
8. Is purchasing a profession? If not, why not? If yes, how will the profession, and the people practicing it, change over the next decade?
9. In what ways might e-commerce influence the role of supply managers in their own organizations? In managing supply chains or networks?

References

Dobler, D. W. and D. N. Burt, *Purchasing and Supply Management.* 6th ed. New York: McGraw-Hill, 1996.

Ellram, L. M. and L. M. Birou. *Purchasing for Bottom Line Impact: Improving the Organization Through Strategic Procurement.* Burr Ridge, IL: Irwin Professional Publishing, 1995.

Handfield, R. B. and E. L. Nichols, Jr., *Introduction to Supply Chain Management,* New York: Prentice Hall, 1998.

Heinritz, S. F., P. V. Farrell, L. Giunipero, and M. G. Kolchin, *Purchasing: Principles and Applications.* 8th ed. Englewood Cliffs, N.J.: Prentice Hall, 1991.

Leenders, M. R. and D. L. Blenkhorn, *Reverse Marketing,* New York: The Free Press, 1988.

Leenders, M. R. and A. E. Flynn, *Value-Driven Purchasing—Managing the Key Steps in the Acquisition Process,* Burr Ridge, IL: Irwin Professional Publishing, 1995.

Monczka, R. M. and R. J. Trent, *Purchasing and Sourcing Strategy: Trends and Implications,* Tempe, AZ: Center for Advanced Purchasing Studies, 1995.

Monczka, R. M., R. J. Trent, and R. B. Handfield, *Purchasing and Supply Chain Management.*

Tully, S. "Purchasing's New Muscle," *Fortune,* Feb. 20, 1995.

Watts, C. A., K. Y. Kim, and C. K. Hahn, "Linking Purchasing to Corporate Competitive Strategy," *International Journal of Purchasing and Materials Management,* 31, no. 2, (Spring 1995), pp. 3–8.

Zenz, G. J., *Purchasing and the Management of Materials,* 7th ed. New York: John Wiley & Sons, 1994.

CASE 1–1
COMMERCIAL LAUNDRY PRODUCTS

Joan Walters, purchasing manager at Commercial Laundry Products (COLP), was reviewing quotes she had just received for cardboard boxes. She was trying to determine whether opportunities for savings existed once all coin-operated laundry products were consolidated at her plant.

COLP was a wholly owned subsidiary of Linden Chemicals and manufactured and distributed industrial laundry and cleaning products. A specialty line for COLP was comprised of eight laundry products sold in coin-operated vending machines located in laundromats. These products, referred to as "coin-ops," were provided by laundromat owners as a service to customers. They included detergents, bleaches, and fabric softeners.

Currently, 9 million of the 10 million coin-op product boxes sold were co-packaged. COLP provided the laundry product and the co-packager packaged the required quantities and shipped finished products into the distribution system. The co-packagers passed on to COLP the costs of the packaging materials, processing labor, and the transportation costs, while charging a negotiated profit margin.

Of the eight different products comprising the coin-op line, only three were currently packaged in-house. The plan was to move the full line in-house and to discontinue the use of co-packagers.

Purchasing Cardboard Boxes. Cardboard boxes were supplied by printers who printed, die cut, scored, and glued the boxes before delivery. Key components of the price were the number of colors used in printing and the quantity of the order. The fewer the colors and the larger the quantity, the lower the per unit price. In the past year COLP was paying $49/M for its boxes and was being charged $30/M for the co-package boxes. Joan felt that there might be some savings generated from economies of scale if all the boxes were printed by one supplier. The cost savings generated by large lot orders would be an important component to the plan they were developing to move all operations in-house.

Joan asked local printers to quote prices for four possible order quantities: 500,000; 750,000; 1,500,000; and 2,000,000.

The Purchasing Decision. Joan knew she could construct an order using any combination of the individual product packages that she required. The printer would design a printing plate with a specified combination of the boxes using the four basic colors. Given the standardized dimensions, the "number up" (i.e., the number of boxes) on each printed sheet was 20.

The following is an example of how she could construct an order for four different product boxes and still order a total quantity of 750,000 boxes.

Specifications of the printing plate used to print 37,500 sheets: 8 hot water detergent boxes; 3 cold water detergent boxes; 6 bleach boxes; and 3 fabric softener boxes for a total of 20 boxes per sheet. The order would result in a total quantity of 300,000 hot water detergent boxes; 112,500 cold water detergent boxes; 225,000 bleach boxes; and 112,500 fabric softener boxes for a total of 750,000 boxes. The printing cost would be based on the 750,000 volume.

Joan had asked local printers to quote prices for four possible order quantities: 500,000, 750,000, 1,500,000, and 2,000,000. Joan looked at the last quote submitted and the best of the three quotes she had requested. She now had enough information to determine the possible cost savings. She knew, however, that the final calculation of savings depended on her decision concerning order quantities. Obviously, she could achieve the highest cost savings by ordering the entire year's forecasted demand of 10 million boxes but she was concerned about the storage costs for this amount of inventory plus the possibility of damage to the cardboard boxes. In addition, with eight products, there was always the possibility that forecasted demand would be incorrect and she would be left with excess inventory. There was also a chance that marketing would make changes to the product mix or box designs within a year's time frame, making old boxes obsolete. Flexibility was important.

Excel Printers, an outstanding local supplier, had provided the most competitive quotes of the three received. It had quoted as follows:

Order Quantity	Price / 1000
500,000	$29.50
750,000	$26.87
1,500,000	$24.77
2,000,000	$23.93

CASE 1–2
CUSTOM EQUIPMENT

It was July 2, and Matt Roberts had just been given his first assignment, the "Wire Management Program" (WMP), by the purchasing manager of Atlanta-based Custom Equipment Inc. The purpose of the WMP was to reduce the supplier base for the company's wire and cable requirements. As a newly hired purchasing agent, Matt wondered how to proceed.

Custom Equipment. Custom Equipment Inc. (CE) was a relatively new division of Custom Equipment Global, a multinational electrical engineering and technology company. CE generated sales of $66 million in the past year, and had forecast growth of 25 percent for each of the upcoming four years.

CE's products were divided into assembly line equipment and press automation equipment. Assembly line products included units such as framers, in which a vehicle frame was fed onto a line and welded in specified areas. Press automation products were units built to move vehicle frames, doors, and hoods between machines already installed within the customer's assembly process. The machines were built in Atlanta, tested, approved, disassembled into sections, shipped to the customer's facility, and then re-assembled.

All machines at Custom Equipment were handbuilt. Most units were unique due to the requirements of the manufacturer and the intended purpose of the machines. Each machine was comprised of steel, mechanical, electrical, and hydraulic parts. Wires and cables were purchased in lengths and installed throughout the unit. With automotive design changes occurring annually, CE was constantly reconditioning previous builds or bidding on new lines. CE prided itself on customer satisfaction. In the automotive industry, a key factor was on-time delivery of equipment required to begin production.

CE's Purchasing Department. The purchasing department at CE was composed of six purchasing agents and one manager. Responsibilities were divided into commodity groups. These groups consisted of: electrical, mechanical, hydraulic/pneumatic, robots/weldguns, affiliate-produced parts/fabricated components, and steel/other metals. Matt was hired recently to replace two retiring purchasing agents.

Matt Roberts. Matt held an undergraduate business degree from a well-known business school. Upon graduation, Matt had worked for a year as an inventory analyst for a multinational manufacturing organization. He had applied to CE after visiting its display booth at a local manufacturing trade show. Matt was eager to make an early contribution at CE and he believed that the WMP presented an excellent opportunity.

Wire Management Program (WMP). Matt's manager had recently initiated the WMP believing that CE could improve value for all of its wire and cable requirements from volume leverage. Rationalizing the supplier base would also save time currently spent processing multiple supplier invoices. A stronger relationship could be fostered with the chosen supplier, which could help increase the priority of CE orders and open further opportunities for cost savings. Also, transportation costs could be reduced because all items would be arriving from a single source. Finally, sourcing from a single supplier would allow the purchasing agent to focus on issues involving higher dollar values.

Matt's manager had given him the impression that the WMP should be implemented before the end of October.

Manufacturing Components. Last year CE's total component purchases totaled $32 million. CE had a total supplier base of 3,000 companies, of which less than 5 percent were regular suppliers. The first reason for having such a large number of suppliers was that newly hired purchasing agents usually had previously-established relationships with certain suppliers. The second reason was that some suppliers specialized in certain products.

When CE was awarded a job, it needed to be thoroughly designed and tested within the engineering department's computer-aided design (CAD) system. Part of this process consisted of determining every component that would be required to complete the job. Required components, which were divided into hydraulic, mechanical, and electrical categories, were entered into a Bill of Materials (ingredient list). The Bill of Materials created a demand for specific parts within Custom Equipment's computer system. Purchasing agents identified requisitions related to their commodity group and satisfied them by creating purchase orders. There was usually some variation between actual requirements and initial expectations. When components were over-ordered, they needed to be returned to the supplier or held in inventory until a need arose. Returning products was usually time-consuming and obviously did not add any value. Keeping over-ordered material tied up company funds. When needed items were under-ordered or forgotten, they would need to be ordered immediately. Recently, many items were labeled as "rush," causing pressure on the purchasing agents to help resolve the problem through expediting.

Each assembly line and press automation product was divided into cells. Cells consisted of numerous components. Ninety-eight percent of component orders were job-specific. Some jobs were comprised of more than 10 separate cells, which entailed many engineers entering materials required for their designated cell. Certain parts were common across cells, but the entry time varied. A significant problem was that there could be numerous orders each day for 10 feet of the same wire, creating unnecessary ordering and processing costs, since each line on the purchase order had to be entered, received, and processed individually. This was often the cause of administrative problems and headaches, because a purchase order for electrical items could contain more than 100 items.

When a project-related item was received, it was kept in an unlocked receiving area until it was needed for the job. Custom Equipment's carrying costs amounted to 15 percent per annum. There were some incidences of workers "borrowing" items required for their jobs, which had not been ordered or which had not yet arrived. This created shrinkage problems, with no direct accountability. Also, in a pinch, the receiving area might issue parts from another job to one with a more urgent requirement; however, approval had to be obtained from the project manager.

The bottom line was that material availability was important because each job cell built on the previously completed cell. Missing components could significantly delay the production of later cells.

Wires and Cables. Wires and cables were considered commodity products within the electrical industry. Wires were fabricated from copper rods rolled into a desired thickness and then covered with a protective coating. Cables were made by combining two or more copper wires, separated by insulation, and using an outer covering or jacket. Wire differed from cable primarily in the number of conductors, jacketing, insulation, and resistance to external factors.

Occasionally, situations arose in which a product was specified by the end-user. In these instances, CE engineers were forced to use the specified product, which might only be available through nonstandard vendors. Specified products occurred more often with motor cables than with wires.

Although current supply processes were generally accepted, Matt felt that the WMP gave him an ideal opportunity to analyze what changes would be possible. He knew, however, that buy-in from key users would be required before implementing any significant changes.

Electrical Component Suppliers. Custom Equipment's wire and cable requirements for any one job were typically purchased from 3–6 different electrical suppliers. The suppliers' product lines contained significant overlap, which led to the desire of reducing the base to a single source. The amount of wire and cable purchased last year was approximately $700,000. Wire and cable purchases were predicted to increase at the same rate as corporate sales.

Matt asked some shop floor employees about CE's current six suppliers. The employees volunteered both positive and negative comments regarding the various suppliers. Matt considered these comments as "unofficial" past-performance reviews. However, he got the impression that some employees seemed to prefer certain suppliers because of friendships outside of work or because of similar nationalities. He was hesitant to consider all comments given due to these potential biases. He was also skeptical about some of the comments of the purchasing agents for similar reasons.

Matt discovered that the Receiving Manager had been keeping some records of suppliers' delivery performance for the last 30 months because of CE's ISO 9001 certification requirements. Criteria such as delivery, product returns, and overall supplier service were tracked and kept within the records of the Receiving Department. With these records, in conjunction with his conversations with the Receiving Manager, Matt believed he could develop an objective assessment of the suppliers' past performance. There had been no significant quality problems with any of CE's current suppliers according to the Receiving Manager. He believed that the vendors possessed relatively uniform quality.

The Next Step. Matt's boss had created the Wire Management Program to seek benefits from reducing the number of wire and cable suppliers. Matt's initial thought was that a single supplier could provide the best prices for CE's annual requirements. He realized that there were arguments both in favor and against using this approach. He would have to analyze the capabilities and managerial abilities of each company in order to reach a decision.

Matt began to think about possible methods to reduce the total number of wire and cable suppliers. CE had established strong relationships with some of the suppliers, and he therefore wanted to give all interested companies an opportunity to present their case. Whatever he chose, he would need to justify his recommendation to his manager and CE's engineers and other employees.

CASE 1–3
THE PURCHASING CO-OP (R)

In May, Margaret Warren, owner and manager of M-Powered Ideas of St. Thomas, Ontario, reflected upon the successful performance of the small business owners purchasing co-operative she had helped organize four months earlier. Margaret was considering how the co-op, which she used to purchase essential oils used for the production of her Utopia Soap products, should grow and what membership benefits to promote.

Margaret Warren and M-Powered Ideas. Margaret started M-Powered Ideas in January 1997 to offer small-office desktop publishing services. In addition, M-Powered Ideas faxed newsletters and announcements for the Western Ontario District of the Purchasing Management Association of Canada. Prior to starting M-Powered Ideas, Margaret was employed as a professional purchasing agent for Victoria Hospital in London, Ontario.

Several summers earlier, Margaret visited an herb farm in California and came across a handmade-soap maker with whom she spoke at length. Intrigued by the chemical blending and creativity involved in the soap-making process, she purchased several books on soap making and immediately began experimenting with soap formulations that were produced in 1-pound batches. Margaret shared her creations with family and friends who kept returning, even offering to pay for more soap. Soon after, she began to show and sell her line of fragrant handmade soaps outside of this group of family and friends. Margaret created the brand name "Utopia Soap" for her product and produced it under the umbrella name of M-Powered Ideas.

Utopia Soap. As sole operator of Utopia Soap, Margaret opened a workshop in her back yard where all soap production took place. Her soaps started with a special combination of coconut, olive and palm oils—the base oils; the blending of additives and fragrances resulted in numerous soap blends. For example, one standard soap produced and labelled "Jasmine Dream" contained an infusion of dried calendula blossoms in olive oil. Other standard blends were likewise descriptively labelled (e.g., "Seabreeze," "Winery Weekend," "Berry Fresh" and "Manly") and were typically offered on a year-round basis. In addition to these standard blends, Margaret offered specialty products such as an emu oil soap and custom blended soaps. The average production cost per bar of soap was $1.[1]

Sales of Utopia Soap for the previous year amounted to $10,000. Approximately 70 percent of annual sales were for standard soaps. Additionally, 40 percent of annual sales came from Ontario retailers such as gift shops, craft stores, health-food stores, and bed-and-breakfasts, as the soaps were primarily viewed as gift items or skin-care products. All soaps were sold to retail and wholesale customers for $2.99, with retailers typically selling the product with a $1 markup (Margaret also retailed a small percentage of Utopia Soap herself at $3.99). Despite the relatively small volume of soap sales, Margaret anticipated a 25 percent growth in sales during the current year with a goal of reaching $100,000 in annual sales at the end of the next three years. Based upon the past two years of sales, Margaret planned for 80 percent of this year's soap business occurring between mid-April and mid-November.

Materials Purchasing. Margaret's current equipment limited her to batches of about 20 pounds, yielding 75 bars of soap.

Materials used in the production of standard soap, such as base and essential oils, Margaret normally purchased every five weeks. Base and essential oils accounted for approximately 90 percent of soap production cost (see Exhibit 1). Given that a 467 millilitre bottle of essential oil, for example, might cost $100, Margaret's material purchases averaged $200 an order, with average shipping costs of $10. Shipping lead times from vendors averaged two to three days. On average, she kept approximately eight weeks of finished goods inventory on hand of standard soap products. Materials for custom soaps were purchased once orders were confirmed. Margaret found that some suppliers were quite unresponsive from a service standpoint to requests, for example, for detailed product information and expedited shipments.

EXHIBIT 1   Production Cost Breakdown by Category

Category	Percentage
Base oils	60
Essential and Fragrance oils	30
Labor	4
Packaging	1
Overhead	5

Source: Margaret Warren, owner

---

[1]All amounts in Canadian dollars unless otherwise stated.

The Purchasing Cooperative. Margaret recognized last fall that one way to gain purchasing clout with suppliers would be through the formation of a purchasing cooperative. Margaret's own experience with purchasing cooperatives started with the London Public Purchasing Co-op. This consisted of publicly funded agencies collaborating to purchase commodity type items ranging from copier paper to electrical and plumbing parts. Some of the co-op contracts Margaret packaged and negotiated ran into the million-dollar range. While nothing on that scale would be needed, Margaret approached members of the Local Business Women's Association (LBWA) in November to pitch the formation of a purchasing cooperative for commodity items like essential and fragrance oils. Margaret identified several individuals who sold products in retail locations similar to those where she sold Utopia soap (i.e., those with similar raw material needs) and convinced five other small business operators of the benefits in forming a purchasing cooperative. These five LBWA members included an emu farmer, a rhea farmer, an herb gardener, a jam and preserve maker, and a skin-care products producer. All co-op members agreed to aggregate their monthly purchases into a single order with the first, for essential oils, placed in January. Since then, monthly co-op orders have ranged between $800 and $1,000 with a $15 shipping charge shared among members.

While specific cost savings for all co-op members were not regularly collected, Margaret estimated that the co-op members each had reduced purchasing-related costs by about 20 percent. More important for the co-op members was the recognition that while their combined ordering volumes allowed for some purchasing discount volumes to be achieved, the materials vendors they had dealt with since the co-op's origin appeared more responsive to servicing specific member requests. On one recent order, a fragrance oil vendor, atypically, charged the co-op for a litre but redistributed the product into two half-litre bottles for the two co-op members using the oil.

Margaret recognized the knowledge of materials management practices, production techniques, and the local retail market that co-op members were now sharing. She liked the fact that each member was willing to share responsibility on an agreed-upon rotation basis in the management of the co-op's primary activities of obtaining price quotes, aggregating ordering needs, planning case splits, placing orders, paying vendors, invoicing co-op members, and making delivery arrangements. The current co-op members were considering the possibility of extending the type of materials purchased collaboratively (e.g., currently oils and packaging) to photocopying services, and the printing of brochures and business cards—all applicable to the needs of the members. Margaret mulled over how the purchasing co-op she had organized should grow.

2 OBJECTIVES AND ORGANIZATION FOR EFFECTIVE PURCHASING AND SUPPLY MANAGEMENT

Chapter Outline

Key Questions for the Purchasing Decision Maker

SHOULD WE
- Separate sourcing and materials management functions?
- Combine the supply and logistics functions?
- Use cross-functional sourcing teams?

HOW CAN WE
- Get others in the organization to recognize the key purchasing decision authority areas?
- Gain the maximum benefits from our organization structure?
- Use cross-functional teams to make better sourcing decisions?

Every organization in both the public and private sector is in varying degrees dependent on materials and services supplied by other organizations. No organization is self-sufficient. Even the smallest office needs space, heat, light, power, communication and office equipment, furniture, stationery, and miscellaneous supplies to carry on its activities. Purchasing and supply management is, therefore, one of the basic, common functions of every organization. One important management challenge is ensuring effective use of the resources and capabilities of the supply organization and the supply chain and supplier network to maximize the supply contribution to organizational objectives.

Advantages of a Professional Purchasing Staff

In very small companies, the owner/manager is often responsible for all of the management functions, including operations, marketing, finance, and purchasing. As companies grow, delegation of various functional responsibilities to others takes place. It is theoretically possible to let each person in an organization be responsible for acquiring his or her needs from outside suppliers. However, creation of a special group or department staffed with supply professionals has many potential advantages:

1. It is easier to standardize.
2. It cuts down on duplication and allows for effective and efficient development and use of electronic supply systems.
3. It provides clout. Purchasing can enter into contracts that provide for pricing based on the organization's total requirements. Clout can be used to obtain supplier concessions, such as lower prices, faster deliveries, better quality, or improved service. There also may be freight savings because shipments can be made in carload or truckload quantities.
4. It prevents interdepartmental or business unit competition in periods of material shortages.

5. It is administratively more efficient for suppliers, since they can focus their selling efforts on the purchasing manager.

6. It provides better control over purchase commitments. Since a large percentage of a firm's cash outflow goes for purchases, the aggregate commitment at any specific point in time can be managed.

7. It is easier to prevent bribery or other unethical practices.

8. It enables the development of specialization and expertise in purchasing decisions and is a better use of management time.

9. It is essential for strategic supply management.

In practice, therefore, it has been proven that assigning the supply function to purchasing professionals, properly trained and charged with the appropriate responsibilities and authority, can contribute more efficiently and effectively to organizational goals and strategies than assigning supply responsibilities to those for whom supply is a secondary responsibility. Consequently, this chapter addresses the organizational issues faced by supply professionals.

Objectives of Purchasing/Supply Management

The standard statement of the overall objectives of the purchasing function is that it should obtain the *right materials* (meeting quality requirements), in the *right quantity,* for delivery at the *right time* and *right place,* from the *right source* (a supplier who is reliable and will meet its commitments in a timely fashion), with the *right service* (both before and after the sale), and at the *right price* in the short and long term. The purchasing decision maker might be likened to a juggler, attempting to keep several balls in the air at the same time, for the purchaser must achieve these seven *rights* simultaneously. It is not acceptable to buy at the lowest price if the goods delivered are unsatisfactory from a quality/performance standpoint, or if they arrive two weeks behind schedule, causing a shutdown of a production line. On the other hand, the *right* price may be a much higher than normal price if the item in question is an emergency requirement on which the buyer cannot afford the luxury of adhering to the normal lead time. The purchasing decision maker attempts to balance the often-conflicting objectives and makes trade-offs to obtain the optimum mix of these seven rights.

Nine Goals of Purchasing

A more specific statement of the overall goals of purchasing would include the following nine goals:

1. *Provide an uninterrupted flow of materials, supplies, and services required to operate the organization.* Stock-outs or late deliveries of materials, components and services can be extremely costly in terms of lost production, lower revenues and profits, and diminished customer goodwill. For example, (1) an automobile producer

cannot complete the car without the purchased tires; (2) an airline cannot keep its planes flying on schedule without purchased fuel; (3) a hospital cannot perform surgery without purchased surgical tools; and (4) an office cannot be used without purchased maintenance services.

Minimum Inventory

2. *Keep inventory investment and loss at a minimum.* One way to ensure an uninterrupted material flow is to keep large inventory banks. But inventory assets require use of capital that cannot be invested elsewhere, and the cost of carrying inventory may be 20 percent to 50 percent of its value per year. For example, if purchasing can support operations with an inventory investment of $10 million instead of $20 million, at an annual inventory carrying cost of 30 percent, the $10 million reduction in inventory represents a savings of $3 million, in addition to freeing $10 million in working capital.

Improve Quality

3. *Maintain and improve quality.* To produce the desired product or service, a certain quality level is required for each material input; otherwise the end product or service will not meet expectations or will result in higher-than-acceptable costs. The internal cost to correct a substandard quality material input could be huge. For example, a spring assembled into the braking system of a diesel locomotive costs less than $5. However, if the spring turns out to be defective when the locomotive is in service, the replacement cost is in the thousands of dollars, caused by tear down required to replace the spring, the lost revenue to the railroad because the locomotive is not in service, and the possible loss of locomotive reorders. The need to improve supplier quality continually so our products and services can compete effectively on a worldwide basis has caused renewed attention to purchasing's quality objective.

Develop Suppliers

4. *Find or develop competent suppliers.* In the final analysis, the success of the purchasing department depends on its skill in locating or developing suppliers, analyzing supplier capabilities, selecting the appropriate supplier, and then working with that supplier to obtain continuous improvements. Only if the final selection results in suppliers who are both responsive and responsible will the firm obtain the items and services it needs at the lowest ultimate cost. For example, if a computer system is purchased from a supplier who later goes out of business and is not able to perform the long-term maintenance, modification, and updating of the system, the initial favorable price turns out to be a very high life-cycle cost, due to the supplier's inability to make good on the original commitment.

Standardize

5. *Standardize, where possible, the items bought.* The best item possible, from an overall company viewpoint, for the intended application should always be bought. However, supply should constantly strive to standardize its capital equipment, materials, maintenance repair,

and operating (MRO) and services purchases wherever and whenever possible. For materials, standardization can provide opportunities for lower prices through volume purchase agreements and lower inventory and tracking costs while maintaining service levels. In the case of capital equipment, standardization results in reduction in MRO inventories and reduced costs for training staff on equipment operation and maintenance.

Achieve Lowest Total Cost

6. *Purchase required items and services at lowest total cost.* The purchasing activity in the typical organization represents the largest share of that organization's total costs. Consequently, the profit-leverage effect of the purchasing activity, as discussed in the previous chapter, can be very significant. The most convenient method to compare competing proposals from suppliers is on the basis of price. However, the responsibility of the purchasing function is to obtain the needed goods and services at the lowest total cost of ownership, which necessitates consideration of other factors, such as quality levels, warranty costs, inventory and spare parts requirements, downtime, etc., which in the long term might have a greater cost impact on the organization than the original purchase price.

Develop Cross-Functional Relationships

7. *Achieve harmonious, productive working relationships with other functional areas within the organization.* The actions of supply managers cannot be effectively accomplished without the cooperation of other departments and individuals within the organization. For example, operations must provide purchasing with information concerning volumes and delivery dates in a timely fashion if purchasing is expected to locate competent suppliers and make advantageous purchase agreements. Engineering and operations must be willing to consider the possible economic advantages of using substitutes and different suppliers. Purchasing must work closely with quality control in determining inspection procedures for incoming materials, in communicating to suppliers the changes needed in the event that quality problems are found, and assisting in evaluating the performance of current suppliers. Suppliers expect to be paid on schedule and the accounts payable department must adhere to agreements with suppliers regarding supplier payment terms in order to maintain good long-term supplier relations. Furthermore, purchasing should expect to work with other functions, such as engineering, marketing and operations, on cross-functional teams involved with a wide variety of projects, ranging from product design to cost reduction, and quality or delivery improvement initiatives.

Reduce Administrative Costs

8. *Accomplish the purchasing objectives at the lowest possible level of administrative costs.* It takes resources to operate the purchasing department: salaries, communications expenses, supplies, travel costs, computer costs, and accompanying overhead. If purchasing procedures are not efficient, purchasing administrative costs will be

excessive. The objectives of purchasing should be achieved as efficiently and economically as possible. If the firm is not realizing its purchasing objectives due to inadequate analysis and planning, perhaps additional personnel or streamlined processes are needed. But supply managers should be continually alert to improvements possible in purchasing methods, procedures, and techniques. For example, opportunities to reduce transaction costs include automating requisition systems through e-mail and company intranet systems, and using purchasing cards and electronic ordering systems for small value purchases. Companies with efficient purchasing processes can create competitive advantage through reduced costs, improved flexibility and reaction time, while allowing supply personnel to concentrate on value-added activities.

**Improve
Competitive
Position**

9. *Improve the organization's competitive position.* Supply relationships must seek to provide competitive advantage. Securing a low-cost source of supply represents one area where supply can help the organization gain a competitive edge. However, other opportunities exist, such as access to new technologies, flexible delivery arrangements, fast response times, access to high-quality products or services and product design and engineering assistance. Companies that are successful in the long run must constantly look for opportunities in the supply chain to provide a superior value proposition for their customers, and supply represents a key area for such opportunities. Chapter 18 discusses the potential contributions of purchasing and supply management to the overall strategy of the organization and specific internal supply strategies for strengthening the organization's competitive position.

Purchasing's Prime Decision Authority

Four Key Areas   The purchasing/supply department must have prime decision authority in four key areas if it is to contribute effectively to organizational goals and strategies. In organizations using cross-functional sourcing teams, the team itself may exercise these prerogatives in its role as decision maker. However, many organizations do not use teams and the purchasing/supply department must then have the prime decision authority in these areas:

Select the Supplier. Purchasing/supply should be the expert in knowing, or determining, which supplier has the capability to provide the needed products or services and how to analyze supplier reliability.

Use Whichever Pricing Method is Appropriate. This also includes determining the total cost of ownership in order to determine the optimal price and terms of the agreement. This is one of the main expertise areas of purchasing; it must have room to maneuver if it is to achieve the lowest ultimate price and total cost of ownership.

Question the Specifications. Purchasing should have the right to question specifications and to suggest substitutes that will do the same job, and it has the responsibility to bring these alternatives to the attention of the user or requisitioner. The final decision on accepting a substitute will be made by the user.

Monitor Contacts with Potential Suppliers. Purchasing must be in the communication loop with potential suppliers. When users contact a potential supplier directly, without purchasing's knowledge, this provides the supplier with an opportunity to influence the product or service specifications to the supplier's advantage. Alternatively, requisitioners sometimes make commitments to suppliers that prevent purchasing from arriving at agreements that will give the buying firm the best value. If supplier technical personnel need to talk directly with engineering or operating personnel in the buyer's firm, purchasing should be involved and monitor the outcome.

These areas of prime purchasing responsibilities and authority should be established as matters of company policy, approved by the chief executive officer, so that purchasing can play its proper role on the management team. Of course, should unique expertise exist elsewhere in the organization, purchasing managers should ensure such expertise is properly exploited to the organization's advantage.

Organizational Structures

Managing the balance between the competitive environment, corporate strategy, and organizational structure is an ongoing process for every company. Senior management selects strategies designed to address competitive challenges and adopts an appropriate corporate organizational structure to complement the company's strategy.

Compared to organizations of the past, corporate organization structures are leaner and flatter and are more adaptive and flexible. Rigid functional structures have been replaced with a greater dependence on cross-functional teams that overlay the functional organization to push decisions lower in the organizational hierarchy.

Almost every company has a separate supply function as part of its organizational structure. A study done by the Center for Advanced Purchasing Studies (CAPS) in 2000, *Major Structural Changes in Supply Organizations,* found, that in large companies, supply organizational structures had to be congruent with the overall corporate organizational structure.[1] In other words, the

---

[1]Michiel R. Leenders, and P. Fraser Johnson, *Major Structural Changes in Supply Organizations* (Tempe, AZ: Center for Advanced Purchasing Studies, 2000).

The CPO's Challenge

chief purchasing officer (CPO) does not normally have full freedom to select the organizational structure that he or she might want for the supply function. Rather, the challenge for the CPO is to manage the supply organization to deliver the maximum benefits within the predefined structure. For example, a chief executive might decide that a decentralized organizational structure is appropriate in order to allow flexibility in responding to customer requirements. In such a situation, the supply organization would also be decentralized to the various business units to fit the corporate organizational model.

The organizational structure of the supply function influences how purchasing executes its responsibilities, how it works with other areas of the firm, and the skills and capabilities needed by the supply personnel. Regardless of the structure adopted, work must be assigned to ensure the efficient and effective delivery of goods and services to the organization. This requires managing personnel and delegating responsibilities. Managing the people in the supply organization to their full potential can represent one of the most significant challenges for most companies.

Organization for Purchasing and Supply Management

Once the corporate organizational structure is set, no matter what organizational design is chosen, delegation takes place within it. Whether the organization structure is based on functions, products or business processes is immaterial; what really matters is that work must be assigned and executed in accordance with strategic plans and organizational goals. It follows logically that organizational planning and delegation are important segments of the integration of strategic goals and organizational designs.

Key Aspects of Supply Organizational Design

The following sections describe the key aspects of supply organizational design, including the role of the chief purchasing officer, purchasing status in the organization and its reporting relationship, purchasing relationships with other areas of the firm, and specialization in the purchasing function.

The Chief Purchasing Officer (CPO)

The chief purchasing officer's responsibilities may be divided and apportioned among subofficials and departments, but the functional responsibility and authority of the chief purchasing officer (CPO) should be definitely recognized. Moreover, functionalization implies that all the responsibilities reasonably involved in the purchasing function must be given to the CPO, covering the relevant supply network links as well as the full range of organizational needs. The essential principle is that there are certain universally recognized duties pertinent to this function and that these duties should definitely be placed in a separate group equal in status with the other major functions of the organization.

TABLE 2–1   **Title of the Chief Purchasing Officer**

Title of CPO	*Percent of Firms*
Purchasing Agent	0%
Materials Manager	3
Director of Materials	6
VP of Materials Management	6
Manager of Purchasing	14
VP of Purchasing	18
Director of Purchasing	22
Other	31

The individual who holds the top purchasing position in a large organization in North America probably will have the title of Director of Purchasing, Vice President of Purchasing, or Manager of Purchasing. The title of Purchasing Agent rarely is used in large organizations for the CPO, although it is not unusual for the Purchasing Agent title to be used for people in mid- to lower-level buying positions in large firms or for the CPO at small and medium size firms. Table 2–1 shows the titles used for the CPOs in 308 large firms in the 1995 CAPS study.[2]

The CPOs in the 1995 CAPS study tended to be well educated, with 94 percent of them holding a college degree, including 39 percent with a graduate degree. These numbers are almost the same as those from an earlier CAPS study in 1988.[3]

Purchasing Reporting Relationships

Purchasing's Status in the Organization

The executive to whom the CPO reports gives a good indication of the status of purchasing and the degree to which it is emphasized within the organization. If the chief purchasing officer has vice presidential status and reports to the CEO, this indicates that purchasing has been recognized as a top management function. The lower that purchasing reports in the organization, the less influence supply is likely to have on corporate strategy.

Table 2–2 shows the reporting relationship of purchasing in close to 300 major organizations.[4] In many firms, purchasing reports to the executive immedi-

---

[2]Harold E. Fearon and Michiel R. Leenders, *Purchasing's Organizational Roles and Responsibilities* (Tempe, AZ: Center for Advanced Purchasing Studies, 1995).

[3]Harold E. Fearon, *Purchasing Organizational Relationships* (Tempe, AZ: Center for Advanced Purchasing Studies, 1988).

[4]Harold E. Fearon and Michiel R. Leenders, *Purchasing's Organizational Roles and Responsibilities* (Tempe, AZ: Center for Advanced Purchasing Studies, 1995).

TABLE 2–2   Purchasing Reporting Relationships, 1988 and 1995

	Percent of Firms	
Position to Whom the CPO Reports	*1988*	*1995*
President	16%	16%
Executive VP	19	15
Senior VP/Group VP	*	19
Financial VP	7	10
Manufacturing/Operations VP	24	15
Materials/Logistics VP	8	7
Engineering VP	1	1
Administrative VP	13	9
Other (many of whom were VPs)	12	8

*Category not identified in study

ately in charge of the manufacturing function, since the major share of purchasing activity is directed at satisfying production requirements. In other firms, purchasing might report to an administrative vice president along with MIS, personnel, and other functions common to all departments. Or, purchasing may report to the chief financial officer, based on immediate impact on cash flows and the large number of dollars tied up in inventory. In a heavily engineering-oriented firm, the reporting relationship might be to the chief of engineering to get closer communication and coordination on product specification and quality control matters.

Factors that influence the level at which the purchasing function is placed in the organizational structure cover a broad spectrum. Among the major ones are:

Factors Influencing Purchasing's Level in the Organization

1. The amount of purchased material and outside services costs as a percentage of either total costs or total income of the organization. A high ratio emphasizes the importance of effective performance of the purchasing function.

2. The nature of the products or services acquired. The acquisition of complex components or extensive use of subcontracting represents a difficult purchasing problem.

3. The extent to which supply and suppliers can provide competitive advantage.

The important consideration in determining to whom purchasing should report relates to where it will be most effective in realizing its contribution to the organization's objectives. Purchasing should report at a level high enough in the organization so that the key supply aspects of strategic managerial decisions will receive proper consideration.

Supply Relationships with Other Areas of the Firm

Purchasing must have a close working relationship with several other areas of the firm. For example, it depends on operations to provide realistic plans so that purchases can be made within normal supplier lead times to obtain the best ultimate value. It depends on engineering to evaluate the cost, quality and delivery advantages of using alternate materials. It depends on marketing/sales for long-term sales forecasts so that realistic material supply strategies can be developed. It depends on accounting to pay invoices in a timely fashion to take advantage of cash discounts and maintain good supplier relationships. In addition, if organized as separate departments and not a responsibility of purchasing, close cooperation is needed between receiving, stores, inventory control, traffic, and investment recovery, since they all impact on the ability of purchasing to do an effective job.

This is not a one-way street. The other functions within the firm have a right to expect that their supply needs will be met in a timely and cost-effective manner. Also, they expect to get reliable and timely information, as needed, from purchasing.

Cross-Functional Cooperation Is Essential

In organizations anxious to explore the full benefits of supply chain management innovations, cross-functional cooperation is essential. Focusing on total organizational success instead of functional territories directs everyone's attention to external customer satisfaction. Purchasing and supply expertise is vital in effective supply chain management and is more likely to be appreciated by the other team players than in the more traditional functional "silo" context.

Nevertheless, it is useful to examine some of the interfaces between purchasing and the key relationships with other functions in the organization.

Purchasing and Design Engineering. Close to 80 percent of the value of any given requirement is established during the first few phases in the standard acquisition process: recognition of need and translation of needs into commercial equivalents. Therefore, close cooperation between design engineering and purchasing to assure proper specifications is essential. The design needs to be manufacturable, but also procurable and appropriate to end customer needs in value and satisfaction. It is obvious that such close liaison also needs the proper involvement of marketing, operations, and finance/accounting to recognize these opportunities and constraints. It is during the design phase that all of these varied interests need to be appropriately incorporated, something that is unlikely to happen unless the various functional experts can represent their points of view well and are able to work effectively as a team. Too frequently, the failure to include supply considerations properly at the design stages results in inadequate product or service performance, costly delays, rework and end user dissatisfaction. A recent survey of both design engineers and purchasers working within the same organization disclosed that close cooperation between these two groups still has some ways to go. Table 2–3 presents the results.[5]

Importance of Cooperation at the Design Stage

---

[5]Design News/Purchasing Survey, *Purchasing,* May 1, 1997, pp. 32S17–32S17.

TABLE 2–3 **Purchasing and Design Engineering Relationship**

	Responses	
	Purchasers	Design Engineers
How much do purchasing and engineering interact during design?		
Extensively	42%	22%
Moderately	58	69
Not at all	0	9
At what stage do you work with your engineering/purchasing department?[†]		
Concept stage	54	33
Initial stage	55	68
When design is complete and approved	19	38
Don't work with them	2	5
What does engineering expect from purchasing?[†]		
Supplier qualification	84	65
Supplier selection	84	62
Price negotiation	91	91
Delivery terms negotiation	84	82
Quality problem resolution	74	48
What does purchasing expect from engineering?[†]		
Detailed parts specifications	100	95
Performance specifications	77	80
Supplier recommendations	45	67
Supplier selection	16	36
Who makes the initial contact with suppliers in a design project?[†]		
Engineering	55	77
Purchasing	45	29
Who has final approval of suppliers for product design?		
Engineering	17	35
Purchasing	19	8
Joint approval	64	57

[†]Totals add up to more than 100% due to multiple responses.

Integrated Logistics Is the Challenge

Purchasing and Operations. In most organizations, close purchasing-operations coordination is essential to operational excellence. In manufacturing companies, especially, the total task of integrated logistics—meeting end-customer demands on the one side and using the supply networks on the other, while managing material and information flow, equipment, people and space effectively—represents an incredible challenge. Meeting quality, delivery, quantity, cost, flexibility, and continuity objectives profitably and competitively requires a great deal of strategic as well as tactical skills of both operations and supply managers.

Purchasing and Marketing/Sales. Since purchasing and marketing are mirror images of each other, it stands to reason that there may be benefits

Purchasing and Marketing Are Mirror Images

from greater integration of the two functions. Although research indicates that purchasing is not typically included in marketing planning, purchasing and marketing often serve on new product development teams in organizations. Purchasing can offer information on current and future market conditions and negotiation expertise, and marketing can keep purchasing up-to-date on marketing campaigns, special promotions, and sales forecasts, and involve purchasing in meetings with end customers to help purchasing better understand customer needs. One study identified negotiation and customer service as two critical success factors in *both* buying and selling, and a good place to begin gaining the benefits of shared training.[6]

Goal Congruence Needed

Purchasing and Accounting/Finance. Purchasing and accounting/finance interact in the areas of accounts payable, planning, and budgeting. Purchasers often complain that accounting focuses too much on the bottom line and not enough on meeting the payment terms of the contract. The buying organization is not living up to the terms of the agreement if it fails to pay invoices in a timely manner. Improved communication between purchasing and accounting/finance and greater goal congruence can help to alleviate some of the problems. Purchasing can help finance by providing funds flow forecasts, focusing on inventory minimization and providing market information.

Specialization within the Purchasing/Supply Function

Four Areas of Specialization

If the purchasing organization is to contribute well to organizational goals and objectives, it needs to be staffed by professionals with clearly defined responsibilities. Specialization within the purchasing department allows staff to develop expertise in particular areas and may require the creation of specialized groups within the supply organizational structure. Obviously, in a small firm, where there is a one-person purchasing department, no such specialization is possible. Most large purchasing organizations consist of four general areas of specialization: sourcing and commodity management, materials management, administration, and purchasing research.

Sourcing and Commodity Management. These personnel locate potential suppliers, analyze supplier capabilities, select suppliers, and determine prices, terms, and conditions of supplier agreements; they create contracts and purchase orders. This activity is normally further specialized by type of commodity to be purchased; such as raw materials (which may be further specialized); fuels; capital equipment; office equipment and supplies; and MRO supplies. Figure 2–1 presents a job description for a commodity specialist at Deere & Company.

---

[6]Alvin J. Williams, Larry Giunipero and Tony L. Henthorne, "The Cross-Functional Imperative: The Case of Marketing and Purchasing," *International Journal of Purchasing and Materials Management,* Summer 1994, p. 33.

FIGURE 2–1

Commodity Specialist Job Description for Deere & Company

Job Title: Commodity Specialist

Department: Supply Management

Job Function: Locate sources for and procure materials, products, supplies or services to support the assigned commodity requirements of the enterprise. Manage the relationships with suppliers.

Primary Duties:

1. Manage source selection and development through a team process, including the evaluation of cost, quality and manufacturing systems.
2. Develop and manage internal and external supplier/customer relationships, including strategic alliances where appropriate.
3. Lead and/or participate in simultaneous engineering teams; facilitate the integration of suppliers into the product delivery process (PDP).
4. Evaluate the cost effectiveness of designs, procure tooling, and qualify processes to assure the product meets specifications.
5. Make recommendations for design change and/or influence design through personal or supplier involvement.
6. Develop and execute supply management strategies to manage cost, quality, and continuous improvement.
7. Develop material control and logistics objectives.
8. Act as a primary communications link between tactical and strategic purchasing functions and business units; participate in team activities.

Project Buying. A variation of commodity management is project buying, where the specialization of buying and negotiation is based on specific end products or projects, requiring the buyer to be intimately familiar with all aspects of the project from beginning to end. Project buying might be used in the purchasing organization of a large general contractor, where the purchasing for each job is part of a self-contained, temporary organization. At the completion of the project, the buyer then would be reassigned to another project. The United States Defense Acquisition University trains special project managers who are responsible for the proper acquisition and development of new military equipment initiatives. Such projects may last as long as 20 years.

Materials Management. This group manages the contract after it is signed and directs the flow of materials and services from the supplier, and keeps track of the supplier's delivery and quality commitments so as to avoid any disruptive surprises. If problems develop, the materials management group pressures and assists the supplier to resolve them. Materials management activities are frequently handled at the local plant or office level and involve regular communication with suppliers concerning requirements, such as order quantities and delivery dates. Figure 2–2 presents a job description for a supply management planner.

Administration. This group handles the physical preparation and routing

FIGURE 2–2

Supply Management Planner Job Description for Deere & Company

Job Title: Supply Management Planner

Department: Supply Management

Job Function: To expedite, schedule and/or analyze requirements for purchased materials in accordance with established requirements and inventory control criteria. May interact with suppliers to establish procedural agreements, obtain delivery commitments, and resolve quality problems.

Primary Duties:

1. Manages specific supplier performance and feedback, along with managing day-to-day business plan and relationships with supplier.
2. Plans and/or executes inventory goals by product/supplier and plans/develops delivery system to meet material control objectives (i.e., JIT delivery, P.O.U.D., EDI).
3. Schedules material based on requirements, and expedites deliveries that are delinquent or expected to be delinquent. Tracks and resolves problems with inbound shipments.
4. Interprets systems output to determine items requiring follow-up to suppliers on materials ordered to assure on-time delivery.
5. Involved with the day-to-day problem resolution/corrective action with suppliers; to scrap, return, reclaim or replace rejected material. Responsible to bring products within specifications.
6. Acts as the primary communications link between tactical and strategic purchasing functions and business unit; participates in supply management team activities.
7. Costs and implements current part revisions, including tooling, as part of the decision-processing activity. Also reads and reacts to engineering decisions.
8. Conducts price/economic order quantity analysis and compares multiple quotes, including piece price, freight, duty, performance systems and supplier rating. Also investigates invoice price errors.

of the formal purchase documents, manages the department budget, keeps the necessary data required to operate the department, and prepares reports needed by top management and purchasing. These personnel will likely handle operation of the information systems, including EDI and business-to-business Internet systems.

Purchasing Research. Purchasing researchers work on special projects relating to the collection, classification, and analysis of data needed to make better purchasing decisions. Activities include studies on use of alternate materials, long-range demand, price and supply forecasts, and analysis of what it should cost an efficient supplier to produce and deliver a product or service.

This group is also responsible for performing benchmarking studies. For example, the global purchasing processes and systems group at Cable and Wireless plc, in the United Kingdom, benchmarks its purchasing processes to identify opportunities to improve its supply systems.[7]

Purchasing Activities and Responsibilities

In the last decades, purchasing has assumed greater responsibilities in a wide range of areas, including those not seen as traditional purchasing activities, as companies strive to leverage profit opportunities and create competitive advantage through their supply practices. The 1988 *Purchasing Organizational Relationships*[8] study done by the Center for Advanced Purchasing Studies (CAPS) and the follow-up study, *Purchasing's Organizational Roles and Responsibilities*[9] done in 1995, found that the role of the purchasing department increased over the seven-year period between the two studies. (See Table 2–4.)

The 1995 CAPS study on roles and responsibilities also addressed the role of purchasing in major corporate initiatives, in an attempt to measure the level of involvement of the function in strategic issues. In terms of corporate procurement, outsourcing is the one area in which purchasing was found to have above a moderate involvement and the expectation for a significantly increased role.

In terms of non-supply-oriented corporate activities, purchasing still has a significant way to go before it is meaningfully involved. It was found that purchasing's involvement in information systems planning, corporate strategic planning, new product development, risk management, and finan-

---

[7]Michiel R. Leenders, and P. Fraser Johnson, *Major Changes in Supply Chain Responsibilities* (Tempe, AZ: Center for Advanced Purchasing Studies, 2001).

[8]Harold E. Fearon, *Purchasing Organizational Relationships* (Tempe, AZ: Center for Advanced Purchasing Studies, 1988).

[9]Harold E. Fearon and Michiel R. Leenders, *Purchasing's Organizational Roles and Responsibilities* (Tempe, AZ: Center for Advanced Purchasing Studies, 1995).

TABLE 2–4 **Functions that Report to Purchasing**

Function	1988	1995
Scrap/surplus disposal	57	63
Materials and purchasing research	*	60
Inbound traffic	40	51
Stores/warehousing	34	41
Inventory control	37	41
Material planning	*	40
Outbound traffic	31	39

*Category not identified in study

Limited Involvement in Non-Supply-Oriented Activities

cial and technology planning is low, and its involvement in governmental relations, countertrade, marketing planning, and corporate mergers and alliances is slight.[10] Interestingly, respondents to the survey indicated an expectation of significant increases in future involvement in corporate activities (except for governmental relations). Whether or not reality will bear this expectation out only time will tell. For the present, purchasing is not perceived as the strategic player many professionals in the field feel it should be.

Purchasing Activities

Today's supply management organization has a great many more responsibilities then the traditional "buying" activities once associated with the function. The activities handled by the supply function vary from firm to firm, even within the same industry. However, regardless of company size, there are a number of activities common to most supply organizations. These are provided in Table 2–5.

In addition to the responsibilities listed in Table 2–5, purchasing may have responsibilities for a number of other activities such as: stores and warehousing, in-plant materials movement, quality assurance, and accounts payable.

Purchasing's Role in Non-Traditional Purchases

In some organizations, purchasing activities are limited to production-related materials and services, leaving responsibility for nonproduction materials and services in the hands of users. Nonproduction purchases can represent considerable annual expenditures at most companies and includes computers and software, travel, real estate, construction services, utilities and insurance. The CAPS 1995 report on nontraditional purchases also confirmed purchasing's low involvement in many areas of corporate procurement. Fifty-nine percent of total purchase dollars were spent by departments other than purchas-

---

[10]Harold E. Fearon and Michiel R. Leenders, *Purchasing's Organizational Roles and Responsibilities* (Tempe, AZ: Center for Advanced Purchasing Studies, 1995).

TABLE 2–5   Purchasing Activities

Area of Responsibility	Activities
Purchasing/Buying	• Creating contracts and supply agreements for materials, services, and capital items • Managing key purchasing processes related to supplier selection, supplier evaluation, negotiation, and contract management
Purchasing Research	• Identifying better techniques and approaches to supply management, including benchmarking processes and systems • Identifying medium- and long-term changes in markets, and developing appropriate commodity plans to meet future needs • Identifying supply chain trends and opportunities for better materials and services
Inventory Control	• Managing inventories and expediting material delivery • Establishing and monitoring vendor-managed inventory systems
Transportation	• Managing inbound and outbound transportation services, including carrier selection
Environmental and Investment Recovery/Disposal	• Managing supply chain related activities to assure compliance with legal and regulatory requirements and with company environmental policies • Managing disposal of surplus materials and equipment
Forecasting and Planning	• Production planning and forecasting of short-, medium- and long-term requirements
Outsourcing and Subcontracting	• Evaluating potential suppliers, negotiating contracts • Supporting the transition from internal production to external supply and vice versa
Nonproduction/Nontraditional Purchases	• Managing cost-effective delivery of nonproduction and nontraditional purchases, such as office supplies, security services, janitorial services, advertising and insurance
Supply Chain Management	• Implementing and managing key supplier relationships and supplier partnerships, including supplier development and participation on cross-functional teams • Developing strategies that use the supply network to provide value to end customers and contribute to organizational goals

ing, including large amounts for capital equipment, utilities, and insurance.[11] Organizations should not ignore the opportunities to use the skills of their purchasing group in the acquisition of nontraditional materials and services.

The Influence of Industry Sector on Purchasing Activities

Industry sector influences purchasing responsibilities. Firms that manufacture discrete goods face a significant number of dynamic, product-related pressures that affect the purchasing function which are less likely to occur

---

[11]Harold E. Fearon and William A. Bales, *Purchasing of Nontraditional Goods and Services* (Tempe, AZ: Center for Advanced Purchasing Studies, 1995).

Purchasing Plays Key Role in Discrete Goods Industries

in commodity-oriented process industries. These pressures include changing consumer preferences, product innovation, and relatively short product life cycles. Electronic equipment, automobile manufacturers, apparel and furniture industries are all examples of discrete goods industries. For example, automobile manufacturers update most car models every four years, working with key suppliers several years in advance as part of the product development process. Purchased materials and services also represent a high percentage of the cost of sales for firms in discrete goods industries. For example, purchased materials and services can represent 80 percent of the average cost of an automobile. Consequently, firms in discrete goods industries are likely to have purchasing departments that play a key role in each step in the materials cycle, from product design to production.

Purchasing Plays a Support Role in Process Industries

The role of purchasing in process industry firms, such as oil and gas, chemicals, glass and steel industries, is typically different compared to firms in discrete goods industries. Many process industry firms have two supply organizations: a specialized supply group, such as a commodity trading department, that frequently handles purchasing for important raw materials; and a purchasing group responsible for the acquisition of materials, supplies, and services that support the operation of facilities. For example, it is common practice for crude oil acquisition in most large integrated oil companies to be handled by a commodity trading group, while other purchases are handled by the purchasing organization. As a result, although the cost of purchased materials and services might represent a substantial portion of the total cost of sales, the purchasing function for firms within processing industries is frequently excluded from the acquisition of the single most important raw material.

In the public, not-for-profit and service sectors, most purchases are for end use within the organization itself, with the exception of purchases for resale, such as in distribution and retail. In fast-growing organizations, capital purchases may represent a large percentage of total acquisition expenditures.

Supply Organizational Structures for Single Business Unit Firms

The size and activities of the purchasing function in a single business unit organization will depend on a number of factors, such as the size of the company and the nature of its business. Figure 2–3 provides an example of a purchasing organization in a typical medium-sized, single business unit enterprise. Obviously, in small companies where the purchasing staff consists of only one or two individuals, the staff is expected to be flexible in terms of their capabilities and skills. Specialization will occur as the organization gets larger and the company can afford to hire additional supply personnel.

FIGURE 2–3

Example of a Typical Purchasing Organization in a Medium-Sized Company

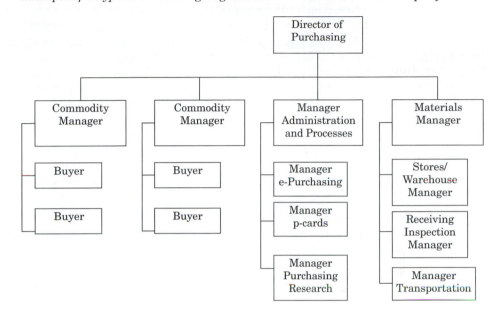

Supply Organizational Structures for Multibusiness Unit Firms

Supply organizational options can be viewed as a continuum, centralized at one extreme and decentralized at the other. The overall corporate structure sets the framework for the purchasing structure, whether centralized, hybrid or decentralized. Each organization structure carries certain advantages while simultaneously offering certain disadvantages. Tables 2–6 and 2–7 summarize the potential advantages and disadvantages of decentralized and centralized purchasing organizational structures.[12]

Hybrid Purchasing Organizational Structures

It is clear from Tables 2–6 and 2–7 that the advantages and disadvantages of both centralized and decentralized supply organizational structures are significant. In multiplant/multibusiness unit organizations, different divisions or business units often sell different products or services requiring a different mix of purchased items. Often a profit-center management motivation and control technique is used in which the division manager is given

---

[12]Michiel R. Leenders, and P. Fraser Johnson, *Major Structural Changes in Supply Organizations* (Tempe, AZ: Center for Advanced Purchasing Studies, 2000).

TABLE 2–6   **Potential Advantages and Disadvantages of Centralization**

Advantages	Disadvantages
• Greater buying specialization	• Narrow specialization and job boredom
	• Lack of job flexibility
• Ability to pay for talent	• Corporate staff appears excessive
• Consolidation of requirements—*clout*	• Tendency to minimize legitimate differences in requirements
• Coordination and control of policies and procedures	• Lack of recognition of unique needs
• Effective planning and research	• Focus on corporate requirements, not on business unit strategic requirements
	• Most knowledge sharing one-way
• Common suppliers	• Even common suppliers behave differently in geographic and market segments
• Proximity to major organizational decision makers	• Distance from users
• Critical mass	• Tendency to create organizational silos
• Firm brand recognition and stature	• Customer segments require adaptability to unique situations
• Reporting line—*power*	• Top management not able to spend time on suppliers
• Strategic focus	• Lack of business unit focus
• Cost of purchasing low	• High visibility of purchasing costs

Capture Benefits of Both Structures

total responsibility for running the division, acts as president of an independent firm, and is judged by profits made by the division. Since material purchases are the largest single controllable cost of running the division and have a direct effect on its efficiency and competitive position, the profit-center manager may insist on having direct authority over purchasing. This has led firms to adopt decentralized-centralized purchasing, or a hybrid organizational structure, in which the purchasing function is partially centralized at the head office and partially decentralized to the business units. Often there is a corporate purchasing organization that works with the business unit purchasing departments in those tasks which are more effectively handled on a corporate basis: (1) establishing policies, procedures, controls, and systems, (2) recruiting and training of personnel, (3) coordinating the purchase of common-use items in which more "clout" is needed, (4) auditing purchasing performance, and (5) developing corporatewide supply strategies. Therefore, hybrid organizational structures attempt to capture the benefits of both centralized and decentralized structures by creating an organizational structure that is neither completely centralized nor decentralized. (See Figure 2–4)

TABLE 2–7   Potential Advantages and Disadvantages of Decentralization

Advantages	Disadvantages
• Easier coordination/communication with operating department	• More difficult to communicate among business units
• Speed of response	• Encourages users not to plan ahead
	• Operational versus strategic focus
• Effective use of local sources	• Too much focus on local sources—ignores better supply opportunities
	• No critical mass in organization for visibility/effectiveness—"whole person syndrome"
	• Lacks clout
• Business unit autonomy	• Suboptimization
	• Business unit preferences not congruent with corporate preferences
	• Small differences get magnified
• Reporting line simplicity	• Reporting at low level in organization
• Undivided authority and responsibility	• Limits functional advancement opportunities
• Suits purchasing personnel preference	• Ignores larger organization considerations
• Broad job definition	• Limited expertise for requirements
• Geographical, cultural, political, environmental, social, language, currency appropriateness	• Lack of standardization
• Hide the cost of supply	• Cost of supply relatively high

FIGURE 2–4

Potential Advantages of the Hybrid Structure

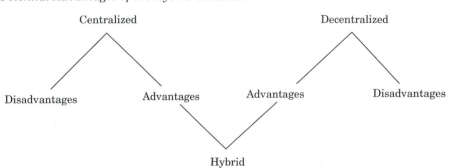

The popularity of the hybrid structure was reflected in the 1995 CAPS study, *Purchasing's Organizational Roles and Responsibilities.* It found that 68 percent of the firms reported using a hybrid structure, up from 61 percent in the 1988 CAPS study.[13] Meanwhile, the 1995 study also reported that firms using centralized supply structure declined from 27 percent to 22 percent, and the popularity of the decentralized structure declined from 12 percent to 10 percent.

Figure 2–5 provides one example of the hybrid organizational structure for the purchasing function at Thomson Multimedia, a large international consumer electronics manufacturer, whose brands include RCA.[14]

Managing Organizational Change in Purchasing

Firms frequently make major changes to their purchasing organizational structure. A finding from CAPS research on purchasing organizations was that, over a seven-year period, 41 percent had changed purchasing organization structures.[15]

CAPS conducted a study in 2000, in part, to understand: (1) Why are so many structural changes in supply organizations at large companies? and (2) If the hybrid organizational structure is theoretically so attractive, then why do so many large firms not use this structure and/or move out of it?[16] The results of the study had several important findings. First, the research found that each of the organizational structure changes studied was the result of a change in the overall corporate organizational structure. In none of the situations did the CPO have free choice to select the supply organizational structure that he or she deemed appropriate for the circumstances. Rather the supply organizational structure was forced to be congruent with **Supply** the overall corporate structure. The challenge for supply executives, there-**Structure** fore, was not to craft an organizational structure based on the needs of the **Follows** organization but rather expect to be handed an organizational structure by **Corporate** senior management. In these circumstances the management challenge be-**Structure** comes to maximize the benefits of the organizational structure while minimizing the disadvantages.

Change Secondly, there are a number of implementation issues that need to be **Management** considered when making a major organizational structure change in supply. **Required** Major organizational structure change affects the lives of many people and

---

[13]Harold E. Fearon and Michiel R. Leenders, *Purchasing's Organizational Roles and Responsibilities* (Tempe, AZ: Center for Advanced Purchasing Studies, 1995).

[14]Michiel R. Leenders, and P. Fraser Johnson, *Major Changes in Supply Chain Responsibilities* (Tempe, AZ: Center for Advanced Purchasing Studies, 2001).

[15]Johnson, P.F.; Leenders, M.R.; Fearon, H.E., "Evolving Roles and Responsibilities of Purchasing Organizations," *International Journal of Purchasing and Materials Management,* vol. 34, no. 1 (Winter 1998), pp. 2–11.

[16]Michiel R. Leenders, and P. Fraser Johnson, *Major Structural Changes in Supply Organizations* (Tempe, AZ: Center for Advanced Purchasing Studies, 2000).

FIGURE 2–5

Organization Structure of Thomson Multimedia

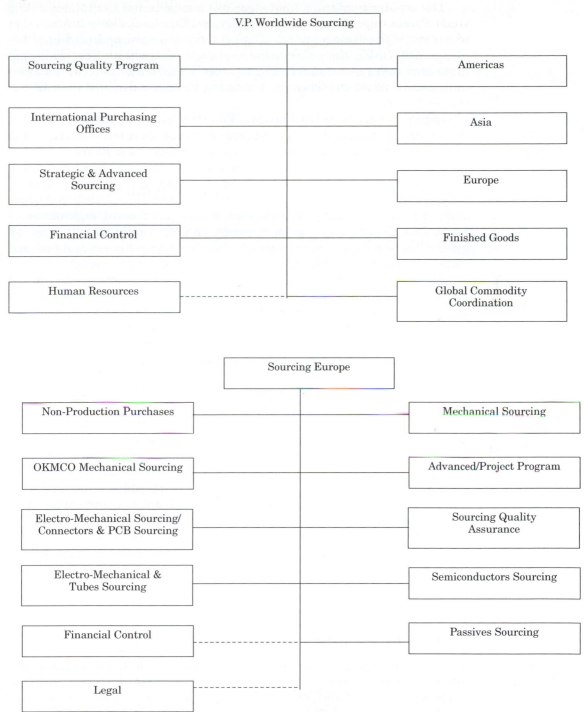

creates an atmosphere of apprehension among the staff. Implementing change places significant pressures on the CPO, who not only has to worry about managing the day-to-day affairs of the purchasing department but also implementing the organizational change successfully. The challenges associated with these issues frequently contribute to the need to seek assistance from consultants when implementing a major structural change.

Two Key Issues: Talent and Information Technology

Changes Toward Centralization. Two issues were identified concerning implementing structural changes toward centralization: sources of supply talent, and information technology. In the process of moving toward centralization, the source of supply talent at all levels of the supply function was a significant challenge. When moving out of the decentralized mode, the organization may not have experienced senior corporate-level supply personnel. How and where to develop such organizational talent represented an important implementation issue. Some firms placed a greater priority on CPO credibility within the organization, as opposed to previous supply experience. Others identified new CPOs with previous supply experience to handle the change process.

The move toward centralization also created implementation issues at the middle- and junior-level staff. The CAPS study found that a move toward increased centralization required the addition of staff with specialized skills in areas such as contracting. Quite often the existing supply talent in the decentralized organization was perceived to lack the required training or experience needed in the new centralized environment.

One Key Issue: Dismantling Supply

Changes Toward Decentralization. The CAPS research identified one implementation issue unique to the sites in the study moving toward decentralization: how to dismantle the centralized supply unit effectively. Several different approaches were identified in the study. For example, Ontario Hydro created a shared services function that was responsible for negotiating corporatewide agreements and establishing and maintaining corporate purchasing policies, while the business units were responsible for materials management activities. The approach taken by Hoechst was to create a separate legal entity, Hoechst Procurement International, which would also offer purchasing services to other companies on a fee-for-service basis. The key objective in both situations was to preserve at least some of the organization's core supply capabilities and talent, while adapting to the new structural requirements of the company.

Teams and Teaming

Reasons for Teams

The use of teams has become a popular approach in many companies. Teams are being used in a number of different functional areas and for a variety of purposes, such as quality, cost, or delivery improvement initiatives, product development, process engineering, and technology management.

Organizations seek to combine the flexibility of decentralized purchasing and the buying power and information sharing of centralized purchasing through the use of teams—a number of people working together on a common task. Purchasing teams can provide superior results, compared to individual efforts, as a result of the range of skills, knowledge, and capabilities of team members. They also promote interfunctional cooperation and communication, thereby facilitating consensus in the organization. A survey of senior purchasing executives identified "ability to work in teams" as one of the five most important skills required of a world-class purchasing/supply management professional.[17]

Teams can be project-oriented or ongoing. Project teams are brought together to achieve a specific goal or outcome, such as completion of a capital project or an e-commerce initiative. Ongoing teams continue indefinitely, such as a sourcing team that selects and manages supply relationships for a particular commodity or product.

Types of Supply Teams

Various types of purchasing and supply management teams are used, including cross-functional teams, teams with suppliers, teams with customers, teams with both suppliers and customers, supplier councils (key suppliers), purchasing councils (purchasing personnel only), commodity management teams (purchasing personnel only), and consortiums (pool buying with other firms). The 1995 CAPS study on organizational roles found that all these teaming techniques were used to some degree by the respondents, and their use was expected to increase, with the highest expected increase in teams with suppliers and cross-functional teams.[18] A Michigan State University (MSU) study found that 80 percent of firms studied planned to emphasize the use of cross-functional sourcing teams over the next three years.[19]

Cross-Functional Teams

Reasons for Cross-Functional Teams

Cross-functional teams consist of personnel from different functions brought together to achieve a specific task. Cross-functional team tasks can be a specified project or consist of a continuous assignment. The MSU research showed the five main reasons firms commit resources to cross-functional team development are to (1) achieve time-reduction targets, (2) get cross-boundary ownership of tasks and problems, (3) promote innovation and synergy, (4) improve organizational goal achievement, and (5) promote professional development of team members.

Three important cross-functional teams for purchasing are sourcing, new product development and commodity management.

---

[17]Larry C. Giunipero and Dawn H. Percy, "World-Class Purchasing Skills: An Empirical Investigation," *The Journal of Supply Chain Management,* Fall 2000, pp. 4–13.

[18]Harold E. Fearon and Michiel R. Leenders, *Purchasing's Organizational Roles and Responsibilities* (Tempe, AZ: Center for Advanced Purchasing Studies, 1995).

[19]Robert M. Monczka and Robert J. Trent, "An Action Plan for Creating Effective Teams," *NAPM Insights,* March 1993, p. 22.

TABLE 2–8 **Team Assignments**

Sourcing Team Assignment	Percentage of Teams Pursuing Assignment
Develop cost-reduction strategies	74%
Evaluate and select suppliers	73%
Support sourcing requirements for items with established production specifications	67%
Support sourcing requirements during new product development	56%
Perform supplier development activities	47%
Support product design	44%
Perform value analysis activities	40%
Develop local sourcing strategies	38%
Negotiate corporatewide purchase agreements	38%
Identify common purchased items between corporate business units	36%
Develop sourcing strategies for the entire business unit	36%
New technology development	34%
Develop corporatewide sourcing strategies	26%

Cross-Functional Sourcing Teams. A cross-functional sourcing team "consists of personnel from at least three functions brought together to achieve a purchasing- or material-related assignment. This includes assignments in which the team must consider purchasing goals or decisions involving supply base management."[20] Cross-functional sourcing teams can focus on a wide range of tasks. Table 2–8 lists the percentage of sourcing teams working on various assignments from a survey of 107 cross-functional sourcing teams at 18 U.S.-based companies.[21]

New Product Development Teams. Effective new product development processes can better an organization's competitive position. Cross-functional teams can benefit the product development process in a number of ways, including shorter development cycle times, improved quality, and reduced development costs. These goals are attained because the process is concurrent rather than sequential. Rather than each functional area performing its task and passing the project off to the next functional area, the key functional groups—usually design, engineering, manufacturing, quality assurance, purchasing, and marketing—work on the new-product development simultaneously. Because a large percentage of a product's cost is purchased mate-

Concurrent Processes Improve Competitive Position

---

[20]Robert J. Trent, "Understanding and Evaluating Cross-Functional Sourcing Team Leadership," *International Journal of Purchasing and Materials Management,* Fall 1996, p. 36.

[21]Robert J. Trent and Robert M. Monczka, "Effective Cross-Functional Sourcing Teams: Critical Success Factors," *International Journal of Purchasing and Materials Management,* Fall 1994, pp. 3–11.

rials, early supplier involvement is needed. A survey conducted by *Purchasing Magazine* found that 70 percent of respondents said that their company is involving purchasing in new product launch efforts, while 45 percent indicated that their company has plans to increase purchasing's involvement in new product design.[22]

Cross-Functional Teams at Harley-Davidson

One company that successfully uses cross-functional teams for sourcing and product development is Harley-Davidson, the motorcycle manufacturer. There is a different cross-functional team responsible for each line of Harley-Davidson motorcycles. The platform teams are responsible for the life cycle of their particular product line. Each platform team consists of a program manager who is generally from the design community, as well as a manufacturing lead, a purchasing lead, and a marketing lead. Once the platform team decides, based on information from many sources, what the general design and style of the bike will be, the project is then turned over to the company's engineering center of expertise. The center of expertise is a cross-functional team itself. It consists of purchasing professionals, engineers, suppliers and others who work together to integrate all design components in a cost-effective, high-quality manner. Once the design is done, the platform team is responsible for getting the end product into the hands of customers. It also is responsible for accumulating and analyzing field reports, surveys of owner satisfaction levels, and marketing information.[23]

Commodity Management Teams. Commodity management teams are formed when expenditures are high and the commodity is complex and important to success. These are generally permanent teams that provide increased expertise, more interdepartmental coordination and communication, better control over standardization programs, and increased communication with suppliers.

Cross-Functional Teams at Cessna Aircraft

Commodity management teams develop and implement commodity strategies aimed at achieving the lowest total cost of ownership. These teams engage in a number of activities, including supply base reduction, consolidation of requirements, supplier quality certification, managing deliveries and lead times, cost savings projects, and management of supplier relationships.

Cessna Aircraft Company created full-time cross-functional commodity teams as part of a major change in its supply organization. Each team had representatives from seven different functional areas – purchasing, manufacturing, engineering, product design engineering, reliability engineering, product support, and finance. The mandate of the commodity teams was to drive supplier improvements and integration of suppliers into Cessna's design and manufacturing processes. Each commodity management team had strategic plans that were tied to the CEO's strategic objectives and

---

[22]"Companies Get Purchasing Pros into the Design Stage," *Purchasing,* Aug. 24, 2000, p. 26.

[23]"How Harley-Davidson Uses Cross-Functional Teams," *Purchasing,* Nov. 4, 1999, p. 144.

were updated yearly. The plan provided the long-term objectives, short- and long-term targets, and key processes and resource process maps.[24]

Managing Cross-Functional Teams

Changing to a team-based workplace can represent a significant change for those involved and requires a significant level of commitment and training by both the company and the individual team members. A Michigan State University study of 108 cross-functional sourcing teams at 18 U.S. firms found that most teams failed to meet the performance expectations of team members and executive management.[25]

Research by Murphy and Heberling found that the organizations in their study that successfully implemented multidisciplinary teams adhered to the following eight principles:[26]

Eight Principles of Successful Teams

1. There was a cultural change throughout the organization, from top management to the individual worker.

2. They were product, or goal focused; organized for customer satisfaction rather than functional success.

3. Upfront planning involved all functional areas from the start.

4. They put the right people (right qualifications), in the right place (on a team that needed their skills), at the right time (when those skills were needed).

5. They relied upon teamwork, creating a sense of belonging to something special, and a high level of communication between functional areas.

6. They successfully empowered, with decisions being delegated and made at the appropriate level.

7. They used seamless management tools, with all functional members included as integral team members and project leaders responsible for the life of the entire project.

8. They achieved integration among all functional areas and various teams throughout the project life cycle.

Leading cross-functional teams presents a unique set of challenges for purchasers. For example, cross-functional sourcing teams bring together

---

[24]James P. Morgan, "Cessna Charts a Supply Chain Flight," *Purchasing,* Sep. 7, 2000, pp. 42–61.

[25]Robert M. Monczka and Robert J. Trent, "An Action Plan for Creating Effective Teams," *NAPM Insights,* March 1993, p. 22.

[26]David J. Murphy and Michael E. Heberling, "A Framework for Purchasing and Integrated Product Teams," *International Journal of Purchasing and Materials Management,* Summer 1996, pp. 11–19.

**Role of the
Team Leader**

personnel from a range of disciplines, such as engineering, operations, and sales. Furthermore, some personnel may only be assigned to the team temporarily, and team members may have other responsibilities that compete for their time and attention. Robert Trent conducted a study that examined the critical role that team leaders play and the challenges that they face in a cross-functional sourcing team environment. He identified ten responsibilities and requirements that a sourcing team leader must satisfy to be effective:[27]

1. Work with the team to establish and commit to performance goals
2. Secure individual member involvement and commitment
3. Manage internal team conflict
4. Help maintain team focus and direction
5. Secure required organizational resources
6. Prevent team domination by a member or function
7. Deal with internal and external obstacles confronting the team
8. Coordinate multiple tasks and manage the status of team assignments
9. Clarify and help define each member's role
10. Provide performance feedback to members

Teams with Supplier Participation

Supplier participation in cross-functional sourcing teams depends on the nature of the assignment. For example, it makes sense to include suppliers in teams assigned to develop supplier capabilities or improve supplier responsiveness, but not on teams assigned to evaluate and select new suppliers.

**Early Supplier
Involvement at
Boeing**

Involving suppliers in cross-functional teams at the product design stage can produce substantial benefits and is common in discrete goods manufacturing industries, such as automotive and consumer electronics. The development of the Boeing 777 commercial aircraft made extensive use of supplier participation on cross-functional teams, enabling successful design and production in record time. Automotive manufacturers periodically give suppliers primary responsibility for designing major components, such as seating systems.

Confidentiality is perhaps the biggest obstacle to supplier participation, particularly when new product design is involved. Some firms ask suppliers to sign confidentiality agreements to minimize the potential effect of this obstacle on the team's effectiveness.

---

[27]Robert J. Trent, "Understanding and Evaluating Cross-Functional Sourcing Team Leadership," *International Journal of Purchasing and Materials Management,* Fall 1996, pp. 29–36.

Teams with Customer Participation

End Customer Involvement in Teams

Some organizations include end customers in their teams, in an effort to truly be customer-driven. For example, when a commercial airframe maker designs a new passenger aircraft, it makes sense to have potential airline customers participate in the design team. They know best the characteristics a new aircraft must have from the airline perspective, given its anticipated passenger loads, route structures, maintenance plans, and passenger service strategies. However, research has found that purchasing does not participate very frequently on teams involving customers.[28]

Colocation of Purchasers with Internal Customers

Locating buyers with internal customers, for example engineering, can help to break down barriers between functions as individuals get to know, and learn to work with, each other. Also, internal customers are more likely to involve purchasing in decisions if the buyer is readily accessible when questions arise. Buyers can "sell" other departments on their worth by providing information on markets, suppliers, and specific commodities.

Supplier Councils

A Tool for Managing Supplier Relationships

A number of large firms, such as General Motors and Boeing, use supplier councils as a means of managing their supplier relationships. Supplier councils usually consist of 10 to 15 senior executives from the company's preferred supplier base, along with six to eight of the buying firm's top management. Supplier councils usually meet two to four times per year and deal with purchasing policy issues at the buying firm with the objectives of developing relationships and improving communication with the supply base. Supplier councils allow suppliers to be proactive participants in the supply management activities at the buying firm and can be useful forums to communicate strategies to key suppliers, identify problems with the supply base early on, and agree upon competitive targets in areas such as cost, quality, and delivery improvements.

Purchasing Councils

Purchasing councils are generally comprised of senior purchasing staff from the company and are established to facilitate coordination among the business units, divisions or plants. Many firms use purchasing councils as a means of sharing information among decentralized units, or coordinating activities focused on a specific problem that might involve several purchasing

---

[28]Harold E. Fearon and Michiel R. Leenders, *Purchasing's Organizational Roles and Responsibilities* (Tempe, AZ: Center for Advanced Purchasing Studies, 1995).

Corporate Purchasing Council at Wellman

groups. The goals of the council are to manage buyer-supplier relationships properly and to encourage continuous improvement.

A good example of a purchasing council is at Wellman, a manufacturer and distributor of polyester fibers and PET resins. Wellman had a decentralized purchasing organization, where plant purchasing reported to the local manager at each site. The corporate purchasing council was created, consisting of site purchasing leadership. It concentrated on standardizing purchasing processes, aggregating requirements and leveraging volume for lower prices, standardizing goods and services among sites to the fullest practical extent, and simplifying and streamlining the materials process. This included formulating annual business plans for purchasing, with specific objectives.

Consortiums

A purchasing consortium "consists of two or more independent organizations that join together, either formally or informally, or through an independent third party, for the purposes of combining their individual requirements for purchased materials, services and capital goods to leverage more value-added pricing, service, and technology from their external suppliers than could be obtained if each firm purchased goods and services alone."[29] Purchasing consortia are a form of collaborative purchasing which is used by both public and private sector organizations as a means of delivering a wider range of services at a lower total cost. Purchasing consortia can take one of several forms, ranging from informal groups that meet regularly to discuss purchasing issues, to the creation of formal centralized consortia for the purpose of managing members' supply activities.

Consortia are quite common in not-for-profit organizations, particularly educational institutions and health-care organizations. For example, a survey of 221 purchasing managers at community hospitals in the United States found that $128 billion, or about 72 percent of their total expenditures on supplies, services, and materials, were purchased through Group Purchasing Organizations (GPOs), such as AmeriNet and Premier Inc., in 1999.[30] A 1997 CAPS study on consortium purchasing in large private sector manufacturing and service organizations found that 28 of the 131 firms that responded to the survey, or 21 percent, were involved in one or more purchasing consortia.[31]

---

[29]T.E. Hendrick, *Purchasing Consortiums: Horizontal Alliances Among Firms Buying Common Goods and Services* (Tempe, AZ: Center for Advanced Purchasing Studies, 1997).

[30] "Group Purchasing Cut Hospital Costs in 1999," *Healthcare Financial Management,* p. 21.

[31]T.E. Hendrick, *Purchasing Consortiums: Horizontal Alliances Among Firms Buying Common Goods and Services* (Tempe, AZ: Center for Advanced Purchasing Studies, 1997).

Cost savings are a primary motivation for the creation and participation in purchasing consortia. Savings in the health-care field have been reported in the 10 percent to 15 percent range, while the respondents to the CAPS study reported average annual dollar savings of 13.4 percent.[32, 33] While cost is an important reason why firms use purchasing consortia, research has found that a number of other factors can also influence consortia use: opportunities for staff reductions, product and service standardization, improved supplier management capabilities, specialization of staff, better customer service, higher profile of the consortium, expanded role of purchasing, and transition of products through ABC categories (higher volumes of B and C category items).[34]

Concerns about Consortia

Despite the benefits, firms hesitate to participate in consortia as a result of concerns in the following areas.[35, 36]

- Anti-Trust Issues: For large firms, there may be concern that collaboration might be viewed as anti-competitive by the U.S. Department of Justice's Anti-Trust Division and/or the Federal Trade Commission. Frequently, however, safeguards can be put in place to address such regulatory issues.

- Concern that the consortium may become unmanageably large and coordination costs: The consortium organization is sometimes viewed as another layer of bureaucracy.

- Fear that if the consortium offers "open enrollment" that it will bring together buyers with widely diverse needs and philosophies towards buyer-seller relations, resulting in untenable complexity and disfunction.

- Fear that the competition might be allowed to join.

- Disclosure of sensitive information: Due in part to concerns that sensitive competitive information may fall into the hands of the competition, most items purchased through consortia are nonstrategic, such as MRO components and routine services.

---

[32] "Group Purchasing Cut Hospital Costs in 1999," *Healthcare Financial Management,* p. 21.

[33] T.E. Hendrick, *Purchasing Consortiums: Horizontal Alliances Among Firms Buying Common Goods and Services* (Tempe, AZ: Center for Advanced Purchasing Studies, 1997).

[34] P. Fraser Johnson, "The Pattern of Evolution in Public Sector Purchasing Consortia," *International Journal of Logistics: Research and Applications,* vol. 2, no. 1, 1999, pp. 57–73.

[35] T.E. Hendrick, *Purchasing Consortiums: Horizontal Alliances Among Firms Buying Common Goods and Services* (Tempe, AZ: Center for Advanced Purchasing Studies, 1997).

[36] P. Fraser Johnson, "The Pattern of Evolution in Public Sector Purchasing Consortia," *International Journal of Logistics: Research and Applications,* vol. 2, no. 1, 1999, pp. 57–73.

- Supplier resistance: Strong suppliers may resist participating in consortium arrangements.
- Availability of suitable distribution channels: Some firms believe that existing distributors provide adequate pricing and service arrangements.
- Firm currently has preferred relationships with suppliers/free riding: The unequal size of member organizations can create difficulties with respect to the allocation of benefits.
- Uncertainty: Some firms were not convinced that costs would decline and were concerned regarding service levels.
- Standardization and compliance: Some firms believed that they had unique requirements and the consortiums would not be able to address their specific needs. Meanwhile the costs of standardizing products and services required substantial time and effort.
- Governance: Loss of control and reporting relationships were concerns. Accommodations can be made, such as setting up advisory committees and rotating member positions on the board of directors for the consortium.

Successful consortia are able to address these hurdles by successfully achieving the following six objectives:

Six Objectives of a Consortium

1. Reducing total costs for the consortium members through lower prices, higher quality, and better services.
2. Eliminating and avoiding all real and perceived violations of antitrust regulations.
3. Installing sufficient safeguards to avoid real and perceived threats concerning disclosure of confidential and proprietary information.
4. Mutual and equitable sharing of risks, costs, and benefits to all stakeholders, including buying firms/members, suppliers, and customers.
5. Maintaining a high degree of trust and professionalism of the consortium stakeholders.
6. Maintaining a strong similarity among consortium members and compatibility of needs, capabilities, philosophies, and corporate cultures.

Conclusion

There is not one perfect organizational structure for any supply organization. The purchasing organizational structure will likely be made to fit the overall corporate structure and the challenge for supply executives is to maximize the benefits of their organizational structure, whether it be centralized, decentralized, or hybrid.

Many purchasers can expect to work on cross-functional sourcing teams, particularly in new product development. Cross-functional teams overlay the functional organizational structure and bring together personnel with diverse skills and capabilities. Participation on teams necessitates joint decision making, including supply-related matters.

No matter where the supply function is situated on the organization chart, each individual member of the purchasing department has the opportunity to improve relations with internal customers and suppliers. Major research into organizational issues over the last decade has provided useful insights into innovative attempts to integrate the supply function and suppliers more effectively into organizational goals and strategies.

Questions for Review and Discussion

1. What are the specialized functions within purchasing? Is this idea used in a small organization? How?

2. What factors influence whether the purchasing organizational structure is centralized, hybrid or decentralized?

3. Where should the purchasing function report in the organization structure?

4. What is included in the buyer/planner position, and why is it used?

5. Discuss the specific objectives of purchasing. Relate these to (1) a company producing washing machines, (2) a large, fast-food restaurant chain, and (3) a hospital.

6. What is materials management; how is it used; and why is it used?

7. What decision authority must purchasing have if it is to be truly effective? What will happen if purchasing does not have this authority?

8. What implementation factors would you consider when asked to change the purchasing organization from a decentralized structure to a centralized structure? What factors would you consider moving from centralized to decentralized?

9. How is team buying likely to affect the purchasing/supply function over the next decade?

10. Why and how would you go about setting up a consortium for the purchase of fuel oil, furniture, corrugated cartons, or office supplies?

References

Design News/Purchasing Survey, *Purchasing,* May 1, 1997, pp. 32S17–32S17.

Healthcare Financial Management, "Group Purchasing Cut Hospital Costs in 1999," p. 21.

Fearon, H.E., *Purchasing Organizational Relationships,* Tempe, AZ: Center for Advanced Purchasing Studies, 1988.

Fearon, H.E. and W.A. Bales, *Purchasing of Nontraditional Goods and Services,* Tempe, AZ: Center for Advanced Purchasing Studies, 1995.

Fearon, H.E. and M.R. Leenders, *Purchasing's Organizational Roles and Responsibilities,* Tempe, AZ: Center for Advanced Purchasing Studies, 1995.

Giunipero, L.C. and D.H. Percy, "World-Class Purchasing Skills: An Empirical Investigation," *The Journal of Supply Chain Management,* Fall 2000, pp. 4–13.

Hendrick, T.E., *Purchasing Consortiums: Horizontal Alliances Among Firms Buying Common Goods and Services,* Tempe, AZ: Center for Advanced Purchasing Studies, 1997.

Johnson, P.F., M.R. Leenders, and H.E. Fearon, "Evolving Roles and Responsibilities of Purchasing Organizations," *International Journal of Purchasing and Materials Management,* vol. 34, no. 1 (Winter 1998), pp. 2–11.

Johnson, P.F., "The Pattern of Evolution in Public Sector Purchasing Consortia," *International Journal of Logistics: Research and Applications,* vol. 2, no. 1, 1999, pp. 57–73.

Leenders, M.R. and P.F. Johnson, *Major Structural Changes in Supply Organizations,* Tempe AZ: Center for Advanced Purchasing Studies, 2000.

Leenders, M.R. and P.F. Johnson, *Major Changes in Supply Chain Responsibilities,* Tempe AZ: Center for Advanced Purchasing Studies, 2001.

Monczka, R.M. and R.J. Trent, "An Action Plan for Creating Effective Teams," *NAPM Insights,* March 1993, p. 22.

Morgan, J.P., "Cessna Charts a Supply Chain Flight," *Purchasing,* Sep. 7, 2000, pp. 42–61.

Murphy, D.J. and M.E. Heberling, "A Framework for Purchasing and Integrated Product Teams," *International Journal of Purchasing and Materials Management,* Summer 1996, pp. 11–19.

Purchasing, "How Harley-Davidson Uses Cross-Functional Teams," Nov. 4, 1999, p. 144.

Purchasing, "Companies Get Purchasing Pros into the Design Stage," Aug. 24, 2000, p. 26.

Trent, R.J., "Understanding and Evaluating Cross-Functional Sourcing Team Leadership," *International Journal of Purchasing and Materials Management,* Fall 1996, p. 36.

Trent, R.J. and R.M. Monczka, "Effective Cross-Functional Sourcing Teams: Critical Success Factors," *International Journal of Purchasing and Materials Management,* Fall 1994, pp. 3–11.

Williams, A.J.; L. Giunipero, and T.L. Henthorne, "The Cross-Functional Imperative: The Case of Marketing and Purchasing," *International Journal of Purchasing and Materials Management,* Summer 1994, p. 33.

Case 2–1
Goodlife Club

Sally Newton was the only purchasing person of Goodlife Club, a fitness club with 19 centers scattered around Texas. In February, she was thinking of how to handle the resistance coming from some center managers, especially the "alliance" of three Dallas centers to the newly introduced centralized purchasing system which she had designed one month ago.

Goodlife Club. Goodlife Club was founded 10 years ago and owned by Jim Stewart, a business graduate from Austin. At the age of 25, he opened his first fitness center in Austin. Over the past 10 years, the club had been growing gradually and, currently, it had 19 centers scattered around Texas (see Exhibit 1). The head office, however, remained in Austin.

Sally Newton. Sally Newton was 24. Right after her completion of a diploma in psychology from a junior college in Austin, she joined Goodlife Club in January as the purchasing person of the club. Her

Exhibit 1   **Locations of the 19 Fitness Centers of Goodlife Club**

Location	Number of Centers
Austin	5 (including the head office)
Amarillo	1
Corpus Christi	1
Dallas	3
Galveston	1
Houston	3
Lubbock	2
San Antonio	2
Waco	1
Total	19

job responsibilities included the administration of purchasing and inventory control. Before her college studies, she had had a number of years of work experience in various areas but none of them specifically related to purchasing or inventory control. As she herself said, "This is my first job in this area."

The Purchase System in Goodlife before Sally Newton. "If there was really a purchasing system in Goodlife before Sally came, I could only say it was a 'very, very loose' one," one staff member commented.

Goodlife needed many different kinds of items to keep its centers running. They ranged from parts for machines and equipment like bike parts and suntan bulbs to stationery supplies and toiletries. Before Sally joined the club, each center was responsible for its own purchasing. Most centers did not keep any inventory and purchased items needed on an ad hoc basis (i.e., buy when needed at a nearby store). In the head office, there had been a part-time employee performing the purchasing and inventory control job but only for the head office. She did not purchase items for the other 18 centers but kept records for them.

Sally Newton's New Centralized Purchasing System. During the first week in Goodlife, Sally examined the two binders which were left by the part-time employee she replaced. She was surprised to find that the club was using the center-based ad hoc purchasing system and thought that a centralized one might work in this situation. She talked to her boss about this idea and her boss encouraged her to investigate further.

She then did some research work on it and found that a centralized purchasing system could really save considerable money for the club. For example, she had found a supplier that would reduce the cost of toiletry purchases by nearly 50 percent if the club bought in bulk through it. Therefore, along with searching for more suppliers for different items, she spent time on developing the details of the centralized purchasing system.

Basically, the new system that Sally had designed centralized all purchases in the head office. Instead of each center buying its own requirements, the center manager was asked to fill in an order form and fax it to the head office. The deadline was 5 o'clock on Monday every week—and the

items requested would be sent to the requesting center on the following Monday. Sally had the authority to disapprove or reduce the amount requested if she thought it was not justified. However, each center was allowed to have a petty cash fund of $100 for meeting any urgent purchases.

By the end of January, Sally finished the plan, which was immediately approved by her boss. She notified all 19 centers by memo explaining the reasons for the new purchasing system and the details of it.

Resistance from Center Managers. After about one month of implementation, Sally was a bit frustrated by the resistance from some of the center managers. Some managers did not use the order form but just called in right away when they needed some items. The most difficult one was that the three fitness centers in Dallas "joined" together and resisted changing to the new system.

Sally believed the three Dallas center managers had gotten together after her January memo and decided to purchase their needs collectively in Dallas without using Sally's centralized purchasing system. She had no proof of this, but neither had she received any purchase requests from any Dallas center.

As far as the other centers were concerned, Sally did not know whether she was purchasing all of their requirements or not. She had received some requisitions from each and tried to satisfy these orders as best as she could. She had, moreover, not been able to meet her own deadline of a one-week turnaround in all cases. She had been very busy trying to meet the various requests she had received and had not really had the time to assess how well her system was performing.

CASE 2–2
DUCHESS UNIVERSITY

In April, the Purchasing Department at Duchess University lost three of its fourteen employees because of death and personal reasons. Jim Haywood, head of the Purchasing Department, saw these unexpected personnel changes as an opportunity to address an issue that had bothered him for a while:

"Should I reorganize the structure of the department and, if so, how?"

Company Background: Duchess University
Duchess University was a public institution with about 3,000 full-time employees and about 25,000 students, which provided undergraduate and graduate education in all major academic disciplines. The total university budget was about $500 million and purchases were about $120 million. Currently, the University faced major challenges: increased demand for university education; at the same time many faculty members were nearing retirement and it was difficult to find replacements at acceptable costs. Moreover, the government had reduced its grants in recent years and had put a cap of 2 percent on tuition increases for the next five years, thus, constraining the University's major revenue generators.

The Purchasing Department. The Web site of the Purchasing Department stated its mission: "Our objective is to look after your needs. We want to provide you with the right goods or services, at the right time, at the right price, and on a continuing basis." To accomplish its goals, the department (1) purchased goods and services such as computer and business products, lab supplies, photocopiers, furniture, and travel for the University; (2) managed central supplies, which were bought in bulk, stored, and redistributed, as required; (3) was responsible for ensuring the economic and timely delivery of goods and services; (4) maintained an asset inventory; and (5) managed the disposal of goods.

Exhibit 1 provides the department organization chart. Junior buyers had a purchasing limit for a single purchase of $2,000; employees at the senior buyer level, $25,000. Purchasing managers had a purchasing limit of $50,000. Jim Haywood noted that the current department structure was a result of "patching up" in the last four years, in which the department had been extremely busy. In addition to its daily tasks, the department had to absorb the continuous introduction of software systems. The

EXHIBIT 1   Purchasing Department Organization Chart

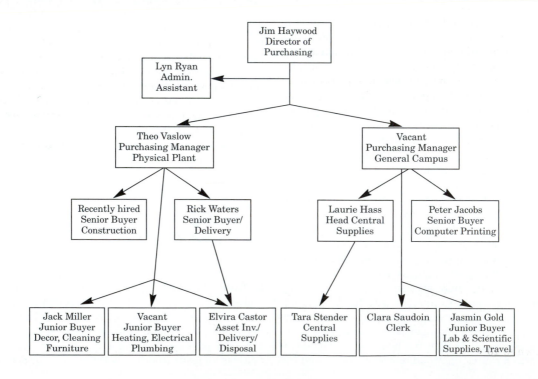

consistent work overload had prevented Jim Haywood from attending to his non-daily responsibilities, including a systematic revision of the department structure.

Jim Haywood. Jim Haywood had assumed the position of Director of Purchasing six years earlier after working 17 years in the University's financial services area. As Director of Purchasing, he still reported to the Director of Financial Services, with whom he had a good relationship. When Jim took over the Purchasing Department, it was in turmoil: The previous Director had taken early retirement after senior management had voiced distrust in the department, and purchasing agents had strongly resisted changes to improve the department's efficiency. Moreover, the department staff was dispersed in two buildings.

When Jim came in, his goals included the reduction of the middle management layer (that is, the purchasing managers), the introduction of an online purchasing system, the integration of the department in one location, and the benchmarking of the department's performance. For the most part, Jim had achieved these goals. By January of the current year, through intra-university transfers, early retirement, and attrition, the number of purchasing agents had been reduced to two from six, and the total number of employees was 14, down from 20 in six years. PeopleSoft, a software package for business process applications, was in use. So far, however, PeopleSoft supported the current work processes, but reengineering to optimize PeopleSoft had yet to get under way. Moreover, all employees worked now in one location. Finally, Jim had introduced a Center for Advanced Purchasing Studies (CAPS) benchmarking system.

The Current Situation. At the end of April, Jim Haywood faced the following situation:

- In April, one purchasing manager had died; furthermore, a senior buyer had left after her husband was transferred, and a junior buyer had left after her husband retired. Jim had hired a replacement for the senior buyer position, but the replacement would not arrive until late May. He had not yet decided what to do with the remaining two vacant positions. Right now, his staff was down to 10 employees.

- CAPS showed that the Purchasing Department had significantly improved over the past six years. For example, the total revenue per professional employee of $50 million was above the benchmark value of $30 million. Similarly, the total amount of purchases per buyer of $12 million had steadily improved over time and was now at the benchmark value. CAPS, however, also indicated that the department was still performing below average on several other parameters, such as cycle time and the number of suppliers per employee.

- After the consistent work overload during the previous four years, there was now an opportunity for reevaluating the department and catching up on non-daily responsibilities. Among other things, Jim reevaluated his goals for the department and its restructuring:

  > "First, I want to reconsider the people issues in our department. I need to find a way to foster the careers of my employees. They have been with me for a long time, know what they do, and deserve recognition. Second, I still see room for improving the 'value added' in the department. We do too much work that does not increase our effectiveness. Third, we have to react to a current budget cut of 2 percent and future anticipated budget cuts between 3 percent and 5 percent."

  To share these goals and to get input on how to achieve them, Jim had already met with his superior. He had also had meetings with his three remaining senior employees—Theo Vaslow, Rick Waters and Peter Jacobs—both individually and as a group. In addition, a staff meeting with all employees had taken place.

- In these meetings, several issues surfaced. Jim, as well as the purchasing agent Theo Vaslow, felt that they had to do too much supervising. Despite the reductions in personnel, the morale in the Purchasing Department was good. Most employees had been with the department for more than 10 years, and generally employee commitment to their department and their jobs was high. Jim generally viewed his employees as high performers who had done their best to keep the Purchasing Department running in extremely busy times because of the introduction of software systems. Some employees at the junior buyer level, however, had indicated their frustration about the lack of promotion opportunities, as promotions to the senior buyer level led to salary increases of about 25 percent.

- On the basis of the meetings, Jim had generated a task list for achieving the goals, which is shown in Exhibit 2. Jim felt that now the goals and the task list were complete, but he was not sure how to implement them. He wondered to what extent restructuring the department would address issues on the task list.
- In September, the Purchasing Department would face an upgrade of PeopleSoft. Moreover, the department would have to gear up for web-based processing of purchasing requisitioning that would start within the next year. Jim stated:

> "Like in previous years, it is going to be tough. We will have to work very hard just 'to keep the train on the tracks' while implementing the new systems."

What Was Next? Jim wanted to restructure the department before September. He asked himself: "What exactly should the outcome of the restructuring of the department be? And, if I changed the structure, how should I do it?"

EXHIBIT 2   **Task List for the Purchasing Department**

Duchess University
Purchasing Organizational / Responsibilities Review

Task	Expected Outcome
• Eliminate the reprocessing of data.	• Free up people power; reduce costs.
• Analyze the purchasing data.	• Maximize purchasing effectiveness.
• Analyze the data from central supplies.	• Maximize purchasing effectiveness.
• Review the supplier master file.	• Save costs because of early payments.
• Eliminate forms (paperwork).	• Reduce costs.
• Update authorizations and limits system.	• Ensure functioning of the department.
• Train new university employees.	• Utilize resources outside the department on purchasing processes.
• Further develop the Web site by integrating. software solutions	• Reduce costs and speed up processes.
• Train purchasing employees on PeopleSoft.	• Improve effectiveness of personnel.
• Increase the number of systems contracts.	• Reduce costs.
• Review systems contracts that have ended.	• Reduce costs.
• Standardize purchasing processes across buyers.	• Achieve uniform best practices.
• Segregate procurement from non-procurement activities.	• Improve daily operations.
• Rewrite job descriptions.	• Reflect past changes. Gain promotion compensation.

3 PROCEDURES AND INFORMATION FLOWS

Chapter Outline

Key Questions for the Purchasing Decision Maker

SHOULD WE
- Make greater use of blanket orders, systems contracting, or procurement cards to simplify and improve the purchasing process?
- Adopt an invoiceless payment system?
- Consider using a third-party supplier for MRO requirements?

HOW CAN WE
- Handle small orders more efficiently?
- Obtain better and more complete information from other functions within the organization?
- Communicate more effectively with our internal customers (the departments we serve)?

Five Reasons to Develop a Sound Purchasing Process

The purchasing/supply management area requires a wide range of standard operating procedures to deal with the normal daily tasks. The large number of items, the large dollar volume involved, the need for an audit trail, the severe consequences of poor performance, and the potential contribution to effective organizational operations inherent in the function are five major reasons for developing a sound system. The acquisition process is closely tied to almost all other functions included in an organization and also to the external environment, creating a need for complete information systems and cross-functional cooperation. The Internet and the availability of integrated software packages has had a substantial impact on the acquisition process and its management. Supply managers need to stay abreast of technological developments and be able to assess the fit of each new tool with the organization's goals and strategy. Considerable management skill is required to ensure continuing effectiveness.

Steps in the Purchasing/Supply Management Process

The purchasing system is basically a communications process. Determining what needs to be communicated, to whom, and in what format and time frame is at the heart of an efficient and effective purchasing and supply management process. It is essential for purchasing and supply professionals to determine when and where in the process they can add value and when and where they can extricate themselves from the transactions that are best left to others. The fundamental steps in a sound purchasing process, and the rationale for each, are described below. Once the basic process is understood, it is easy to see opportunities for applying technology tools to increase efficiency by streamlining the process without sacrificing effectiveness. Computerized purchasing systems, e-procurement and electronic business-to-business (B2B) systems are addressed in Chapter 4.

The essential steps in the purchasing process are:

1. Recognition of need.
2. Description of the need, with an accurate statement of the characteristics and amount of the article, commodity, or service desired.
3. Determination and analysis of possible sources of supply.
4. Determination of price and terms.
5. Preparation and placement of the purchase order.
6. Follow-up and/or expediting the order.
7. Receipt and inspection of goods.
8. Clearing the invoice and paying the supplier.
9. Maintenance of records and relationships.

Customizing the Process to the Purchase Category

The way in which this process is operationalized depends in part on the nature of the purchase. The flowchart in Figure 3–1 demonstrates one way in which an organization might customize the purchasing process based on different categories of purchases. In this example, the first cut is determining whether or not the purchase is strategic. While the exact definition may vary from organization to organization, a general description might be that a strategic purchase is one that is critical to the mission of the organization. This definition allows for high- and low-dollar value purchases that are mission critical. For these purchases it makes sense to spend more time, money, and resources in the sourcing process. For nonstrategic purchases (the right column of the flowchart), the first cut is made based on a small dollar threshold. A second cut is made based on the availability of a pre-qualified supplier. Other ways to categorize purchases are discussed in Chapter 6.

1. Recognition of Need

Any purchase originates with the recognition of a definite need by someone in the organization. The person responsible for a particular activity should know what the individual requirements of the unit are—what, how much, and when it is needed. This may result in a material requisition from inventory. Occasionally, such requirements may be met by the transfer of surplus stock from another department or division. Sooner or later, of course, the purchase of new supplies will become necessary. Some purchase requisitions originate within the production or using department. Requests for office equipment of all sorts might come from the office manager or from the controller of the company. Some requests come from the sales or advertising departments or from research laboratories. Frequently, special forms will indicate the source of requisitions; where this is not the case, distinctive code numbers for each supply department may be used. A typical requisition is shown in Figure 3–2.

The supply department is responsible for helping to anticipate the needs of using departments. The supply manager should urge not only that the requirements be as nearly standard in character as possible and that a

FIGURE 3–1

A Sample Sourcing Process Flowchart

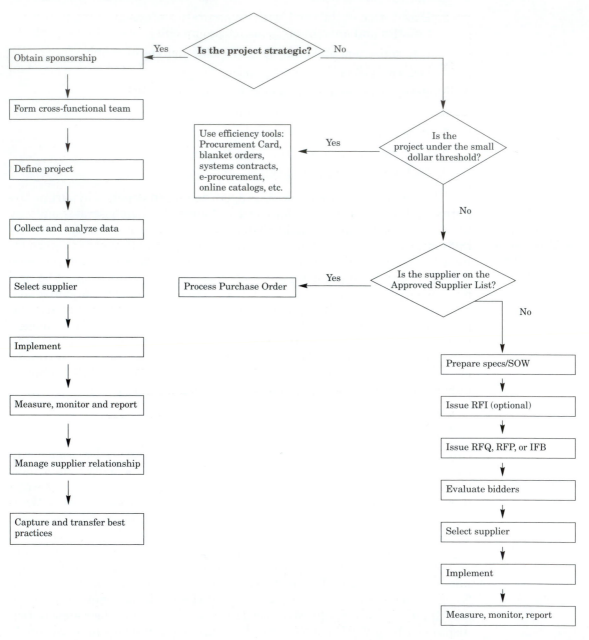

FIGURE 3–2

Purchase Requisition

Purchase Requisition

Department requisitioning ——————————————— Number ——————

Budget account ———————————————————— Date ——————

Quantity required	Unit	Description

Required date ————————————————————————————

Notify in event of problems ——————————————————————

Special delivery instructions ——————————————————————

————————————————
Requisitioning authority

Instructions: Complete in duplicate. Send original to Purchasing Department, requisitioner keep file copy.

minimum of special or unusual orders be placed, but also that requirements be anticipated far enough in advance to prevent an excessive number of "rush" orders. Also, because the supply department is in touch with price trends and general market conditions, the placing of forward orders may be essential to protect against shortage of supply or increased prices. This means that supply should inform using departments of the normal lead time, and any major changes, for all standard purchased items. Early purchasing involvement and early supplier involvement (ESI), often as

Greatest Opportunity to Affect Value

members of new product development teams, brings in information that may result in cost avoidance/reduction, faster time to market, and greater competitiveness. As discussed in Chapter 2, many organizations are turning to cross-functional teams to bring different functional areas, and suppliers, into the process as early as possible. Because the greatest opportunity to affect value is in the need-recognition and description stages (product conception and design), the supply manager and supplier can contribute more in the need-recognition and description stages than later in the acquisition process. (See Chapter 5 for additional information on value creation.)

Emergency and Rush Orders. Frequently, an excessively large number of requisitions will be received marked "rush." Rush orders cannot always be avoided; emergencies do arise which justify their use. Sudden changes in style or design and unexpected changes in market conditions may upset the most-carefully-planned material schedule. Breakdowns seemingly are inevitable, with an accompanying demand for parts or materials which are not carried in stock.

Unjustified Rush Orders

There are, however, so-called rush orders that cannot be justified on any basis. They consist of those requisitions which arise because of (1) faulty inventory control, (2) poor production planning or budgeting, (3) an apparent lack of confidence in the ability of the supply department to get material to the user by the proper time, and (4) the sheer habit of marking the requests "rush." Whatever the cause, such orders are costly. This higher cost is due in part to the greater chance of error when the work is done under pressure. Rush orders also place an added burden on the seller, and this burden must directly or indirectly find its way into the price paid by the buyer.

Reducing the Number of Rush Orders

What can be done to reduce the seriousness of the problem? For an excessive number of rush orders that are not actually emergency orders, the solution is a matter of education in the proper supply procedure. In one company, for example, when a rush requisition is sent, the department issuing the order has to explain to the general manager the reason for the emergency requirement and secure approval. Furthermore, even if the requisition is approved, the extra costs, so far as they can be determined, are charged to the department ordering the material. The result has been a marked reduction in the number of such orders. The use of pre-approved suppliers and online catalogs may also mitigate the problem by reducing the lead time for order processing and by allowing users to issue requests against an existing contract directly with the supplier.

Small Value Purchase Orders. Small orders are a continuing matter of concern in every organization. Most requisitions follow Pareto's law, which

Pareto's Law

says that about 70 percent of all requisitions amount to only about 10 percent of the total dollar volume. (Pareto's Law, also known as ABC analysis, is discussed in detail in Chapter 6, "Quantity and Delivery.") When organizations analyze their purchases, many find, as Scott Paper did, that 90 percent of the transactions account for 10 percent of the dollars. At Scott Paper, of the 90 percent, 65 percent was for MRO (maintenance, repair, and operations) items, and 28 percent for general and administrative expenses, with an average transaction amount of $700.[1] Many organizations spend as much to process the transaction for a $500 purchase as for a $5,000 one. One important consideration is the cost of the system set up to handle small orders versus the cost of the items themselves. Because the lack of a small item may create a nuisance totally out of proportion to its dollar value, assured supply is usually the first objective to be met.

Handling Small Value Purchase Orders

Many approaches can be used to address the small order question. Typically they involve simplifying or automating the process or consolidating purchases to reduce the acquisition cycle time (time from need recognition to payment), reduce administrative cost, and free up the buyer's time for higher-value or more critical purchases. A few examples are:

1. Use the "stockless buying" or "systems contracting" concept. This has been used most widely in the purchase of MRO items. (See explanation later in this chapter.)

2. A procurement credit card is provided to internal customers who use it to purchase directly from established suppliers.

3. Purchasing sets up blanket orders against which internal customers issue release orders; suppliers provide summary billing.

4. Electronic linkage is made with major suppliers either through an Electronic Data Interchange (EDI) system or an Internet-based electronic procurement system. Ordering and reordering occurs automatically. (See Chapter 4.)

5. Reverse auctions in which the buyer pre-qualifies suppliers and invites them to an online auction, during which bidders submit bids and the contract to supply for a period of time is awarded.

6. Authority levels and bidding practices are adjusted, and telephone and fax are used for ordering.

7. Integrated suppliers are used to provide a variety of supplies.

8. Low-value order placement is outsourced to third parties.

9. If the fault lies with the using department, perhaps persuasion may be employed to increase the number of standardized items requested.

10. Another possibility is for the supply department to hold small requisitions as received until a reasonable total, in dollars, has been accumulated.

---

[1] Jim Miller, "Purchasing Gets a New Charge," *Procurement Card Guide: Supplement to NAPM Insights,* June 1995, p. 8.

11. Establish a requisition calendar, setting aside specific days for the requisitioning of specific supplies, so that all requests for a given item are received on the same day. The calendar also may be so arranged that practically all the supplies secured from any specific type of supplier are requisitioned on the same day.

12. Invoiceless payments (self-billing) are arranged, or blank checks are sent with orders.

13. Users place orders directly.

Blank Check Purchase Order. This method for combating the small order problem often is referred to as the "Purchase Order Draft" or POD system or Kaiser Check System. The blank check purchase order (PO) is a special form in which the supplier is sent a check along with the PO (see Figure 3–3). When the merchandise is shipped, the supplier enters the amount due on the check and cashes it. This system has certain built-in safeguards: the check can be deposited only to the supplier's account; it must be presented for deposit within a set number of days (normally 60 or 90 days); and the check (it's really a bank draft) clearly is marked "not good for an amount over $1,000." Obviously the maximum amount limit is set to fit the particular buying organization's needs; typically it is $1,000, but some companies set a lower amount, for example, $500, and some go as high as $5,000. The risk to the buyer is small under these restrictions. The advantages are that it cuts down paperwork on the low-dollar purchases; it saves postage, for the check goes in the same envelope as the PO; it saves envelopes; the buyer can negotiate a larger cash discount in return for instant payment; and it saves time (and personnel) in the accounts payable function. But probably the major advantage is that this system requires complete shipment—*no back orders are allowed* (referred to as "fill or kill"), and the supplier is notified either by the PO or by an attached instruction sheet that whatever amount is shipped closes the order and the supplier pays itself only for that amount actually shipped. Thus the supplier has a real incentive to ship the order complete—and most normally do—since payment is immediate for items shipped. This also cuts down on the number of receiving reports, inventory entries, and payments.

Advantages of Blank Check Purchase Orders

Corporate Purchasing Cards. Corporate purchasing or procurement cards are credit cards that are issued to internal customers (users) in the buying organization. The cards can also be merged with technology to be electronic commerce compatible and data sensitive to capture important information for buying organizations.[2] Procurement cards are used primarily to reduce administrative costs and cycle time for low-dollar value, indirect

---

[2]"The Power of Purchasing and Supply Management," supplement to *Purchasing Today* reprinted from *Fortune Magazine,* Oct. 26, 1998, p. S4.

FIGURE 3–3

Blank Check Form

FUND	DEPT	DIV	C C	W O	ACCT NO.

CASH PURCHASE ORDER
MARICOPA COUNTY
DEPARTMENT OF MATERIALS MANAGEMENT
MATERIALS MANAGEMENT CENTER, 320 W. LINCOLN
PHOENIX, ARIZONA 85003

SEE ATTACHED INSTRUCTIONS

MARICOPA COUNTY ARIZONA

CASH PURCHASE ORDER This number MUST appear on ALL documents.	C.P.O. No. X 00057
DATE	
CONTRACT NO.	

V E N D O R

DELIVERY INSTRUCTIONS
SHIP
TO
ON OR BEFORE

ITEM	CATALOG NO. REQ/ITEM NO.	DESCRIPTION	QUANTITY AND UNIT OF ISSUE	UNIT PRICE	EXTENDED PRICE

IMPORTANT

TO AVOID INVOICING, THE VENDOR MUST ITEMIZE THIS SALE IN THE SPACE PROVIDED BELOW

ALL DISCREPANCIES MUST BE RECONCILED WITH THE DEPARTMENT OF MATERIALS MANAGEMENT BEFORE THIS ORDER IS FILLED PLEASE CALL– (602) 262-3244

LESS CASH DISCOUNT	%	—
ON $ TAX	%	+
BUYER	TOTAL	

NEW 6 78 20-05-11

VENDOR MUST COMPLETE THIS SECTION

ITM	QUANTITY	UNIT PRICE	AMOUNT
INVOICE #		CASH DISCOUNT ______ %	—
		TAX ______ %	+
		TOTAL	

91-170
1221

TREASURER OF MARICOPA COUNTY
PHOENIX, ARIZONA
CASH PURCHASE ORDER

WARRANT & CLAIM No. X 00057

FUND
VOID 90 DAYS AFTER
DATE
AMOUNT
$

NOT VALID FOR MORE THAN $500.00

PAY TO THE ORDER OF

DRAWN BY MARICOPA COUNTY BOARD OF SUPERVISORS

MATERIALS MANAGEMENT DEPARTMENT AUTHORIZED SIGNATURE	CONTROLLER'S DEPARTMENT AUTHORIZED SIGNATURE

⑈90000057⑈ ⑆122101706⑆ 212 001⑉000212⑈

Source: Maricopa County Department of Materials Management, Phoeniz, AZ.

(nonproduction) materials, supplies, and services transactions. Holders of the card are given dollar limits and lists of preferred suppliers with whom purchasing has already negotiated prices and terms. Purchasing cards automate many aspects of the purchasing system, thereby eliminating purchase orders and individual invoices, and ensuring suppliers of fast payment, two or three days versus thirty-plus in a typical system. By moving the transaction activities to the user department, the purchasing cycle time is reduced and so is the cost of processing the transaction. Also, buyers (and accounts payable) are freed from the day-to-day transactions related to small-value purchases and can concentrate on higher-value purchases and supply management issues.

Risks, Controls, and Benefits of Procurement Cards

The primary perceived risk of purchasing cards is loss of control. Management wants assurance that only authorized persons will be issued the cards, and that only appropriate purchases will be made from preferred suppliers. In response to these concerns, card issuers have instituted controls which (1) determine, at the point of sale, if the purchase meets preset dollar limits per card, (2) limit the number of transactions per day, (3) limit the value of a single transaction, and (4) determine if it is an approved supplier. While retail acceptance of the purchase cards is widespread worldwide, industrial suppliers have been slower to sign up for the programs. But the promise of fast payment and the potential for increased volume is leading to wider acceptance by industrial suppliers. A cross-industry comparison of 28 industries ranging from aerospace to transportation to engineering/construction to municipal governments performed by the Center for Advanced Purchasing Studies (CAPS) indicates that, on average, 10.4 percent of purchases are made through a procurement card, up from 3.7 percent in 1998.[3] Average use by industry varies widely from only 0.7 percent of transactions via a P-Card in Engineering and Construction (February 1999 data) to 40.2 percent in DOE Contractors (March 1999 data).[4]

The most sophisticated card programs are able to: (1) track and report sales tax information for audit purposes, (2) identify whether the supplier is a minority business owner, (3) capture specific product information, (4) dictate a cost center that should be charged for the purchase, and (4) include different types of purchases, including travel and entertainment expenses and fleet expenses.[5]

2. Accurate Description of Desired Commodity or Service

No purchaser can be expected to buy without knowing exactly what the internal customers want. For this reason, it is essential to have an accurate description of the need, the article, the commodity, or the service requested.

---

[3]Center for Advanced Purchasing Studies, "Cross-Industry Comparison of Standard Benchmarks," Spring 2000, p. 2.

[4]ibid.

[5]"The Power of Purchasing and Supply Management," supplement to *Purchasing Today* reprinted from *Fortune Magazine,* Oct. 26, 1998, p. S4.

Purchasing and the user, or the cross-functional sourcing team, share responsibility for accurately describing the item or service needed. It is at this point in the process that costs are driven in the final cost of ownership. If the user/buyer writes unclear or ambiguous descriptions, or over-specifies materials or quality levels, this will lead to unnecessary expenditures.

Early Purchasing Involvement

The purchaser should question a specification if it appears that the organization might be served better through a modification. An obvious case is the one where market shortages exist in the commodity requested and a substitute is the only reasonable alternative. Because future market conditions play such a vital role, it makes sense to have a high degree of interaction between the purchasing and specifying groups in the early stages of need definition. At best, an inaccurate description may result in some loss of time; at worst it may have serious financial consequences and cause disruption of supply, hard feelings internally, lost opportunity for a product or service improvement, and loss of supplier respect and trust.

Because the purchasing department is the last one to see the specification before it is sent on to the supplier, the need for a final check here is clear. Such a check is not possible if purchasing department personnel have no familiarity with the product or service requested. Any questions regarding the accuracy of the requisition should be referred back to the requisitioner or sourcing team and should not be settled unilaterally in the supply department.

Importance of Uniform Terms of Description

The terms used to describe desired articles or services should be uniform. The importance of proper nomenclature as a means of avoiding misunderstanding cannot be overemphasized. The most effective way to secure this uniformity is to maintain in the supply office a file listing the articles usually purchased. Such files may be kept in various ways. Some organizations have found it worthwhile to maintain a general catalog, which lists all the items used, and a stores catalog, which contains a list of all of the items carried in stock. Such catalogs may be kept in loose-leaf form, in a card index, or by a computer listing. If such catalogs are adequately planned and properly maintained, they tend to promote the uniformity in description. They also tend to reduce the number of odd sizes or grades of articles requisitioned, and they facilitate accounting and stores procedures. However, unless such catalogs or their equivalents are properly planned, maintained, and actually used, they can be confusing and expensive beyond any benefits which could be derived from them.

The following information should be included on the requisition (see Figure 3–2):

1. Date.
2. Number (identification).
3. Originating department.
4. Account to be charged.
5. Complete description of material or service desired and quantity.
6. Date material or service needed.

7. Any special shipping or service-delivery instructions.

8. Signature of authorized requisitioner.

Some organizations include spaces on the requisition form for "suggested supplier" and "suggested price."

Flow of the Purchase Requisition. At a minimum, at least two copies of the requisition should be made: the original to be forwarded to the supply department and the duplicate retained by the issuer. In electronic purchasing systems, the need for audit trails and proper authorization remain but are, obviously, handled differently. It is a common practice to allow only one item to appear on any one purchase requisition, particularly on standard items. In the case of some special items, such as plumbing fittings not regularly carried in stock, several items may be covered by one requisition, provided they are for delivery at the same time. This simplifies recordkeeping because specific items are secured from different suppliers, call for different delivery dates, and require separate purchase orders and treatment. In the case of firms operating with a computerized material requirements planning (MRP) system, the requisitions will be automatically computer generated.

It is important for the purchasing department to establish who has the power to requisition. Under no circumstances should the purchasing department accept requisitions from anyone other than those specifically authorized. Just as important is that all sales personnel know definitely that a requisition is not an order.

All requisitions should be checked carefully before any action is taken. The requested quantity should be based on anticipated needs and should be compared to economical purchasing quantities. The delivery date requested should allow for sufficient time to secure quotations and samples, if necessary, and to execute the purchase order and obtain delivery. If insufficient time is allowed, or the date would involve additional expense, this should be brought to the attention of the requisitioner immediately.

Procedures for Handling Requisitions

The procedure for handling requisitions on receipt in the purchase office is of sufficient importance to warrant citing an example from one organization. After being time-stamped, the proper specification card is attached to each individual requisition. If a contract already exists, the buyer marks all items covered by the contract, placing on the requisition the word *contract,* the name of the firm with which the order is to be placed, the price, terms, the FOB point (See Chapter 10, "Purchasing Logistics Services"), the total value, and the payment date, for the controller's information. The purchase order is then prepared, carefully checked with the specification card, the price, terms, and so on, before the order finally is mailed, faxed, or electronically transmitted to the supplier selected.

When items are not covered by contract, the buyer has three options for soliciting business from potential suppliers: issuing a (1) Request for Quotation (RFQ), (2) Request for Proposal (RFP), or (3) Invitation for Bid (IFB).

Three Options for Solicitation: RFQ, RFP, and IFB

The descriptions used in this text work off the assumption that an RFQ will be issued in situations where the buyer and internal user can clearly and unambiguously describe the need, for example by using a grade of material or commonly accepted terminology. In these cases, an RFQ would basically bring the comparison to one of price. When the buyer has a more complex requirement and wants to draw on the supplier's expertise in developing and proposing a solution, an RFP or IFB would be more appropriate than an RFQ. Also, if the buyer is planning to use negotiation as the tool for determining price and terms, then an RFP would be appropriate. If, however, the buyer is planning to use a competitive bid process without the opportunity to negotiate after bid receipt, then an IFB might be more appropriate. Since there are no commonly accepted definitions of these terms, it is important for buyers to communicate clearly to potential suppliers the process that will be followed to analyze and select a supplier(s). Many organizations use different solicitation tools depending on the complexity of the purchase, the dollar value, and the degree of risk they wish the supplier to bear.

Requests for Quotation

Requests for Quotations (RFQ) will be sent out on standard inquiry blanks provided for this purpose. Where quotations are to be requested, a list of the names of potential suppliers will be written on the back of the requisitions. Standard inquiry forms are prepared, checked, signed, and mailed, faxed, or electronically transmitted to potential suppliers. When the quotations are received from the various suppliers, they will be entered on the quotation sheet and the buyer determines the supplier with whom the business is to be placed. The purchase order then is prepared and placed with the chosen supplier.

Requests for Proposal

Requests for Proposals (RFP) typically include a more detailed package describing the needs of the buying organization and providing potential suppliers the opportunity to propose solutions to meet the requirements. For example, a buyer may issue an RFP for photocopying services for the entire organization, including convenience copiers for each department and high-speed, high-volume copiers to be run by either in-house staff or supplier personnel. The RFP may provide potential suppliers the opportunity to propose multiple solutions to the buyer.

Invitation for Bid

An Invitation for Bid (IFB) is similar to an RFP in terms of the bid specification package that is developed and sent to suppliers. It is important to communicate to suppliers how the final selection will take place. Will this be a sealed competitive bid in which the contract will be awarded based on the lowest bid? Will the bids be the starting point from which negotiations will take place?

Benefits of Traveling Requisitions

Use of the Traveling Requisition. To reduce operating expenses, some companies with manual purchasing systems have found it desirable to use the so-called traveling requisition for recurring requirements of materials and standard parts. The traveling requisition is a cardboard form used when a particular item must be purchased repeatedly for a given department. The traveler contains a complete description of the item and is sent to purchasing when a resupply of the item is needed by the user, indicating quantity and date needed. Purchasing writes the PO, enters data on supplier, price, and PO number on the traveler, and sends it back to the requisitioner, who puts the card in the files until a subsequent resupply is needed. As many as 24 to 36 purchases can be triggered by this traveler card. Use of the traveler eliminates the recopying of routine description data and substitutes for 24 to 36 individual purchase requisitions, saving paperwork and time. It also provides a complete, cumulative purchase history and use record on one form.

When parts or material covered by the traveling requisition are being ordered, the inventory control clerk inserts the date, the date required, the name of the department for which the request is made and the quantity, and obtains an authorized signature prior to sending the requisition to the purchasing department. If a computerized inventory control system is used, much of the work of the inventory clerk will be done automatically by computer. After selecting the supplier, the buyer fills in the supplier's code number, quantity, required date, unit price, and his or her name and date, and returns the card to the using department or inventory control department (after the PO is issued), where it is filed until another quantity is needed.

Bill of Material Used for Standardized Items

Use of the Bill of Materials Requisition. A second variation is the bill of material (B/M). It is used by firms who make a standard item over a relatively long period of time as a quick way of notifying purchasing of production needs: A B/M for a toaster made by an appliance manufacturer would list the total number or quantity, including an appropriate scrap allowance, of parts or material to make one end unit, for example, a two-slice toaster. Production scheduling then merely notifies purchasing that it has scheduled 18,000 of that model into production next month. Purchasing then will "explode" the B/M (normally by a computerized system) by multiplying through by 18,000 to determine the *total* quantity of material needed to meet next month's production schedule. Comparison of these numbers with quantities in inventory will give purchasing the open-to-buy figures. In a firm which has developed a totally integrated materials computer system, in which long-term agreements containing supplier and pricing information have been entered into the database, the computer will generate order releases to cover the open-to-buy amounts. Use of the B/M system is a means of simplifying the requisitioning process where a large number of frequently needed line items is involved.

Blanket and Open-End Orders. The cost of issuing and handling purchase orders may be reduced when conditions permit the use of blanket or open-end orders. A blanket order usually covers a variety of items. An open-end order allows for addition of items and/or extension of time. MRO items and production line requirements used in volume and purchased repetitively over a period of months may be bought in this manner.

Releases are Issued Against the Blanket Order

All terms and conditions involving the purchase of estimated quantities over a period are negotiated and incorporated in the original order. Subsequently, releases of specific quantities are made against the order. In some instances, it is possible to tie the preparation of the releases into the production scheduling procedures and forward them to the purchasing department for transmission to the supplier, or the release may go from production scheduling direct to the supplier. It is not unusual for an open-end order to remain in effect for a year, or until changes in design, material specification, or conditions affecting price or delivery make new negotiations desirable or necessary. Figure 3–4 shows a form used to authorize release of materials on a blanket order.

Stockless Buying or Systems Contracting. Systems contracting or stockless buying is a more sophisticated merging of the ordering and inventory functions than blanket contracts. Systems contracts rely on periodic billing procedures; allow non-purchasing personnel to issue order releases; employ special catalogs; require suppliers to maintain minimum inventory

FIGURE 3–4

Blanket Order Release

RAYTHEON

RAYTHEON COMPANY
SORENSEN OPERATION
SOUTH NORWALK, CONN.

BLANKET ORDER RELEASE
THIS NUMBER MUST APPEAR ON ALL DOCUMENTS AND PACKAGES

REQUISITION NO.	REQUISITIONED BY	UNIT	RELEASE DATE	PURCHASE ORDER NO.	RELEASE NO.
TO		SHIP VIA UPS		ACCOUNT NO.	
		SHIP MATERIAL TO ABOVE ADDRESS UNLESS INDICATED OTHERWISE BELOW SORENSEN		PROD. SHOP ORDER NO.	
				DELIVER MATERIAL TO (INTERNAL)	

DELIVERY AT DESTINATION	VENDOR CODE	MATERIAL CODE	TAXABLE	YES	NO	EXEMPTION NO.
	620393				X	5151175

RECEIVED Date	RECEIVED Quantity	Item	Quantity Ordered	DESCRIPTION	Part Number	Qty	Net Unit Price	

x INDICATES CONFIRMING ORDER DATE YOUR	BLANKET ORDER TERMS AND CONDITIONS APPLY		TOTAL
RECEIVING DEPARTMENT USE ONLY			

Source: Raytheon Company

levels, but normally do not specify the volume of contract items a buyer must buy; and improve inventory turnover rates.

Systems Contracting for MRO Purchases

This technique has been used most frequently in buying stationery and office supplies, repetitive items, maintenance and repair materials, and operating supplies (MRO). This latter class of purchases is characterized by many different types of items, all of comparatively low value and needed immediately when any kind of a plant or equipment failure occurs. The technique is built around a blanket-type contract which is developed in great detail regarding approximate quantities to be used in specified time periods, prices, provisions for adjusting prices, procedures to be followed in picking up requisitions daily and making delivery within a short time (normally 24 hours), simplified billing procedures, and a complete catalog of all items covered by the contract.

Generally the inventory of all items covered by a contract is stored by the supplier, thus eliminating the buyer's investment in inventory and space. Requisitions for items covered by the contract go directly to the supplier and are not processed by the purchasing department. The requisition is used by the supplier to pull stock, to pack, to invoice, and as a delivery slip. The streamlined procedure reduces paper-handling costs for the buyer and the seller and has been a help in solving the small order problem.

Some organizations use an electronic system in systems contracting which requires a data transmission terminal. The buyer or requisitioner simply indicates each item needed and the quantity required, which is transmitted electronically to the supplier's computer.

In some firms with large volume requirements from a specific supplier, that supplier stores items in the customer's plant, as though it were the supplier's warehouse. The buyer's contact with the supplier is by computer, through a computer modem. The system would work as follows:

Steps in Computerized Systems Contracting

1. The buyer places the blanket order for a family of items, such as fasteners, at firm prices.

2. The supplier delivers predetermined quantities to the inventory area set aside in the buyer's plant. The items are still owned by the supplier.

3. Buyer inspects the items when they are delivered.

4. The computer directs storage to the appropriate bin or shelf.

5. Buyer places POs through the computer terminal, thus relieving the supplier's inventory records.

6. Pick sheets are computer prepared. Buyer physically removes the items from the supplier's inventory.

7. Supplier submits a single invoice monthly for all items picked.

8. Buyer's accounting department makes a single monthly payment for all items used.

9. Computer prepares a summary report, at predetermined intervals, showing the items and quantity used, for both the buyer's and supplier's analysis, planning, and restocking.

Benefits of Systems Contracting

Systems contracting has become popular in nonmanufacturing organizations as well. It is no longer confined to MRO items and may well include a number of high-dollar volume commodities. The shortening of the time span from requisition to delivery has resulted in substantial inventory reductions and greater organizational willingness to go along with the supply system. The amount of red tape has become minimal. Because the user normally provides a good estimate of requirements and compensates the supplier in case the forecast is not good, the supplier risks little in inventory investment. The degree of cooperation and information exchange required between buyer and seller in a systems contract often results in a much warmer relationship than is normally exhibited in a traditional arm's-length trading situation.

Third-Party MRO Suppliers. Some firms have developed contracts with third-party suppliers to provide all of their MRO requirements for the entire company or for a major division. For example, AT&T announced in early 1996 an aggressive program, titled the "Industrial MRO Global Procurement" program, designed to shave 20 percent a year off their industrial MRO purchases. Under this program, which will take several years to be fully implemented, AT&T plans to reduce its 8,500 MRO suppliers to only 4. It focuses primarily on items used to maintain AT&T buildings and equipment, such as electrical, plumbing, and hardware items, but it also includes commodities such as tools and abrasives. AT&T hopes to obtain better service and quality, as well as better pricing for its approximately $400 million of MRO items used each year.[6]

3. Selection of Possible Sources of Supply

Supplier selection constitutes an important part of the purchasing process and involves the location of qualified sources of supply and assessing the probability that a purchase agreement would result in on-time delivery of satisfactory product and needed services before and after the sale. This step is discussed in detail in Chapters 7 and 8.

Among the basic records, computerized or hard copy, in a well-organized supply office should be:

1. Outstanding contracts against which orders are placed as required.

2. A commodity classification of items purchased.

3. A record of suppliers.

---

[6]Diane Trommer, "AT&T Cuts MRO Vendors from 8,500 to Four," *Electronic Buyer's News,* Jan. 22, 1996, p. 52.

FIGURE 3–5

Quotation Request

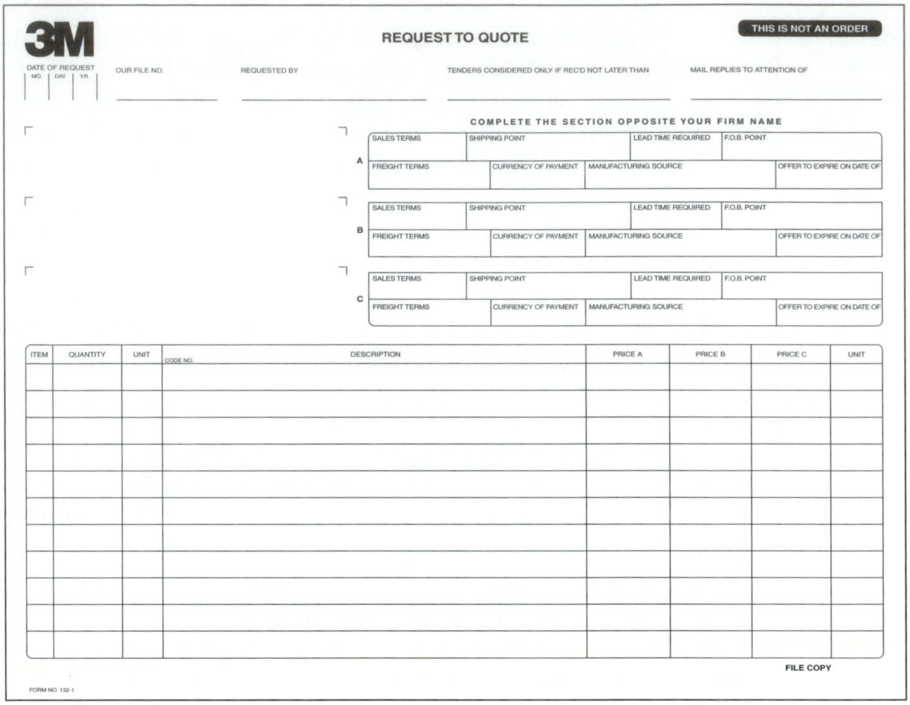
3M

REQUEST TO QUOTE

THIS IS NOT AN ORDER

DATE OF REQUEST MO. DAY YR. | OUR FILE NO. | REQUESTED BY | TENDERS CONSIDERED ONLY IF REC'D NOT LATER THAN | MAIL REPLIES TO ATTENTION OF

COMPLETE THE SECTION OPPOSITE YOUR FIRM NAME

A: SALES TERMS | SHIPPING POINT | LEAD TIME REQUIRED | F.O.B. POINT | FREIGHT TERMS | CURRENCY OF PAYMENT | MANUFACTURING SOURCE | OFFER TO EXPIRE ON DATE OF

B: SALES TERMS | SHIPPING POINT | LEAD TIME REQUIRED | F.O.B. POINT | FREIGHT TERMS | CURRENCY OF PAYMENT | MANUFACTURING SOURCE | OFFER TO EXPIRE ON DATE OF

C: SALES TERMS | SHIPPING POINT | LEAD TIME REQUIRED | F.O.B. POINT | FREIGHT TERMS | CURRENCY OF PAYMENT | MANUFACTURING SOURCE | OFFER TO EXPIRE ON DATE OF

ITEM	QUANTITY	UNIT	CODE NO. DESCRIPTION	PRICE A	PRICE B	PRICE C	UNIT

FILE COPY

FORM NO. 132-1

Source: 3M

With many commodities which are in constant use by an organization, particularly those for which there is an open and free market on which quotations can be obtained at practically any hour of the day, no problem is involved. Bids are often called for, however, on merchandise of common use, such as stationery. A typical quotation form is illustrated by Figure 3–5.

4. Determination of Price and Terms

Analysis of the quotes and the selection of the supplier lead to the placing of an order. Since analysis of bids, quotations, and proposals and the selection of the supplier are matters of judgment, it is necessary only to indicate here that they are logical steps in purchasing. Some organizations use a simple bid analysis form (see Figure 3–6) to assist in analyzing the bids or quotations, but there is no uniform practice. And many purchases are placed through methods other than bidding, for example, from price lists or through negotiation. Determination of price and terms, through a variety of methods, is discussed in detail in Chapter 9.

FIGURE 3–6

Bid Analysis Form

TELEPHONE BID RECORD ARIZONA STATE UNIVERSITY		VENDOR	VENDOR	VENDOR
DATE	BY / PURCHASE REQUISITION	QUOTED BY	QUOTED BY	QUOTED BY
QUANT.	DESCRIPTION	BID AMOUNT	BID AMOUNT	BID AMOUNT
101422-9 2/80	TOTAL			
	DELIVERY TIME			
	TERMS			
	F. O. B. POINT			

Source: Arizona State University

5. Preparation of the Purchase Order

Documentation Required

The placing of an order usually involves preparation of a purchase order form (see Figure 3–7), unless the supplier's sales agreement or a release against a blanket order is used instead. Failure to use the proper contract form may result in serious legal complications. Furthermore, the transaction may not be properly recorded. Therefore, even where an order is placed by telephone, a confirming written order should follow. At times, when emergency conditions arise, it may be expedient to send a truck to pick up items without first going through the usual procedure of requisition and purchase order. But in no instance—unless it be for minor purchases from petty cash—should materials be bought without documentation, written or computer-generated.

Purchase Orders versus Sales Order Forms

All companies have purchase order forms; in practice, however, all purchases are not governed by the conditions stipulated on the purchase order but many are governed by the sales agreement submitted by the seller. Because every company naturally seeks to protect itself as completely as possible, responsibilities which the purchase order form assigns to the source of supply are, in the sales agreement, often transferred to the buyer. Naturally, a company is anxious to use its own sales agreement when selling its products and its own purchase order form when buying.

Determining Applicable Documentation

Some purchasers assert that they will not make any purchase except on their own order form. If the seller strenuously objects to any of the conditions contained in the order form and can present good reasons for the modification of such provisions, a compromise is effected. In a strong sellers' market, however, it may be difficult to adhere to this rule. Also, some suppliers refuse to sell except when the buyer signs their sales order form. If there is no alternative source, as, for example, when a company holds a patent on an article, the value of which is so outstanding that no substitute is acceptable, then the purchaser has no choice in the matter. But, ordinarily, the choice as to which document shall actually be used depends somewhat on the comparative strength of the two parties, the character of the commodity being purchased, the complexity of the transaction, and the strategy used in securing or placing the order.

A good deal of confusion seems to prevail on this whole matter. A buyer may freely sign a sales representative's order form (which, though it may bind the purchaser, legally it is not likely to be binding on the supplier until later confirmed by its home office) and then send a purchase order to the supplier, expecting it to govern. Or a buyer, subsequent to mailing or faxing a purchase order, may receive in reply not an acceptance but a sales order, which really is a counteroffer and not an acceptance.

Point of Contract Formation

However, in the case of low-dollar-value POs, having a legally binding agreement may not be of great importance, for the likelihood of subsequent legal action is slight. For this reason, and to save the cost of handling extra paperwork, many firms do not even use an acknowledgment or acceptance

FIGURE 3-7
Purchase Order

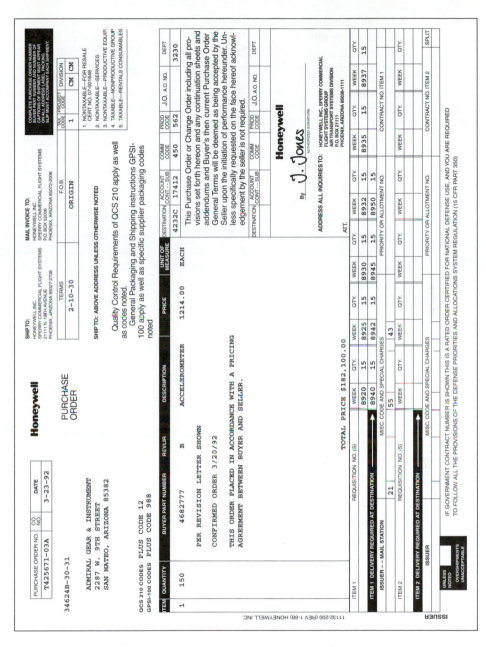

Source: Honeywell Flight Systems Division

copy as part of the purchase order packet on orders under a certain dollar amount, for example, $5,000. This means that they do not have a legally binding contract until the materials arrive. However, the cost of legal action to force delivery on small-value POs would be prohibitive.

Form of the Purchase Order. Purchase order forms vary tremendously as to format and routing through the organization. The essential requirements on any satisfactory purchase order form are the serial number, date of issue, the name and address of the supplier receiving the order, quantity and description of the items ordered, date of delivery required, shipping directions, price, terms of payment, and conditions governing the order.

Typical Conditions Included on a Purchase Order

These conditions governing the relations between the buyer and the seller are important, and the question of what should and what should not be included is subject to a good deal of discussion. What actually appears on the purchase order form of any individual company is usually the result of experience. The items included in the conditions might:

1. Contain provisions to guard the buyer from damage suits caused by patent infringement.

2. Contain provisions concerning price, such as, "If the price is not stated on this order, material must not be billed at a price higher than last paid without notice to us and our acceptance thereof."

3. Contain a clause stating that no charges will be allowed for boxing, crating, or drayage.

4. Stipulate that the acceptance of the materials is contingent on inspection and quality.

5. Require in case of rejection that the seller receive a new order from the buyer before replacement is made.

6. Precisely describe quality requirements and the method of quality assurance/control.

7. Provide for cancellation of the order if deliveries are not received on the date specified in the order.

8. Contain conditions stating that the buyer refuses to accept drafts drawn against the buyer.

9. Have some mention of quantity relating to overshipments or undershipments of the quantities called for. In certain industries it is hard to control definitely the amount obtained from a production run, for example, printing, and in such instances overruns and underruns are usually accepted within certain limits.

10. Provide for matters of special interest to the company, governing such matters as arbitration and the disposition of tools required in making parts.

Processing a Purchase Order

Individual companies differ widely both in the number of copies of a purchase order issued and in the method of handling these copies. In a typical example, the distribution may be as follows: The original is sent to the supplier, sometimes accompanied by a duplicate copy to be returned by the supplier as an acceptance copy to complete the contract.

One copy is filed in the numerical PO file maintained by the purchasing department; another may be maintained in the supplier file. In some companies, the purchasing department does not maintain hard copies of POs; instead the copies are photographed and kept in microfilm or microfiche form. One copy is sent to the accounting department for use in the accounts payable process. A copy is sent to the stores department so it can plan for the receipt of the materials. A separate copy may be sent to the receiving department (if receiving and stores are organizationally separate), where it will be filed alphabetically by supplier and used to record quantities actually received when the shipment arrives. If the material is to go through incoming inspection (which normally would be raw material and production parts), a copy would be routed there also.

All the copies of the purchase order, though essentially identical and all prepared in one operation, are by no means identical in form. For instance, the supplier's acceptance copy may contain an acceptance statement not reproduced on any of the other copies. Only the receiving department's copy may provide for entering the receiving data. The purchasing department copies may provide space for data regarding delivery promise, invoices, and shipments. Pricing information normally is eliminated from the receiving copy, due to its confidential nature.

Managing Purchase Order Information

As might be expected, purchase orders are filed in various ways. It is important to be able to locate the documents any time they are wanted. So far as possible, too, all papers relating to a particular purchase order should be attached to one copy or, if necessary to file some elsewhere, cross-referenced so they can be found quickly. Nothing reflects more unfavorably on a supply department than to have inquiries made by users, production, stores, engineering, or accounting personnel concerning information answerable only from the purchase order and to find the purchasing personnel cannot answer the questions promptly and authoritatively.

One method of filing the purchase orders, where two copies are kept, is to file one numerically by the purchase order number, and to file the second, together with the accompanying requisition and correspondence, alphabetically by supplier's name. Still another procedure is to file one alphabetically by supplier, and the second copy in a tickler file under the date the acceptance copy should be received from the supplier. In case acceptance is not received according to the time due, this fact is noted on this copy of the purchase order, follow-up is instituted in an effort to get the acceptance, and the purchase order is moved ahead to a second "acceptance date." When the order is finally accepted, the tickler copy is again moved, this time being filed under the date either by which final follow-up is desirable or by which the shipment is due.

**Securing a
Valid Contract**

Giving or sending a purchase order does not constitute a contract until it has been accepted. The usual form of acceptance requested is that of an "acknowledgment" sent by the supplier to the purchasing department. Just what does constitute mutual consent and the acceptance of an offer is primarily a legal question. Generalizations concerning the acceptance of offers, as any lawyer will indicate, are likely to be only generalizations with many exceptions.

One further reason for insisting on securing an acceptance of the purchase order is that, quite aside from any question of law, unless the order is accepted, the buyer can only assume that delivery will be made by the requested date. When delivery dates are uncertain, definite information in advance is important if the buyer is to plan operations effectively.

6. Follow-Up and Expediting

After a PO has been issued to a supplier, the buyer may wish to follow up and/or expedite the order. At the time the order is issued, an appropriate follow-up date is indicated. In some firms, purchasing has full-time follow-up and expediting personnel.

**Follow-Up
Routine**

Follow-up is the routine tracking of an order to ensure that the supplier will be able to meet delivery promises. If problems—for example, quality or delivery—are developing, the buyer needs to know this as soon as possible so that appropriate action can be taken. Follow-up, which requires frequent inquiries of the supplier on progress and possibly a visit to the supplier's facility, will be done only on critical, large-dollar and/or long lead-time buys. The follow-up often is done by phone to get immediate information and answers, but some firms use a simple form, often computer generated, to request information on expected shipping date or percentage of the production process completed as of a certain date. Figure 3–8 shows a follow-up form.

**Expediting
Applies
Pressure**

Expediting is the application of pressure on a supplier to get it to meet the original delivery promise, to deliver ahead of schedule, or to speed up delivery of a delayed order. It may involve the threat of order cancellation or withdrawal of future business if the supplier cannot meet the agreement. Expediting should be necessary on only a small percentage of the POs issued, for if the buyer has done a good job of analyzing supplier capabilities, only reliable suppliers—ones who will perform according to the purchase agreement—will be selected. And if the firm has done an adequate job of planning its material requirements, it should not need to ask a supplier to move up the delivery date except in unusual situations. Of course, in times of severe scarcity the expediting activity assumes greater importance.

7. Receipt and Inspection of Goods

The proper receipt of materials and other items is of vital importance. Many organizations have, as a result of experience, centralized all receiving under

FIGURE 3–8

Follow-Up Form

aps.

PURCHASE ORDER FOLLOW-UP
(Please Rush Reply)
PURCHASING DEPARTMENT • P.O. BOX 21666 • PHOENIX, ARIZONA 85036

Date _____
This is our _____ Request
Please Answer Immediately

REPLY TO ITEMS CHECKED BELOW BY
☐ This Form   ☐ Wire   ☐ Phone

Our Purchase Order No.	Request for Quotation No.	Your Invoice No.	Date	Amount	Your Reference

☐ 1. RUSH SHIPMENT. ADVISE EARLIEST DATE.
☐ 2. WHEN WILL SHIPMENT BE MADE? IF SHIPPED. ADVISE METHOD.
☐ 3. PLEASE TRACE SHIPMENT.
☐ 4. IF SHIPMENT HAS BEEN MADE, MAIL INVOICE, TODAY.
☐ 5. PLEASE MAIL RECEIPTED FREIGHT BILL.
☐ 6. WHY DID YOU NOT SHIP AS PROMISED? ADVISE WHEN YOU WILL SHIP.
☐ 7. WILL YOU SHIP ON DATE SHOWN ON PURCHASE ORDER?
☐ 8. RELEASE SHIPMENTS AS SHOWN UNDER REMARKS.
☐ 9. PLEASE MAIL US ACCEPTANCE COPY OR OUR PURCHASE ORDER.
☐ 10. PLEASE ACKNOWLEDGE OUR ORDER.
☐ 11. PLEASE MAKE YOUR SHIPPING DATE MORE SPECIFIC.
☐ 12. WHEN WILL BALANCE OF ORDER BE SHIPPED.
☐ 13. WHEN WILL PRICES BE SUBMITTED? PLEASE RUSH.
☐ 14. PLEASE MAIL SHIPPING NOTICE.
☐ 15. PLEASE INDICATE OUR PURCHASE ORDER NUMBER ON PAPERS REFERRED TO OR ATTACHED.

☐ 16. WE HAVE NO RECORD OF TRANSACTION COVERED BY INVOICE. ADVISE DATE OF SHIPMENT, NAME OF PERSON PLACING ORDER AND FURNISH SIGNED DELIVERY RECEIPT COPY.
☐ 17. INVOICE RETURNED HEREWITH.
☐ 18. INVOICE IS REQUIRED IN _____ COPIES.
☐ 19. PRICE OR DISCOUNT IS NOT IN ACCORDANCE WITH QUOTATION.
☐ 20. TERMS ON INVOICE ARE NOT IN ACCORDANCE WITH THE PURCHASE ORDER.
☐ 21. ENCLOSED INVOICE SENT TO US IN ERROR.
☐ 22. DIFFERENCE IN QUANTITY.
☐ 23. UNIT PRICE INCORRECT.
☐ 24. EXTENSION INCORRECT.
☐ 25. PURCHASE ORDER NO. LACKING OR INCORRECT.
☐ 26. SALES TAX DOES NOT APPLY – See reverse side of Purchase Order.
☐ 27. SHOULD BE BILLED F.O.B. DESTINATION.
☐ 28. HAVE YOU CONSIDERED THIS ORDER COMPLETE?
☐ 29. _____

Reply: _____

Vendor
By _____

Purchasing
By _____

510-00J

SEND WHITE AND PINK COPIES WITH CARBON INTACT. WHITE COPY IS RETURNED WITH REPLY.

Source: Arizona Public Service Company

one department, the chief exceptions being large organizations with multiple sites. Receiving is so closely related to purchasing that, in many organizations, the receiving department is directly or indirectly responsible to the purchasing department. In firms where just-in-time inventory management systems have been implemented, materials from certified suppliers or supplier partners bypass receiving and inspection entirely and are delivered directly to the point of use. Further discussion of these arrangements is presented in Chapter 6, "Quantity." Receiving also may be bypassed for small-value purchases.

Reasons for Receiving

The prime purposes of receiving are:

1. To confirm that the order placed some time ago has actually arrived.
2. To check that the shipment arrived in good condition.
3. To ensure the quantity ordered has been received.

4. To forward the shipment to its proper next destination, be it storage, inspection, or use.

5. To ensure that proper documentation of the receipt is registered and forwarded to the appropriate parties.

In checking the goods received, it sometimes will appear that shortages exist either because material has been lost in transit or because it was short-shipped. Occasionally, too, there is evidence that the shipment has been tampered with or that the shipment has been damaged in transit. In all such cases, full reports are called for, going to both the traffic department and the purchasing department.

Receiving Procedures

Normally one copy of the PO form, often with the quantity column masked out to force a count, is used for receiving. Receiving information then must be supplied to the purchasing department to close out the order, to inventory control to update the inventory files, and to accounts payable for the invoice clearance and payment. Some organizations use a separate receiving-slip form, rather than a copy of the PO, on which receiving records the date of receipt, supplier name, description of materials, and the receiving count. In organizations with an integrated computer materials system, receiving counts are entered directly into the computer data file.

Sometimes suppliers are negligent about invoicing goods shipped, and it may be necessary to request the invoice to complete the transaction. On the other hand, payment of an invoice prior to the receipt of material is often requested. The question then is: When invoices provide for cash discounts, do you pay the invoice within the discount period, even though the material may not actually have been received, or do you withhold payment until the material arrives, even at the risk of losing cash discounts?

Reasons to Withhold Payment until Goods Arrive

The arguments for withholding payment of the invoice until after the goods have arrived are as follows:

1. Frequently the invoice does not reach the buyer until late in the discount period and, on occasion, may even arrive after it. This situation arises through a failure on the part of the supplier (a) to mail the invoice promptly, especially where due allowance is not made for the Saturdays, Sundays, or holidays which elapse between the dating of the invoice and its processing and mailing; and (b) where the supplier is, in terms of mailing time, several days away from the buyer.

2. It is unsound buying practice to pay for anything until an opportunity has been given for inspection. The transaction has not, in fact, been completed until the material or part has actually been accepted, and payment prior to this time is premature. In fact, legally, the title to the goods may not have passed to the buyer until acceptance of them.

3. In any event, the common practice of dating invoices as of the date of shipment should be amended to provide that the discount period runs from receipt of the invoice or the goods, whichever is later.

Reasons to Process Payment before the Goods Arrive

The arguments in favor of passing the invoice for payment without awaiting the arrival, inspection, and acceptance of the material are several:

1. The financial consideration may be substantial.

2. Failure to take the cash discounts as a matter of course reflects unfavorably on the credit standing of the buyer.

3. When purchasing from reputable suppliers, mutually satisfactory adjustments arising out of unsatisfactory material will easily be made, even though the invoice has been paid.

Payment in Computerized Systems

Some organizations, particularly those with integrated computer purchasing systems, question whether they need to receive an invoice at all, since the invoice provides no information that they do not already have and it is another piece of paperwork that costs money to handle. They notify their suppliers that payment, under the agreed-on cash discount schedule, will be made in a set number of days from receipt of satisfactory merchandise (and they may specify that payment will be made only after the complete shipment has been received). They simply then compare, in their computer system, the PO, the receiving report, and the inspection report; if they agree, then the computer simply prints a check at the receipt date plus the agreed-on payment term. Obviously, this requires that the receiving report be accurate; that the PO be fully priced, including taxes and cash discount terms; and that purchases be made FOB destination, since there is no way to enter in freight charges. The PO then is the controlling document. An additional enhancement is use of an electronic funds transfer (EFT) system, where the buyer transmits payment information from its computer through a telephone modem to the bank's computer, and the funds are transferred to the supplier's bank account by account number and PO number.

8. Clearing the Invoice and Payment

The invoice constitutes a claim against the buyer and needs to be handled with care. Invoices commonly are requested in duplicate. Often invoices must show order number and itemized price for each article invoiced.

Procedure relating to invoice clearance is not uniform. In fact, there is a difference of opinion on whether the checking and approval of the invoice is a function of the supply department or the accounting department. Clearly, the invoice must be checked and audited. Many concerns maintain that because the work is accounting in character, the accounting department should do it. The arguments are that it relieves the purchasing department of the performance of a task not value-adding; that it concentrates all the accounting work in a single office; and that it provides a check and balance between the commitment to buy and the payment to the supplier.

The prime argument for having invoices checked in the purchasing department is that this is where the original agreement was made. If discrepancies exist, immediate action can be taken by purchasing.

Where the invoice normally is handled by the accounting department, the following procedure is typical:

1. All invoices are mailed in duplicate by the supplier directly to the accounts payable department, where they are promptly time-stamped. All invoices then are checked and certified for payment, except where the purchase order and the invoice differ.

2. Invoices at variance with the purchase order on price, terms, or other features are referred to the purchasing department for approval.

Because the time required in purchasing to resolve minor variances might be more valuable to the organization than the dollar amount in dispute, many organizations use a decision rule that calls for payment of the invoice as submitted, providing the difference is within prescribed limits, for example, plus or minus 5 percent or $25, whichever is smaller. Of course, accounts payable should keep a record of the variances paid by supplier account to identify suppliers who are intentionally short-shipping.

If any of the necessary information is not on the invoice or if the information does not agree with the purchase order, the invoice is returned to the supplier for correction. Ordinarily, the buyer insists that, in computing discounts, the allowable period dates from the receipt of the corrected invoice, not from the date originally received.

In every instance of cancellation of a purchase order involving the payment of cancellation charges, accounting requires from the purchasing department a "change notice" referring to the order and defining the payment to be made before passing an invoice for such payment.

In cases where purchasing does the invoice checking, the following procedure applies: After being checked and adjusted for any necessary corrections, the original invoice is forwarded to the accounting department to be held until the purchasing department authorizes its payment. The duplicate invoice is retained by the purchasing department until the receiving department notifies it of the receipt of the materials. As soon as the purchasing department obtains this notification in the form of a receiving report, it checks that report against the invoice. If the receiving report and the invoice agree, the purchasing office keeps both documents until it receives assurance from inspection that the goods are acceptable. The purchasing department then forwards its duplicate copy of the invoice and the report from the receiving department to the accounting department, where the original copy of the invoice is already on file.

9. Maintenance of Records

After having gone through the steps described, all that remains for the completion of any order is to update the records of the supply department. This operation involves little more than assembling and filing the purchasing department's copies of the documents relating to the order and transferring to appropriate records the information the department may wish to keep. The former is largely a routine matter. The latter involves judgment as to what records are to be kept and also for how long.

Most companies differentiate between the various forms and records as to their importance. For example, a purchase order constitutes evidence of a contract with an outside party and, as such, may well be retained much longer (normally seven years) than the requisition, which is an internal memorandum.

Basic Purchase Records

The minimum, basic records to be maintained, either manually or by computer, are:

1. PO log, which identifies all POs by number and indicates the open or closed status of each.
2. PO file, containing a copy of all POs, filed numerically.
3. Commodity file, showing all purchases of each major commodity or item (date, supplier, quantity, price, PO number).
4. Supplier history file, showing all purchases placed with major large-total-value suppliers.

Additional record files may include:

1. Labor contracts, giving the status of union contracts (expiration dates) of all major suppliers.
2. Tool and die record showing tooling purchased, useful life (or production quantity), usage history, price, ownership, and location. This information may avoid being billed more than once for the same tooling.
3. Minority and small business purchases, showing dollar purchases from such suppliers.
4. Bid-award history file, showing suppliers asked to bid, amounts bid, number of no bids, and the successful bidder, by major items. This information may highlight supplier bid patterns and possible collusion.

Policy and Procedure Manual

Carefully prepared, detailed statements of organization, of duties of the various personnel, and of procedures and data systems (including illustrative forms used, fully explained) are of great value. A manual is almost an essential for the well-conceived training program for junior members. Furthermore, it adds an element of flexibility in facilitating the transfer of personnel from one job to another in case of vacation, illness, or temporary workload imbalances. Finally, the manual is useful in explaining to those not in the function what and how things are done.

Some managers feel that because their departments are not as large as those in bigger companies, there is no special need for a manual. They feel that everyone knows all that would be put in a manual anyway and hence there is no need for writing it all down. This argument overlooks the benefits gained in the actual task of preparing the manual.

Preparation of the Manual

The preparation of a manual is time-consuming and somewhat tedious, to be sure, but well worth the cost. Unless the work is carefully planned and well done, accurate, and reasonably complete, it might almost as well not be done at all. Careful advance planning of the coverage, emphasis, and arrangement is essential, as well as including a clear definition of the purposes sought in issuing the manual and the uses to which it is to be put, for both of these have a bearing on its length, form, and content.

Very early in the project, the preparer must decide whether the manual is to cover only policy or is to include also a description of the organization and the procedures, and, if the latter, in how much detail. A collection of manuals now in use should be the starting point. Fortunately, excellent sample manuals that can serve as guides are available from any number of organizations.

When the general outline has been determined, the actual writing may be started. This work need not be done all at one time but section by section as the opportunity presents itself. It also is well to have the work thoroughly discussed and carefully checked, not only by those within the department itself, but by those outside, such as engineering and production personnel, whose operations are directly affected. When a section is completed, that portion may provide the basis for a department discussion forum, not only for the sake of spotting errors and suggesting modifications before the material is actually reproduced, but also to ensure that everyone understands its contents. This should be done prior to issue. When reproduced, a loose-leaf form may be found preferable because it allows for easy revision. Another worthwhile step is to have the chief executive of the organization write a short foreword, endorsing the policy and practices of the department and defining its authority.

Common Subjects in a Manual

While many subjects might be covered in the manual, some of the more common are: authority to requisition, competitive bidding, approved suppliers, supplier contacts and commitments, authority to question specifications, purchases for employees, gifts, blanket purchase orders, confidential data, rush orders, supplier relations, lead times, determination of quantity to buy, over and short allowance procedures, local purchases, capital equipment, personal service purchases, repair service purchases, authority to select suppliers, confirming orders, unpriced purchase orders, documentation for purchase decisions, invoice clearance and payment, invoice discrepancies, freight bills, change orders, samples, returned materials, disposal of scrap and surplus, determination of price paid, small order procedures, salesperson interviews, and reporting of data.

Information Systems

Purchasing procedures are established basically to process inputs of information from outside the purchasing and supply function and to produce outputs of information needed by other functions and institutions outside the purchasing function. Few business functions have the breadth of contacts both within the firm and with the external environment that the well-operated purchasing and supply function has.

Internal Information Flows to Purchasing

Every functional activity within the firm generates information to, and/or requires information from, the purchasing system. Figure 3–9 diagrams the information flows to purchasing. The information sent to purchasing falls into the following two major categories:

Catgories of Internal Information

1. Statements of needs for materials and services obtained from inside the firm.
2. Requests for information available within purchasing or obtainable from outside the firm.

A brief description of the information flows charted in Figure 3–9 follows.

Planning. This function provides purchasing with information important in obtaining the long-term future requirements of the firm for facilities, materials, and services. Competent planning is of special importance in preparing for future construction needs and for raw materials or components in tight or diminishing supply.

Sales Forecasting. Well-developed sales forecasts are one of the most helpful tools available to purchasing in planning strategies. Business operations

FIGURE 3–9

Internal Information Flows to Purchasing

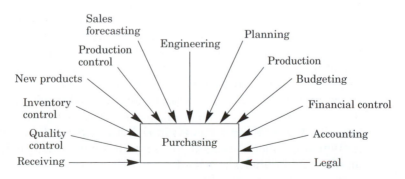

usually achieve the greatest degree of operating efficiency when orderly planning permits orderly acquisition and scheduling of requirements. When purchasing has adequate advance notice of kinds of materials likely to be required and approximate quantities, it is in a favorable position to obtain the optimum balance between the conditions in the marketplace and the needs of the firm.

Budgeting and Financial Control. The information provided by the budgeting function helps in coordinating the information from planning and sales forecasting and brings into focus any constraints imposed by the financial control function. Such constraints may apply to the operating expenses of the purchasing system as well as to the possibilities of following other than a buy-as-required inventory policy.

Accounting. The accounting function supplies information on payments to suppliers, cost studies for make-or-buy decisions, and comparison of actual expenditures to budget.

Legal. Because the purchasing function is the major activity authorized to commit the firm to contracts for materials and services, the legal function provides information regarding contracts and procedures.

Engineering. The basic responsibility of engineering is to provide information on what types of materials are needed and the specification of the qualities needed. The acknowledged right of purchasing to challenge specifications usually promotes greater efficiency in the organization.

Production and Production Control. The production function frequently provides information on the quality requirements for materials. The production control and scheduling function provides information on what materials are needed and in what quantities for a given time period covered by a production cycle. Properly compiled, such information provides a useful tool in planning purchasing and supply operations.

Inventory Control. This function provides basic information on what needs to be purchased or ordered at any given time. The use of economic order quantities will be determined by the inventory policy, which governs the investment in inventory at any given period. An inventory policy may be influenced by the financial resources of the firm, future plans, current market conditions, and lead time in the purchase of materials.

Quality Control and Receiving. Both of these functions provide information which determines if the suppliers have furnished materials of the quality and quantity specified. Such information is essential to the proper performance of the purchasing function.

New Products. The importance of new product development to the success of a company has increased greatly in recent years. Unless information about new product development reaches purchasing at the inception of the project, the full contribution possible from purchasing seldom will be realized.

External Information Flows to Purchasing

The efficiently operated purchasing department is one of the firm's major contact points with the external world and, as such, is a receiving point for a flow of information from sources outside the firm. Much of this information is essential to the operation of the firm. Figure 3–10 shows the nature of the information. A brief explanation of each of the major types of information coming from external sources follows:

Categories of External Information

General Market Conditions. Competent purchasing executives and buyers become specialists on general market and business conditions. Suppliers' salespeople, purchasing trade publications, various Institute for Supply Management (formerly the National Association of Purchasing Management) publications and services, and local purchasing association meetings and publications provide a constant stream of information about prices, supply and demand factors, and competitors' actions.

Sources of Supply. Suppliers' salespeople, advertising media of all types, special promotions, exhibits at trade shows and conventions, and credit and financial reports provide information initiated by suppliers and aimed at their customers and potential customers.

Suppliers' Capacity, Suppliers' Production Rates, and Labor Conditions in the Suppliers' Plants and Industries. Information flows on these factors are of great importance in determining inventory policy and assuring continuity of supply and production.

FIGURE 3–10

External Information Flows to Purchasing

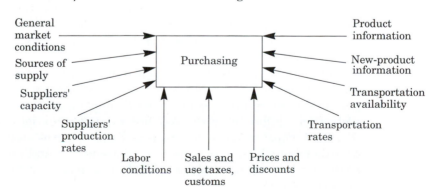

Prices and Discounts, Customs, Sales and Use Taxes. Information of any nature regarding prices is important to the effective functioning of purchasing. Much of the price information is obtained directly from suppliers or salespeople representing potential suppliers. The services of consultants specializing in economic trends frequently are useful in determining price trends, particularly of commodities. Both the customs and tax fields are rapidly changing, requiring continuous monitoring.

Transportation Availability and Rates. The types, availability, and rates of transportation services have had an increasingly important bearing on the cost of materials within recent years. Whether problems involving transportation are the direct responsibility of a logistics department is not the critical point. It is how the information, which is of importance in its effect on costs of material, is used by purchasing.

New Product and Product Information. The great emphasis on creating new products and services has placed a heavy burden on the purchasing function. Purchasing must process the information about products and services received from the outside in such a way that the appropriate function within the firm will be alerted to any product information, whether it be new or old, which can be useful in improving effectiveness, reducing costs, or aiding in developing new products or services for the firm.

Internal Information Flows from Purchasing to the Organization

There are very few functions of a business which are not concerned to some degree with the information that flows or can be generated from purchasing. Figure 3–11 diagrams the major types of information that flow from purchasing to the organization:

Purchasing Feeds Information to Other Functions

General Management. Purchasing personnel have daily contact with a wide spectrum of the marketplace, and if properly qualified by education, ability, and experience, are in an advantageous position to collect up-to-the-minute information about current market and business conditions. These data, when correlated and refined, can provide top management with information valuable in the operation of the company.

Engineering. The engineering function requires much information from the marketplace. While there are situations which warrant the engineers making their own direct contacts with suppliers in order to obtain product and/or price information or place orders, such situations should be the exception. Competent purchasing specialists, or a cross-functional team, can provide more effective service by better sourcing and negotiation of lower prices than an engineer whose special competence is concerned with an engineering specialty.

FIGURE 3–11

Internal Information Flows from Purchasing

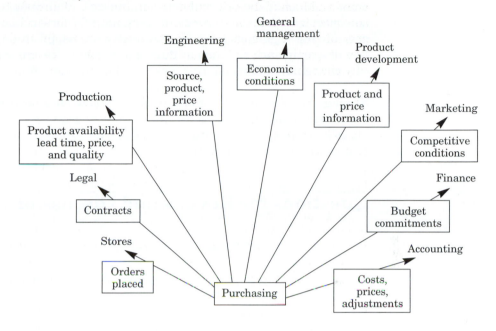

Product Development. Product development departments, regardless of whether they are part of the engineering or the marketing functions, benefit from new materials information and price information the purchasing function can provide from its contacts in the marketplace. A purchasing function that recognizes its obligation to maximize information flow to new product activities performs a valuable service.

Marketing. The purchasing department is a target for the sales and promotion plans of many different suppliers from many industries. Perceptive purchasing personnel frequently can provide information on new types of selling campaigns which have value to the marketing function of their own firm.

Production. The production function depends on purchasing for information about materials, material availability, material delivery lead times, material substitutes, and help in locating sources of supply for production equipment. Production also can be aided by purchasing with information about new maintenance, repair, and operating supply items.

Legal. The purchasing department furnishes the legal department with much of the information needed for drawing contracts for all types of materials purchased under a blanket contract, a stockless buying arrangement, long-term agreements, and EDI systems.

Finance and Accounting. Purchasing is in a position to provide the finance and accounting functions with information basic to budget development and administration and determining cash requirements. Material and transportation costs and trends in costs, need for forward buying because of possible shortages resulting from greater demand, or anticipated interruption of supply, such as happens during a major strike, are some of the kinds of information purchasing provides to aid in planning financial operations.

Stores. The formulation of an inventory policy for a store's department is dependent on information concerning lead times and availability of materials, price trends, and substitute materials. The purchasing department is the best source of such information.

Questions for Review and Discussion

1. Outline and discuss the steps involved in a sound purchasing procedure.
2. Where, and how, should invoices be cleared for payment within an organization?
3. What contribution to purchasing efficiency might be effected through the use of (1) a corporate purchasing card, (2) the bill of material, and (3) systems contracting?
4. What approaches, other than the standard purchasing procedure, might be used to minimize the small order problem?
5. What records are needed for efficient operation of the purchasing function? Specifically, how can needed data be obtained and maintained?
6. How do follow-up and expediting procedures differ?
7. What items should be covered in a policy manual? Write a proposed policy statement for three of the items.
8. Are rush orders ever justified? When? How should they be handled?
9. What should be the information flows between purchasing and (1) internal organizational activities and (2) external activities?

References

Glossary of Key Purchasing and Supply Terms, compiled by the National Association of Purchasing Management, 2000.

Griffiths, D., *NAPM InfoEdge: Managing Small-Dollar Purchases,* Tempe, AZ: National Association of Purchasing Management, January 1996.

NAPM Supply Management Series: Purchasing and Supply Management Policy and Business Management Guide, Tempe, AZ: National Association of Purchasing Management.

Procurement Card Guide, supplement to *Purchasing Today,* March 1998.

CASE 3–1
MIKE WESLEY

In April, Mike Wesley, the purchasing manager at Wesley Printing, was reviewing a coordination problem the company had experienced with a recent print job. Late delivery to an important customer had been avoided only as a result of special measures taken by company staff. However, these actions, while necessary under the circumstances, resulted in significant cost overruns. Mike knew that the company could not afford to encounter such problems in the future.

Wesley Printing. Wesley Printing was a specialty printer producing pressure-sensitive and glue-applied paper labels for customers primarily in the food and beverage industry. Founded in 1905, the company was owned and managed by several descendants of the founder.

Wesley Printing competed on the basis of product quality and customer service. As a unionized shop, its cost structure was higher than that of many of its competitors. Several of Wesley's larger competitors preferred high volume jobs, where customers typically made sourcing decisions on the basis of price. Smaller printing companies did not have the experience or resources to deal with difficult printing processes. Wesley emphasized a high level of service to its customers, working closely with them to achieve their objectives, willing to go out of its way to satisfy the customer, and being flexible in meeting very short lead times.

Meeting deadlines was very important to Wesley's customers. A shortage of labels at a customer's production line could result in downtime or expensive rework. The costs caused by such delays could be charged back to the printer, and the disruption to schedules made repeat business unlikely.

Wesley's Organization. Wesley Printing was organized on the basis of functional groups. On the administration side, there were the sales, finance and accounting, purchasing, and estimating departments. On the operations side, there was the art department, where customer-provided artwork was retouched and adjusted; the camera department, which photographed the artwork on the large "process camera" in order to make the films; the plate department, where the films were used to produce printing plates for the presses; the press department, where the actual printing took place; the bindery department, where large sheets of labels were sheared or die-cut to correct size and shape; and finally the shipping and receiving department. A customer order moved sequentially through these departments, scheduled by the production manager. Scheduling was sometimes difficult because it was common for last-minute changes in customer requirements to make schedule alterations necessary.

The Fine Foods Job

Monday, April 14. On Monday, April 14, the sales representative handling the Fine Foods account received a request for a quote on an unusual job. Instead of the usual flat label, Fine Foods wanted 60,000 small folded booklets, with a hole in one corner, through which passed a loop of string to enable it to be hung from the necks of condiment bottles. It was a rush job that had to be ready for a 7 a.m. production run the Tuesday of the following week, so that the client could have samples ready for a new product launch at a trade show. No schedule slippage could be tolerated.

The sales representative passed the order to the estimator, together with a sample booklet, in order to have a quotation prepared. The estimator knew that the job could be laid out such that an attachment on the press could fold the booklet as it was printed. Wesley did not have a drill suitable for making the holes, nor did they have equipment to insert the strings, so the estimator secured a quote from an outside bindery for those two parts of the job. The outside bindery agreed to complete its work by the following Monday morning if the job went ahead.

The finished quote was returned to the sales representative and a copy filed. The sales representative took the quote to the production manager to get a schedule commitment that the job would be done by Friday noon, in time to go to the outside bindery. The production manager agreed the commitment could be made.

Tuesday, April 15. The sales representative returned the quote to Fine Foods on Tuesday morning, and the client gave the job to Wesley, agreeing to send the artwork to arrive on Wednesday. The quote having been accepted, the file copy of the estimate and job specifications were retrieved and passed to the production manager, who scheduled the job and generated instructions for each production department. When the file was transferred, the sample was no longer in it. The production manager contacted the purchasing manager to have a purchase order prepared for the work to be done by the outside bindery. The purchasing manager sent the PO to the bindery, all the while assuming a simple flat tag was involved.

Wednesday, April 16. The artwork arrived and was duly processed by the art and camera departments. When the resulting films arrived at the plate maker, he laid the plates out in such a way that the booklets would not fold correctly if the press attachment was used. They would now have to be folded on a special folding machine, which Wesley did not have.

Thursday, April 17. The plates were sent to the press on Thursday afternoon for the print run, which was scheduled for the night shift. When the night shift press operator mounted the plates, he did not set up the folder attachment because the machine could not do the job properly. He assumed that alternate arrangements had been made for folding.

Friday, April 18. The full print run was completed in the morning and sent to Wesley's bindery, where the large sheets were cut to size, tied in blocks, and put in cartons for shipping to the outside bindery. The shipper, who prepared the shipment and assembled the paperwork instructions to go to the outside bindery, did not notice that the still unfolded booklets were not accompanied by any instructions for the bindery to fold them. The cartons of labels were sent to the outside bindery on Friday at noon.

Late Friday afternoon, the purchasing manager received a phone call from the manager of the bindery stating that the job arrived unfolded, that he had not contracted to fold them, and because he did not have the proper folding equipment, he intended to return the job. Mike and the sales representative were the only people in the office at that time and they both realized that if that happened, it would be impossible to meet the client's deadline.

Mike pleaded with the bindery manager to find some way to fill at least part of the order. The bindery manager agreed that if he could find enough labor to work around the clock all weekend, he could probably have a quarter of the order hand-folded and assembled by Monday evening. The sales representative called his contact at Fine Foods and imparted the news that, due to production difficulties, they would not be able to ship the full order on time, and would he be able to get by with a quarter of it? The customer replied that a quarter would not be enough, but he could get by with a third. Mike called the bindery manager and with more difficult persuasion got him to increase the quantity to a third.

Crews of people worked around the clock, hand-folding 20,000 little booklets. They were drilled and strung and were ready late Monday night. The Fine Foods account sales representative picked the booklets up from the bindery and personally delivered them to the production line at Fine Foods 150 miles away, a little before 7 o'clock the next morning.

After the Storm. Now that the emergency had passed, Mike felt it was important to find and correct whatever had gone wrong in their procedures that allowed such a slip-up to occur. He felt it was necessary to be able to assure both Fine Foods and the outside bindery that Wesley knew not only what had gone wrong, but also how to prevent it from happening again. This was the only way to assure both the customer and the supplier that they would not experience this kind of difficulty with Wesley in future dealings. It was also important for Wesley to prevent errors like this from happening again as all the extra costs involved in filling this order had caused a significant loss on the job.

Mike questioned how this had happened. The missing sample booklet was later found on the estimator's desk, but Mike felt that this was not the fault of a single person. All over the shop, mistakes had been made and not caught or corrected. Under pressure to be more efficient, Wesley was now turning out more work with fewer people than they had in the past. Mike wondered if production pressures no longer allowed the employees time to notice errors of omission. Wesley had recently completed all the documentation requirements to receive ISO 9000 certification, but that had not prevented this problem. Mike wondered what actions should be taken to prevent this kind of problem from happening again.

Case 3–2
UIL Inc.

In October, Jim Sinclair, materials manager for UIL Inc., was troubled by the amount of time consumed by processing rush orders. Jim wondered if inventory cages, eliminated several years earlier, would have to be reimplemented in some form, or whether he should try something different.

UIL. UIL manufactured custom equipment for a large variety of industries worldwide. UIL was a wholly-owned subsidiary of Marin Inc., a large holding company. UIL functioned as an independent profit center responsible for its own purchasing, manufacturing, and sales functions. Capital was allocated to UIL from Marin on the basis that a levy would be charged to UIL's bottom line based on a percentage of capital utilized. Managers were then measured on their ability to maximize the final profit figure after the payments for use of capital had been paid to the parent. Otherwise, managers were free to make decisions regarding regular operations.

Current Materials Requisition System. The UIL production operation required the requisition of a varied group of materials, ranging from items consumed on a regular basis, to items purchased sporadically, if not on a one-time basis. Under the current system, when workers on the plant floor required additional supplies, they would arrange for their requisition via Jim, the materials manager. Jim then had to issue a purchase order to a supplier to receive delivery of the required items.

The highest volume of orders existed in the Welding, Hardware, and Maintenance/Repair/ Operating (MRO) areas. In these areas, individual items were inexpensive, often costing less than one dollar. Currently, items were held in stock with the quantity maintained within a minimum-maximum range. A computer system was used to track the number of items in stock and was supposed to indicate when inventory levels fell below the minimum level, thereby triggering an order by the materials manager.

Growth in the Number of Purchase Orders (POs). Unfortunately, because inventory items in the three groups were so numerous yet inexpensive, employees were not motivated to keep inventory records current, and stock-outs were frequent. These items, although trivial when available, would stop an area of operation when required. As a result, the materials manager was forced to issue a rush order to restock the supply. Lately, however, these rush orders had become a significant portion of the POs being issued and were consuming increasingly more of the materials manager's time. This was further aggravated by the portion of spend that this large number of POs represented. Jim's analysis showed that:

Percentage of Total Spend	Spend Percentage of Total POs Issued
less than 1%	accounted for 25%
less than 4%	60%
less than 8%	73%
less than 30%	94%

Elimination of Inventory Cages. The traditional method of handling high volume, low cost items, was with the use of inventory cages on the shop floor. An employee was assigned to a fenced-in inventory holding area or "cage" where production workers were able to request the items required. The cage manager would then be responsible for maintaining inventory levels of the items in the cage, giving the materials manager advanced notice of when orders would be required, and providing insight into ideal lot sizes. The cage manager could also maintain a degree of control as to the usage of the items.

Several years ago, Jim chose to eliminate the cages, citing the high cost of maintaining an employee to handle the inventory, particularly when the items being handled represented such a small cost to the company. Unfortunately, soon after the cages were eliminated, the instances where rush purchase orders to cover stock-outs began to rise. Jim felt that the problem had grown to such proportions that he was not able to dedicate sufficient time to the remainder of the purchases, items that represented a much more significant proportion of total spend.

As a result, he concluded that the cages, in some form, might have to be reimplemented.

Outsourcing as an Alternative. In October, Jim began exploring the alternative of allowing his suppliers to maintain inventory levels of the items in the three high-volume groups: MRO, Welding, and Hardware. This would be done by issuing a blanket purchase order for all of the items required in the class each month. All items in the class would be ordered from the same supplier under a single purchase order, resulting in a single invoice at the end of the month. This would reduce the number of purchase orders to 12 per year, per group, for a total of 36 transactions. In the period from January to October, this would have eliminated 637 transactions out of a total of 3,454 in this eight-month period.

Jim identified several disadvantages to the system. Currently, items within a class were purchased from many different suppliers, thereby providing an opportunity to shop around for the best quality and price. Under the proposed system, all the items would be purchased from the same supplier for a given class of products.

As well, it was the supplier that would come to the company premises and restock items. This presented the risk that the supplier would be motivated to overstock the shelves and poorly manage the inventory or even allow portions of the inventory to become obsolete. Poor management of inventory was even more likely because liability is-

sues determined that the inventory would have to become the property of UIL at the time of delivery to the site, resulting in carrying costs to UIL. Jim felt that this risk could be minimized by setting minimum-maximum levels as before, and that he could still monitor the purchases being made, even if it was one month after-the-fact on the invoice.

The greatest benefit Jim recognized was the savings associated with not needing to hire someone to work in the cage. The suppliers would take on that responsibility and had already committed themselves to not raising their prices, despite the extra service provided. There was a risk, however, that over time, prices would rise due to the extra costs incurred by offering the materials handling service. Jim could supply the parts he required, and if a relationship with one of the suppliers he selected deteriorated, he could replace them. But, he was a bit worried that they would become dependent on one supplier's line of products, making a change to a new supplier more difficult.

The Decision. Jim had already interviewed several potential suppliers for the three product groups and was comfortable with his options. He was still not sure, however, if handing over this materials handling function was a good idea. He knew that the standard cage method was a better alternative than the system currently used, but he had to decide if perhaps costs could be reduced further by this new option.

Case 3–3
Artsell Inc.

It was 10 a.m., Wednesday, December 22, and Tom Pepper, Services Manager at the Artsell Inc., Texas plant, had just returned from a meeting with Carrie Denton, Purchasing Agent. She had informed him that the purchasing system, which he had recommended, was inadequate for invoicing. With a team meeting scheduled for noon, he knew that he had little time to decide what to do.

Artsell Inc. Artsell Inc. was a complex international firm with an emphasis on developing unique products for sale internationally. Artsell provided more than 50,000 products in the industrial, business, service, resource, and consumer marketplace. The Texas plant had about 2000 employees and a sales volume of almost $1 billion.

The Manufacturing Area. Tom Pepper became the manufacturing services manager two years ago, after 15 years with Artsell. As manufacturing services manager, Tom was responsible for overseeing the maintenance of equipment, lighting, janitorial work; supporting the various manufacturing groups; and handling shipping and receiving. Overall, there were approximately 280 employees in Tom's area. (See Exhibit 1 for an organization chart.)

The Maximo System Decision. About one year ago, the newly appointed plant manager, Stan Kurgan, approached Tom Pepper to discuss his mandate. He made it clear to Tom that maintenance was spending a lot of money, and the system in use was not adequately tracking the maintenance situation at Artsell. Tom recognized that there were a few options available, and from the options he chose to implement a new purchasing system called Maximo, which would track supply requirements and notify the accounting system of any requirements needs (Exhibit 2). This decision was made last spring, based largely on the fact that the Maximo system was currently in use in the Pennsylvania plant, and they were eager to pass along the system at a minimal cost to Artsell. Tom also saw Maximo as a better system because the existing system lacked the required integrity. Maximo would, however, require interfacing with the Pur Pay accounting system in order to allow for invoicing payment.

After deciding on the Maximo system, Tom appointed Casey Zimmerman from the Information Technology (IT) area to head up the project of planning and implementing this new system. Casey took ownership of the task and completed large portions of the test and development stages. He was the most knowledgeable on the subject of the Maximo implementation and integration at the time when he became sick in the early summer.

While Casey was aware of the need for an interface to the Pur Pay accounting system, his absence resulted in the split of his duties between other workers. One of the people who took over made the decision that because the Pur Pay system was outdated and would be replaced by People Soft in another year or so, spending time on developing the interface was not cost effective. As a result, they did not develop the interface. The developer thought it would be much easier for accounting to manually match the invoices than for IT to develop the interface. With the Maximo roll-out date set for January 1, it was the discovery that Maximo was not interfacing with Pur Pay that prompted the meeting between Carrie Denton, a purchasing agent (See Exhibit 3) and Tom.

As Tom sat back to think about his 10 a.m. meeting, his stomach once again began to turn:

Carrie: What do you mean there's no interface to Pur Pay? How do you expect us to pay invoices?

Tom: It was too much work to develop an interface, and our resources were better used in other areas. It only requires one extra step from the accounting department—why are you so worried about this? We've already spent $30,000 to $50,000 on this project, plus two full-time staff for six months. We can't spend any more on this.

Carrie: One extra step? Do you know what kind of work that would require for 200 invoices a day? This is not going to happen. We don't have the human power or the time for this, and clearly it is just not possible. Are you forgetting that the agreement that we made with the IT department clearly stated that the interface was a requirement of purchasing? Fix this, and fix it before we go live, because my department will not do this.

Invoicing Requirements. Prior to Maximo, producing invoices was done by the Pur Pay system by matching all invoice, receipt information, and PO information. Payment was then performed through an interface into the system that Maximo was chosen to replace. Maximo was to be used to generate a Requirement Replenishment Listing to Pur Pay. This would, in effect, place orders for supply requirements automatically into Pur Pay, where a purchase order would be issued. In addition, Maximo was chosen to allow for additional functionality in the area of work orders and stock-to-inventory items.

EXHIBIT 1   Reporting Structure at the Artsell Texas Plant

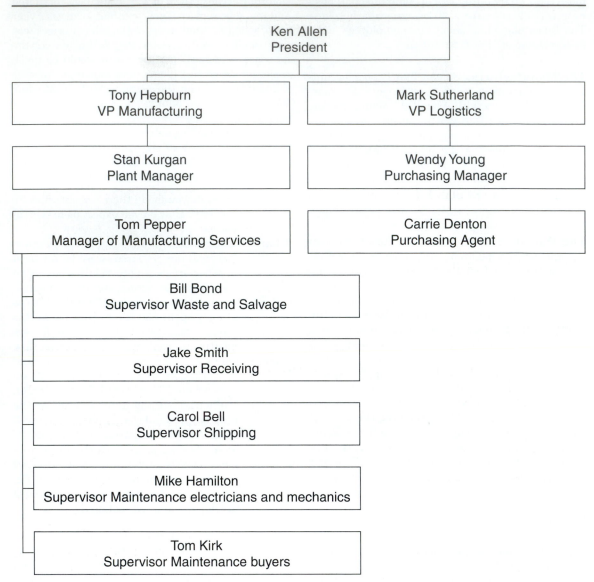

Alternatives Available. Tom thought about the situation and came to the conclusion that there were three options which he could choose from.

Accounting Personnel Manually Match Invoices. The first option involved arguing with up-per management to get the accounting people to do the manual matching of invoices. This would involve just a few more steps in the process, and he thought accounting could handle it. After all, in two years, People Soft was expected to replace Pur Pay, and the problem would be solved. Tom estimated

EXHIBIT 2   Artsell Inc.

ARTSELL SYSTEMS

MAXIMO   **PUR PAY**

- Generate List of Supply Requirements based on supply amounts on-hand.
- Send requirements listing to Pur Pay

- Receipt of goods sent into Maximo

- Generate Purchase Order to supplier

- Performance of invoice matching to Purchase Order and Goods Receipt

EXHIBIT 3 Artsell Inc.

JOB DESCRIPTION—PURCHASING AGENT

Effectively manage the procurement component of the Supply Chain in support of Plant and Facilities Engineering and Plant Maintenance businesses. Provide timely and accurate order management, including required follow-through, from receiving the client's order to payment of the supplier's invoice. Work with the Engineering and Manufacturing clients to understand their business plans and their expectations of the Purchasing department. Co-ordinate Purchasing efforts with other Logistics and Admin staff groups who also support Engineering and Maintenance. Work with suppliers to utilize their technology to deliver innovative solutions and lowest total delivered cost. Initiate and manage to completion procurement projects that will result in process, productivity, and cost improvements. Utilize the computer to prepare analysis to support improvement proposals.

that it would cost approximately $30,000 per year for each of the full-time clerical staff that would be required to perform this matching.

Customization. The second option was to develop the link into Pur Pay to allow the system to interface. Tom estimated that this would involve the time of one full-time person for at least another six months, and Tom was certain that they would have to hire externally for this position.

Procurement Card. The third option was to use a procurement card whereby the supplier would enter the data into one of the two systems for matching to the invoice, based on certain levels of cards. The procurement card was to be used, much like a credit card, with the bank handling the cards, and generating invoices to the suppliers through a means similar to a monthly credit card statement. The first type of card would be for personal use, the second would require all information to be entered, and the third would be a blanket type in which the supplier would have to list purchase order references and transaction dates. Tom contacted the bank manager, who indicated that the bank would handle all design aspects for the cards. All of the input would need to be reviewed by management, and Tom assumed that they could use internal people to fill this need. The software for this option would cost each supplier anywhere from $250 to $500 for the software and installation.

The Decision. Tom could just imagine the result if he chose the wrong option, especially since he had recommended Maximo in the first place. With only two hours until the team meeting, Tom knew he had to come up with a clear decision in a very short time. He wondered what choice he should recommend to his team.

4 TECHNOLOGY AND E-COMMERCE

Chapter Outline

Key Questions for the Purchasing Decision Maker

SHOULD WE:

- Use e-procurement tools, including auctions and reverse auctions, for some or all of our purchases?
- Adopt an electronic bill presentment and payment system?
- Make greater use of the computer and the Internet to simplify and improve the purchasing system?

HOW CAN WE:

- Decide which technology tools are most appropriate for the organization's categories of purchases?
- Make the purchasing and supply management process more efficient using technology?
- Use technology to control maverick spending, e.g. spending that is done outside of established purchasing procedures?

E-Commerce Growth Expected

Within the past 25 years, we have witnessed a remarkable development of hardware and software used in aiding the recording, transmission, analysis, and reporting of information in the operation of complex business systems. The development of the Internet and the millions of documents available on the World Wide Web have had an astounding impact on people's ability to access information instantaneously. Even though there are still many unanswered questions when it comes to the lasting impact of the Internet, it is clear that all processes and procedures used to perform tasks in all areas of business, including supply management, will be impacted.

Most people in organizations recognize the strategic importance of information and knowledge management. The Internet, which was initially seen primarily as a tool for information sharing, is now seen as having tremendous potential for electronic commerce. According to International Data Corporation, online business-to-business Internet-based purchases tallied $32 billion in 1998 and are projected to reach $331 billion by 2002.[1] Forrester Research in Cambridge, Massachusetts, estimates even more explosive growth with business-to-business buying reaching $2.72 trillion by 2003.[2] Yet, in April 2001, the NAPM-Forrester Research Report on eBusiness, which measures the adoption of Internet-based procurement and tracks online activity for both manufacturing and nonmanufacturing organizations, reported that most organizations were still in the early stages of adoption. At that time, the most widely adopted uses of the Internet in procurement were:

---

[1]Cherish Caroway Whyte, "We're Not There Yet!" *Purchasing Today,* January 1999, p. 40.
[2]Ibid.

- Purchasing indirect materials (70.9 percent of those surveyed reported buying some indirect materials online),
- As part of a Request for Proposal (RFP) process (48.8 percent),
- To identify new suppliers (80.7 percent), and
- To collaborate online with suppliers (42.8 percent).[3]

Technology is a tool that can improve efficiency and effectiveness when applied appropriately to a process. Therefore, the decision maker must carefully assess the process to determine when and where the application of technology is most appropriate and what technology should be selected. If the process itself is flawed then a process improvement program must be undertaken before the process is automated.

This chapter starts with a brief glossary of key terms and a detailed description of available technology. It also addresses the potential ways that technology and Web-based applications might contribute to the efficiency and effectiveness of the purchasing process. Lastly, the implications of technology and e-commerce for supply management are discussed.

Glossary of Terms

Applications software are programs that manipulate data for a specific purpose, such as maintaining the open order file or taking supplier performance statistics and formatting them into a supplier performance evaluation analysis and report.

Auction (see also online auction). A seller with goods to sell invites multiple buyers to bid against each other at a set time and place to purchase the goods.

Bar code is a series of parallel rectangular bars and spaces arranged in a predetermined pattern to encode letters, numbers, and special characters.

Business-to-Business (B2B). Electronic commerce between business entities.

Business-to-Consumer (B2C). Electronic commerce between businesses and consumers.

Business-to-Government (B2G). Electronic commerce between businesses and government agencies.

Data aggregators develop a library of product specifications from a variety of suppliers and then license organizations to use the product specifications and assist in developing the transaction data.

Decision-Assisting (Decision-Support) Systems process data to assist purchasing management in selecting from among alternatives.

Digital signatures. Short units of data bearing mathematical relationships to the data in the document's content that are transmitted using public key cryptography (PKI) programs. These programs create a pair of keys (one public key and one private key), and what the public key encrypts only the private key can decrypt. Alternatively, what the private key encrypts only the public key can decrypt. This assures confidentiality of information, and the digital signature allows the receiver to verify the sender of the data.

Document Type Definitions (DTDs). Definitions of industry-specific data elements needed to execute specific transactions.

E-commerce is a broad term meant to include any type of trading or business transaction that is handled electronically. This may be done through the use of the technology of the computer, including such tools as EDI, the Internet, intranets and/or extranets, to streamline and enhance commercial transactions of both private and public sector entities.

---

[3]NAPM-Forrester Research, *Report on eBusiness, www.napm.org*, April 27, 2001.

ERP Software Systems provide a corporate platform for information technology and include financial and manufacturing applications. Examples include SAP, Oracle, J. D. Edwards, and PeopleSoft.

Electronic Data Interchange (EDI) is a closed system (e.g., not Web-based) requiring a Value-Added Network (VAN) to allow both buyer and seller to obtain and provide much more timely and accurate information.

Electronic or online catalog is a digitized version of a supplier's catalog that allows buyers to view detailed buying and specifying information about the supplier's products and/or services through their computers' browsers.

E-Marketplaces are Web sites on which member companies buy and sell their goods and exchange information.

E-procurement applications are Web-based tools used to improve the efficiency and effectiveness of indirect or MRO purchases.

Expert systems provide decision-making assistance via an interactive question-and-answer session with a human.

eXtensible Markup Language (XML). A computer language that uses identifying tags that allow information exchange without having to reformat the data for retrieval and viewing.

Extranet. An organization's Web site that provides a limited amount of accessibility to persons outside the organization and often is used to link with actual and potential suppliers.

Firewall. Protective software used to prevent unauthorized access to confidential records.

Internet. The physical global network of computers, information servers, telephone lines, satellite links, signal routers, and the name and address codes that allow access to the World Wide Web. It is run mostly on a not-for-profit basis cooperatively by local and international organizations.

Intranet. A private Internet set up by a company to share data with workers and provide access to the larger Internet.

Mobile Commerce or M-Commerce. Electronic commerce conducted via wireless devices.

Online reverse auction or e-auction. A buyer wishes to purchase goods and invites multiple sellers to bid against one another using the Internet as the auction arena.

Purchasing operating systems process data for the routine operations of the department, such as maintaining the status of purchasing actions; generating POs, change orders, and requests for quotation; filing and sorting supplier lists; and maintaining commodity, price, and supplier history files.

Systems software. A group of programs provided by the computer manufacturer that runs the computer—starts it and makes the components work together.

World Wide Web (www). A term used to describe the network of billions of graphic hypertext documents or Web pages which are accessed from Web sites and hyperlinks connecting pages and Web sites.

Computer Use in Purchasing and Supply Management

Once the purchasing process is clearly understood in the context of the need for audit control of expenditures, approval requirements within the organization, and the differences between and among different categories of purchases, supply managers can turn their attention to process improvements. Some process improvement tools, including blanket orders, systems contracting, and procurement cards, were discussed in Chapter 3. The focus of this section is on process improvements that may be made through technology and Web-based applications.

Opportunities for Process Improvements with Technology

From the description of the steps in the purchasing and supply management process in Chapter 3, and the rationale behind these steps, it is relatively easy to identify points in the process where automation or computerization might improve the process. Figure 4–1 shows the activities in the purchasing process which can be assisted or performed by a computerized or electronic system.

Benefits of Computerization

Figure 4–2 is a diagram of a simplified automated purchasing system. Five basic benefits obtained from computerization are:

1. A reduction in clerical manual effort to a minimum, reduction or elimination of duplicate data entry, and usually fewer errors and decreased processing or cycle time.

2. Information from records is often more accurate and available almost instantly, resulting in better negotiation preparation, prices, and quality. Speedier communication also makes international suppliers more viable.

3. Operating performance is improved through better control, not only by the timely availability of information for sound decision making, but also by the flexibility afforded by the ease of handling vast quantities of detail, thus providing new tools for the buyer and manager. Buyers are freed from repetitive tasks and have more time for more value-adding tasks. Purchasing is also better able to improve the integration of purchasing and supply management processes with other processes within the organization and with the supply network.

4. Supplier relationships may be improved because of faster, more accurate information flows (about requirements, schedules, orders, invoices, and so forth), and the availability of the buyer to spend more time in face-to-face discussions with suppliers about important issues.

5. The firm's capability to reduce the total cost of doing business may be enhanced by enabling just-in-time systems with associated lead time and inventory reductions, bar-coding system applications, integrated manufacturing between buyer and seller, and electronic funds transfer.

It is no easy task, however, to decide which of the many available tools will best serve the organization's purposes, especially when technology is changing rapidly.

Software

Systems Software Defined

To operate the computer, two types of software are needed. The first is the *systems software,* a group of programs provided by the computer manufacturer that runs the computer—starts it and makes the components work together. They do things such as copy information from one storage disk to

FIGURE 4–1

Steps in Purchasing Cycle: Examples of the Potential Contribution of a Computerized Purchasing System

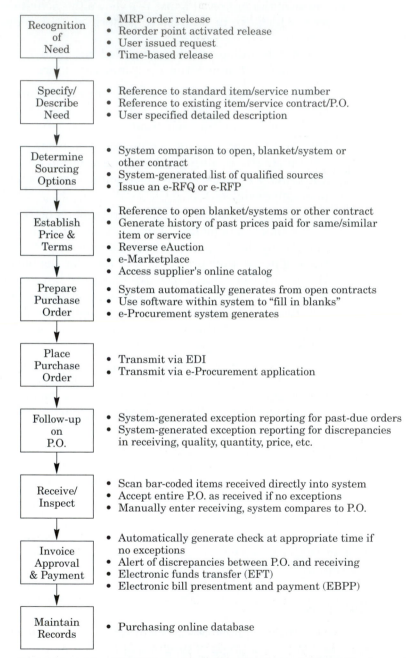

Recognition of Need	• MRP order release • Reorder point activated release • User issued request • Time-based release
Specify/ Describe Need	• Reference to standard item/service number • Reference to existing item/service contract/P.O. • User specified detailed description
Determine Sourcing Options	• System comparison to open, blanket/system or other contract • System-generated list of qualified sources • Issue an e-RFQ or e-RFP
Establish Price & Terms	• Reference to open blanket/systems or other contract • Generate history of past prices paid for same/similar item or service • Reverse eAuction • e-Marketplace • Access supplier's online catalog
Prepare Purchase Order	• System automatically generates from open contracts • Use software within system to "fill in blanks" • e-Procurement system generates
Place Purchase Order	• Transmit via EDI • Transmit via e-Procurement application
Follow-up on P.O.	• System-generated exception reporting for past-due orders • System-generated exception reporting for discrepancies in receiving, quality, quantity, price, etc.
Receive/ Inspect	• Scan bar-coded items received directly into system • Accept entire P.O. as received if no exceptions • Manually enter receiving, system compares to P.O.
Invoice Approval & Payment	• Automatically generate check at appropriate time if no exceptions • Alert of discrepancies between P.O. and receiving • Electronic funds transfer (EFT) • Electronic bill presentment and payment (EBPP)
Maintain Records	• Purchasing online database

Source: Adapted from Lisa Ellram and Laura Birou, *Purchasing for Bottom-Line Impact: Improving the Organization through Strategic Procurement* (Burr Ridge, IL: Irwin Professional Publishing, 1995), p. 135.

FIGURE 4–2

Simplified Flowchart of an Automated Purchasing System

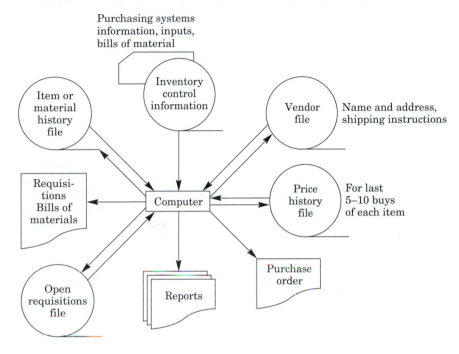

another and cause the printer to work. The systems software currently is very adequate for the tasks at hand.

Applications Software Defined

Second is the *applications software,* which are the programs that manipulate data for a specific purpose, such as maintaining the open order file or taking supplier performance statistics and formatting them into a supplier performance evaluation analysis and report. There are a number of "off-the-shelf" purchasing software packages available. The software is constantly changing and improving, and the published guides to current programs appear frequently.[4] These software programs may be designed for the exclusive use of purchasing, or they may be a module in an enterprise resource planning system designed to link together all of an organization's business processes.

Systems Growth Expected

According to a study by Monczka and Trent, systems growth is expected in two areas.[5] The first is in systems that increase purchasing process efficiency, and the second is in systems that improve the productivity and effectiveness of

---

[4]See, for example, "1999 Purchasing Software Buyers' Guide," *Purchasing,* July 15, 1999, *http://www.manufacturing.net/magazine/purchasing.*

[5]Robert M. Monczka and Robert J. Trent, *Purchasing and Sourcing Strategy: Trends and Implications* (Tempe, AZ: Center for Advanced Purchasing Studies, 1995), p. 63.

buying personnel and units. Implementation in the first area is more easily done because the software is available and it requires fewer resources. Development in the second area is slower because it requires a larger budget and more external MIS support.

Application Service Providers (ASP)

Web-hosted Applications

Organizations are moving more toward function- or task-specific software packages such as warehouse, transportation management, or supply chain management software. The organization rents the software from an application software provider, or ASP, and accesses it via the Internet rather than purchasing and installing the software on in-house computers. These are also referred to as Web-hosted applications. Problems with integrating the online software with in-house software continue to plague users. In 1999, AMR Research projected that sales of supply chain management (SCM) software would grow from 14 percent of the $78 billion business software market to 26 percent in 2004.[6] SCM software includes logistics, transportation, warehousing, and inventory management.

Hypertext Markup Language (HTML) versus eXtensible Markup Language (XML)

Advantages and Obstacles to XML Adoption

When the Internet was first developed, HTML was used to arrange text and images on Web browsers. However, HTML is unable to distinguish between computer data presentation and the data itself. This means that HTML is good for sending electronic documents, but inadequate for direct data exchanges between computers on the Web. XML, which gained World Wide Web Recommendation status in February 1998, uses identifying tags that allow information exchange without having to reformat the data for retrieval and viewing. One obstacle to widespread XML adoption is the lack of standard tags and Document Type Definitions (DTDs) for defining industry-specific data elements needed to execute specific transactions. As of May 2001, XML had not been universally adopted as the standard, although many efforts were under way to speed up adoption. The major benefit of a standard language is an Internet that doesn't discriminate between different computers and software.

Efficiency Improvements through Technology

Purchasing Operating Systems. Purchasing operating systems process data for the routine operations of the department, such as maintaining the

---

[6]"Supply Chain Management: ERP Software Sales Expected to Plummet."*Logistics Management & Distribution Report,* July 2000, p. 18.

Manage Routine Purchasing Operations

status of purchasing actions; generating POs, change orders, and requests for quotation; filing and sorting supplier lists; and maintaining commodity, price, and supplier history files. Typically, those purchasing functions having large volumes of repetitive data are most likely to use these systems. The greater accuracy of high-quality data throughput and turnaround effectiveness justify their use.

Provide Reporting Formats

Management Reporting Systems. These systems process data, often drawing on data files set up for the purchasing operating systems files, and then report these data to management. Examples are the supplier and buyer performance evaluation reports.

Provides a Corporate Platform for IT

Enterprise Resource Planning (ERP) Software. ERP Software Systems, such as SAP, Oracle, J. D. Edwards, and PeopleSoft, provide a corporate platform for information technology and include financial and manufacturing applications. All the rage in the 1990s, ERP Systems commanded roughly 64 percent of the enterprise application software market in 1999. AMR Research of Boston predicts the ERP portion of the market will plummet to 28 percent by 2004.[7] The enterprise application software market also includes enterprise relationship management, supply chain management, and electronic commerce programs.

Commonly Used Technology Tools

There are a number of technological tools used in everyday purchasing operations, including fax machines, fax/modem cards, Internet fax, e-mail, and voice mail. While these tools are widely used in personal as well as business arenas, it is worth commenting on a few aspects of each.

Fax Use Exploding in Latin America

Facsimile Transmissions. In the 1980s, the fax machine took over in many workplaces as the first choice in communications equipment. Although e-mail has probably surpassed the fax in most workplaces in the United States, fax usage is exploding in Latin America and is very strong in Europe where Internet access is expensive and not always readily available.[8] Use of the fax machine reduces the purchase cycle time and provides an easy, relatively cheap means of communication. This helps organizations achieve the speed which is so essential to being competitive in today's world. Many organizations, however, do not track the costs of faxes and may be spending far more than they realize. Costs can get out of hand, just as they have for some organizations using overnight delivery services. Using the fax machine as a substitute for proper planning is never advised.

Fax/Modem Use in the Purchasing Process

Fax/Modem. The computer fax/modem card allows the user rapid transfer of data, graphics, and images using the computer and a conventional telephone

---

[7]Ibid.

[8]Bob Mueller, "Competing Technologies: No Match for Fax," *Purchasing.com,* February 22, 2001.

line. The fax/modem can be used by purchasers for the conventional receipt and transmission of a fax, electronic mail (e-mail) with suppliers, and transmission of data files which can be downloaded and manipulated in spreadsheets or word processors without rekeying the data as required by conventional fax machines. Fax/modems are more cost effective than fax machines because of the faster rates of data transmission.

Cost Advantages of MFPs

Multifunction Products (MFP). MFPs combine fax as a feature on machines that print, scan, and tie into computer networks. One type of MFP is the Internet fax which attaches a TIFF image to an e-mail message. The message can be viewed using graphics software, and because it is electronic, it can be viewed, stored, retrieved, and forwarded electronically. This eliminates the paper copy, unless the recipient chooses to print the file, and takes advantage of local telephone charges through an Internet service provider.

Use of E-mail in the Purchasing Process

Electronic Mail (E-mail). E-mail allows users to transmit messages back and forth within the organization and to external parties. E-mail can be used to communicate with suppliers, and, in some cases, is a means for suppliers to access and respond to requests for proposals (RFPs). The state of Oregon created the Vendor Information Program (VIP) that provides electronic access to the state's RFPs 24 hours a day, seven days a week. Computer centers are available statewide for those suppliers lacking their own computer equipment. They estimate that within the first year, the VIP program saved $60,000 in paper and postage and $500,000 in personnel, and reduced prices paid $12.8 million over the previous year as a result of increased competition.[9]

Advantages and Disadvantages of Voice Mail

Voice Mail. Voice mail is another communication tool that can, if used properly, save time, provide accurate information, improve communications between buyers and internal customers and suppliers, and cut down on "telephone tag." At its best, voice mail allows callers to communicate detailed information which the receiver can then respond to, in detail, or act on, without requiring a response. The voice mail industry reports that more than half of all business calls convey information one-way, therefore not requiring person-to-person communication. At its worst, voice mail turns both parties into receptionists who spend time copying down phone messages and then taking their turn at "telephone tag."

Effectiveness Improvements

Alternative Actions are Selected

Decision-Assisting (Decision-Support) Systems.   These systems process data to assist purchasing management in selecting from among alternatives. They do not merely present or analyze data, but rather they in-

---

[9]Jill Sunkel, "RFP—ASAP!," *NAPM Insights,* July 1993, p. 40.

corporate information into an analytical framework utilizing techniques such as mathematical relationships, simulations, or other algorithms. The outcome is definitive in nature and presents the results in either a deterministic or probabilistic fashion. Decision-assisting systems typically select alternative actions; management then considers the recommendation of the model with other variables (that may not be quantifiable) in arriving at a final decision. Examples are quotation analysis, price discount analysis, synthetic pricing, forecasting, and forward buying and futures trading models.

Expert Systems. Expert systems are computer programs that mimic the problem-solving behavior of human experts. Computer models are constructed using artificial intelligence programming languages to replicate the knowledge base and "rules of thumb" or heuristics human experts would use in making decisions. Expert systems provide decision-making assistance via an interactive question-and-answer session with a human. Expert systems make recommendations based on their previously created knowledge base, the question-and-answer session with the human decision maker, and available external databases. Few expert systems have been developed for use in purchasing decision making, but the potential is there since such systems are designed to improve the quality of decision making when decisions are characterized as dynamic, time-dependent, or complex, as many purchasing decisions are. Areas of potential growth are the development of supplier evaluation and selection expert, priority purchase processing expert, material price forecast expert, and capital asset buying adviser.

Global Databases. Firms with extensive international operations can benefit from developing global databases which allow the firm to consolidate volumes and sourcing strategy. Developing these databases is difficult because of the significant investment, unreliable or nonexistent information networks in some countries, differing technical standards between countries, regulatory obstacles, and internal organizational obstacles. Considering the difficulties in coordinating efforts across multiple business units in North America, it is easy to imagine the further complications that arise when different countries, languages, cultures, and business cultures come into play. Some companies have adopted and implemented one ERP system throughout global operations as a key step in the development of global processes.

Buyer Workstations. Buyer personal computer (PC) workstations integrate a number of elements to create a total systems package that can result in increased effectiveness and productivity. The ideal technical components of a buyer workstation are (1) an automated transaction system, linked to mainframe computer databases, which performs routine purchasing activities, (2) access to decision-support software, (3) an expert systems element, and (4) personal productivity improvement software, word processing, spreadsheets, graphics, and database managers.

Expert Systems Mimic Human Problem-Solving

Global Databases Key to Developing Global Processes

Systems Integration Possible with Buyer Workstations

EDI Systems Require a Value-Added Network

Electronic Data Interchange (EDI) with Suppliers. With the growth of microcomputer usage in supply management in the 1980s, an exciting and challenging development was the capability of direct electronic transmission of data and standard business forms between a buying firm and its suppliers. Known as electronic data interchange or EDI, these are closed systems (i.e., not Web-based) requiring a Value-Added Network (VAN). EDI allows both buyer and seller to obtain and provide much more timely and accurate information, permitting greater administrative efficiency through paperwork reduction, as well as raising the quality level of decisions made. Such applications have been in place for many years, although on a limited scale. In 1995 Monczka and Trent reported that 75 percent of the business units they surveyed had EDI capability with suppliers.[10] The real growth of EDI comes in the increasing volume of transactions handled electronically (see Figure 4-3).

Reasons for EDI Growth

There are several reasons why EDI growth occurred, although at a slower pace than originally projected. First, the use of EDI became a routine way of doing business, especially in manufacturing. The technology was readily available and third-party networks were established, making EDI feasible for small as well as large firms. Second, the drive to reduce cycle time supported the implementation of EDI. Third, EDI fostered closer buyer-supplier relationships by facilitating the exchange of information between buyer and seller and handling many of the routine transactions, thereby freeing the buyer to spend time with suppliers on more value-adding activities.

Electronic data interchange (EDI) has become the preferred way of doing business in many organizations. As the cost of buying and operating a microcomputer continues to fall, EDI is not limited to only large organizations. It is well within reach of the small purchaser and supplier as well. Firms that can exploit the strategic contribution of EDI, particularly in the area of critical information exchange rather than the basic electronic order processing function, stand to gain the most.[11]

Bar Coding and EDI

Large databases with accurate and timely information are required for EDI applications (and Web-based applications discussed later in this chapter). For example, in inventory control or order generation such things as part numbers, current on-hand levels, and on-order quantities are essential. Bar coding or automatic identification systems replace data key entry with automatic data capture at the point of transaction and direct transmission to a computer or storage device.

---

[10]Robert M. Monczka and Robert J. Trent, *Purchasing and Sourcing Strategy,* p. 64.
[11]Ibid.

Bar Code Defined

A bar code is a series of parallel rectangular bars and spaces arranged in a predetermined pattern to encode letters, numbers, and special characters. A scanner "reads" the information by passing a light beam across the bar code, sensing the width of the bars and transmitting the information into the computer, where it is decoded.

In purchasing, bar coding is particularly useful in receiving inbound materials and order generation. The benefits in receiving are quick and accurate data entry, and faster checking and clearing of shipments. Automatic tracking of shipments throughout the system is simplified, and the receiving dock operates in a Just-in-Time, (JIT) mode. The benefits of bar coding in order generation are labor savings, fewer errors and corrections, fewer disruptions due to material unavailability, and less need for safety stocks.

The availability of the microcomputer in purchasing provides the capability of expanding such applications nationwide for any American Standard Code for Information Interchange (ASCII) dumb terminal, including almost all microcomputers, that has appropriate communications software. A telephone modem now can communicate over the phone lines to another computer, which may be thousands of miles away. The cost of the communications software and telephone modem that make the computer and telephone signals compatible can be less than $200. The transmission of signals is very rapid.

With such a direct communications linkup with a supplier, the buyer can obtain price quotes, determine availability of items in a supplier's stock, transmit a PO, obtain follow-up information, provide the supplier information about changes in purchase requirements caused by schedule revisions, obtain service information, and send letters and memos—all instantly.

Technology Enables Process Improvements

The development of EDI marked the beginning of an era where computer technology enabled closer, faster relationships with suppliers. At every point in history, technology has been used as a tool to enable process improvements. When the telegraph was new technology, it revolutionized business because it enabled faster communication and wider dissemination of information. In the early twenty-first century, supply managers, like all managers, are grappling with the impact of the Internet and Web-based applications on business processes. The demand for closer relationships with suppliers and other members of supply networks, and the need for accurate information available in real time, put incredible pressure on business process managers to use Web-based applications. It is predicted that the changes brought about because of the Internet will result in far-reaching changes in the way buyers and suppliers cope with their administrative paperwork requirements.

XML versus EDI

In the early twenty-first century, one dilemma for those with well-developed EDI systems is whether or not they should migrate them to a Web-based

FIGURE 4–3

EDI Benefits

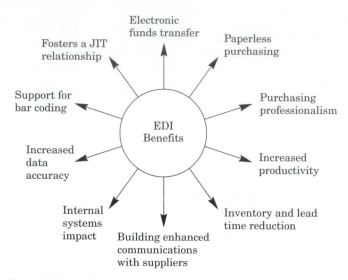

Source: Robert M. Monczka and Joseph R. Carter, *Electronic Data Interchange: Managing Implementation in a Purchasing Environment* (East Lansing, MI: Graduate School of Business Administration, Michigan State University, 1987), p. 4.

Example of EDI- and XML-Supported Transactions at SciQuest.com, Inc.

system (see Figure 4-4). For example, Rob Fusillo, CIO of SciQuest.com Inc., a scientific products e-marketplace, estimates that transaction costs could be cut by 50 percent if EDI-based transactions and VANs could be eliminated and XML used exclusively.[12] XML-enabled solutions may also be more accessible to smaller organizations that have typically been hindered by a lack of IT staff, computing resources, and funds for EDI systems and VANs. Fusillo of SciQuest.com Inc. reported that of the 1,000 buyers and sellers using the exchange, about 15 percent of the information comes from large corporations that transfer data to the e-marketplace using the EDI format. The exchange has to support XML and EDI as well as nonautomated formats such as fax and e-mail. Because many large organizations have invested heavily in EDI, and XML has not been adopted as the standard language, most estimates are that EDI will not disappear any time soon.

Four Choices: XML versus EDI

Those faced with the XML versus EDI question have at least four choices:

1. Maintain existing EDI applications and VANs while investing in technologies that process XML-defined content for new projects.
2. Deploy a dedicated EDI-to-XML translation tool.

_____

[12]Anne Chen, "Getting to XM," *eWeek,* August 6, 2000, *http://www.zdnet.com/ecommerce/stories/main*, found April 27, 2001.

FIGURE 4–4

EDI vs. XML

	EDI	XML
Optimized for:	Compressed messages	Easy display and programming
Requires:	Dedicated EDI server	Web server
Server cost:	$10,000 - $100,000	$5,000
Uses:	Value-added network	Existing Internet connection
Message format:	Months to master	Learned in hours
Requires:	C++ programmers	JavaScript, Visual Basic, Python or Perl script writers
Readable by:	Machine	Human and machine

Source: Gartner Goup, found in Anne Chen, "Getting to XML," *eWeek,* August 6, 2000.

3. Deploy an enterprise integration server platform to perform the EDI-to-XML integration.
4. Use a third-party integration broker to handle transformation and routing.

Intranets and Extranets

Internet and Intranet Example BNSF

An *intranet* is a private Internet set up by a company to share data with workers and provide access to the larger Internet. An *extranet* is an organization's Web site that provides a limited amount of accessibility to persons outside the organization, and often is used to link with actual and potential suppliers. Companies with e-procurement applications use the company Intranet as the means of accessing the application. For example, at Burlington Northern Santa Fe (BNSF) Railway, employees bring up the BNSF home page and click on "BNSF SourceNet" to access the shopping menu which asks, "Where do you want to shop?" Buyers can then search by name, by product family, by supplier name, or by description, adding to their shopping carts until done, and then click on the checkout icon. The software sends the order to the back shop system and launches (eXtensible Markup Language) XML over the Internet to the supplier.[13]

Internet Uses for Purchasers

Purchasers can use the Internet to search, retrieve, and read computer files worldwide; exchange e-mail globally; search and retrieve "shareware," "freeware," and commercial software; search databases of organizations, individuals, and government sources; and search and purchase items from electronic catalogs, suppliers, and distributors. As the legal and commercial role of the Internet is clarified, purchasers are finding it to be a tool of great importance. (See Chapter 12: Legal Aspects of Purchasing for a discussion of the legal issues in e-commerce.)

---

[13]Cade Metz, "Purchasing Power, BNSF: Making the trains run on time," *PC Magazine,* October 31, 2000, found at *www.zdnet.com / ecommerce / stories / main.*

In early 1996 one study concluded: "Based on our surveys and analysis of Internet domain distribution, online service customers, and other available surveys, we conclude that the prospects for commercial consumer use of the Internet are vastly overstated. . . . and there is little commerce actually consummated via the Internet, as even those enterprises that accept orders via it rely on non-Internet-based payment methods."[14]

By 2001 there still was not a high volume of business conducted over the Internet. In supply management the focus was on integrating e-procurement with the organization's inventory and financial operations. Real-time updates to inventory systems and automatic electronic payments are already in use in some organizations. However, e-procurement is not for everyone.

Four Issues in E-procurement Implementation

Forrester Research described four main problems related to the purchasing process that can hinder an organization's ability to successfully implement e-procurement. These are:[15]

1. The requirement for explicit approval (e.g., manual sign-off) prior to making an online purchase.

2. Reliance and comfort with fax and e-mail lead to clumsy links between buyers and suppliers.

3. Transaction-by-transaction review prior to payment rather than paying on proof of shipment.

4. Haphazard review of buying and supplying behavior that leaves people unsure of the degree of success of e-procurement.

E-Procurement Applications

E-procurement applications are Web-based tools used to improve the efficiency and effectiveness of purchasing. Thus far, e-procurement has been used primarily for the purchase of indirect or MRO items. Indirect purchases are all those items that an organization purchases to run the business but that do not end up in an end-product that is sold to customers. Commonly referred to as MRO (maintenance, repair, and operating supplies), these C-items (See ABC analysis or Pareto Analysis) typically consume about 20 percent of the annual spend (expenditures on purchases) and account for roughly 80 percent of the purchase orders processed by the buying organization. The costs associated with processing these purchases can easily exceed the value of the item purchased. For example, the U.S. federal govern-

Indirect Materials Purchased via E-procurement

---

[14]Diane Trommer, "Study: Intranet's the Place to Be," *Electronic Buyer's News,* January 8, 1996, pp. 84 and 87.

[15]NAPM and Forrester Research, *Report on e-Business,* April, 2001, *www.napm.org.*

The U.S. Government and BNSF Examples

ment partnered with Visa International to achieve its goal of conducting 80 percent of its purchases electronically by 2001.[16]

Burlington Northern Santa Fe (BNSF) Railway, for example, initiated its e-procurement application in May 2000 with 30 employees using the application to purchase goods from Boise Cascade. BNSF's goal was for 2,000 employees to have access to 17 different suppliers' catalogs by the end of 2000.[17]

Recent surveys report that organizations increasingly buy indirect materials online. Most organizations surveyed bought some indirect materials, and organizations purchasing large volumes tend to use the Internet more often than those buying small volumes. Whether the optimistic forecasts of some will materialize is an interesting question because forecasts for EDI implementation historically also were wildly optimistic. The basic idea behind e-procurement is for the employees of the buying organization (the one wanting to purchase MRO supplies) to use a Web-based package through which they use browsers to access suppliers' digitized online catalogs, select items, and communicate purchase orders directly to designated suppliers. The e-procurement system includes a workflow automation system that accepts the requisitions, applies policy rules, routes the orders for approvals, sends the orders to the appropriate supplier, and tracks order status.[18] A reporting module captures data on spend levels with different suppliers.

Types of E-procurement Applications

E-procurement applications can take a number of forms:

1. The buying organization can purchase and install on its servers a package from a solutions provider. In 2001, two of the major providers were Ariba and CommerceOne. Given the volatility of the market, it is difficult to predict which providers will survive.

2. The buying organization can use a third-party to host the e-procurement application for the organization. In this case, the entire application resides outside of the buyer's firewall. (A firewall is protective software used to prevent unauthorized access to confidential records.[19]

3. An e-marketplace serving multiple buyers and multiple sellers, often in the same industry, can purchase and operate the e-procurement application.

4. "Content Vendors" may supplement the e-procurement package by creating supplier catalogs or providing access to existing ones.

An interesting twist on e-procurement is the approach taken by Wells Fargo financial services company.[20] Wells Fargo employees access the e-procurement

---

[16]"The Power of Purchasing and Supply Management," a Special Supplement to *Purchasing Today,* reprinted from *Fortune* magazine, October 26, 1998, p. S4.

[17]Metz.

[18]David Koltermann, *Electronic Trading-Hubs: Types and Issues,* unpublished paper, The University of Western Ontario, March 2000, p. 4.

[19]*NAPM Glossary of Key Purchasing and Supply Terms, www.napm.org*, April 24, 2001.

[20]*www.wellsfargo.com*

application via Web browsers through the company's intranet. In addition, for a monthly fee, Wells Fargo customers can access the Wells Fargo e-procurement application via the company's financial portal to purchase MRO supplies from the suppliers with whom Wells Fargo has negotiated discounted prices.

Benefits of E-procurement

Whatever form it takes, the main benefits expected from e-procurement are:

1. Employees will use the suppliers with whom contracts and relationships are established rather than engaging in rogue or maverick buying,
2. Cycle time will be reduced in the process of purchasing indirect items and replenishing supplies,
3. Communications will be faster and less manually or paper-intensive, and
4. Transaction costs will be lowered.

Gaining these benefits, however, is not a given. Even in organizations that have attempted to control and contain processing costs and prices of MRO or indirect purchases through supply-base rationalization, single sourcing, and corporate-wide contracts, opportunities for abuse abound. In many organizations, employees who are scattered around the country, and sometimes the world, engage in "maverick" or "rogue" buying, meaning they ignore corporatewide contracts and purchase from local retailers. This behavior often results in the organization as a whole paying more for MRO items than they would if everyone ordered against the contract. Even with an e-procurement application, employees may resist using it unless such use is mandated by management.

BNSF Example Continued

For example, despite having a corporatewide contract with Boise Cascade for office supplies, many of BNSF's employees located in 28 states and 2 Canadian provinces made purchases from other office suppliers. According to Jeff Campbell, vice president and chief sourcing officer at BNSF, "When we went into our general ledger system, we found we were spending $3 million a year with Boise and $8 million with other places."[21] In May 2000, BNSF automated its indirect purchases through an e-procurement application using Clarus, a Web-based package. Now, employees are required to purchase office supplies through the company intranet which, through an interface with the Clarus system, routes purchase orders to Boise Cascade. Since BNSF Purchasing has already negotiated terms and conditions with Boise Cascade, the items can be shipped against the contract. Campbell says, "By deploying one deeply discounted, corporatewide contract with Boise Cascade and requiring all of our employees to use Clarus, we're seeing great savings. Paying list price or even 10 to 20 percent off with various shops can't compare with buying from the corporate catalog online at 50 to 60 percent off."[22]

---

[21]Metz, op. cit.
[22]Metz, op. cit.

Steps in Setting Up an E-procurement System

Setting up an e-procurement system for indirect materials. Setting up an e-procurement system typically follows these steps:

1. A solutions provider is selected and the type of relationship determined (purchase a software package, use a third party, or join an e-marketplace).

2. The buyer(s) determines how many suppliers and which suppliers to keep in its supply base for indirect purchases.

3. The buyer(s) negotiates terms and conditions with the chosen suppliers, including deeply discounted prices in return for volume.

4. Digitized versions of the suppliers' catalogs are loaded alongside the e-procurement application.

5. Employees use computer browsers to search the catalogs of designated suppliers, select items for purchase, and create requisitions (also through the browser), and a purchase order (PO) is generated.

6. The PO is streamed directly into the supplier's inventory application and the order is processed, the goods are shipped.

7. Invoicing and/or payment is made, sometimes through an electronic bill presentment and payment process.

Implementation Challenges

Digital Signatures Valid

Not all organizations have successfully implemented an electronic procurement system for every step of the purchasing process. Two typical sticking points are (1) the approval process and (2) the invoicing and payment process. Now that digital signatures can be used to form a legally valid contract, some organizations have incorporated them into their computerized purchasing process. This can eliminate the sometimes lengthy delays that can occur securing the appropriate signatures to authorize a purchase. However, there are still technical hurdles to be overcome before electronic signatures will be feasible for many users because many browsers contain minimal authentication features, some companies are developing pen-based and other types of technologies to facilitate online contracting, and a number of companies already provide digital signature products using public key infrastructure (PKI).

On the other end of the process—invoicing and payment—delays are again common as accounts payable (AP) ensures that the funds were indeed authorized, the goods received, and the invoice prepared for the correct amount. Computerizing this part of the process provides an opportunity for the buyer to work internally to ensure that his or her finance and accounting managers pay according to the contract terms. In a manual system, any discrepancies between or among the invoice, receiving, and the PO can result in delays in paying the supplier. Adding to these delays is the delay caused by many organizations paying later than the agreed-upon terms.

Externally, there may be difficulty in finding e-commerce-enabled suppliers or suppliers may be in the early stages of digitizing their catalogs.

Role of Purchasing in E-Procurement

Purchasing's Decision-Making Role in E-procurement

From a supply management standpoint, the important thing to remember about e-procurement is that the buyer still plays a critical decision-making role in the process. The organization still benefits from having supply personnel with the investigative and analytical skills to source, evaluate, and select suppliers; the influencing and persuading skills to negotiate the best deal for the organization, and a strategic and long-term planning approach to anticipate and prevent problems down the road. The transactional side of indirect purchases, not the decision-making side, is streamlined and responsibility for actually placing orders delegated to the user whenever possible.

Electronic or Online Supplier Catalogs

Two Types of Data in Online Catalogs

An online catalog is a digitized version of a supplier's catalog that allows buyers to view detailed buying and specifying information about the supplier's products and/or services through their computers' browsers. Product catalogs include two types of information: (1) product specification data, and (2) transaction data. Product specification data are all the bits of information describing the products; transaction data are price, shipping and billing addresses, and quantity discounts. Product specification data is the same for all buyers, but transaction data must be customized to reflect the pricing and other terms and conditions negotiated with the supplier. For example, Business Depot, Dell Computer, and Cisco all provide customized versions of their catalogs for different buyers who have contracts with them.

When transitioning to an e-procurement application, ensuring online catalog accessibility is critical to the success of the program. This issue of catalog accessibility may become a factor in the supplier selection decision. The dilemma for the buyer is that the existing supplier, if there is one, may not have a digitized catalog. In this case the buyer has to decide if he or she wants to continue doing business with the supplier. If so, the buyer has to take into account conversion time for the supplier to get the catalog online. If the buyer does not already have a relationship with a supplier, then the supplier selection decision can include a criterion that the supplier be e-commerce-enabled. However, the best supplier may not be e-enabled and the buyer may be making a mistake to put too much weight on this criterion.

Options for Digitizing Catalogs

Suppliers have a number of options available to digitize their catalogs. The same solutions provider that the buyer's organization uses can typically take the supplier's catalog, manual or electronic, and convert it to a format suitable to their server. Or the supplier can purchase an out-of-the box software package and make the conversion themselves or purchase the services of the software provider. If the buyer doesn't have an existing relationship with a supplier and does not wish to develop one, a data aggregator may be the answer. Data aggregators develop a library of product specifications from a variety of suppliers and then license organizations to use the product specifications and assist in developing the transaction data. Another approach is to use a catalog network in which a host company collects all the catalogs and customizes the transaction data for each buyer. The buyer can either pull the catalogs onto his or her server or access them from the host company. In some cases, the vendor will allow the buyer to "punch out" or access a supplier-hosted catalog.

General Electric Co. announced in early 1996 that it was setting up a private online system that lets suppliers enter bids for GE business.[23] Suppliers could obtain specifications, determine contractual requirements, and then submit their bids online. In 1997, TPN Register was formed as a joint venture between GE Global eXchange Services, an electronic commerce service provider, and Thomas Publishing Company, publisher of the *Thomas Register of American Manufacturers.*[24] By 2001 TPN Register provides an interactive catalog management service and, through TPN Marketplace™, claims to provide a faster, simpler, more customized, and more economical approach to catalog management than traditional catalog software solutions.[25]

Tyco Electronics Example of a Company-Specific Catalog

Company-Specific Catalogs. Some companies have developed electronic catalogs of their products. For example, AMP (now part of Tyco Electronics, the largest passive components supplier in the world) announced in early 1996 it would have an electronic catalog available on the Internet containing "extensive information on 30,000 AMP products . . . Information will continuously expand to cover all engineering and specifying needs." They estimated it would save users as much as 45 minutes compared to searching paper catalogs.[26] By April 2001, AMP had more than 135,000 products available via its online catalog, as well as downloadable customer drawings, test reports, product and application specifications, and CAD (computer assisted design) models. Authorized customers could also access real-time information on pricing, product availability, order status, sample requests, and shopping cart features.[27]

Thomas Register Online

---

[23]"Let's Go Surfing Now, Says GE to Its Contractors," *Investor's Business Daily,* January 9, 1996, p. A-9.

[24]*www.tpn.com*, April 27, 2001.

[25]Ibid.

[26]AMP news release, "AMP Launches Global Electronic Service Via Internet; Customer Service, Sophisticated Technology Are Keys to Success," issued January 12, 1996.

[27]*www.tycoelectronics.com*, April 24, 2001.

Industrywide Informational Databases

Thomas Publishing Company, which has published the hard-copy *Thomas Register of American Manufacturers* since 1905, began publishing it on CD-ROM in 1993 and made the information available over the Internet in 1995 (thomas-register.com).[28] While there is a fee for buying the print and CD-ROM versions of the Register, the online database is available free of charge to anyone with Internet access. As of August 2000, the database provided access to 168,000 U.S. and Canadian companies, 63,669 product and service headings, 135,415 trademarks and brand names, and 785,543 CAD drawings available for online searching 24 hours a day, seven days a week for free. It also links by product and company to more than 7,782 online catalogs or suppliers' Web sites.

Thomas Publishing also maintains four other sites: TREMnet.com, the Thomas Register of European Manufacturers, and TFIRnet.com, the Thomas Food Industry Register Buying Guide. TREMnet.com provides access to 180,000 industrial suppliers, organized by 10,000 industrial product classifications, in 6 languages, and from 17 European Union countries. TFIRnet.com provides access to more than 22,000 U.S. and Canadian suppliers of food products, ingredients, and supplies under 5,800 product categories. ThomasRegional.com provides instant access to comprehensive buying information on more than 520,000 industrial distributors, manufacturers, and service companies in 6,000 categories. Thomas Publishing's site AERnet.com, the American Export Register, provides information and listings of export companies.

Auctions and Reverse Auctions

In an auction, a seller has goods it wishes to sell and invites multiple buyers to bid against each other at a set time and place to purchase the goods. In a reverse auction, a buyer has goods it wishes to purchase and invites multiple sellers to bid against one another to sell their goods to the buyer. An online reverse auction or e-auction uses the Internet as the auction arena. The April 2001 NAPM-Forrester Research *Report on eBusiness* reported that only 15 percent of survey respondents bought products or services through an online auction.[29] The report also found that manufacturers used online auctions almost three times as often as nonmanufacturers, and large-volume buying organizations used them more than twice as often as small-volume buying organizations.

Characteristics of Effective Online Auctions

Online auctions have been most effective when (1) the good or service has the characteristics of a commodity, e.g. there is a clear and unambiguous

---

[28]Thomas Publishing Company news release, "Thomas Publishing Launches New Online Corporate Purchasing Network," issued December 6, 1995.

[29]NAPM-Forrester Research *Report on eBusiness.*

specification; (2) there are multiple suppliers available and willing to compete for the business; and (3) the organization has access to the technology necessary to run the auction. Third-party software providers can run the auction and some are now making software available for lease or purchase.

The purchasing process itself remains essentially the same as a non-Internet-based bidding process. Potential sources must be identified, prequalified, and invited to bid. A clear specification and the process for submitting bids must be communicated to all bidders. The actual auction event can be conducted in a number of ways, including open offer negotiations, private offer negotiations, and posted price.

Open Offer Negotiations. Suppliers can select the items they want to place offers on, see the most competitive offers from other suppliers for each item, and enter as many offers as they want up until a specified closing time. The names of suppliers will not be identified.

Private Offer Negotiations. Suppliers receive from the buying organization offers that include target price and quantity. Suppliers select the item(s) they wish to bid on and enter an offer by a specific time. The buyer evaluates each supplier's offer and enters a "Status" for each item. The levels of "Status" are:

Accepted: the supplier is awarded the contract, contingent on final qualification.
Closed: the supplier may no longer submit offers for the item in question.
BAFO: the supplier who receives electronically the Best and Final Offer status may submit one more offer for the item.
Open: the supplier may submit another offer.

Bidding may be continued for as many rounds as necessary to accept or close all items.

Posted Price. The buyer indicates the price that is acceptable. The first supplier that meets this price gets the award.

Growth of E-Marketplaces Slow

E-Marketplaces

Business-to-business e-marketplaces are Web sites on which member companies buy and sell their goods and exchange information. Various forms of e-marketplaces rose and fell at a rapid rate, including industrywide marketplaces, also known as public exchanges such as Chemdex or Covisint, and private exchanges such as the short-lived one set up by Dell Computers. Thus far, both buyers and sellers have been reluctant to participate in e-marketplaces. Recent surveys indicate that only a small percentage of organizations were buying goods or services through online marketplaces in the early twenty-first century.

Implications for Purchasing

Clearly these are exciting times for both those responsible for developing supply strategy and those tasked with implementation. In an environment of rapidly changing technology, it is difficult to predict exactly what the landscape will look like for supply managers in the future. It is, therefore, important to identify the key questions that decision makers in supply management must answer before embarking on an e-commerce path. These include:

1. Should we be a leader or a follower?
2. What should be acquired through e-commerce?
3. What tools should we use to acquire those items?
4. Who should we use as a service provider?
5. Should we enter into an alliance, and if so, what type, or work privately?

Should we be a leader or a follower? The management of each organization must decide if it wishes to be an early adopter of new technology, or if it prefers to see what emerges as the norm or standard. Early adopters of e-commerce tools often report that, despite the difficulties encountered, there are advantages to being further along than later adopters. Those who choose to wait tend to believe that the high risks and costs associated with adopting new technology in its infancy far outweigh whatever competitive advantages that might be gained. Decision makers must assess a number of factors, including the organization's risk aversion and success level with technology implementation in the past, before moving forward.

What should be acquired through e-commerce? Should the organization purchase indirect materials, direct materials, or both through e-commerce tools? To date, the majority of electronic purchase transactions have been for indirect materials or MRO (maintenance, repair, and operating supplies), which are typically low-value, low-risk purchases. Organizations that have enjoyed the benefits of buying indirect or MRO items through e-procurement are turning their attention to direct materials. However, recent surveys indicate that only a small number of organizations buy direct materials online. Supply managers must consider the characteristics of each category of purchase (see Chapter 6 for a discussion of purchases categories) to determine which goods or services might be successfully procured online. This analysis should include careful consideration of the existing and desired buyer-supplier relationship to ensure that the method of procurement does not adversely harm the relationship.

What tools should we use to acquire those items? A number of tools are available for streamlining the purchasing process. These range from lower technology tools, such as procurement cards, to high-technology tools, such as online reverse auctions, online catalogs, and e-marketplaces. A decision to adopt e-commerce for procurement does not necessarily mean that all the available tools will be adopted. The manager must determine the appropriateness of the tool to the type of material or service under consideration, the nature of the buyer-supplier relationship, and the comfort level of the internal stakeholders and the suppliers.

Who should we use as a service provider(s)?   If the decision is made to use a third-party service provider, a careful assessment must be made of the available providers. On the technical side, several critical issues are: compatibility with, or ease of migration from, existing software; scalability (can it grow with your needs); the supplier's technical reputation and experience with supply chain management; and expertise of the staff. Some of the key considerations beyond the technical issues are the long-term viability of the provider, user-friendliness of the software, fee structure, and service and support –offline and online.

Should we enter into an alliance, and if so, what type, or work privately?[30]   There are a number of options available for e-commerce applications to supply management. Electronic purchasing can be done through a buyer-controlled system or through a neutral, third-party-controlled catalog aggregation site known as an e-marketplace or trading hub. The decision to join a trading hub requires careful consideration given their infancy, instability, and volatility. A number of factors must be considered, including the technical standards (interoperability and ease of data exchange), the degree of trust (confidence in the provider, confidentiality of information, system reliability, and uptime), and the cost and benefits of membership. On the seller side, the benefits may include improved service quality from more accurate and timely order processing, increased revenues from market expansion, and lower costs. For the buyer, participation in e-hubs may reduce transaction costs, increase competition through reduced search costs, and ultimately lead to lower materials costs.

Conclusion

As purchasing and supply managers continue to transition to a more strategic role in many organizations they also will continue to test and apply new technologies to the supply process. One of the exciting areas for newcomers to supply management is the appropriate application of technology. Although current surveys indicate that overall e-commerce adoption has been

---

[30]Koltermann, p. 1.

slower than anticipated due to the difficulties of internal and external integration and the lack of data standards, the future holds much promise for technology-enabled process improvements. The challenges are great, but those who see the opportunity for cost reductions, faster cycle times, and improved communication flows will continue to seek ways to use these new tools to their best advantage.

Questions for Review and Discussion

1. What is EDI? How has it changed buyer-seller relationships?
2. In a company not now using the computer for purchasing, where would you start and what would you need to do to develop an integrated computer purchasing/supply system?
3. In a company not now using the Internet for purchasing, where would you start and what would you need to do to develop an integrated e-commerce strategy for the purchasing and supply management process?
4. How does the use of an e-procurement system change the nature of the skills and knowledge required of supply management personnel?
5. What kinds of software are needed for computer applications in purchasing? What is presently available?
6. What is the application of bar coding in the purchasing system?
7. What are some of the major obstacles to faster adoption of e-commerce in supply management? What can be done to overcome these obstacles?
8. What should be considered before switching from an existing EDI system to a Web-based system?
9. Why has there been difficulty in developing successful B2B exchanges or e-marketplaces? How do you think these issues will be resolved?
10. What possible improvements in purchasing and supply could the Internet offer in the future?

References

Carter, P., J. R. Carter, R. M. Monczka, T. H. Slaight, and A. J. Swan, *The Future of Purchasing and Supply: A Five- and Ten-Year Forecast,* Tempe, AZ: Center for Advanced Purchasing Studies, 1998.

Emmelhainz, M., A. *EDI: A Total Management Guide,* 2nd ed. New York: Van Nostrand Reinhold, 1993.

Fawcett, S. E., "Information Technology in Purchasing," Chapter 7 *in The Supply Management Environment,* Tempe, AZ: National Association of Purchasing Management, 2000.

Koltermann, D., *"Electronic Trading-Hubs: Types and Issues,"* unpublished paper, The University of Western Ontario, March 2000.

McKinsey & Company and CAPS Research, *E-markets White Paper,* Tempe, AZ: Center for Advanced Purchasing Studies, *www.capsresearch.org*, May 1, 2001.

NAPM — Forrester Research, *Report on eBusiness,* updated every three months, www.napm.org.

Trent, R. J. and M. G. Kolchin, *Reducing the Transactions Costs of Purchasing Low Value Goods and Services,* Tempe, AZ: Center for Advanced Purchasing Studies, 1999.

ZDNet, *www.zdnet.com*. An excellent source of information for those interested in buying, using, or learning more about technology.

Case 4–1
Somers Office Products Inc.

George Bellows, purchasing manager of Somers Office Products (Somers), in Calgary Alberta, was considering whether he needed to switch suppliers. Fairmont Canada, one of Somers's primary suppliers, had just announced that they were being acquired by MSC Inc., a direct competitor of Somers.

Somers Office Products Inc. Somers Office Products had been established as a dealer in stationery in 1920 and had functioned as a family business until 1975, when it was acquired by the current management group. Somers operated two retail outlets, but the bulk of its sales were to commercial customers. The company continued to be privately owned and operated at a profit. It operated a warehouse and total employment was about 80 people, most of whom were in sales.

The company had three product segments: office supplies, office furniture, and office design services. Office supplies constituted the largest segment and included items such as stationery, paper, and forms. One of the fastest growing lines was computer supplies, such as printer cartridges.

Suppliers. The office supplies industry was very price competitive and the trend for resellers, such as Somers, was for a higher level of use of wholesalers, rather than direct purchases from manufacturers. Large wholesalers, who could generally offer pricing levels similar to those received directly from the manufacturers, competed on the basis of value-added services, such as next-day delivery.

As a reseller, Somers purchased office supplies through a variety of channels but relied on two distributors, Fairmont Canada and Roancroft Stationers. Fairmont Canada specialized in computer supplies and had annual sales of $150 million (CAD). Roancroft, a large U.S.-based company with sales of $3.5 billion (USF), provided Somers with a wide range of office supplies. Both suppliers had invested heavily in technology that provided opportunities for customers to view catalogs and to place orders online.

Distribution. Somers provided its customers with catalogs that were regularly supplemented with fliers. Somers' office supply orders were, for the most part, met from inventory. The company had a fill rate of almost 98 percent and thus provided a very high service level to its customers.

To achieve a high level of customer service without maintaining excessive inventory levels, Somers had developed close working arrangements with Roancroft and Fairmont Canada. For example, while Somers maintained approximately 4,500 items in inventory, Roancroft maintained inventories in over 25,000 items. Somers supplied catalogues to its customers that included products supplied by Roancroft, and customer orders were sent from Somers to Roancroft on a daily basis by electronic data interchange (EDI). Any orders sent by 4:30 p.m. would be delivered to Somers (or directly to a customer, if required) by 10 a.m. Customer orders were then combined at the Somers warehouse and shipped the following day.

Fairmont Canada provided Somers with access to more than 100 manufacturers and stocked over $20 million of products in inventory. Orders received by 5 p.m. were shipped that day.

Fairmont Canada Acquisition. On April 3, MSC Inc., a direct competitor of Somers, announced that it was acquiring Fairmont Canada, a subsidiary of the U.S.-based Fairmont Inc. At the same time, it was also announced that Roancroft was acquiring the U.S. wholesale operations of Fairmont Inc.

Recently, Fairmont Inc. had expanded its activities to direct, end-user sales through a subsidiary that sold computer supplies through e-catalogs over the Internet. Many resellers considered this expansion of Fairmont Inc. as direct competition with their own activities and believed that Fairmont Inc. had gained an unfair advantage in the marketplace.

The Decision. The extent to which Fairmont Canada would pursue direct sales activities was still unclear to George, who was concerned that terminating its relationship with the supplier would require restructuring of processes and client relationships. One option available to Somers was to use Wahby International, a U.S.-based supplier of computer supplies that George had been using on a limited basis. Wahby provided catalogs with Internet ordering and order-tracking capabilities and had entered into a partnership with FedEx to provide a very high level of shipping response capability. The company stated in its corporate mission a total commitment to support its resellers and that it avoided any direct sales to end users. Wahby had sales of $1 billion (USF), but unfortunately, it did not have a strong presence in Canada, and George

was concerned about leaving the company exposed to a single supplier of computer supplies.

George knew that Wayne Fitzsimmons, president of Somers, would expect a strategy to be developed quickly in reaction to the news concerning Fairmont Canada. Meanwhile, Somers was considering its own expansion into e-commerce as a defensive move against the new competition in the field and as a means to lower its costs. However, the establishment of a Web site catalog was still in the planning stage and an upgrade of their computer system would be needed.

CASE 4–2
CABLE AND WIRELESS plc (A)

Ninian Wilson, procurement process manager for Cable and Wireless plc in London, England, was evaluating his options for the company's first ever e-auction. It was July 10, and Ninian needed to settle on both the commodity and the e-auction service provider that he should use for the pilot project.

Cable and Wireless plc. Cable and Wireless plc (C&W) was a leading global telecommunications company. Its core business unit, C&W Global, was a provider of Internet protocol (IP) and data services to business customers in the key markets of the United States, Europe and Asia. C&W's global infrastructure provided a high-performance network that delivered integrated Internet, data, voice, and messaging communications to its customers. Its annual revenues were £9 billion and the company employed 55,000 people.

C&W had recently undertaken a thorough review of its assets and business strategy. As a result, management had sold a number of nonstrategic businesses and planned to reinvest the proceeds in network development and expansion in its IP and data services area, where it saw long-term growth opportunities.

The E-Procurement Initiative. Earlier in the year, an executive level group, the eGo team, had been formed to help guide C&W's transformation into an e-business. Don Reed, CEO Global Services, was the executive sponsor of the team, which focused on the e-enabling of C&W's customers, employees, partners, and suppliers and the links between these parties. The eGo team had a number of projects and initiatives under way, including e-procurement.

The goals of the e-procurement initiative were to (1) provide C&W employees with desktop e-transacting capabilities; (2) empower the procurement organization with e-enabling capabilities, such as e-auctioning; (3) free up supply resources through removal of non-value-adding activities, such as manual data rekeying; (4) reduce acquisition costs; and (5) reduce maverick buying. To develop an understanding of the full costs, benefits, and implications of implementing an e-procurement capability, a pilot project, called ¥ε$, was initiated. Six C&W executives sat on the e-procurement steering committee, including Martin Ward, the Senior Vice President of Purchasing. Ninian Wilson was the program director for the e-auction component of the pilot.

Commodities Under Consideration. Ninian's plan was to organize an online, real-time bid competition for a suitable commodity. He hoped that running an e-auction would provide insights into the reverse auction process and quantify cost-savings opportunities. Ninian commented, "The potential benefit is a cut in the price of a contract by as much as 20 to 30 percent, and this pilot will help us prove this."

As a starting point, Ninian looked at contracts that were coming to the end of their term and needed to be renewed. He identified archival services and marketing paper as potential candidates for the e-auction pilot.

Archival Services. C&W had six suppliers providing record storage services for its various operations in the U.K. representing a total annual cost of £133,000. Each of the suppliers were located in the greater London area and provided the same basic services: labeling, delivery, next-day retrieval, and storage. Several vendors had indicated that they would need price increases for the next contract.

Wendy Ellis, the commodity manager, had issued an RFQ two months prior, with the intention of consolidating requirements with a single vendor. Concerned that not all of the current vendors provided fireproof storage, Wendy added this feature to the RFQ, which she felt would add about £1,000 per year to the total cost. Each of the six current suppliers was asked to quote on C&W's archival storage requirements, and Clauws Records Services had submitted the lowest bid at a price of £423,000 for a 36-month contract.

Marketing Paper. C&W purchased approximately £4 million in paper worldwide used for marketing and sales literature. Its large spend in this area and the wide geographic coverage meant that C&W dealt with a number of paper merchants directly.

Ninian was aware that the contract for C&W's U.K. requirements for marketing paper was due to be revisited within the next month, and based on current prices, represented an annual spend of approximately £1.2 million. C&W did not currently have contracts in place for its requirements in Europe, the United States or Asia and purchased its marketing paper in these regions from a large number of suppliers. However, the current U.K supplier, Engler Paper, had expressed an interest in working with C&W to expand its supply relationship to other regions.

Ninian felt that he could conduct an e-auction for C&W's global requirements or focus on its U.K. requirements only. He had identified seven potential suppliers, including two that had experience with e-auctions.

E-Auction Service Providers. Ninian recognized that if he proceeded with an e-auction, he would have to make arrangements with an online bid service provider. His initial investigation had uncovered a large number of auction service providers that used a variety of different approaches. Eventually he narrowed his alternatives to two service providers.

IA-TECH was a U.S.-based e-procurement solutions provider with one of the three most popular types of software. It was one the world's largest providers of e-auction services and had conducted more than 250 reverse auctions for a number of firms in North America and Europe. IA-TECH proposed that it would charge a flat fee of £12,000 to conduct the auction for archival services, £25,000 for U.K. marketing paper, and £50,000 for C&W's total corporate requirements for worldwide marketing paper. IA-TECH's proposals were based on a maximum of six bidders.

e-Procure Systems was a relatively new e-auction service provider based in the U.K. e-Procure Systems had developed its own software and had conducted about 50 reverse auctions. It offered C&W two different pricing schemes. One option was a tiered commission structure of 3 percent for the first £500,000 of the contract, 2 percent for the second £500,000, 1 percent for the next £500,00 and .5 percent thereafter. Alternatively, e-Procure Systems also offered a risk-reward pricing structure, where it would take a fee of 15 percent of total savings from the e-auction over the existing cost.

Each of the service packages from IA-TECH and e-Procure Systems included training, support, and consulting, customization and auction marketing. In order to proceed, Ninian knew that he needed to establish parameters for the e-auction service arrangement and select a service provider.

Finalizing the E-Auction. Ninian had several concerns. While he was satisfied that e-auctions could be useful for some commodities, he was uncertain which commodities were best suited for this procurement technique. Ninian was also uncertain as to how the suppliers would respond and knew that the suppliers would have to cooperate for the e-auction to be successful. Furthermore, Ninian needed to decide on the appropriate number of suppliers and determine which ones were best suited to participate.

Finally, this would be Ninian's first experience with an e-auction and, if he did decide to proceed, he knew it would be important to map out a game plan carefully. Not only did he need a commodity strategy, but he would also need to select an online bid service provider.

Ninian had a meeting with the e-Procurement Steering Group in two weeks, when he would be expected to present his recommendations.

CASE 4–3
ESTABLISHING E-BUSINESS STANDARDS AT DEERE & COMPANY*

By the beginning of April 2000, Deere & Company, headquartered in Moline, Ill., had made the decision to shift Deere's $7 billion supply chain to an e-business model by 2003. Paul Morrisey, Manager of E-Business and Supply Management, was responsible for helping to establish common technology standards for the entire Deere supply chain. He needed to develop a preliminary plan for the establishment of those standards for a meeting with his boss in two weeks. Paul wondered what it would take to reach an agreement with suppliers and whether Deere was in a position to manage the supply chain electronically.

Deere & Company. The 163-year-old Deere & Company was the only agricultural equipment company in the United States to have never changed hands. It was a highly decentralized company that operated more than 60 business units, sold products in more than 160 countries, and had 39,000 employees. In 1999, annual sales revenue had declined to $11.7 billion from a 1998 level of $13.8 billion. Even worse, profits had declined to $239 million from a 1998 level of $1.021 billion.

The company operated three different types of businesses. First, and largest, was Equipment Operations, consisting of agricultural, construction and forestry, and commercial and consumer lawn care. Second was Support Operations, comprised of power systems such as engines and transmissions, and service parts for Deere equipment. The third area was Financial Services — consisting of credit, which made financing and leasing agreements — and health care, which managed health care systems for 1,400 companies.

Each of Deere's 14 divisions currently purchased products independently, although there was a corporate coordinator of purchasing for some products

---

* This case written by professor Steve Maranville is reproduced with the permission of Deere & Company and NAPM.

who operated in an advisory capacity. Electronic Data Interchange (EDI) had been in place since the early '90s with 2,000 Deere suppliers representing 90 percent of domestic orders. However, there was a lack of global commonality in systems used. Every operating unit had developed its own method of using technology with suppliers.

Earlier, at Deere's annual meeting with major suppliers, Paul had heard complaints about the co-ordination problems in supply that existed within Deere. One supplier commented, "I get calls from 50 different people at Deere and they want 50 different things." A second major supplier said, "It's like there are 14 different companies all operating under the Deere name. If you want us to help you, help yourselves first."

Because Deere had no common, corporate supplier database, different divisions were purchasing the same products from the same supplier at different prices. Suppliers were successfully taking advantage of Deere's inability to coordinate purchase quantities.

Paul Morrisey. In more than 20 years, Paul Morrisey had moved successfully through a series of positions in manufacturing management at Deere. He came to corporate headquarters five years ago. Just before assuming his present position he completed a stint in marketing. For the past several months he'd been working on Deere's Internet and supply chain strategies. He believed that movement to e-business required a fundamental shift in thinking that had to be reflected in supply management processes. If done correctly, it could establish a sense of continuity throughout the supply chain. Paul had said, "We have to rethink our processes. We need to ask what would we do if we were a brand new company, rather than continuing to do what we've always done."

Movement Toward an E-Business Model. Paul Morrisey's vision for an e-business integration of Deere's supply chain was:

"...a pull system without much inventory. We have to figure out how to enable the supply chain to respond to a customer's needs quickly. As we fill the order we should collect additional information about the customer and mine the data to anticipate future customer needs. We need to fill the customer's order quicker than our competitors. And, we have to recognize that technology isn't the solution, it's the tool."

Paul categorized suppliers into three levels. The lowest level includes those suppliers with which Deere shares only information — communication, even if electronic, is at a fundamental level. The second level of suppliers are more sophisticated and are able to conduct e-commerce business transactions. The highest level includes those suppliers that are integrated partners and collaborate with Deere on product design. Only a very select group of suppliers were, or would be, brought to this level.

Different divisions at Deere had varying levels of technology in place. However, there were efforts in progress to establish common enterprise standards for EDI and to implement core transactions at all units. Notably, a common supplier database that was intended to be corporate-wide and used by all divisions was being developed. Previously, each individual unit had developed databases. This decentralization of data resulted in a lack of awareness about the overall nature of the business that Deere was doing with various suppliers. Paul believed that a transition from Deere's traditional purchasing model to strategic supply management via e-business would require the changes shown in Exhibit 1.

Approximately 70 percent of Deere's product content was purchased, amounting to $7.1 billion in material. Management had set a goal for supply management to reduce the cost of purchased goods and services by $1.1 billion over the next three years.

There were 1,200 supply management employees worldwide. Seventy-eight percent of the work force was located in North America. In 1999, 82 percent of purchases originated in the United States, Europe accounted for 13 percent; South America for 2 percent; India, China, Africa, and Australia combined for another 2 percent; and Mexico accounted for the remaining 1 percent. While Deere's offshore purchases were small, efforts were under way to source more on the global market.

Development of a Common Technology. To help Deere establish technological standards for the entire company and its supply chain, the Deere Electronic Commerce Council was formed with the mission to ". . .drive global enterprise connectivity between Deere, its customers, and supply chain using secured, industry-standard information technology." Specific objectives were to move to 100 percent paperless, Web-based transactions, Web-based supplier collaboration on product development, and Web-based procurement.

In the past, not only had Deere failed to coordinate technological standards among its suppliers, it had failed to do so within its own company. The result was that some suppliers had to deal with different Deere divisions in different ways. Now, in order to integrate its supply chain, Deere had to establish common standards while resisting a Deere-specific solution. In other words, it had to develop or choose standards that could be used by suppliers on an industry-wide, or even multi-industry basis.

While some industry standards were available, they were far from complete. In addition, the software technology for fully integrating supply chains wasn't immediately available. Paul Morrisey believed there were pockets of good technology, but there was nothing to make it all come together. Deere had established initiatives to work with SAP, IBM, and Microsoft to develop applications for business-to-business Internet platforms, data warehousing, and Internet security.

As Paul thought about what he had to do, he realized he also would have to educate the leadership of the company on what was possible, bring business processes and technological systems into synch, and accomplish a cultural change among management that would allow Deere to operate in new ways.

Paul thought to himself that the difference between adopting the technology and changing the underlying culture is just like the difference between learning how to drive a different car and learning how to drive on the other side of the road. Learning how to drive a new car is a new skill, but learning how to drive on the other side of the road is a cultural change. Deere had to learn how to drive on the other side of the road. It wasn't about the technology; it was about being the best at what we do.

As he thought about these concerns, he reminded himself that his plan and recommendations were due to his boss in two weeks.

EXHIBIT 1   Establishing E-Business Standards at Deere and Company

Transitioning from Purchasing to Strategic Supply Management

Traditional Purchasing Structure	*Strategic Supply Management*
Cost, quality, delivery	Total cost management
Coordinated purchasing	Strategic sourcing
Little assistance to suppliers	Supplier development
Deere product designs	Supplier integration in designs
Buy/sell relationships	Management relationships
Management of functions	Management of processes
Systems designed for internal use	Global integration of systems

5 QUALITY SPECIFICATION AND INSPECTION

Key Questions for the Supply Decision Maker

SHOULD WE
- Change our specification method?
- Initiate a QFD program?
- Certify suppliers?

HOW CAN WE
- Improve customer satisfaction with quality?
- Reduce the costs of quality?
- Achieve zero defects?

Quality has always been one of the key issues in supply management. The traditional definition of quality meant meeting specifications or conformance to specifications. In the total quality management context, the definition was enlarged to represent a combination of corporate philosophy and quality tools directed towards satisfying customer needs. With influence over materials and services from suppliers, the purchasing function plays a key role in the final quality of the final product or service.

Even in its simplest definition, quality continues to represent significant challenges; in its broader context it may well determine an organization's ability to survive and prosper in the years ahead. In this chapter, quality will be discussed in a supply management context. It starts with the determination and description of need and concludes with quality measurement and total quality management.

Determination of Need

Every acquisition is intended to fill a need inside the purchaser's organization. Effective supply requires a full understanding of the function the acquisition is to fulfill; how the need is described and how its quality is determined and measured. Together these various activities determine *what* is to be acquired and whether what is supplied meets requirements.

Quality Concerns Drive Supply Initiatives

Quality has taken on a special meaning in the past decades. While new concepts such as MRP and just-in-time production have revolutionized the quantity, delivery, and inventory aspects of materials management, they have also required a new attitude toward quality. When no safety stock is available and required items arrive just before use, their quality must be fully acceptable. This extra pressure, along with all the other good reasons for insisting on good quality, has sparked major efforts by purchasers to seek supplier quality assurance. In many cases, these efforts have involved supplier certification programs or partnerships, including the establishment of satisfactory quality control programs at the premises of those who supply the suppliers. Renewed interest in quality has reinforced the need for a team buying approach to purchasing, the trend to supplier rationalization, cooperative buyer-supplier relations, longer-term contracts, and a reevaluation of the role of the price-quality trade-off in purchase decisions.

To understand the role of quality in procurement, it is necessary to determine how needs are defined, what constitutes a "best buy," and what action purchasers take to ensure that the right quality is supplied.

Every organization can be viewed as a transformation process with inputs and outputs. Before the input can be acquired effectively and efficiently, it is necessary to identify exactly what is needed and why. This identification is often complicated because different people in the organization share in the responsibility of preparing and questioning specifications, and because considerations external to the organization may have a major influence as well. Furthermore, no common agreement exists as to the meaning of ideas such as function, quality, reliability, and suitability.

Determination of Need is a Three-Step Process

The first phase in any acquisition is to determine what is needed and why. Actually, this should be a three-step process. First, the organization's needs are established by focusing on the needs of its customers. Second, it is determined what the market can supply. Third, a conclusion is reached as to what constitutes good value under the circumstances. Frequently, steps one and two and, occasionally, all three steps are performed concurrently. The danger in proceeding through these steps too quickly is that vital information and analysis may be lost. Obviously, in complex purchases the process may well go through these steps iteratively before a final decision is reached.

Needs Can Be Categorized

Every organization's needs can be divided into a variety of categories. Traditional standard ones include: raw materials, purchased parts, MRO items, packaging, services, tools, resale items, and equipment. A different way is to separate requirements that will become part of the product or service that is provided to the organization's customers, as opposed to requirements that are needed to maintain the processes the organization uses to produce and distribute its goods and services to its customers. These can simply be identified as external (production or direct) and internal (nonproduction indirect or MRO) requirements. Both should be customer driven and congruent with the organization's objectives and strategies.

The quality concept argues that an organization's products or services are inseparable from the processes used to produce them. Just focusing on the product or service without examining the process that produces it is likely to miss the key to continuous improvement. If the process is not in statistical control and targeted for continuous improvement, the quality of the products or services produced is likely to suffer. This applies equally to the supply function as to the operations function of any organization.

Actually, every organization can be seen as part of a chain of organizations that has suppliers to one side and customers to the other. In further

FIGURE 5–1

The Transformation and Value-Added Chain

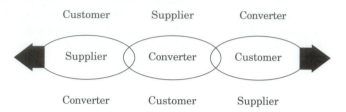

<table>
<tr><td>Customer</td><td>Supplier</td><td>Converter</td></tr>
<tr><td>Supplier</td><td>Converter</td><td>Customer</td></tr>
<tr><td>Converter</td><td>Customer</td><td>Supplier</td></tr>
</table>

Three Roles of Every Organization

detail, every organization, by definition, performs three roles: customer, converter, and supplier (see Figure 5–1). As a converter, every organization needs to add value as its part of the chain.

The same idea can be applied on a micro level inside every organization. Each department or function itself is part of an internal chain performing the same three roles: customer, converter, and supplier to other internal functions and, in some cases, to external customers and suppliers. Here, also, the value-added concept is important. Each department or function must add value and strive to minimize the cost of doing so by process control and continuous improvement in congruence with organizational goals and strategies.

Even in those organizations where traditional functions such as purchasing, production, and sales have given way to teams and functional boundaries have blurred or disappeared, the need for quality remains and the group must assume collective responsibility for it.

A continuous examination of the current and future needs of internal and external customers should result in the identification of current and future requirements to be procured. In theory, this sounds fairly simple; in practice all kinds of difficulties exist.

Identifying Value Opportunities

Moreover, it has become generally recognized that about 70 percent of the opportunity for value improvement lies in the first two phases of the acquisition process: (1) need identification and (2) description. Therefore, great attention needs to be paid to ensure that value opportunities are not overlooked (see Figure 5–2).

Early Supply and Supplier Involvement

Ways to Achieve Early Supply Involvement

Given the high opportunity to affect value during the need identification and description stage, it is essential that supply considerations are brought to bear on decisions during these two stages. Early supply involvement and early supplier involvement (ESI) help assure that what is specified is also procurable and represents good value. Various organizational approaches, such as staffing the supply area with engineers, colocating purchasing people in the engineering or design areas, and using cross-functional teams on new product development, have been used to address effective early supply involvement.

FIGURE 5–2

Opportunity to Affect Value during the Six Steps of the Acquisition Process

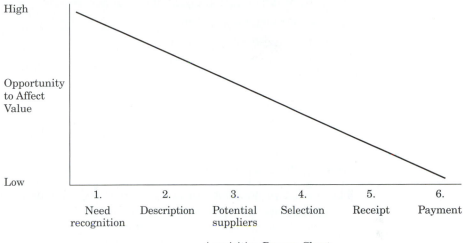

Acquisition Process Chart

Methods of Description

The using, requesting, or specifying department must be capable of reasonably describing what is required to be sure of getting exactly what is wanted.

Purchasing's Role in Describing Need

Although the prime responsibility for determining what is needed usually rests with the using or specifying department, the supply department has the direct responsibility of checking the description given. Purchasers should, of course, not be allowed to alter arbitrarily the description or the quality. They should, however, have the authority to insist that the description be accurate and detailed enough to be perfectly clear to every potential supplier. The buyer also must call to the attention of the requisitioner the availability of other options that might represent better value.

The description of an item may take any one of a variety of forms or, indeed, may be a combination of several different forms. For our discussion, therefore, *description* will mean any one of the various methods by which a buyer conveys to a seller a clear, accurate picture of the required item. The term *specification* will be used in the narrower and commonly accepted sense referring to one particular form of description.

Methods of Description

The methods of description ordinarily used may be listed as follows and will be discussed in order:

1. By brand
2. "Or Equal."

3. By specification.

    a. Physical or chemical characteristics.

    b. Material and method of manufacture.

    c. Performance or function.

4. By engineering drawing.

5. By miscellaneous methods.

    a. Market grades.

    b. Sample.

6. By a combination of two or more methods.

Description by Brand

There are two questions of major importance in connection with the use of branded items. One relates to the desirability of using this type of description and the other to the problem of selecting the particular brand.

Description by brand or trade name indicates a reliance on the integrity and the reputation of the supplier. It assumes that the supplier is anxious to preserve the goodwill attached to a trade name and is capable of doing so. Furthermore, when a given requirement is purchased by brand and is satisfactory in the use for which it was intended, the purchaser has every right to expect that any additional purchases bearing the same brand name will correspond exactly to the quality first obtained.

Reasons to Describe by Brand Name

There are certain circumstances under which description by brand may be not only desirable but also necessary:

1. When, either because the manufacturing process is secret or because the item is covered by a patent, specifications cannot be laid down.

2. When specifications cannot be laid down with sufficient accuracy by the buyer because the supplier's manufacturing process calls for a high degree of that intangible labor quality sometimes called *expertise* or *skill,* which cannot be defined exactly.

3. When the quantity bought is so small as to make the setting of specifications by the buyer unduly costly.

4. When, because of the expense involved or for some similar reason, testing by the buyer is impractical.

5. When users have real, even if unfounded, preferences in favor of certain branded items, a bias the purchaser may find almost impossible to overcome.

Objections to Buying by Brand Name

On the other hand, there are objections to purchasing branded items, most of them turning on cost. Although the price may often be quite in line with the prices charged by other suppliers for similarly branded items, the whole price level may be so high as to cause the buyer to seek unbranded substitutes or even, after analysis, to set its own specifications. There are many articles on the market which, in spite of all the advertising, have no brand discrimination at all. Thus, the purchaser may just as well prefer using trisodium phosphate over a branded cleaning compound costing 50 to 100 percent more.

A further argument, frequently encountered, against using brands is that undue dependence on brands tends to restrict the number of potential suppliers and deprives the buyer of the possible advantage of a lower price or even of improvements brought out by competitors.

"Or Equal"

It is not unusual, particularly in the public sector, to see requests for quotations or bids which will specify a brand or a manufacturer's model number followed by the words "or equal." In these circumstances, the buyer tries to shift the responsibility for establishing equality or superiority to the bidder without having to go to the expense of having to develop detailed specifications.

Description by Specification

Specification constitutes one of the best known of all methods employed. A lot of time and effort has been expended in making it possible to buy on a specification basis. Closely related to these endeavors is the effort toward standardization of product specifications and reduction in the number of types, sizes, and so on, of the products accepted as standard.

It is becoming common practice to specify the test procedure and results necessary to meet quality standards as part of the specification as well as instructions for handling, labeling, transportation, and disposal to meet environmental regulations.

Advantages of Buying with Specifications

Traditional advantages of buying with specifications include:

1. Evidence exists that thought and careful study have been given to the need and the ways in which it may be satisfied.

2. A standard is established for measuring and checking materials as supplied, preventing delay and waste that would occur with improper materials.

3. An opportunity exists to purchase identical requirements from a number of different sources of supply.

4. The potential exists for equitable competition. This is why public agencies place such a premium on specification writing. In securing bids from various suppliers, a buyer must be sure that the suppliers are quoting for exactly the same material or service.

5. The seller will be responsible for performance when the buyer specifies performance.

Limitations of Buying with Specifications

Eight limitations in using specifications are:

1. There are many items for which it is practically impossible to draw adequate specifications.

2. Although a saving may sometimes be realized in the long run, the use of specifications adds to the immediate cost.

3. The specification may not be better than a standard product, readily available.

4. Compared with purchase by brand, the immediate cost is also increased by the necessity of testing to ensure that the specifications have been met.

5. Carelessness in drawing specifications may give the purchaser a false sense of security.

6. Unduly elaborate specifications sometimes result in discouraging possible suppliers from placing bids in response to inquiries.

7. Unless the specifications are of the performance type, the responsibility for the adaptability of the item to the use intended rests wholly on the buyer.

8. The minimum specifications set up by the buyer are likely to be the maximum furnished by the supplier.

Specification by Physical or Chemical Characteristics. Specification by physical or chemical characteristics provides definitions of the properties of the materials the purchaser desires. They represent an effort to state in measurable terms those properties deemed necessary for satisfactory use at the least cost consistent with quality. For example, muriatic acid:

Appearance	*Clear*
Color—APHA	40–50
HCl	31.5%
Free Cl	Nil
Organics	5–7 ppm
Fe	0.8 ppm
Ni	Nil
Arsenic	Nil

Specification by Material and Method of Manufacture. The second type of specification prescribes both the material and method of manufacture. Outside of some governmental purchases, such as those of the armed forces, this method is used when special requirements exist and when the buyer is willing to assume the responsibility for results. Many organizations are not in this position, and, as a result, comparatively little use is made of this form of specification.

Specification by Performance or Function. The heart of performance specification is the understanding of the required functions. It is not easy to think of the basic function the item must perform. We tend to speak of a box instead of something to package in, a bolt instead of something that fastens. We think of a steak instead of something to eat, and a bed instead of something to sleep on.

Why make an issue of this? It seems so simple as to be hardly worth mentioning. But, actually, this is the heart of a sound need definition. Here lie the major clues for improving value. A casual bypassing of the function needed frequently results in improper specification. For example, a hose will be too short, a lining will shrink, a bolt shear, a motor burn out, a paint peel, a machine vibrate, a vessel burst, a part won't fit, an insurance policy won't cover, and a host of other troubles of this sort arise. Many of these troubles will result from underestimating the function required or from negligence, error, or oversight because certain functional needs have been forgotten or overlooked. It is no coincidence that value analysis and value engineering concentrate on proper function definition as their basis.

Function Definition Is the Basis of Value Analysis and Value Engineering

The answer to this problem, one will say, is to buy quality. If the item is not of sufficient quality to perform the task required of it, it does not fulfill the function. Moreover, quality can be a cloak for various inadequacies. Buying the best-quality high-alloy screws will not help if bolts were needed in the first place.

If the basic functional need is defined as a sheet metal screw, instead of a need to fasten together two sheets of metal of certain physical and chemical characteristics, the first basic step in sound acquisition is missed. Also missed is the opportunity to investigate such alternatives as bolts, rivets, and spot welds, to name just a few.

Verb-Noun Combinations Best Define Function

Describing functions as verb-noun combinations—"provide torque, transmit current, contain liquid, and so on"—forces clear thinking about the intended function. Separating functions into primary and secondary categories also identifies what is really needed versus what might be deleted. In addition, once the function is properly identified, it is possible to establish its worth by comparison to other ways of achieving the same function. For example, special-alloy, custom-shaped fuel tanks for a small navy boat were replaced by four mild steel drums, reducing cost by about 90 percent. The four mesh screens on an industrial motor were needed to "exclude matter" and "permit access." The value of these functions was estimated at 20 percent of the existing cost. A more detailed look at value analysis and value engineering is provided in Chapter 13. Nevertheless, at this point the usefulness of functional identification needs to be recognized.

Performance Based Specifications Call for Supplier Expertise

Performance or function specification in combination with a Request for Proposal (RFP) is employed to a considerable extent, partly because it throws the responsibility for a satisfactory product back to the seller. Performance specification is results and use oriented, leaving the supplier with the decisions on how to make the most suitable product. This enables the supplier to take advantage of the latest technological developments and to substitute anything that exceeds the minimum performance required.

A specification for missile silo doors required that they be able to withstand the impact of a tree or telephone pole that might be moving at hurricane speeds. This required the contractor to construct a telephone-pole hurling machine!

The satisfactory use of a performance specification, of course, is absolutely dependent on securing the right kind of supplier. It should be noted that it may be difficult to compare quotations and the supplier may include in the price a risk allowance.

Description by Engineering Drawing. Description by a blueprint or dimension sheet is common and may be used in connection with some form of descriptive text. It is particularly applicable to the purchase of construction, electronic and electrical assemblies, machined parts, forgings, castings, and stampings. It is an expensive method of description not only because of the cost of preparing the print or computer program itself but also because it is likely to be used to describe an item that is quite special as far as the supplier is concerned and, hence, expensive to manufacture. However, it is probably the most accurate of all forms of description and is particularly adapted to purchasing those items requiring a high degree of manufacturing perfection and close tolerances.

Miscellaneous Methods of Description

There are two additional methods of description, description by market grades and description by sample.

Description by Market Grades. Purchases on the basis of market grades are confined to certain primary materials. Wheat and cotton[1] have already been referred to in this connection; lumber, steel, copper, and other commodities will suggest themselves. For some purposes, purchase by grade is entirely satisfactory. Its value depends on the accuracy with which grading is done and the ability to ascertain the grade of the material by inspection.

Furthermore, the grading must be done by those in whose ability and honesty the purchaser has confidence. It may be noted that even for wheat and cotton, grading may be entirely satisfactory to one class of buyer and not satisfactory to another class.

---

[1]For agricultural raw materials, such as wheat and cotton, the grades are established by the U.S. Department of Agriculture. They include all food and feed products, the standards and grades for which have been established in accordance with the Federal Food and Drug Act, the Grain Standards Act, and other laws enacted by Congress. As will be noted later, establishing grades acceptable to the trade is essential to the successful operation of a commodity exchange.

Description by Sample. Still another method of description is by submission of a sample of the item desired. Almost all purchasers use this method from time to time but ordinarily—there are some exceptions—for a minor percentage of their purchases, and then more or less because no other method is possible.

Good examples are items requiring visual acceptance, such as wood grain, color, appearance, smell, and so on.

Combination of Descriptive Methods

An organization frequently uses a combination of two or more of the methods of description already discussed. The exact combination found most satisfactory for an individual organization will depend, of course, on the type needed by the organization.

Sources of Specification Data

Speaking broadly, there are three major sources from which specifications may be derived: (1) individual standards set up by the buyer; (2) standards established by certain private agencies, either other users, suppliers, or technical societies; and (3) governmental standards.

Individual Standards. Individual standards require extensive consultation among users, engineering, purchasing, quality control, suppliers, marketing, and, possibly, ultimate consumers. This means the task is likely to be arduous and expensive.

Individual Standards May be Costly

A common procedure is for the buying organization to formulate its own specifications on the basis of the foundation laid down by the governmental or technical societies. To make doubly sure that no serious errors have been made, some organizations mail out copies of all tentative specifications, even in cases where changes are mere revisions of old forms, to several outstanding suppliers in the industry to get the advantage of their comments and suggestions before final adoption.

Standard Specifications. If an organization wishes to buy on a specification basis, yet hesitates to undertake to originate its own, it may use one of the so-called standard specifications. These have been developed as a result of a great deal of experience and study by both governmental and nongovernmental agencies, and substantial effort has been expended in promoting them. They may be applied to raw or semimanufactured products, to component parts, or to the composition of material. The well-known SAE steels, for instance, are a series of alloy steels of specified composition and known properties, carefully defined, and identified by individual numbers.

Advantages of Standard Specifications

When they can be used, standard specifications have certain advantages. They are widely known and commonly recognized and readily available to every buyer. Furthermore, the standard should have somewhat lower costs of manufacture. Finally, because they have grown out of the wide experience of producers and users, they should be adaptable to the requirements of many purchasers.

Standard specifications have been developed by a number of nongovernmental engineering and technical groups. Among them may be mentioned the American Standards Association, the American Society for Testing Materials, the American Society of Mechanical Engineers, the American Institute of Electrical Engineers, the Society of Automotive Engineers, the American Institute of Mining and Metallurgical Engineers, the Underwriters Laboratories, the National Safety Council, the Canadian Engineering Standards Association, the American Institute of Scrap Recycling Industries, the National Electrical Manufacturers' Association, and many others.

While governmental agencies have cooperated closely with these organizations, they have also developed their own standards. The National Bureau of Standards in the U.S. Department of Commerce compiles commercial standards. The General Services Administration coordinates standards and federal specifications for the nonmilitary type of items used by two or more services. The Defense Department issues military (MIL) specifications.

The American National Standards Institute (ANSI) is a private, nonprofit organization that administers and coordinates the U.S. voluntary standardization system. Its mission is to enhance U.S. global competitiveness and the American way of life by promoting, facilitating and safeguarding the integrity of the voluntary standardization system.[2]

Developed by ANSI, NSSN, A National Resource for Global Standards, contains more than 250,000 references to standards from more than 600 developers worldwide. ANSI provides access to various U.S. and global standards on its Web site and can be a valuable resource for purchasers who need access to various standards.[3]

Government, Legal and Environmental Requirements. Federal legislation concerning environmental factors, employee health and safety, and consumer product safety requires vigilance on the part of purchasing personnel to be sure that products purchased meet government requirements. The Occupational Safety and Health Administration (known as OSHA) of the U.S. Department of Labor has broad powers to investigate and control everything from noise levels to sanitary facilities in places of employment. The Consumer Product Safety Act gives broad regulatory power to a commission to safeguard consumers against unsafe products. Purchasing people have the responsibility to make sure that the products they buy meet the requirements of the legislation. Severe penalties, both criminal and civil, can be placed on violators of the regulations.

---

[2]American National Standards Institute, *www.ansi.org*, January 2001.

[3]See *www.nssn.org* or *www.ansi.org*.

Types of Loss Exposure

Loss Exposure. There are selective buying situations where the specifications may well expose the buying organization to risk. Robert S. Mullen, Director of Purchasing at Harvard University, cited the instance of a purchase of fireproof mattresses, costing only about $1,000 more in total, to avoid a multimillion dollar suit in case of student injury or death. Environmental risks represent another category.

Another form of loss exposure is related to the possibility of pilferage. The attractiveness of the requirements to consumers and the ease of resale may be reasons for theft. An alert purchaser can significantly cut down on losses by purchasing in smaller quantities, insisting on tamper-proof packaging, choosing the appropriate transportation mode, following the advice of security experts, and making sure that quantities are carefully controlled throughout the acquisition and disposal process.

Standardization and Simplification

The terms *standardization* and *simplification* are often used to mean the same thing. Strictly speaking, they refer to two different ideas. *Standardization* means agreement on definite sizes, design, quality, and the like. It is essentially a technical and engineering concept. *Simplification* refers to a reduction in the number of sizes, designs, and so forth. It is a selective and commercial problem, an attempt to determine the most important sizes, for instance, of a product, and to concentrate production or use on these wherever possible. Simplification may be applied to articles already standardized as to design or size or as a step preliminary to standardization.

The challenge in an organization is where to draw the line between standardization and simplification, on the one hand, and suitability and uniqueness, on the other. Clearly, as economic and technological factors change, old standards may no longer represent the best buy. Frequently, by stressing standardization and simplification of the component parts, rather than the completed end product, production economies may be gained combined with individuality of end product. Simultaneously, procurement advantages are gained in terms of low initial cost, lower inventories, and diversity in selection of sources. The automotive industry, for example, has used this approach extensively to cut costs, improve quality, and still give the appearance of extensive consumer options.

Global Standardization at Sasib

Sasib, a manufacturer of equipment for the food and beverage industry headquartered in Italy, found that product standardization was an important issue for its large global customers, such as Coca Cola and Heineken. The chief purchasing officer described the importance of standardization and the role of supply: "Standardization is important to us, not just for leveraging purchases across the group, but also in terms of our ability to design and build a product for our customer that is consistent, regardless of where it is manufactured. We also want to be able to exchange and optimize manufacturing capacity. For example, we need to develop the flexibility to build machines in the U.S. that are designed in Europe and vice versa. More importantly, our customers are expecting standardization across our product lines. This can only be done if we use the same suppliers who can provide support everywhere in the world. Consequently, we use top-quality suppliers with global supply and service networks. Previously, the companies were dealing with local suppliers. Even in situations where divisions used common suppliers, prices and specifications differed substantially."[4]

Quality, Suitability, and Best Buy

Practitioners often use the term *quality* to describe the notions of function, suitability, reliability and conformance with specifications, satisfaction with actual performance, and best buy. This is highly confusing.

Quality

**Quality:
Conformance
or
Performance?**

Quality in the simplest sense refers to the ability of the supplier to provide goods and services in conformance with specifications. The area of inspection, discussed at the end of this chapter, covers this interpretation. Quality may also refer to whether the item performs in actual use to the expectations of the original requisitioner, regardless of conformance with specifications. Thus, it is often said an item is "no good" or of "bad quality" when it fails in use, even though the original requisition or specification may be at fault. The ideal, of course, is achieved when all inputs acquired pass this use test satisfactorily.

Suitability

**Suitability
Refers to
Fitness for Use**

Suitability refers to the ability of a material, good, or service to meet the intended functional use. In a pure sense, suitability ignores the commercial considerations and refers to fitness for use. In reality, that is hardly practiced. Gold may be a better electrical conductor than silver or copper but is far too expensive to use in all but special applications. That is why chips are wired with gold and houses with copper. The notion of "best buy" puts quality, reliability, and suitability into a sound procurement perspective.

"Best Buy"

The decision on what to buy involves more than balancing various technical considerations. The most desirable technical feature or suitability for a given use, once determined, is not necessarily the desirable buy. The distinction is

---

[4]Michiel R. Leenders and P. Fraser Johnson, *Major Structural Changes in Supply Organization* (Tempe, AZ: Center for Advanced Purchasing Studies, 2000).

between technical considerations which are matters of dimension, design, chemical or physical properties, and the like, and the more inclusive concept of the "best buy." The "best buy" assumes, of necessity, a certain minimum measure of suitability but considers ultimate customer needs, cost and procurability, transportation, and disposal as well.

If the cost is so high as to be prohibitive, one must get along with an item somewhat less suitable. Or if, at whatever cost or however procurable, the only available suppliers of the technically perfect item lack adequate productive capacity or financial and other assurance of continued business existence, then, too, one must give way to something else. Obviously, too, frequent reappraisals are necessary. If the price of copper increases from $1 a pound to $1.50 or more, its relationship to aluminum or other substitutes may change.

"Best Buy" Is Always a Compromise

The "best buy" is a combination of characteristics, not merely one. The specific combination finally decided on is almost always a compromise because the particular aspect of quality to be stressed in any individual case depends largely on circumstances. In some instances the primary consideration is reliability; questions of immediate cost, or facility of installation, or the ease of making repairs are all secondary. In other instances the lifetime of the item of supply is not so important; efficiency in operation becomes more significant.

The decision on what constitutes the best buy for any particular need is as much conditioned by marketing as by procurement and technical considerations. It should be clear that to reach a sound decision on the best buy requires all relevant parties—marketing, engineering, operations and supply—to work closely together. The ability and willingness of all parties concerned to view the trade-offs in perspective will significantly influence the final decisions reached.

Service and "Best Buy"

Sometimes the service the supplier performs is as important as any attribute of the product itself. Service may include design, recordkeeping, transportation, storage, disposal, installation, training, inspection, repair, and advice, as well as a willingness to make satisfactory adjustments for misunderstandings or clerical errors. Some purchasers include the supplier's willingness to change orders on short notice and be particularly responsive to unusual requests as part of their evaluation of the service provided. To cover some types of service, suppliers issue guarantees, covering periods of varying length. The value of such guarantees rests less on the technical wording of the statement itself than on the goodwill and reliability of the seller.

Many suppliers specifically include the cost of service in the selling price. Others absorb it themselves, charging no more than competitors and relying on the superior service for the sale. One of the difficult tasks of a buyer is to get only as much of this service factor as is really needed without paying for

Factoring in Service Requirements

the excessive service the supplier may be obliged to render to some other purchaser. In many instances, of course, the servicing department of a manufacturing concern is maintained as a separate organization. The availability of service is an important consideration for the buyer in securing the "best buy" at the outset.

Determining the "Best Buy"

It is generally accepted that the final verdict on technical suitability for a particular use should rest with those involved in using, engineering, specifying, or resale. Supply's right to audit, question, and suggest must be recognized along with the need for early involvement of procurement during the design phase.

Cross-Functional Teams May Determine "Best Buy"

Supply fails to live up to its responsibility unless it insists that economic and procurement factors be considered, and unless it passes on to those immediately responsible for specification suggestions of importance that may come as a result of its normal activities. The buyer is in a key position to present the latest information from the marketplace that may permit modifications in design, more flexibility in specifications, or changes in manufacturing methods that will improve value for the ultimate customer. Cross-functional teams are preferable to an adversarial approach to "best buy" determinations.

Total Quality Management (TQM)

Total quality management is a philosophy and system of management focused on customer satisfaction. In TQM the customer can be internal or external and is anyone in the supply chain who receives materials from a previous step in the chain. TQM begins with top management's developing its vision for total quality, providing the commitment and support to strive for the realization of this vision, and reviewing and encouraging progress toward this achievement. According to the U.S. General Accounting Office, four important features of TQM are:

Four Features of TQM

1. Quality must be integrated throughout the organization's activities.
2. There must be employee commitment to continuous improvement.
3. The goal of customer satisfaction, and the systematic and continuous research process related to customer satisfaction, drives TQM systems.
4. Suppliers are partners in the TQM process.[5]

---

[5]F. Ian Stuart and P. Mueller, Jr., "Total Quality Management and Supplier Partnerships: A Case Study," *International Journal of Purchasing and Materials Management*, vol. 30, no. 1, Winter 1994, pp. 14–21.

Quality Is the Integrating Force

TQM stresses quality as the integrating force in the organization. For TQM to work, all stages in the production process must conform to specifications that are driven by the needs and wants of the end customer. All processes, those of the buyer and the suppliers, must be in control and possess minimal variation to reduce time and expense of inspection. This in turn reduces scrap and rework, increases productivity, and reduces total cost.[6] However, TQM is more than a philosophy and involves the use of several tools, such as quality function deployment (QFD) and statistical process control, in order to achieve performance improvements.

The following sections describe how quality management techniques are used and how they apply to the supply function.

Quality

Quality Dimensions

Considerable interest in the use of quality as a competitive tool has reawakened management appreciation of the contribution quality can make in an organization. On the supply side, how well suppliers perform may be crucial to the buying organization's own success in providing quality goods and services. A variety of surveys tend to show that, in many organizations, at least 50 percent of the quality problems stem from goods and services supplied by suppliers. Moreover, new management tools and techniques like MRP, JIT, and stockless purchasing all require that what is delivered by a supplier conform to specifications. Furthermore, it is not realistic to insist that suppliers supply high-quality goods without ensuring that the buying organization's own quality performance is beyond reproach. This applies to the procurement organization, its people, policies, systems, and procedures as well. Quality improvement is a continuing challenge for both buyer and seller. Moreover, close cooperation between buying and selling organizations is necessary to achieve significant improvement over time.

Eight Dimensions of Quality

Quality is a complex term, which, according to Professor David Garvin of the Harvard Business School, has at least eight dimensions. These are:

1. *Performance.* The primary function of the product or service.
2. *Features.* The bells and whistles.
3. *Reliability.* The probability of failure within a specified time period.
4. *Durability.* The life expectancy.
5. *Conformance.* The meeting of specifications.
6. *Serviceability.* The maintainability and ease of fixing.

---

[6]Ibid.

7. *Aesthetics.* The look, smell, feel, and sound.

8. *Perceived Quality.* The image in the eyes of the customer.

Obviously, from a procurement point of view, the ninth dimension should be "procurability"—the short- and long-term availability on the market at reasonable prices and subject to continuing improvement.

Reliability

Reliability Is the Mathematical Probability of Function

Reliability is the mathematical probability that a product will function for a stipulated period of time. Complexity is the enemy of reliability because of the multiplicative fact of probabilities of failure of components. The distribution of failures is normally considered to be exponential, with failures occurring randomly. This facilitates calculations by making the reliabilities of the components additive. Testing is also more flexible because of the time-numbers trade-off. The same inference may be drawn from 20 parts tested for 50 hours as for 500 parts tested for 2 hours. Exceptions like the Weibull distribution (which accounts for the aging effect) and the bathtub curve (which recognizes the high probability of early failure, a period of steady state, and a higher probability of failure near the end of the useful life) can also be handled, but they require more complex mathematical treatment.

From a procurement standpoint, it is useful to recognize the varying reliabilities of components and products acquired. Penalties or premiums may be assessed for variation from design standard depending on the expected reliability impact.

The Cost of Quality

Traditional View of Quality

The old-fashioned management perspective was that the quality—cost curve was similar to the economic order quantity curve, or broadly U-shaped (see Figure 5–3). Under this notion, it was considered acceptable to live with a significant defect level because it was assumed that fewer defects would increase costs.

New View of Quality

Thanks to the contribution of leaders like Deming, Juran, Shingo, and Crosby, a new perspective on quality and its achievability has emerged. This view of quality argues that every defect is expensive and prevention or avoidance of defects lowers costs (see Figure 5–4).

Interestingly enough, it used to be that purchasers were willing to pay more for higher quality products or services, recognizing the benefits to the purchaser's organization, but also assuming that the supplier might have to incur higher costs to achieve better quality. If quality were "inspected in," this would indeed be a higher-cost solution. Deming argues that the stress in quality should be in making it right the first time, rather than inspecting quality in. Making it right the first time should be a lower-cost solution.

FIGURE 5–3

The Traditional View of the Quality-Cost Trade-off

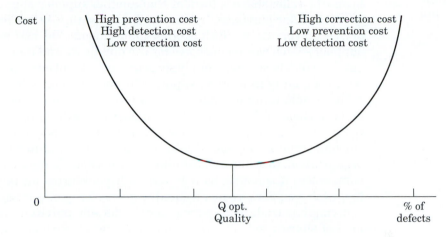

FIGURE 5–4

The Current View of the Quality-Cost Trade-off

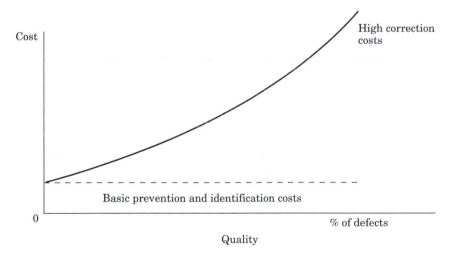

Therefore, it is not unreasonable for a purchaser and seller to work together on achieving both improved quality and lower costs!

Three Quality Challenges for Supply

Quality presents three real challenges for supply. The first is learning how to apply quality principles to purchasing's own performance. The second, how to work cooperatively with suppliers on continuing quality improvement. And the third is how to deal with supplier rationalization and all that it implies.

**Quality and
Single Versus
Multiple
Sourcing**

Many of purchasing's policies and procedures have been designed on the principle that competition is at the heart of the buyer-seller relationship. What keeps the seller sharp is the fear that another supplier might take away sales to a particular purchaser by offering better quality, better price, better delivery, better service, or a host of other inducements. The assumption was that a supplier switch was inexpensive for the purchaser and that multiple sourcing gave the purchaser both supply security and control over suppliers. The emergence of quality as a prime supply criterion challenges this traditional competitive view. It argues that it is very difficult to find a high-quality supplier and even more difficult to create a supplier who will continually improve quality. In fact, it may require very extensive work of various experts in the purchasing organization, along with the appropriate counterparts in the selling organization, to achieve continuing improvement in quality. Under these circumstances it is not realistic to use multiple sources for the same end item, to switch suppliers frequently, and to go out for quotes constantly. But single sourcing has traditionally created considerable purchaser nervousness. The idea of sharing key organizational information with suppliers so that they can better plan, design, and service the purchaser's requirements is scary for procurement experts whose skills were honed on a competitiveness philosophy. The heart of a new approach to quality centers on understanding the tools, techniques, and mathematics of quality.

Perhaps the traditional view of quality stems from an economic environment of high demand and low worldwide competition, in which defects were tolerated. Perhaps this was further abetted by an incomplete grasp of the real costs of quality and of poor quality. Unfortunately, in many organizations these costs are well hidden and, therefore, difficult to consider in decision making. Five major cost categories applicable to quality are prevention, appraisal, internal failure, external failure, and morale.

**Five Quality-
Related Cost
Categories**

Prevention Costs. Prevention costs relate to all activities that eliminate the occurrence of future defects. These include such diverse costs as various quality assurance programs; precertifying and qualifying suppliers; employee training and awareness programs; machine, tool, material, and labor checkouts; preventive maintenance; and single sourcing with quality suppliers, as well as the associated personnel, travel, equipment, and space costs.

Appraisal Costs. Appraisal costs represent the costs of inspection, testing, measuring, and other activities designed to ensure conformance of the product or service. Appraisal costs might occur at both the seller's and buyer's organizations as each uses a variety of inspection systems to ensure quality conformance. If appraisal requires setting aside batches, or sending product to a separate inspection department, detection costs should include extra handling and inventory tie-up costs aside from the inspection cost itself in terms of space, people, equipment, materials, and associated reporting systems. (The advantages of using the supplier's QC reports and making it right the first time are evident.)

Internal Failure Costs. Internal failure costs are the costs incurred within the operating system as a result of poor quality. Included in internal failure costs are returns to suppliers, scrap and rework, and all associated costs such as extra transportation and management time to expedite replacement materials.

External Failure Costs. External failure costs are incurred when poor quality goods or services are passed on to the customer and include costs of returns, warranty costs, and management time handling customer complaints. Unfortunately, when poor quality parts are incorporated in assemblies, disassembly and reassembly costs may far outweigh the cost of the original part itself. When a defective product gets into the hands of customers or their customers, the possibility of consequential damages arises because a paper roll did not meet specifications, the printer missed an important deadline, a magazine did not reach advertisers and subscribers on time, and so on. There may be health or safety consequences from defective products. These costs are the most expensive because of the possible effects on individual customer goodwill and lost sales and profits. The loss of customers, the inability to secure new customers, and the penalties paid to keep existing customers; all are also part of external failure costs.

Morale Costs. One cost seldom recognized in an accounting sense is the morale cost of producing (or having to use) defective products or services. Aside from the obvious productivity impact, it may remove the incentive for the employees in the organization to keep searching for continuing improvement and they may develop a laissez-faire attitude.

An Overall Quality-Cost Perspective. In fact, it is so unpleasant to detail the costs of defective quality that the temptation is strong to ignore them. And that is exactly what many organizations have done for many years. They have also built these costs into internally accepted standards. As a consequence, the opportunity to improve quality is great in most organizations.

Quality Contributes Much to Final Product Cost

Some organizations have attempted to quantify the total cost of quality, and the outcome of such studies suggests that 30 to 40 percent of final product cost may be attributable to quality. Obviously, there is a huge incentive to tackle quality as a major organizational challenge.

Continuous Improvement

Kaizen Equals Continuous Improvement

Continuous improvement, sometimes called by its Japanese name, *kaizen,* refers to the relentless pursuit of product and process improvement through a series of small, progressive steps and is an integral part of TQM. Continuous improvement should follow a well-defined and structured approach and incorporate problem-solving tools, such as Pareto analysis, histograms, scatter diagrams, check sheets, fishbone diagrams, control charts, run charts, and process flow diagrams.

The Deming Wheel

The *plan-do-check-act cycle,* sometimes called the Deming Wheel, provides a good model for conducting continuous improvement activities. The data is collected and the performance target is set in the plan phase. Countermeasures are implemented in the do phase. Evaluation and measuring results of the countermeasures are performed in the check phase. The improvement is standardized and applied to other parts of the organization in the act phase.

Continuous Improvement at Honda

Honda's BP Program is an example of applying a continuous improvement philosophy to supplier management. BP stands for best position, best productivity, best product, best price, and best partners. The BP is a 13-week process that focuses on waste elimination and is based on the principle that the people that perform the work are the greatest source of improvement ideas and creativity. Like all Honda improvement initiatives, BP follows Deming's plan-do-check-act cycle.[7]

The Malcolm Baldrige National Quality Award and ISO 9000

The Baldrige Award Diffuses TQM Practices

The annual Malcolm Baldrige National Quality Award is intended to recognize U.S. organizations that excel in quality achievement and quality management, motivate U.S. companies to improve quality and productivity, provide standardized quality guidelines and criteria for evaluating quality improvement efforts, and provide guidance to U.S. organizations striving to make improvements by describing how winning organizations were able to achieve their successes. The diffusion of TQM practices is one of the most important aspects of the Baldrige Award, and the organization sends out more than 200,000 criteria packages each year.

The Baldrige Award evaluates both quality management programs and achievement of results, with heavy emphasis on total corporate financial performance. Some companies, such as Honeywell, Motorola, Southwest Bell and Cummins Engine, have required their suppliers to use modified versions of the Baldrige criteria for quality measurement and evaluation.[8]

---

[7]Dave Nelson, Rick Mayo and Patricia Moody, *Powered By Honda* (New York, NY: John Wiley & Sons, 1998).

[8]Sime Curkovic and Robert Handfield, "Use of ISO 9000 and Baldrige Award Criteria in Supplier Quality Evaluation," International Journal of Purchasing and Materials Management, Spring 1995, pp. 2–11.

In Canada, the government has initiated its own national quality awards program and, of course, in Japan, the Deming Prize carries a tremendous amount of international prestige.

ISO 9000 Quality Standards[9]

Internal and External Benefits of ISO 9000 Certification

The International Organization for Standardization (ISO) in Geneva, Switzerland, tries to provide common standards across the world. The American National Standards Institute (ANSI) and the Canadian Standards Association (CSA) are North American members. The ISO 9000 quality standards were first adopted in 1987 and revised in 1994, and they evolved quickly in Europe and later became popular in North America. By 2001, more than 300,000 organizations worldwide had been certified.[10] Respondents to a survey by Dun & Bradstreet and Irwin Professional Publishing identified significant internal and external benefits of ISO 9000 registration. The two most significant internal benefits were better documentation (87 percent) and greater quality awareness by employees (82.9 percent). The three most significant external benefits were higher perceived quality (83.3 percent), competitive advantage (69.6 percent), and reduced customer quality audits (56.1 percent).[11]

Applicability to All Sectors of the Economy

In December 2000, ISO announced significant revisions to its 9000 series, creating ISO 9000:2000. The traditional criticism of the ISO 9000 series since its initial release was that it did not check for actual customer satisfaction, nor did registration necessarily guarantee a quality product or service. The revisions aim to specifically address these weaknesses and make ISO 9000 relevant for organization in all sectors—services and manufacturing, profit and nonprofit organizations.

The most significant change in ISO 9000:2000 is the integration of ISO 9001, ISO 9002 and 9003 into the new ISO 9001:2000. This is the only standard in the ISO 9000 family against which third-party certification can be carried. ISO 9004:2000, which is meant to be implemented following ISO 9001:2000, is a guideline standard that provides guidance for continuous improvement of quality management systems to achieve sustained customer satisfaction.

Major Changes in ISO 9000

The major changes in the revised ISO 9000 standards are increased focus on top management commitment and customer satisfaction, the emphasis on processes within the organization, and the introduction of continual improvement concepts. The revisions of ISO 9001:2000 and ISO 9004:2000 are based on eight quality management principles that reflect what the organizing committee considered best management practice: customer-focused

---

[9]Information about the International National Standards Organization can be found on their Web site at *www.iso.ch*.

[10]International Standards Organization, *www.iso.ch*, February 2001.

[11]Haily Lynne McKeefry, "Study: ISO Benefits Boom," *Electronics Buyers News,* July 1, 1996, p. 40.

organization, leadership, involvement of people, process approach, system approach to management, continual improvement, factual approach to decision making, and mutually beneficial supplier relationships.[12]

Quality Function Deployment (QFD)

Quality Function Deployment (QFD) is an important aspect of TQM and represents a method for developing new products that seeks to respond to pressures to introduce higher quality new products at less cost and in less time. QFD, which has been used successfully by Toyota and many others, is based on teamwork and customer involvement and integrates marketing, design, engineering development, manufacturing, production, and purchasing in new product development from the conception stage through final delivery. Through coordination and integration, rather than the traditional sequential development approach, QFD allows the end customer's needs and wants to be communicated at the product development stage and then drives the design and production stages. More time is spent upfront in product development, but by accurately defining customer needs and wants, the total time spent on the design cycle is reduced because fewer design changes are made in later stages of the process. The four integrated stages of the QFD process are:

Four Stages of the QFD Process

1. *Product planning,* to determine design requirements.
2. *Parts deployment,* to determine parts characteristics.
3. *Process planning,* to determine manufacturing requirements.
4. *Production planning,* to determine production requirements.

Suppliers Role in Each Stage

Suppliers can also play a role in each of these stages in the following manner.

1. *Product planning.* Provide expertise in analyzing customer requirements and generating a list of new product ideas.
2. *Parts deployment.* Provide alternative design concepts and estimate the manufacturing costs of various parts.
3. *Process planning.* Suppliers can determine their own existing processes' constraints.
4. *Production planning.* Help develop performance measurement criteria for production planning.

Benefits of QFD

Using the QFD methodology, buyer and supplier integration into the process can benefit the organization by (1) reducing or eliminating engineering changes during product development, (2) reducing product development cycle time, (3) reducing startup cycle time, (4) minimizing product failures and

---

[12]International Standards Organization, *www.iso.ch*, February 2001.

repair costs over the product life, and (5) creating product uniformity and reliability during production.[13]

Integration of Functions and Processes Is Critical to Global Competitiveness

From the perspective of supply management, well-functioning buyer-supplier relationships are a key contribution that purchasers and supply managers can make to the organizations' TQM and QFD efforts. Supply base rationalization and closer relationships with key suppliers through partnering arrangements or strategic alliances go hand in hand with quality initiatives (see Chapter 8). The importance of matching purchasing performance measures to the strategic initiatives of the organization is also important if TQM and QFD are to be successful. For example, if purchasing's performance is measured on the basis of reduction in materials costs and operating efficiency rather than the quality of supplier relations, purchasers may be more inclined to buy on the basis of price alone, thereby undermining the quality initiatives of the firm. Integration of functions and processes throughout the firm, and with key suppliers, is a critical component of global competitiveness.

Inspection and Testing

Inspection and testing may be done at two different stages in the acquisition process. Before commitment is made to a supplier, it may be necessary to test samples to see if they are adequate for the purpose intended. Similarly, comparison testing may be done to determine which product is better from several different sources. After a purchase commitment has been made, inspection may be required to ensure that the items delivered conform to the original description.

Testing and Samples

Testing products may be necessary before a commitment is made to purchase. The original selection of a given item may be based on either a specific test or a preliminary trial.

When suppliers offer samples for testing, the general rule followed by purchasers is to accept only samples that have some reasonable chance of being used. Buyers are more likely to accept samples than to reject them because they are always on the lookout for items that may prove superior to those in current use. For various reasons, however, care has to be exercised. The samples cost the seller something and the buyer will not wish to raise false hopes on the part of the salesperson. Sometimes, too, the buyer lacks adequate facilities for testing and testing may be costly to the buyer. To meet

---

[13]A. Ansari and Batoul Modarress, "Quality Function Deployment: The Role of Suppliers," *International Journal of Purchasing and Materials Management,* vol. 30, no. 4, Fall 1994, pp. 28–35.

Samples: To Pay or Not to Pay?

these objections, some organizations insist on paying for all samples accepted for testing, partly because they believe that a more representative sample is obtained when it is purchased through the ordinary trade channels and partly because the buyer is less likely to feel under any obligation to the seller. Some organizations pay for the sample only when the value is substantial; some follow the rule of allowing whoever initiates the test to pay for the item tested; some pay for it only when the outcome of the test is satisfactory. The general rule, however, is for sellers to pay for samples on the theory that, if sellers really want the business and have confidence in their products, they will be willing to bear the expense of providing free samples.

Determining Appropriate Type of Test

Use and Laboratory Tests. The type of test given also varies, depending on such factors as the attitude of the buyer toward the value of specific types of tests, the type of item in question, its comparative importance, and the buyer's facilities for testing. At times a use test alone is considered sufficient, as with paint and floor wax. One advantage of a use test is that the item can be tested for the particular purpose for which it is intended and under the particular conditions in which it will be used. The risk that failure may be costly or interrupt performance or production is, however, present. At other times a laboratory test alone is thought adequate and may be conducted by a commercial testing laboratory or in the organization's own quality control facility. For retailers, a test may be given in one or more stores to establish whether consumer demand is sufficient to carry the product.

The actual procedure of handling samples need not be outlined here. It is important to make and keep complete records concerning each individual sample accepted. These records should describe the type of test, the conditions under which it was given, the results, and any representations made about it by the seller. It is sound practice to discuss the results of such tests with supplier representatives so that they know their samples have received a fair evaluation.

Inspection

The ideal situation for inspection is, of course, one in which no inspection is necessary. This is possible because the quality assurance effort cooperatively mounted by the purchaser and the supplier has resulted in outstanding quality performance and reliable supporting supplier-generated records. Because not all organizations have reached this enviable goal, examining some of the more common ideas surrounding inspection and quality control is useful.

Purpose of Inspection

Just as the purpose of adequate description is to convey to the supplier a clear idea of the item being purchased, so the purpose of inspection is to assure the buyer that the supplier has delivered an item that corresponds to the description furnished. When new suppliers are being tried, their products or services must be watched with particular care until they have proved themselves dependable. Unfortunately, too, production methods and skills, even of old suppliers, change from time to time; operators become careless, errors are made, and occasionally a seller may even try to reduce production costs to the point where quality suffers. Thus, for a variety of reasons, it is poor policy for a buyer to neglect inspection methods or procedures. There is no point in spending time and money on the development of satisfactory specifications unless adequate provision is made to see that these specifications are lived up to by suppliers.

Determining Type of Inspection, Frequency, and Thoroughness

The type of inspection, its frequency, and thoroughness vary with circumstances. In the last analysis, this resolves itself into a matter of comparative costs. How much must be spent to ensure compliance with specifications?

In setting specifications, it is desirable to include the procedure for inspection and testing as protection for both buyer and seller. The supplier cannot refuse to accept rejected goods on the ground that the type of inspection to which the goods would be subjected was not known or that the inspection was unduly rigid. Supplier and purchaser need to work out both the procedure for sampling and the nature of the test to be conducted. This way both supplier and purchaser should achieve identical test results, no matter which party conducts the test. Whereas in some situations purchasers may be more sophisticated in quality control and, in others, the suppliers, it is sensible for both sides to cooperate on this issue.

Reasons to Use Commercial Labs

Commercial Testing Labs and Services. The type of inspection required may be so complicated or expensive that it cannot be performed satisfactorily in the buyer's or seller's own organization. In such cases it may be attractive to use the services of commercial testing laboratories, particularly in connection with new processes or materials or for aid in the setting of specifications. Also, the use of an unbiased testing organization may lend credibility to the results. For example, air, water, and soil samples are often sent to commercial labs to test for compliance with EPA standards.

Furthermore, standard testing reports of commonly used items are available from several commercial testing laboratories. They are the commercial equivalent of Consumer's Reports and can be a valuable aid.

Quality Assurance and Quality Control

The responsibility of a quality assurance group is not confined to the technical task of inspecting incoming material or monitoring in-house production. Obviously, it plays a key role in supplier certification. The quality group can initiate material studies. It can be called on to inspect samples provided by suppliers. Frequently it must investigate claims and errors, both as to incoming items and as to outgoing or finished products. It may examine material returned to stores to determine its suitability for reissue. Similarly, it may be called on to examine salvage material and to make a recommendation as to its disposition. Other duties include quality assurance and attendant efforts to help suppliers and their suppliers to design, implement, and monitor continuous quality improvement programs.

Determining Structure and Location of Quality Assurance

The structure and location of the quality assurance function constitute a relevant problem of administration. In most cases, the work of inspection is performed by a separate department whose work may be divided into three main parts: the inspection of incoming materials, the inspection of materials in the process of manufacture, and the inspection of the finished product. The assignment of this work to a separate department is supported partly on the ground that if the inspectors of materials in process and of the finished product report to the executive in charge of operations, there may be occasions when inspection standards are relaxed in order to cover up defects in production.

Inspection Methods. The current high interest in quality fueled by concern for customer satisfaction, cost, competitiveness, employee morale, and technological requirements reinforces the need for appropriate inspection methods.

Zero Defects Programs

A substantial specialized body of literature is available on the subject of quality control and inspection methods. In this text only some of the basic quality control concepts will be indicated. Although the mathematics for statistical quality control have been well established for decades, their application has not been as widespread as might have been desirable. Over the past 30 years, various forms of *zero defects programs* have been initiated. The original efforts were largely attributable to defense and space programs, where the consequences of part failures were obviously very serious. Current thinking on quality reinforces the zero defects target as suppliers and purchasers both seek this goal for mutual benefit. If a purchaser could be certain that everything supplied by a supplier were defect-free, it would eliminate the need for overordering and for further inspection and enable immediate use of the materials or parts supplied. At the same time, the purchaser could concentrate its efforts on ensuring that its own goods or services meet with desired quality targets. Such an ideal situation does not evolve without extensive management efforts. The procurement role in seeking supplier cooperation in the pursuit of the zero defect objective should not be minimized.

Similarly, materials personnel must be thoroughly familiar with the inspection methods commonly used inside their organization and by suppliers, so that they can reinforce their organization's quality efforts appropriately.

Build in Quality, Don't Inspect It In

Inspection is expensive. If a part is of acceptable quality, inspection does not add to its value. Inspection represents a delay, a further addition of cost, and a possibility of error or damage in handling. It is obviously preferable to make it right in the first place rather than "inspect the quality in" by separating the acceptable from the unacceptable parts, which is wasteful. Moreover, experience in organizations that have successfully pursued quality improvement programs shows significant productivity improvements have occurred simultaneously.

Because almost all output results from a manufacturing or transformation process of some sort, process control is the preferred approach to controlling product quality. Process control is a key aspect of TQM and is described in the following section.

Process Control[14]

In processes using repetitive operations, the quality control chart is invaluable. The output can be measured by tracking a mean and dispersion. The X bar chart is useful for charting the population means and the R bar chart the dispersion.

Statistical Quality Control

Dr. W. Edwards Deming, the well-known American quality control specialist, assisted Japanese manufacturers in instituting *statistical quality control* (SQC) beginning in the 1950s. Dr. Deming showed that most processes tend to behave in a statistical manner, and that understanding how the process behaves without operator interference is necessary before controls can be instituted. Managing quality using SQC techniques involves sampling processes and using the data to statistically establish performance criteria and monitor processes.

Process Capability Focuses on Consistency

Process capability refers to the ability of the process to meet specifications consistently. Because no process can produce the same exact results each time the activity is performed, it is important to establish what kind of variability is occurring and eliminate as much variability as possible. A process capability study identifies two types of variability, (1) the common causes or random variability, and (2) special causes. *Statistical process control* (SPC) is a technique that involves testing a random sample of output from a process in order to detect if nonrandom changes in the process are occurring.

Statistical Process Control Defined

Common Causes of Variability

Common causes of variability may be machine, people, or manufacturing related. For instance, machine lubrication, tool wear, or operator technique would be common causes that result in inconsistent output. These common causes are often a natural part of the system and do not fluctuate. The only way to reduce common causes is to change the process. The output distribution about the mean quality level, taking into consideration common causes, results in the natural capability for a particular process.

Special Causes of Variability

Special causes or outside, nonrandom problems such as wear and tear on machinery, material variation, or human error, must also be identified and eliminated; otherwise the output will fall outside the acceptable quality range. Statistical process control procedures are primarily concerned with detecting and eliminating special causes.

Stable Process Defined

In determining whether or not a process is stable, the supplier must determine what the natural capability of the process is, and whether or not the upper and lower specification limits meet the specifications of the buyer.

---

[14]Michiel R. Leenders and Anna E. Flynn, *Value-Driven Purchasing: Managing the Key Steps in the Acquisition Process* (Burr Ridge, IL: Irwin Professional Publishing, 1995).

When a process is "under control," the supplier can predict the future distributions about the mean. For a process to be capable and in control, all the special causes of variation in output have been eliminated and the variation from common causes has been reduced to a level that falls within the acceptable quality range specified by the buyer.

A process is capable when the process is in control, stable, and predictable and when the process averages a set number of standard deviations within the specifications.

$\bar{X}$ and R charts are used widely to help control processes. Upper and lower control limits can be set so that operator action is required only when the process or machine starts to fall outside of its normal desirable operating range. Figure 5–5 illustrates this "wandering" type of behavior at a steel mill. The rolling operation controls the thickness of the steel and each hour the operator collects data and puts it on the $\bar{X}$ bar chart by calculating the

Purpose of Upper and Lower Control Limits

FIGURE 5–5

Control Chart

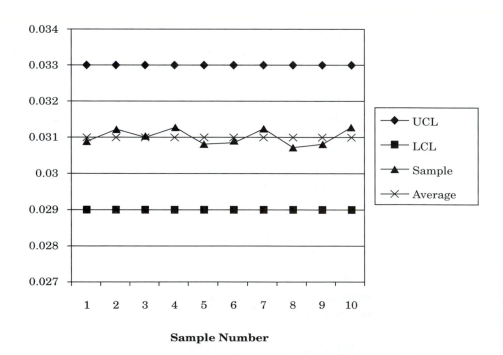

Control Chart

Sample Number

means of samples taken from the process. An R chart is the plot of the range within each of the samples. If the mean or range falls outside their acceptable limits, the process is stopped and action is taken to determine the cause for the shift so that corrections can be made.

The control chart uses random sampling techniques and is well suited to most manufacturing and service operations producing large output and where it is not necessary to screen every item produced, for example, stamping steel parts or processing applications in an insurance office.

Process Capability Measurement

In supplier selection and ongoing supplier performance evaluation, the buyer is concerned with determining and ensuring that the supplier is able to meet the quality specifications. One important tool is measuring the capability of the process(es) used by the supplier and comparing that capability to the quality specifications set by the buyer. As long as the buyer's quality specifications fall within the process capability of the supplier, the buyer should be reasonably certain of receiving satisfactory items. If, however, the buyer specifies a narrower quality range than the supplier's process is capable of achieving, the buyer will probably have to worry more about inspection, rework, and scrap.

The first step in quality assurance is making sure that the supplier's process capability and the buyer's quality range mesh. If the natural range of the supplier's process is wider than the range of the buyer's quality requirements, then the buyer must negotiate with the supplier to have the supplier narrow the natural range through process improvements such as operator training or machine improvements. If it is not economically feasible or the supplier is unable or unwilling to make improvements for some reason, then the buyer may seek another supplier rather than incur the extra cost of inspection, rework, and scrap.

Cpk.[15] The Cpk statistic is used to measure and describe machine or process capability relative to specification requirements by determining the percentage of parts that a process can produce within design specifications. Cpk is defined as the *lower* of either of the following:

$$\frac{\text{Upper Tolerancde Limit -}\bar{X}}{\text{Process Spread}} \quad \text{or} \quad \frac{\bar{X}\text{ - Lower Tolerance Limit}}{\text{Process Spread}}$$

$\bar{X}$ is the process mean and the process spread is equal to three standard deviations of the output values, or the spread on one side of the process average. The higher the Cpk, the more capable the process is of producing parts that are consistently within specification.

Screening.   There are basically two major types of quality checks on output. One is to inspect every item produced. The other is to sample.

---

[15]Michiel R. Leenders and Anna E. Flynn, *Value-Driven Purchasing: Managing the Key Steps in the Acquisition Process* (Burr Ridge, IL: Irwin Professional Publishing, 1995).

It is traditionally held that 100 percent inspection, or screening, is the most desirable inspection method available. This is not true. Experience shows that 100 percent inspection seldom accomplishes a completely satisfactory job of separating the acceptable from the nonacceptable or measuring the variables properly. Actually, 200 or 300 percent inspection or even higher may have to be done to accomplish this objective. Depending on the severity of a mistake, an error of discarding a perfectly good part may be more acceptable than passing a faulty part. In some applications, the use of such extreme testing may increase the cost of a part enormously. For example, in certain high-technology applications, individual parts are required to be accompanied by their own individual test "pedigrees." Thus, a part which for a commercial application might cost $0.75 may well end up costing $50 or more and perform the identical function.

"Poka Yoke" Devices

One of the many contributions of Shigeo Shingo in Japan was the development of foolproof, simple "poka yoke" devices which permit inexpensive, rapid 100 percent inspection to ensure zero defects. A simple example would be a small gate on an output conveyor. All parts too small or too large would be automatically identified and removed.

Sampling. The alternative to inspection of every item produced is to sample. How a sample is taken will vary with the product and process. The purpose is always to attempt to secure a sample that is representative of the total population being tested. Random sampling is one commonly used technique.

Random Sampling

The method of taking a random sample will depend on the characteristics of the product to be inspected. If it is such that all products received in a shipment can be thoroughly mixed together, then the selection of a sample from any part of the total of the mixed products will represent a valid random sample. For example, if a shipment of 1,000 balls of supposedly identical characteristics is thoroughly mixed together and a random sample of 50 balls is picked from the lot and inspected and 5 are found to be defective, it is probable that 10 percent of the shipment is defective.

If the product has characteristics which make it difficult or impractical to mix together thoroughly, consecutive numbers can be assigned to each product, and then, through the use of tables of random sampling numbers (of which there are several) or a standard computer program, a sample drawn by number is chosen for detailed inspection.

General Rule of Random Sampling

The general rule which the statisticians believe should be observed when drawing a random sample is: Adopt a method of selection that will give every unit of the product to be inspected an equal chance of being drawn.

Sequential Sampling. Sequential sampling may be used to reduce the number of items to be inspected in accept–reject decisions without loss of accuracy. It is based on the cumulative effect of information that every additional item in the sample adds as it is inspected. After each individual item's inspection, three decisions are possible: to accept, to reject, or to sample another item. A. Wald, one of the pioneers of sequential sampling development, estimated that, using his plan, the average sample size could be reduced to one half as compared to a single sampling plan.

Procedure for Sequential Sampling

In a simple version of sequential sampling, 10 percent of the lot is inspected, and the whole lot is accepted if the sample is acceptable. If the sample is not acceptable, an additional 10 percent may be inspected if the decision to reject cannot be made on the basis of the first sample.

Inspection Computer Programs. Many quality control computer programs are available. They have resolved the tedium of extensive calculations and charts and provide a range of applications. All computer manufacturers and many service companies maintain these programs for use by customers. Standard programs, for example, select sampling plans, calculate sample statistics and plot histograms, produce random selection of parts, plot operating characteristics (OC) curves, and determine confidence limits.

Supplier Certification

No matter how perfect the description of the need, the purchaser still needs to worry about whether the supplier will supply what is really required. Normally, this involves quality assurance programs, testing, inspection, and quality control.

Supplier Quality Capability Surveys

Usually, before a new supplier is given an order, and often before a supplier is allowed to quote, the purchaser conducts a quality capability or quality assurance survey on the supplier's premises. The purpose is to ensure that the supplier is capable of meeting the specifications and quality standards required. Whereas this practice started in the military field, it is now common in all high-technology areas and in most larger organizations.

This survey, normally conducted by engineering, manufacturing, purchasing, and quality control personnel, will examine not only the supplier's equipment, facilities, and personnel, but also the systems in place to monitor and improve quality. Also examined are the supplier's efforts to seek cooperation and compliance in quality standards from its suppliers and the supplier's commitment to ongoing quality improvement.

It is desirable to have continuing involvement with suppliers to evolve common quality standards, to agree on inspection methods, and to work out ways and means of improving quality while decreasing inspection and overall cost.

Clearly, the question as to whether to purchase only from certified suppliers extends well beyond quality considerations alone. In organizations pursuing partnerships with suppliers, quality certification is usually the first category of interorganizational alignment. It is evident in many industries that a minimum level of quality capability will be a standard requirement for any supplier and that corporate survival may depend on it.

The obvious target in improving quality is to have the right quality by making it right the first time, rather than inspecting the quality in. It is this

Quality Improvement in Supply Management

pressure to create quality at its source that is behind all quality improvement programs. The same philosophy should also apply to the supply department itself and the purchaser's own organization. It is very difficult for a purchaser to insist that suppliers meet stringent quality requirements when it is obvious to the suppliers that the purchasing organization itself shows no sign of a similar commitment. The smartest thing for any purchasing department wishing to start a quality drive is to apply quality standards to its own performance on all of the phases in the acquisition cycle in which it is involved. Not only will this create familiarity with statistical quality control and quality standards in the purchasing department itself, but it also gives purchasing the right to ask for similar commitment by others.

Adjustments and Returns

Prompt action for adjustments and returns made necessary by rejections are a responsibility of the purchasing department, aided by the using, inspection, or legal departments.

Any nonconforming product, material, or equipment must be locked up to avoid the possibility of inadvertent processing, pilferage, or additional damage while its disposition is being deliberated. Some organizations use a material review board to decide how to deal with specific nonconforming materials.

Options for Dealing with Non-Conforming Materials

The actual decision as to what can or should be done with material that does not meet specifications is both an engineering and a procurement question. It can, of course, be simply rejected and returned at the supplier's expense or held for instructions as to its disposition. In either case the buyer must inform the supplier whether the shipment is to be replaced with acceptable material or to consider the contract canceled. Not infrequently, however, a material may be used for other than the originally intended purpose or substituted for some other grade. It is also possible that some private readjustment is called for. A third alternative is to rework the material, deducting from the purchase price the cost of the additional processing involved. Also, particularly in the case of new types of equipment or new material to which the purchaser is not accustomed, the supplier may send a technical representative to the buyer's organization in the hope that complete satisfaction may be provided.

Allocating Costs Between Buyer and Seller

A problem growing out of inspection is that of the allocation, between buyer and seller, of costs incurred in connection with rejected material. The costs incurred on rejected materials may be divided into three major classes: (1) transportation costs, (2) testing costs, (3) contingent expense.

The practice of allocating these costs varies considerably. The practice is affected to some degree by the kind of material rejected, trade customs, the essential economies of the situation, the buyer's cost accounting procedure, and the positions of strength of each organization. In practically all cases reported, transportation costs both to and from the rejection point are charged back to the supplier. Very few companies report inspection or testing costs as items to be charged back to the supplier. Such costs are ordinarily borne by the buyer and are considered a part of purchasing or inspection costs.

In many cases, contracts or trade customs provide that the supplier will not be responsible for contingent expense, yet this is perhaps the greatest risk and the most costly item of all from the buyer's standpoint. Incoming materials that are not of proper quality may seriously interrupt production; their rejection may cause a shortage of supply which may result in delay or actual stoppage of production, extra handling, and other expense. Labor and/or equipment time may be expended in good faith on material later found to be unusable. It is, in general, however, not the practice of buyers to allocate such contingent costs to the supplier. Some buyers, however, insist on agreements with their suppliers to recover labor, equipment, or other costs expended on the material before discovery of its defective character.

In a partnership mode, or with special quality programs in place at both the purchaser's and supplier's organizations, the frequency of defective materials or services decreases drastically. And the resolution of difficulties arriving from defective or late deliveries is usually handled in a highly professional and efficient manner, avoiding the nastiness of blame avoidance and litigation threats.

Questions for Review and Discussion

1. Why use supplier certification?
2. What constitutes a best buy?
3. How could a quality philosophy be applied to a purchasing department?
4. What are the various costs associated with quality, and why is it difficult to determine the magnitude of some of these costs?
5. Why should a purchaser be familiar with the mathematics of quality control and inspection?
6. What are the trade-offs between 100 percent inspection and sampling?
7. What is quality function deployment (QFD)? What role do buyers and suppliers play in QFD?
8. What are the advantages of using functional specifications?
9. Why was Deming so insistent on single sourcing?
10. Why should a purchaser be concerned about function?

References

American National Standards Institute, www.ansi.org, January 2001.

Ansari, A. and B. Modarress, "Quality Function Deployment: The Role of Suppliers," *International Journal of Purchasing and Materials Management,* vol. 30, no. 4, Fall 1994, pp. 28–35.

Choi, T. Y. and M. Rungtusanatham, "Comparison of Quality Management Practices: Across the Supply Chain and Industries," *The Journal of Supply Chain Management,* Winter 1999, pp. 20–27.

Curkovic, S. and R. Handfield, "Use of ISO 9000 and Baldrige Award Criteria in Supplier Quality Evaluation," *International Journal of Purchasing and Materials Management,* Spring 1995, pp. 2–11.

International Standards Organization, www.iso.ch, February 2001.

Leenders, M. R. and A. E. Flynn, *Value-Driven Purchasing: Managing the Key Steps in the Acquisition Process,* Burr Ridge IL: Irwin Professional Publishing, 1995.

Leenders, M. R. and P. F. Johnson, *Major Structural Changes in Supply Organizations,* Tempe AZ: Center for Advanced Purchasing Studies, 2000.

McKeefry, H. L., "Study: ISO Benefits Boom," Electronics Buyers News, July 1, 1996, p. 40.

Nellore, R., K. Soderquist, G. Siddall and J. Motwani, "Specifications—Do We Really Understand What They Mean?", *Business Horizons,* November–December 1999, pp. 63–69.

Nelson, D., R. Mayo and P. Moody, *Powered By Honda,* New York, NY: John Wiley & Sons, 1998.

Stuart, F. I. and P. Mueller Jr., "Total Quality Management and Supplier Partnerships: A Case Study," *International Journal of Purchasing and Materials Management,* vol. 30, no. 1, Winter 1994, pp. 14–21.

CASE 5–1
ST. ANN'S HOSPITAL

In late February, Hal Watkins, Director of Purchasing for St. Ann's Hospital, was trying to decide on a supplier for disposable surgical drapes. Both of St. Ann's major suppliers felt the contract was rightfully theirs, and Hal was unsure how to proceed.

St. Ann's. St. Ann's was a publicly funded teaching hospital which maintained 24 operating rooms and 910 beds. Like most hospitals, St. Ann's had experienced substantial budget cuts during the past decade and was under a great deal of financial pressure.

In order to maintain some control over costs, the hospital had limited the annual operating room budgets of its surgeons. The doctors had fixed an-nual budgets for surgical procedures to cover personnel, equipment, and supplies. This policy provided a substantial incentive to the doctors to watch their own costs, because once the funds had been used up the doctor could not perform any more surgery and could not, therefore, collect any more fees.

Purchasing. The purchasing department employed 15 people and had responsibility for buying all of the hospital's medical and nonmedical supplies. Hal Watkins, the director, had been hired the previous August. Annual purchases of operating room supplies amounted to $1.5 million. Of that total, about $800,000 were purchased from Tyler Medical Supplies, $500,000 from Alpha Products, and the remainder from the other two suppliers of medical products.

In choosing medical supplies, St. Ann's relied on two evaluations: a clinical evaluation by the affected medical staff, and a financial evaluation by the Purchasing Department. Traditionally, the clinical evaluation had dominated purchase decisions. If a doctor wanted a particular product, purchasing ordered it. Under this system, the hospital was purchasing relatively small volumes from a great many suppliers.

Now, however, with budgets as tight as they were, the balance was shifting. For the past several years, St. Ann's had operated through "prime vendor agreements." The agreement with Alpha expired two months ago and was being renegotiated. Tyler's agreement ran for another four years. According to the terms of these agreements, the vendor would provide volume incentive rebates of about 1.5 to 2 percent on purchases of products covered by the agreement in exchange for preferred or exclusive rights to provide those products.

Because the rebates were based on volume, Purchasing had to convince the doctors to use the products covered by the agreements, rather than continuing to order whatever they chose. They accomplished this by returning the amount of the rebate to the doctors' operating room budgets to use for anything (except personnel) they chose.

Disposable Surgical Drapes. Surgical drapes are used during surgery to cover the patient. They are large sheets with small areas, or incises, cut out to expose the area where the incision is to be made for the particular surgical procedure. In the past, St. Ann's had been using reusable cloth drapes but felt that a cost savings might be achievable by switching to the recently developed disposable drapes.

Although the financial analysis was favorable toward disposable drapes, a clinical evaluation of the product had to be conducted before a final decision was made. St. Ann's decided to test Alpha Products' disposable drapes.

The clinical evaluation was very positive, and St. Ann's had decided to switch to disposable drapes. At this point, competitive bids were sought from the market to determine which company would win the $400,000 contract. Alpha was unhappy with the decision to go for bids. Even though it had been made clear that no permanent commitment was being made to purchase disposable drapes from them when they were selected as the test product, Alpha felt that because their product had been successful in the clinical setting, they should receive the contract.

When Hal Watkins took over as purchasing manager six months ago, the bids had been sitting untouched for about two months. His first task was to review the background material on the disposable drapes and the prime vendor agreements and to assess the bids. Hal found that the bid from Tyler products was lower and felt that if the product were clinically acceptable, it should be chosen. Four months ago, in October of last year, he got agreement from the Operating Room Chief of Staff to run a three-month test of the Tyler product, beginning on December 1.

The clinical evaluation of Tyler's product was mixed. It met the minimum requirements for drapes—it fully covered the patients and the incises were properly placed—but the nursing staff said they preferred the Alpha product. They felt that it unfolded more easily, and that the incises on the Tyler product tore frequently, causing them to have to discard the drape because the sterile field would be compromised.

On February 27, Hal received the final terms of the new prime vendor agreement with Alpha. Much to his surprise, Alpha had made substantial improvements to their rebate offers. With these new terms, Alpha's bid on the disposable drapes contract looked much more competitive, although it was still 5 percent higher.

Hal's Dilemma. Hal was unsure how to proceed. He was uncomfortable bringing this new information into the decision at this stage. On the basis of the original bids, Tyler's product was the clear winner, in spite of the nursing staff's preference for Alpha drapes, because the price difference was just too great. Furthermore, Tyler was aware of the outcome of the clinical test and expected to be awarded the contract because the product had met the required specifications at a substantially lower price.

On the other hand, given that Alpha had renegotiated the prime vendor agreement, and as a result was more competitive with Tyler on this product, Hal knew the pressure from the nursing staff to choose the product they preferred would be substantial.

It was six months since Hal had taken over as Director of Purchasing. Most of the issues that were unresolved when he arrived had by now been finalized, and Hal was anxious to resolve this one as well. He knew that both Alpha and Tyler would be expecting to hear the good news from him soon.

CASE 5–2
DORMAN PRINTING INC.

On January 25, Alex Szabo, the Purchasing Manager of Dorman Printing Inc., received a call from Print Shop Manager Dave Wilson. Dave complained that the ink that had been purchased from Mareden Ltd. one week ago dried too slowly and was causing printing quality problems. Alex Szabo decided to visit the print shop to see what was happening in order to decide what action to take concerning the supply relationship with Mareden Ltd.

Background. Dorman Printing Inc. (Dorman), a small printing firm with 43 employees, produced tag labels for the food packaging industry. Printing was a very competitive business, and price and quality were the major customer concerns. Manufacturing and distribution were not complex and the expenditures in these areas were relatively minor compared to costs of supplies. Consequently, purchasing played a key role in maintaining cost and quality.

Alex had more than 25 years experience in the printing industry and had worked for Dorman for more than 20 years. He had built very good relations with his suppliers. "When I was young, we worked together," he said, "and now when I am older, we are still together. They have never caused any problems." Alex believed such stable relations had a special benefit and felt that he could rely on his suppliers whenever Dorman had an urgent or unexpected demand for supplies.

However, Alex never stopped looking for alternative suppliers because of the cost and quality pressures. Alex commented that, "Anyway, business is business. I must compare price and quality among potential suppliers all the time. There is always someone who comes to me promising to offer better products with competitive prices."

Mareden Ltd. Mareden Ltd. (Mareden) was one such new supplier. Alex came across its sales manager, John Field, at a trade show. Alex was attracted by John's proposal to provide "good" quality ink at a price about 5 percent lower than his current supplier. Examining Mareden's products briefly, Alex found no problems and asked for some samples to take back to the shop.

The results of the test production were good and Alex, therefore, ordered one week's ink supply from Mareden. According to his experience, there were often some new problems that emerged in the normal manufacturing process, thus he felt it would be safe to order only a small amount at the beginning.

Production Problem. After visiting the print shop, Alex could easily see the trouble that the ink caused. The printing presses were jamming and scrap rates were high. However, production could not be delayed because the client was waiting for delivery of the labels. He, therefore, asked Dave Wilson to stop the current production run and start over again using ink from another supplier. Alex then called one of his major suppliers and asked him to ship ink to Dorman. The replacement ink arrived the following day.

Alex phoned John Field the next day and told him the news. John apologized for causing the problem and promised to ask his technicians to check what happened as soon as possible. John indicated that he considered his product to be high quality and he had never encountered such a problem with any of his existing customers.

The Decision. Alex had to decide what to do about the situation with Mareden. Although he had serious doubts about their credibility at this point, Dorman spent approximately $800,000 per year on ink and Alex did not want to miss an opportunity for large cost savings. Furthermore, Alex was aware that Dorman was about to spend approximately $1,500,000 on a new press. The president had indicated to Alex that Dorman needed to specify the characteristics of the major inputs, such as ink, when setting the specifications for the new equipment.

6 QUANTITY AND DELIVERY

Chapter Outline

Key Questions for the Supply Decision Maker

SHOULD WE
- Change the way we forecast?
- Initiate a stockless purchasing system?
- Purchase our A items differently?

HOW CAN WE
- Improve our inventory management?
- Obtain supplier cooperation for JIT?
- Make lot sizing decisions better?

Factors Affecting Quantity and Delivery Decisions

Continuous improvement; speed to market; customer, employee, and supplier satisfaction; and global competitiveness require dedication to productivity and value-adding activities. These organizational goals drive management attitudes to quality, quantity, and delivery, with profound impact on the acquisition process. With respect to quantity and delivery considerations, the most telling evidence comes from inventory reduction and the drive to increase frequency of deliveries, while decreasing the amount delivered at one time. Accompanying efforts in setup time reduction, just-in-time (JIT) systems, stockless systems, order cost reduction, EDI and e-commerce are all part of the same drive.

The decisions of *how much* to acquire and *when* logically follow clarification of *what* is required. The natural response is to say "buy as much as you need when you need it." Such a simple answer is not sufficient, however. Many factors significantly complicate these decisions. First, managers must make purchase decisions before, often a long time before, actual requirements are known. Therefore, they must rely on forecasts, not only of future demand, but also of lead times, prices, and other costs. Such forecasts are rarely, if ever, perfect. Second, there are costs associated with placing orders, holding inventory, and running out of materials and goods. Third, materials may not be available in the desired quantities without paying a higher price or delivery charge. Fourth, suppliers may offer reduced prices for buying larger quantities. Fifth, shortages may cause serious consequences.

In many organizations the decision of how much to purchase and when is made more important by the close relationship between purchase quantity and scheduled use. It is necessary to distinguish between how much to buy in an individual purchase or release and what portion of total requirements to buy from an individual supplier. This chapter deals only with individual order quantities; the allotment to suppliers is discussed in Chapters 7 and 8.

Time-Based Strategies and Quantity Decisions

Quantity and delivery go hand in hand. Order less, deliver more frequently; order more, deliver less frequently. Every supplier performance evaluation scheme includes quantity and delivery as standard evaluation criteria. To ensure timely delivery, recognition needs to be given to the times required to complete each of the steps in the acquisition process discussed in Chapter 3. The ability to compress these times by doing them in parallel, by eliminating time-consuming and nonvalue-adding activities, by doing steps faster, and by eliminating delays can provide significant benefits. Much of the reengineering work in the supply area has focused on the acquisition process to make it more responsive and to reduce cycle time.

For the supply management function, the time-based strategies that are of importance in the quantity decision are ones that relate directly to the flow of materials, inventories (raw material, work-in-process, and finished goods) and related information and decisions. Competitive advantage accrues to organizations that can (1) successfully reduce the time it takes to perform activities in a process (reduce cycle time) and (2) coordinate the flow of resources to eliminate waste in the system and ensure that materials and equipment arrive on time or just-in-time in economically sized batches.

Long cycle times can occur in the design and development process, in the material acquisition to distribution of finished goods process, and in administrative support cycles (e.g., accounts payable, purchase order development/release cycle). Some of the causes of long cycle times are waiting and procrastination, poorly engineered designs, the accumulation of batches prior to movement, inefficient and long physical flows with backtracking, and poor communication. Long cycle times can impact decisions about *how much* to buy. Compressed cycle times and coordination of material and information flows can result in materials arriving just-*on*-time (e.g., when they were scheduled to arrive), or just-*in*-time (just prior to actual use or need). Material Requirements Planning-type (MRP) programs can be used to plan the timing and quantity of purchased materials and internally manufactured materials.

Causes and Consequences of Long Cycle Times

There are many causes for poor material flow coordination, including late, early, or no deliveries, low fill rate, material defects, scrap, uneven batch sizes, long lead times, production schedule changes, downtime, long setup/changeover times, infrequent updates of MRP systems, forecasts, and on-hand inventory accounting systems. Greater coordination of material and information flows both within the buying firm and its customers and between the buying firm and its suppliers (and their suppliers) can result in lower inventories and improvements in return on assets (see example in Chapter 1).

Classification of Purchases

Type of Requirement

A variety of classification systems are available to help in inventory control and in quantity and timing decisions. A basic distinction is between direct purchases (used in products or services subsequently sold to customers) and indirect purchases (consumed internally by processes or management systems). Another distinction is between types of requirement; for example, energy, raw materials, parts and subassemblies, MRO items, resale items, packaging, services, or tools and capital goods.

Frequency of Purchase

A second way to classify requirements is by the frequency with which they are purchased. Some items, often of a capital nature, are obtained infrequently whereas others may be bought on a repetitive basis. A number of purchase quantity rules are in use for repetitive purchases; they will be discussed later in this chapter. Quite different decision criteria are appropriate for infrequent purchases.

Stock Items

A third classification is whether or not purchases are for stock replenishment. Presumably, most stock items require repetitive purchases and the risk of buying too much would be viewed quite differently from overbuying on nonrepetitive purchases.

Physical or Chemical Nature

A fourth classification is based on the physical or chemical nature and dimensions of the purchased items. Requirements could be solids, liquids, or gases. Some might be quite unstable, volatile, perishable (or even dangerous) and thus require quite different handling, storage conditions, and purchase quantity rules than more stable or safer materials. Similarly, the nature of the packaging material and the size and shape of the package will affect the purchaser's ability to store items and hence the desired purchase quantity.

Transport Type

A fifth classification is based on transport type. Items shipped a short distance by the purchaser's own truck might be purchased in much smaller quantities than those coming a long distance by common carriers or by ship.

ABC Classification

Monetary Value

A final classification is based on monetary value. In the nineteenth century, the Italian Vilfredo Pareto observed that, regardless of the country studied, a small portion of the population controlled most of the wealth. This observation led to the Pareto curve whose general principles hold in a wide range of situations. In materials management, for example, the Pareto curve usually holds for items purchased, number of suppliers, items held in inventory, and many other aspects. The Pareto curve is often called the 80-20 rule, or more usefully, ABC analysis, which results in three classes, A, B, and C, as follows:

Class	Percentage of Total Items Purchased	Percentage of Total Purchase Dollars
A	10	70–80
B	10–20	10–15
C	70–80	10–20

These percentages may vary somewhat from organization to organization, and some organizations may use more classes. The principle of separation is very powerful in materials management because it allows concentration of management efforts in the areas of highest payoff. For example, a manufacturer with total annual purchases of $30.4 million had the following breakdown:

ABC Analysis Example

Number of Items	Percentage of Items	Annual Purchase Value	Percentage Annual Purchase Volume	Class
1,095	10.0%	$21,600,000	71.1%	A
2,168	19.9	5,900,000	19.4	B
7,660	70.1	2,900,000	9.5	C
10,923	100.0%	$30,400,000	100.0%	

A similar analysis of the organization's suppliers or inventories would be expected to show a similarly high portion of total value from a relatively small number of suppliers and items, respectively.

Purchase value is a combination of unit price and number of units so it is not sufficient to classify either high-priced or high-unit volume items as A's on that basis alone. Annual value must be calculated and a classification into three groups on this basis, as shown below, is a good starting point.

Category	Unit Value	Annual Volume	Annual Value
A	high	high	high
A	medium	high	high
A	low	very high	high
B	high	low	medium
B	medium	medium	medium
B	low	high	medium
C	medium	low	low
C	low	medium	low
C	low	low	low

Usage of ABC Analysis

How can a supply manager use such a classification? It pays to spend far more managerial time and effort on A and B items than on C items. Because supply assurance and availability are usually equally important for all items, it is common to manage C items by carrying inventories, by concentrating a wide variety of requirements with one or a few suppliers, by stockless buying agreements or systems contracting, by procurement cards, by placing transaction responsibility with the end user, and by reviewing the items infrequently. These techniques reduce paperwork and managerial effort (for most items) but maintain a high service coverage. A items are particularly critical in financial terms and are, therefore, barring other considerations, normally carried in small quantities and ordered and reviewed frequently. B items fall between the A and C categories and are well suited to a systematic approach with less frequent reviews than A items. It should be noted that some B or C items may require A care because of their special nature, perishability, or other considerations.

Forecasting

Forecasting is very much a part of the supply management picture and directly affects both quantity and delivery. Forecasts of usage, supply, market conditions, technology, price, and so on, are always necessary to make good decisions. The problem is how to plan to meet the needs of the future, which

Responsibility for Forecasting

requires answers to questions, such as: Where should the responsibility for forecasting future usage lie? Should the supply management group be allowed to second-guess sales, production, or user forecasts? Should suppliers be held responsible for meeting forecasts or actual requirements? Should the supply manager be held responsible for meeting actual needs or forecasts?

In most manufacturing organizations the need for raw materials, parts, and subassemblies is usually derived from a sales forecast, which is the responsibility of marketing. In service organizations and public agencies, the supply function often must both make forecasts and acquire items. In resale, the buyer may have to assess the expected sales volume (including volumes at reduced prices for seasonal goods), as well as make purchase commitments recognizing seasons. Whatever the situation, missed forecasts are quickly forgotten but substantial overages or shortages are long remembered. Supply managers are often blamed for overages or shortages no matter who made the original forecast or how bad the forecast was.

Unreliable Nature of Forecasts

The real problem with forecasts is their unreliability. Forecasts will usually be wrong, but will they exceed or fall short of actual requirements and by how much? In a chemical company the marketing group's demand forecast for a consumer product resulted in the following usage estimates for a basic petrochemical commodity:

Year	Barrels
1	70,000
2	120,000
3	190,000
4	280,000

At $60 per barrel for this petrochemical (at the time of the decision), this was a significant purchase. Discussion with the marketing group revealed considerable uncertainty regarding this forecast (see Figure 6–1). In five years demand could be as low as 70,000 or as high as 600,000 barrels. This wide range of possible requirements made the procurement plan far more difficult because it had to be prepared to recognize all possible outcomes. For example, a take-or-pay commitment for 100,000 barrels per year after the

FIGURE 6–1

Forecasts Showing Uncertainty

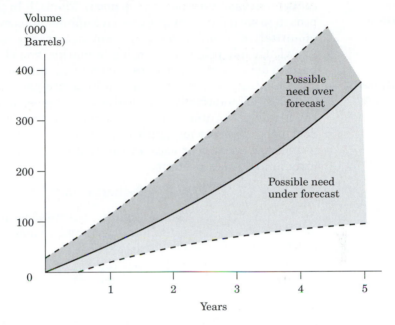

first year was obviously not acceptable because actual needs might be well below that level. Simultaneously, provisions had to be found for substantial increases in requirements should actual needs greatly exceed the forecast.

To a supplier, a substantial variation from forecast may appear as a procurement ploy. If demand falls below forecast, the supplier may suspect that the original forecast was an attempt to obtain a favorable price or other concessions. Should demand exceed forecast, supplier costs may well increase because of overtime, rush buying, and changed production schedules. Purchasers need to share forecast uncertainty regularly with suppliers so that their quotations may take uncertainty into account. Such sharing is obviously impossible if buyers themselves are not aware of the uncertainty and its potential impact on the supplier. Forecasts should also be updated regularly. In the preceding chemical company example, quarterly updates for the next year and annual updates beyond that would be appropriate.

Forecasting Techniques

There are many forecasting techniques that have been developed and an extensive literature that describes them. This section will review some briefly but will not describe any technique in detail.

One of the most common classes is the *qualitative* approach of gathering opinions from a number of people and using these opinions with a degree of

**Delphi
Technique**

judgment to give a forecast. Market forecasts developed from the estimates of sales staff, district sales managers, and so on, are an example. Such forecasts may also flow from the top down. The Delphi technique is a formal approach to such forecasting. Collective opinion forecasts lack the rigor of more quantitative techniques but are not necessarily any less accurate. Often, knowledgeable people with intimate market knowledge have a "feel" that is hard to define but which gives good forecasting results.

**Quantitative
Forecasting**

Quantitative forecasting attempts to use past data to predict the future. One class of quantitative forecasting techniques, *causal models,* tries to identify leading indicators, from which linear or multiple regression models are developed. A carpet manufacturer might use building permits issued, mortgage rates, apartment vacancy rates, and so on, to predict carpet sales. The model might take the form:

Carpet sales next month

$= A + B$ (building permits last month)
$+ C$ (building permits two months ago)
$+ D$ (mortgage rate)
$+ E$ (vacancy rate)
$+ F$ (carpet sales last month)

where A−F are the derived regression constants. Standard computer programs are used to develop and test such models. Chosen indicators are usually believed to cause changes in sales, although even good models do not prove a cause-and-effect relationship. Indicator figures must be available far enough ahead to give a forecast that allows time for managerial decisions.

**Time Series
Forecasting**

The third quantitative forecasting class assumes that sales (or other items to be forecast) follow a repetitive pattern over time. The analyst's job in such *time series forecasting* is to identify the pattern and develop a forecast. The six relevant aspects of the pattern are constant value, trend, seasonal variations, other cyclical variations, random variations, and turning points. These features are illustrated in Figure 6–2.

Inventories

Many purchases cover repetitive items often held in inventory. Thus, inventory policy has a great influence on purchase quantity decisions. The questions of how much to order, when, and how much to carry in stock are key decisions subject to continuous improvement examination along with the focus on quality and customer, employee, and supplier satisfaction. It is important in making delivery, inventory, or purchase order size decisions to understand why inventories exist and what the relevant trade-offs are.

Inventory management is complicated by the rapidly changing environment within which inventory and purchasing planning is carried out. In-

FIGURE 6–2

Illustration of Some Forecasting Terms

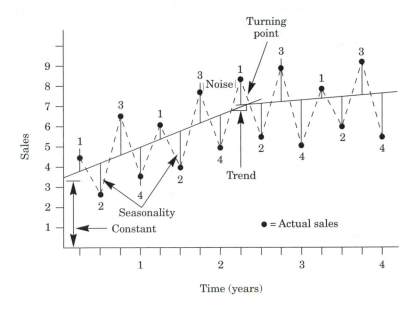

ventories always seem to be too big, too small, of the wrong type, or in the wrong place. With changing economic conditions, what is too little in one period may easily become too much in the next.

Efforts to Reduce Inventories
Because of the high cost of carrying inventory, many systems have been developed to reduce stocks. Japanese manufacturers have spearheaded such efforts in mass production industries. Suppliers, often located very near the plant, deliver items directly to the point of use in the plant at very frequent intervals. The use of kanbans and a variety of just-in-time inventory management schemes has revolutionized manufacturing thinking about all forms of inventories. Nevertheless, it is useful to understand the nature and costs of inventories so that appropriate policies and procedures can be developed for specific organizational needs. North American organizations have begun to rely heavily on material requirements planning systems that have similar goals of reducing inventories wherever possible by having accurate, timely information on all aspects of the users' requirements, thorough coordination of all departments, and rigorous adherence to the system.

Like purchases, inventories may be classified in a variety of ways including ABC analysis (see Figure 6–3), nature of the items carried, and frequency of use. Computer systems allow extensive automation of purchasing and inventory control. Control of all items is improved and managerial time is freed for the negotiations, value engineering, research, and other managerial tasks necessary to deal effectively with A and B items.

FIGURE 6–3

ABC Classification of Inventory

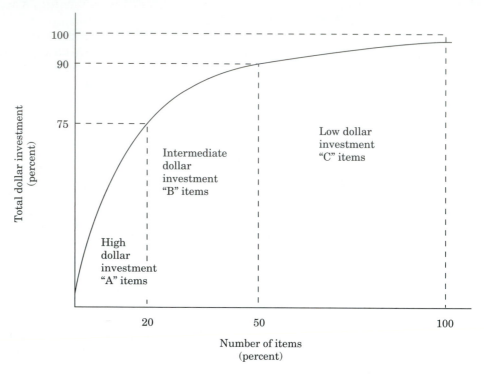

Inventory Costs

Purposes of Inventory

Inventories exist for many purposes including:

To provide and maintain good customer service.

To smooth the flow of goods through the productive process.

To provide protection against the uncertainties of supply and demand.

To obtain a reasonable utilization of people and equipment.

For every item carried in inventory, the costs of having it must be less than the costs of not having it. Inventory exists for this reason alone. Inventory costs are real but are often not easy to quantify accurately. The relevance of cost elements in a given situation depends on the decisions to be made. Many costs remain fixed when the order size of only one item is doubled, but the same costs may well become variable when 5,000 items are under consideration. The main types of inventory costs are described in the following sections.

Carrying, Holding, or Possession Costs. These include handling charges; the cost of storage facilities or warehouse rentals; the cost of equip-

Types of Carrying Costs

ment to handle inventory; storage, labor, and operating costs; insurance premiums; breakage; pilferage; obsolescence; taxes; and investment or opportunity costs. In short, any cost associated with having, as opposed to not having, inventory is included.

The cost to carry inventory can be very high. For example, recent estimates of the annual cost to carry production inventory ranged from 25 to 50 percent of the value of the inventory. Many firms do not do a very good job of estimating carrying costs. While there are several methods for calculating inventory carrying costs, the basic elements are (1) capital costs, (2) inventory service costs, (3) storage space costs, and (4) inventory risk costs.[1]

Once the firm has estimated its carrying costs as a percentage of inventory value, annual inventory carrying costs can be calculated as follows:

Calculating Annual Inventory Carrying Costs

(carrying cost per year) = (average inventory value)
$\times$ (inventory carrying cost as a % of inventory value)

Average inventory value = (average inventory in units) $\times$ (material unit cost)

$$CC = Q/2 \times C \times I$$

where

CC = carrying cost per year

Q = order or delivery quantity for the material, in units

C = delivered unit cost of the material

I = inventory carrying cost for the material, as a percentage of inventory value

Types of Ordering Costs

Ordering or Purchase Costs. These include the managerial, clerical, material, telephone, mailing, fax, e-mail, accounting, transportation, inspection, and receiving costs associated with a purchase or production order. What costs would be saved by not ordering or by combining two orders? Header costs are those incurred by identifying and placing an order with a supplier. Line item costs refer to the cost of adding a line to a purchase order. Most orders will involve one header and several line item costs. Electronic data interchange (EDI) and Internet-based ordering systems try to reduce ordering or purchase costs significantly as well as reduce lead time at the same time.

Types of Setup Costs

Setup Costs. These refer to all the costs of setting up a production run. Setup costs may be substantial. They include such learning-related factors as early spoilage and low production output until standard rates are achieved as well as the more common considerations, such as setup employees' wages and other costs, machine downtime, extra tool wear, parts (and

---

[1]Doug M. Lambert, James R. Stock and Lisa M. Ellram, *Fundamentals of Logistics Management* (Burr Ridge, IL: Irwin McGraw-Hill, 1998).

equipment) damaged during setup, and so on. Both the purchaser's and vendors' setup costs are relevant. It should be pointed out that the reduction of setup costs and times permits smaller production runs and hence smaller purchaser order quantities and more frequent deliveries.

Types of Stockout Costs

Stockout Costs. These are the costs of not having the required parts or materials on hand when and where they are needed. They include lost contribution on lost sales (both present and future), changeover costs necessitated by the shortage, substitution of less suitable or more expensive parts or materials, rescheduling and expediting costs, labor and machine idle time, and so on. Often, customer and user goodwill may be affected, and occasionally penalties must be paid. The impact of stockouts on customers will vary. In a seller's market, an unsatisfied customer may not be lost as easily as in a buyer's market. In addition, each individual customer will react differently to a shortage.

In many organizations stockout costs are very difficult to assess accurately. The general perception, however, is that stockout costs are substantial and much larger than carrying costs. Stockout costs, here discussed as they relate to inventory, are similar for late delivery or quantity shortfalls.

Price Variation Costs. Suppliers often offer items in larger quantities at price and transportation discounts. Purchases in small quantities may result in higher purchase and transportation costs, but buying in larger quantities may result in significantly higher holding costs. The price discount problem will be discussed in Chapter 9.

Identifying, Collecting, and Measuring Inventory Costs

Many inventory costs may be hard to identify, collect, and measure. One can try to trace the individual costs attributable to individual items and use them in decision making. Usually such costs will be applicable to a broader class of items. A second approach is to forecast the impact of a major change in inventory systems on various cost centers. For example, what will be the impact on stores of a switch to systems contracting for half of the C items? Or, what would be the impact of a just-in-time system on price, carrying, ordering, and stock-out costs? Because most inventory models are based on balancing carrying, order, and stockout costs to obtain an optimal order and inventory size, the quality and availability of cost data are important considerations.

The Functions of Inventory

The following classification of inventory functions reveals the multipurpose roles played by inventories.

Transit or Pipeline Inventories. These inventories are used to stock the supply and distribution pipelines linking an organization to its suppliers and customers as well as internal transportation points. They exist because of the need to move material from one point to another. Obviously, transit inventories are dependent on location and mode of transportation. A decision to use a distant supplier with rail transport will probably create a far larger raw materials transit inventory than one to use a local supplier with truck delivery.

In *just-in-time* (JIT) production a variety of means are used to reduce transit inventories, including the use of local suppliers, small batches in special containers, and trucks specifically designed for side loading in small quantities.

Transit Inventories and JIT

Cycle Inventories. These stocks arise because of management's decision to purchase, produce, or sell in lots rather than individual units or continuously. Cycle inventories accumulate at various points in operating systems. The size of the lot is a trade-off between the cost of holding inventory and the cost of making more frequent orders and/or setups. A mathematical description of this relationship, the economic order quantity, will be discussed later. In JIT, the need for cycle inventories is reduced by setup cost and time reduction.

Holding Costs versus Order and Setup Costs

Buffer or Uncertainty Inventories or Safety Stocks. Buffer or uncertainty inventories or safety stocks exist as a result of uncertainties in demand or supply. Raw material, purchased parts, or MRO buffer stocks give some protection against the uncertainties of supplier performance due to shutdowns, strikes, lead-time variations, late deliveries to and from the supplier, poor-quality units that cannot be accepted, and so on. Work-in-process buffer inventories protect against machine breakdown, employee illness, and so on. Finished goods buffers protect against unforeseen demand or production failures.

Management efforts to reduce supply uncertainties may have substantial payoffs in reduced inventories. Options may include: using local sources, reducing demand uncertainty, reducing lead time, having excess capacity, or reducing stockout costs. Buffer inventory levels should be determined by balancing carrying cost against stockout cost.

Reducing Supply Uncertainties

Buying in expectation of major market shortages is a longer time-frame variation of buffer inventory. It may require large sums and top management strategic review. Chapter 8 discusses forward buying more fully.

Another class of buffer stock is that purchased in anticipation, but not certainty, of a price increase. In this case the trade-off is between extra carrying costs and avoidance of higher purchase cost. This trade-off can be structured as shown in Figure 6–4. Obviously, intermediate levels of price increase and the timing of increases will also be identified. Other buffer stock trade-offs can be structured similarly.

Anticipation or Certainty Inventories. Anticipation or certainty stocks are accumulated for a well-defined future need. They differ from buffer stocks in that they are committed in the face of certainty and therefore have

FIGURE 6–4

Decision to Inventory in Anticipation of a Possible Price Increase

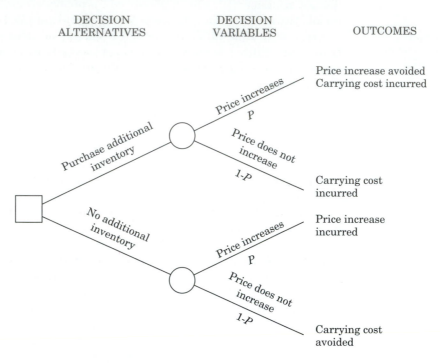

less risk attached to them. Seasonal inventories are an excellent example. The stocking of commodities at harvest time for further processing during the year is a typical example. Reasons for anticipation stocks may include strikes, weather, shortages, or announced price increases.

Reasons for Anticipation Inventories

The managerial decision is considerably easier than with buffer stocks because the certainty of events makes probability estimates unnecessary. Unfortunately, in times of shortages and rapid price increases, organizations may not be able to commit enough funds to meet the clear need for more anticipation stocks. Public organizations working under pre-established budgets may not be able to obtain authorization and funds. Many organizations that are short of working capital may be similarly frustrated.

Decoupling Inventories. The existence of decoupling inventories at major process linkage points makes it possible to carry on activities on each side of the point relatively independently of each other. The amounts and locations of raw material, work-in-process, and finished goods decoupling inventories depend on the costs and increased operating flexibility benefits of having them.

All inventories perform a decoupling function, whether they be transit, cycle, buffer, or certainty inventories. When the prime purpose is to decouple, and space and time have been designed into the process to accommodate them, it is appropriate to recognize decoupling inventory as a unique category of its own.

The ability to plan independently of the short-run behavior of suppliers or customers is highly valued by most North American and European managers. It gives flexibility and independence to both parties and is an excellent area for negotiations. Many contracts specify that a supplier maintain a certain finished goods inventory. The appropriate size of such inventory depends on the situation.

Why Classify Inventories by Function

By examining the functions of inventory it is clear that they are the result of many interrelated decisions and policies within an organization. At any time, any of the inventory functional types will be physically indistinguishable from the others. Frequently, a particular item may serve many of the functions simultaneously. Why, then, classify inventories by function? The answer lies in the degree of controllability of each class. Some inventories are essentially fixed and uncontrollable whereas others are controllable. (In the long term, of course, all inventories are controllable.) A management directive to reduce total inventories by 20 percent could, because of purchasing and marketing policies and prior commitments on cycle and seasonal inventories, reduce decoupling and buffer inventories to nearly zero with potentially disastrous results. Proper inventory management requires a thorough understanding of both the forms and the functions of inventory.

The Forms of Inventory

Five Forms of Inventory

Inventories may be classified by form as well; indeed this classification is much more common. The five commonly recognized forms are (1) raw materials, purchased parts, and packaging; (2) work-in-process; (3) finished goods; (4) MRO items; and (5) resale items. Scrap or obsolete materials, although technically regarded as inventory, will not be considered here (see Chapter 11 dealing with investment recovery).

Raw materials, purchased parts, and packaging for manufacturers are stocks of the basic material inputs into the organization's manufacturing process. As labor and other materials are added to these inputs, they are transformed into work-in-process inventories. When production is completed, they become finished goods. In general, the forms are distinguished by the amount of labor and materials added by the organization. The classification is relative in that a supplier's finished goods may become a purchaser's raw materials.

For resource industries, service organizations, and public organizations, MRO inventories may be substantial. In resource industries, a significant portion of such inventory may be maintenance or repair parts to support the heavy capital investment base.

In resale organizations the main categories are goods for resale and inventories to maintain building and equipment.

For many consumer goods industries, such as food and beverage, packaging represents a major purchase inventory category with substantial environmental implications.

Inventory Function and Form Framework

Combining the five forms and five functions of manufacturing inventory gives the 25 types of inventory that make up the inventory profile of an organization. They are presented in Figure 6–5 along with some of the managerial decision variables affecting each type. Not all inventory types will be present to the same extent in each organization; indeed some may be completely absent. The 25 types make inventory control a more complex but a more easily focused task.

Controlling Inventory through Process Management[2]

Decisions in Various Functions Influence Inventory Behavior

The behavior of inventories is a direct result of diverse policies and decisions within an organization. User, finance, production, marketing, and purchasing decisions can all have crucial influences on stock levels. Long-term fixed marketing or procurement policies may render finished goods transit, raw materials transit, and cycle inventories quite inflexible, whereas short-term production scheduling may provide a great amount of flexibility of work-in-process inventories. Long-term supply contracts coupled with falling demand may lead to raw materials accumulation. To be effective, managers must recognize the behavior and controllability of each type of inventory in both the short and long terms. For effective supply management they must also coordinate the policies and decisions of all functional areas.

Often managers use various informal rules of thumb in their decision making. A common one is turnover in number of times per year. The rule of thumb would dictate that as the use doubles, inventories should also double. However, a closer look must be taken at the components of that inventory.

Understanding the Components of Inventory Should Drive Decisions

Cycle inventories, produced in economic order lots (see the next section), increase proportionally to the square root of demand so, as demand doubles, cycle inventories should rise by a factor of only about 1.4. Ordering raw materials or storing them may have quite different cost structures from setting up machines, issuing production orders, or storing finished goods.

Transit inventories depend on supply and distribution networks. A change in the distribution system to accommodate extra volume could more than double or even reduce finished goods transit inventory. Anticipation stocks vary with the pattern of demand, not demand itself. Decoupling inventories may remain unchanged. Buffer inventories may increase or decrease in response to demand and supply instabilities. Many of these effects

[2]For a good discussion of ways to manage inventory by managing supply processes, see Alan R. Raedels, *Value-Focused Supply Management: Getting the Most Out of the Supply Function* (Burr Ridge, IL: Irwin Professional Publishing, 1995).

FIGURE 6–5

Inventory Forms and Functions

Inventory Function	Raw Materials, Purchased Parts, and Packaging 1	Work-in-Process 2	Finished Goods 3	MRO 4	Resale 5
1 Transit (pipeline)	**Logistics Decisions**				
	Design of supply system, supplier location, transportation mode	Design of layout and materials handling system	Design of plant location and product distribution system	Supplier location, transportation mode, small shipments	Warehouse location, distribution, transportation mode
2 Cycle (EOQ, lots)	**Product/Process Design Decisions**				
	Order size, order cost	Lot size, setup	Distribution costs, lot sizes	OEM or not and order size	Order size and order cost
3 Buffer (uncertainty)	**Management Risk Level Decisions and Uncertainty**				
	Probability distributions of price, supply and stock-out, and carrying costs	Probability distributions of machine and product capabilities	Probability distributions of demand and associated carrying and stockout cost	Probability distributions of breakdowns during use	Probability distributions of demand associated with carrying and stock-out costs
4 Anticipation (price) (shortage)	**Price/Availability/Decisions and Uncertainty, Seasonality, Capacity**				
	Know future supply and demand price levels	Capacity, production costs of hire, fire, transfer, overtime, idle time, etc.	Demand patterns (seasonal)	Maintenance planning projects	Supply and demand patterns and price levels
5 Decoupling (interdependence)	**Production Control Decisions**				
	Dependence/ independence from supplier behavior	Dependence/ independence of successive production operations	Dependence/ independence from market behavior	Stock at vendor or at user	Stock at vendor or buyer stock

will balance each other but the point remains: Rules of thumb are crude ways of controlling inventory levels. Even if they seem to work, managers never know if they are the best available. Any set of rules must be interpreted intelligently and reevaluated periodically.

Inventory Reduction Efforts

It is clear from the earlier discussion that the Japanese efforts to reduce all forms of inventories have addressed all of the functions described above. For example, transit times and inventory levels have been reduced by having suppliers located nearby, or by sharing inbound freight with other local companies or several suppliers. Cycle inventories have been brought down by reducing setup times, and decoupling inventories by better planning and better quality. To reduce inventory held because of uncertainty in supply and demand (buffer or safety stocks), the firm must reduce uncertainty in the supply process. Quantity (or demand) uncertainty can be reduced by process improvements that reduce incoming defects and quantity variations from suppliers as well as less variation and higher yield rates in internal processes. Timing uncertainty can be reduced by reducing replenishment lead time, by shortening process lead times, and ensuring on-time delivery. It is a continuing challenge to search for better ways to control inventories.

Managing Supply Chain Inventories

Decisions regarding what inventory to have in the supply chain and where to have it have important implications for customer service, working capital commitments, and ultimately profitability. Companies such as Dell, Wal-Mart and Saturn have demonstrated the opportunities to combine lean supply chains with high levels of customer service.[3]

Information Technology Issues

Supply chain inventory management involves managing information flows and establishing operational design of the physical flow of the goods and services. Managing information flows with supply chain partners is not an easy task. While information technology can be used to link customers quickly and efficiently, firms are frequently required to make major investments in new systems to ensure compatibility. A lack of common standards for electronic commerce has resulted in a number of initiatives, such as the Voluntary Interindustry Commerce Standards (VICS) Association's Collaborative Planning and Replenishment (CPFR) Committee. The CPFR Committee has created guidelines to explain business processes, supporting technology, and change management issues associated with implementing

---

[3]Morris A. Cohen, Hau L. Lee and Don Willen, "Saturn's Supply-Chain Innovation," High Value in After-Sales Service," *Sloan Management Review,* Summer 2000, p. 93; Joan Magretta, "The Power of Virtual Integration: An Interview with Dell Computer's Michael Dell," *Harvard Business Review,* March-April 1998, pp. 73–84.

collaborative supply chain relationships.[4] (See Chapter 4 for a more detailed examination of e-commerce issues in supply chain management.)

However, coordinating information technology standards and software compatibility is just part of the challenge. Because most suppliers frequently deal with multiple customers, as opposed to focusing on a dominant downstream supply chain partner, issues relating to confidentiality must be addressed, affecting what information should be shared and when it should be communicated.

Operational Design Issues

Operational design issues relate to production and fulfillment activities and can affect performance factors such as lead times, quality, and lot sizes. For example, flexible manufacturing processes that can respond quickly to customer orders may allow reductions in safety stock. Identifying appropriate modes of transportation is also important. Rail may provide the lowest cost, but trucking provides faster door-to-door service and opportunities to reduce transit inventories.

Finally, inventory fulfillment policies should take into account market conditions and the impact on supplier operations. Broad policies such as "we keep four weeks of inventory for all A items" ignores variability of demand or supply for product groups or families. It may be necessary to develop policies within group classifications to ensure that appropriate levels of safety stock are maintained.

Establishing order policies based on lot sizing rules, such as full truckloads to minimize shipping costs, can lead to large fluctuations in demand at the supplier level. This phenomenon is known as the "bullwhip effect."[5] It can be addressed by sharing forecasts with suppliers so that they can plan production and have appropriate inventory available while keeping their costs low.

Stockless Purchasing Systems

The terms *stockless purchasing* and *systems contracting* are often used interchangeably. Actually, stockless purchasing systems are a special subset of systems contracts where the purchaser's stock is taken over by a supplier. The supplier's delivery system is so reliable and fast that there is no need for any safety stock on the purchaser's premises. Typical applications include, but are not limited to, office, electrical, plumbing, and building maintenance supplies of a relatively standard nature. Coupled with Internet-based ordering systems and catalogs, EDI, and direct delivery to the place of use, the stockless systems not only help reduce inventory levels but also purchasing, receiving, handling, invoicing, and payment costs.

---

[4]CPFR, *www.cpfr.org,* March 2001.

[5]Hau L. Lee, V. Padmanabhan and Seungjin Whang, "The Bullwhip Effect in Supply Chains," *Sloan Management Review,* Spring 1997, pp. 93–102.

Determining Order Quantities and Inventory Levels

In the following sections, some relatively simple theoretical models used to determine order quantities and inventory levels are discussed. The application of these models depends on whether the demand or usage of the inventory is dependent or independent. Dependent demand means the item is part of a larger component or product, and its use is dependent on the production schedule for the larger component. Hence, dependent demand items have a *derived demand.* Independent demand means the usage of the inventory item is not driven by the production schedule and is determined directly by customer orders.

Managing Independent Demand—Economic Order Quantity Models for Cycle Inventories

Fixed Quantity Models

The classic trade-off in determining the lot sizes in which to make or buy cycle inventories is between the costs of carrying extra inventory and the costs of purchasing or making more frequently. The objective of the model is to minimize the total annual costs. In the very simplest form of this model, annual demand *(R)*, lead time *(L)*, price *(C)*, variable order or setup cost *(S)*, and holding cost percentage *(K)* are all constant now and in the future. When inventory drops to the reorder point *(P)*, a fixed economic order quantity *(Q)* is ordered, which arrives after lead time *(L)*. Back orders and stock-outs are not allowed.

Total cost is given as purchase cost, plus setup or order cost, plus holding cost, or:

$$TC = RC + \frac{RS}{Q} + \frac{QKC}{2}$$

Determining EOQ

Using differential calculus, the minimum value of Q (also known as the EOQ) is found at:

$$Q_{opt} = \sqrt{\frac{2RS}{KC}}$$

This is the value at which order cost and carrying cost are equal. Figures 6–6 and 6–7 show how costs vary with changes in order size and how inventory levels change over time using this model. As an example of the use of the model, consider the following:

EOQ Example   **FIGURE 6–6**

Material Carrying and Order Costs

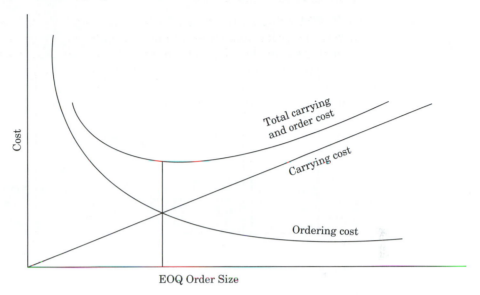

R = annual demand = 900 units
C = delivered purchase cost = $45/unit

K = carrying cost percentage = 25 percent
S = order cost = $50/order
L = lead time = 10 working days

$$Q_{opt} = \sqrt{\frac{2RS}{KC}}$$ = 89 units

The reorder point, P, is the lead time, L, times daily demand.

$$P = \frac{LR}{250} = \frac{10 \times 900}{250} = 36 \text{ (assumes 250 working days)}$$

This model suggests an order of 89 units whenever the inventory drops to 36 units. The last unit will be used just as the next order arrives. Average inventory will be 89/2 = 44.5 units. In practice, it might be advisable to keep some safety stock that must be added to the average inventory. Also, the bottom of the cost curve (see Figure 6–6) is relatively flat (and asymmetric) so that there might be advantages in ordering 96 (eight dozen) or 100 units instead. In this case these quantities would cost approximately an additional $2.50 and $6.25, respectively, out of a total annual cost of about $41,500. These costs are the additional ordering and carrying costs resulting from the additional units ordered.

FIGURE 6–7

Simple Fixed Quantity Model

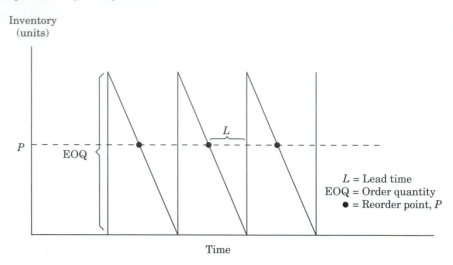

The assumptions behind the EOQ model place some rather severe restrictions on its general applicability. Numerous other models have been developed which take into account relaxation of one or more of the assumptions. The reader may wish to refer to books on inventory management for a more extensive discussion.

Fixed Period Models

In many situations, ordering every so often rather than whenever the stock reaches a certain level is desirable from an operations viewpoint. The scheduling of workload is easier when employees can be assigned to check certain classes of inventory every day, week, month, and so on.

In fixed quantity models, orders are placed when the reorder point is reached, but in fixed period models, orders are placed only at review time. The inventory level must, therefore, be adjusted to prevent stockouts during the review period and lead time.

Determining the Optimal Order Period

Fixed period models attempt to determine the optimal order period. The minimum cost period can be determined as follows. There are R/O cycles per year and therefore T (the fraction of the year) is O/R. This value of O can then be substituted in the EOQ formula to give:

$$T_{opot}R = \sqrt{\frac{2RS}{KC}} \ or \ T_{opt} = \sqrt{\frac{2S}{RKC}}$$

For the example used on the previous page:

$$T_{opt} = \sqrt{\frac{2 \times 50}{900 \times 0.25 \times 45}} = 0.1 \ \ or, \ \ 10 \ times \ per \ year$$

Fixed Period Model Example

For a year of 250 working days, this is 25 working days or once every five weeks. The optimum order quantity, EOQ, is RT_{opt} or 90 units. This is the same result as before. Organizational procedures may make a review every four weeks or monthly more attractive. In this case T would change to 0.08 and O to 72 at an additional cost of $23.77 per year over the optimum value.

Probabilistic Models and Service Coverage

The aforementioned models assume that all parameters are known absolutely. It is far more common to have some variation in forecast demands, lead times, and so on. Probabilistic lot size models take these variations into account. The models are more complex than the deterministic ones above, but the probabilistic approach gives much more information on likely outcomes.

Service Coverage Definitions

Buffer or Safety Stocks and Service Levels. For buffer or safety stocks, the major decision variable is how much buffer inventory to carry to give the desired service coverage. The service coverage can be defined as the portion of user requests served. If there are 400 requests for a particular item in a year and 372 were immediately satisfied, the service coverage would be 93 percent.

Service coverage can also be defined as the portion of demand serviced immediately. If the 372 orders in the above example were for one unit each and the 28 other, unserviced ones, for five units each, the service coverage could be defined as $372/[372 + (28 \times 5)]$ or 73 percent. It is obviously important to understand exactly what is meant by service coverage in an organization.

Holding a large inventory to prevent stockouts, and thus to maintain a high service coverage, is expensive. Similarly, a high number of stockouts is costly. Stockout costs are often difficult and expensive to determine but nevertheless real. Setting service coverage requires managers to make explicit and implicit evaluations of these costs so that the appropriate balance between carrying and stockout can be achieved.

Critical Fractile

In independent demand situations, the appropriate service coverage can be determined by the following ratio called the *critical fractile:*

$$Critical \ fractile \ = \frac{C_v}{C_v + C_o}$$

$$C_v = cost \ of \ understocking \qquad C_o = cost \ of \ overstocking$$

For illustrative purposes, assume that management has estimated the following costs and probabilities of customer action as a result of a stockout:

	Cost	Probability	Expected Value
Back order placed	$10	0.50	$5.00
Order canceled (lost contribution)	50	0.45	22.50
Customer's business lost forever	600	0.05	30.00
Miscellaneous costs (expediting, etc.)			25.00
Total			$82.50

Determining Desired Service Coverage

Management further estimates that holding a unit of this item for one time period costs $4. The desired service coverage is thus:

$$\frac{C_v}{C_v + C_o} = \frac{\$82.50}{\$82.50 + \$10.00} = .89 \ \ or \ 89\%$$

Because of the expense and difficulty of obtaining these costs and probability estimates for individual items, managers often set service coverage arbitrarily, typically about 95 percent, implying a ratio of stockout to holding costs of about 19 to 1. In practice, setting and managing service coverage is difficult because of the complexity of item classification, function, and interdependence. Service coverage need not be as high on some items as on others, but an item that may be relatively unimportant to one customer may be crucial to another. If the customer is an assembly line, a low service coverage on one component makes higher service coverage on others unnecessary. Also, some customers will tolerate much lower service coverage than will others. Within an organization, customers are internal departments, and

Relationship Service Coverage and Required Inventory Investment

service coverage attained is one measure of supply management's effectiveness. It is useful to stress that service coverage and inventory investment required are closely related. It becomes expensive to achieve very high service coverage, and a high service coverage expectation without the necessary financial backup can lead only to frustration. Procurement is, of course, also interested in service coverage as it pertains to supplier performance.

Service coverage can be used to determine the appropriate level of buffer inventory. The situation is shown in Figures 6–8 and 6–9. Four situations can arise as shown from left to right in Figure 6–8.

Determining Level of Buffer Inventory

1. Only some of the buffer inventory was used.

2. No buffer inventory remained but there was no stockout.

3. There was a stockout.

4. All the buffer inventory remained.

Figure 6–9 starts with an EOQ model except that it is not certain how many units will be used between placing and receipt of an order. Figure 6–9 targets desired service coverage at 95 percent, given the standard deviation

FIGURE 6–8

Fixed Order Quantity Model with Buffer Inventory and Variation in Demand

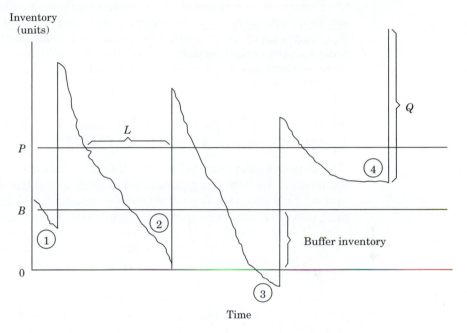

FIGURE 6–9

Determination of Buffer Inventory to Achieve Desired Coverage

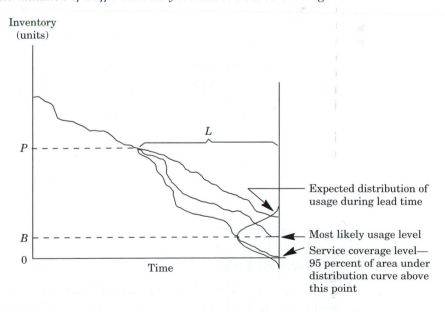

of average daily demand, an assumption of a normal demand distribution, and a most likely usage level.

The complexity of probabilistic models increases greatly when lead times, usable quantities received, inventory shrinkage rates, and so on also vary under conditions of uncertainty, when non-normal distributions are observed, and when the variations change with time. Simulation models and other more advanced statistical techniques can be used to solve these complex situations.

Managing Dependent Demand—Material Requirements Planning (MRP)

One of the assumptions behind the lot-sizing models just described is that demand for the item being purchased or made is independent of all other demands. This situation is true for most manufacturers' finished goods. However, subassemblies, raw materials, and parts do not exhibit this independence. Demand for these items is dependent on the assembly schedule for finished goods. Similarly, many MRO items depend on maintenance schedules. Recognition of the existence of demand dependence lies behind the technique known as material requirements planning (MRP).

MRP Systems Meet the Needs of Master Schedule

MRP systems attempt to support the activities of manufacturing, maintenance, or use by meeting the needs of the master schedule. In order to determine needs, MRP systems need an accurate bill of materials for each final product or project. These bills can take many forms but it is conceptually advantageous to view them as structural trees. Several general types of structural trees can be identified. Process industries, such as oil refiners and drug and food manufacturers, generally take a few raw materials and make a much larger number of end products. Discrete goods manufacturer/assemblers, such as the automobile companies, make a number of components, purchase others, and assemble them into end products. Assemblers, such as electronics companies, buy components and assemble them into finished goods. Schematic diagrams of these structural types are shown in Figure 6–10. Each type of firm can use MRP profitably but the greatest benefits usually accrue to the middle group because of the greater complexity of its operations.

Goals of MRP

The goals of MRP are to minimize inventory, to maintain high service coverage, and to coordinate delivery schedules and manufacturing and purchasing activities. These aims often conflict in other systems, but under MRP are achievable simultaneously. This feature, and the ability of modern MRP systems to allow rapid re-planning and rescheduling in response to the changes of a dynamic environment, are responsible for the attractiveness of MRP.

Structural Trees

Consider the manufacture of a final product A made up of three units of B and two of C. Each B is made up of two units of C and one of D. This struc-

FIGURE 6–10

Structural Tree Types

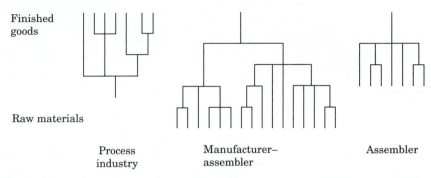

Finished goods

Raw materials

Process industry   Manufacturer–assembler   Assembler

FIGURE 6–11

Structural Tree for the Manufacture of A

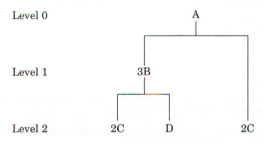

Level 0   A

Level 1   3B

Level 2   2C   D   2C

tural relationship is shown in Figure 6–11. C and D might be raw materials, or purchased parts, or subassemblies. Components of any subassemblies made in-house should be included in the structural tree.

Principle of Low-Level Coding

The structural tree is divided into levels and clearly shows the dependent demand feature. MRP systems calculate requirements for components in each level starting from the top down. C occurs twice, once as a component of B and once as a component of A. Consequently it could be placed in either (or both) level 1 or level 2. Demand for C cannot be calculated properly before demand for B is determined. Therefore, according to the MRP principle of low-level coding, C is placed only in level 2.

The MRP Plan

The top row of Figure 6–12 shows the master production schedule for A derived from the demand figures supplied by the marketing department.

MRP Plan for A

	Week:	0	1	2	3	4	5	6	7	8	9	10
Level 0	demand		20	30	0	50	25	10	15	20	5	25
	scheduled											
item A:	receipts		25	0	0	30	25	10	15	20	5	25
lead time:												
1 week	on hand	45	50	20	20	0	0	0	0	0	0	0
	order											
	release		0	0	30	25	10	15	20	5	25	—
Level 1	demand		0	0	90	75	30	45	60	15	75	—
item B:												
3 per A	scheduled		0	0	20	75	30	45	60	15	75	—
lead time:	receipts											
2 weeks	on hand	70	70	70	0	0	0	0	0	0	0	—
	order											
	release		20	75	30	45	60	15	75	—	—	—
Level 2	demand		40	150	120	140	140	60	190	10+	50+	—
item C:												
2 per A +	scheduled		30	75	105	140	140	60	190	10+	50+	—
2 per B	receipts											
lead time:												
2 weeks	on hand	100	90	15	0	0	0	0	0	—	—	—
	order											
	release		105	140	140	60	190	10+	50+	—	—	—
Level 2	demand		20	75	30	45	60	15	75	—	—	—
item D:	scheduled											
1 per B	receipts		30	60	25	45	60	15	75	—	—	—
lead time:												
3 weeks	on hand	10	20	5	0	0	0	0	0	—	—	—
	order											
	release		45	60	15	75	—	—	—	—	—	—

The schedule is divided into weekly periods and may result from firm orders or forecasts. Figure 6–12 also gives the current inventory status, the expected receipts from previous orders, and the required lead times to make or purchase A, B, C and D. Given this information, managers can derive a schedule for the release of shop orders for production of A. Using these derived numbers and similar logic, schedules for release of shop or purchase orders for B, and, subsequently, C and D can be obtained. The schedules and their derivation are also shown in Figure 6–12.

Meaning of Symbols in MRP

The time periods (buckets) are typically weeks although, in principle, longer or shorter periods could be used. Use of very short periods makes the system effectively bucketless. The example makes a clear distinction between "0" and "—." The symbol "0" represents a conscious decision to require, make, or hold no items. The symbol "—" means that the appropriate values are not yet known because the demand figures that will generate a value lie beyond the current 10-week time horizon. Indeed, the values for D show that to ensure continued supply of A, no inventories, and no expediting, a time horizon of at least six weeks is required. A new set of forecasts and an updated master production schedule will be required within four weeks.

Negative inventory values, not found in this schedule, would indicate a stock-out and signal management to take appropriate action.

Three Principles of MRP

This example illustrates the three basic principles and three inputs of MRP. Dependence of demand has been discussed. The second principle is the netting of inventory and the expected receipt of open orders to give the row labeled "on hand." The third principle is the time phasing, which uses information on lead times and needs to put the shop or purchase orders in the right time bucket.

MRP Inputs

Three Inputs of MRP

There are three basic MRP inputs. The whole system is driven by the requirements forecast by time period (the master production schedule) for the item in level 0. The structured bill of materials is the second input. The third input is the file that contains information on inventories, open orders, and lead times so that the quantity and timing of orders can be calculated.

The logic of MRP allows simultaneous determination of how much and when to order. The calculations hinge on the assumptions that all information is accurate and known with certainty, that material will be ordered as required, that the plant has the capacity to produce infinite quantities, and that ordering or setup costs are not significant. These assumptions do not generally hold.

MRP Lot Sizing

Figure 6–12 assumes that shop or purchase orders will be released only in the exact quantities required. Although this lot-for-lot order size rule minimizes inventory, it may give high setup or order costs. If, for A, the setup cost is $20 per order and the annual carrying cost is $26 per unit, the derived EOQ is 40 units (based on annualizing the 10-week demand of 200 units). The revised order release schedules for A and B are shown in Figure 6–13.

Trade-off Between Carrying and Setup and Ordering Costs

Because the demand for B, C, and D is dependent on the scheduled order release for A, changing the lot-sizing rule for A has a marked effect on the demand pattern for B and other dependent items. The above example used an EOQ lot-sizing rule. Is it the appropriate one? The EOQ approach assumes a steady demand, but the demand for A is quite lumpy. Several algorithms and heuristics have been developed to deal with this problem. They make the same trade-off between carrying and setup or ordering cost as the EOQ approach but typically identify the number of future periods' requirements to make or buy each setup or order, a number which varies with

FIGURE 6–13

MRP Order Release Plan for A and B Using EOQ Lot Sizing for A

Week:		1	2	3	4	5	6	7	8	9	10
A demand		20	30	0	50	25	10	15	20	5	25
scheduled-											
receipts		25	0	0	40	40	0	0	40	0	40
on hand	45	50	20	20	10	25	15	0	20	15	0
order											
release		0	0	40	40	0	0	40	0	40	—
B demand		0	0	120	120	0	0	120	0	120	—
scheduled											
receipts		0	0	50	120	0	0	120	0	120	—
on hand	70	70	70	0	0	0	0	0	0	0	0
order											
release		50	120	0	0	120	0	120	—	—	—
Net requirement		0	0	0	30	25	10	15	20	5	25
Cycle number 1:											
Period numbers					1	2	3	4			
$H(t-1)R_t$					0	12.5	10	22.5			
Cycle number 2:											
Period numbers								1	2	3	4
$H(t-1)R_t$								0	10	5	37.5
Cycle number 3:											
Period numbers											1
Requirement											
schedule		0	0	0	65	0	0	40	0	0	25+
Order											
schedule		0	0	65	0	0	40	0	0	25+	—

fluctuating demand. The algorithms and heuristics define rules on which the decision is based.

Procedure for Incremental Order Quantity Heuristic

For illustrative purposes, the procedure for the incremental order quantity heuristic will be described using the demand pattern for A already described, R_t as period demand, t as period number, S as setup cost, and H as period holding cost. The first week with a net positive order requirement is week three. Therefore, the first cycle will begin in week three and it will be renumbered as period one. S has already been incurred but items made and used in period one will incur no holding cost. The question is, should the 25 units of A required for period two also be made in period one? The heuristic uses the rule:

If $S \le H(t-1)R_t$, a new cycle will begin in period t;

if not, the existing cycle will continue.

For A with setup costs of $20, holding costs of $0.50 per week, and a one-week lead time, the schedule shown in Figure 6–13 is calculated. Cycle 1 ends in period 3 because, for period 4, $H(t − 1)R_t = (0.50)(4 − 1)(15) = 22.5$, which exceeds S. According to this schedule, 65 units of A would be ordered in week three, 40 units in week 6, and at least 25 units in week 9. The even spacing of these orders is a result of the demand pattern and costs, not of the heuristic itself.

The following table compares the costs over the 10-week period for A using six different lot-sizing rules. Even though 10 weeks is insufficient time to draw firm conclusions, it is clear that there are cost differences and that, for this example, the algorithms and heuristics seem to perform better than lot-for-lot or EOQ.

Lot-Sizing Rule	*Setups*	*Inventory*	*Costs*
Lot-for-lot	7	90	$ 185.00
EOQ	4	175	167.50
Incremental order quantity[6]	3	165	142.50
Silver and Meal[7]	3	165	142.50
Part-period balance[8]	4	145	152.50
Wagner-Whitin algorithm[9]	3	165	142.50

Lot-Sizing Rules

Lot-sizing rules remain an area of active research because the best (lowest cost) rule in any case depends on setup costs, order costs (and their ratio), the variability of demand, the length of the planning horizon, and the size of the planning period. As Orlicky[10] has pointed out, "if the requirements data are changed, *the example can be rigged so as to produce practically any results desired.*" Even the Wagner-Whitin algorithm, which is an optimizing one, has its drawbacks, so there is no one best model even for individual situations. Materials managers must evaluate several models and find one that seems to give acceptable, although perhaps not optimal, results over a long period.

---

[6]J. R. Freeland and J. L. Colley, "A Simple Heuristic Method for Lot Sizing in a Time-Phased Reorder System," *Production and Inventory Management,* first quarter, 1982; W. J. Boe and C. Yilmaz, "The Incremental Order Quantity," *Production and Inventory Management,* second quarter, 1983.

[7]E. A. Silver and H. C. Meal, "A Heuristic for Selection Lot Size Quantities for the Case of a Deterministic Time-Varying Demand Rate and Discrete Opportunities for Replenishment," *Production and Inventory Management,* second quarter, 1973.

[8]See for example, R. L. La Forge, "MRP and the Part-Period Algorithm," *Journal of Purchasing and Materials Management,* winter 1982, and references therein.

[9]H. M. Wagner and T. M. Whitin, "Dynamic Version of the Economic Lot Size Model," *Management Science,* No. 1, 1958; R. A. Kaimann, "A Fallacy of 'E.O.Q.ing,' " *Production and Inventory Management,* first quarter, 1968.

[10]J. Orlicky, *Material Requirements Planning* (New York, NY: McGraw-Hill, 1975), p. 136.

This example examined the effect on item A only. The lower-level items could be treated similarly. In the preceding example, the extreme lumpiness for B, C, and D, derived from the calculation for A, results in lot-for-lot order quantities being optimum in many cases. Again the appropriate lot sizes will depend on the specific features of B, C, and D. In a multiproduct plant, with many common parts, demand for B, C, or D may be affected by other end products. The complex and dynamic nature of this environment makes the lot-sizing decision a challenge.

Safety Stock. The calculations in Figure 6–12 show inventory at 0 after the starting stocks have been drawn down. Because lead times, forecasts, and so on are known to be at least occasionally wrong, it makes sense to carry some safety stock to ensure that production can continue. Inventories can be kept low by carrying safety stock only at the finished goods level and expending extra effort to reduce lead-time uncertainties. Proper planning for safety stock will ensure that it is accounted for at the master production schedule level so that balanced sets of components are produced.

When and Where to Hold Safety Stock

One area of uncertainty that warrants special mention is that of a reject allowance. If a purchased or fabricated part is known to contain a certain portion of unacceptable units, the MRP-generated order should be scaled up accordingly.

Reject Allowance

Infinite Capacity. As presented earlier, MRP places no restrictions on the number of units of any item that the plant or a supplier can produce in a time bucket. Clearly, however, plants do have capacities. The situation is very complex in job shops making a constantly changing mix of many products with many common subunits, and with the same machines and workers making many different items. Even though MRP will give a time-phased output plan, it may not be a feasible one. The job of scheduling work on the shop floor, and of dealing with absenteeism, breakdowns, poor quality, and unexpected delays, remains. A long time horizon and the use of anticipation inventories help, but they have their own costs. Clearly, more is needed to overcome this basic flaw in MRP logic. Modern MRP systems have ways of doing so.

Modern MRP Systems and Capacity Requirements Planning (CRP)

Three Stages of MRP Implementation

Modern MRP systems are more complex than the simple logic presented in Figure 6–12. The implementation of materials requirements planning is a three-stage process. (1) Class C is the basic open-ended MRP system, (2) Class B is a closed-loop system that includes shop floor control and capacity requirements planning, and (3) Class A or MRP II (manufacturing resource planning) brings the remainder of the firm's planning processes and accounting information into the planning system.

Closed-Loop MRP

The most significant advance in MRP systems has been the addition of capacity requirements planning (CRP). CRP performs a similar function for manufacturing resources that MRP performs for materials. When the MRP system has developed a materials plan, CRP translates the plan into the required human and machine resources by workstation and time bucket. It then compares the required resources against a file of available resources. If insufficient capacity exists, the manager must adjust either the capacity or the master production schedule. This feedback loop to the master production schedule results in the term *closed-loop MRP* to describe this development.

The CRP module is often linked to a module that controls the manufacturing plan on the shop floor. The goal is to measure output by work center against the previously determined plan. This information allows identification of trouble spots and is necessary on an ongoing basis for capacity planning.

MRP System Updates

MRP systems must be updated frequently to ensure that decisions are made on the basis of consistent, complete, and accurate data. The updating can be either partial or complete. Complete regenerations of large systems are time-consuming and expensive, so, typically, such updates are done infrequently (weekly), often at night. Reliance on such a regenerative system leads to slow response to environmental changes and to poor information and large deviations from plan late in the regenerative time period. In contrast, net change systems are updated partially to show the net effects of change whenever new data are entered. The nervousness and incompleteness of such systems can create suboptimal production plans. Insertion of dampeners to filter out relatively minor changes reduces the nervousness. Most systems offer a combination of net-change and regenerative modes. Many modern systems also have modules that connect to the accounting system and which help in developing product costs and budgeting.

MRP System Redefined

A modern MRP system is thus a lot more than simply a device to calculate how much material to obtain and when to do so. It is an information and communication system that encompasses all facets of the organization. It provides managers with performance measures, planned order releases (purchase orders, shop orders, and rescheduling notices), and the ability to simulate a master production schedule in response to proposed changes in production loading (by, for example, a new order, delayed materials, a broken machine, or an ill worker). The integration required of such systems forces organizations to maintain highly accurate information, abandon rules of thumb, and use common data in all departments. The results are reduced inventory levels, higher service coverage, ready access to high-quality information, and, most importantly, the ability to replan quickly in response to unforeseen problems.

Not all organizations have been successful in implementing MRP systems. Implementation may take years and involve major investments in training, data preparation, and organizational adjustments as well as in software, computer time, and possibly hardware. However, most organizations with successfully implemented systems feel that the reduced inventory, lead times, split orders and expediting, increased delivery promises met, and discipline resulting from MRP make the investment worthwhile.

Distribution Requirements Planning (DRP)[11]

Application of MRP Logic to the Distribution Function

Distribution requirements planning (DRP) and distribution resource planning (DRP II) are applications of the time-phasing logic of MRP to the distribution function. The purpose of DRP is to forecast the demand by distribution center to determine the master scheduling needs. DRP, unlike order point-based distribution systems, attempts to anticipate future needs throughout the distribution chain and plan deliveries accordingly.

Purchasing Implications of MRP

The tight control required by MRP means that purchasing records regarding quantities, lead times, bills of material, and specifications must be totally accurate. Also, purchasing and the stores function will become more centralized, and access to stores must be more tightly controlled.

The on-time delivery required of MRP needs cooperation from suppliers. Purchasers must, therefore, educate their suppliers to the importance of quantity, quality, and delivery promises to the purchaser. Such education should enable purchasers to reduce their safety stock. Educational efforts become easier as more suppliers adopt MRP themselves.

Purchasing's Role in an MRP System

Many MRP systems have purchasing modules that perform many of the routine clerical purchasing tasks. The purchaser's job becomes more analytical and professional. The long-term nature of the MRP planning horizon, typically a year, means longer term planning for purchasing and the negotiation of more long-term contracts with annual volume-based discounts. These contracts have more frequent order release and delivery, often in nonstandard lot sizes. Quantity discounts on individual orders become much less relevant in favor of on-time delivery of high-quality product.

Purchasers must understand the production processes both of their own organizations and of their suppliers. The tighter nature of MRP-using organizations increases the responsibility on purchasing to be creative and flexible in providing assistance to minimize the inevitable problems that will occur in supply lines. The MRP system provides purchasers with an information window to production scheduling so they are better able to use judgment in dealing with suppliers. Because of the reduced resource slack that results from MRP, purchasers must incorporate de-expediting into their

---

[11]Alan R. Raedels, *Value-Focused Supply Management: Getting the Most Out of the Supply Function* (Burr Ridge, IL: Irwin Professional Publishing, 1995).

activities as well as the more usual expediting role. The integrating and forward-looking nature of MRP means an increase in specialization in the purchasing department. Also, specialization will be based on finished product line outputs rather than on raw material inputs.

In contrast to MRP, just-in-time production methods can achieve many of the goals of MRP in conjunction with MRP or on a stand-alone basis.

Enterprise Resource Planning (ERP) Systems

Integration Role of ERP Systems

Many companies use enterprise resource planning systems, such as SAP, J.D. Edwards and PeopleSoft, to integrate business systems and processes. ERP systems are software that allows all areas of the company—manufacturing, finance, sales, marketing, human resources, and purchasing—to combine and analyze information. It can provide a link from customer orders through the fulfillment processes. Therefore, fully implemented ERP systems allow purchasing to be aware of orders received by sales, manufacturing to be aware of raw material delivery status, sales to understand product or service lead times and availability, and financial transactions and commitments to be communicated directly into the financial accounting system.

Installing an ERP system can be expensive, typically costing a *Fortune 500* company license fees in the tens of millions of dollars, plus approximately five times that level in consulting fees.[12] The benefits from ERP systems come from elimination of costly manual systems and standardization of data.

Some ERP systems use Web-enabled systems that allow supply chain partners to exchange information, such as orders, forecasts, production plans, inventory levels and fill rates, via the Internet. These systems provide real-time communication, lower information processing costs, and the use of consistent data among buyers and sellers. A thorough discussion of e-purchasing applications is provided in Chapter 4.

Just-in-Time (JIT)

Many successful organizations use a radically different philosophy popularly and descriptively termed *just-in-time (JIT)*. JIT production means that components and raw materials arrive at a work center exactly as they are needed. This feature greatly reduces queues of work-in-process inventory.

Goals of JIT

The goals of JIT production are similar to those of MRP—providing the right part at the right place at the right time—but the ways of achieving these

---

[12]Vincent A. Mabert, Ashok Soni and M.A. Venkataramanan, "Enterprise Resource Planning Survey of U.S. Manufacturing Firms," *Production and Inventory Management Journal,* second quarter 2000, pp. 52–58.

goals are radically different and the results impressive. Whereas MRP is computer based, JIT is industrial engineering based. JIT focuses on waste elimination in the supply chain, and there are many JIT features that are good practice in any operation, public or private, manufacturing or nonmanufacturing.

Process Design

In JIT, product design begins with two key questions—will it sell and can it be made easily? These questions imply cooperation between marketing and operations. Once these questions have been answered positively, attention turns to design of the process itself. The emphasis is on laying out the machines so that production will follow a smooth flow. Automation (often simple) of both production and materials handling is incorporated wherever possible. Frequently, U-shaped lines are used, which facilitate teamwork, worker flexibility, rework, passage through the plant and material and tool handling. In process design, designers strive to standardize cycle times and to run a constant product mix, based on the monthly production plan, through the system. This practice makes the production process repetitive for at least a month. For example, a manufacturer of three products (or models) A, B, and C of equal cycle time and monthly demands of 1,000, 2,000, and 500, respectively, might have a production schedule of BABABCB or BBBBAAC repeated 500 times in the month.

Setup and Order Costs in JIT System

The ability to smooth production, as in the above example, implies very low setup and order costs to allow the very small lot sizes, ideally one. JIT treats setup and order costs as variable rather than as the fixed ones implied by the EOQ equation. By continuously seeking ways to reduce setup times, the Japanese were the first to have managed impressive gains. Setups, which traditionally required three to four hours, have been reduced to less than 15 minutes in some JIT facilities. These dramatic improvements have been achieved by managerial attention to detail on the shop floor; the development and modification of special jigs, fixtures, tools, and machines; and thorough methods training. Setup simplification is aided by their willingness to modify purchased machines, their acquisition of machines from only a few sources, and their frequent manufacture of machines in-house-often special purpose, light, simple, and inexpensive enough to become a dedicated part of the process. Order costs, conceptually similar to setup costs, have similarly been reduced.

Three Quality Principles Behind JIT

One of the necessary corollaries of having components and materials arrive just as they are needed is that the arriving items must be perfect. In JIT, a number of interrelated principles are used to ensure high-quality output from each step in the production process.

The Maker Is Responsible for Quality

First, responsibility for quality rests with the maker of a part, not with the quality control department. In addition, workers and managers habitually seek improvement of the status quo, striving for perfection. Quality improvements are often obtained from special projects with defined goals, measures of achievement, and endings. Also, workers are responsible for correcting their own errors, doing rework, and so on.

Quality Is Built-In

Second, the use of production workers instead of quality control inspectors builds quality in rather than inspecting it in. This feature and the small lot sizes allow every process to be controlled closely and permit inspection of every piece of output. Workers have authority to stop the production line when quality problems arise. This aspect signifies that quality is a more important goal of the production system than is output.

Compliance Is Required

Third, JIT insists on compliance to quality standards. Purchasers reject marginally unacceptable items and visit supplier plants to check quality on the shop floor for themselves. Because such visits are frequent, JIT manufacturers document their quality in easily understood terms and post the results in prominent places. This process forces the manufacturer to define quality precisely.

Quality Control Measures

JIT control of quality is helped by the small lot sizes that prevent the buildup of large lots of bad items. JIT tends to have excess production capacity so that the plants are not stressed to produce the required quantities. In the same vein, machines are maintained and checked regularly and run no faster than the recommended rates. Plant housekeeping is generally good. The quality control department acts as a quality facilitator for production personnel and suppliers, giving advice in problem solving. This department also does some testing, but the tests tend to be on final products not easily assignable to a single production worker, or special tests requiring special equipment, facilities, knowledge, or long times not available to personnel on the shop floor. Automatic checking devices are used wherever possible. Where necessary, sample lots are chosen to consist of the first and last units produced rather than a larger, random sample. Analytical tools include the standard statistical techniques, often known by workers, and cause-and-effect diagrams to help solve problems.

JIT requires great dedication by both workers and managers to hard work and helping the organization. By Western standards, JIT workers must be flexible. They are trained to do several different jobs and are moved around frequently. The workers are responsible for quality and output. Workers continuously seek ways to improve all facets of operations and are rewarded for finding problems which can then be solved. The JIT plant has a high proportion of line workers that add value in the production process and correspondingly fewer staff personnel. The environment is much like many quality-of-work-life programs—consensus decision making involves and commits everyone.

Pull System

Sequential JIT is a term applied to production systems where each operation is part of the sequence and where the withdrawal of product by the subsequent operations signals the need to start the operation. This is the typical "pull system."

JIT Redefined

In summary, JIT is a mixture of high-quality working environment, excellent industrial engineering practice, and a healthy focused factory attitude that operations are strategically important. The order and discipline are achieved through management effort to develop streamlined plant configurations that remove variability. The JIT system has often been described as one that pulls material through the factory rather than pushing it through. The use of a kanban system as a control device illustrates this point well.

Kanban Systems. Kanban is a simple but effective control system that helps make JIT production work. Kanban is not synonymous with JIT, although the term is often incorrectly so used and the two are closely related. *Kanban* is Japanese for *"card";* the use of cards is central to many Japanese control systems, including the one at Toyota, whose kanban system has received much attention.

Kanban Means Card

Kanban systems require the small lot size features of JIT and discrete production units. The systems are most useful for high-volume parts used on a regular basis. They are much less useful for expensive or large items which cost a lot to store or carry, for infrequently or irregularly used items, or for process industries that don't produce in discrete units.

Two Types of Kanban Systems

Two types of kanban systems exist—single card and double card. In double-card systems, two types of cards (kanban) exist—conveyance (C-kanban) and production (P-kanban). Single-card systems use only the C-kanban. The two-card system's operation uses the following rules.[13]

Rules for Double Card Kanban Systems

1. No parts may be made unless there is a P-kanban authorizing production. Workers may do maintenance, cleaning, or work on improvement projects until a P-kanban arrives rather than making parts not yet asked for. Similarly, C-kanban controls the transport of parts between departments.

2. Only standard containers may be used, and they are always filled with the prescribed small quantity.

3. There is precisely one C-kanban and one P-kanban per container.

The system is driven by the user department pulling material through the system by the use of kanban. The main managerial tools in this system are the container size and the number of containers (and therefore kanban) in the system. The control is very precise, flexible, and responsive. It prevents an unwanted buildup of inventory.

Deliberate Inventory Level Reduction

Inventories often exist to cover up problems in supply or inside the organization. For example, a buffer inventory can protect a user from poor quality or unreliable delivery from a marginal supplier. In JIT, the deliberate lowering of inventory levels to uncover such malpractices forces an organization

---

[13]R.J. Schonberger, *Japanese Manufacturing Techniques: Nine Hidden Lessons in Simplicity* (New York, NY: Free Press, 1982).

Reducing Inventory to Uncover the Root Course of Malpractices

to identify and solve the underlying problems or causes for high and undesirable inventories. This deliberate inventory reduction is often seen by some managers as a form of organizational suicide, a willingness to put continuity of supply, service, or operation at risk. However, enough organizations have experimented with this concept (and survived) to show the merits of this practice. Diagrammatically, this lowering of inventory levels is frequently shown as a seascape of inventory with sharp rocks of different heights underneath representing the problems or malpractices that need to be exposed sequentially.

JIT Implications for Supply Management

Supply Requirements for Successful JIT

There are a number of implications of JIT for supply management. One of the obvious includes the necessity to deal with suppliers of high and consistent quality and with reliable delivery. This implies that concentrating purchases with fewer nearby suppliers may be necessary. The frequent delivery of small orders may require a rethinking of the inbound transportation mode. For example, it is normal to have a trucker follow a standard route daily to pick up, from 6 to 20 different suppliers, small lots in a specially designed side-loading vehicle. Having delivery arranged directly to the place of use eliminates double handling. Special moving racks designed for proper protection, ease of counting, insertion, and removal also help improve material handling. A lot of supplier training and cooperation is required to assist in the design and operation of an effective JIT system.

In the minimum sense, JIT can refer to arranging for delivery just before a requirement is needed. In this context, JIT has wide applicability beyond manufacturing—in public, service, and other nonmanufacturing organizations. Reliability of delivery reduces the need for buffer or safety stock, with the benefits that arise out of such inventory reduction.

Achievable Dimensions of JIT

JIT has become sufficiently entrenched as a concept that its applicability is not in question, only the extent to which it should be applied. Research by McLachlin and Piper has shown that a full-blown JIT-based operating system has 11 achievable dimensions:[14] (1) setup time reduction, (2) small-lot production, (3) small-lot transportation, (4) multiprocess handling through automation, (5) zero-defect quality control, (6) equipment maintenance, (7) leveling (and mixing) of production, (8) withdrawal by subsequent processes, (9) in-house modification and production of equipment (10) JIT supply arrangements, and (11) employee involvement in continuous improvement. This provides a checklist for purchasers seeking suppliers with JIT capability. They should be cautioned, however, that in this research little evidence of widespread adoption of zero-defect quality control and employee involvement in continuous improvement was found.

---

[14]Ron McLachlin and Chris Piper, "Just-in-Time Production," *Business Quarterly,* Summer 1990, pp. 36–42.

Buyer-Supplier Relations in JIT Systems

In JIT there is a close cooperation between supplier and purchaser to solve problems, and suppliers and customers have stable, long-term relationships. In keeping with the JIT philosophy, suppliers, usually few in number, are often located close to their customers to facilitate communication, on-time delivery of small lots of parts, low pipeline and safety stocks, and low purchasing costs. The situation in many JIT companies is much like extensive backward vertical integration. The organizations avoid formal ownership ties but achieve many of the same ends by close coordination and systems integration that smooth operations. The job of a purchaser in the JIT environment is one of a facilitator, negotiator, communicator, and developer rather than of an expediter.

Research into communication links between purchaser and supplier in a JIT environment considered written exchanges, computer-to-computer hookups, telephone exchanges, and one-on-one and group meetings. Findings showed more information was supplied to JIT suppliers than to others. Also, manufacturers believed open and reliable communications led to improved quality, while similar suppliers' communications led to improved cost and delivery performance.[15]

Implementing Lean Supply

Eliminating Waste Through Continuous Improvement

Lean production, sometimes called "Big JIT," was pioneered by Toyota and focuses on eliminating waste through continuous improvement. Lean production principles foster low-cost production systems that are more flexible and responsive to customer needs.[16] A number of organizations, such as Lockheed Martin, Boeing and the Chrysler division of DaimlerChrysler, have been working with their suppliers to implement lean supply management principles.[17]

Lean Supply Management at Chrysler

Chrysler sends teams into key supplier's plants for a full week to assist with making changes from a traditional production-line process to a lean manufacturing approach. The intent is to teach suppliers about lean production concepts and implement cost savings in manufacturing operations. The Chrysler team includes a facilitator from purchasing, the engineer responsible for the design of the product involved, the quality specialist responsible for the supplier's plant, the receiving "customer," and the buyer. The Chrysler team helps the supplier identify waste and inefficiencies, and

---

[15]Leslie Richeson, Charles W. Lackey and John W. Starner Jr., "The Effect of Communication on the Linkage between Manufacturers and Suppliers in Just-in-Time Environment," *International Journal of Purchasing and Materials Management,* Winter 1995, pp. 21–30.

[16]James P. Womack and Daniel T. Jones, "From Lean Production to the Lean Enterprise," *Harvard Business Review,* Vol. 27, no. 2, 1994, pp. 93–103.

[17]Tom Stunza, "Prepping the Supply Base for Leaner Supply Systems," *Purchasing,* Vol. 128, No. 9, 2000, pp. 62–68; Kevin R. Fitzgerald, "Chrysler Training helps Suppliers Trim the Fat," *Purchasing,* September 4, 1997, pp. 73–74.

together the group reengineers the process, trains the workers, and makes refinements. On the final day all the team members, from both Chrysler and the supplier, report the results to the supplier's top management.[18]

Questions for Review and Discussion

1. Of what interest is ABC analysis?
2. What is a master production schedule and what role does it perform?
3. Why is it expensive to carry inventories?
4. In a typical fast-food operation, identify various forms and functions of inventory. How could total investment in inventories be lowered? What might be the potential consequences?
5. What is stockless purchasing?
6. What is a kanban and why is it used?
7. What problems do inaccurate usage forecasts create for buyers? For suppliers?
8. What is the difference between JIT and MRP?
9. Why would anyone prefer to use a fixed period reordering model over a fixed quantity one?
10. Why is it difficult to achieve organizationwide dedication to employee involvement in continuous improvement?

References

CPFR, *www.cpfr.org,* March 2001.

Cohen, M. A.; H. L. Lee and D. Willen, "Saturn's Supply-Chain Innovation, High Value in After-Sales Service," *Sloan Management Review,* Summer 2000, p. 93.

Fitzgerald, K. R., "Chrysler Training Helps Suppliers Trim the Fat," *Purchasing,* Sep. 4, 1997, pp. 73–74.

Lambert, D. M.; J. R. Stock and L. M. Ellram, *Fundamentals of Logistics Management,* Burr Ridge, IL: Irwin McGraw-Hill, 1998.

Lee, H. L., V. Padmanabhan and S. Whang, "The Bullwhip Effect in Supply Chains," *Sloan Management Review,* Spring 1997, pp. 93–102.

---

[18]Kevin R. Fitzgerald, "Chrysler Training helps Suppliers Trim the Fat," *Purchasing,* September 4, 1997, pp. 73–74.

Mabert, V. A.; A. Soni and M.A. Venkataramanan, "Enterprise Resource Planning Survey of U.S. Manufacturing Firms," *Production and Inventory Management Journal,* Second Quarter 2000, pp. 52–58.

Magretta, J., "The Power of Virtual Integration: An Interview with Dell Computer's Michael Dell," *Harvard Business Review,* March–April 1998, pp. 73–84.

McLachlin, R. and C. Piper, "Just-in-Time Production", *Business Quarterly,* Summer 1990, pp. 36–42.

Orlicky, J., *Material Requirements Planning,* New York, NY: McGraw-Hill, 1975, p. 136.

Raedels, A. R., *Value-Focused Supply Management: Getting the Most Out of the Supply Function,* Burr Ridge, IL: Irwin Professional Publishing, 1995.

Richeson, L., C. W. Lackey and J. W. Starner Jr., "The Effect of Communication on the Linkage between Manufacturers and Suppliers in Just-in-Time Environment," *International Journal of Purchasing and Materials Management,* Winter 1995, pp. 21–30.

Schonberger, R.J., *Japanese Manufacturing Techniques: Nine Hidden Lessons in Simplicity,* New York, NY: Free Press, 1982.

Stunza, T., "Prepping the Supply Base for Leaner Supply Systems," *Purchasing,* Vol. 128, No. 9, 2000, pp. 62–68.

Womack, J. P. and D. T. Jones, "From Lean Production to the Lean Enterprise," *Harvard Business Review,* Vol. 27, No. 2, 1994, pp. 93–103.

CASE 6–1
ROGER GRAY

Late in the afternoon of August 23, Roger Gray, purchasing manager at Anderson Plastics, watched as his boss angrily left the room. It was the second time in a week that Roger had been blamed when the plant had run out of raw materials, and he wondered how he should address the materials management problems at the California plant.

Anderson Plastics Inc. Anderson Plastics Inc. was a large multinational supplier of plastic compounds, which constituted the raw material for a number of different plastic materials, such as polypropylenes, polyethylenes, styrenes, and nylons. These compounds were used to manufacture a variety of products, such as automotive bumpers and dashboards, helmets, packing material and hard-shell suitcases.

The company had pursued a growth strategy, mainly through acquisitions, during the last decade. Currently, Anderson Plastics operated 13 manufacturing plants in North America, Europe, Latin America and the Asia-Pacific region with a combined sales volume of about $1 billion. The company employed approximately 2,200 people worldwide.

Anderson Plastics. The California manufacturing plant was 110,000 sq. ft. in size and sat on about 14 acres of industrial land with access to a rail siding. A total of 74 people worked at the plant.

During the last decades, Anderson and its customers had moved to just-in-time systems (JIT), which required Anderson to work closely with customers to schedule delivery of raw materials. The result had been a trend toward lower supply chain inventories. However, this also increased the risk of stockouts, which could result in expensive downtime for Anderson's customers.

Purchasing & Materials Management. Until two years ago, purchasing at Anderson Plastics had been a non-centralized function, where each department was responsible for ordering its own raw materials. Because of materials management problems, such as excess inventory for some products while experiencing frequent stock-outs of others, management decided to make a change. Therefore, Roger Gray, a production supervisor at the plant with 16 years experience, was moved over to take control of a newly created centralized purchasing function for the plant.

The materials management system in place at Anderson Plastics had not yet been properly integrated with other parts of the Anderson Plastics organization or its suppliers. Roger had found the materials management system to be unreliable, frequently contributing to stock-outs. While it was good at processing regular shipments, it could not handle unexpected requirements adequately. In addition, a parallel 'handwritten' system was in effect, which required Gray to spend two to three hours a day filling out forms. In his first year, Gray developed a series of spreadsheet applications to automate some of the repetitive and error-prone tasks.

As the plant expanded, the number of products that Roger had to keep track of rose from 250 to 550. Even with his new spreadsheet applications, it became increasingly difficult for Roger to manage inventory levels accurately.

Roger was severely criticized when a stockout occurred, even though he believed that most of the time it was not his fault. Often, the materials management system was a couple of days behind real-time and so it didn't reflect current inventory levels. At other times, transportation problems, especially the chronic unreliability of the U.S. rail system, caused shipments to be delayed. The plant only had a 10-silo capacity for raw materials and also used rail cars full of material as temporary warehouses when necessary. Roger felt that inventory levels were high, but he had never been criticized for carrying 'too-much' inventory.

The Two Recent Incidents. Both of this week's stock-outs were typical. The first had occurred because production had not informed Roger that a prime customer had suddenly ordered twice its usual requirement a week earlier and had failed to record the quantities withdrawn from inventory properly. Thus, Roger's record showed a significant amount of inventory still on hand.

Today's incident had involved a shipment by rail from Texas that should have arrived four days ago, but which had been mysteriously delayed in transit. The supplier had shipped on the proper date and was not at fault.

CASE 6–2
CONNECTICUT CIRCUIT
MANUFACTURERS

It was the morning of February 1, when Jack Veber, Senior Buyer at Connecticut Circuit Manufacturers (CCM), received a phone call from a large customer complaining that an order had not been delivered on time. Since this was not the first such occurrence, Jack knew that he would be expected to present recommendations that addressed this problem at the general management meeting the following day.

Connecticut Circuit Manufacturers. Connecticut Circuit Manufacturers was established in June 1980 and specialized in circuit board design and assembly. CCM manufactured two product lines: Contract Products and Design Products.

CCM had manufactured Contract Products since the company first began operation in 1980. Contract Product customers provided the design of the circuit board and CCM manufactured the circuit board in specified quantities. CCM expected to sell 4,000 – 5,000 units of Contract Products. Sales of Contract Products had grown consistently at 10 percent per year, and this growth rate was expected to continue in the next three years.

Design Products were introduced seven months ago. For Design Products, CCM was responsible for the design of the circuit board as well as for production. As with Contract Products, Design Products were manufactured in quantities specified by the customer. Annual sales of Design Products for the current year were expected to be 500–1,000 units. The company anticipated a rapid 40 percent per annum growth rate of this product line in the next three years.

Management of CCM had been the same since the company was founded in 1980. All members of the management team were middle-aged entrepreneurs who spent the majority of their time exploring new opportunities for the company. Management was very open with employees and encouraged them to voice concerns and recommendations that related to company improvement and growth.

The manufacturing of circuit boards was a competitive industry, and margins on a single circuit board were small. CCM had three local competitors who manufactured high quality circuit boards at competitive prices.

Production. CCM assembled circuit boards in batches, and production lot sizes were based on confirmed customer orders. Assembly operations varied among products and were based on design specifications and material requirements.

A range of raw materials were used in circuit board assembly, including integrated circuits, resistors, printed circuit boards, connectors, cables and fasteners. Consequently, the production department at CCM worked very closely with the buying group with respect to inventory management. It was the buyer's responsibility to ensure that all supplies required for production were available in inventory.

Recently, production reached full capacity with a single shift. The company was growing and expectations were for rapid growth due to the introduction of Design Products. CCM added a second shift in February that increased capacity to 7,000 units.

Twelve suppliers were currently providing CCM with the commodities required for circuit board production. The majority of these suppliers had enjoyed a long-term relationship with CCM. However, management felt that under current market conditions, additional suppliers could be developed to provide similar levels of quality, price, and service.

The CCM Supply Group. Jack Veber was hired as Senior Buyer by CCM on November 30. In his new role, Jack Veber was responsible for ensuring that all resistors and cables were available when needed for production. Jack Veber spent the majority of his time managing relationships with suppliers and keeping track of customer orders and deadlines. In order to keep inventory costs down, Jack Veber had to make sure that excess inventory of these items was kept to an absolute minimum.

Prior to coming to CCM, Jack Veber spent five years as an intermediate buyer at a large local manufacturer. His responsibilities at his previous employer included purchasing all commodities for two specific customers. Jack Veber gained experience in purchasing all types of commodities and claimed this was the main reason he was offered the position as Senior Buyer at CCM.

Along with Jack Veber, another Senior Buyer and one Junior Buyer handled purchasing at CCM. The other Senior Buyer was Al Cooper who had been with CCM for 15 years. His responsibilities included purchasing all types of integrated circuits and connectors and printed circuit boards. As integrated circuits and printed circuit boards were expensive to keep in inventory, Al Cooper spent the majority of his time keeping track of integrated circuit board requirements for production and managing existing relationships with integrated circuit board suppliers.

Tim LeBlanc was the Junior Buyer. He started with CCM two years ago, immediately after graduating with a purchasing degree from a local college. Due to limited experience, Tim LeBlanc had minimal purchasing responsibility. His main role was to assist the Senior Buyers by providing them with required production information. Tim was also responsible for purchasing all types of screws, nuts and washers. Ideally, as Tim gained experience, he would be given more purchasing responsibility.

In February, CCM had five customers. Three of these customers were regular Contract Product customers and two were Design Product customers. Contract Product customers had an ongoing business relationship with CCM. These customers tended to be sensitive to product quality, price, and on-time delivery.

Design Product customers were mainly conscious of product quality and customer service. The main features of customer service as defined by these customers were on-time delivery and effective customer relations. The company also hoped to attract new customers for its Design Products and expected that Design Product business would lead to additional Contract Product business.

The General Management Meeting. As part of becoming better acquainted with CCM's requirements, Jack Veber had gathered some information and created summary tables provided in Exhibits 1 and 2. He did not know yet whether these might be useful in rethinking CCM's supply strategy and execution.

The phone call he received earlier that morning was from Customer E complaining about a late de-

livery. Several weeks earlier, a similar phone call was received from Customer A.

Jack Veber had a meeting with upper management the next day at the general management meeting. Upper management was already aware of the complaint made by Customer A and would most likely be made aware of Customer E's complaint before tomorrow's meeting. Jack Veber was eager to determine what factors might have led to the delivery problems but had no specific information yet. During the general management meeting, Jack Veber planned to present his analysis and provide recommendations that would reduce the possibility of similar problems occurring in the future.

EXHIBIT 1   Connecticut Circuit Manufacturers

Annual Component Purchases

Item Name	Annual Orders (parts)	Buyer	Total Annual Purchases
Integrated Circuits	50,000	Cooper	$250,000
Resistors	500,000	Veber	$50,000
Printed Circuit Boards	7,000	Cooper	$105,000
Connectors	14,000	Cooper	$35,000
Cables	8,000	Veber	$24,000
Screws, Nuts, Washers	448,000	LeBlanc	$15,680

EXHIBIT 2   Connecticut Circuit Manufacturers

Annual Purchases For Each Customer

Item Name	Customers					
	A^*	B	C	D	E^*	Total
Integrated Circuits	15	10	20	3	25	73
Resistors	15	40	18	12	10	95
Printed Circuit Boards	4	3	5	1	7	20
Connectors	2	4	3	1	5	15
Cables	2	2	2	0	4	10
Screws, Nuts, Washers	8	12	10	10	10	50
Total # Items	46	71	58	27	61	263
Total Material Value	$135,000	$50,000	$80,000	$14,680	$200,000	$479,680

*Design Product Customers

CASE 6–3
ABBEY PAQUETTE

As it approached 5 P.M. on Friday, August 15, Abbey Paquette, Purchasing Agent for the Chicago-based Pentz International Inc., contemplated the events of the last five days. Abbey and her team had spent a week collecting information that might help them respond to a request that had come directly from the company president to make a drastic reduction in the $2.5 million annual inventory carrying cost. Abbey was now wondering how to proceed.

Company Background. In the mid-1920's, a group of five talented young engineers developed and refined a process to extrude aluminum tube into a continuous helical fin over a variety of liner tubes. The resulting bimetal fin tubing worked as an extremely effective component in large-scale heat exchangers. The extended heat transfer surface of these tubes enabled the group's heat exchanger products to find applications in the pulp and paper, power generation, electrical transmission and distribution, and other process-related industries.

In 1928, based on the success of the group's heat exchanger products, Pentz International Inc. (PII) was established in Chicago, Illinois. As the combination of the fin-tube and time-proven heat exchanger designs gained wider recognition, PII's business grew in both the United States and international markets. By the 1980's PII's heat transfer products were being used in a wide variety of industrial applications all over the world, including hydroelectric installations in Australia, electric transmission and distribution systems in Europe, giant water-pumping systems in the United States, and in several waste-to-energy facilities in the Middle East.

PII had operated as a distinct entity under various ownerships during the company's growth and evolution. In September 1990, PII was acquired by Belgian-based Redmain Industries and became a member of the Redmain Heat Transfer Group. Redmain Industries was one of the largest privately held corporations in Europe, with over 15,000 employees worldwide. Under Redmain ownership, PII became a world-leading designer and manufacturer of a wide range of specialized heat transfer equipment. Employment at the plant grew to 240 people, and current year sales were forecasted to be $50 million.

Purchasing at PII. Abbey Paquette was responsible for purchasing and materials management activities at the plant. She negotiated contracts with suppliers, scheduled deliveries, and managed raw material inventories. A major challenge presented by these responsibilities was carrying sufficient inventories to ensure that material was always available for manufacturing operations. Abbey recognized, however, that holding material in inventory unnecessarily could be expensive for the company.

Edict from the New President. Abbey had arrived at the office early Monday morning and was surprised to find many people already hard at work. She checked her e-mail, as she did first thing every morning, and discovered a personal e-mail from Isaac Chisholm, PII's new President, that simply read:

> "Presently this site's annual inventory carrying costs are close to two and a half million — this number should be reduced to zero by year-end. Please get back to me with some suggestions on how we may approach this goal. I offer my full support in this initiative."

Isaac Chisholm had taken over as President of PII on August 3 with a mandate to improve PII's poor financial performance. Within just a few days several drastic changes were already apparent.

After reading the e-mail, Abbey's heart sank as she began to think about what an enormous request had just been made. She realized that the fact that inventory levels had been allowed to reach such levels reflected very poorly on her and, consequently, Abbey was anxious to solve the problem. Her immediate reaction was to contact the company's other purchasing agent, Karen Black. Karen and Abbey agreed that they needed to clear their schedules and dedicate the following week entirely to identifying what could be done. They enlisted the support of the Production Manager, Kathleen Deholihan, and the Accounting Manager, Marty Sullivan.

The Investigation

Carrying Costs. The group met with the company Controller, David Ellis, on Tuesday morning. During the meeting, David explained to the team that the term "carrying cost" referred to money that was tied up in inventory but that could otherwise be applied to other "value-added activities." It also included, according to David, other costs such as handling, storage, and obsolescence. He indicated that PII used a rate of 20 percent for calculating inventory holding costs. David went on to point out that the value of the materials and the length of time in inventory contributed to inventory carrying costs.

David also reminded Abbey and the others that PII incurred costs each time an order was placed. He estimated that the variable costs of placing an order with a supplier were about $50.

Inventory Tracking and Control. When the team began to investigate the present inventory tracking and control procedures, Abbey and Karen were shocked to discover that the database from which they drew their inventory information and based decisions for new component orders was filled with outdated and inaccurate information. It was discovered that the inventory clerk had been fired a few months earlier and had not been replaced. Instead, the forklift drivers who "pulled" components from the warehouse for use in manufacturing were expected to enter the information into the database regarding what they had removed from stock.

One of the forklift drivers, Rick, indicated that when things were busy in production, he just jotted information on a pad of paper what had been pulled, and then entered the information when things slowed down a bit. He admitted that, at times, engineers and other line operators pulled parts themselves without recording the information.

Recognizing that the existing inventory data was suspect, the team decided to dedicate two full days, Wednesday and Thursday, to completing an inventory count. When the count was completed the team discovered a number of inventory record errors, including several charges to inventory carrying costs for items that were no longer in stock.

Supplier Agreements. After a grueling couple of days involved in the inventory count, the team turned their attention to analyzing supplier agreements. Abbey and Karen found that many of the supplier agreements were based on large batch orders. For example, PII ordered component BD-517 from a local supplier at a cost of $26.75 each, with a minimum order quantity of 2,000 pieces. However, weekly usage of the BD-517 was approximately 500 pieces.

Developing a Plan

By Friday, Abbey felt that the team had accomplished a lot since Monday. She now had to turn her attention to deciding what steps needed to be taken next. Long hours had been spent updating the database, but Abbey knew that rehiring a clerk would not be possible in the present environment and, consequently, she wondered what she should do in order to improve the situation. She also recognized that in order to reduce inventory carrying costs PII's investment in raw materials would have to be reduced. Before she could go home to her family and relax for the weekend, Abbey knew she had to come up with a definitive plan of action that she could present to Isaac Chisholm Monday morning.

CASE 6–4
CORN SILK

On January 7, Kim Hutton, Commodity Purchasing Manager for Corn Silk Inc. (CSI), a wet corn mill located in Iowa, had just heard that plant production was scheduled to operate at 70 percent of capacity for the next three months. Having already signed the contracts to purchase corn for full production capacity, and concerned about available storage bin capacity, she had only a week to decide on a course of action.

Company Background. CSI started its Iowa plant in 1858 and built additional plants in the West subsequently. Through the process of wet milling, CSI transformed corn into both consumer and industrial products. Each day thousands of bushels of corn were processed into such items as corn starches, corn syrups, gluten feed, gluten meal and corn oil.

The Iowa plant employed 100 people and had remained profitable over the years. This plant handled purchases and sales for its smaller Minnesota counterpart. Maximum daily production capacity at Iowa was 50,000 bushels/day. Minnesota was 30,000 bushels/day. Major customers included large soda and food companies. The company dealt with 800 suppliers.

As the primary raw material was corn, CSI dealt with the uncertainties of the agricultural industry. Prices depended largely upon uncontrollable variables, such as weather and corn market prices.

Kim Hutton. As a Commodity Purchasing Manager, Kim handled all corn purchases for the Iowa and Minnesota plants. She ensured prompt corn delivery and maintained supplier relations. The production plans and storage capacities of the two plants affected her purchase quantities.

Normally, Ms. Hutton made her purchases month by month. For example, in September she bought the full amount of corn needed for production in October. However, an exception was made for the months of January until March because most suppliers took their holidays after the harvest ended and before the spring planting. Exhibit 1 provides a list of January–March purchase commitments.

Many factors influenced her daily buying decisions, including price and quality. Delivery was especially important as Kim's priority was to keep the two plants in operation. Quantities were purchased by month on a full production basis, without input from the sales department. Daily purchases were made from a suppliers list, while futures were bought through the Chicago Board of Trade, with the use of her desktop computer. On average, Kim acquired and facilitated the delivery of $40 million worth of corn per year for the Iowa plant, at an average cost of $2.50/bushel, and $27 million worth of corn for the Minnesota sister plant.

The Dilemma. Kim was first alerted to the problem on January 7, after overhearing a conversation between two sales managers that both the Iowa and Minnesota plants would be operating at 70 percent for the following three months. Further investigation confirmed that this was indeed the plan.

Normally, the plant had capacity for four days worth of storage. However, according to the daily report, during the last two days production had only reached 89 percent of capacity, revealing that she would have to include this unused corn in her calculations of available storage capacity. Being the first week of January Kim had already signed the contracts to purchase corn based on a 100 percent production capacity for the three-month period ending March 31.

It was industry policy for suppliers to charge producers $30/ hour in 'demurrage' fees after two hours if their truck waited at the facility to unload. Incidents of delayed truck deliveries would cause Kim's costs to increase drastically.

To have the extra corn held in storage would cost $0.03/bushel per month. Otherwise, Kim could attempt to "wash the contract," selling the corn at the current spot price. Whether this resulted in a gain or loss depended on the current supply and demand for corn.

Finally, Kim wondered about the plausibility of deferring every supplier's deliveries by 30 percent. This alternative would allow Kim to have corn lined up for coming months. However, it was common knowledge that suppliers preferred a high turnover rate, as it prevented rotting of the corn seed. Supplier relationships were important to CSI and Kim questioned how they would react to a significant change in delivery schedules.

Kim wondered what action she should take. Financial issues, such as carrying costs, had to be weighed against the value of long-term supplier relationships. Deciding which suppliers to deal with and the nature of any proposed changes would influence her ability to meet future requirements. In the meantime, she was all too aware that a decision had to be made quickly before CSI started incurring demurrage costs.

EXHIBIT 1   Corn Purchase Commitments for January–March

Supplier Name	Purchase Commitments In Tonnes[*] as at Jan. 7		
	Jan. 1–Jan. 25	*Jan.26–Feb. 22*	*Feb.23–Mar 29*
A	7794.90	2735.03	44.66
B	389.31	2141.87	9195.09
C	2848.63	1143.81	48.15
D	2019.21	14932.83	1965.61
E	12539.64	3573.38	1648.35
F	3599.73	78.51	21478.92
G	33.82	204.71	3515.09
H	247.68	40.26	468.84
I	2515.22	2293.26	340.09
J	555.89	35.62	7112.46
K	115.61	270.22	857.20
L	33.76	431.42	28.69
M	426.92	38.06	12.44
N	912.56	32.51	10954.61
O	77.26	1548.00	965.62
P	899.10	37.94	3756.00
Q	75.02	189.51	431.00
R	290.19	498.18	577.25
S	10365.45	74.59	6.79
T	660.38	4101.44	254.00
U	1125.18	876.24	508.00
V	130.41	2324.65	40.70
W	552.19	214.89	
X	37.31	709.63	
Y		81.31	
Z		49.02	
Total	48245.37	38656.89	64209.56

[*]1 Tonne = 39.368 Bushels

7 SUPPLIER SELECTION

Chapter Outline

Key Questions for the Purchasing Decision Maker

SHOULD WE
- Use teams to select suppliers?
- Use one or more suppliers?
- Switch from informal to formal supplier evaluation?

HOW CAN WE
- Analyze suppliers better?
- Create new sources of supply?
- Avoid ethical difficulties?

Sourcing and Supplier Selection

Effective sourcing decisions form the basis of creating a sound supply base for any organization. In this and the next chapter the major factors influencing supplier choice and development are discussed. This chapter focuses on finding and evaluating suppliers and examining issues of supplier number, location and size, and ethics. The next chapter examines make or buy, outsourcing, supplier relations, strategic sourcing, and supply chain management.

The Supplier Selection Decision

The Weighting of Objectives Varies Depending on the Nature of the Buy

The decision to place a certain volume of business with a supplier should always be based on a reasonable set of criteria. The art of good purchasing is to make the reasoning behind this decision as sound as possible. Normally, the purchaser's perception of the supplier's ability to meet satisfactory quality, quantity, delivery, price, and service objectives will govern this decision. Some of the more important supplier attributes related to these prime purchasing objectives may include past history, facilities and technical strength, financial status, organization and management, reputation, systems, procedural compliance, communications, labor relations, and location. Obviously, the nature and the amount of the purchase will influence the weighting attached to each objective and hence the evidence that needs to be provided to support the selection decision. For example, for a small order of new circuit boards to be used by engineers in a new product design, the quality and rapid delivery are of greater significance than price. The supplier should probably be local for ease of communication with the design engineers and have good technical credentials. On the other hand, a large printed circuit board order for a production run would have price as one of the key factors, and delivery should be on time, but not necessarily unusually fast. Thus, even on requirements with identical technical specifications, the weighting attached to the supplier selection criteria may vary. It is this sensitivity to organizational needs that separates the good buyer from the average. The one result every buyer wishes to avoid is unacceptable supplier performance. This may create costs far out of proportion to the size of the original purchase; it upsets cross-functional relations; and it strains supplier goodwill and ultimate customer satisfaction.

Risk Assessment and Risk Management

Supply Decisions Must Fit the Organization's Risk Profile

Risk management is the way in which an organization's management makes decisions about the risks it is willing to take in light of the expected returns. A company's risk management process should identify and communicate the organizational risk and return expectations, monitor and measure risks taken, control risk, and provide for corrective action when necessary. Overall, the process needs to be structured to aggregate individual risks to determine if an organization is at an acceptable risk level companywide. Risk management includes actions that avoid risks, mitigate risks, transfer risk, insure against risk, limit risk, or explicitly take the risk.[1] For the buyer or supply manager, it is essential to consider each decision in the context of the organization's risk profile.

Risk Assessment Is a Factor in Supplier Selection

Research into the risk assessment behavior of buyers shows that the perceived risk of placing business with an untried and unknown supplier is high. Likewise, the perceived risk associated with routine, repetitive purchases is much less than the risk of new or less standard acquisitions. In general, the risk is seen to be higher with unknown materials, parts, equipment, or suppliers and with increased dollar amounts. Buyers can take a number of actions to avoid, mitigate, transfer, limit, or insure against risk. For example, a buyer may attempt to transfer risk by asking for advice, such as engineering judgment; or by seeking additional information, including placing a trial order; or by hedging in the commodities market. The buyer may require bid bonds, performance bonds, or payment bonds to insure against risk; or avoid risk by not doing business with suppliers in certain countries; or mitigate risk by dual or multiple sourcing rather than single sourcing. The buyer may limit risk by negotiating payment terms that allow progress payments when certain milestones are met, but withhold a percentage of the payment until completion and acceptance of the service provided. When a buyer takes an action such as selecting a supplier, or switching suppliers, or agreeing to certain terms and conditions, he or she should take these actions with the explicit understanding of both the risk at which the decision puts the organization, the return expected, and the balance between the two. The buyer's assessment of the trade-off between risk and reward in isolation and in the aggregate should guide the buyer's decisions.

According to Cynthia Glassman, a principal with Ernst & Young's Risk Management and Regulatory Practice, there are internal and external factors

---

[1]Cynthia Glassman, "The Last Word: An Evolution in Risk Strategy," *The RMA Journal,* October 2000, found on Ernst & Young's Web site, *www.ey.com*, April 17, 2001.

Internal and External Factors Affect Risk Profile

that affect an organization's risk profile. External factors include changes in the economy, competitive factors, legislative and regulatory changes, and the availability of new technology. In late 2000, the growth of Internet applications led to an expected boom in e-commerce, which led many business people to jump on the e-business train. The unexpected bust of many dot.coms led to a "wait-and-see" attitude among more cautious managers. Internal factors include changes in organization or leadership, new strategies, new products or variations on old ones, and the use of new technology, distribution channels, or processes. In late 2000, a number of organizations retooled the purchasing process by applying new technology to gain efficiencies. These new strategies included e-procurement systems for purchasing indirect materials, reverse auctions, and online bidding (See Chapter 4 for more detail).

Portfolio Analysis

One approach to risk management is to categorize purchases according to a portfolio matrix (see Figure 7–1) which characterizes goods or services that fall

FIGURE 7–1

Supply Risks and Dollars Extended

RISKS

High

High	**Bottleneck**	**Strategic**
	▪ Unique Specification ▪ Supplier's technology is important ▪ Production-based scarcity due to low demand and/or few sources of supply ▪ Substitution is difficult ▪ Usage fluctuates and is not routinely predictable ▪ Potential storage risk	▪ Continuous availability is essential to the operation ▪ Custom design or unique specifications ▪ Supplier technology is important ▪ Few suppliers with adequate technical capability or capacity ▪ Changing source of supply is difficult ▪ Substitution is difficult.
Low	**Non-Critical** ▪ Standard specification or "Commodity" type items ▪ Substitute products readily available ▪ Competitive supply market with many suppliers	**Leverage** ▪ Unit cost management is important because of volume of usage. ▪ Substitution is possible ▪ Competitive supply market with several sources

Low

| Low | **VALUE** | High |

Source: Adapted from Peter Kraljic, "Purchasing Must Become Supply Management," *Harvard Business Review,* September–October 1983.

in each quadrant. From this analysis the actual goods and services purchased by an organization can be placed in the appropriate quadrant, and decisions can then be made as to the most appropriate tools for each type of transaction.

Decision Trees

Decision Making Under Uncertainty

The supplier selection decision can be seen as decision making under uncertainty and can be represented by a decision tree. Figure 7–2 shows a very simple, one-stage situation with only two suppliers seriously considered and two possible outcomes. It illustrates, however, the uncertain environment present in almost every supplier choice and the risk inherent in the decision. To use decision trees effectively, the buyer must identify the options, the criteria for evaluation, and assess the probabilities of success and failure. This simple tree could apply to a special one-time purchase without expectation of follow-on business for some time to come.

The more normal situation for repetitive purchases is shown in Figure 7–3. Whether the chosen source performs well or not for the current purchase under consideration, the future decision about which supplier to deal with next time around may well affect the present decision. For example, if the business is placed with supplier C and C fails, then this may mean that only A could be considered a reasonable source at the next stage. If having A as a single source, without alternatives, is not acceptable, choosing C as the supplier at the first stage does not make any sense.

It is necessary to consider the selection decision as part of a chain of events, rather than as an isolated instance. This addition of a time-frame—past, present, and future—makes the sourcing decision even more complex. However, as

FIGURE 7–2

A Simple One-Stage Supplier Selection Decision

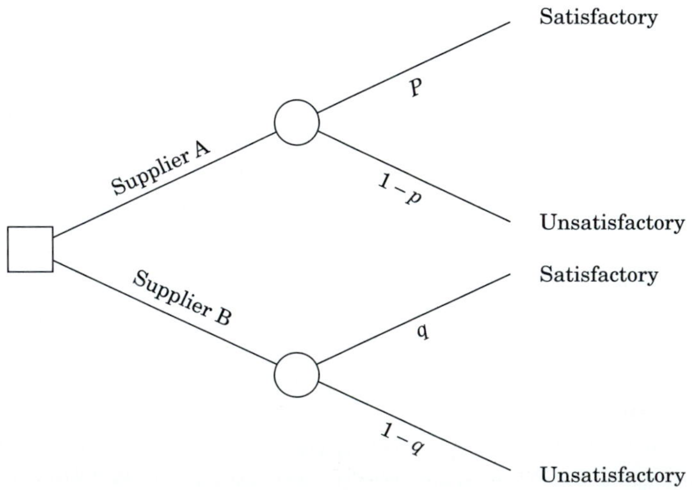

FIGURE 7–3

Simplified Three-Stage Decision Tree for Supplier Selection

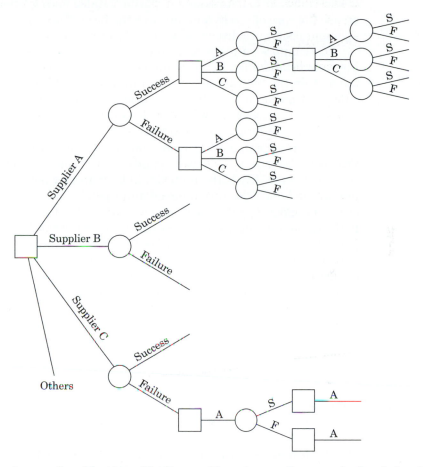

long as the objective of finding and keeping good sources is clearly kept in mind, the decision can be evaluated in a reasonable business context.

Sources of Information about Suppliers

Knowledge of sources is a primary qualification for any effective buyer. The normal principal sources consist of catalogs (online, printed, and microfilm), trade journals, advertisements of various sorts, supplier and commodity directories, the Internet, sales interviews, colleagues, professional contacts, and the purchasing department's own records.

Many Types of Catalogs Exist

Catalogs. Catalogs of the commonly known sources of supply, covering the most important materials in which a company is interested, are essential in any well-managed purchasing department. The value of such catalogs depends largely on the form in which they are presented, the readiness with which the material contained in them is available, and the use which is made of such information. Advances in online catalog management continue to increase the ease of access and improve the form of presentation. Catalog management issues are discussed in detail in Chapter 4.

Distributors' catalogs contain many items from a variety of manufacturing sources and offer, to a certain extent, a directory of available commodities within the distributors' fields. Equipment and machinery catalogs provide information as to the specifications of, and the location of a source of supply for, replacement parts as well as new equipment. Catalogs frequently provide price information. Many supplies and materials are sold from standard list prices, and quotations are made by quoting discounts only. Catalogs are also reference books called for by department heads and engineers.

The availability of the material in the catalogs is largely a matter of the manner in which they are indexed and filed, a not-so-simple task even with online catalogs. Catalogs are issued in all sorts of sizes and formats, which make them difficult to handle. Proper indexing of catalogs is essential. Some firms use online catalogs or computer or microfilm files, others loose-leaf ledgers with sheets especially printed for catalog filing; others use a form of a card index. Indexing should be according to suppliers' names as well as products listed. It should be specific, definite, and easily understandable.

Online Catalogs

Online catalogs (discussed in Chapter 4) are increasingly used by buyers. The advantage of online catalogs is that both buyers and internal customers have ready access to them, and they can be customized to include the prices and other terms and conditions negotiated by the buyer with the seller. As discussed in Chapter 4, management of online catalog content is as serious an issue as management of hard-copy catalogs. Managing the customized content of the catalogs is a separate issue from accessing and managing the generic catalog information available to all buyers.

Content and Advertising Useful

Trade Journals. Trade journals also are a valuable source of information as to potential suppliers. The list of such publications is, of course, very long, and the individual items in it vary tremendously in value. Yet, in every field there are worthwhile trade magazines, and buyers read extensively those dealing with their own industry and with those industries to which they sell and from which they buy. These journals are utilized in two ways. The first use is a study of the text, which not only adds to a buyer's general information but suggests new products and substitute materials. The trade gossip provides information about suppliers and their personnel. The second use has to do with advertising. A consistent perusal of the advertisements in such publications is a worthwhile habit cultivated by all keen buyers.

Trade Directories. Trade directories are another useful source of information. They vary widely in their accuracy and usefulness, and care must be exercised in their use. Trade registers, or trade directories, are volumes that list leading manufacturers, their addresses, number of branches, affiliations,

Directories are Sorted by Commodity, Manufacturer, and Trade Name

products, and, in some instances, their financial standing or their position in the trade. They also contain listings of the trade names of articles on the market with names of the manufacturers, and classified lists of materials, supplies, equipment, and other items offered for sale, under each of which is given the name and location of available manufacturing sources of supply. These registers, then, are so arranged that they may be consulted either by way of the commodity, the manufacturer, or the trade name.

Such standard directories as, for example, *Thomas Register of American Manufacturers, MacRae's Blue Book* and the Kompass publications in Europe, not to mention the more specialized directories, serve a useful purpose. Many trade directories, including the *Thomas Register,* are available online. The Yellow Pages of telephone directories provide lists of local suppliers.

Trade directories of minority- and women-owned business enterprises can assist purchasers with a goal or requirement to increase the percentage of contracts awarded to these firms. For example, Pro-Net (*www.pronet.sba.gov*) is an online database maintained by the U.S. Small Business Administration (SBA) containing information on small, disadvantaged, 8(a), and women-owned businesses. Searches can be based on SIC Codes, keywords, location, quality certifications, business type, and ownership race and gender. *TRY US Resources* was established in 1968 to foster minority economic development through the publication of directories of minority- and women-owned business (*www.tryusdir. com*). A number of organizations also certify businesses as minority- and women-owned, including the Women's Business Enterprise National Council (WBENC), *www.wbenc.org*; the National Women Business Owners Corporation (NWBOC), *www.wboc.org*; the National Minority Supplier Development Council (NMSDC), *www.nmsdcus.org*; and in the public sector, the Office of Small Disadvantaged Business Utilization (OSDBU), *www.sbu.gov/GC/OSDBU.html*.

Sales Representation. Sales representatives may constitute one of the most valuable sources of information available, with references to sources of supply, types of products, and trade information generally. An alert buyer makes it a point to see as many sales representatives as possible without neglecting other duties. It is essential to develop good supplier relations that begin with a friendly, courteous, sympathetic, and frank attitude toward the supplier salesperson. The buyer should endeavor not to waste any time. After the visit, a record is made of the call, together with new information obtained.

Salespersons are Valuable Information Sources

Some purchasers make it a point to see personally every sales representative who calls at the office; others, because of lack of time and the pressure of other duties, are unable to follow such a rule, but they do make sure that someone interviews every visitor in order that no one may go away feeling rebuffed.

Ethical Dealings between Sales Representatives and Purchasers

Most organizations have policies and procedures concerning the relations between the purchasing office and suppliers' representatives. Purchasing and materials management associations in many countries around the world

Courtesy, Honesty, and Fairness are Hallmarks of Good Buyers

have adopted their own codes of ethics governing the relationship between supplier and purchaser. All of them are based on the requirement that both supplier and purchaser need to deal ethically with one another to ensure a sound basis for business dealings. Thus, courtesy, honesty, and fairness are stressed and buyers are urged to behave in such a fashion as to reflect the organization's wishes. Normally, this includes seeing suppliers without delay, to be truthful in all statements, to cover all elements of procurement in order that the final understanding may be complete, to not ask suppliers to quote unless they have a reasonable chance at the business, to keep specifications fair and clear and competition open and fair, to respect the confidence of suppliers with regard to all confidential information, not to take advantage improperly of sellers' errors, to cooperate with suppliers in solving their difficulties, and to negotiate prompt and fair adjustment in cases of dispute. It is also expected that a buyer be courteous in stating rejection of bids with explanations that are reasonable, but not to betray confidential information, to answer letters promptly, and to handle samples, tests, and reports with prompt, complete, and truthful information. Lastly, all codes of ethics stress a need to avoid all obligations to sellers except strict business obligations. A more complete treatment of ethics is included at the end of this chapter.

Keeping Purchasing in the Supplier Selection Loop

Occasionally, sales representatives attempt to avoid the purchasing department because they believe it may be to their advantage to do so. If the supplier secures an order without the knowledge and agreement of purchasing, internal dissension may be created, as well as resentment against the sales representative. The short-term gain may turn into a long-term loss. Although purchasing personnel are expected to be well acquainted with the organization's operation, equipment, materials, and its varied requirements, and to be qualified to pass on the practicality of suggestions and proposals that may be made by sales representatives and technical people, the purchaser does not, as a rule, have the background that constitutes the basis for the technical person's special knowledge. Therefore, it is often necessary to refer such proposals to others better qualified to handle them. However, the best way for a new supplier to reach the right people in any organization is through purchasing. In situations where cross-functional sourcing teams are used, different team members may manage the supplier relationship for their primary area of concern. The team approach lessens the fears of individual members that others will make decisions that are not in their best interests.

In a partnering relationship or a buyer-supplier alliance, discussed in Chapter 8, it is normal to have a substantial amount of regular direct contact between supplier personnel and nonpurchasing people in the buyer's organization. Direct contacts are not normally part of the supplier selection decision but are essential to the effective execution of the contract and maintenance of a superior working relationship.

Supplier and Commodity Files. Information from any source, if of value, should be recorded. One such record has already been mentioned, the index accompanying the catalog file. Another common record is the supplier file, commonly on small cards or a simple computer file, classified by name of supplier. Such files contain information concerning the address of the supplier, past orders placed with the company, supplier performance evaluation records, and other pertinent information of any sort that might be of value to the buyer.

Another valuable record is a commodity file, in which material is classified on the basis of the product. The information in such files relates to the sources from which the product has been purchased in the past, perhaps the price paid, the point of shipment, and a cross-reference to the supplier file. Miscellaneous information is also given, such as whether specifications are called for, whether a contract already exists covering the item, whether competitive bids are commonly asked for, and other data which may be of importance. Accompanying files dealing with sources are, of course, those relating to price and other records. Some of these have already been discussed in earlier chapters, and others will be discussed later. The information management aspects of enterprise resource planning (ERP) systems and e-procurement systems are discussed in Chapter 4.

The Internet

Internet Resources Abound

The Internet and the World Wide Web provide a rapidly growing and ever-changing body of information for purchasers. The challenge for most buyers is not finding information, but identifying, sorting, analyzing, and using relevant information. The following brief list contains Web addresses for some sites of interests to purchasers.

Internet—World Wide Web Sites—Purchasing Chemical Abstracts *www. acs.org* This is the home page of the American Chemical Society. There is also a members-only section which requires a membership/access fee.

NAPM Home Page *www.napm.org* This is the home page for the National Association of Purchasing Management in the United States. Many of the resources are available to members only. The site includes the monthly manufacturing and nonmanufacturing Reports on Business, considered leading indicators of economic activity in the United States.

PMAC *www.pmac.ca* This is the home page for the Purchasing Management Association of Canada.

Ivey Purchasing Managers Index *www.iveypmi.uwo.ca* The Richard Ivey School of Business at the University of Western Ontario initiated a Canadian Purchasing Managers Index in 2000. The index includes goods, services, and government. It is released seven days after the first working day of each month at 10 a.m. Eastern Standard Time on the Ivey Web site.

Government of Canada *www.canada.gc.ca/* The main home page of all Web sites for the Canadian government. From here you can go to any Canadian government department having a Web page. If you are looking for information on the North American Free Trade Agreement, look under Foreign Affairs.

Primark Financial Information Division *www.primark.com* Provides financial information on U.S. and international companies through flexible delivery platforms.

United States Securities and Exchange Commission *www.sec.gov* All companies in the United States that file their quarterly 10Q and annual 10K reports are on this database. As of May 1996, all public companies are required to file electronically. These are big reports full of interesting information, mainly financial in nature, although you never know what might be included.

Dun & Bradstreet *www.dnb.com* Provides basic company reports online for a fee. No financial information is available online; it reports the company's location and products.

Thomas Register of American Manufacturers *www.thomasregister. com* This is the no-charge (yes, free) online version and allows you to look up sources with a simple two-word search. It provides company names, addresses, and telephone numbers, but no detail on the company and what other products they produce. It includes listings for more than 156,000 companies in the United States and Canada and more than 7,700 online supplier catalogs and Web links. Order Online is Thomas Register's electronic commerce service.

WorldPages.com *www.worldpages.com* An Internet and Yellow Pages directory company with listings in the United States and Canada and links to more than 350 international directories. It also links to a directory of toll-free (800/888) numbers in the United States.

World Wide Yellow Pages *www.yellow.com/* This is exactly what it says, a worldwide listing of companies. It is not complete; lots of companies are not listed but more are being added all the time.

Ziff Davis Media Publications *www.zdnet.com* An excellent resource for online magazines (e-zines) with up-to-the-minute information on e-commerce.

Visits to Suppliers. Some supply executives feel that visits to suppliers are particularly useful when there are no difficulties to discuss. The supply manager can talk with higher executives rather than confining discussion to someone who happens to be directly responsible for handling a specific complaint. This helps to cement good relations at all levels of management and may reveal much about a supplier's future plans that might not otherwise come to the buyer's attention. Such a visitation policy does raise certain problems not found in the more routine types of visits, such as who should make the visits, how best to get worthwhile information, and the best use of the data once obtained. Experience has indicated that in order to get the best results from such trips, it is desirable (1) to draw up in advance a general outline of the kinds of information to be sought; (2) to gather all reasonably available information, both general and specific, about the company in advance of the trip; and (3) to prepare a detailed report of the findings, once the visit is completed. When the visits are carefully planned, the direct expense incurred is small compared with the returns.

Samples. In addition to the usual inquiries concerning the potential supplier and a plant visit, samples of the supplier's product can be tested. Some thought may well be devoted, therefore, to the problem of how to handle what may be called the "sample problem." Frequently, a sales representative for a new product urges the buyer to accept a sample for test purposes. This raises questions as to what samples to accept, how to ensure a fair test of those accepted, who should bear the expense of testing, and whether or not the supplier should be given the results of the test. (See "Testing and Samples" in Chapter 4.)

Colleagues. Frequently, colleagues inside the organization in nonsupply positions may be valuable sources of information about potential sources of supply. Purchase requisitions may contain an empty space for the requisitioner to identify potential sources.

References. Often buyers will include a request for references in the RFQ, RFP, or IFB. Because the supplier will likely give references who will give positive feedback, it is the job of the interviewer to get the needed information. First, make sure that the reference is a company of similar size and objectives. Second, talk to people with firsthand knowledge of the supplier's performance. Third, ask open-ended questions that allow the reference to describe the performance of the supplier and the relationship. For example, a new customer might be asked about the implementation process: "Did it go smoothly? Tell me about a time when things weren't going according to plan. How did the supplier deal with the problem or change?" A veteran customer might be asked about the supplier's actions to stay competitive or to continuously improve: "Tell me about a time when the supplier initiated an

(Margin headings:)

Guidelines for Site Visits

Decisions About Samples

Effective Use of References

improvement that also benefited you (the customer)?" Past customers might be asked about the transition process to another supplier: When you switched suppliers, how did the original supplier handle the transition of information? materials? etc.?"[2]

Narrowing the List

Matching Evaluation to Type of Purchase

From any or all of these various sources of information, the buyer is able to make up a list of available suppliers from whom the necessary items can be acquired. The next step is to reduce this list to workable length, retaining only the most likely sources of supply. From this short list, the best source (or sources, if more than one are to be used) must be selected. Obviously, the extent to which the investigation and analysis of sources is carried will depend on the cost and the importance of the item involved. Many items are so inexpensive and are consumed in such small quantities as to render any studied investigation unwise.

In reducing the number of potential suppliers to a practical list or in passing on the desirability of a new supplier (either for a new product or for one already being used), it is obvious that an adequate study must be made of each supplier's qualifications. The investigation required may be drawn out and extensive. It may well require joint inquiry by the buyer, cooperating with representatives of using and technical departments such as engineering, quality control, systems, and maintenance on an informal or formal team or task force.

Supplier Evaluation

Existing and Potential Sources

The evaluation of suppliers is a continuing task. Current suppliers have to be monitored to see if expected performance materializes. New sources need to be screened to see if their potential warrants serious future consideration. Because most organizations tend to place a significant portion of repetitive business with the same suppliers, evaluation of current sources will be discussed first.

Informal and Formal Evaluation of Current Suppliers

Two Types of Current Suppliers

A current supplier is one that has passed through earlier supplier screening efforts and subsequently received, at a minimum, one order. Most buyers would tend to separate current suppliers into at least two categories. Some

---

[2]Chuck Stefanosky, "Don't be Afraid to Dig Deep," *Purchasing Today,* November 1999, pp. 10–11.

suppliers are still so new to the supplier force that it is not clear just how good they are. The second group constitutes "established suppliers" who over the past have proven to be reliable, good sources. Both groups are evaluated continuously, formally and informally. Nevertheless, it is common practice to pay extra special attention to those new sources who have not yet established a proven track record of satisfactory performance over time under a variety of market conditions.

Informal Evaluation. Informal evaluation includes assessments of personal contacts between supplier and personnel in the purchaser's organization in all functions where such contact takes place. "How are things going with supplier X?" is a typical question that can and should be asked by supply personnel when in contact with others in their own organization. Similarly, street talk obtained at professional meetings, conferences, and from the media can be useful in checking out and comparing such personal impressions. A knowledgeable buyer will have accumulated a wealth of such information on suppliers and will always be on the alert for signs that new information may affect the overall assessment of a supplier. In fact, in most small organizations almost all evaluation of current sources is carried out informally. When users and buyers are in daily personal contact and feedback on both satisfactory and unsatisfactory supplier performance is quick, such informality makes a lot of sense.

Size of the Organization Affects Type of Evaluation

In larger organizations, however, communication lines are stretched, purchasers and users may be in totally different locations, and large contracts may be agreed to by a head office purchasing group or a prime contractor located at one of the main using locations, while daily supplier contact is handled at various locations. If suppliers are also large, requirements in different locations of the country or the world may be met with varying degrees of success by different plants belonging to the same supplier. As the buying organization grows larger, therefore, the need to have a more formal system for evaluating current sources also increases.

Executive Round Table Discussions. One simple semiformal supplier evaluation tool is the regular, annual discussion between top managers in the purchaser's organization and those of the supplier. Normally, these top-level discussions are confined to major suppliers of major or strategic requirements. The presence of top executives of both sides lends weight to the occasion and permits discussion of past performance; future expectations; economic, social, and technological trends; long-term plans; and so on, in a high-level context. The person in charge of the supply function normally makes the arrangements for such sessions and invites the appropriate executives to take part. These round table discussions can help cement relationships between the purchaser and supplier at a high level, and when repeated over time can provide invaluable information for both sides. They would normally, but not exclusively, take place on the purchaser's premises.

A Form of Semi-Formal Evaluation

Obviously, the number of such high-level sessions must be limited. Equivalent lower-level sessions for suppliers further down on the priority list also have considerable merit and permit a regular update in a broader context than the normal supplier-purchaser contacts geared to specific current orders.

Formal Supplier Evaluation and Rating.   In evaluating current sources, the obvious question is "How well did the supplier do?" As orders are delivered, it should be possible to keep track of whether quality, quantity, price, delivery, and service objectives and other terms and conditions were met. Most formal supplier rating schemes attempt to track actual performance over time. Thus, corrective action can be taken as needed. Also, when the time for placing another order arrives, the past record can be used to assess whether the same supplier should again be seriously considered or not.

Factors Included In Formal Rating Systems

Most formal supplier rating schemes track supplier performance on quality, price, delivery, and service. A very simple scheme for smaller organizations might include a notation only as to whether these factors were acceptable or not for specific orders received. More detailed evaluations include a summary of supplier performance over time.

Quality Performance

It is normal to track a supplier's quality performance very closely and in sufficient detail to enable the pinpointing of corrective action. In many organizations, only certified suppliers are considered for potential future business, and extensive evaluations on quality and other dimensions of supplier attributes and performance are carried out accordingly (see Chapter 5).

Delivery Performance

Delivery performance of a current supplier is fairly easily tracked if good records exist of delivery promises and actual receipts and few modifications have been made on an informal basis. In a JIT mode, nonperformance on delivery is just as critical as unsatisfactory quality, and actual delivery is closely monitored.

Example of Delivery Evaluation

Top rating:	*a.* Meets delivery dates without expediting.
	b. Requested delivery dates are usually accepted.
Good:	*c.* Usually meets shipping dates without substantial follow-up.
	d. Often is able to accept requested delivery dates.
Fair:	*e.* Shipments sometimes late, substantial amount of follow-up required.
Unsatisfactory:	*f.* Shipments usually late, delivery promises seldom met, constant expediting required.

Price Performance

Actual price performance of a supplier is easily tracked, as discrepancies between agreed-to prices and those actually invoiced by suppliers should normally be brought to purchasing's attention anyway. Price ratings of suppliers are, therefore, often of a comparison type, actual price versus target, or actual price versus lowest price received from other suppliers supplying the same requirement.

Service Performance

It is in the service area that perhaps most judgment is called for. Opinions need to be collected on the quality of technical assistance, supplier attitude and response time to requests for assistance, support staff qualifications, and so on. It is normal, therefore, to have a relatively simple rating scheme for service, such as outstanding, acceptable, and poor, along with explanations regarding specific incidents to explain these ratings.

Other Evaluation Criteria

Accompanying the trend to supplier base reduction, strategic sourcing, and closer relations with key suppliers is the growing sophistication in supplier performance rating. In the IPC case at the end of this chapter, for example, continuous improvement is tracked along with more traditional factors. In other cases, suggestions for product or service redesign, value-chain improvements, willingness to work on supply-chain teams, assistance in disposal, or the development of anything that would provide better value for the ultimate customer may be tracked and become part of the permanent record.

Weighted Point Evaluation Systems. Many organizations rate suppliers by assigning points and scales to each factor and each rating. Where several sources supply the same goods or services, such schemes permit cross-comparisons. Outstanding performance of a supplier can then be rewarded with additional business, while poor performance may result in the development and implementation of a performance improvement plan, or lead

Example of a Formal Evaluation Instrument

to less business with the supplier, or possibly dropping a supplier altogether. The IPC case at the end of this chapter provides a good example of a weighted point evaluation system and how it applies to a specific supplier. (See page 287)

Process for Developing a Weighted Point Evaluation Process

Several issues are of concern with weighted point evaluation systems. The typical process for developing a weighted point evaluation system is to (1) identify the factors or criteria for evaluation, (2) determine the importance of each factor, and (3) establish a system for rating each supplier on each factor. The relevant factors or decision criteria should be determined in the context of the purchase. Clearly, most organizations track major suppliers much more closely than those sources deemed to have less impact on organizational performance. Some organizations use annual dollar volume as a guide toward such categorization, for example, identifying A, B, and C sources, much the same as inventories can be classified using the Pareto distribution (see Chapters 3 and 5). Some organizations add a special category of "critical" goods or services regardless of dollar volume, where unsatisfactory performance by a supplier might result in serious problems for the organization. The purpose of such categorization is to fit each category with an appropriate supplier rating scheme. For example, for a high-value, high-volume purchase over a long-term contract, the buyer may include factors such as the supplier's management, human resources, and information systems fit. For a C-item (low dollar

Classifying Suppliers to Track Performance

value, high volume), the critical factors may be delivery, availability, convenience, and price. There are a number of ways to assign weight to the factors. One is to assign percentages to each factor for a total of 100 percent. Another approach is to assign each factor a weight of 1, 2, or 3, where 1 equals critical to the organization's success, 2 equals neutral, and 3 equals noncritical. The latter approach may result in weighting all factors of highest importance rather than truly determining the key factors that should drive the decision-making process.

Obviously, the selection of the factors, weights, and form of measurement will require considerable thought to ensure congruence between the organization's priorities for this product class and the rating scheme's ability to identify superior suppliers correctly. For different product classes, different factors, weights, and measures should be used to reflect varying impact on the organization.

Online Performance Tracking

In a fully computerized system, all supplier performance data would be entered as orders were received, and the buyer (and the supplier in some cases) should have online access so as to be able to discuss the supplier's performance at any time. Suppliers need to be informed periodically as to how they stand on the rating scale. Improved performance on the part of the supplier often results from the knowledge that its rating is lower than some competitor's or falls short of a set target.

The Evaluation of Potential Sources

Obviously, the evaluation of an existing supplier is substantially easier than the evaluation of a potential source. Because checking out a potential supplier often requires an extensive amount of time and resources, it should be done only for those suppliers on the short list who stand a serious chance of receiving a significant order. Where such a potential supplier competes with an existing supplier, the expected performance of the new source should, hopefully, be better than that of the existing one.

Common Evaluation Factors

In evaluating potential sources, the most common major factors are technical or engineering capability, manufacturing or distribution strength, financial strength, and management capability.

The use of trial orders has been mentioned as a popular means of testing a supplier's capability, but popular as this may be, it still begs the question as to whether the trial order should have been placed with a particular source at all. Even though a supplier may complete a trial order successfully, it may not be an acceptable source in the long run.

Two Key Questions in Evaluation

The evaluation of potential sources, therefore, attempts to answer two key questions:

1. Is this supplier capable of supplying the purchaser's requirements satisfactorily in both the short and long term?

2. Is this supplier motivated to supply these requirements in the way the purchaser expects in the short and long term?

The first question can be largely answered on a technical basis. The second probes the human side. Why should supplier personnel give special attention to this purchaser's requirements?

Technical, Engineering, and Manufacturing Strengths

Current and Future Capabilities

Technical and engineering capability, along with manufacturing strengths, impinge on a number of concerns for the purchaser. The most obvious first factor is the quality capability of the supplier. Chapter 5 has already discussed a variety of means of evaluating potential suppliers, including the quality capability survey. It is possible, however, that a company capable of meeting current quality standards may still lack the engineering and technical strengths to stay with new technological advances. Similarly, manufacturing may lack capacity, or the space to expand, or the flexibility to meet a variety of requirements. Presumably, the reason for selecting one supplier over another is because of greater strengths in areas of importance to the purchaser. The evaluation of the supplier, therefore, should focus not only on current capability, but also on the supplier's future strengths. Only in very large organizations might the procurement group have sufficient technical strength to conduct such supplier evaluations on its own. It is normal that other functions such as engineering, manufacturing, using departments, or quality control provide expert assistance to assess a potential supplier on technical and manufacturing strengths.

Should the supplier be a distributor, the stress might be more on distribution capability. The nature of the agreements with the distributors supplying manufacturers, their inventory policies, systems capability and compatibility, and ability to respond to special requirements would all be assessed, along with such technical strengths of the personnel as might be necessary to assist the purchasing organization to make the right choices among a series of different acceptable options.

A number of distributors have moved strongly into systems contracts used even as substitutes for internal MRO staffing, permitting organizations the option of outsourcing the total MRO supply function and reducing the total supply base drastically.

Management and Financial Evaluation

As the tendency toward greater reliance on single sources for a longer period of time continues, along with greater interest in materials requirements, just-in-time production, and strategic sourcing, a potential supplier's management strengths take on added significance. From the procurement point of view, the key question is: "Is the management of this supplier a corporate

Measuring a Supplier's Management Strength

strength or a weakness?" This will require a detailed examination of the organization's mission, its corporate values and goals, its structure, qualifications of managers, management controls, the performance evaluation and reward system, training and development, information systems, and policies and procedures. It is also useful to have an explanation as to why the supplier's management believes it is managing well and an indication of its most notable successes and failures. A functional assessment of strengths and weaknesses in areas like marketing, supply, accounting, and so on, will substantiate the overall picture. For example, consider a contract where the supplier spends a substantial percentage of total contract volume on raw materials and parts with outside suppliers or subcontractors. An evaluation of this supplier's procurement system, organization, procedures, and personnel is vital and can best be carried out by competent procurement staff in the organization that is letting the contract.

An assessment of this sort will require submission of documentation by the supplier as well as personal visits by qualified personnel from the buying organization. In some very large organizations considering the letting of large contracts, a task force or a special new-supplier team is required to submit a formal report detailing the management strengths and weaknesses of potential suppliers, and this evaluation may well carry the project.

Measuring a Supplier's Financial Strength

The financial strengths and weaknesses of a supplier obviously affect its capability to respond to the needs of customers. There are often substantial opportunities for negotiation if the purchaser is fully familiar with the financial status of a supplier. For example, the offer of advance payment or cash discounts may have little appeal to a cash-rich source but may be highly attractive to a firm short of working capital. A supplier with substantial inventories may be able to offer supply assurance and a degree of price protection at times of shortages that cannot be matched by others without the materials or the funds to acquire them.

The buyer must determine the extent of the financial assessment appropriate for each purchase. A couple of questions that might help make the decision are: (1) "Is the supplier strategically important to us?" If so, a full financial analysis would be necessary. (2) "Is the product or service being purchased considered strategic?" and (3) "Are there other short-term alternatives available?" If another supplier, product, or service can be quickly substituted then the buyer can reduce the expense of a full evaluation.[3]

Individual financial measures that may be examined include, but are not limited to, credit rating, capital structure, profitability, ability to meet interest and dividend obligations, working capital, inventory turnover, current ratio, and return on investment. Presumably, financial stability and strength are indicators of good management and competitive ability. Financial state-

---

[3]Marc Ensign, "Breaking Down Financial Barriers," *Purchasing Today,* July 2000, p. 12.

Applicable Financial Ratios

ments, therefore, are a reasonable source of information about a supplier's past performance. Whether the supplier will continue to perform in the same manner in the future is an assessment the purchaser must make, taking all available information, including the financial side, into account. Some of the financial ratios that a buyer may want to take a look at include profit and loss, inventory turnover, account receivables turns, and current ratio. This information is available from Dun & Bradstreet. Some online resources for financial information are: *www.hoovers.com* and *www.dnb.com* (Dun & Bradstreet).

Financial Ratio	Possible Interpretation
Profit/Loss	If the profit margin is below the industry average, the supplier may be unable to invest in processes, equipment or people.
Inventory Turnover	If the company has poor inventory turnover, it is tying up assets that could better be put to research and development, capital investment, and employee salaries, and some of the inventory may be obsolete.
Receivables Turnover	If receivables are too high, then the supplier is financing its customers and its money is not available for other uses. Also, many of the receivables may be uncollectable.
Current Ratio	Current assets compared to current liabilities. Indicates the likelihood of a cash flow problem.

Assigning Weight to Evaluation Factors

There is general agreement among procurement executives that a supplier's management capability and financial strength are vital factors in source evaluation and selection. Even after a satisfactory evaluation of management, financial, and technical strengths of a supplier has been completed, the question remains as to what weight should be accorded to each of the various dimensions. Also, should the purchaser take the initiative in insisting that the supplier correct certain deficiencies, particularly on the management or financial side?

Many examples exist that illustrate the need for supplier strength. These are normally related to the long-term survival of the company. Small suppliers are frequently dependent on the health, age, and abilities of the owner-manager. Every time this individual steps into an automobile the fate of the company rides along. The attitudes of this individual toward certain customers may be very important in supply assurance.

Relationships and Communication Channels and Key Components

Most long-term and significant supplier-purchaser relationships are highly dependent on the relationships and communication channels built by the respective managers in each organization. Unless each side is willing and able to listen and react to information supplied by the other side, problems are not likely to be resolved to mutual satisfaction.

Additional Source Selection Considerations

One might think that after a supplier had been found who could meet all the requirements, the search would be over. Such is not the case. Shall the buyer, in buying a given item, rely on a single supplier or utilize several? Shall the buyer buy directly from manufacturers or through distributors? Shall the buyer give preference to local sources, consider minority groups, and address environmental and political concerns? Should a buyer take an active role in developing new sources or even try to have the requirements made in-house? To make a final selection of source, it may be necessary to consider these questions. In doing so, it shall be assumed that adequate investigation has been made of the supplier's financial standing, general reputation for fairness, and capacity to meet the requirements as to quality, quantity, delivery, and service, and that prices are not unreasonable.

Single versus Multiple Sourcing

Should the buyer rely upon a single supplier or utilize several? The answer to this question must be the very unsatisfactory one, "It all depends."

Arguments Favoring a Single Source

Briefly, the arguments for placing all orders for a given item with one supplier are as follows:

1. Prior commitments, a successful past relationship, or an ongoing long-term contract with a preferred supplier might prevent even the possibility of splitting the order.

2. The supplier may be the exclusive owner of certain essential patents or processes and, therefore, be the only possible source. Under such circumstances the purchaser has no choice, provided that no satisfactory substitute is available.

3. A given supplier may be so outstanding in the quality of product or in the service or value provided as to preclude serious consideration of buying elsewhere.

4. The order may be so small as to make it not worthwhile to divide it.

5. Concentrating purchases may make possible certain discounts or lower freight rates that could not be had otherwise.

6. The supplier will be more cooperative, more interested, and more willing to please if it has all the buyer's business.

7. When the purchase of an item involves a die, tool, mold charge, or costly setup, the expense of duplicating this equipment or setup is likely to be substantial.

8. Deliveries may be more easily scheduled.

9. The use of just-in-time production, stockless buying or systems contracting, or EDI are more likely to be successful in a single source arrangement for a specific item.

10. Effective supplier relations require considerable resources and time. Therefore, the fewer suppliers the better.

11. Single sourcing is a prerequisite to partnering.

Arguments Favoring Multiple Sourcing

On the other hand, there are arguments for multiple sourcing—provided, of course, that the sacrifice is not too great:

1. It has been traditional practice to use more than one source, especially on the important requirements, even though in the United States single sourcing has been the trend for years.

2. Knowing that competitors are getting some of the business may tend to keep the supplier more alert to the need for giving good prices and service.

3. Assurance of supply is increased. Should fire, strikes, breakdowns, or accidents occur to any one supplier, deliveries can still be obtained from the others for at least part of the needs.

4. The purchasing organization has developed a unique capability of dealing with multiple sources.

5. To avoid supplier dependence on the purchaser.

6. To obtain a greater degree and volume of flexibility, because the unused capacity of all the suppliers may be available.

7. Even in situations involving close and cooperative supplier relationships, it is possible to make backup arrangements so that supplier X specializes in product Q and backs up supplier Y, who specializes in product R and backs up supplier X.

8. Strategic reasons, such as military preparedness and supply security, may require multiple sourcing.

9. Government regulations may insist that multiple suppliers, or small or minority sources, be used. If there is high risk associated with a small or single-minority source, multiple sourcing may be necessary.

10. Sufficient capacity may not be available to accommodate the purchaser's current or future needs.

11. Potential new or future suppliers may have to be tested with trial orders, while other sources receive the bulk of the current business.

12. Volatility in the supply market makes single sourcing unacceptably risky.

Genuine concern exists among supply executives as to how much business should be placed with one supplier, particularly if the supplier is small. It is feared that sudden discontinuance of purchases may put the supplier's survival in jeopardy, and, yet, the purchaser does not wish to reduce flexibility by being tied to dependent sources. One simple rule of thumb traditionally used was that no more than a certain percentage, say 20 or 30 percent, of the total supplier's business should be with one customer. An interesting situation exists in the early twenty-first century with the failure of so many technology companies. The decision of which technology platform to build an e-commerce structure on is a high-risk decision when it is unclear which suppliers will survive the industry shakeout. For example, Staples Inc., the office supply retailer and a leading e-commerce innovator, selected two technology platforms, Microsoft Corporation's Site Server Commerce Edition 3.0 and IBM Web Sphere, for its Web sites. In a year or so the company will standardize on one platform. Meanwhile, both suppliers work to out-perform the other on speed and cost of delivering a capability.[4]

Choosing an IT Supplier at Staples, Inc.

How to Divide Business Among Suppliers

If a decision is made to divide an order among several suppliers, there is then the question of the basis on which the division is to be made. The actual practice varies widely. One method is to divide the business equally. Another is to base the allocation on geographical coverage. Another is to place the larger share with a favored supplier and give the rest to one or more alternates. In the chemical industry, as in a number of others, it is common practice to place business with various suppliers on a percentage-of-total-requirements basis. Total requirements may be estimated, not necessarily guaranteed, and there may not even be a minimum volume requirement. Each supplier knows what its own percentage of the business amounts to but may not be aware of who the competition is or how much business each competitor received if the number of sources exceeds two. There is no common practice or "best" method or procedure, although renewed interest in single sourcing is consistent with a number of current trends, especially the quality movement, partnerships, and strategic sourcing.

Manufacturer or Distributor?

The question sometimes arises whether to purchase from the manufacturer directly or from some trade channel such as a wholesaler, distributor, or even a retailer. Occasionally, pressure is brought to bear, particularly by various types of trade associations, to induce the purchaser to patronize the wholesaler, distributor, or mill supply house. The real issue involved here is often closely related to buying from local sources. The question is not primarily one of proximity to the user's plant but rather one of buying channels.

Reasons for Using a Wholesaler

The justification for using trade channels is found in the services which they render. If wholesalers are carrying the products of various manufacturers and spreading marketing costs over a variety of items, they may be able to lay down the product at the buyer's plant at a lower cost, particularly when the unit of sale is small and customers are widely scattered or when the demand is irregular. Furthermore, they may carry a stock of goods greater than a manufacturer could afford to carry in its own branch warehouse and, therefore, be in a better position to make prompt deliveries and

---

[4]Lauren Gibbons Paul and Lisa Vaas, "Leaders of a New Pack, No. 1: Staples — Click or Brick, Your Pick," *eWeek,* November 13, 2000, *www.zdnet.com/ecommerce/stories.*

to fill emergency orders. Also, they may be able to buy in car- or truck-load lots, with a saving in transportation charges, and a consequent lower cost to the buyer.

Local sentiment may be strongly in favor of a certain distributor. Public agencies are particularly susceptible to such influence. Sometimes firms that sell through distributors tend, as a matter of policy, to buy whenever possible through distributors.

Reasons for Bypassing a Wholesaler

On the other hand, some large organizations often seek ways of going around the supply house, particularly where the buyer's requirements of supply items are large, where the shipments are made directly from the original manufacturer, and where no selling effort or service is rendered by the wholesaler. Some manufacturers operate their own supply houses to get the large discount. Others have attempted to persuade the original manufacturers to establish quantity discounts—a practice not unlike that in the steel trade.

Reasons for Establishing Special Services

Still others have sought to develop sources among small manufacturers that do not have a widespread distribution organization. Some attempts have been made to secure a special service from a chosen distributor, such as an agreement whereby the latter would add to its staff "two people exclusively for the purpose of locating and expediting nuisance items in other lines." A similar arrangement might place a travel agency employee directly on the purchaser's premises to improve service.

Systems contracting and stockless purchasing systems depend heavily on concentrating a large number of relatively small purchases with a highly capable distributor.

Ultimately, every participant in the value chain needs to add value. This guiding principle should apply also to the selection of nonmanufacturers in the distribution network.

Geographical Location of Sources

Preference for Local Sources

Shall purchases be confined as largely as possible to local sources, or shall geographical location be largely disregarded? Most buyers *prefer* to buy from local sources.

Dependable Service

This policy rests on two bases. The first is that a local source can frequently offer more dependable service than one located at a distance. For example, deliveries may be more prompt both because the distance is shorter and because the dangers of interruption in transportation service are reduced. Knowledge of the buyer's specific requirements, as well as of the seller's special qualifications, may be based on an intimacy of knowledge not possessed by others. There may be greater flexibility in meeting the purchaser's requirements; and local suppliers may be just as well equipped as to facilities, know-how, and financial strength as any of those located at more distant points. Thus, there may well be sound economic reasons for preferring a local source to a more distant one. In just-in-time production systems, proximity of the supplier's plant to that of the purchaser is vital. Organizations such as the automotive companies, for example, have thus found themselves encouraging suppliers to relocate plants closer to automobile assembly operations.

Community Commitment

A second basis for selecting local sources rests on equally sound, although somewhat less tangible, grounds. The organization owes much to the local community. The facility is located there, the bulk of the employees live there, and often a substantial part of its financial support, as well as a notable part of its sales, may be local. The local community provides the company's personnel with their housing, schools, churches, and social life. Executives are constantly asked by local business owners or managers at local professional and social gatherings why they are not receiving any business. To recognize these facts is good public relations.

Therefore, if a local source of supply can be found that can render a buyer as good a value as can be located elsewhere, it should be supported. Moreover, buyers should attempt to develop local sources when potential exists.

Complications of Local Sourcing

This policy has two complicating elements. One is supply's primary responsibility to buy well. Emotion should rarely supplant good business judgment, for to do so, in the long run, is to render the local community a poor service indeed. A second complication arises through the difficulty of defining "local." Technological changes have affected not only the size and distribution of the centers of population but also the commercial and business structure, resulting in, among other things, a widening of market areas and hence the sources from which requirements can be obtained. Therefore, what once might properly have been called local has, for many areas and many items, become state, provincial, or national. There is no easy rule by which a buyer can decide the economic boundaries of the local community. As e-commerce activities grow, the boundaries of time and space will shrink even more. As it becomes easier to access information about potential suppliers and to move information between and among organizations it may also become easier to do business with international suppliers. (See also Chapter 14 about buying internationally.)

Supplier Size

Should a purchaser have the option of buying from a large, medium, or small supplier, which size of supplier should be favored? This also depends on the size of the purchasing organization. A matrix of relative sizes can be developed (see Figure 7–4).

Implications of Supplier Size

The size and nature of the requirement may also affect the decision, as it is general wisdom that the larger the requirement, the larger the supplier should be. Generally, smaller suppliers tend to be local for those smaller requirements where flexibility, speed of response, and availability tend to be more important than price. Larger suppliers tend to be more appropriate for high-volume requirements where technology, quality, and total cost of own-

FIGURE 7–4

Relative Purchaser and Supplier Size

Purchaser Size	Supplier Size
Small	Small
	Medium
	Large
Medium	Small
	Medium
	Large
Large	Small
	Medium
	Large

ership may be critical. And medium suppliers fall in-between. The trouble with generalizations is that exceptions abound. Small suppliers tend to fill niches that the larger ones cannot or may have chosen not to cover. According to Hispanic Business Magazine, the leaders of its Fastest-Growing 100 Companies focus on a strategy of concentrating on, and filling, one niche in the marketplace. Take, for example, Cube Corporation, a facilities and building management company providing services to the U.S. federal government. Most of CEO Jack Mencia's competitors got into this area as a sideline when the construction market weakened. Although Mencia didn't gross $1 million until year three, by making this niche his company's core business, Cube Corporation earned $50 million in 2000.[5]

Cube Corp. Example of a Niche Business

Small suppliers have traditionally shown a loyalty and service deemed impossible from larger suppliers, but the customer service focus of many larger organizations is trying to attack this perception. Small suppliers tend to depend on the management of a key owner-manager, and this person's health and attitude will affect the risk of doing business. Larger organizations tend to have greater stability and greater resources, reducing the day-to-day risk of supplier performance.

Technology and the Small Suppliers

Government pressure for minority sources has renewed interest in the large purchaser–small supplier interface and the role of education, assistance, and continuing watchfulness on the part of the purchaser to help the supplier succeed. Advances in technology present both opportunities and challenges to small business owners. On the one hand, the Internet is available to anyone with a computer and a modem. On the other hand, many small business owners fear that the cost and resources needed to operate in the world of e-commerce will leave them out of the game. Joe Villarreal, CEO of VCI Inc., an information technology services company serving the federal government, sees the Internet as an equalizer in the long run, even though

[5]Joel Russell, "Pick a Niche and Fill It," *Hispanic Business,* July/August 2000, p. 44.

many small businesses are forced to adapt rapidly to a paperless business process.[6] (See Chapter 4 for more detail).

Joint Purchasing with Supplier

Risks and Rewards of Joint Purchasing

Sometimes a purchaser becomes involved with buying certain requirements for suppliers, believing it can purchase more effectively and efficiently than they can. Because the suppliers would realize substantial savings, some of these must be passed along to the purchaser. Although the purchaser will incur some additional expense, there would be a net gain to both parties in the transaction. The close relationship that would exist between the suppliers and purchasers, furthermore, would enable purchasers to know more about the production costs of suppliers and to ascertain whether or not they were paying a fair price for the products. The purchaser would, moreover, be sure of the quality of the materials used and would increase buying power. However, the supplier may claim that quality difficulties stem from the poor quality of material supplied. With a reduction in the number of buyers in the market for the raw materials, there would be less false activity and thus greater price stability. This last reason is rather important. Not infrequently, when a large company requests bids from individual suppliers, they in turn enter the material markets to make inquiries about prices and quantities available. If six suppliers are bidding on an offer, their preliminary inquiries for material required to fill the prospective order will be multiplied six times.

Purchasing for Company Personnel

Another problem faced by most purchasing departments is that of the extent to which it is justified in using its facilities to obtain merchandise for employees of the organization or for its executives at better terms than they could individually obtain through their own efforts. Some companies not only sell their own merchandise to their employees at a substantial discount and also allow them to buy at cost any of the merchandise bought by the company for its own use, but they go even further and make it possible for employees to obtain merchandise that the company itself neither makes nor uses.

Reasons for Purchasing for Employees

There are some reasons why a company should pursue a policy of employee purchasing. Under certain circumstances, of course, it is imperative that a company make some provision for supplying its employees with at least the necessities of life, a condition particularly true in remote mining and lumbering locations. A policy of employee purchasing, it is also argued, provides the means for increasing real wages at little or no cost to the company. It may increase the loyalty of the employees to the organization and thus form a part of the fringe benefits. Employees often feel they are entitled to any considerations or advantages the company can obtain for them. Fur-

---

[6]Ibid., p. 52.

thermore, whatever the procurement manager may think about the general practice, it is often somewhat difficult to refuse a request from a top executive to "see what can be done about a discount."

Reasons against Purchasing for Employees

Many companies, on the other hand, have steadfastly refused to adopt such a policy. There is some question of just how much prices are really reduced compared with the prices of the chain store, the supermarket, the discount store, and other low-cost distribution outlets. Some ill will toward the company may be aroused because the ordinary retailer is likely to feel that the company is entering into direct competition, or at least is bringing pressure to grant discounts to the organization's employees.

Unfortunately, few people realize how difficult it is for a purchasing department to handle numerous small requests of a personal nature. It is a time-consuming and unrewarding task because a complete market search is almost impossible, and any quality, price, or service troubles arising from the purchase are always brought back to those involved.

Social, Political, and Environmental Concerns

Non-economic Factors Defined

Non-economic factors may have a significant bearing on procurement sourcing decisions. These include social, political, and environmental concerns. In a 2000 CAPS study, Carter and Jennings defined the purchasing manager's involvement in the socially responsible management of the supply chain as "a wide array of behaviors that broadly fall into the category of environmental management, safety, diversity, human rights and quality of life, ethics, and community and philanthropic activities."[7]

Social. Most organizations recognize that their existence may affect the social concerns of society. Some social problems can be addressed through supply policy and actions. For example, it is possible to purchase from social agencies employing recovering addicts, former prisoners, or the physically and mentally handicapped, certain items or services which assist in the employment of these people. It is possible to purchase from suppliers located in low-income areas or certain geographical areas of high unemployment. The U.S. government has tried in a variety of ways to encourage purchasing from small, woman-owned or minority suppliers by requiring that, on public contracts, a certain percentage of total value be placed with such suppliers. Companies in the private sector often engage in these actions voluntarily out of a sense of corporate social responsibility and to gain strategic advantage.

Strategic Advantage of Supplier Diversity

For example, Detroit's big three automotive manufacturers have positioned supplier diversity as a strategic advantage because they see the connection between from whom they buy and to whom they sell. By helping to develop

---

[7]Craig R. Carter and Marianne M. Jennings, *Purchasing's Contribution to the Socially Responsible Management of the Supply Chain* (Tempe, AZ: Center for Advanced Purchasing Studies, 2000), p. 7.

the economy of the ethnic community through its supplier development programs, it is also increasing the purchasing power of the members of ethnic communities.[8]

Importance of Supplier Development Initiatives

Most larger organizations recognize the problems and opportunities present through the exercise of purchasing power in the social area. It is not easy for a hard-nosed purchasing manager, used to standard low-risk, reputable sources and extensive competition, to consider dealing with the high-risk sources often represented by this class. Most purchasing managers agree that the "deal" must make good business sense and that an arrangement based on charity will sooner or later collapse. Without purchasing's initiative to seek out those suppliers who might have reasonable potential, it is unlikely that much can or will be accomplished. Too many of the potential sources are small, have few resources, and possess low marketing skills. Recognition of supplier weaknesses and the willingness to be of assistance are, therefore, necessary ingredients. Normally, sources like these will be local, allowing for personal contact, watchfulness, and support through the development stage. Supplier development is addressed in greater detail in Chapter 8.

Political. The basic question in the political area is: Should the acquisition area be seen as a means of furthering political objectives? Public agencies have long been under pressure of this sort. "Buy local" is a common requirement for city and state purchasing officials. "Buy American" is a normal corollary requirement. The attempt by the Canadian government to direct the Department of Supply and Services to spread purchases across the country, approximately in line with population distribution, is another example. For military purposes, the U.S. government has a long-standing tradition of support and development of a national supply base to afford security protection in the case of conflict.

Pressure to Buy Locally

The question always arises as to how much of a premium should be paid to conform with political directives. Should a city purchasing agent buy buses from the local manufacturer at a 12 percent premium over those obtainable from another state or other country?

For private industry, political questions are also present. Should the corporation support the political and economic aims of the governing body? Governments have little hesitation on large business deals to specify that a minimum percentage should have domestic content. In the aerospace and telecommunications industry, for example, foreign orders are often contingent on the ability to arrange for suitable subcontracting in the customer's home country. It is interesting that governments have no fear to tread where private industry is forbidden to walk. Multinationals often find themselves caught in countries with different political views. American companies for

---

[8]Ginger Conrad, "Effective M/WBE Supplier Development," *Purchasing Today,* May 2000, p. 6.

many years have not been allowed to trade with Cuba. American subsidiaries in other countries face strong national pressure to export to Cuba the same products that the American parent is not allowed to sell from American soil. The same holds for purchasing from countries with whom trade is not encouraged by the government. American subsidiaries frequently find themselves caught between the desire of the local government to encourage local purchases and the U.S. government, which encourages exports from the parent or the parent's suppliers. The growing role of government in all business affairs is likely to increase difficulties of this kind in the future. Their resolution is far from easy and will require a great deal of tact and understanding.

Minority and Women Business Enterprise (M/WBE) Sourcing. Government legislation requiring suppliers on government contracts to place a percentage of business with designated minority suppliers or woman-owned businesses has forced many purchasers to undertake searches for such suppliers. Most purchasers have found they had to initiate assistance and educational programs to make their minority sourcing programs work. For example, for fiscal year 1998 the U.S. Department of Energy (DOE) awarded $224 million to such firms out of a total of $16 billion in contracting opportunities. In 2000, the secretary of the DOE established a mentor-protégé program in which prime contractors help energy-related small minority businesses increase their capabilities in return for subcontracting credit and other incentives.[9] In one sense, these early reverse marketing efforts provided useful insights into the process of developing partnerships with larger suppliers as well.

There are a number of resources and publications available to link buyers and minority and women business owners including:

- The U.S. Small Business Administration (SBA), specifically its 8(a) Business Development Program, (*www.sba.gov*)
- The National Minority Supplier Development Council and its regional Purchasing Councils, (*www.nmsdcus.org*)
- *Minority Business Entrepreneur (MBE)* magazine, *www.mbemag.com*
- *Hispanic Business* magazine, *www.HispanicBusiness.com*

Environmental. Environmental considerations impact every phase of the acquisition cycle, from need definition to disposal. Public awareness of the desirability of the ideal goal—zero environmental impact—has grown in the past decades. Consequently, supply's role in helping to achieve this goal needs to be examined carefully. In a CAPS study on *Environmental Supply Chain*

Role of Government in Business Decisions

Department of Energy Example

M/WBE Resources

---

[9]Patricia Guadalupe, "New DOE Contracts," *Hispanic Business,* July/August 2000, p. 22.

Management, Carter and Narasimhan reported that environmental supply chain management strategies are in their infancy, with most efforts focused on avoiding violations rather than including environmental considerations in supply decisions.[10]

Two Problems Associated with Environmental Issues

The first issue is: Should our organization purchase materials, products, or equipment that may directly or indirectly increase environmental concerns? Should the purchasing group raise the environmental questions when others in the organization fail to do so? The second issue is: Should we purchase from sources, domestic or international, that we know are not following sound environmental practices? These are not easy questions answered glibly out of context. It is possible to evade the issue by putting government in the control seat, saying, "As long as government allows it, it must be all right." A practical consideration is that government may shut down a polluting supplier with little notice, endangering supply assurance.

Available Resources

There are many resources available to the environmentally conscious supply manager. The National Recycling Coalition (*www.nrc-recycle.org*) in the United States provides resources to procurement and contracting officials who are interested in purchasing environmentally preferable computers and information technology equipment. They have made available several Requests for Proposals (RFPs) from different agencies that demonstrate how to contract for proper recovery and recycling of electronic equipment.

Hierarchy of Attack

Another area of concern is packaging, a huge U.S. waste disposal problem of about 60 million tons/year containing: paper (50 percent), glass (22 percent), metal (11 percent), plastics (12 percent), and other (5 percent). The EPA has identified its preferred hierarchy of attacking this waste problem as: (1) source reduction—design or use less, (2) reuse—multiple use of same package or container, (3) recycle—reprocess into raw material, (4) incinerate—at least extract energy, but create CO_2 pollution at a minimum, (5) landfill—require space and transportation to store with potential impact on land and water.

Minimize Environmental Impact

Obviously, suppliers can aid substantially in addressing these priorities in helping to minimize the environmental impact of purchaser's and their customers' requirements (see also Chapter 10, "Investment Recovery"). In many organizations, purchasing's role as an information link between environmentally affected individuals and functions and suppliers in the handling of waste and hazardous materials has been established already. U.S. federal regulations, for example, for chemicals as to (1) transportation, (2) use, and (3) disposal of hazardous materials, have created a need for comprehensive hazardous materials management and information systems (HMMIS). Workplace right-to-know-legislation and emergency-preparedness requirements further reinforce the need for HMMIS.

---

[10]Joseph R. Carter and Ram Narasimhan, *Environmental Supply Chain Management* (Tempe, AZ: Center for Advanced Purchasing Studies, 1998).

Design for Recycling

New environmental legislation is continually tightening standards and addressing new issues. For example, "designing for recycling" requires manufacturers of appliances and automobiles to design their products for ease of disassembly to allow for recovery of useful materials. In the automobile industry, this represents a particularly difficult challenge. Much of the weight-reduction emphasis to improve government-required fuel ratings has come about by the substitution of lightweight, but difficult to retrieve and recycle, plastics for heavier but easily recycled metal parts.

Environmental Programs

There are a number of environmental programs that affect the purchasing and supply function including Industrial Voluntary Environmental Programs, Voluntary Environmental Protection Agency (EPA — U.S.) Programs, and ISO 14000. The ISO 14000 certification program, developed along the lines of ISO 9000, is a process for certifying the environmental management system of an organization. In a recent study by CAPS Research, *ISO 14000: Assessing its Impact on Corporate Effectiveness and Efficiency,"* respondents from plants that are certified reported that, other than lead times, certification has a large, positive impact on the perceived efficiency and effectiveness of the organization's environmental management system.[11]

An Industrial Voluntary Program is initiated by an industry group to encourage commitment on the part of member companies to continually improving its health, safety and environmental performance. For example, in 1990 the American Chemistry Council (formerly Chemical Manufacturers Association [CMA]) initiated Responsible Care®, an environmental, health, and safety performance improvement initiative. The vision of the initiative is "no accidents, injuries, or harm to the environment."[12] It has reported a 50 percent reduction in the industry's total emissions, a decrease in worker injury and illness rates, and the establishment of community advisory panels in CMA member plant communities.[13] Currently, 45 countries have embraced Responsible Care® and are advancing it under the guidance of the International Council of Chemical Associations (ICCA).[14] Why should supply

Chemical Industry Voluntary Program

managers in the chemical industry be involved in efforts to reduce toxic release inventory (TRI) emissions? The costs associated with these emissions include costs from excess raw materials, lost product for sale, labor and production capacity required to generate waste, disposal costs, and waste management costs. The Pollution Prevention Code of the initiative lists a hierarchy of activities including source reduction, recycle/reuse, energy recovery, and treatment; areas in which supply managers may be able to add value.

---

[11]Steven A. Melnyk, Roger Calantone, Rob Handfield, Robert Sroufe, and Frank Montabon, *ISO 14000: Assessing its Impact on Corporate Effectiveness and Efficiency* (Tempe, AZ: Center for Advanced Purchasing Studies, 1999).

[12]Responsible Care® Progress Report 2000, July 24, 2000, p. 4.

[13]Elena R. Moshinsky, "Trends: Purchasing and the Environment," *Purchasing Today,* July 1998, p. 36.

[14]Responsible Care® Progress Report 2000, July 24, 2000, p. 30.

Voluntary Programs Sponsored by the EPA

In the United States, the Environmental Protection Agency (EPA) runs a number of voluntary programs. For example, the Environmental Accounting Project, begun in 1993, provides tools for calculating the environmental costs of non-prevention approaches and the economic benefits of pollution prevention. The project makes available a number of case studies, benchmarking projects, and calculation and spreadsheet tools for conducting environmental cost analysis for business decision making. The tools and reports are available from the project's Web site, *www.epa.gov/opptintr/acctg/earesources.htm*.

There may be opportunities in the environmental arena for purchasers who are at the forefront of environmental awareness. By being ahead of, rather than behind, legislative requirements, opportunities to tap government financial support and public recognition for innovative experiments may exist. The simple fact is that almost every supplier selection decision is likely to be impacted by environmental considerations.

Ethics

Purchasing represents the exchange of money for goods and services. Often, a very large amount of money is involved in this exchange. It is, therefore, vital that the transactions associated with the procurement process be carried out at the highest ethical level. Unfortunately, temptation is always present where large amounts of money are involved. Sometimes suppliers will go to considerable lengths to secure business and resort to unethical practices, such as bribes or large gifts. Sometimes unscrupulous purchasers take advantage of their privileged position to extract personal rewards that are unethical as well as illegal. Clearly, both suppliers and purchasers are responsible for ensuring that unethical conduct is not tolerated. On the purchasing side, both PMAC and ISM have Codes of Ethics and Principles and Standards of Purchasing Practice which guide the professional behavior of their members. (See Figure 7–5 and Figure 7–6.)

Equal Treatment of Customers, Employees, and Suppliers

Most larger organizations in their policies and procedures will deal specifically with standards of behavior of purchasing personnel and their relations with suppliers. Many organizations are moving to a congruent position that equates the treatment of customers, employees, and suppliers as identical. Simply stated: "Every customer, employee, and supplier of this organization is entitled to the same level of honesty, courtesy, and fairness."

Buyers are urged to behave in such a fashion as to reflect the organization's wishes.

Gifts and Gratuities

How shall the purchasing manager deal with the problem of excessive entertainment and gifts in any one of their varied and subtle forms? Here is a

FIGURE 7–5

Excerpts from the PMAC Code of Ethics

Precepts

Members shall not use their authority or office for personal gain and shall seek to uphold and enhance the standing of the purchasing profession and the Association by:

a. **Maintaining an unimpeachable standard of integrity** in all their business relationships both inside and outside the organizations in which they are employed;

b. **Fostering the highest standards of professional competence** amongst those for whom they are responsible;

c. **Optimizing the use of resources** for which they are responsible so as to provide the maximum benefit to their employers;

d. **Complying with the letter and spirit of:**

  (i) The laws of the country in which they practice,

  (ii) The Association's "Principles and Standards of Purchasing Practice," and any other such guidance on professional practice as may be issued from time to time,

  (iii) Contractual obligations; and

e. **Rejecting and denouncing any business practice that is improper.**

Rules of Conduct

A member will adhere to the following rules of conduct:

a. *Declaration of Interest*

A member shall immediately declare to the member's employer any personal interest that may impinge upon, or that others may reasonably deem to impinge upon, a member's impartiality on any matter relevant to the member's duties.

b. *Confidentiality and Accuracy of Information*

A member shall respect the confidentiality of information received in the course of the member's duties and shall not use this information for personal gain. In the course of the member's duties, the member shall only provide information that is true and fair and not designed to mislead.

c. *Fair Competition*

While considering the advantages to the member's employer of maintaining a continuing relationship with a supplier, a member shall avoid any arrangement that might prevent the effective operation of fair competition.

d. *Business Gifts and Hospitality*

To preserve the image and integrity of the member, the member's employer, and the profession, a member shall not accept business gifts other than items of small intrinsic value. Reasonable hospitality is an accepted courtesy of a business relationship. A member shall not accept gifts or hospitality with such frequency and of a nature whereby the member might be, or others might deem the member to be, influenced in making a business decision as a consequence of accepting the gifts or hospitality.

e. *Discrimination and Harassment*

No member shall knowingly participate in acts of discrimination or harassment toward any person with whom the member has business relations.

f. *Environmental Issues*

A member shall recognize the member's responsibility to environmental issues consistent with the corporate goals or mission of the member's organization.

g. *Interpretation*

When in doubt on the interpretation of the Professional Code of Ethics, a member shall refer to the Ethics Committee of the member's institute or corporation.

FIGURE 7–6

ISM Principles and Standards of Purchasing Practice

1. Avoid the intent and appearance of unethical or compromising practice in relationships, actions, and communications.
2. Demonstrate loyalty to the employer by diligently following the lawful instructions of the employer, using reasonable care and only authority granted.
3. Refrain from any private business or professional activity that would create a conflict between personal interests and the interests of the employer.
4. Refrain from soliciting or accepting money, loans, credits, or prejudicial discounts, and the acceptance of gifts, entertainment, favors, or services from present or potential suppliers that might influence, or appear to influence, purchasing decisions.
5. Handle confidential or proprietary information belonging to employers or suppliers with due care and proper consideration of ethical and legal ramifications and governmental regulations.
6. Promote positive supplier relationships through courtesy and impartiality in all phases of the purchasing cycle.
7. Refrain from reciprocal agreements that restrain competition.
8. Know and obey the letter and spirit of laws governing the purchasing function and remain alert to the legal ramifications of purchasing decisions.
9. Encourage all segments of society to participate by demonstrating support for small, disadvantaged, and minority-owned businesses.
10. Discourage purchasing's involvement in employer-sponsored programs of personal purchases that are not business related.
11. Enhance the proficiency and stature of the purchasing profession by acquiring and maintaining current technical knowledge and the highest standards of ethical behavior.
12. Conduct international purchasing in accordance with the laws, customs, and practices of foreign countries, consistent with United States laws, your organization policies, and these Ethical Standards and Guidelines.

Approved 1/92

---

practice that seeks, through gifts, entertainment, and even open bribery, to influence the decision of persons responsible for making a choice between suppliers.

Such attempts to influence decisions unfairly are directed not only toward supply personnel. Managers, supervisors, and others in production, marketing, information systems, engineering, or elsewhere who are directly responsible for, or largely influence, decisions regarding types of materials or services to be procured are also approached. In such cases, even though the purchaser is not directly influenced, the buyer's task is affected. So serious do some organizations consider this whole problem that they forbid any employee to receive any gift, no matter how trivial, from any supplier, actual or potential.

It is, of course, difficult to distinguish always between legitimate expenditures by suppliers in the interest of goodwill, and illegitimate expenditures made in an attempt to place the buyer under some obligation to the supplier. In these borderline cases, only ordinary common sense can provide the answer.

The Institute for Supply Management (formerly NAPM) and the Purchasing Management Association of Canada (PMAC) in their codes of ethics strongly condemn gratuities. It is true, however, that every year a small number of cases are uncovered of individuals who do not abide by this code, thereby placing the whole profession under suspicion. Part of the blame

Distinguishing between Legitimate and Illegitimate Expenditures by Suppliers

must clearly lie with those who use illegal enticements to secure business. For example, a salesperson calls on a purchaser and invites him or her out to lunch so they may discuss a transaction without losing time or as a matter of courtesy. Such action is presumed to be in the interests of goodwill, although the cost of the lunch must be added to the selling price. An attractive but inexpensive gift may be given by the supplier's company to adorn the desk of the buyer. The supplier's name appears on the gift, and therefore it is construed as advertising. The sales representative may send a bottle of wine or sporting event tickets after a deal has been completed.

It is but a step from this type of effort to entertaining a prospective buyer at a dinner, followed perhaps by a theater party. The custom of giving simple gifts may develop into the providing of much larger ones. It is difficult to draw the line between these different situations. In some organizations, the purchasing manager or buyer not infrequently refuses to allow sales personnel to pay for luncheons or at least insists on paying for as many luncheons as do prospective sellers.

Aside from its economic aspects, the practice of commercial bribery is involved in many legal cases. Fundamentally, the rulings on commercial bribery rest on the doctrine of agency. Any breach of faith on the part of the agent, who has always been recognized by law as keeping a fiduciary position, is not permitted; therefore, the agent's acceptance of a bribe to do anything in conflict with the interests of its principal is not permitted by law.

Commercial Bribery and Its Consequences

The evils of commercial bribery are more far-reaching than would at first appear. Although originating with only one concern, bribery is rapidly likely to become a practice of the entire industry. A producer, no matter how superior the quality of goods or how low its price, is likely to find it extremely difficult to sell in competition with concerns practicing bribery. The prices paid by the buyer who accepts bribes are almost certain to be higher than they would be under other circumstances. Defects in workmanship or quality are likely to be smoothed over by the buyer who accepts bribes hidden from his or her employer. Materials may be deliberately damaged or destroyed to make products of some manufacturers who do not offer bribes appear unsatisfactory. There is no point in going further into an analysis of this practice. It takes many forms, but regardless of the guise in which it appears, there is nothing to be said for it.

Even though bribery is outlawed in North America, it may flourish in other parts of the world, legally or not. The spectacular revelations about the bribery involved in sales of U.S. aircraft to other countries during the mid-1970s were a sad reminder of the pervasiveness of such practices in our world. (See, also, Chapter 14 on international buying and the Foreign Corrupt Practices Act.)

Trade Relations

Under what circumstances, if at all, shall trade relations or reciprocity be practiced? A workable, though none too exact, definition of *reciprocity* is as follows: "Reciprocity is the practice of giving preference in buying to those suppliers who are customers of the buying company, as opposed to suppliers who do not buy from the company." This broad statement, however, is scarcely the form in which the problem arises. Much fruitless criticism has been advanced on the part of those who apparently do not fully realize that so far as purchasing departments, at least, are concerned, reciprocity is not a debatable policy to the extent that it involves purchasing requirements under conditions which will result in higher prices or inferior service. Purchasing directors do debate the issue as to how far it should be practiced, *assuming that conditions of price, service, and quality are substantially the same.*

The Case Against Reciprocity

The case against any general use of reciprocity rests on the belief that the practice is at variance with the sound principles of either buying or selling. The sale of a product or service must be based on the qualities of the product sold and of the service attending the transaction. There is only one permanent basis for a continuing customer-supplier relationship: the conviction on the part of the buyer that the product of a particular seller is the one best adapted to the need and is the best all-around value available. As long as the sales department concentrates its attention on this appeal, it will find and retain permanent customers.

Few purchasers would object to reciprocal buying on the basis that quality, service, and price must be equal. In practice, abuse is practically certain to creep in. For instance, buyers are urged to buy from X, not because X is a customer, but because X is Y's customer and Y is our customer, and Y wants to sell to X.

The normal expectation of a seller using reciprocity as an argument is that the purchaser is willing to grant price, quality, or delivery concessions. In North America, reciprocity is on shaky legal grounds, and the U.S. Supreme Court has upheld the Clayton Act under Section 7 that reciprocity may be restrictive to trade and create unfair competition.[15]

International Purchasing and Reciprocity

On an international scale, a form of reciprocity is practiced widely by governments who insist on "offsets." For example, a foreign company may receive a government contract on the condition that it meets stringent local content requirements. Thus, the supplier is forced to develop new sources, often at substantial cost, to secure the business. Furthermore, such foreign contracts often involve barter because the purchaser insists on paying with raw materials or locally manufactured goods.

Overall Supplier Selection Considerations

Before a purchaser can make a final supplier choice, a decision on all the important questions of policy just discussed must be reached: whether to patronize a single or several sources of supply; whether to buy directly from the

---

[15]The Case is *FTC v. Consolidated Foods* (1965), 380 U.S. 592.

manufacturer or through a distributor; whether to buy wholly from local sources; to what extent, if at all, to practice reciprocity; what weight to give social, political, and environmental concerns; and how to deal with the problem of commercial bribery. Having formulated a policy with reference to these matters, the basis has been laid for settling the specific issues as they arise later on.

Additional sourcing factors are raised in the next chapter, and these also require resolution before a specific sourcing decision can be made. Major topics yet to be covered include make or buy and outsourcing, as well as supplier relations, strategic sourcing, reverse marketing, and supply chain management.

Questions for Review and Discussion

1. Where does the borderline fall between gratuities and bribery?
2. Why should a purchasing department not buy items for personal use by employees of the organization?
3. Why is the trend toward single sourcing? What are the disadvantages to this trend?
4. What is a weighted point evaluation system? Why is it used?
5. Why might purchasing from distributors or wholesalers be preferable to buying directly from the manufacturer?
6. What are the advantages of purchasing from small local sources?
7. When might it be appropriate to conduct an informal, rather than a formal, supplier evaluation?
8. What are the similarities and differences between evaluating new and existing sources of supply?
9. Why is purchasing focusing more attention on a supplier's management as part of the evaluation process? How might this evaluation be conducted?
10. How might social, political, or environmental issues impact a purchaser's supplier selection decision?

References

Bakos, J. Yannis and Erik Brynjolfsson, *Incomplete Contracts, Trust and Long-Term Supplier Relationships: From Vendors to Partners: Information Technology and Incomplete Contracts in Buyer-Supplier Relationships,* Center for Coordination Science Technical Report, MIT

Sloan School of Management, Cambridge, Massachusetts, Journal of Organizational Computing, 1993.

Carter, Craig R. and Marianne M. Jennings, *Purchasing's Contribution to the Socially Responsible Management of the Supply Chain,* Tempe, AZ: Center for Advanced Purchasing Studies, 2000.

Carter, Joseph R. and Ram Narasimhan, *Environmental Supply Chain Management,* Tempe, AZ: Center for Advanced Purchasing Studies, 1998.

Cavinato, Joseph L. and Ralph G. Kauffman, Editors in Chief, *The Purchasing Handbook,* 6th edition, The McGraw-Hill Companies, 2000, Chapter 11, Identification and Evaluation of Sources, pp. 235–276.

Conrad, Ginger, "Effective M/WBE Supplier Development," *Purchasing Today,* May 2000, p. 6.

Cooper, Robert W., Gary L. Frank, and Robert A. Kemp, *NAPM Management Issues Series: Ethical Issues, Helps, and Challenges for the Professional in Purchasing and Materials Management,* Tempe, AZ: NAPM, 1995.

Curkovic, Sime and Robert Handfield, "Use of ISO 9000 and Baldrige Award Criteria in Supplier Quality Evaluation," *International Journal of Purchasing and Materials Management,* Spring 1996.

DePaul University Institute for Business & Professional Ethics (*www.depaul.edu/ethics/*). This site links to DePaul's ethics publications including *The Online Journal of Ethics* and *The Newsletter of the Institute for Business & Professional Ethics.*

Ethics Policy Statement for Purchasing, Supply, and Materials Management, NAPM TECHNotes, 1995.

Krause, Daniel R. and Robert B. Handfield, *Developing a World Class Supply Base,* Tempe, AZ: Center for Advanced Purchasing Studies, 1999.

McIvor, Ronan and Marie McHugh, *Partnership Sourcing: An Organization Change Management Perspective,* Journal of Supply Chain Management, 2001.

National Minority Supplier Development Council (NMSDC), *www.nmsdcus. org.*

CASE 7–1
LANCASTER LIFE INSURANCE CO.

Glenn Williamson, Purchasing Manager at Lancaster Life Insurance Co., had failed to award one of Lancaster's long-time group insurance clients a printing contract. Six months later, the printer was threatening to change insurers, and Lancaster's sales representative covering the printer was on the phone demanding action.

Lancaster Life Insurance Co. Lancaster had premiums of $1.5 billion and earnings of $65 million during the past year. Lancaster's products were distributed by 2,261 of the company's own sales representatives through the head office and

155 regional offices. The company's annual report stated that such key profitability ratios as mortality experience, interest rate spreads, and loss ratios were at satisfactory levels. Nevertheless, the economic climate had caused a considerable slowing of business growth. The following table shows premiums and earnings contributions by product line.

Product Line	Premiums ($ millions)	Earnings Contribution ($ millions)
Individual insurance	618	24.1
Retirement products	456	11.8
Employee benefits[*]	326	11.6
Reinsurance and other	109	17.0
Total	1,509	64.5

[*]Group insurance (typically includes some combination of health, vision, dental coverage, etc. as well as life insurance)

Group Insurance Products. Group insurance was essentially a commodity product, purchased by a firm to include in its employee benefit package. Clients purchased group insurance on the basis of price for a given level of service quality. Its smaller margins and lack of customer loyalty meant that group insurance was considered by the sales force to be a tougher business than individual insurance. Approximate commissions on a group policy were in the 3 percent range, compared to 7 percent on an individual policy. While individuals changed life insurers relatively infrequently, businesses, especially larger ones, were a much less stable customer base.

Purchasing Department. Lancaster's highly centralized purchasing department fell under the umbrella of Corporate and Administrative Services. The purchasing department bought all non-computer-related supplies, from business forms to photocopiers to company cars, for the entire Lancaster organization and its sister firms. Total purchases amounted to about $100 million per year. Glenn Williamson managed a staff of 18 general buyers and specialized forms managers.

Supplies used on a regular basis, or "stock" purchases, were stored in a central warehouse. Regional offices ordered supplies on a rotating sched-

ule, and shipments were made to 10 to 12 offices per day. Williamson valued the inventory in the warehouse at approximately $2 million. The purchasing department was responsible for the acquisition of $20 million of supplies annually. The forms managers oversaw the printing and inventory levels of approximately 3,500 different business forms and advertising brochures.

The purchasing department viewed itself as providing a service to head office and the regional offices, its major clients. The main goal of the department was to obtain the best value for its purchasing dollar. Williamson defined this as getting the necessary quality for the lowest possible price and worked continuously to reduce costs without sacrificing quality. For the past 10 years, suppliers had been chosen on the basis of a bidding process to encourage competitive pricing and service. Under this process, suppliers were encouraged to quote their best price for a predetermined level of quality and service, and the lowest price won the contract.

In Lancaster's experience, centralized purchasing was much more cost-effective than having regional offices buying their own supplies. As Williamson explained, "Who is going to get the better price—an office administrator buying one photocopier or an experienced purchaser buying 20 photocopiers?"

Because Lancaster provided life insurance to so many different people, Williamson was very conscious of the public relations responsibilities of the purchasing department. "The suppliers are all existing clients or potential clients. We need to be seen as giving people a fair chance."

Master Printer Inc. Master Printer had supplied advertising brochures to Lancaster for many years. Williamson described the historical relationship:

They used to just walk into the Marketing Department and walk out with the contract. No competition. Nothing. So they could charge what they liked. Now, I'm not saying they were gouging us. Their quality and service were always very good. They just were not pricing competitively. Then, 10 years ago, the purchasing department got more teeth, and we started getting quotes from the suppliers. Within two years, Master Printer's sales to

Lancaster dropped to about 20 percent of their previous levels. The company wasn't doing well, so then a couple of years ago it came under new ownership.

We got a call from the group rep covering them last spring, asking why Master Printer had not been awarded a particular contract. I guess their management was upset at not getting it and was turning up the heat on the sales rep. Maybe threatening not to renew their $100,000 plus policy. So I told the rep that their bid was $6,000 higher than the five other bids. Everyone else was bidding around $22,000. Anyway, it seemed to satisfy him. That was the last I heard of it.

Reciprocal Buying. Reciprocal buying issues, or the pressure to purchase from a particular supplier in order to ensure that the supplier also remained a group or personal client, were not new in the business. The pressure on the purchasing department from sales reps and their managers was, however, becoming stronger and more frequent as the recession deepened and competition, particularly for group business, intensified. "Times are tough," commented Williamson. "They want the policy, and some of those reps will promise anything to get it. So where does that leave us?"

Williamson found that Lancaster's policy with respect to reciprocal buying offered little concrete guidance: "It says 'All other things being equal, we will favor our clients,' but what are 'all other things'? And if we are only going to buy from our clients, then do we tell that to all potential bidders? And if we do that, then why would a non-client bid? So up go the prices."

On Tuesday morning, November 17, the sales representative covering Master Printer phoned again for Glenn Williamson. Master Printer's management was going to take its insurance business somewhere else. This was *Lancaster's* client and *his* client, and who did the idiots in purchasing think they were? He worked his butt off and here was Williamson driving away his clients! What was Williamson going to do about it? How did Williamson plan to get his client back? He was going to take this as high as he needed to go. He wanted action *now*.

CASE 7–2
QUOTECH INC.

"Should we go with Castle Metal's lower quote, or favor Marmon Keystone's proven reliability?" pondered Emily Trent, Purchasing Agent for Quotech Inc., a Cleveland-based manufacturer of materials handling equipment. It was May 1 as she prepared for her meeting the next day with Larry Pilon, sales representative from Marmon Keystone. At stake was an order for up to $700,000 of tubing that needed a decision within a week.

United Dominion Industries and Quotech Inc. Quotech Inc. was one of three companies comprising the Materials Handling Division (MHD) of Halgus Holdings (HH). HH total sales for last year were $2.15 billion, producing $98.4 million in net income. The Materials Handling Division represented approximately 18 percent of HH's sales.

Last year, the MHD reported a profit of $42 million on sales of $388 million, compared to the preceding year's figures of $38.9 million and $349 million respectively. Most of the growth in sales and earnings was attributable, however, to recent acquisitions. According to the company annual report, last year had been a disappointing year for HH, despite double-digit sales growth from its existing operations as well as from newly acquired companies. HH had suffered price erosion in its markets. The situation made cost-reduction measures vital for HH. Nicholas Whitehead, the president of HH, had gone on record as saying, "There are definitely opportunities for supply chain savings."

Last year, HH adopted the PEP program designed to achieve additional improvement in the company's operations. Cost reduction and containment were identified as key components of the PEP initiative, responsible for the maintenance of HH's competitive position.

Purchasing at Quotech. In addition to Emily, the Purchasing Department at Quotech comprised Frank Wilson, Director of Purchasing, and Rhonda Bates, Buyer. Together, they were responsible for deciding on Quotech's $17 million in manufacturing component purchases. HH's company structure and its PEP initiative called for close coordination between operating units within a division. As such, the purchasing personnel at Quotech were in close touch with their counterparts in Canada and Virginia. Doing so had proven a good strategy, as purchase consolidation measures and the consequent increase in volume-based buying power had squeezed savings of $500,000 in the first quarter of 2000 alone. Given company objectives, and the success in achieving reduction in costs, the reliance on a consolidated purchase ordering process was expected to continue.

The Sourcing Selection Issue. The issue currently demanding Emily's attention was the sourcing of the division's requirement for 2 7/8″ tubing. She was the lead buyer for the division. The tubing in question was a standard material for a variety of products. While not a mission-critical component, tubing that did not meet vendor specifications could cause equipment malfunction. Furthermore, like most manufacturing components, the supplier's inability to meet production demands on a timely basis could result in costly assembly line shutdowns. As such, the role of the supplier was not trivial. While each of the three companies comprising the division had historically sourced its purchases independently, top management's cost reduction imperative had changed this practice. As such, the current order was worth up to $700,000 and represented a consolidated purchase meant to satisfy all companies' tubing requirements for the coming year.

Quotech's Current Supplier: Marmon Keystone. Marmon Keystone was part of the U.S.-based Marmon Group of companies. Its local arm was based in Akron and had been a supplier of components to Quotech for the past decade. Emily had been very satisfied with Marmon Keystone, thanks to Doug Elliott, its sales representative. Doug made it a point to visit with Emily at appropriate intervals, inquiring about Quotech's sourcing needs, if any. Over the course of their relationship, Doug had become a trusted partner supplier to Emily, making good on Marmon Keystone's promises of reliable product quality and on-time delivery, two attributes that were very important to Quotech.

As it was not possible to develop detailed product specifications for every component, and a lot depended on the supplier's ability to provide components based on an "eyeball" evaluation at the vendor's plant premises, Doug Elliott had built an enviable record for himself and his firm. Quotech's Supplier Performance Tracking System indicated that over the last three years, there was evidence of just one MGA (product return) to Marmon Keystone, which was rectified immediately. Furthermore, Marmon Keystone had, in effect, taken on Quotech's inventory handling by performing the warehousing function on behalf of Quotech. This service spared Emily a big headache and saved Quotech a significant amount annually. One incident, particularly, stood out in Emily's mind as she evaluated Marmon Keystone. On one of his visits, Doug had noted the low inventory on an unrelated component and suggested filling the order. This proactive commitment to Quotech's interest on his part was yet to be imitated by any other suppliers.

Two years ago, when Doug Elliott was promoted to the position of General Manager at Marmon Keystone, he specifically instructed his replacement, Larry Pilon, to "take special care of this account." Larry had been true to his word and had continued the tradition of value creation and vendor satisfaction that his predecessor had displayed. This prompted Emily to attribute Marmon Keystone's success as a supplier to institutional rather than person-specific reasons. With annual sales of almost $300,000 to Quotech, it was not surprising that Marmon Keystone was among its top 20 suppliers, while Quotech was probably among Marmon Keystone's top 10 customers.

Castle Metals. Castle Metals had come to the attention of Emily through John Stevenson, the purchasing manager at the Canadian company. Emily knew very little about Castle Metals. Records indicated that the firm did not appear among the top 50 suppliers to the Toronto plant. Further investigation into the Canadian company's purchases last year indicated $300,000 from Marmon Keystone.

Neither Quotech nor the Canadian company had any history of dealing with Castle Metals.

However, both firms had different sourcing needs in that the Canadian company was more of a "specialty shop" requiring multiple variations of basic components in small quantities. In contrast, Quotech had standard sourcing requirements and tended to purchase higher quantities of more standardized components. It was felt that Castle Metals could serve both companies' diverse needs from its Mississauga, Ontario plant. Moreover, Castle Metals' bid for the tubing had undercut Marmon Keystone's by $18,000. To Emily's surprise, John Stevenson and her Virginia counterparts believed Castle Metals should be the supplier for the 2 7/8″ tubing. While surprised by the decision, she nevertheless realized that it could be based on the need to source products from multiple suppliers to "keep them honest."

Conclusion. Emily considered the sourcing decision as well as the "consolation" she could award the "losing" firm. Her records indicated that the Canadian location sourced $240,000 in components and the Virginia plant also had further tubing requirements. Given that both Castle Metals and Marmon Keystone had branches in all three locations, the possibility existed that she could use either as a supplier for those requirements. "What do I tell Larry?" thought Emily, as she planned for the meeting.

CASE 7–3
BID EVALUATION

On August 4, Matt Roberts, Custom Equipment's (CE) newly hired buyer, was preparing for a meeting with the Purchasing Manager the following day. He had received four bids for CE's cable and wire business and was wondering if the bid evaluation criteria he had developed earlier were still appropriate and what action to recommend next.

Bidding Process. Given his limited experience at CE, Matt decided that going out for bid would be

the best idea because he was not personally familiar with any of the electrical suppliers that sold wire and cable to CE.

The package that Matt had distributed contained a list of all wire and cable products used annually and a usage forecast for the coming year. Suppliers were asked to provide pricing, terms, delivery method, and their current stock situation of products of concern to CE. Pricing and ability to accommodate CE's requirements were important considerations, as were return policies. Suppliers were asked to include any innovative ideas on how to improve service to CE.

Ten potential electrical suppliers had been asked to bid for CE's entire yearly wire and cable requirements. Suppliers invited to participate in the Wire Management Program (WMP) were chosen based on CE's confidence in their ability to quote all of CE's requirements for wire and cable. All suppliers were local, so distance to CE's plant was not considered to be a factor.

Completed bids were submitted to CE from the four most capable suppliers because the other six suppliers could not adequately satisfy all of CE's needs. Although Matt believed the other six companies to be quite capable, most claimed that they could not satisfy all of CE's requirements. Licensing agreements, the size of the company, and willingness to stock certain products could be reasons for this. However, Matt believed four bids still made for a competitive bid environment.

Some suppliers had asked about the possibility of supplying alternative products with nearly identical features, especially as a substitute to CE's request for 'Newflex' cable. Due to licensing agreements, only Premier Cable Corporation (PCC), Bannister Electric, and Eastern Electric could supply Newflex. Some suppliers, such as State Electric, could supply "Kelvin" cable as an alternative to Newflex. Many large customer companies purchased Kelvin cable in place of Newflex, claiming Kelvin to be more effective in high-intensity applications.

The CE bid also included a list of currently held obsolete stock in CE's warehouse. Due to changes in customer specifications, CE's warehouse contained some wire and cable stock that was no longer used for its projects. The stock still had resale value, and

Matt's manager wanted the bidding electrical companies to submit a buy-back value as part of their quotes. She estimated the value of the inventory to be $5,000.

From his discussions with CE's Receiving Manager with regard to the performance records kept for ISO 9001 purposes, Matt had completed an analysis and comparison of the suppliers prior to receiving the submitted bids (See Exhibit 1). He had also developed the criteria with which to evaluate the submitted bids. Matt had also assigned weights to each criterion (See Exhibit 2). Given the nature of CE's business, Matt wanted the evaluation to be a realistic reflection of what was most critical to CE's operations. He took the total value of each bid, separated it into wire and cable, respectively, and created a bid summary with which to analyze the pricing of each bid (See Exhibit 3).

EXHIBIT 1   Supplier Overview

		Vendor		
Vendor Aspects	*PCC*	*Eastern*	*State*	*Bannister*
Target market (small, regional)	Specialized	Med.–Large	Small–Medium	Med.–Large
Supply	Custom	Volume	Custom/Volume	Volume
Positioning (quality, leader)	Service	Availability	Service	Availability
Cost base	1 location	3 locations	1 location	Many locations
Sales	$14 mil/year	$117 mil/year	$51 mil/year	$225 mil/year
MRP	No	Yes	No	Yes
Reputation	Good	Good	Very Good	Good
Payment terms	Net 15 days	Net 45 days	Net 30 days	Net 30 days
Management	Fair/Weak	Good	Good	Good
ISO certification	Began Process	Certified	Registered	Certified

EXHIBIT 2   Criteria for Bid Evaluation

Criteria	*Weight*	*PCC*	*Eastern*	*State*	*Bannister*
Past performance[*]	20	17	14	16	0
Price	35	30	27	24	33
Terms	15	10	13	12	12
Delivery (from order to arrival)	15	10	12	15	0
Future EDI & EFT	10	0	10	10	10
Inventory buy-back[**]	5	2	5	5	4
TOTAL	100	69	81	82	59

[*]As judged by the Receiving Manager.

[**]Inventory buy-back was a figure based on the number of dollars willing to credit for current CE wire and cable stock.

EXHIBIT 3   **Bid Summary**

Bidder	Wire Products[*]	Cable Products[*]	Buy-back of CE's stock	Total
Premier Cable Corp.	$322,762	$519,435	$(2,000)	$840,197
Eastern Electric	$295,841	$558,233	$(5,000)	$849,074
State Electric	$305,593	$577,152	$(5,000)	$877,745
Bannister	$285,090	$538,791	$(4,000)	$819,881

[*]All prices fixed for one year, unless there is a fluctuation of greater than $0.10/lb. in the price of copper.

Electrical Component Suppliers. Below are descriptions of the four electrical suppliers that submitted completed bids to Custom Equipment.

Premier Cable Corporation (PCC). PCC was a small electrical supplier that specialized in cable and cable accessories. It had been servicing the automotive and robotics industries for nine years. PCC's reputation was based on its service. It had a five-year relationship with CE and was currently supplying CE with all of its Newflex cable requirements.

PCC wanted to continue to supply CE with Newflex cable in the future. However, it was worried about bidding against larger suppliers on commodity wire products because it did not possess the economies of scale of the larger suppliers. The president was quoted as saying, "It's hard to do both high-end cable and commodity wire products together." Because of its size, PCC had no intention of installing any new computer systems in the coming year, and it also did not have much use for CE's obsolete stock wires and cables.

Delivery from PCC's facility was made through a courier. CE received delivery of its orders 3–4 days from order placement. PCC could provide 24-hour service if necessary, but at an extra cost. Many Newflex cables were held in stock at PCC. Non-stocked cables could be couriered overnight from the Newflex manufacturing plant in New Jersey. Because many of CE's requirements were urgent, it was reassuring to have PCC as a supplier. The owner and sales representative wore beepers on the weekends in case of customer emergencies.

PCC's sales representative provided great service and returned all calls promptly, according to comments from some CE buyers. Another buyer had also informed Matt that PCC's delivery times were fair for non-rush items. The organization was very responsive and interested in pleasing its customers. One of PCC's customers that Matt had spoken with described the company as "service-oriented . . . cost issues come later. They're willing to work with pricing. . . . quality is never an issue."

Eastern Electric. Eastern Electric (Eastern) was a well-established electrical distributor located about 30 miles away. It was a large organization that desired all of CE's electrical business. Eastern's top priority was product availability, which it met with its size and dealer network. Eastern's pricing was competitive, and its management team was professional and friendly. It was sometimes difficult to get a hold of the inside sales representative. Response time to requests had occasionally been slow in the past. On average, delivery took 2–3 days from order. CE could receive up to three deliveries from Eastern each day because it operated its own fleet of delivery trucks; however they usually contained the components ordered a few days prior. Eastern's size and detailed order fulfillment processes could impede its ability to process rush orders.

Matt visited Eastern Electric's central wire warehouse and was impressed by the amount of products it held in stock, including Newflex cable. It had the latest computer systems. Eastern Electric had not been a major player in CE's wire and cable business in the past, although it supplied many other electrical components on a daily basis.

Bannister. Bannister was a very large wire and cable supplier that began operations in the early 1950s. It had not done any recent business with Custom Equipment, for which Matt could not find any specific reason. Therefore, CE's Receiving Manager had no current records of performance. Order fulfillment was performed through the use of courier delivery services. Some of Bannister's key customers were very large prominent customers. These companies used large quantities of wire and cable.

The sales representative was friendly but gave a lot of "general" answers to Matt's questions. He seemed interested in obtaining CE's business but unfamiliar with basic inventory concepts, which surprised Matt. Matt got the initial impression that CE would not be the Bannister representative's most valued customer.

By chance, Matt met and spoke with a former employee of Bannister a few days later, who described the organization as being "too big . . . not fast . . . everything needs to be documented and this can cause problems with rush deliveries. However, it prides itself on product availability and competitive pricing."

State Electric. State Electric was a small electrical supply company that had been dealing with CE for eight years. Its founder and its sales representative had both originally been employed by Eastern Electric but had resigned 11 years ago to start State Electric. State was currently supplying CE with most of its wire requirements.

State's primary focus was service. Delivery times were excellent, usually same-day or next day for stock items, according to CE's Receiving Manager. Otherwise, delivery would usually take 2–3 days. State was recently planning to implement new computer systems to serve its customers better. Its outside sales representative was always available to answer questions or give advice, and he personally visited Custom Equipment every few days. Matt observed that his presence was well appreciated by CE's engineers and employees, and everyone seemed to like him.

Of the four bidding suppliers, State could not supply Newflex cable. Instead, it wanted to supply CE with Kelvin cable, which was more expensive but supposedly equally effective. Some concern arose regarding this replacement cable because it had not been fully tested on a CE job as of yet. State held two "lunch and learn" seminars at CE to educate the engineers and purchasing agents about the Kelvin company and its products. These helped to familiarize all concerned with Kelvin products

and gave the engineers at CE an opportunity to inspect the products and ask technical questions.

Another potential difficulty with Kelvin cable was that there were numerous jobs with Newflex as the customer-specified cable. If CE wanted to use Kelvin products, it would need written permission from the customer. CE would first have to try the Kelvin cable on a non-specified job. To help convince CE to try the new cables, the representatives from State and Kelvin together agreed to supply an entire job with Kelvin products free of charge. This offer was significant considering that the cable for an average CE project cost between $8,000–$12,000.

Selection Criteria. Even before the bids had been sent out, Matt had identified a set of evaluation criteria and weights. Now that he had received the bids Matt wondered if the need criteria and weights needed revision, and which supplier he should recommend to the Purchasing Manager at the next day's meeting.

CASE 7–4
INDUSTRIAL PRODUCTS CORPORATION (IPC)

Maggie Agnelli, the packaging purchasing manager for IPC, wondered what she should say in tomorrow's meeting with the plant manager of Branco, a major supplier. In the last three quarters, Branco's quality performance rating had shown a steady decline. It was essential for Maggie to get the plant manager's cooperation to avoid future problems.

IPC. IPC, a diversified manufacturing organization offering a wide range of products to both industrial and consumer markets, employed approximately 1,100 people. Sales were $100 million a year, and the company had a long-standing track record of successful business performance.

Quality Control. Contributing to the success of IPC was a commitment to strict quality standards in purchasing. Coordination between the supplier and IPC's plant was crucial to avoid production

Exhibit 1   Supplier Performance Scoring Criteria

Quality

Item	Grade	Criteria
Rejected and nonconforming	4	No rejected or nonconforming shipments.
	3	Up to 5% of shipments nonconforming.
	2	>5–10% of shipments nonconforming.
	1	>10–20% of shipments nonconforming.
	0	>20% of shipments nonconforming.
Process capability, data/samples	4	Less than 1% outside control limits and samples/data received for all shipments.
	3	Up to 5% outside limits and 90–99% of shipments have samples/data.
	2	5–10% outside limits and 80–90% of shipments have samples/data.
	1	10–20% outside limits and 70–80% of shipments have samples/data.
	0	More than 20% outside limits and <70% of shipments have samples/data.

Delivery

Item	Grade	Criteria
Quantity	4	All correct quantities (within tolerance).
	3	Up to 5% shipments incorrect (within tolerance).
	2	>5–10% shipments incorrect (within tolerance).
	1	>10–20% shipments incorrect (within tolerance).
	0	>20% shipments incorrect (within tolerance).
Time	4	All shipments on time (within tolerance).
	3	Up to 5% of shipments outside tolerance.
	2	>5–10% of shipments outside tolerance.
	1	>10–20% of shipments outside tolerance.
	0	>20% of shipments outside tolerance.
Paperwork	4	No missing lot numbers, packing lists, invoice errors, or other required documentation.
	3	Up to 5% of shipments have errors.
	2	>5–10% of shipments have errors.
	1	>10–20% of shipments have errors.
	0	>20% of shipments have errors.

slowdowns. Contact was maintained directly between plant personnel and sales representatives. When a problem in the manufacturing plant arose due to the supplier's product, the appropriate sales representative was immediately notified by fax via a standard form called "Nonconformance Action Report" completed by the plant operator closest to the problem. The sales representative was required to return, by fax, a standard "Feedback Form" to acknowledge the problem and explain how it was to be solved.

Supplier deviations from standard, as reported on the Nonconformance Action Report, were also forwarded to each purchasing manager. The supply assistant compiled these forms, together with information collected on a number of other supplier performance criteria, such as accuracy of the quantity delivered, shipments on time, and accuracy of paperwork (see Exhibit 1). Each quarter, each purchasing manager used the information collected to compute a "Supplier Performance Rating." Suppliers were all rated on the same scoring criteria.

EXHIBIT 1   *(Concluded)*

Delivery

Shipment condition	4	All shipments received in expected condition.
	3	Up to 5% of shipments have damaged pallets, inadequate packaging or damaged cartons.
	2	>5–10% of shipments are damaged as above.
	1	>10–20% of shipments are damaged as above.
	0	>20% of shipments are damaged as above.

Continuous Improvement

Item	Grade	Criteria
Corrective action	4	Nonconformance Action Report/Supplier's response and implementation within 30 days.
	3	Nonconformance Action Report/Supplier's response and implementation within 31–60 days.
	2	Nonconformance Action Report/Supplier's response within 30 days.
	1	Nonconformance Action Report/Supplier's response within 31–60 days.
	0	No response within 60 days.
Cost, lead time, lot size reduction	4	Major reduction in unit cost, lead time, and lot size.
	2	Minor reduction in unit cost, lead time, and lot size.
	0	No reduction in unit cost, lead time, and lot size.

The criteria and scoring system implemented by IPC was developed internally and reflected the key aspects of supplier performance deemed to be important by IPC management. Vendors received a copy of the scoring criteria so that they were fully aware of how they were evaluated. At the end of each quarter, they were advised of their rating. IPC maintained detailed documentation of supplier activity and variance from norms.

The rating criteria included three categories: quality, delivery, and continuous performance, with quality accounting for the largest portion—50 percent of the total rating. Within each category there was a list of items. Each item was scored according to the supplier's provision of that item, on a scale from 0 to 4. Scores were then weighted and totaled. A total performance rating for the quarter was derived by summing categories (see Exhibit 2 for Branco's scoring sheet). The supplier's maximum possible score was 4. An overall rating of 3 was considered the minimum acceptable performance rating.

Branco. Maggie had been watching Branco's performance ratings for the last three quarters with some concern. Although the problems incurred each quarter were rectified by Branco, the next quarter brought even more problems. As a result, Branco's performance rating had dropped further each quarter. Finally, in the most recent quarter, Branco's rating dropped below the minimum acceptable standard of 3 (see Exhibits 2 and 3). When Branco's sales representative, Lonnie Crowbak, received the rating, she had called Maggie immediately, and she was just as concerned. They agreed that a meeting was necessary right away, and that IPC's production manager, Bill White, and Branco's plant manager, Joe Kakavalakus, must attend. They agreed to meet at IPC.

Branco was the supplier of packing cartons for IPC's abrasive products. The packing cartons were an odd size and required custom specifications. As a result, it had been necessary for Branco to customize production operations to meet the unique requirements of IPC. Branco, however, had become the only supplier of all custom packing cartons to IPC. As a result, IPC could not source a custom product from a different supplier easily or quickly. Branco delivered on a daily basis, and its yearly sales to IPC amounted to about $280,000. Custom work required a substantial commitment from both parties. The relationship of trust and certainty between IPC and Branco had taken a long time to solidify.

Quality problems were costly for IPC. A number of Branco's orders had included defective cartons due to overlapping flaps. Nonconformance problems such as this were typically not identified until a production run had started, and equipment stalls occurred. Production used a fully automated line process, and a stall at one end resulted in a slow-down throughout. Because the defective cartons would not affect the end product to the customer, IPC continued the run in order to meet customer deadlines. However, the last Branco shipment of defective packing cartons resulted in a 30 percent production loss for an entire day's (two shifts) production. At full production, IPC ran 2,000 cartons per hour, with three operators at $18 per hour each.

The Meeting with Branco. Over the last few years, Maggie felt things had changed drastically in the industry. At one time, as a purchaser, she might have demanded that the supplier make changes, "or else." This was no longer the case. Maggie reflected, "In such a tight market, you just don't drop suppliers. Relationships are everything."

In the meeting tomorrow morning, Maggie felt it was essential that she impress upon Lonnie and Joe her desire to continue a strong relationship. Yet, she would somehow have to convince Joe that something had to change at his end, without confronting him. Maggie wondered, "What should my agenda be for this meeting? What should I say?"

EXHIBIT 2   Scoring Sheet

Supplier Performance Rating
Branco
For Past 3 Months

Category	Item Description	Item Score	Item Weight	Category Score	Category Weight	Total Score
Quality	Rejected and nonconforming	3	0.65	1.95		
	Process capability, data/samples	2	0.35	0.70		
				2.65	0.50	1.33
Delivery	Quantity	4	0.30	1.20		
	Timely deliveries	4	0.30	1.20		
	Paperwork	4	0.20	0.80		
	Shipment condition	4	0.20	0.80		
				4.00	0.30	1.20
Continuous improvement	Corrective action response	3	0.50	1.50		
	Cost, lead time, lot size reduction	0	0.50	0.00		
				1.50	0.20	0.30
Total						2.83

EXHIBIT 3   Branco's Performance Rating

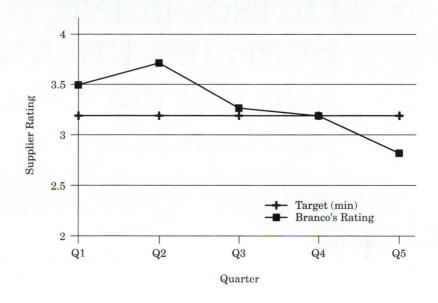

8 OUTSOURCING, SUPPLIER RELATIONS, AND SUPPLY CHAIN MANAGEMENT

Key Questions for the Purchasing Decision Maker

SHOULD WE
- Change our stance on make or buy?
- Use one or more suppliers?
- Outsource something we have been making?

HOW CAN WE
- Improve our relations with suppliers?
- Create new sources of supply?
- Develop partnerships or alliances with our key suppliers?

It has been long-standing wisdom in the procurement field that the key strategic decisions in supply management center on which supplier to pursue and what kinds of relations to maintain with suppliers. Strategic supply management is founded on the conviction that a significant competitive edge can be gained from the suppliers an organization has developed and its supply systems and supplier relations. Any organization's desire to satisfy its customers and to provide continuing improvement in its customer service is dependent on its suppliers to help it accomplish this goal. (See Figure 8–1.)

Supply and Demand Management are Critical

Supplier performance has a greater impact on the productivity, quality, and competitiveness of the organization than most managers realize. Recent trends to buy instead of make, to outsource instead of continuing to make, to improve quality, to lower inventories, to integrate supplier and purchaser systems, and to create cooperative relations such as partnerships have underlined the need for outstanding supplier performance.

In the supply chain management perspective, the link between the buying organization and its direct suppliers (and their suppliers) is obviously one of the two primary external ones. The other link, between the buying organization and its customers, continues the chain on the exit, or distribution, side. The ability of any organization to connect these two external links through its internal organization will, to a large extent, determine the effectiveness of its total supply chain. Figure 8–2 provides a simplified overview of these links. Because in any chain, the weakest link determines the strength of the whole chain, it is important that the strength of each link be equal and congruent. It is also a relatively simple perspective that greater strength in any one link can create a customer-dominant, internally dominant, or supply-dominant organization.

Achieving Competitive Advantage Through Supply Management

In this chapter, the prime perspective is to develop a supply link that will provide a short- and long-term strategic competitive advantage.

FIGURE 8–1

Customer Service Inputs

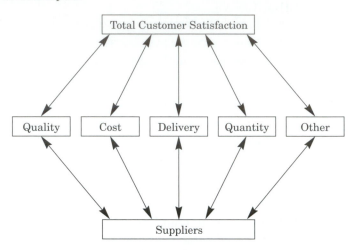

Depending on the nature of the purchase—whether it is a repeat, a modified repeat, or a new requirement; the size of the dollar amount involved; and the market conditions—the criticality or impact of the supplier choice may vary and the acquisition process and final decision may change. Whereas in the past most buyers felt that the supplier selection decision should be purchasing's domain, today's trend to team purchasing recognizes that it is necessary to bring together key organizational resources outside and inside of the supply area to achieve sound supplier choices. Moreover, the trend to fewer suppliers, longer-term contracts, e-procurement, and continuing improvement in quality, price, and service requires much closer coordination and communication between various people in both the buying and selling organizations. Therefore, improving buyer-seller relationships is a key concern.

Outstanding supplier performance normally requires extensive communication and cooperation between various representatives of the buying organization and the selling organization over a long period of time. In full recognition of this, progressive procurement organizations are pursuing ways and means of limiting their total number of suppliers and maximizing the results from fewer key suppliers. Bringing new suppliers on-stream is expensive and is often accompanied by a period of learning and aggravation for both sides. Frequent supplier switching for the sake of a seemingly lower price may not result in obtaining the best long-term value. As quality improvement programs and just-in-time production efforts take hold, proximity of the supplier's premises to those of the purchaser becomes a significant consideration. An imaginative and aggressive supplier development effort, both with existing and new sources, holds high promise as a review of exist-

Trends in Supplier Management

Limited Number of Suppliers and Closes Relationships

FIGURE 8–2

Simplified Supply Chain Perspective Showing the Three Core Links

ing suppliers discloses gaps and as new technology evolves into new requirements. System and philosophical compatibility between purchaser and supplier has become more vital as ways and means are found to shorten the time taken from requisition to actual receipt of the order.

These exciting new approaches to supplier choice and relationships between suppliers and purchasers are in stark contrast to the old-fashioned, hard-nosed way of procurement. It used to be reasonably common that suppliers were dropped with little notice when they failed to provide the lowest quote on an annual contract. The ideas of sharing information and assisting suppliers to improve quality, quantity, delivery, price, and service performance are no longer seen as novel, but more a necessity for world-class performance.

Make or Buy

Trend toward Outsourcing

A critical strategic decision for any organization centers on the issue of make or buy. The whole character of the organization may be colored by the organization's stance on this decision. It is one of vital importance to an organization's productivity and competitiveness. Managerial thinking on this issue has changed dramatically in the last few years with increased global competition, pressures to reduce costs, downsizing, and focus on the firm's core competencies. The trend is now toward outsourcing or seeking outside suppliers for services or goods that have been provided in-house.

Traditionally, the make option tended to be favored by many large organizations, resulting in backward integration and ownership of a large range of manufacturing and subassembly facilities. Major purchases were largely confined to raw materials, which were then processed in-house. New management trends favoring flexibility and focus on corporate strengths, closeness to the customer, and increased emphasis on productivity and competitiveness reinforce the idea of buying outside. It would be very unusual if any one organization were superior to competition in all aspects of manufacturing or services. By buying outside from capable suppliers those requirements for which the buying organization has no special manufacturing or service advantage, the management of the buying organization can concentrate better on its main mission. This philosophy has already resulted in substantial downsizing and has created an expanded scope for purchasing in the process. With the world as a marketplace, it is the purchaser's responsibility to search for or develop world-class suppliers suitable for the strategic needs of the buying organization.

A recent North American phenomenon has been the tendency to purchase services outside that were traditionally performed in-house. These include security, food services, and maintenance, but also computer programming, training, engineering, accounting, legal, research, personnel, and even contract logistics and purchasing. Thus, a new class of purchases involving services has evolved. (For a detailed description of the purchase of services, see Chapter 17.)

The make-or-buy/outsource decision is an interesting one because of its many dimensions. Almost every organization is faced with it continually. For manufacturing companies, the make alternative may be a natural extension of activities already present or an opportunity for diversification. For nonmanufacturing concerns, it is normally a question of services rather than products. Should a hospital have its own laundry, operate its own dietary, security, and maintenance services, or should it purchase these outside? Becoming one's own supplier is an alternative that has not received much attention in this text so far, and yet it is a vital point in every organization's procurement strategy.

What should be the attitude of an organization toward this make-or-buy issue? Many organizations do not have a consciously expressed policy but prefer to decide each issue as it arises. Moreover, it can be difficult to gather meaningful accounting data for economic analysis to support such decisions.

Key Question in Make or Buy   If it were possible to discuss the question in the aggregate for the individual firm, the problem should be formulated in terms of: What should our organization's objective be in terms of how much supply value should be added in-house as a percentage of final product or service cost and in what form? A strong supply group would favor a buy tendency when other factors are not of overriding importance. For example, one corporation found its supply ability in international markets such a competitive asset that it deliberately divested itself of certain manufacturing facilities common to every competitor in the industry.

Reasons for Make instead of Buy

There are many reasons that may lead an organization to produce in-house rather than purchase. These include:

1. The quantities are too small and/or no supplier is interested in providing the goods.

2. Quality requirements may be so exacting or so unusual as to require special processing methods that suppliers cannot be expected to provide.

3. Greater assurance of supply or a closer coordination of supply with the demand.

4. To preserve technological secrets.

5. To obtain a lower cost.

6. To take advantage of or avoid idle equipment and/or labor.

7. To ensure steady running of the corporation's own facilities, leaving the suppliers to bear the burden of fluctuations in demand.

8. To avoid sole-source dependency.

9. Competitive, political, social, or environmental reasons may force an organization to make even when it might have preferred to buy. When a competitor acquires ownership of a key source of raw material, it may force similar action. Many countries insist that a certain amount of processing of raw materials be done within national boundaries. A company located in a high-unemployment area may decide to make certain items to help alleviate this situation. A company may have to further process certain byproducts to make them environmentally acceptable. In each of these instances, cost may not be the overriding concern.

10. Finally, there is a purely emotional reason. The management of some organizations appears to take pride in size.

Reasons for Buying Outside

There are many reasons why an organization may prefer to purchase goods or services outside. These include:

1. The organization may lack administrative or technical experience in the production of the items or services in question.

2. Excess production capacity may force the organization to go into the market and even into competition with its former suppliers. This may affect relations with other suppliers or customers as well.

3. Frequently, certain suppliers have built such a reputation for themselves that they have been able to build a real preference for their component as part of the finished product. Normally, these are branded items which can be used to make the total piece of equipment more acceptable to the final user. The manufacturers of construction or mining equipment frequently let the customer specify the power plant brand and see this option as advantageous in selling their equipment.

4. The challenges of maintaining long-term technological and economic viability for a noncore activity.

5. A decision to make, once made, is often difficult to reverse. Union pressures and management inertia combine to preserve the status quo.

6. It is difficult to determine the true long-term costs of the make decision. Experience has made it amply clear that once management has definitely committed itself to a policy of procurement by manufacture, it is not difficult for costs to be figured to justify both the original decision and a continuance of the practice.

7. There is more flexibility in selecting possible sources and substitute items.

8. Organizations have to determine where their value-added activities are part of their core business and where they wish to distinguish themselves from others. The last decade has seen an increasing willingness to reexamine past make-or-buy decisions in the light of today's competitive environment. The net result has been a substantial shift into the buy or outsource option, suggesting that significant market opportunities existed to do better.

9. Superior supply management expertise.

10. Acquisition generally requires less overhead.

Role of Supply in Make or Buy Decision

Thus, it becomes increasingly evident that the make-or-buy decision is often a difficult one and that the decision to make, once made, is likely to place the organization in a position from which it is difficult to withdraw. It is supply's responsibility to ensure that the buy alternative is seriously investigated before a make decision is ever made.

The Gray Zone in Make or Buy

A Range of Options May Exist

Research by Leenders and Nollet[1] suggests that a "gray zone" may exist in make-or-buy situations. There may be a range of options between 100 percent make or 100 percent buy. This middle ground may be particularly useful for testing and learning without having to make the full commitment to make or buy. Particularly in the purchase of services, where no equipment investment is involved, it may be that substantial economies accrue to the organization that can substitute low-cost internal labor for expensive outside staff or low-cost external labor for expensive inside staff.

Further research into the role of manufacturing engineering suggests an interesting make-or-buy implication. To what extent should the purchasing company's engineering group get involved in specifying processes and work layouts for a subcontractor or a supplier? Thus, the purchaser's own manufacturing engineering group can combine its efforts with an outside supplier who basically supplies space, equipment, and labor. Whether a lack of manufacturing engineering strength on the part of the supplier is a desirable longer-term situation is open to debate. Moreover,

---

[1]M. R. Leenders and J. Nollet, "The Gray Zone in Make or Buy," *Journal of Purchasing and Materials Management,* Fall 1984, pp. 10–15.

overspecification of processes and equipment by the buyer's manufacturing engineers may prevent innovative process or product solutions by the suppliers.

Given the changing emphasis toward buying outside or outsourcing, the middle ground or gray zone in make or buy may offer valuable opportunities or superior options for both purchaser and supplier.

Subcontracting

Subcontractor Defined

A special class of the make-or-buy spectrum is the area of subcontracting. Common in military and construction procurement, subcontracts can exist only when there are prime contractors who bid out part of the work to other contractors; hence the term *subcontractor*. In its simplest form, a subcontract is a purchase order written with more explicit terms and conditions. Its complexity and management varies in direct proportion to the value and size of the program to be managed. The management of a subcontract may require unique skills and abilities because of the amount and type of correspondence, charts, program reviews, and management reporting which are necessary. Additionally, payment may be handled differently and is usually negotiated along with the actual pricing and terms and conditions of the subcontract.

Aerospace and Construction Typically Subcontract

The use of a subcontract is appropriate when placing orders for work that is difficult to define, will take a long period of time, and will be extremely costly. For example, aerospace companies subcontract many of the larger structural components and avionics. Wings, landing gears, and radar systems are examples of high-cost items which might be purchased on a subcontract. A similar form of subcontracting is often used in the construction industry, where a building contractor might subcontract the electrical or plumbing work of a building or project.

Subcontract Administration

In the aerospace industry, the subcontract is normally administered by a team which might include: a subcontract administrator (SCA); an equipment engineer; a quality assurance representative; a reliability engineer; a material price/cost analyst; a program office representative; and/or an on-site representative.

Managing the subcontract is a complex activity that requires knowledge about performance to date as well as the ability to anticipate actions needed to ensure the desired end results. The SCA must maintain cost, schedule, technical, and configuration control from the beginning to the completion of the task.

Cost Control of the Subcontract

Cost control of the subcontract begins with the negotiation of a fair and reasonable cost, proper choice of the contract type, and thoughtfully imposed incentives. Schedule control requires the development of a good master schedule which covers all necessary contract activities realistically. Well-designed written reports and recovery programs, where necessary, are essential. Technical control must be instigated to ensure that the end product conforms to all the performance parameters of the specifications that were established when the contract was awarded. Configuration control ensures that all changes are documented. Good configuration control is essential to "after-market" and spares considerations for the product. Unlike a normal purchase order of minimal complexity, where final close-out may be accomplished by delivery and payment, a major subcontract involves more definite actions to close. These actions vary with the contract type and difficulty of the item/task being procured. Quite often, large and complex procurements require a number of changes during the period of performance. These changes result in cost claims which must be settled prior to contract closure. Additionally, any tooling or data supplied to the contractor to support the effort must be returned. All deliverable material, data, and reports must be received and inspected. Each subcontract's requirements will vary in the complexity of the closure requirements; however, in all cases a subcontract performance summary should be written to provide a basis for evaluation of the supplier for future bidder or supplier selection. Such a report also is necessary in providing information for subsequent claims or renegotiation.

Outsourcing[2]

Outsourcing Defined

Outsourcing is a type of make-or-buy decision that has gained prominence in the 1990s. Organizations outsource when they decide to buy something they had been making in-house. Outsourcing is basically a reversal of a previous make decision. For example, a company whose employees clean the buildings may decide to hire an outside janitorial firm to provide this service. That a huge wave of outsourcing and privatization (in the public sector) has hit almost all organizations during the last decade is evident. In the urge to downsize, "right size," and eliminate headquarters staff, and to focus on value-added activities and core competencies in order to survive and prosper, public and private organizations have outsourced an extremely broad range of functions and activities formerly performed in-house. Some activities, such as janitorial, food, and security services, have been outsourced for many years. Information Systems (IS) is one activity that has received much attention recently as a target for outsourcing. It has been estimated that worldwide outsourcing of the IS function was about $50 billion in the mid-1990s and growing rapidly. The contract logistics industry is expected to triple in size to $50 billion in annual revenue in the year 2000.[3] According to

Worldwide Outsourcing Growing Rapidly

---

[2]This section is based in large part on research done by Michiel R. Leenders, Randy P. Kudar, Anna E. Flynn, and Douglas Clark, "Fleet Management's Contribution and Outsourcing," an unpublished research report for the National Association of Fleet Administrators, 1995.

[3]Jon Bigness, "In Today's Economy, There Is Big Money to Be Made in Logistics," *The Wall Street Journal,* September 6, 1995, p. A1.

a survey conducted by Dun & Bradstreet and The Outsourcing Institute in 1997, the functions most likely to be outsourced were: information technology (30 percent); human resources (16 percent); marketing/sales (14 percent); finance (11 percent); administration (9 percent); and all other functions (22 percent).[4]

Approaches to Outsourcing

Other popular outsourcing targets are mail rooms, copy centers, and corporate travel departments. An entire function may be outsourced, or some elements of an activity may be outsourced and some kept in-house. For example, some of the elements of information technology may be strategic, some may be critical, and some may lend themselves to cheaper purchase and management by a third party.[5] Identifying a function as a potential outsourcing target, and then breaking that function into its components, allows the decision makers to determine which activities are strategic or critical and should remain in-house, and which can be outsourced on a commodity-like basis.

The growth in outsourcing in the logistics area is attributed to transportation deregulation, the focus on core competencies, reductions in inventories, and enhanced logistics management computer programs. Lean inventories mean there is less room for error in deliveries, especially if the organization is operating in a just-in-time mode. Trucking companies have started adding the logistics aspect to their businesses—changing from merely moving goods from point A to point B to managing all or a part of all shipments over a longer period of time, typically three years, and replacing the shipper's employees with their own. Logistics companies now have complex computer tracking technology that reduces the risk in transportation and allows the logistics company to add more value to the firm than it could if the function were performed in-house. Third-party logistics providers track freight using electronic data interchange technology and a satellite system to tell customers exactly where its drivers are and when the delivery will be made. In a just-in-time environment, where the delivery window may be only 30 minutes, such technology is critical.

Hewlett-Packard Outsourcing Example

For example, Hewlett-Packard turned over its inbound, raw materials warehousing in Vancouver, Washington, to Roadway Logistics.[6] Roadway's 140 employees operate the warehouse 24 hours a day, seven days a week, coordinating the delivery of parts to the warehouse and managing storage. Hewlett-Packard's 250 employees were transferred to other company activities. Hewlett-Packard reports savings of 10 percent in warehousing operating costs.

---

[4]Michael Patton, "The Ongoings of Outsourcing," *Outsourcing Guide:* Supplement to *Purchasing Today,* August 1998, p. 5.

[5]Mary C. Lacity, Leslie P. Willcocks, and David F. Feeny, "IT Outsourcing: Maximize Flexibility and Control," *Harvard Business Review,* May–June 1995, pp. 86–87.

[6]Jon Bigness, *The Wall Street Journal,* op. cit.

FIGURE 8–3

Reasons for Outsourcing

	Reasons for Outsourcing
1995	1998[7]
Cost reduction	Reduce and control operating costs
Head-count reduction	Improve company focus
Focus on core competencies	Gain access to world-class capabilities
Acquire and deploy peripheral knowledge or process technology	Free internal resources for other purposes
	Resources are not available internally
Minimize inventory and materials handling,	Accelerate reengineering benefits
Reduce development and production cycle times	Function difficult to manage/out of control
	Make capital funds available
Improve efficiency	Share risks
Reaction to positive media reports	Cash infusion

[7]Survey of Current and Potential Outsourcing End-Users, The Outsourcing Institute Membership, 1998, *www.outsourcing.com.*

Reasons for Outsourcing

Figure 8–3 lists some of the main reasons for outsourcing in 1995 compared with 1998. At the beginning of the outsourcing trend in the late 1980s and early 1990s, companies were focused on reducing costs, which resulted in massive downsizing. Outsourcing provided a means to achieve the goal of cost reduction through head-count reduction along the promise, if not delivery, of equal or improved service quality. In the late 1990s and early 2000, the major downsizing was completed and a tight labor market in the United States made the quest for talent more difficult than it had been in decades. The 1998 survey reflects this situation in that several of the driving forces behind outsourcing were related to the organization's ability to attract the necessary talent.

Risks of Outsourcing

Figure 8–4 lists some of the associated risks of outsourcing. One of the drawbacks to outsourcing in the eyes of some is the layoffs that often result, and even in cases where the service provider (third party) hires former employees, they are often hired back at lower wages with fewer benefits. Outsourcing is perceived by many unions as efforts to circumvent union contracts. The United Auto Workers Union has been particularly active in trying to prevent auto manufacturers from outsourcing fleet operations. These risks haven't really changed over time. However, as organizations have gained more experience in making outsourcing decisions and crafting outsourcing contracts, many decision makers have become better at applying sourcing and contracting expertise to these decisions. From writing the statement of work or request for proposal to defining the terms and conditions, the success of an outsourcing agreement lies in the details.

FIGURE 8–4

Risks of Outsourcing[8]

Loss of control

Higher exit barriers

Exposure to supplier risks: financial strength, loss of commitment to outsourcing, slow implementation, promised features not available, lack of responsiveness, poor daily quality

Unexpected fees or "extra use" charges

Difficulty in quantifying economies

Conversion costs

Supply restraints

Attention required by senior management

Possibility of being tied to obsolete technology

Concerns with long-term flexibility and meeting changing business requirements

---

[8]Information drawn from the following sources: Leenders, et al., "Fleet Management's Contribution and Outsourcing," op. cit. pp. 38–40; "Making Way for the Virtual Enterprise," *Purchasing,* December 15, 1994, p. 18; and Mary C. Lacity and Rudy Hirscheim, *Information Systems Outsourcing* (New York: John Wiley & Sons, 1993).

Outsourcing Purchasing and Logistics

Saturn Example

The purchasing function has also come under scrutiny in some organizations as a target for outsourcing. For example, when Saturn Corporation streamlined its supply management operations, it determined that supply could add the most value in the management of production materials, and that a distributor could add the most value in the area of nonproduction-related materials.[9] Saturn's purchasing management team supported the idea of outsourcing nonproduction purchasing as a way to minimize the number of suppliers, develop partnering relationships, minimize problems, and reduce the accounts and administrative paperwork. A cross-functional management team drawn from purchasing, manufacturing and product engineering, finance, materials management, and the United Auto Workers Union evaluated hundreds of potential suppliers before selecting Cameron & Barkley (CAMBAR). CAMBAR, chosen to act as the outside purchasing arm of Saturn Corporation, orders, inventories, delivers, and pays suppliers. CAMBAR is also responsible for quality control, material warranty, and assistance in supplier selection. CAMBAR also agreed to achieve a 5 percent annual cost reduction, which it shares with Saturn, through increased efficiency and organization and supplier price reductions. EDI is used for ordering, receiving, and payment via electronic funds transfer (EFT). Daily requirements are transmitted seven times a day via EDI transmissions, and orders are shipped from the distributor's warehouse, 10 miles from the plant.

---

[9]Fred Gardner, "Saturn's Better Idea: Outsource Purchasing," *Electronic Business Buyer,* September 1993, pp. 136–41.

**Little
Outsourcing of
Supply
Activities**

In a CAPS study on outsourcing done in 1997, it was found that there was little outsourcing of typical supply management activities. For MRO activities, 65–75 percent of respondents reported no or a slight degree of outsourcing; for strategic purchases, 70–90 percent; and the percentage for nonstrategic, non-MRO activities fell between the two. The activities most likely to be outsourced were inventory monitoring, order placement, and order receiving, with more than 40 percent of respondents expecting increased outsourcing in inventory monitoring and order placement. Survey respondents also reported that they believe internal supply groups outperform third-party groups for strategic purchases, but the two offer more comparable service on nonstrategic purchases.[10]

**Logistics
Activities and
the Logistics
Function
Widely
Outsourced**

Many tasks associated with the logistics function as well as the entire function itself have been heavily outsourced. The tasks typically outsourced include freight auditing, leasing, maintenance and repair, freight brokering, and consulting and training. A quick Internet search reveals a host of companies offering integrated logistics services. The term *integrated logistics* had its origin in organizations in which distribution of the finished goods was a major activity compared with manufacturing and supply. In the theoretical sense, it obviously makes sense to look at the total supply chain in an integrated way and ensure that the logistics are fully integrated. The problems with integrated logistics do not lie with its conceptualization but its practicality. Like supply chain management, weak links in the total chain make it difficult to achieve effective integration across the whole. Wal-Mart is one retailer that certainly has shown that aggressive management of the logistics function can achieve significant competitive advantage in retailing. Undoubtedly, as awareness of opportunities in the logistics function and its integration within the total supply chain become more obvious, significant further developments will take place (see also Chapter 9 on transportation and logistics).

The Outsourcing Matrix. The decision to outsource or not depends on a number of financial and nonfinancial variables and the particular situation of the organization. In every organization, a type of outsourcing matrix may exist as follows.[11] (See Figure 8–5.)

**Factors
Affecting the
Outsourcing
Decision**

Thus, quadrant 1 represents functions, tasks, and activities that definitely should be in-house and are currently performed in-house. Quadrant 2 represents functions, tasks, and activities that should be done in-house but that are currently outsourced. Quadrant 3 represents functions, tasks, or activities that should be outsourced but are currently done in-house. Quadrant 4 represents tasks, functions, and activities that should be outsourced and are.

---

[10] Lisa M. Ellram and Arnold Maltz, *Outsourcing: Implications for Supply Management* (Tempe, AZ: Center for Advanced Purchasing Studies, 1997), p. 9.

[11] Leenders, et al., "Fleet Management's Contribution and Outsourcing," p. 50.

FIGURE 8–5

The Outsourcing Matrix

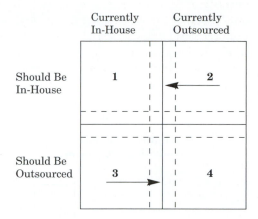

Quadrants 1 and 4 are the two stable quadrants where things are the way they should be. Quadrants 2 and 3 are not congruent, and pressures in each quadrant will exist to correct the situation for economic and/or noneconomic reasons. Smart managers should correct these situations quickly and try to avoid getting into quadrants 2 and 3 in the first place. The dotted lines in the quadrants indicate that a fuzzy zone exists where the best decision may not be all that evident. The greatest amount of judgment is required around the center of the matrix.

For any one organization the symmetry suggested by the diagram in Figure 8–5 may not exist. Figure 8–6 shows three possibilities with varying ratios of in-house and outsourced tasks in an organization.

For example, quadrant 1 (in-house) could be huge compared to quadrant 4 (outsourcing), or vice versa. Hopefully, both quadrants 2 and 3 (possibly reflecting dubious decisions in the past) should be significantly smaller than quadrants 1 or 4.

Outsourcing Example: Fleet Ownership and Management

Deciding what represents a core competency to an organization is not always an easy task, nor is the decision always the same for a specific function. For example, ownership and management of an in-house fleet of vehicles may be subject to the decision to outsource or maintain in-house. In an organization where the sales force is large, the cars for salespeople may be seen as an extension of the sales force and part and parcel of the company's ability to outperform the competition in personal sales. Many of the functions of fleet management may be outsourced—leasing rather than owning vehicles, maintenance, resale of vehicles—but the contact with the drivers may be retained as an in-house function because keeping the drivers (sales force) happy is critical to the success of the organization. In a utility company, the mechanical expertise needed to maintain specialty vehicles may be seen as part of the company's core competency, whereas the maintenance of the au-

FIGURE 8–6

The Outsourcing Matrix—Three Common Possibilities

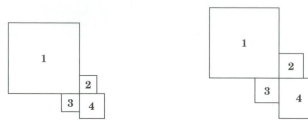

Possibility 1— Almost no outsourcing makes sense

Possibility 2— A reasonable balance between in-house and outsourcing

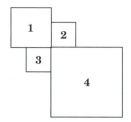

Possibility 3— Outsourcing dominant

tomobile fleet may not. The outsourcing decision is a function of many factors, and each organization must assess these factors based on the goals and objectives and long-term strategy of the organization. Those functions or activities falling within the dotted lines, especially closer to the center of the diagram, require more careful analysis and judgment than those outside of this area.

Another way of analyzing whether or not outsourcing makes sense is depicted in the flowchart in Figure 8–7.[12]

Purchasing's Role in Outsourcing

Supply Managers Can Add Value to the Out-sourcing Decision

Research indicates that purchasing has had relatively moderate involvement in the outsourcing decisions made by many organizations. However, given the nature of the decision, purchasing should, by rights, be heavily in-

---

[12]Adapted from Mary C. Lacity and Rudy Hirscheim, *Information Systems Outsourcing* (New York: John Wiley & Sons, 1993).

FIGURE 8–7

The Outsourcing Decision

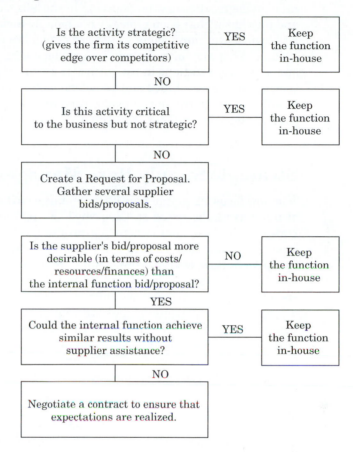

volved in outsourcing.[13] Supply managers believe they can add value to the outsourcing decision in the following ways:

- Providing a comprehensive, competitive process
- Identifying opportunities for outsourcing
- Aiding in selection of sources
- Identifying potential relationship issues
- Developing and negotiating the contract
- Ongoing monitoring and management of the relationship.[14]

---

[13]Harold E. Fearon and Michiel R. Leenders, *Purchasing's Organizational Roles and Responsibilities* (Tempe, AZ: Center for Advanced Purchasing Studies/National Association of Purchasing Management, 1995), p. 23.

[14]Ibid, p. 11.

In fact, in some cases, such as information systems outsourcing which has grown rapidly in the last few years, purchasing was not involved to any significant degree. Because outsourcing in the '90s focused primarily on services, and purchasing has been typically not heavily involved in service acquisitions, it is logical that purchasing would not play a large role in the outsourcing decision.[15] This may or may not change, depending on the role of purchasing/supply in organizations in the future. In terms of purchasing's value proposition, appropriately skilled and knowledgeable supply managers should be able to affect value in the initial exploration of alternatives leading up to an outsourcing decision and not after the decision has already been made.

Strategic Supply Base Management

The new focus on suppliers is based in large part on the profit leverage effect of purchasing discussed in Chapter 1. A 1995 article in *Fortune* magazine states: "When the goal is boosting profits by dramatically lowering costs, a business should look first to what it buys."[16] Manufacturers spend an average of 55 cents of every revenue dollar on purchasing goods and services, and only about 6 cents on labor and 3 cents on overhead. Service organizations spend about 15 cents of every sales dollar on purchasing goods and services, a much smaller percentage, but still a potentially lucrative area to focus on when cutting costs. The realization that supply management offers one of the best opportunities to reduce costs and improve profitability is sweeping across businesses in the United States, Canada, and other parts of the globe. Cost reductions can be realized by improving supply's internal systems (Chapter 3), by performing value analysis on acquired goods and services (Chapters 9 and 13), by improving the acquisition of commodities (Chapter 13), and by improving management of the supply base (Chapters 7 and 8).

According to a CAPS study, *The Future of Purchasing and Supply: A Five- and Ten-Year Forecast,* there is growing realization on the part of executives that suppliers can have an impact on long-term innovation and growth by providing access to new resources and enhancing sales.[17]

The focus on sourcing and supply management strategy is driven by trends that will impact effectiveness in the year 2000 and beyond. Monczka has identified seven trends that will impact performance in the areas of organization, people, systems, measurements, and procurement/sourcing

Seven Trends Impact Performance

---

[15]Harold E. Fearon and William A. Bales, *Purchasing of Nontraditional Goods and Services* (Tempe, AZ: Center for Advanced Purchasing Studies/National Association of Purchasing Management, 1995), p. 8.

[16]Shawn Tully, "Purchasing's New Muscle," *Fortune,* February 20, 1995, p. 75.

[17]Phillip L. Carter, Joseph R. Carter, Robert M. Monczka, Thomas H. Slaight, and Andrew J. Swan, *The Future of Purchasing and Supply: A Five- and Ten-Year Forecast* (Tempe, AZ: Center for Advanced Purchasing Studies, 1998), p. 20.

FIGURE 8–8

The Impact of Year 2000 Trends on Procurement / Sourcing Strategies

Trend	Procurement / Sourcing Strategies
Globalization	• Integrate procurement/customer strategies • Build competitive advantages with key suppliers on quality, cost, delivery, time, etc. • Modify supply base structure/channels
Information technology	• Link strategies worldwide • Link electronically to critical suppliers
External customer focus	• Integrate the supply base into the external customer product/value supply chain
Product/Process technology	• Strategic supplier alliances with leading product/process technology suppliers
Increasing job complexity	• Require comprehensive supply base/sourcing strategies and measure performance against the strategy goals
Environmental/Legal issues	• Incorporate environmental considerations in commodity strategies
Reengineering	• Reengineer external processes • Modify outsourcing patterns

strategies. Figure 8–8 is excerpted from Monczka's work and shows the trends and strategies that impact suppliers and supply base management.[18]

Purchaser-Supplier Relations

When one organization supplies another with goods or services, the nature of the relationship between the two organizations is a major influencer of the ultimate value and customer satisfaction achievable. Supply management is, therefore, not simply engaged in the exchange of money for goods and services, but also in the management of the buyer-seller relationship. This factor is the driving force in the trend toward use of the term *supply management,* rather than purchasing.

Use of Term Supply Management

In this section, the nature of supplier goodwill is discussed along with the qualifications of good and preferred suppliers, partnerships, strategic alliances, and supply chain management.

---

[18]Robert M. Monczka, "Purchasing 2000: Building the Infrastructure," NAPM Annual International Purchasing and Materials Management Conference Proceedings, 1994, p. 240.

Supplier Goodwill

Good sources of supply are one assurance of good quality today, and progressive thinking and planning is a further assurance of improved quality tomorrow. Superior sources of supply, therefore, are an important asset to any organization.

It has long been considered sound marketing policy to develop goodwill on the part of customers toward the seller. This goodwill has been cultivated through the development of trademarks and brands, through extensive advertising, through missionary efforts as well as through regular calls by sales personnel, and through the many other devices which have appealed to the imaginations of marketing managers. These days these efforts are often lumped together under the term *relationship marketing*. Sellers are jealous of this goodwill, considering it one of their major assets. It has real commercial value and is so recognized by courts of law.

Buyer-Supplier Goodwill Should be Cultivated

Goodwill between a purchasing organization and its suppliers needs to be just as carefully cultivated and just as jealously guarded. When purchasers are as aggressive in their attempts to maintain proper and friendly relations with suppliers as marketing managers are in their relations with customers, congruence in supply-chain linkage may be achieved. Because strategic plans are so often based on the assumption that supply sources will be cooperative, it makes sense to ensure that such cooperation will be forthcoming.

Progressive companies have started to measure supplier goodwill on a regular basis using third-party research organizations to conduct surveys. The president of one electronics firm flatly stated: "No company can be world class if it does not measure on a regular basis the satisfaction level of its key suppliers and try to improve constantly on its relations with its suppliers."

One of the interesting outcomes of supplier satisfaction surveys is the general finding that suppliers believe that the best purchasers are those who know more about the supplier's business than the supplier's own employees.

A Purchaser-Supplier Satisfaction Model

Assessment Can Take Many Forms

Certainly one of the major assessments a purchaser must make is whether the current relationship with a supplier is a satisfactory one or not. This relationship is highly complex, and different people inside the purchasing organization may have different perceptions of it. In the simplest form, with a new supplier just after a relatively small order has been placed but no deliveries have yet been made, it may consist only of an assessment of the agreement just reached and the buyer's quick impression of the sales representative. For a long-term supplier of major needs, the assessment will be based on past and current performance, personal relationships with a number of personnel in both organizations, and even future expectations. Such assessments may well change as a result of competitive action in the marketplace. What may look like a good price deal today may not look so attrac-

FIGURE 8–9

A Simple Purchaser-Supplier Satisfaction Model

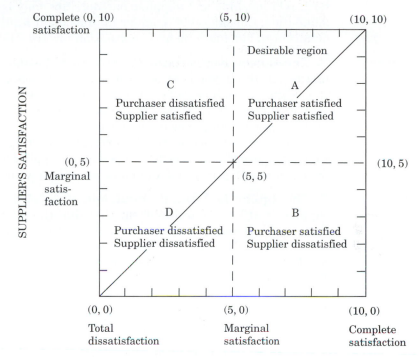

PURCHASER'S SATISFACTION

tive when information comes to light that a fully competent competitor could have supplied the same materials or items for substantially less.

The model in Figure 8–9 provides a simple framework for clarifying the current purchaser-supplier relationship in terms of satisfaction and stability. The assumptions behind it are:

Assumptions Behind Satisfaction Model

1. That satisfaction with a current supplier relationship can be assessed, however crudely, at least in macro terms, whether it is satisfactory or not.

2. That an unsatisfied party (seller or purchaser or both) will attempt to move to a more satisfactory situation.

3. That attempts to move may affect the stability of the relationship.

4. That attempts to move may fall in the win-lose, as well as the lose-lose, lose-win, and win-win categories.

5. That purchaser and seller may well have different perceptions of the same relationship.

6. That many tools and techniques and approaches exist that will assist either party in moving positions and improving stability.

Buyer and Seller Satisfied

A. The Upper Right-Hand Quadrant. (5,5–10,5–10,10–5,10) Region. Considerable satisfaction exists on both sides and stability is likely. Long-term relationships and supplier partnerships may be built on this kind of foundation. Considerable room for improvement is still possible within this quadrant in moving from a (5,5) situation toward a (10,10) objective.

Only Buyer Satisfied

B. The Lower Right-Hand Quadrant. (5,0–10,0–10,5–5,5) Region. In this region the buyer is at least marginally satisfied, but the seller is not. This is the mirror image of the C region, and the seller is likely to initiate action for change which may end up subsequently in any of the four regions. Stability is not likely over the long run.

The above comments are, of course, general in nature. It is entirely possible for a powerful purchaser or a powerful supplier to maintain a B or C region position respectively for a long time with a weak counterpart.

Only Supplier Satisfied

C. The Upper Left-Hand Quadrant. (0,5–5,5–5,10–0,10) Region. The supplier is at least marginally satisfied, but the purchaser is not. The purchaser will attempt to improve the buying situation. If this is done at the expense of the seller, a see-saw may be created whereby the purchaser's efforts result in the supplier's moving down the satisfaction scale into the D region. The assumption is that the most dissatisfied party is the most likely instigator of change. It is also possible that such instigations may reduce satisfaction for both parties so that both end up in the D region. Hopefully, changes might result in both parties moving into the A region.

Neither Buyer Nor Seller Satisfied

D. The Lower Left-Hand Quadrant. (0,0–5,0–5,5–0,5) Region. Both parties agree that significant dissatisfaction exists on both sides. This kind of situation is not likely to be stable for any length of time because each side will be striving to improve at least its own satisfaction.

Fairness or Stability Line

The Diagonal Line. The diagonal in the diagram may be seen as a "fairness or stability" line. As long as positions move along this line, both purchaser and supplier are at least equally well off. Its end points of (0,0) and (10,10) represent two extremes. The (0,0) position is completely undesirable from either standpoint and is a "total war" picture, which is extremely unstable. It represents an unlikely starting point for any long-term stable position because memories of this unhappy state of affairs are likely to prevent substantial improvements. The obvious solution is disassociation and the seeking of a new source by the purchaser.

Ideal, But Rarely Attainable Level

The (10,10) position represents a utopian view rarely found in reality. It requires a degree of mutual trust and sharing and respect that is difficult to achieve in our society of "buyer beware" and where competition and the price mechanism are supposed to work freely. In some partnerships, a relationship close to the (10,10) state has been developed. Buyers are willing to share risks and information with the seller, and the seller is willing to open the books for buyer inspection. Problems are ironed out in an amicable and mutually acceptable manner and both parties benefit from the relationship.

Minimum Acceptable Level

The middle position of (5,5) should really be considered as a minimum acceptable goal for both sides, and few agreements should be reached by the purchaser without achieving at least this place. Adjustments in positions should, hopefully, travel along the diagonal and toward the (10,10) corner. Substantial departures from the diagonal raise the difficulty that the agreement may be seen as less beneficial to one party than the other, with the possibility of jealousy and the attempt by the less-satisfied party to bring the other down to a more common denominator. The region of greatest stability will, therefore, lie close to the (5,5)–(10,10) portion of the diagonal line.

Buyer's and Seller's Perceptions May Diverge

Perceptions. This model becomes more complex when the perceptions of both parties are considered, both with respect to their own position and the other side's. For example, the purchaser's perception may be that the relationship is in the A region. The supplier's perception may or may not match this view. Let us look at the congruent side first.

Buyer and Seller Have Same Perception

Congruent Situations. Where both buyer's and supplier's perceptions agree, congruence exists and both parties would record their own and the other side's satisfaction on the same place on the chart. This does not necessarily mean that both parties are satisfied with the situation. Both at least have the same starting point, and mutual agreement on this is useful. For example, take an (8,6) situation, and both buyer and seller agree that the buyer is better satisfied with the current arrangement than the seller. Chances that both will be willing to work toward a corrective solution are reasonable (see Figure 8–10).

Buyer and Seller Have Differing Perceptions

Noncongruent Perceptions. Lack of congruence in perceptions of relative positions will present a problem in itself. Take, for example, the situation where the buyer's perceptions of the situation is (2,8), but the seller's perception is (9,1) (see Figure 8–10). The buyer thinks the supplier has a pretty good deal but is quite dissatisfied with the purchaser's situation. The seller's opinion is the exact opposite. So both parties are dissatisfied, but their actions are likely to lead to even further dissatisfaction on the other side. This would normally be a highly unstable situation. It may be possible to settle differences of perception through discussion among the managers involved. Such resolution will be necessary before any attempts can be undertaken to improve the position of either side.

Using the Framework. This model is based on the assumption that both purchaser and seller are capable of expressing a view on the degree of satisfaction that exists with a relationship. Essential elements of this relationship would include perceptions on quality, prices paid, service, and delivery; performance on the purchaser's side and promptness of payment, accessibility, fairness, and professionalism on the supplier's side; and whether the demands and cooperation of the other party are reasonable in

FIGURE 8–10

Purchaser-Supplier Satisfaction Model Showing (1) Congruent (2) Noncongruent Perceptions

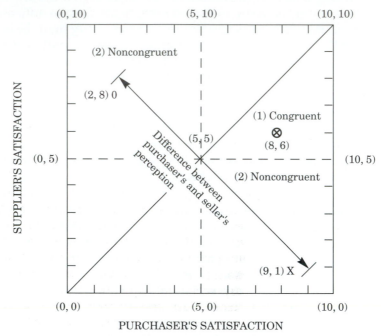

0 = Purchaser's perception of position of both parties.
X = Seller's perception of position of both parties.

view of the circumstances. Personality and philosophical factors and organizational values are also components. These measures are, of course, difficult to quantify, but ranking of relative positions compared to other suppliers (or customers) may well be possible. Even though absolute quantification is difficult, this model may be useful in a number of ways.

Model May Be Used to Develop Improvement Plans

From a supply point of view, it is possible to assess the total package of current supplier relationships and to determine how many fall inside the desirable region and how many outside. A significant percentage of unsatisfactory or marginal situations will mean a substantial amount of work to restructure current arrangements. The supply perception of a relationship may be shared with a supplier to check on congruence and as a starting point for mutual diagnosis and plan for change. Even the process of attempting to assess contracts and suppliers against the model's framework may be useful in establishing the key variables which are relevant for the particular commodity under study. Finally, the severity of the situation is a good indicator of the need for action and the tools and techniques which might be applied.

For example, a purchaser may wish to work harder at a (1,5) than a (5,5) situation of equal dollar value and corporate impact.

Tools and Techniques for Moving Positions. A number of supply management and marketing means may be used to shift positions on the satisfaction chart. The use of some of these will adversely affect the perceptions of the other party, and these might be called "crunch" tools or negative measures. Others are likely to be viewed in less severe terms and might be considered "stroking" methods or positive approaches. For example, crunch tools for the purchaser include:

Negative Measures to Shift Satisfaction Levels

1. Complete severance of purchases without advance notice.
2. Refusal to pay bills.
3. Refusal to accept shipments.
4. Use or threat of legal action.

For the supplier, examples would include:

1. Refusal to send shipments as promised.
2. Unilateral price increase without notice.
3. Insistence on unreasonable length of contract, take-or-pay commitments, onerous escalation clauses, or other unreasonable terms and conditions and use of take-it-or-leave-it propositions.

Stroking techniques by the purchaser would include:

Positive Measures to Shift Satisfaction Level

1. Granting of substantial volumes of business, long-run commitments, or 100 percent requirements contracts.
2. Sharing of internal information on forecasts, problems, and opportunities to invite a mutual search of alternatives.
3. Evidence of willingness and ability to work toward changed behavior in the purchasing organization to improve the seller's position.
4. Rapid positive response to requests from suppliers for discussions and adjustments in price, quality, delivery, and service.

On the supplier side, examples could be:

1. Willingness and ability to make rapid price, delivery, and quality adjustments in response to purchase requests without a major hassle.
2. Invitation to the purchaser to discuss mutual problems and opportunities.
3. The giving of notice substantially in advance of pending changes in price, lead times, and availability to allow the purchaser maximum time to plan ahead.

It is interesting that stroking techniques are more likely to be used in the A region, further strengthening the stability of the relationship, whereas

The Process and the Results Impact Perception

the use of crunch tools may well accomplish short-term objectives but may impair future chances of a desirable stable relationship.

The perception of a relationship is based on both the results obtained and the process by which they have been achieved. For example, a price concession grudgingly granted by a supplier and continually negatively referred to by supplier's personnel may create less satisfaction for the purchaser than one more amicably reached. Crunch methods pleasantly applied may be far more palatable than the same tool used in a hard-nosed way. For example, an unavoidable price increase can be explained in person by a supplier's sales manager well in advance more palatably than by a circular letter after the increase has been put into effect. A supply manager can visit a supplier's plant to determine ways and means of solving a quality problem and explain that no deliveries can be accepted until the problem is solved, instead of sending back shipment after shipment as unacceptable. The results–process combination puts a heavy emphasis on managerial judgment and capability to accomplish change effectively.

Purchaser-Supplier Relationship Management

Team Approach to Long-Term Relationships

The discussion on the satisfaction-stability framework underlines the need for extensive communications and communication skills for both parties in the buying-selling relationship. The whole art of supplier relationship management from a supply perspective is to bring both sides into an effective working relationship. This will require substantial coordination work inside the purchaser's organization to ensure that the people most vitally concerned with a particular supplier's performance are fully involved in the planning and execution of a program leading to the desired long-term relationship. Therefore, the team approach to long-term supplier relations is probably the only reasonable option. In such team acquisition, the buyer or supply manager usually plays the coordinator and project manager role.

Internal Cooperation and a Strategic Approach Key to Supplier Relationship Management

Without internal cooperation and a congruent strategic internal approach to the improvement of supplier relations, supplier relationship management is impossible. The members of the internal team are the ones who have to deal directly with their appropriate counterparts on the supplier side. The necessity for good management of this interface is obvious. Immediate and concerted action needs to be taken when either side detects problems or sees opportunities. Awareness of the full details of each side's situation, aspirations, strengths, and weaknesses is necessary for any team member to be able to assess the impact of changes, problems, or opportunities on the other side. Simply stated, the seller's and purchaser's personnel need to understand their own organizations and the other's very well so that both sides can work on continuing improvement for mutual benefit. Such understanding can come only through exposure, discussion, mutual problem solving, and willingness to investigate every aspect of a meaningful relationship frankly. Given that in many organizations it is difficult for individual employees in different functional areas to work well together toward a common goal, it is easy to appreciate the challenge posed by adding the supplier's organization to this set. It may well be that the development of superior supplier relations will be the most critical challenge for supply managers in the decades ahead.

Moreover, the ability to develop effective working relationships with suppliers will be dependent on supply's ability to develop effective working relationships internally. Thus, supply's status within the organization and the availability of qualified supply personnel will be key determinants of the organization's ability to get the most out of its supplier force.

Partnerships and Strategic Alliances

Buyer-supplier relationships fall somewhere on a continuum from traditional, adversarial relationships to fully integrated, seamless relationships, as depicted in Figure 8–11.

Operational and Strategic Needs Are Unmet

Unacceptable Suppliers. Unacceptable suppliers fail to meet the operational and strategic needs of the buying organization. Discontinuing business with unacceptable suppliers and substituting better ones is the normal action required. A special case exists where such a discontinuance may create even greater problems for the purchasing organization. A typical example is a sole-supply situation, as in the case of a patented or OEM part where the supplier takes undue advantage of its privileged position. Even then, when discontinuance in the short term may not be feasible, in the long term it may be, if the supply organization has diligently worked on finding an appropriate substitute or developing another source of supply. Another exception is a new source of supply that is still learning how to satisfy the purchasing organization's requirements and is assiduously working to achieve significant improvement.

Current Operational Needs Met

Acceptable Suppliers. Acceptable suppliers meet current operational needs as required by contract. Acceptable suppliers provide a performance that other purchasers could easily match and, hence, acceptable suppliers provide no basis for competitive edge.

Value-Added Services Provided

Good Suppliers. Good suppliers are somewhat better than acceptable suppliers in that they also offer the potential of value-added services in addition to products. To move a supplier from acceptable to good will require a substantial amount of purchaser and supplier effort.

Some Strategic Needs Met

Preferred Suppliers. Purchasers have a system or process orientation with preferred suppliers, and this integration avoids unnecessary duplication and speeds up transactions, which normally are handled on an electronic basis. Both parties work toward mutual improvements to eliminate nonvalue-adding activities. Preferred suppliers meet all operational and some of the strategic needs of the buying organization.

FIGURE 8–11

Buyer-Supplier Relationship Investment versus Rewards Obtained

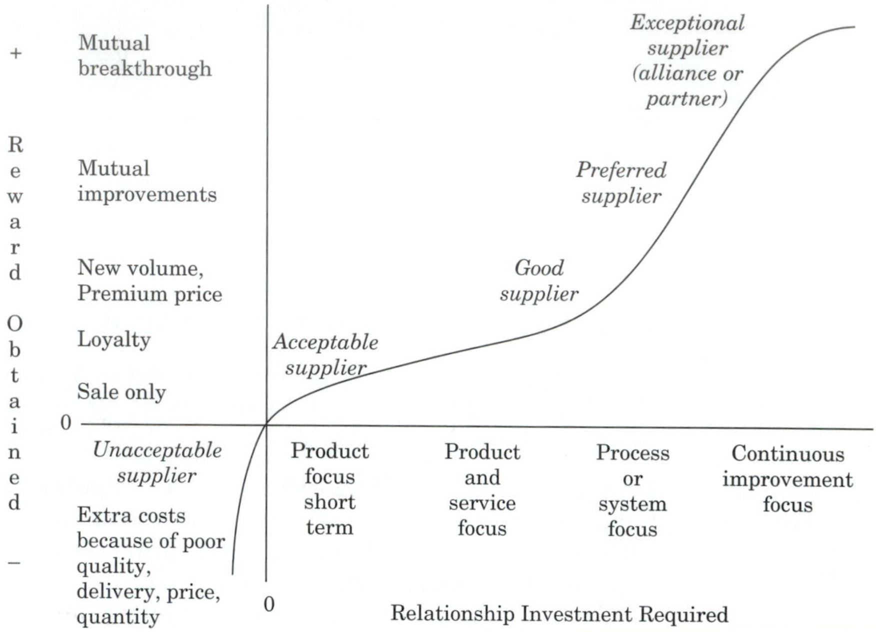

*Adapted from C. Michael Stralkowski and S. Alexander Billon, "Partnering: A Strategic Approach to Productivity Improvement," *National Productivity Review,* Spring 1988.

Operational and Strategic Needs Anticipated

Exceptional Suppliers. Exceptional suppliers anticipate the operational and strategic needs of the purchaser and are capable of meeting and exceeding them. With exceptional suppliers, mutual breakthroughs may be a source of significant competitive advantage. Exceptional suppliers, like exceptional customers, need to be treasured. They can serve as an example of what is possible: an opportunity to experiment with new and different approaches to supply base management and as an early indicator of future supply management and supplier relationship direction and goals.

Figure 8–11 reminds us that it may require a substantial amount of work on the part of both the supplier and the purchaser to obtain the big rewards of mutual breakthrough. Patience and persistence are required to sustain the investment in relationship building. The lack of evidence of substantial reward in the earlier stages may be disappointing for those who are interested only in the short haul. A similarity exists in athletic training. World and Olympic records are seldom obtained by those not willing to commit fully beforehand to the intensive and extensive training and developmental program.

Supplier Relationships at Disneyland

Leslie Monroe, Contract Coordinator at Disneyland in Anaheim, California, reports that:

"The innovation that is most common at Disneyland isn't about systems or processes or contracts; the true innovation is in the relationships we are building with key suppliers of goods and services. I need to understand my supplier's business as much as he or she needs to understand mine. We are working together to identify cost savings and value-creating opportunities, including alternative products, process changes, or any number of areas that positively impact the bottom line without sacrificing quality, safety, or the environment."[19]

In full recognition that exceptional suppliers are scarce and that substantial investment is required in creating a superior buyer-supplier relationship, a large number of purchasers have started to create preferred suppliers, partnerships, or strategic alliances. These are a logical evolution arising from supplier rationalization efforts.

Single Source Relationships Must Add Value

The danger in single-sourcing lies in becoming puppets of suppliers. Suppliers know that customers depend on them, and they may charge excessively or let quality or delivery slip, or slow down or stop continuing improvement programs. As an aside, it is ironic that many purchasers who buy from other divisions within a multidivisional organization find that these divisions give their captive in-house customers low priority. This is where careful supplier relationship management becomes important. It requires an understanding and identification of value. Value is the ultimate long-term life cycle cost and benefit to the user of the product or service acquired. It does not necessarily mean lowest purchase price, or lowest investment in inventory, or fastest delivery time, or lowest delivery cost, or longest life, or highest disposal value, or even the highest attainable quality; it is an optimal amount cutting across all of these. The purchase price frequently is one important part of this total. It is the duty of the supply manager to make sure that the purchase represents exceptional long-term value. Moreover, in the establishment of preferred suppliers or partnerships it is normal to agree on future quality, delivery, and price goals, in full recognition of learning curve theory and the commitment of both buyer and seller to continuous improvement.

Supplier Partnerships at Alberto Culver

At Alberto Culver, a personal-care products company, partnerships consist of multi-year contracts with key suppliers which include a goal for the contract term and a performance-based incentive rebate. A target level for quality and on-time delivery performance is negotiated and performance is measured monthly. The rebate is adjusted accordingly and paid annually. When targets are exceeded, Alberto Culver encourages its supplier partners to return the rebate to their employees as bonuses. The two work jointly toward continuous improvement and agree to higher performance targets each year with the ultimate goal of attaining a specific goal by the end of the contract period.[20]

---

[19]Leslie R. Monroe, "The Relationships We Build," *Purchasing Today,* February 1999, p. 68.

[20]Judy K. Spencer, "Set a Target Level," *Purchasing Today,* February 1999, p. 68.

Terms Defined

Buyer-Supplier Partnerships and Strategic Alliances. In the last decade, a large number of organizations have started to create "partnerships" with their suppliers. The term *partnership* gives lawyers discomfort, because in the legal sense it has certain obligations which are not necessarily part of a standard buyer-seller partnership. Unfortunately, considerable confusion exists regarding the meaning of partnership, and the selling community has further compounded these difficulties by making it part of a standard sales pitch to any customer. To avoid some of this confusion, some purchasers have chosen the term *preferred suppliers;* others, *strategic alliances* or similar terms.

The interest in buyer-supplier partnerships was fanned in the 1980s by the study of Japanese companies who maintained very close relationships with their suppliers. This was seen as one of the key elements in the achievement of quality, fast delivery, and continuous improvement. Early adopters in North America included companies like Xerox, Honeywell, Polaroid, Motorola, IBM, and the automotive companies, to name just a few. This move into a partnership mode really represents a substantial paradigm shift from the traditional buying-selling mode. A summary of some of the key differences is shown in Figure 8–12.

Partnership Example at CompUSA

In the late 1990s, buying organizations continued to develop closer relationships or partnerships with suppliers. For example, CompUSA initially formed a partnership with Wallace, a large printing company, to print and replenish forms to 210 retail stores. Next, CompUSA consolidated its requirements for other supplies and purchased them from Wallace at a lower cost. Wallace prints a quarterly catalog of supplies it provides to CompUSA as well as some items it replenishes from other suppliers. In the first year, supply expenditures were reduced by 32 percent.[21]

SEMATECH's Partnering Perspective. SEMATECH originally was created through a joint effort of the American electronics industry giants and the U.S. federal government to assist the electronics industry and its suppliers to be world class. It has evolved into an international consortium though which member companies cooperate pre-competitively in key areas of semiconductor technology to accelerate the development of advanced manufacturing technologies needed to build powerful semiconductors.[22] SEMATECH identified quality as the key driver of competitiveness and partnering as the means to achieve quality. Their interpretation of partnering extends to customers, employees, and suppliers. On the supplier side, SEMATECH identified two classes of partnership. Every supplier should be treated as a "basic partner" with mutual respect, honesty, trust, open and frequent communica-

Two Classes of Partners: Basic and Expanded

---

[21]Becky S. Moore, "Increased Service," *Purchasing Today,* February 1999, p. 68.
[22]Corporate Information, International SEMATECH, *www.sematech.org*, April 17, 2001.

tion, and understanding of each other as the minimum guidelines governing the relationship.

SEMATECH identified the need for an "expanded partnership" with selected key suppliers. Expanded partnering builds on basic partnering, is a long-term relationship process, provides focus on mutual strategic and tactical goals, and may include customer/supplier team support to promote mutual success and profitability. Therefore, in addition to basic partnering guidelines, expanded partnering has a long-term view, must have continuing improvement as an objective, and evidence of it must exist. The partners must have a passion to help each other succeed, place a high priority on the relationship, and include shared risks, opportunities, strategies, and technology road maps. It is expected that most organizations would have a limited number (6 to 20) of expanded partnerships.

An expanded partnership would normally have a top executive assigned to it. This executive would meet at least two to four times per year with his or her counterpart in the selling organization, who would monitor internal progress on joint projects and smooth the way for changes necessary for success. In addition, there should be regular monthly meetings planned for buyer-seller representatives and daily and weekly contact on project teams and other activities, involving a substantial number of people from various functions in the buying and selling organizations.

FIGURE 8–12

View of Buyer-Supplier Relationship: A Paradigm Shift

Traditional	Partnership
Lowest price	Total cost of ownership
Specification-driven	End customer-driven
Short term, reacts to market	Long term
Trouble avoidance	Opportunity maximization
Purchasing's responsibility	Cross-functional teams and top management involvement
Tactical	Strategic
Little sharing of information on both sides	Both supplier and buyer share short- and long-term plans
	Share risk and opportunity
	Standardization
	Joint ventures
	Share data

Early Supplier Involvement (ESI)/Early Purchasing Involvement (EPI). The opportunity to affect value in the acquisition process is greater in the early stages (need recognition and description) than in the later ones. (See Chapter 5, Figure 5–2.) Involving the supplier and the buyer in these early stages can lead to improvements in processes, design, redesign, or value analysis activities. The drive to cut cycle time, improve competitiveness, and reduce costs compels many organizations to include supplier(s) on cross-functional teams. A supplier may participate with the hope of securing the business, or as part of an ongoing partnering/alliance relationship. Confidentiality issues often must be dealt with upfront, and it must be clear to the supplier(s) if involvement guarantees the business or not.

Greatest Opportunity to Affect Value is in Need Recognition and Description

Benefits of Partnering

The benefits from partnering come from intercorporate closeness. The philosophy is similar to design for manufacturability or design for assembly, where internal barriers are removed between design, marketing, manufacturing engineering, quality assurance, procurement, and operations to avoid functional suboptimization. The removal of functional barriers, avoiding "throwing the design over the wall," helps speed the introduction of new designs and achieves significant quality and cost improvements. The same idea extended makes suppliers part of the process—it could be called "design for procurability." Others call it "early supplier involvement" or ESI. Moreover, if suppliers involve their suppliers in the process, the purchasing organization has access to a wide pool of talent all focused on the needs of its customers. When the supplier is making investment decisions, hiring decisions, new product or process or system decisions, these can be made keeping the customer-partner's future needs in mind. It is this latent potential for improvement that the partnership tries to tap.

Partnerships may be seen as an alternate solution for the make option in the make-or-buy decision. Similarly, a partnership could be a substitute for vertical integration. A partnership attempts to unlock the benefits from shared information without the disadvantages of ownership.

Partnerships require hard work on both sides to make them effective. They require a tolerance toward mistakes and a real commitment to make the relationship work. The key idea is that each partner might enhance its own competitive position through the knowledge and resources shared by the other.

Partnerships Require Organizational Commitment

Concerns about Partnerships. There are serious concerns about the idea of partnerships. Not all purchasers believe that cooperative relationships are better than the competition-based culture upon which most traditional procurements tools and techniques are based. The idea that at least one partner might wish to take advantage of the preferred status and let the commitment and relationship slide is a serious concern. In a technology-driven world, intellectual rights to new technology are extremely valuable and the preservation of secrecy a vital concern. Whether purchasers or suppliers, or either, can be trusted with information that might shape competitive strategy in years to come needs to be weighed very carefully.

Similarly, whether cutting off the option to "shop around" is in the best long-term interest of the purchaser will depend on its customer satisfaction-driven strategies. Clearly, the decision to enter into a partnership mode is an organizational commitment, not just a procurement one, and is of key strategic importance.

Limitations of Partnering

Case research in Manchester, United Kingdom, with 11 companies showed the limitations of partnering were:[23]

- A lot of time was spent in establishing the relationship; this was expressed as "a lot of time for nothing" by more than one company.
- The arrangement sometimes tended to limit the possibility of exploiting more attractive marketplace opportunities.
- Unequal treatment sometimes resulted when more than one product was procured from the same supplier.
- More than one company said that the customer tried to use the partnership to cut the price.
- Joint product development caused some conflict over ownership and intellectual property rights. This is critical in high-technology industries when seeking to obtain funding for research.
- Where purchasing volumes were small, establishing a partnership arrangement with a supplier was perceived as much more difficult, simply because the potential for mutual advantage was much less.
- In the case of small companies, linking a higher proportion of the business to one of a few customers was a risk in terms of market security.

Soft Factors Influence Partner Selection

From a supplier selection perspective, what is interesting about selecting potential partners is the focus on soft as well as hard factors. All of the traditional hard factors of quality, delivery, cost, environment, safety and continuing improvement, financial and management stability, and technological accomplishment still continue. But, for potential partners, soft factors also become important like: congruence of management values on issues like customer satisfaction, concern for quality, employee involvement, supplier relationships, and personal compatibility between functional counterparts. Vital questions are: "Can we work well together? Can we respect and trust each other? Do we like each other?" Questions like these are not answered easily and quickly.

Five Phases to Partnership

Developmental Path to Partnership. It is, therefore, more likely that potential partners are found among the organization's best current suppliers. The idea that buyer and seller might grow into a partnership mode has been advanced in a variety of academic and practitioner circles. A fairly typical

---

[23]A. Adacum and B. G. Dale, "Supplier Partnering: Case Study Experience," *International Journal of Purchasing and Materials Management,* Winter 1995.

FIGURE 8–13

The Developmental Path to Partnership

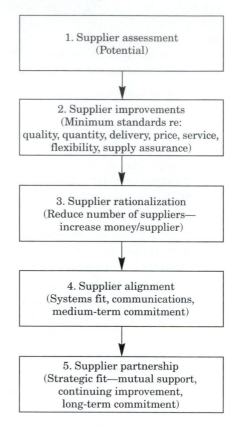

route to partnership might follow five phases, as suggested in the developmental path to partnership shown in Figure 8–13.

Whether a partnership is working well or not from a purchaser's perspective can be summarized as in Figure 8–14.

Partnering Strategies and Outcomes. Developing partnering-type relationships takes time, and some organizations may be ill prepared for the amount of time it does take before seeing the desired results. Graham, Daugherty, and Dudley found that organizations in their study reported accelerated success in implementing six strategies and achieving six outcomes after three years of a partnering relationship.[24] The six strategies are:

Six Strategies

---

[24]T. Scott Graham, Patricia J. Daugherty, and William N. Dudley, "The Long-Term Strategic Impact of Purchasing Partnerships," *International Journal of Purchasing and Materials Management,* Fall 1994, pp. 14–15.

FIGURE 8–14

Some Indicators of a Successful Partnering Effort

- Formal communication processes
- Commitment to supplier's success
- Mutual profitability
- Stable relationships, not dependent on a few personalities
- Consistent and specific feedback on supplier performance
- Realistic expectations
- Employee accountability for ethical business conduct
- Meaningful information sharing
- Guidance to supplier in defining improvement efforts
- Non-adversarial negotiations and decisions based on total cost of ownership

---

Source: SEMATECH.

1. Decreased average delivery lot size.
2. Decreased total number of suppliers.
3. Decreased average number of sources used per purchased item.
4. Increased average contract/agreement length.
5. Increased average frequency of delivery to the plant.
6. Increased supplier involvement in quality certification programs.

Six Outcomes   The six outcomes are:

1. Improved quality of the supplier's operations/processes.
2. Improved quality of incoming goods.
3. Decreased supplier's total cost.
4. Decreased buying organization's total cost.
5. Improved supplier's ability to handle buyer-initiated changes to the agreed-to delivery date.
6. Improved buyer's ability to handle supplier-initiated changes to the agreed-to delivery date.

As might be expected, rewards increased over time. In this study, respondents reported greater success in implementing strategies than achieving outcomes, a result attributed by the authors to a "lag effect."

Another interesting question is what happens over a longer period of time. Do benefits continue to accelerate, or does the law of diminishing returns set in? Companies like Honda, that have maintained partnering-type relationships with some suppliers since the late 1970s, have clearly found a

Long-Term Impact of Partnering   way to continue generating benefits for both parties. Whether all companies can sustain the relationship over the long term probably depends on many variables, including what the original goals of the partnership were, the level of commitment of both sides to continuing to develop the relationship, and the specific situation of the companies and industry. Thinking about the longer term at the initial stages of the relationship may help to prevent dissatisfaction in the long run.

Strategic Alliances

Strategic alliances in a procurement sense represent special arrangements with key suppliers that make a strategic difference to both buyer and seller. The term "expanded partnership" used by SEMATECH might fit this category. They arise from the conviction of both buyer and seller that it is in the interest of both to formalize the relationship beyond the standard buying-selling mode.

Frequently, these alliances are technology-based and require substantial investment of both buyer and seller to achieve major market breakthroughs. Obviously, as major cornerstones of corporate strategy, these alliances are of major concern to top management and reinforce the perspective that suppliers and supplier relationships are of strategic concern to any organization.

Enhancing the Prospects for Success

In their breakthrough research on problems in alliances, Stuart and McCutcheon identified three "prior conditions scales": (1) outlook, (2) power, (3) gains; and two "alliance-building process scales": (1) info share, and (2) help gap.[25] They found that "to enhance the prospects for success":

1. *Identify supplier firms in which a philosophical match exists* between the two firms' managements on such issues as views toward quality and productivity improvement. Such a fit is possible despite differences in the parties' size and power.

2. *Create an interorganizational task force to establish clear expectations* of the information required for successful problem identification and resolution, the level of technical expertise available from both parties, and how the benefits from such improvements are to be measured and then shared in a mutually agreeable manner.

3. *Slightly exceed the expectations* established in item 2 above.

Colocation/In-plants

As organizations look for ways to do more work with fewer people and achieve the productivity and competitiveness goals of the firm, they are increasingly looking to suppliers for expertise and assistance. Having a key supplier locate personnel in a department in the buying organization who can function as buyer, planner, and salesperson can improve buyer-seller

---

[25]F. Ian Stuart and David McCutcheon, "Problem Sources in Establishing Strategic Supplier Alliances," *International Journal of Purchasing Materials Management,* Winter 1995, pp. 6–8.

communications and processes, absorb work typically done by the firm's employees, and reduce administrative and sales costs.

Reverse Marketing/Supplier Development

Reverse Marketing Defined

In supplier selection the assumption has so far been made that at least one suitable and willing supplier already exists, and that the purchaser's problem is primarily one of determining who is the best supplier. It is possible, however, that no suitable source is available and that the purchaser may have to create a source. Reverse marketing or supplier development implies a degree of aggressive procurement involvement not normally encountered in supplier selection. For example, it frequently places a purchasing manager in a position where a prospective supplier must be persuaded to accept an order. In this no-choice context, the purchaser does not initiate supplier development as an appropriate technique or tool; it is the only alternative other than making the part in-house.

Reverse marketing/supplier development should take a broader point of view. It defines the need for developing new or existing suppliers as follows: The purchaser is aware that benefits will accrue to both the supplier and the purchaser, benefits of which the supplier may not be aware. These benefits may be limited to the particular order at hand, or they may include more far-reaching aspects, such as technical, financial, and management processes, skills, or quality levels; reduction of marketing effort; use of long-term forecasts or permitting smoother manufacturing levels and a minimum of inventory; and so on.

Purchaser Initiative Is the Hallmark of Reverse Marketing

It is the aggressiveness and initiative by the purchaser that makes the difference (see Figure 8–15). In the normal market context, the purchaser responds to marketing efforts. In reverse marketing, the purchaser, not the marketer, has the initiative and may quote prices, terms, and conditions as part of the aggressive role. This is why the term *reverse marketing* has been chosen as a synonym for supplier development. Numerous examples show that high payoffs are possible from this purchasing initiative, and that suppliers of all sizes may be approached in this fashion.

Reasons for Reverse Marketing

A further reason for reverse marketing is that there are bound to be deficiencies in the normal industrial marketing-purchasing process in which the marketer traditionally takes the initiative. Even when a supplier and a purchaser have entered into a regular buyer-seller relationship, often neither party is fully aware of all the opportunities for additional business that may exist between them. This might arise because of salesperson and buyer specialization, a lack of aggressiveness by the salesperson, or a lack of inquisitiveness by the purchaser.

If gaps are evident even where an established buyer-seller relationship exists, there must be even greater shortcomings where no such relationship has yet been established. For example, a supplier may be unable to cover its

FIGURE 8–15

Supplier Development Initiative with the Purchaser

THE MARKETING CONTEXT

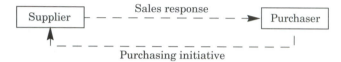

THE SUPPLIER DEVELOPMENT CONTEXT

full market because of geography, limited advertising, or lack of coverage by its sales force, distributors, or agents. Most suppliers have lines of products that receive more management attention and sales push than other products also made or sold by the same company. It is always difficult to keep entirely up-to-date. A time lag may exist between the time of product or service introduction and the time the purchaser finds out about it. By filling these gaps through aggressiveness, the purchaser effectively strengthens this whole process.

One of the most important arguments in favor of reverse marketing not yet mentioned arises from future considerations. If the procurement role is envisaged as encompassing not only the need to fill current requirements but also the need to prepare for the future, reverse marketing can be valuable in assuring future sources of supply.

Three Outside Forces Drive Reverse Marketing

There are at least three outside forces that suggest the increasing necessity for purchaser initiative in the creation of future sources of supply. One of these forces is technological. The increasing rate of development of new products, materials, and processes will tend to make the industrial marketing task even more complex and more open to shortcomings. In addition to this, the stepping-up of international trade will tend to widen supplier horizons and may create a need for purchaser aggressiveness in the development of foreign sources of supply. One of the most demanding and important tasks of management of a subsidiary in an underdeveloped country is the problem of supplier development. Lastly, new management concerns with extracting competitive advantage from the supply chain require purchasers to be more aggressive with suppliers and to develop sources to their expectations.

In their *Reverse Marketing* text,[26] Leenders and Blenkhorn identify the challenges and opportunities inherent in the process of reverse marketing.

---

[26]Michiel R. Leenders and David L. Blenkhorn, *Reverse Marketing: The New Buyer-Supplier Relationship* (New York: Free Press, 1988).

The role of aggressor forces the purchaser to prepare carefully and to identify needs and options, probably with greater precision and detail than under the traditional, more passive, seller-buyer approach. This extra preparation and homework tends to pay off handsomely in large improvements in quality, delivery, price, service, or other objectives the purchaser may be pursuing.

Reverse marketing need not be limited to the creation of new sources but can be applied to existing suppliers where the gap between purchaser expectations and supplier reality is large. In view of the excellent results obtained by those practicing reverse marketing, it is easy to predict increased use of reverse marketing/supplier development in the future.

Supplier Development at Honda

Honda of America Manufacturing Inc. offers a good example of a successful supplier development program.[27] Because purchased parts represent about 80 percent of the cost of a finished Honda automobile, suppliers are clearly of strategic importance. Honda works with suppliers in the following ways to develop world-class suppliers:

- Reduce costs through target costing and providing assistance in meeting the targets.
- Improve quality by working together on quality problems, and through the use of quality circles, with a goal of zero defects. No incoming inspection is done at Honda.
- Develop leading-edge technology by linking Honda research and development with suppliers throughout the new-car development process.
- Teach "self-reliance." Honda's goal is to develop suppliers to the point where they no longer need Honda's help, and may in fact, become teachers in their own organizations and with their own suppliers.

Four Stages in Developing a Globally-Aligned Supplier Network

In a CAPS study, *Developing a World-Class Supply Base,* the authors defined supplier development as "a bilateral effort by both the buying and supplying organizations to jointly improve the supplier's performance and/or capabilities in one or more of the following areas: cost, quality, delivery, time-to-market, technology, environmental responsibility, managerial capability and financial viability."[28] The authors continued to describe four major stages in developing a globally-aligned supplier network as:

1. Identify, assess, and rationalize the supply base,
2. Problem-solving development,
3. Proactive development, and
4. Integrative development.

---

[27]This example is a synopsis of Kevin R. Fitzgerald, "Medal of Excellence: Honda Wins for Superb Supplier Development," *Purchasing,* September 21, 1995, pp. 32–40.

[28]Daniel R. Krause and Robert B. Handfield, *Developing a World-Class Supply Base* (Tempe, AZ: Center for Advanced Purchasing Studies, 1999), p. 8.

Supply Chain Management

Supply chain management is a systems approach to managing the entire flow of information, materials, and services from raw materials suppliers through factories and warehouses to the end customer. Supply chain management is different from supply management. Supply chain management (SCM) emphasizes all aspects of delivering products to customers, whereas supply management emphasizes only the buyer-supplier relationship. SCM represents a philosophy of doing business that stresses processes and integration.

Characteristics of Supply Chain Management

Supply chain management is characterized by a number of factors.[29] Channelwide information sharing and monitoring, inventory management, evaluation of costs, and joint planning occur over an extended, and sometimes indefinite, time period. Coordination of efforts occurs across channel members, across management levels, and across functions, rather than merely focusing on specific buyer-seller transactions as in a traditional system. Compatible corporate philosophies are essential to achieving the necessary levels of planning and coordination. Because of the difficulty of coordinating across channels, a smaller supply base is desirable to allow for closer integration. Some type of channel leadership is also needed, usually a dominant player in the chain, or, in the future, perhaps a cross-organizational team. Sharing of risks and rewards is also necessary to maintain the appropriate level of commitment to the success of the supply chain as a whole. Operations in the SCM approach are faster than in a traditional system. Electronic data interchange can be used channelwide to reduce cycle times, thereby eliminating some of the uncertainty in the system and reducing the inventory base.

Goals of Supply Chain Management

The goals of supply chain management are to reduce uncertainty and risks in the supply chain, thereby positively affecting inventory levels, cycle time, processes, and ultimately end-customer service levels. The focus in SCM is on system optimization. Tools that can assist in systems or supply chain improvements are benchmarking current performance in a particular inventory network, understanding the sources of uncertainty and the impact on upstream and downstream nodes in the supply chain, working to control uncertainty, and planning for changes in policies and procedures that might lead to cost reductions or performance improvements.[30]

SCM Implementation is Difficult

Supply chain management makes a lot of sense conceptually. The difficulty is in implementation. As many organizations have found, it is extremely difficult to make buyer-supplier partnerships or alliances work well.

---

[29]Martha C. Cooper and Lisa M. Ellram, "Characteristics of Supply Chain Management and the Implications for Purchasing and Logistics Strategy," *The International Journal of Logistics Management,* 4, no. 2 (1993), pp. 15–18.

[30]Tom Davis, "Effective Supply Chain Management," *Sloan Management Review,* Summer 1993, pp. 36–37.

Extending the concept across a supply channel and encompassing all the aspects of delivering to the end customer are even more difficult. In many cases, the supply chain management concept is a philosophical change in the way business should be done, but many organizations are still struggling to better manage processes with one supplier. Often a buyer works to get its first-tier suppliers to flow down the practices and ideas to its suppliers and may offer to assist with training.

Supply Network More Accurately Depicts the Process

Supply Networks

The term *supply chain* is obviously a misnomer. If we start off with a purchasing organization as a starting point and work down the supply side, it has a number of suppliers, each of which in turn has its own set of suppliers, and so on. The result is a supply network or a series of chains. This is illustrated in Figure 8–16 for one buying organization and three of its suppliers, tracing through just some of the key requirements generated by the original purchaser (heavier lines indicate a larger volume of business). A supply network can become exceedingly complex very quickly.

The Diminishing Leverage in a Supply Network. Aside from complexity, the diminishing leverage effect of the original purchaser also needs to be emphasized. A number of organizations have attempted to influence the supply management of their first-tier suppliers, for example by specifying from whom they should acquire certain requirements and, possibly, even at what price. A typical example might be a large food company that directs its

FIGURE 8–16

The Complexity of Supplier Networks

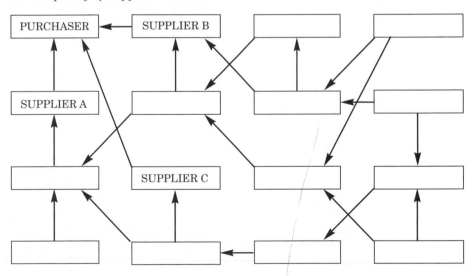

FIGURE 8–17

The Diminishing Leverage in Supply-Chain Management

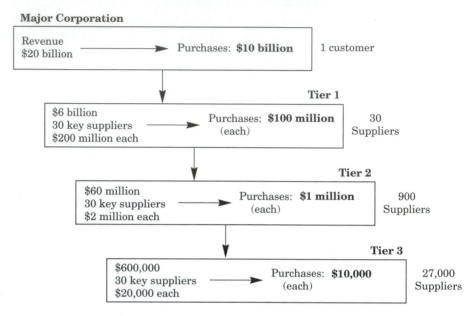

3 Key Assumptions

1. **Purchases 50% of revenue**
2. **30 key suppliers - 60% of purchases**
3. **No common suppliers**

copackers to acquire packaging from the same suppliers with whom the large company has extensive contracts at favorable prices. A multidivisional organization might direct its suppliers to acquire certain requirements from another division or subsidiary of the same parent company. There is a fine line between reciprocity or trade relations in these kinds of deals.

Leverage Dissipates at Third and Fourth Tier

In any case, Figure 8–17 shows that there is likely to be a substantial diminution of the leverage of the original purchaser as more tiers in the supplier network get involved. Therefore, unless there are overlapping suppliers, in which tier 1, 2, 3, and 4 suppliers all deal with the same supplier at a significant volume level, the clout of the original purchaser has largely dissipated at the third- and fourth-tier levels. This in no way suggests that ignoring supply management strategies or practices of first- and second-tier suppliers is wise and has little potential. If we subscribe to the proposition that effective supply management can significantly affect competitive advantage in organizational success, the supply management and, in fact, all of the logistics-related activities of first- and second-tier suppliers are likely to impact the supply chain and supply network of the original purchasing or-

FIGURE 8–18

Supply Chain for a Manufacturer of Consumer Goods Showing Cumulative Effect of Transports and Storages

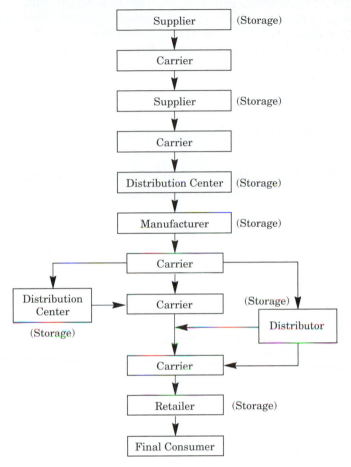

Conclusion: Each final consumer receives a good that has passed through a minimum of five transports and storages.

ganization. Because transportation and inventories are integral to every supply network, the cumulative effect of multiple transports and storages on timeliness and cost can be very high as a percentage of the acquisition cost of the final customer in the chain or network (see Figure 8–18).

Conclusion

The supplier selection decision has become far more complex as environmental, social, political, and customer satisfaction concerns have been added to the traditional factors of quality, delivery, cost, and service. It is no surprise that approaches like supplier rationalization, preferred suppliers, partnerships, strategic alliances, reverse marketing, and supply chain management have gained prominence. The realization that suppliers and the buyer-supplier relationship can make a strategic difference to an organization's capability of providing continuing improvement in customer satisfaction drives the search for new and better ways of managing the relationships between buyers and sellers.

Questions for Review and Discussion

1. Why create a preferred supplier, a partnership, or a strategic alliance?
2. What is reverse marketing and why is it used?
3. What are the advantages of supplier rationalization?
4. Why should any organization switch from making to buying?
5. What are the characteristics of supply chain management? How can supply managers effectively manage the supply chain?
6. What is outsourcing? How might one make the decision to outsource an activity or not?
7. How do you know a partnership is not working?
8. What are the goals of early supplier involvement (ESI)? How does ESI fit in with cross-functional teams?
9. What are the risks and rewards of colocation?
10. What is the relationship between satisfaction and stability in buyer-supplier relations?

References

Adacum A. and B. G. Dale, "Supplier Partnering: Case Study Experience," *International Journal of Purchasing and Materials Management,* Winter 1995.

Biemans, Wim G. and Maryse J. Brand, "Reverse Marketing: A Synergy of Purchasing and Relationship Marketing," *International Journal of Purchasing and Materials Management,* Summer 1995.

Burt, David N. and Michael F. Doyle, *The American Keiretsu,* Homewood, IL: Business One Irwin, 1993.

Carter, Phillip L., Joseph R. Carter, Robert M. Monczka, Thomas H. Slaight, and Andrew J. Swan, *The Future of Purchasing and Supply: A Five- and*

Ten-Year Forecast, Tempe, AZ: Center for Advanced Purchasing Studies/ National Association of Purchasing Management/A. T. Kearney, 1998.

Cooper, Martha C. and Lisa M. Ellram, "Characteristics of Supply Chain Management and the Implications for Purchasing and Logistics Strategy," *The International Journal of Logistics Management* 4, no. 2, 1993.

Cross, John, "IT Outsourcing: British Petroleum's Competitive Approach," *Harvard Business Review,* May–June 1995.

Davis, Tom, "Effective Supply Chain Management," *Sloan Management Review,* Summer 1993.

Dixon, Lance and Anne Millen Porter, *JIT II^R Revolution in Buying and Selling,* Newton, MA: Cahners Publishing Company, 1994.

Ellram, Lisa M. and Arnold Maltz, *Outsourcing: Implications for Supply Management,* Tempe, AZ: Center for Advanced Purchasing Studies, 1997.

Graham, T. Scott, Patricia J. Daugherty, and William N. Dudley, "The Long-Term Strategic Impact of Purchasing Partnerships," *International Journal of Purchasing and Materials Management,* Fall 1994.

Handfield, Robert B., Daniel R. Krause, Thomas V. Scannell, and Robert M. Monczka, "Avoid the Pitfalls in Supplier Development," *MITSLoan Management Review,* Winter 2000, Volume 41, Number 2.

Hendrick, Thomas and Lisa Ellram, *Strategic Supplier Partnering,* Tempe, AZ: Center for Advanced Purchasing Studies/National Association of Purchasing Management, 1993.

Krause, Daniel R. and Robert B. Handfield, *Developing a World-Class Supply Base,* Tempe, AZ: Center for Advanced Purchasing Studies, 1999.

Lacity, Mary, Leslie P. Willcocks, and David F. Feeny. "IT Outsourcing: Maximize Flexibility and Control," *Harvard Business Review,* May–June 1995.

Leenders, Michiel R. and David L. Blenkhorn, *Reverse Marketing: The New Buyer-Supplier Relationship,* New York: Free Press, 1988.

Peisch, Richard, "When Outsourcing Goes Awry," *Harvard Business Review,* May–June 1995.

Ramsey, John, "The Myth of the Cooperative Single Source," *Journal of Purchasing and Materials Management,* Winter 1990.

Stralkowski, Michael C. and Alexander S. Billon, "Partnering: A Strategic Approach to Productivity Improvement," *International Journal of Purchasing and Materials Management,* Winter 1991.

Stuart, F. Ian and David McCutcheon, "Problem Sources in Establishing Strategic Supplier Alliances," *International Journal of Purchasing and Materials Management,* Winter 1995.

Watts, Charles A. and Chan K. Hahn, "Supplier Development Programs," *International Journal of Purchasing and Materials Management,* Spring 1993.

CASE 8–1
SAUCY FOODS LIMITED

Denise Seidel, Corporate Purchasing Manager, Saucy Foods Limited (SFL), wanted to prepare a proposal to manufacture mustard in-house. Mustard, an important ingredient in many of SFL's products, was currently purchased from an outside supplier. She hoped a comprehensive proposal could be prepared in one-month's time for the CEO's approval.

General Company Background. SFL had been in business for more than 20 years. Its products included a wide range of syrups, fudges, cone dips, sauces, mayonnaise, and salad dressings. Its customers were major food chains, hotels, and restaurants in Canada, the United States, and Europe.

SFL believed in continuous improvements to its operations. Over the last two years, it invested more than $2 million in plant facilities, the bulk of it new, state-of-the-art process equipment and process control. All production and process control functions were computerized for maximum efficiency.

SFL employed about 120 people. It had a corporate structure of CEO, President, Executive Vice President, Vice President Export Sales, Vice President Domestic Sales, and National Account Manager, and used a network of food brokers who sold and promoted its products.

The Purchasing Area. Denise was responsible for the purchasing area and reported directly to the CEO. She had an inventory control officer, a buyer, and a receiver under her supervision. The purchases could be classified into four different types: labels, packaging, raw materials, and commodities. Mustard was an important raw material used in many of SFL's products.

Current Practice: Purchasing Mustard Externally. Whenever mustard was required, SFL called its supplier and requested that it prepare the appropriate amount to be picked up by a delivery truck from SFL. The purchase order would be prepared before the truck left for the supplier, normally the next day. The mustard supplier used mustard seed as its raw material and blended in the other ingredients after the seed had been reduced to mustard flour. Every month, SFL purchased 500 drums, or 100,000 liters, of mustard. The cost of the mustard itself was $64 per drum. Freight costs were borne by SFL and amounted to about $8 per drum. SFL workers worked on three eight-hour shifts, five days a week. Each worker was paid about $20 per hour. It took about 10 minutes of a worker's time to handle each drum. This included pouring the mustard into the processing kettle, making sure other added ingredients mixed well, and rinsing the drums. The drums were bulky, and because they could not be used in the plant for other purposes, had to be rinsed for a contractor who took them away. The costs of disposing of the drums in this manner were negligible. Other costs and overhead of purchasing were $0.02 per liter.

Suggested Change: Manufacturing Mustard In-House. Denise proposed that the mustard to be produced at SFL would be composed of roughly 60 percent solid, 20 percent water, and 20 percent vinegar. The solid portion was a spice blend, consisting essentially of mustard flour, salt, and other spices which could be readily bought. Water was not a problem as the city provided a reliable supply. Vinegar was already a raw material that SFL ordered in bulk regularly from suppliers. Denise therefore believed that it was a simple matter for SFL to make the mustard for its own use. SFL only needed to buy the spice blend and add water and vinegar in the right proportions. She approached a supplier who indicated that it could make the spice blend at a delivered price of $0.15 per liter for SFL, including freight. However, it needed time for tests to ensure that the blend would be of the right quality for SFL's use. Vinegar cost SFL $0.1875 per liter delivered in 15,000 liter lots. And SFL was paying $0.025 per liter for water. Denise then checked whether production had the time and equipment to make the mustard. Production felt that the change would not be too drastic and no additional workers would be necessary. However, it would use up more of the existing workers' time. Production calculated that the change would entail a total labor and overhead cost of about $0.105 per liter of mustard using standard cost accounting for labor time and overhead charges.

Denise called an information-gathering and discussion session involving purchasing, production, quality assurance, and distribution to discuss the proposed change. The workers were keen on the idea as this meant that they would no longer have to haul and rinse the bulky drums (water and vinegar could be easily channelled to the mixing containers using existing pipes). However, quality assurance expressed concern about the quality of mustard if produced in-house. Because the mustard was an ingredient in many of SFL's products, such a change might adversely affect the quality and taste of these products.

Denise wanted her proposal for in-house manufacture of mustard to be in the company's best interest and wondered how to proceed.

CASE 8.2
PARON METAL FABRICATING INC.

Donald Mines, Materials Manager at Paron Metal Fabricating Inc. in Lancaster, Pennsylvania, was considering a proposal from his purchasing agent to outsource manufacturing for an outrigger bracket. It was the end of April, and Donald had to evaluate the proposal and make a decision regarding whether to proceed.

Paron Metal Fabricating Inc. Background. Paron Metal Fabricating Inc. (Paron) manufactured trailers for highway transport trucks. The company comprised three divisions, the Trailer, Sandblast & Paint, and Metal Fabricating divisions. Each division operated as a separate profit center, but manufacturing operations between each were highly integrated. The Metal Fabricating Division produced most of the component parts of the trailers; the Trailer Division performed the assembly operations; and the Sandblast & Paint Division was responsible for completing the sandblasting and final painting operation. Paron manufactured approximately 40 trailers per year, with about two-thirds of their annual products produced during the period from November to April.

The Outrigger Bracket. The outrigger bracket, part number T-178, was an accessory that could be used to secure oversized containers. The bracket consisted of four component parts welded together, and each trailer sold by Paron had 20 brackets—10 per side.

The Metal Fabricating Division was presently manufacturing the outrigger bracket. The subassembly parts—T-67, T-75, T-69 and T-77—were processed on a burn table machine, which cut the raw material to size. Although the burn table machine could work with eight burn stations, this machine had only been operating with one station. The final assembly operation, T-70, was performed at a manual welding station.

Manufacturing lead time for the outrigger bracket was two weeks. However, the division had been able to coordinate supply and production with assembly operations. Consequently, finished inventory levels of the outrigger bracket were kept to a minimum. Paron estimated its inventory holding costs were 20 percent per annum.

The Outsourcing Decision. In an effort to reduce costs, the Purchasing Agent, Linda Steadman, who reported to Donald Mines, solicited quotes from three local companies to supply the outrigger bracket. Mayes Steel Fabricators (Mayes), a current supplier to Paron for other components, offered the lowest bid, with a cost of $108.20, FOB Paron.

Donald met with the Controller, Gerald Myers, who provided a breakdown of the manufacturing costs for the outrigger bracket. Looking at the spreadsheet, Gerald commented: "These are based on estimates of our costs from this year's budget. Looking at the material, labor, and overhead costs, I would estimate that the fixed costs for this part are in the area of about 20 percent. Keep in mind that it costs us about $75 to place an order with our vendors." Exhibit 1 provides Paron's internal cost breakdown and details from the quote from Mayes.

Donald expected that Paron would have to arrange for extra storage space if he decided to outsource the outrigger bracket to Mayes, who had quoted delivery lead time of four weeks. Because Mayes was local and had a good track record, Donald didn't expect the need to carry much safety stock, but the order quantity issue still needed to be resolved.

EXHIBIT 1   Manufacturing Costs and Mayes Quote: Outrigger Bracket T-178

Parts	Mayes Steel Fabricators	Paron Manufacturing Costs
T-67	$ 14.60	$ 17.92
T-75	$ 21.10	$ 17.92
T-69	$ 18.50	$ 45.20
T-77	$ 13.00	$ 10.37
T-70	$ 41.00	$ 58.69
Total	$ 108.20	$ 150.10

Paron was operating in a very competitive environment and Donald had been asked by the division general manager to look for opportunities to reduce costs. As he sat down to review the information, Donald knew that he should make a decision quickly if it was possible to cut costs by outsourcing the outrigger bracket.

CASE 8–3
SUPER STAMPS AND PRODUCTS INC. (B)

On Monday, April 24, Al Smith, Director of Manufacturing at Super Stamps and Products Inc., was wondering how to preserve its single-supplier relationship with a key customer, Quality Printers Ltd. Quality Printers Ltd., who recently restructured to conform to ISO 9000 certification standards, had since complained about Super Stamps' excessive nonconformance rate. Mr. Smith needed to determine what action to take during this Thursday's meeting with Quality Printers Ltd.

Company Background. Super Stamps and Products was founded in 1945 as a rubber stamp company. Products and services included office products, industrial products, commercial artwork and graphics services, printing, and engraving. The number of full-time employees had increased in the past year to 165, up from 150, due to the acquisition of two related companies. Super Stamps' organiza-

tional structure was divided into four operating divisions, one of which was the graphics department.

Over the past three years, performance had been relatively stagnant. Although sales volume had increased, it was counteracted with eroded margins from price pressures. These trends were forecasted to continue in the foreseeable future.

Graphics Department. The graphics department employed approximately 25 percent of the total work force and accounted for roughly the same percentage of Super Stamps' revenues. The employees of the graphics department were artists who provided computerized typesetting services and artistic design consultation, and produced plates and dies for printing.

Super Stamps' graphics market was located within a 200-mile radius. Although competition was fierce, due to Super Stamps' quality reputation they were able to charge a premium price. Additionally, accurate delivery was also an important competitive factor.

Present Graphics Ordering Process. Production orders were accompanied by a Graphics Request Form, either printed by the order desk or filled out and faxed to the order desk by a regular customer. The Graphics Request Form included a brief description of the job with arrival dates and desired completion dates. After the Graphics Request Form was completed, a process control sheet was introduced to accompany the order through the various stages of the production process. At each stage, additional loose documents accumulated (pricing sheet, artwork, shipping documents, invoice, etc.).

Exhibit 1   Process Flow Diagram— Rubber Plates and Dies

Artists generate required image
End result is camera-ready artwork

↓

Customer approval

↓

The camera department produces film from
the camera-ready artwork

↓

The photo polymer department manufactures
a polymer die from the film

↓

The die mounting department mounts
the polymer die

↓

The die is shipped
to the customer

Upon receiving the Graphics Request Form and the process control sheet, artists completed the appropriate section of the process control sheet to ensure that all necessary information was available. If more information was required, a telephone call was made to the customer to complete the process control sheet. This check minimized computer time when developing artwork.

Once the section of the process control sheet applicable to the artists was completed, development of the requested graphics design began. Once completed, the design was sent to the customer for approval. If approved, it was used by the camera department to produce film for polymer dies. (See Exhibit 1 for graphics production process.)

When dies were ready for shipping, all applicable documents accompanied the product to the customer. When the product was received, the customer checked the process control sheet, the Graphics Request Form, and the design layout with measurements/dimensions, to investigate if any errors existed. If all seemed well, the customer proceeded to install the dies on the machines, per-

formed a test run, and if the test run passed, fullscale production commenced.

Defects were traditionally measured by the customer only if problems with dies existed. If a defect occurred, Super Stamps' policy was limited to refunding or replacing the dies. Thus, the customer was responsible for production waste if defective dies were operated on large-scale printing runs.

Single Sourcing. At the beginning of May, one year ago, a key customer of the graphics department, Quality Printers Ltd., was being restructured by a new management team. Quality Printers Ltd. was contemplating closing its graphics design facilities and outsourcing jobs to a single supplier. Not only did the restructuring involve downsizing their existing facility, it also involved implementing procedures to attain their ISO 9000 certification. Many companies were eager to attain the ISO 9000 certification as it was a growing trend in the industry for quality-focused organizations.

On May 10 last year, three suppliers submitted proposals to become Quality Printers Ltd's single source, one of which was Super Stamps. Prior to the restructuring, Quality Printers Ltd. outsourced most of its overload jobs to Super Stamps, as it had limited capacity and employed only two artists. Last June, Super Stamps was informed its proposal had been selected, conditional upon further negotiations. During the next three months, Quality Printers Ltd. and Super Stamps worked out the details of the proposed single-sourcing initiative and finalized the deal on September 19.

Key features of the contract included:

1. A one-year trial contract, ending September 19 of the current year, estimated to be about $500,000 in volume.

2. Super Stamps purchased the customer's equipment and leased it back at a low rate.

3. Super Stamps hired the customer's two artists, who would have lost their jobs otherwise, for the duration of the trial contract.

Subsequent Developments. On November 2, Super Stamps shipped defective dies to Quality

Printers Ltd. These dies were not inspected by the customer, resulting in the production of 13,000 defective cartons. Furthermore, November's "nonconformance" rate amounted to 8.5 percent. Quality Printers Ltd., due to its ISO 9000 initiatives, evaluated Super Stamps to a "nonconformance" rate and not the traditional defect rate. A defect rate was measured using only errors applicable to the final, shipped product. The "nonconformance" rate was a combination of the defect rate plus any other errors associated with the order (i.e., errors occurring with invoicing, order desk processing, designs not approved and sent back for redrawing, etc.).

The second complaint occurred in February, when Quality Printers Ltd. complained that the nonconformance rate was still unacceptable at 5 percent. In March, Quality Printers Ltd. became furious when another 10,000 cartons were produced with defective dies, amounting to a $15,000 loss. Upon further investigation of why the problem developed, Mr. Smith found out that when Super

Stamps' artist called Quality Printers Ltd. for information missing from its faxed Graphics Request Form, the employee misunderstood the question and answered incorrectly. However, the customer felt Super Stamps made the mistake and should be liable for the $15,000 loss. Super Stamps did not pay the loss, due to their traditional liability policy which was limited only to refunds and replacements, making the customer responsible for checking quality with test runs.

To add to the problem, the determined nonconformance rate for March remained at 5 percent, regardless of Super Stamps' efforts to decrease it.

Current Situation. The customer had stressed its continued displeasure with Super Stamps' quality levels and now demanded the May nonconformance rate be cut by 50 percent. Mr. Smith was wondering what changes should be presented at this Thursday's meeting with Quality Printers Ltd.

9 PRICE DETERMINATION

Key Questions for the Purchasing Decision Maker

SHOULD WE
- Use competitive bidding as our principal means of price determination?
- Use supplier price lists in determining price to pay?
- Make a cost analysis on all of our large-dollar purchase items?

HOW CAN WE
- Spot and combat price fixing?
- Use the futures market to hedge the purchase of raw materials?
- Know when to take a quantity discount or a cash discount?

Determination of the price to be paid is a major purchasing decision. The ability to get a "good price" is sometimes held to be the prime test of a good buyer. If by "good price" is meant greatest value, broadly defined, this is true.

While price is only one aspect of the overall purchasing job, it is extremely important. The purchaser must be alert to different pricing methods, know when each is appropriate, and use skill in arriving at the price to be paid. There is no reason to apologize for emphasizing price or for giving it a place of importance among the factors to be considered. The purchaser rightly is expected to get the best value possible for the organization whose funds are spent.

Management of Internal and External Costs Contributes to Strategic Goal Attainment
The profit leverage effect of purchasing (discussed in Chapter 1) lays the foundation for the role of purchasing in helping the firm meet strategic goals of continuous improvement, customer service, quality, and increased competitiveness. Leveraging the potential of purchasing requires fully exploiting all opportunities to reduce, contain, or avoid costs, resulting in the lowest total cost of ownership and, hopefully, leading the organization to becoming the low-cost producer of high-quality goods and services. Supply management can contribute to attainment of low-cost-producer status by its management

of internal and external costs. Methods of streamlining the acquisition process and reducing internal costs associated with acquisition were discussed in Chapters 2 and 3. This chapter focuses on managing external costs.

Relation of Cost to Price

Fair Price Defined

Every purchasing manager believes the supplier should be paid a fair price. But what does "fair price" mean? A fair price is the lowest price that ensures a continuous supply of the proper quality where and when needed.

A "continuous supply" is possible in the long run only from a supplier who is making a reasonable profit. The supplier's total costs, including a reasonable profit, must be covered by total sales in the long run. Any one item in the line, however, may never contribute "its full share" over any given period, but even for such an item the price paid normally should at least cover the direct costs incurred.

A fair price to one seller for any one item may be higher than a fair price to another or for an equally satisfactory substitute item. Both may be "fair prices" as far as the buyer is concerned, and the buyer may pay both prices at the same time.

Merely because a price is set by a monopolist or is established through collusion among the sellers does not, in and of itself, make that price unfair or excessive. Likewise, the prevailing price need not necessarily be a fair price, as, for example, when such price is a "black" or "gray" market price or when it is depressed or raised through monopolistic or coercive action.

The purchasing manager is called on continuously to exercise judgment as to what the "fair price" should be under a variety of circumstances. To determine this fair price, he or she must have experience (data) and common sense. In part, of course, accuracy in weighing the various factors which culminate in a "fair and just price" is a matter of capitalizing on past experience and thorough knowledge of the processes used to produce the item, and the costs associated with them, as well as logistics costs such as storage, transportation, and other relevant costs.

Meaning of Cost

Assuming this concept of a fair price is sound, what are the relationships between cost and price? Clearly, to stay in business over the long run a supplier must cover total costs, including overhead, and receive a profit. Unless costs, including profit, are covered, eventually the supplier will be forced out of business. This reduces the number of sources available to the buyer and may cause scarcity, higher prices, less-satisfactory service, and lower quality.

Cost Defined

But what is to be included in the term *cost?* At times it is defined to mean only direct labor and material costs, and in a period of depressed business conditions, a seller may be willing merely to recover this amount rather than not make a sale at all. Or cost may mean direct labor and material costs with a contribution toward overhead. If the cost for a particular item includes overhead, is the latter charged at the actual rate (provided it can be determined), or is it charged at an average rate? The average rate may be far from the actual rate.

Most knowledgeable business people realize that determining the cost of a particular article or service is not a precise process. In manufacturing industries there are two basic classifications of costs—*direct* and *indirect*.

Direct Costs Can Be Assigned to a Unit of Production

Direct costs usually are defined as those that can be specifically and accurately assigned to a given unit of production; that is, direct materials, such as 10 pounds of steel; or direct labor, such as 30 minutes of a person's time on a machine or assembly line. However, under accepted accounting practices, the actual price of the specific material used may not be the cost that is included in figuring direct material costs. Because the price paid for material may fluctuate up or down over a period of time, it is common practice to use a so-called standard cost. Some companies use as a standard cost for materials the last price paid in the immediately prior fiscal period. Other companies use an average price for a specific period.

Indirect Costs May Be Fixed or Variable

Indirect costs are those incurred in the operation of a production plant or process, but which normally cannot be related directly to any given unit of production. Some examples of indirect costs are rent, property taxes, machine depreciation, expenses of general supervisors, data processing, power, heat, and light. Indirect costs often are referred to as overhead. They may be fixed or variable.

Variable and Semi-Variable Costs Defined

Classification of costs into variable, semivariable, and fixed categories is a common accounting practice and a necessity for any meaningful analysis of price/cost relationships. Most direct costs are **variable costs** because they vary directly and proportionally with the units produced. For example, a product that requires 10 pounds of steel for one unit will require 100 pounds for 10 units.

Semivariable costs may vary with the number of units produced but are partly variable and partly fixed. For example, more heat, light, and power will be used when a plant is operating at 90 percent of capacity than when operating at a 50 percent rate, but the difference is not directly proportional to the number of units produced. In fact, there would be some costs (fixed) for heat, light, and power if production were stopped completely for a period of time.

Fixed Costs Do Not Vary with Volume

Fixed costs generally remain the same regardless of the number of units produced. For example, real estate taxes will be the same for a given period of time regardless of whether one unit or 100,000 units are produced. Several accounting methods can be used to allocate fixed costs. A common method is to apply a percentage of direct costs in order to allocate the cost of factory overhead. Full allocation of fixed expenses will depend on an accurate forecast of production and the percentage used. Obviously, as full production capacity is reached, the percentage rate will decline.

Factory overhead often is based on some set percentage of direct labor cost because, historically, labor represented the largest cost element. Al-

Typical Product Cost Buildup

though this rarely is true any longer, standard cost accounting often has not changed. Selling, general, and administrative expense is based on a set percentage of total manufacturing cost. The following example illustrates the typical product cost buildup in a manufacturing setting.

Direct materials	$5,500	
+ Direct labor	2,000	
+ Factory overhead*	2,500	(Given: 125 percent of direct labor)
= **Manufacturing Cost**	**$10,000**	
+ General, administrative, and selling cost	1,500	(Given: 15 percent of manufacturing cost)
= **Total Cost**	**$11,500**	
+ Profit	920	(Given: 8 percent of total cost)
= **Selling Price**	**$12,420**	

*Factory overhead consists of all *indirect* factory costs, both *fixed* and *variable.*

Cost Redefined

We now can define costs as so many dollars and cents per unit based on an average cost for raw material over a period of time, direct labor costs, and an estimated volume of production over a period of time on which the distribution of overhead is based.

If this definition of cost is acceptable, then a logical question is, whose cost? Some manufacturers are more efficient than others. Usually all sell the same item at about the same price. But should this price be high enough to cover only the most efficient supplier's costs, or should it cover the costs of all suppliers? Furthermore, cost does not necessarily determine market price. When a seller insists that the price must be a given amount because of costs, this position is not really justified. In the final analysis, goods are worth and will sell for what the market will pay.

Moreover, no seller is entitled to a price that yields a profit merely because the supplier is in business or assumes risk. If such were the case, every business automatically would be entitled to a profit regardless of costs, quality, or service. Unless a seller can supply a market with goods that are needed and desired by users and can supply them with reasonable efficiency, that seller is not entitled to get a price that even covers costs.

How Suppliers Establish Price

Depending on the commodity and industry, the market may vary from almost pure competition to oligopoly and monopoly. Pricing will vary accordingly. For competitive reasons, most firms are not anxious to disclose just how prices are set, but the two traditional methods are the cost approach and the market approach.

The Cost Approach

Prices Are Related to Costs

The cost approach to pricing says the price should be a certain amount over direct costs, allowing for sufficient contribution to cover indirect costs and overhead and leaving a certain margin for profit. For the purchaser, the cost approach offers a number of opportunities to seek lower-cost suppliers, to suggest lower-cost manufacturing alternatives, and to question the size of the margin over direct costs. Negotiation, used with cost-analysis techniques, is a particularly useful tool.

The Market Approach

Prices Are Not Related to Costs

The market approach implies that prices are set in the marketplace and may not be directly related to cost. If demand is high relative to supply, prices are expected to rise; when demand is low relative to supply, prices should decline. This, too, is an oversimplification. Some economists hold that large multinational, multiproduct firms have such a grip on the marketplace that pure competition does not exist and that prices will not drop even though supply exceeds demand. In the market approach, the purchaser must either live with prevailing market prices or find ways around them. If nothing can be done to attack the price structure directly, it still may be possible to select those suppliers who are willing to offer nonprice incentives, such as holding inventory, technical and design service, superior quality, excellent delivery, transportation concessions, and early warning of impending price and product changes. Negotiation, therefore, may center on items other than price.

The Power of Substitution

Many economists hold that substitution of like but not identical materials or products is one of the most powerful forces preventing a completely monopolistic or oligopolistic grip on a market. For example, aluminum and copper may be interchanged in a number of applications. The aluminum and copper markets, therefore, are not independent of one another. The purchaser's ability to recognize these trade-offs and to effect design and use changes to take advantage of substitution is one determinant of flexibility. Make or buy (or outsource) is another option. If access to the raw materials, technological process, and labor skills is not severely restricted, one alternative may be for an organization to make its own requirements to avoid excess market prices.

Sometimes purchasers use long-term contracts to induce the supplier to ignore market conditions. This approach may be successful in certain instances, but it is normal for suppliers to find ways and means around such commitments once it becomes obvious that the prevailing market price is substantially above that paid by their long-term customers.

Government Influence on Pricing

The government's role in establishing price has changed dramatically. The role of government has been twofold. Not only has the government taken an

active role in determining prices by establishing production quotas and instituting (from time to time) various forms of wage/price controls, but it also
regulates the ways that buyer and seller are allowed to behave in agreeing
on prices. Because other governments are active in price control and have, in
a number of situations, created dual pricing for domestic use and exports, it
is difficult to see how the U.S. and Canadian governments will be able to ignore their position. Prices may be determined by review or control boards or
by strong moral suasion. They are likely to be augmented by governmental
controls like quotas, tariffs, and export permits.

**Some
Governments
Are Active in
Price Control**

Governments influence prices of utilities which offer common services,
such as electricity and water, and set prices on licenses and goods and services provided by government-run organizations, such as postal services. Energy deregulation is still in its infancy but will be an interesting and challenging area for purchasers to watch. The U. S. Postal Service is also
undergoing changes as it forges an alliance with private-industry competitor Federal Express. What these changes will mean in terms of pricing and
negotiation opportunities remains to be seen.

Legislation Affecting Price Determination

United States. The federal government has taken an active interest in how
a buyer and seller agree on a price. The government's position largely has
been a protective role to prevent the stronger party from imposing too onerous conditions on the weaker one or preventing collusion so that competition
will be maintained.

**Two Key U.S.
Laws: Sherman
Antitrust Act
and Robinson-
Patman Act**

The two most important federal laws affecting competition and pricing
practices are the Sherman and Robinson-Patman acts. The Sherman Antitrust Act of 1890 states that any combination, conspiracy, or collusion with
the intent of restricting trade in interstate commerce is illegal. This means
that it is illegal for suppliers to get together to set prices (price fixing) or determine the terms and conditions under which they will sell. It also means
that buyers cannot get together to set the prices they will pay.[1] The Robinson-
Patman Act (Federal Anti-price Discrimination Act of 1936) says that a supplier must sell the same item, in the same quantity, to all customers at the
same price. It is known as the "one-price law." Some exceptions are permitted, such as a lower price (1) for a larger purchase quantity, providing the
seller can cost justify the lower price through cost accounting data, (2) to
move distress or obsolete merchandise, or (3) to meet the lower price of local
competition in a particular geographic area. The act also goes on to state that

---

[1]Even with federal legislation prohibiting price fixing, there are frequent instances where
the Justice Department has charged firms with violations. See, for example, "Nintendo
Settlement over Collusion Suit Is Approved by Judge," *The Wall Street Journal,* October 21,
1991, p. B10; and "Major Gas Makers Convicted by Jury in Price-Fixing Case," *The Wall Street
Journal,* December 24, 1991, p. B4.

Federal Trade Commission Investigates Violations

it shall be illegal for a buyer *knowingly* to induce or accept a discriminatory price. However, the courts have been realistic in their interpretation of the law, holding that it is the job of the buyer to get the best possible price for his or her company, and that as long as he or she does not intentionally mislead the seller into giving a more favorable price than is available to other buyers of the same item, the law is not being violated.

If the buyer feels a seller is violating either the Sherman Act or the Robinson-Patman Act, a charge detailing the violation can be made to the Federal Trade Commission (FTC), which was set up to investigate alleged improprieties. From the buyer's standpoint, bringing a seller's actions to the government's attention has few advantages. Since most of the time government's reaction is relatively slow, the need for the item may be gone and conditions may be substantially changed by the time the complaint is decided. Most sellers would view the lodging of a complaint as a particularly unfriendly act, making it difficult for the organization to maintain a reasonable future relationship with that particular supplier. For this reason, complaints are not common, and most are lodged by public buying agencies rather than corporations.

The birth of the business-to-business e-marketplace Covisint, a consortium of major automotive manufacturers, raised antitrust fears. The FTC reviewed the situation and found that *at the time* (October 2000) the fears were unfounded, but it reserved the right to revisit the issue in the future. The finding also stated that the existing procedures for conducting antitrust analysis were applicable even to a situation in which business would be conducted electronically. Given the state of e-marketplaces at the time this book went to press, the regulatory issues seem to be the least of the problems facing e-marketplace providers (See Chapter 4).

Canadian Law Seeks to Maintain Competition

Canada. Canadian federal pricing legislation differs from U.S. legislation, but it has essentially the same intent. It prohibits certain pricing practices in an attempt to maintain competition in the marketplace and applies to both buyers and sellers. Violation of the statute is a criminal offense. Suppliers or buyers may not "conspire, combine, agree, or arrange with another person" to raise prices unreasonably or to otherwise restrain competition. It does not prevent the exchange of data within a trade or professional association, providing it does not lessen price competition. Bid rigging is a per se violation, which means that the prosecution needs only to establish the existence of an agreement to gain a conviction; there is no requirement to prove that the agreement unduly affected competition. It is also illegal for a supplier to grant a price concession to one buyer that is not available to all other buyers (similar to the U.S. Robinson-Patman Act).

Quantity discounts are permitted, as are one-time price cuts to clear out inventory. As in the United States, the Canadian buyer who knowingly is on the receiving end of price discrimination also has violated the law. With regard to price maintenance and the purchase of goods for resale, it requires that a supplier should not, by threat or promise, attempt to influence how the firms that buy from it then price their products for resale.

Types of Purchases

Analysis of suppliers' costs is by no means the only basis for price determination. What other means can be used? Much depends on the type of product being bought. There are seven general classes:

1. *Raw materials.* This group includes the so-called *sensitive commodities,* such as copper, wheat, and crude petroleum, but also steel, cement, etc.

2. *Special items.* This group includes items and materials that are special to the organization's product line and, therefore, are custom ordered.

3. *Standard production items.* This group includes such items as bolts and nuts, many forms of commercial steel, valves, and tubing, whose prices are fairly stable and are quoted on a basis of "list price with some discount."

4. *Items of small value.* This group includes items of such small comparative value that the expenditure of any particular effort to check price prior to purchase is not justified. Maintenance, repair, and operating supplies (MRO) fall in this class.

The other three classes, which are not discussed in detail here because they either are covered elsewhere in or are outside the scope of this text, are:

5. *Capital goods.* These purchased items are accounted for as a capital asset and expensed out through depreciation, rather than being expensed immediately at the time of purchase or use. The purchase of these equipment and construction items is discussed in Chapter 16, "Capital Goods Acquisition."

6. *Services.* This category of purchases is very broad and includes many types of services, such as advertising, auditing, architectural design, legal, insurance, personnel travel, copying, security, and waste removal. Purchase of services is covered in Chapter 17, "Services Purchasing."

7. *Resale.* This category can be subdivided into two groups: (1) Items that formerly were manufactured in-house but have been outsourced to a supplier and now are brought in complete. An example would be the major appliance maker that markets a microwave oven but no longer manufactures the product. Instead it buys the microwave oven complete, under its own brand name. The decision process for these items is the same as presented in this book. (2) Items sold in the retail sector, such as the clothing sold in the general-line

department stores, the food sold through supermarkets, the tools sold in hardware stores, and the tires, batteries, and accessories sold in gasoline/filling stations. Obviously the dollar amount involved in the purchase of these resale items is tremendous. The people who buy these items typically are called merchandise managers, for they first must decide what will sell. Based on this assessment, they then make their buying decisions. Since this text concentrates on industrial and institutional buying, there is no detailed coverage of merchandise buying, although many of the same purchasing principles and practices apply.

Raw Materials/Sensitive Commodities

Commodity Price Trends Are Followed Closely

For these items, the price at any particular moment probably is less important than the trend of the price movement. The price can be determined readily in most instances because many of these commodities are bought and sold on well-organized markets. Prices are reported regularly in many of the trade and business journals, such as *Iron Age, Chemical Marketing Reporter,* and *The Wall Street Journal.* These publications and other sources also are readily available online, giving the interested buyer instantaneous access.

These quoted market prices also can be useful in developing prices-paid evaluation systems and price indexes for use in price escalator clauses.

Timing a Purchase Based on Price Trends

To the extent that such quoted prices are a fair reflection of market conditions, the current cash price is known and is substantially uniform for a given grade. Yet, it is common knowledge among buyers that such published market quotations usually are on the high side, and the astute buyer probably can get a lower price. A company's requirements for commodities of this sort usually are sufficiently adjustable so that an immediate order is seldom a necessity, and purchase can be postponed if the trend of prices is downward.

The price trend is a matter of importance in the purchase of any type of commodity, but it is particularly important with this group. Insofar as "careful and studious timing" is essential to getting the right price, both the type of information required as a basis for such timing and the sources from which the information can be obtained differ from those necessary in dealing with other groups of items. Commodity study research, discussed in Chapter 13, is particularly useful in buying these items.

Special Items

Products Are Unique

Special items include the large variety of purchased parts or special materials peculiar to the organization's end product or service. Make or buy is always a significant consideration on these items because of their proprietary nature. Prices normally are obtained by quotation because no published price lists are available. Subcontracts are common, and the availability of compatible or special equipment, skilled labor, and capacity may be significant factors in determining price. Because large differences may exist between suppliers in terms of these factors and their desire for business, prices may vary substantially between suppliers. Each product in this group is unique and may need special attention. A diligent search for suppliers willing and able to handle such special requirements, including an advantageous price, may pay off handsomely.

Standard Production Items

The third group of items includes those standard production items whose prices are comparatively stable and are likely to be quoted on a basis of list-less-certain-discounts. This group includes a wide range of items commonly obtainable from a substantial list of sources. The inventory problems related to this class of requirements are largely routine. Changes in price do occur, but they are far less frequent than with raw materials and are likely to be moderate. Prices usually are obtained from online or hard-copy catalogs or similar publications of suppliers, supplemented by periodic discount sheets.

Annual Dollar Volume May Be High

It should not be concluded from this that such purchases are unimportant or that the prices quoted should not be examined with care. Quite the contrary is true. The items are important in themselves; the annual dollar volume of purchases is often impressive; and real attention needs to be paid to the unit price. When a requisition is received by purchasing, the first step commonly would be to refer to past purchase records as the first source of information. If the material in question has been regularly purchased or orders have been placed for it recently, an up-to-date price record and catalog file will give all the information pertaining to the transaction, such as the various firms able to supply the commodity, the firms from which purchases have been made, and the prices paid. This information will be sufficiently recent and reliable to enable the buyer to place the order without extended investigation. However, if the buyer does not feel justified in proceeding on the basis of this information, a list of available suppliers from supplier files, catalogs, and other sources can be assembled and quotation requests can be sent to selected sources.

Methods for Purchasing Standard Items

One of the best sources for current prices and discounts is sales representatives. Few manufacturers rely wholly on catalogs for sales but follow up such material with visits by their salespersons. Online auctions (seller-initiated) or reverse auctions (buyer-initiated) are also being used by some organizations seeking a more efficient means of purchasing standard items (See Chapter 4). Much useful data can be obtained from such visits. The buyer learns of price revisions, which should be noted in the appropriate catalog, ascertains the probable date of publication of new editions, and is assured that the corporation is on the proper mailing lists. In some lines confidential discounts, usually based on quantity, are uncovered. Advance notice of intended price changes sometimes is given. It is the buyer's duty to be alert to the possibilities of such information to take full advantage of them.

A sales representative may quote the buyer a price while in the buyer's office, and the buyer may accept by issuing a purchase order (PO). There likely will be no problem, although legally the salesperson probably doesn't have agency authority, and the offer made by the salesperson does not legally commit the selling company *until* it has been accepted by an officer of the selling company. If the buyer wishes to accept such an offer, and to know that the offer is legally binding, he or she should ask the salesperson to furnish a letter, signed by an officer of the selling company, stating that the salesperson possesses the authority of a sales *agent*.

Small-Value Items

MRO Supplies

The fourth group of commodities for the purpose of price determination includes items of such small value, comparatively speaking, that they do not justify any particular effort to analyze the price in detail. These often are referred to as maintenance, repair, and operating (MRO) supplies. Every purchasing department must buy numerous items of this sort; yet these items do not in themselves justify a catalog file, even when such catalogs are available, nor do they represent enough money to warrant sending out for individual quotations. Actually, the pricing problem on such items is handled in a variety of ways; the following constitutes an excellent summary of these procedures.

As discussed in Chapter 4, a number of organizations have experienced success in procuring MRO items through e-procurement systems. While the actual transaction is handled electronically, most of the advantages come from applying good purchasing practices, such as consolidating and standardizing requirements and reducing the number of suppliers.

Procedures Used to Price MRO Supplies

It is also common practice to send out unpriced orders for such items. Another common practice is to indicate on the order the last price paid, this price being taken from the record of purchases or past purchases if the last purchase was not too far back. Other buyers make a practice of grouping these small items under some blanket order or systems-contract arrangement or on a cost-plus basis with suppliers who undertake to have the materials in inventory when needed, and who are willing to submit to periodic checking as to the fairness of the prices they charge. Procurement cards also are used to allow internal customers to purchase small-value items from designated suppliers. (See Chapter 3 for a discussion of blanket orders, systems contracting, and procurement cards, and Chapter 4 for a discussion on e-procurement.)

In most cases, sources of supply for these items are local, and current prices often are obtained by telephone or fax and then placed on the face of the purchase order so they become a part of the agreement. The most common practice of all, however, is perhaps to depend on the integrity of the suppliers and to omit any detailed checking of the proper price on items of small value. Many purchasing managers believe that their best assurance is the

Methods of Price Control on Small Value Purchases

confidence they have in carefully selected sources of supply, and they feel secure in relying on their suppliers to give them the best available price without requiring them to name the price in advance, and without checking it when the invoice is received.

Another method for controlling prices for these small-dollar items consists of the practice of spot-checking. This means the selection of an occasional item which then is carefully investigated to develop the exact basis on which the supplier is pricing. Discovery of unfair or improper prices by such spot checks is considered a reason for discontinuing the source of supply, who is discovered to be taking advantage of the nature of the transaction in pricing. Perhaps a more effective way to buy items of small value, such as those included in the MRO group, is to use the systems-contracting and third-party supplier techniques described in Chapter 3.

Emergency Requirements

Somewhat similar to the small-value purchase problem is the emergency requirement. Here, as for example with equipment breakdown, time may be of much greater value than money, and the buyer may wish to get the supplier started immediately, even though price has not been determined. The buyer may decide merely to say "start" or "ship" and issue an unpriced purchase order. If the price charged on the invoice is out of line, it can be challenged before payment.

Methods of Price Determination

Prices may be determined in a number of ways, most commonly through evaluating responses to requests for quotations, competitive bidding, or negotiation.

The Use of Quotations and Competitive Bidding (Online or Off-line)

Quotations normally are secured when the size of the proposed commitment exceeds some minimum dollar amount, for example, $1,000. Governmental purchases commonly must be on a bid basis; here the law requires that the award shall be made to the lowest *responsible* bidder. (See Chapter 15, Public Purchasing, for a detailed discussion of competitive bidding). In industrial practice, quotations may be solicited with a view to selecting those firms with whom negotiations as to the final price will be carried on.

The extent to which competitive bidding is relied on to secure an acceptable price varies widely. On the one hand, it is a common practice for buyers of routine supplies, purchased from the same sources time after time, to issue unpriced orders. The same thing occasionally happens in a very strong seller's market for some critical item when prices are rising so rapidly that the supplier refuses to quote a fixed price. Whenever possible, however, price should be indicated on the purchase order. In fact, from a legal point of view, a purchase order *must* contain either a price or a method of its determination for the contract to be binding. When it is decided to ask for competitive bids, certain essential steps are needed. These are a careful initial selection of dependable, potential sources; an accurate wording of the request to bid; submission of bid requests to a sufficient number of suppliers to ensure a truly competitive price; proper treatment of such quotations, once received; and a careful analysis of them prior to making the award.

Essential Steps in Competitive Bidding

Select Possible Suppliers

The first step is to select possible suppliers from whom quotations are to be solicited; this amounts, in fact, to a preliminary screening of the sources of supply. It is assumed that the bidders must (1) be qualified to make the item in question in accordance with the buyer's specifications and to deliver it by the desired date, (2) be sufficiently reliable in other respects to warrant serious consideration as suppliers, (3) be numerous enough to ensure a truly competitive price, but (4) not be more numerous than necessary. The first two of these qualifications have been considered in our discussion of sources. The *number* of suppliers to whom inquiries are sent is largely a matter of the buyer's judgment. Ordinarily, at least two suppliers are invited to bid. More often, three or four are invited to submit bids. A multiplicity of bidders does not ensure a truly competitive price, although under ordinary circumstances it is an important factor, provided that the bidders are comparable in every major respect and provided that each is sufficiently reliable so that the buyer would be willing to purchase from that supplier.

The buyer normally will exclude from the bid list those firms with whom it is unlikely that an order would be placed, even though their prices were low. Sometimes bids are solicited solely for the purpose of checking the prices of regular suppliers or for inventory-pricing purposes. It should be remembered, however, that a company is put to some expense—at times, a very considerable one—when it submits a bid. It should not be asked to bear this cost without good reason. Moreover, the receipt of a request to bid is an encouragement to the supplier and implies that an order is possible. Therefore, purchasers should not solicit quotations unless placement of a purchase order is a possibility.

Inquiries Are Sent to Prospective Bidders

Having decided on the companies that are to be invited to bid, the purchaser in an off-line process sends a general inquiry, in which all the necessary information is set forth. A complete description of the item or items, the date on which these items are wanted, and the date by which the bid is to be returned are included. In many instances, a telephone inquiry is substituted for a formal request to bid.

Subsequent to the mailing of an inquiry but prior to the announcement of the purchase award, bidders naturally are anxious to know how their quotations compare with those of their competitors. Because sealed bids, used in governmental purchasing, are not commonly used in private industry, the purchaser is in a position to know how the bids, as they are received, compare with one another. However, if the bids are examined on receipt, it is important that this information be treated in strictest confidence. Indeed, some buyers deliberately keep themselves in ignorance of the quotations until such time as they are ready to analyze the bids; thus they are in a position

Bids Should Be Kept Confidential

to tell any inquiring bidder truthfully that they do not know how the bid prices compare. Even after the award is made, it probably is the better policy not to reveal to unsuccessful bidders the amount by which they failed to meet the successful bid.

Automation of the Bid Process

In many entities in the public sector, the entire bid process has been automated. Bid packages and specifications are made available online, bidders submit their bids and proposals online, and the bid opening and award is communicated electronically. The cycle time reductions and other cost savings obviously can be great if the automated process is efficient.

This process is quite similar when it is an online bidding situation. In the case of an online auction, the potential sources are also pre-qualified and invited to take part in the online bidding. The auction, or event, is set for a specific date and time period much like the deadline and bid opening deadlines in an off-line process. The success of the auction depends in large part on the quality of the bid specifications and the ability of the person and process to pre-qualify suppliers. Bidders can see, online, the actual bid amounts but not who the bidders are.

Firm Bidding

The reason for the confidential treatment of bid price information is its connection with a problem practically all buyers have to face, namely, that of "firm bidding." Most firms have a policy of notifying suppliers that original bids must be final and that revisions will not be permitted under any circumstances. Exceptions are made only in the case of obvious error.

Particularly in times of falling prices, suppliers, extremely anxious to get business, try by various devices to ensure that their bids will be the lowest. Not infrequently they have been encouraged in this procedure by those purchasers who have acceded to requests that revisions be allowed. Unfortunately, it is also true that there are buyers who deliberately play one bidder against another and who even seek to secure lower prices by relating imaginary bids to prospective suppliers. The responsibility for deviations from a policy of firm bidding must be laid at the door of the purchaser as well as the supplier.

Firm Bidding Is the Fairest Means of Treating All Suppliers Equally

A policy of firm bidding is sound and should be deviated from only under the most unusual circumstances. To those who contend that it is impossible to adopt such a policy, the answer is that it actually is the practice followed in many organizations. The advantage of firm bidding as a general policy, however, needs no particular explanation. If rigidly adhered to, it is the fairest possible means of treating all suppliers alike. It tends to stress the quality and service elements in the transaction instead of the price factor. Assuming that bids are solicited only from honest and dependable suppliers and that the buyer is not obligated to place the order with the lowest bidder, it removes from suppliers the temptation to try to use inferior materials or workmanship once their bid has been accepted. It saves the purchaser time by removing the necessity for constant bargaining with suppliers over price.

Exception to Firm Bidding

An exception to the firm bidding approach is one where the buyer wants both parties (seller and buyer) to have the flexibility to clarify and define specifications and prices further after the initial bids are received. The buyer will notify all the sellers, at the time the initial bid request is made, that after the initial bids are received the buyer may enter into discussions concerning any aspects of the requirement with one or more of the bidders, and then request best-and-final-offers (BAFOS). Some public buying agencies now also are permitted to use this approach.[2]

Occasionally the buyer may, after reviewing the bids submitted, notify the bidders that all bids are being rejected and that another bid request is being issued, or that the item will be bought through a means other than competitive bidding. This may be done if it is obvious that the bidders did not fully understand the specifications, if collusion on the part of the bidders is suspected, or if it is felt that all prices quoted are unrealistically high.

Determination of Most Advantageous Bid

Typically, a bid analysis sheet is used to array the bids of all suppliers and the particulars of each bid (see Chapter 3 for an example), or the bids are viewed electronically in real time during an online auction. But after the bids have been submitted and compared, which should be selected? The lowest bid customarily is accepted.[3] The objective of securing bids from various sources is to obtain the lowest price, and the purpose of supplying detailed specifications and statements of requirements is to ensure that the buyer receives the same items or services irrespective of whom the supplier may be. Governmental contracts must be awarded to the lowest bidder unless very special reasons can be shown for not doing so.

Reasons for Not Accepting the Lowest Bid

However, there are several cases in which the lowest bidder may not receive the order. Information received by the buyer subsequent to the request for bids may indicate that the firm submitting the lowest bid is not reliable. Even the lowest bid may be higher than the buyer believes justifiable. Or there may be reason to believe there was collusion among the bidders.

There are other reasons why the lowest bid is not always accepted: plant management, engineering, or using departments may express a preference for a certain manufacturer's product. Possibly a slight difference in price may not be considered enough to compensate for the confidence ensured by a particular supplier's product. A small difference in price may not seem to justify changing from a source of supply that has been satisfactory over a long period; yet the bid process may have been considered essential in ensuring that the company was receiving the proper price treatment.

Selecting the supplier, once the quotations are received, is not a simple matter of listing the bidders and picking out the one whose price is appar-

---

[2]Ron C. Gauthier, " 'Best and Final' in the Public Arena," *NAPM Insights,* January 1995, p. 33.

[3]This statement is made on the assumption that the lowest bid comes from a reliable supplier; presumably, of course, only reliable firms have been invited to bid.

ently low, because the obvious price comparisons may be misleading. Of two apparently identical bids, one actually may be higher than the other. One supplier's installation costs may be lower than another's. If prices quoted are Free on Board origin, the transportation charges may be markedly different. One supplier's price may be much lower because it is trying to break into a new market or is trying to force its only real competitor out of business. One supplier's product may require tooling which must be amortized. One supplier may quote a fixed price; another may insist on an escalator clause that could push the price above a competitor's firm bid. These and other similar factors are likely to render a snap judgment on comparative price a mistake.

Collusive Bidding

Actions If Collusion Is Suspected

A buyer also may reject all bids if it is suspected that the suppliers are acting in collusion with one another. In such cases the proper policy to pursue is often difficult to determine, but there are various possibilities. Legal action is possible but seldom feasible because of the expense, delay, and uncertainty of the outcome. Often, unfortunately, the only apparent solution is simply to accept the situation with the feeling that there is nothing the buyer can do about it anyway. Another possibility is to seek new sources of supply either inside or outside the area in which the buyer customarily has purchased materials or services. Resorting to substitute materials, temporarily or even permanently, may be an effective means of meeting the situation. Another possibility is to reject all the bids and then to attempt, by a process of negotiation or bargaining with one or another of the suppliers, to reduce the price. If circumstances make the last alternative the most feasible, a question of ethics is involved. Some purchasing officers feel that when collusion among the suppliers exists, it is ethical for them to attempt to force down suppliers' prices by means which ordinarily would not be adopted.

The Problem of Identical Prices

It is not unusual for the buyer to receive identical bids from various sources. Because such bids may indicate intensive competition on the one hand, and discrimination or collusion on the other, the purchaser must take care in handling such situations. Some of the situations that tend to make identical or parallel prices suspect are when:

1. Identical pricing marks a novel break in the historical pattern of price behavior.
2. There is evidence of communication between sellers or buyers regarding prices.
3. There is an "artificial" standardization of the product.
4. Identical prices are submitted in bids to buyers on complex, detailed, or novel specifications.

5. Deviations from uniform prices become the matter of industrywide concern—the subject of meetings and even organized sanctions.

Four Ways to Discourage Identical Pricing

The purchaser can take four different types of action to discourage identical pricing. The first is to encourage small sellers who form the nonconformist group in an industry and are anxious to grow. The second is to allow bidders to bid on parts of large contracts if they feel the total contract may be too large. The third is to encourage firm bidding without revision. And the fourth is to choose criteria in making the award so as to discourage future identical bids. If identical bids have been received, the buyer can reject all bids and then either call for new bids or negotiate directly with one or more specific suppliers. In these circumstances, in the letter to suppliers notifying them that all bids have been rejected, it might be appropriate to make a polite reference to the illegality of all forms of price fixing. However, if it is decided that the contract should be awarded at this time, various alternatives are available. It may be given to:

Awarding a Contract When Identical Bids Were Received

1. The smallest supplier.
2. The one with the largest domestic content.
3. The most distant firm, forcing it to absorb the largest freight portion.
4. The firm with the smallest market share.
5. The firm most likely to grant non-price concessions.
6. The firm whose past performance has been best.

U.S. Government Actions Related to Identical Bids

Executive Order 10936, dated April 24, 1961, directed all federal procurement agencies to report to the U.S. Department of Justice all identical bids over $10,000 per line item. State and local purchasing departments also were asked to report identical bids. However, this program was judged ineffective relative to the administrative resources required; it was revoked on July 6, 1983, by Executive Order 12430, entitled "Reports of Identical Bids," although it was emphasized that there is a continuing need to pursue aggressively "all cases of suspected criminal conduct, noncompetitive practices, kickbacks, and other procurement irregularities." Although the annual report entitled "Identical Bidding in Public Procurement" no longer will be available, the National Association of Attorneys General does publish an "Antitrust Report" summarizing state antitrust cases, their current status, or the final outcome.

Competitive bidding attempts to obtain a fair price for items bought; the forces of competition are used to bring the price down to a level at which the efficient supplier will be able to cover only production and distribution costs, plus make a minimum profit. If a supplier wants the order, that supplier will "sharpen the pencil" and give the buyer an attractive quote. This places a good deal of pressure on the supplier.

Conditions that Ensure an Efficient Bid Process

However, for the bid process to work efficiently, several conditions are necessary: (1) There must be at least two, and preferably several, qualified suppliers; (2) the suppliers must want the business (competitive bidding works best in a buyer's market); (3) the specifications must be clear, so that each bidder knows precisely what is being bid on, and so the buyer can easily compare the quotes received from various bidders; and (4) there must be honest bidding and the absence of any collusion between the bidders. When any of these conditions is absent—that is, a sole-source situation, a seller's market, specifications are not complete or subject to varying interpretations, or suspected supplier collusion—then negotiation is the preferred method of price determination.

Negotiation as a Method of Price Determination

When Is Negotiation Used?

Negotiation is the most sophisticated and most expensive means of price determination. It is used on large-dollar purchases where competitive bidding is not appropriate. Negotiation requires that the buyer sit down across a table with a supplier, and through discussion they arrive at a common understanding on the essentials of a purchase/sale contract, such as delivery, specifications, warranty, prices, and terms. Because of the interrelation of these factors and many others, it is a difficult art and requires the exercise of judgment and tact. Negotiation is an attempt to find an agreement that allows both parties to realize their objectives. It is used most often when the buyer is in a single or sole-source situation; in that case, both parties know that a purchase contract will be issued and their task is to define a set of terms and conditions acceptable to both. Because of the expense and time involved, true negotiation normally will not be used unless the dollar amount is quite large; $50,000 or more is the general minimum set by some organizations. A more extensive treatment of negotiation follows near the end of this chapter.

Reasonable negotiation is expected by buyer and seller alike. It is within reasonable bounds of negotiation to insist that a supplier:

1. Operate in an efficient manner.
2. Keep prices in line with costs.
3. Not take advantage of a privileged position.
4. Make proper and reasonable adjustment of claims.
5. Be prepared to consider the special needs of the buyer's organization.

Everything Is Negotiable

While negotiation normally is thought of as a means of establishing price to be paid, and this is the main focus, many other areas or conditions can be negotiated. In fact, *any* aspect of the purchase/sale agreement is subject to negotiation. A few of these areas are:

1. Quality.
   a. Specification compliance.
   b. Performance compliance.
   c. Test criteria.

       d.   Rejection procedures.

       e.   Liability.

       f.   Reliability.

       g.   Design changes.

  2. Support.

       a.   Technical assistance.

       b.   Product research, development, and/or design.

       c.   Warranty.

       d.   Spare parts.

       e.   Training.

       f.   Tooling.

       g.   Packaging.

       h.   Data sharing, including technical data.

  3. Supply.

       a.   Lead times.

       b.   Delivery schedule.

       c.   Consignment stocks.

       d.   Expansion options.

       e.   Supplier inventories.

       f.   Cancellation options.

  4. Transportation.

       a.   FOB terms.

       b.   Carrier.

       c.   Commodity classification.

       d.   Freight allowance/equalization.

       e.   Multiple delivery points.

  5. Price.

       a.   Purchase order price.

       b.   Discounts (cash, quantity, and trade).

       c.   Escalation provisions.

       d.   Exchange terms (monetary rate fluctuation).

       e.   Import duties.

       f.   Payment of taxes.

       g.   Countertrade credits

Price Haggling Is Not Negotiation

Price Haggling. Negotiating a fair price should not be confused with *price haggling*. Purchasing managers generally frown on haggling and properly so, for in the long run the cost to the buyer far outweighs any temporary advantage. For a purchaser to tell a sales representative that he or she has received a quotation that was not, in fact, received or that is not comparable; to fake telephone calls in the sales representative's presence; to leave real or fictitious bids of competitors in open sight for a sales representative to see; to mislead as to the quantity needed—these and similar practices are illustrations of those unethical actions so properly condemned by the codes of ethics of the Institute for Supply Management (formerly the National Association of Purchasing Management) and the Purchasing Management Association of Canada.

Situation When Price May Be Revised Upward	**Revision of Price Upward.** Negotiation need not result in a lower price. Occasionally, there may be revision upward of the price paid, compared with the supplier's initial proposal. If in the negotiation it becomes clear that the supplier has either misinterpreted the specifications or underestimated the resources needed to perform the work, the buyer will bring this to the supplier's attention so the proposal may be adjusted accordingly. A good contract is one that both parties can live with, and under which the supplier should not lose money, providing its operation is efficient. When a purchaser cooperates in granting increases not required by the original supplier proposal, the buyer then is in a position to request decreases in prices if unforeseen events occur that result in the supplier's being able to produce the material or product at a substantial savings.

Provision for Price Changes

Action in Case of Downward Price Movement	**Guarantee against Price Decline.** For goods bought on a recurring basis and for raw materials, the contract may be written at the price in effect at the time the contract is negotiated. The contract then provides for a reduction during a subsequent period if there is a downward price movement in the marketplace. The contract normally specifies that price movement will be determined by the list price reported in a specific business or trade journal. The buyer is more likely to be influenced by such guarantees when they are offered in an effort to overcome reluctance to buy, induced by a fear that prices are likely to drop still further.
Provides the Opportunity to Go With a Lower-Priced Supplier	**Price Protection Clause.** When a buyer enters into a long-term contract for raw materials or other key purchased items with one or more suppliers, the buyer may want to keep open the option of taking advantage of a lower price offered by a different supplier. This might be done by either buying from the noncontract supplier, or forcing the contract supplier(s) to meet the lower price now available from the noncontract suppliers. Therefore, a price protection clause may be incorporated into the contract specifying that: "If the buyer is offered material of equal quality in similar quantities under like terms from a responsible supplier, at a lower delivered cost to the buyer than specified in this contract, the seller on being furnished written evidence of

this offer shall either meet the lower delivered price or allow the buyer to purchase from the other supplier at the lower delivered price and deduct the quantity purchased from the quantity specified in this contract."

Escalator Clauses Provide for an Increase or Decrease in Price

Escalator Clauses. The actual wording of many escalator clauses provides for either an increase or decrease in price if costs change. Clauses providing for escalation came into common use during many of the hyperinflation years in the 1970s when suppliers believed that their future costs were so uncertain as to make a firm quotation either impossible or, if covering all probable risks, so high as to make it unattractive, and perhaps unfair, to the buyer.

In designing any particular escalator contract, several general and many specific problems—such as the proportion of the total price subject to adjustment; the particular measures of prices and wage rates to be used in making the adjustment; the methods to be followed in applying these averages to the base price; the limitations, if any, on the amount of adjustment; and the methods for making payment—will be encountered. In times of price stability, escalation usually is reserved for long-term contracts, on the principle that certain costs may rise and that the seller has no appreciable control over this rise. In times of inflation, shortages, and sellers' markets, escalation becomes common on even short-term contracts as sellers attempt to ensure themselves of the opportunity to raise prices and preserve contribution margins. Changes in material and direct labor costs generally are tied to one of the published price and cost indexes, such as those of the Bureau of Labor Statistics or one of the trade publications, such as *Iron Age* or the *Chemical Marketing Reporter.* Finding a meaningful index to which escalation may be tied is a real problem in many instances. Because most escalation is automatic once the index, the portion of the contract subject to escalation, the frequency of revision, and the length of contract have been agreed to, the need for care in deciding on these factors is obvious.

Example of an Escalator Clause

The following is an illustrative escalator clause:

Labor

Adjustment with respect to labor costs shall be made on the basis of monthly average hourly earnings for the (Durable Goods Industry, subclass Machinery), as furnished by the Bureau of Labor Statistics (hereafter called the Labor Index). Adjustments shall be calculated with respect to each calendar quarter up to the completion date specified in contract. The percentage increase or decrease in the quarterly index (obtained by averaging the Labor Index for each month of the calendar quarter) shall be obtained by comparison with the Labor Index for the base month. The base month shall be____, 200____. The labor adjustment for each calendar quarter as thus determined shall be obtained by applying such percentage of increase or decrease to the total amount expended by the contractor for direct labor during such quarter.

Materials

Adjustment with respect to materials shall be made on the basis of the materials index for Group VI (Metals and Metal Products), as furnished by the Bureau of Labor Statistics (hereafter called the Materials Index). Adjustments shall be determined with respect to each calendar quarter up to the completion date specified in the contract. The percentage of increase or decrease in the quarterly index (obtained by averaging the Materials Index for each month of the calendar quarter) shall be obtained by comparison with the Materials Index for the base month. The base month shall be____, 200____. The material adjustment for each calendar quarter shall be obtained by applying to the contract material cost the percentage of increase or decrease shown by the Materials Index for that quarter.

A Valid Contract Must Include a Price or Method of Price Determination

A buyer who uses escalator clauses must remember that one legal essential to any enforceable purchase contract is that it contain either a definite price or the means of arriving at one. No contract for future delivery can be enforced if the price of the item is conditioned entirely on the will of one of the parties. The clauses cited earlier would appear to be adequate. So too are those clauses authorizing the seller to change price as costs of production change, provided that these costs can be reasonably determined from the supplier's accounting records.

Most-Favored-Customer Clause. Another commonly used price protection clause (sometimes referred to as a "most-favored-nation clause") specifies that the supplier, over the duration of the contract, will not offer a lower price to other buyers, or if a lower price is offered to others, it will apply to this contract as well.

Discounts

Two Classes of Discounts

Discounts fall into two classes. The first class consists of inside prices and various other forms of price concessions that are not always defensible either legally or commercially. The second class consists of ordinary cash, trade, and quantity discounts which are thoroughly legitimate and fair.

The line of distinction between these two classes is difficult to draw for it is not always easy to define what is legitimate and what is not. Clearly there are certain types of apparent price concessions, such as *inside prices,* which no responsible purchasing agent should even request and which, under most circumstances, should be refused if offered. A supplier who offers an inside price to one buyer will offer a similar or lower price to another. A seller who is not open and honest in pricing policy is not one with whom a purchaser can afford to do business.

The second class of discounts warrants more attention.

Purpose of Cash Discounts

Cash Discounts. Cash discounts are granted by virtually every seller of industrial goods, although the actual discount terms are a matter of individual trade custom and vary considerably from one industry to another. The purpose of a cash discount is to secure the prompt payment of an account.

Most sellers expect buyers to take the cash discount. The net price is commonly fixed at a point that will yield a fair profit to the supplier and is the price the supplier expects most customers to pay. Those who do not pay within the time limit are penalized and are expected to pay the gross price.

However, variations in cash discount amounts frequently are made without due regard for the real purpose for which such discounts should be granted and are used, instead, merely as another means of varying prices. If a buyer secures a cash discount not commonly granted in the past, he or she may be sure that the net result is merely a reduction in the price, regardless of the name used. On the other hand, a reduction in the size of the cash discount is, in effect, an increase in the price.

Formula for Determining Value of a Discount

Cash discounts, therefore, sometimes raise rather difficult questions of price policy, but if they are granted on the same terms to all buyers and if postdating and other similar practices are not granted to some buyers and denied to others, then the purchasing department's major interest in cash discounts is confined largely to being sure they are called to the attention of the proper financial managers. The purchaser ordinarily cannot be held responsible for a failure to take cash discounts because this depends on the financial resources of the organization and is, therefore, a matter of financial rather than purchasing policy. The purchaser should, however, be very careful to secure such cash discounts as customarily are granted. It is a part of the buyer's responsibility to see that inspection is made promptly, that goods are accepted without unnecessary loss of time, and that all documents are handled expeditiously so all discounts quoted may be taken. A discount of 2 percent if payment is made within 10 days, with the gross amount due in 30 days, is the equivalent of earning an annual interest rate of approximately 36 percent. If the buying company does not pay within the 10-day discount period but instead pays 20 days later, the effective cost for the use of that money for the 20 days is 2 percent (the lost discount). Because there are approximately 18 20-day periods in a year, $2\% \times 18 = 36\%$, the effective annual interest rate.

To establish the exact date by which payment must be mailed to deduct the cash discount from the payment amount, and to avoid the confusion which often results from handling incorrectly prepared supplier invoices, some firms include a clause in their purchase order specifying that "determination of the cash discount payment period will be calculated from either the date of delivery of acceptable goods, or the receipt of a properly prepared invoice, whichever date is later."

Finance Policy in the Buying Organization

Some customers will take the cash discount even when they are paying after the discount date. Part of the buyer's responsibility is to ensure that his or her organization lives up to the terms and conditions of the contract. This will mean working with other functional areas to ensure that payment is made in a timely manner. This will be of particular importance in partnering arrangements or alliances.

Trade Discounts. Trade discounts are granted by a manufacturer to a buyer because the purchasing firm is a particular type of distributor or user. In general, they aim to protect the distributor by making it more profitable for a purchaser to buy from the distributor than directly from the manufac-

Manufacturer and Distributor Relationship Influences Trade Discounts

turer. When manufacturers have found that various types of distributors can sell their merchandise in a given territory more cheaply than they can, they usually rely on the distributors' services. To ensure that goods will move through the channels selected, the distributor is granted a trade discount approximating the cost of doing business.

However, trade discounts are not always used properly. Protection is sometimes granted distributors not entitled to it, because the services which they render manufacturers, and presumably customers, are not commensurate with the discount they get. Generally speaking, buyers dealing in small quantities who secure a great variety of items from a single source or who depend on frequent and very prompt deliveries are more likely to obtain their supplies from wholesalers and other distributors receiving trade discounts. With the larger accounts, manufacturers are more likely to sell directly, even though they may reserve the smaller accounts in the same territory for the wholesalers. Some manufacturers refuse to sell to accounts purchasing below a stipulated minimum.

Aftermarket Requirements

Discounts often are available to a buyer who also purchases aftermarket requirements (replacement parts for units already sold). The supplier may put the buyer who wishes to buy items that will be sold to the aftermarket into one of several price classifications: (1) an OEM (original equipment manufacturer) class, (2) a class with its distributors, or (3) a separate OEM aftermarket class. Aftermarket suppliers often do special packaging, part numbering, or stocking, which may justify a special price schedule. The buyer needs to know what price classifications the supplier uses and the qualifications for placing the buyer in a particular classification.

Example of a Multiple Discount

Multiple Discounts. In some industries and trades, prices are quoted on a multiple discount basis. For example, 10, 10, and 10 means that, for an item listed at $100, the actual price to be paid by the purchaser is ($100 − 10%) − 10%($100 − 10%) − 10%[($100 − 10%) − 10%($100 − 10%)] = $100 − $10 − $9 − $8.10 = $72.90. The 10, 10, and 10 is, therefore, equivalent to a discount of 0.271. Tables are available listing the most common multiple discount combinations and their equivalent discount.

Two Types of Savings for Sellers

Quantity Discounts. Quantity discounts may be granted for buying in particular quantities and vary roughly in proportion to the amount purchased. From the seller's standpoint, the justification for granting such discounts is usually that quantity purchasing results in savings to the seller, enabling a lower price to the buyer who has made such savings possible. These savings may be of two classes: (1) savings in marketing or distribution expense and, (2) savings in production expense.[4]

In the late 1940s, the Federal Trade Commission, in administering the Robinson-Patman Act, from time to time proceeded against buyers who were alleged to have knowingly received lower prices from sellers than their competitors. It is obvious that in most cases it would be extremely difficult for the buyer to prove the seller had cost savings that could justify the lower price.

Landmark Court Case

In 1953, in a landmark decision, the U.S. Supreme Court ruled in the case of the Automatic Canteen Company of America that:

1. The mere inducement of receipt of a lower price is not unlawful.
2. It is lawful for a buyer to accept anything which it is lawful for a seller to give.
3. It is only the prohibited discrimination a buyer may not induce or receive.
4. It is not unlawful for a buyer to receive a prohibited discrimination unless he knows or, as a reasonably prudent buyer, should know that the differential is prohibited.

The court concluded that to prove cost justification according to the Federal Trade Commission's accounting standards would place a heavy burden on a buyer—it would require a study of the seller's business and "would almost inevitably," to quote the court, "require a degree of cooperation between buyer and seller, as against other buyers, that may offend other antitrust policies, and it might also expose the seller's cost secrets to the prejudice of arm's-length bargaining in the future." The court added: "Finally, not one, but as here, approximately 80 different sellers' costs may be in issue." The court dismissed the case against Automatic Canteen.

Savings Generated by Securing Large Orders

The savings in marketing or distribution expense arise because it may be no more costly to sell a large order than a small one; the billing expense is the same; and the increased cost of packing, crating, and shipping is not proportional. When these circumstances exist, a direct quantity discount not exceeding the difference in cost of handling the small and the large order is justified.

There may be substantial savings in production costs as a result of securing a large order instead of a small one. For instance, setup costs may be the same for a large order as a small one; material costs may be lower per unit.

From the buyer's viewpoint, the question of quantity discounts is intimately connected with that of inventory policy. While it is true that the larger the size of a given order, the lower the unit price likely will be, the carrying charges on the buyer's larger inventory are more costly. Hence, the savings on the size of the order must be compared against the increased inventory costs.

---

[4]The U.S. Supreme Court in May 1948 ruled in the case of the Morton Salt Company (68 S. Ct.) that no wholesaler, retailer, or manufacturer whose product is sold to the public through these channels may grant quantity discounts unless they can be justified by (*a*) lower costs "due to quantity manufacture, delivery, or sale" or (*b*) "the seller's good faith effort to meet a competitor's equally low price." Furthermore, it ruled that the Federal Trade Commission need not prove that discounts are discriminatory. The burden of proof is on the seller to prove the law is not being violated.

The Price-Discount Problem

Carry Inventory versus Pay Higher Price

A normal situation in purchasing occurs when a price discount is offered if purchases are made in larger quantities. Acceptance of a larger quantity provides a form of anticipation inventory. The problem may be solved in several ways. Marginally, the question is: "Should we increase the size of our inventory so that we obtain the benefits of the lower price?" Put this way, it can be analyzed as a return on investment decision. The simple EOQ model is not of much assistance here because it cannot account for the purchase price differential directly. It is possible to use the EOQ model to eliminate some alternatives, however, and to check the final solution. Total cost calculations are required to find the optimal point.

The following problem is illustrative of the calculation.

Sample Price-Discount Problem
R = 900 units (annual demand)
S = $50 (order cost)
K = 0.25 (carrying cost) or 25 percent
C = $45 for 0–199 units per order
    $43 for 200–399 units per order
    $41.50 for 400–799 units per order
    $40 for 800 and more units per order

Sample Calculations for the Price-Discount Problem

	100	*200*	*400*	*800*
Total annual price paid	$40,500	$38,700	$37,350	$36,000
Carrying cost	562	1,075	2,075	4,000
Order cost	450	225	112	56
Total cost	41,512	40,000	39,537	40,056
Average inventory	$2,250	$4,300	$8,300	$16,000
EOQ	Units 89	92*	93*	94*

*Not feasible

A simple marginal analysis shows that in moving from 100 per order to 200, the additional average investment is $4,300 − $2,250 = $2,050. The saving in price is $40,500 − $38,700 = $1,800, and the order cost saving is $450 − $225 = $225. For an additional investment of $2,050, the savings are $2,025, which is almost a 100 percent return and is well in excess of the 25 percent carrying cost. In going from 400 to 800, the additional investment is $7,700 for a total price and order savings of $1,406.25. This falls below the 25 percent carrying cost and would not be a desirable result. The total cost figures show that the optimal purchase quantity is at the 400 level. The largest single saving occurs at the first price break at the 200 level.

The EOQs with an asterisk are not feasible because the price range and the volume do not match. For example, the price for the second EOQ of 92 is $45. Yet, for the 200 to 400 range, the actual price is $43. The EOQ may be used, however, in the following way. In going from right to left on the table (from the lowest unit price to the highest price), proceed until the first valid EOQ is obtained. This is 89 for the 0 to 199 price range. Then the order quantity at each price discount about this EOQ is checked to see whether total costs at the higher order quantity are lower or higher than at the EOQ. Doing this for the example shown gives us a total cost at the valid EOQ level of 89 of:

Total annual price paid	$ 40,500
Carrying cost	500
Order cost	500
Total Cost	$ 41,500

Attaining Lowest Total Cost

Because this total cost at the feasible EOQ of 89 units is above the total cost at the 200 order quantity level and the 400 and 800 order levels as well, the proper order quantity is 400, which gives the lowest total cost of all options.

Avoiding Large Inventories

The discussion so far has assumed that the quantity discount offered is based on orders of the full amount, forcing the purchaser to carry substantial inventories. It is preferable, of course, from the purchaser's standpoint to take delivery in smaller quantities but to still get the lower discount price. This might be negotiated through annual contracts, cumulative discounts, or blanket orders. This type of analysis also can identify what extra price differential the purchaser might be willing to pay to avoid carrying substantial stocks.

Quantity Discounts and Source Selection

The quantity discount question is of interest to many buyers for a second reason: All quantity discounts, and especially those of the cumulative type, tend to restrict the number of suppliers, thereby affecting the choice of source.

Reasons for Quantity Discounts

Because there is real justification for quantity discounts when properly used, the buyer should obtain such discounts whenever possible. Ordinarily they come through the pressure of competition among sellers. Furthermore, an argument may be advanced that such discounts are a matter of right. The buyer is purchasing goods or merchandise, not crating, or packing materials, or transportation. The seller presumably should expect to earn a profit not from those wholly auxiliary services but rather from manufacturing and selling the merchandise processed. These auxiliary services are necessary; they must be performed; they must be paid for; and it is natural to expect the buyer to pay for them. But the buyer should not be expected to pay more than the actual cost of these auxiliary services.

When an attempt is made to justify quantity discounts on the basis that they contribute to reduced production costs by providing a volume of business large enough to reduce the overhead expenses, somewhat more cautious reasoning is necessary. It is true that in some lines of business the larger the output, the lower the overhead cost per unit of product. It also may be true that without the volume from the large customers, the average cost of production would be higher. However, the small buyers may place a greater total proportion of the seller's business than do the large ones. So far as production costs are concerned therefore, the small buyers contribute even more toward that volume so essential to the per-unit production cost than does the larger buyer.

Time Discounts versus Quantity Discounts

Another contention is that large customers ordering early in the season, or even prior to the time actual production of a season's supply begins, should be granted higher discounts because their orders keep the facility in production. Such a buyer probably may be entitled to a lower price than one who waits until later in the season to order. However, such a discount, because it is justified by the early placement of an order and therefore should be granted to every buyer placing an early order regardless of its size, is not properly a quantity discount but is a time discount.

Quantity Purchased Over a Period of Time

Cumulative or Volume Discounts. Another type of quantity discount is cumulative and varies in proportion to the quantity purchased; however, instead of being computed on the size of the order placed at any one time, it is based on the quantity purchased over a period of time. Such discounts are commonly granted as an incentive to a company for continued patronage. It is hoped they will induce a purchaser to concentrate purchases largely with a single source rather than distributing them over many sources, thus benefiting the company offering the discount. Generally speaking, the purchaser should not scatter orders over a number of sources, for distributing one's orders over many sources is uneconomical and costly. No supplier, under such circumstances, is likely to give the same careful attention to the buyer's requirements as it would if it felt it were getting the larger portion of the purchaser's business.

The use of cumulative discounts must meet the same cost justification rules under the Robinson-Patman Act as other quantity discounts. However, as long as the buyer is not knowingly accepting or inducing discriminatory quantity discounts, then the responsibility for justification rests solely with the seller.

Discriminatory Use of Discounts

Reference has been made to the legitimate and illegitimate use of discounts. There is a reason for cash discounts. Trade discounts, as far as they are necessary to the well-being of a desirable source of supply, have their proper place. Quantity discounts may be earned and justified. However, discounts also may be used illegitimately. They may be used to grant price concessions, to pursue a policy of price cutting under a guise of legitimate business practice, or to play certain types of buyers against others. Indeed, under the Robinson-Patman Act, the buyer as well as the seller may be found guilty of the discriminatory use of quantity discounts.

Contract Cancellation

Legitimate Reasons to Cancel a Contract

In practice, cancellations usually occur during a period of falling prices. At such times, if the price has declined since the placing of the order, some buyers may try to take advantage of all sorts of loopholes in the purchase order or sales agreement to reject merchandise. To avoid completion of the transaction, they take advantage of technicalities which under other circumstances would be of no concern to them whatsoever. One can have sympathy for the buyer with a contract at a price higher than the market price. There is little justification, however, for the purchaser who follows a cancellation policy under this situation. A contract should be considered a binding obligation. The practice referred to is an instance of "sharp practice," which hopefully is becoming less and less prevalent as the years go by. There may be occasions when a buyer justifiably seeks to cancel the contract, but to do so merely because the market price has fallen is not one of them.

In some instances, the buyer knows when the purchase order is placed that the customer for whose job the materials are being bought may unexpectedly cancel the order, thus forcing cancellation of purchase orders for materials planned for the job. This is a common risk when purchasing materials for use on a government contract, for appropriation changes often force the government to cancel its order, which results in the cancellation of a great many purchase orders by firms who were to have been suppliers to the government under the now-canceled government contract. Or, severe changes in the business cycle may trigger purchase-order cancellations. If cancellation is a possibility, the basis and terms of cancellation should be agreed on in advance and made part of the terms and conditions of the purchase order. Problems such as how to value, and what is an appropriate payment for, partially completed work on a now-canceled purchase order are best settled before the situation arises.

Cost Analysis

Rationale for Not Conducting Cost Analysis

Some purchasing managers believe they are not justified in going very far into suppliers' costs. They take this position for several reasons: (1) In many cases suppliers do not know their costs, and it would be useless to inquire about them; (2) the interpretation of cost calls for an exercise of judgment, and differences of opinion would arise even if all the figures were available; (3) some suppliers will not divulge cost information; (4) the seller's costs do not determine market prices; and (5) the buyer is not interested in the supplier's costs anyway; the primary concern is getting the best price consistent with quality, service, and quantity. If a seller offers a price that does not cover costs, either in ignorance or with full recognition of what it is doing, the matter is the seller's problem and not the buyer's.

Rationale for Conducting Cost Analysis

To a considerable extent, much of this reasoning is true. However, there are some limitations. In the first place, unless a buyer has some idea of a supplier's costs, at least in a general way, it is difficult to judge the reasonableness of the supplier's prices. Furthermore, the position that the buyer is neither concerned with nor responsible for suppliers who offer merchandise below cost must recognize two things: first, that the buyer cannot complain if ruinous, vicious price cutting eliminates or handicaps efficient suppliers; and, second, that the buyer cannot maintain an attitude of indifference when the sellers offer merchandise below cost and then become intensely concerned when prices rise materially above cost as suppliers fight for financial survival.

Data is Power in a Negotiation

The party in the strongest position in a negotiation session is the one with the best data. Recognizing the importance of cost, it is common practice for the purchaser to make the best estimate possible of the supplier's costs as one means of judging the reasonableness of the price proposed. When the supplier is given a request for proposal (RFP), which is an invitation to make an offer that both parties agree will be subject to further negotiation, normally the buyer will request that the proposal be accompanied by a cost breakdown. If the supplier has nothing to hide and is confident of the work of its estimating department, it should be willing to supply the requested cost breakdown. But, if a cost breakdown cannot be obtained, then the buyer must do a cost buildup, which is far more time-consuming and difficult to do.

Doing a Cost Buildup: Raw Materials and Components Costs

Many larger firms have cost analysts within the supply area to assist the buyer in analyzing supplier costs in preparation for negotiation. Some companies use cost-based pricing, a cost modeling system used by purchasers to determine total cost. These cost estimates must be based on such data as are available. The prices of raw material entering into the product are commonly accessible and the amounts required are also fairly well known. For component parts, catalog prices often offer a clue. Transportation costs are easily determined. The buyer's own engineers should provide data on processing costs. Burden and general overhead rates can be approximated.

Overhead costs generally consist of indirect costs incurred in the manufacturing, research, or engineering facilities of the company. Equipment depreciation typically is the largest single element in manufacturing overhead. It is important to know how these overhead costs are distributed to a given product. If overhead is allocated as a fixed percentage of direct labor costs and there is an increase in labor costs, overhead costs can be unduly inflated unless the allocation percentage is changed.

The growing tendency for industry to become more capital intensive has increased the relative percentage of overhead versus direct labor and materials. Because some items in the overhead, such as local real estate taxes, are attributable to the location of the supplier and others are properly seen as depreciation or investment at varying technological and economic risk levels, the analysis and allocation of these costs to individual products are particularly difficult.

Tooling and Engineering Costs

Both tooling costs and engineering costs often are included as a part of general manufacturing overhead, but it is wisest to pull them out for analysis as separate items since each may account for a relatively large amount of cost. The buyer wants to know what it should cost a reasonably efficient supplier to build the tooling, to own the completed tooling, its life expectancy (number of units), and whether the tooling can be used with equipment other than that owned by the supplier. Only with such information can the buyer guard against being charged twice for the same tooling. In the case of engineering labor, it usually is quite expensive on an hourly basis and the buyer does not want to pay the supplier for engineering work that really isn't necessary.

General and Administrative Costs

General and administrative expense includes items such as selling, promoting, advertising, executive salaries, and legal expense. Frequently there is no justification for the supplier to charge an advertising allocation in the price of a product manufactured to the buyer's specifications.

Material Costs Estimates

Material costs can be estimated from a bill of material, a drawing, or a sample of the product. The buyer can arrive at material costs by multiplying material quantities per unit by raw material prices. Sometimes a material usage curve will be helpful. The purpose of the curve is to chart what improvement should occur from buying economies and lower scrap rates as experience is gained in the manufacturing process. Use of price indexes and maintenance of price trend records are standard practice.

Direct Labor Estimates

Direct labor estimates are not made as easily as material estimates. Even though labor costs are normally labeled direct for machine operators and assembly line workers, in reality they tend to be more fixed than most managers care to admit. Most organizations prefer not to lay off personnel, and there are strong pressures to keep the so-called direct labor force reasonably stable and employed. This means that inventories and overtime often are used to smooth fluctuations in demand and also that labor cost becomes at least semivariable and subject to allocation.

Factors Affecting Labor Costs

Product mix, run sizes, and labor turnover may affect labor costs substantially. The greater the mix, the shorter the lot size produced, and the higher the turnover, the greater direct labor costs will be. These three factors alone may create substantial cost differences between suppliers of an identical end product. Geographical considerations also play a large part because differences in labor rates do exist between plant locations. Such differences may change dramatically over time, as the rapid increases in direct labor rates in Japan and Germany have demonstrated. The astute cost analyst will estimate the supplier's real labor costs, taking the above considerations into account.

The Learning Curve

Factors Affecting the Learning Curve

The learning curve[5] provides an analytical framework for quantifying the commonly recognized principle that one becomes more proficient with experience. Its origins lie in the aircraft industry in World War II when it was empirically determined that labor time per plane declined dramatically as volume increased. Subsequent studies showed that the same phenomenon occurred in a variety of industries and situations. Although conceptually most closely identified with direct labor, most experts believe the learning curve is actually brought about by a combination of a large number of factors that include:

1. The learning rate of labor.
2. The motivation of labor and management to increase output.
3. The development of improved methods, procedures, and support systems.
4. The substitution of better materials, tools, and equipment or more effective use of materials, tools, and equipment.
5. The flexibility of the job and the people associated with it.
6. The ratio of labor versus machine time in the task.
7. The amount of pre-planning done in advance of the task.
8. The turnover of labor in the unit.
9. The pressure of competition to do tasks better, faster, cheaper.

We know the learning curve happens; its presence has been empirically determined a sufficient number of times that its existence is no longer in doubt. The reasons for it sound plausible enough; yet it still is not possible to determine in advance just what the learning rate should be for a brand new product or a novel task.

Implications of the Learning Curve

The learning curve has tremendous implications for cost determination, management by objectives, and negotiation. For example, take a 90 percent learning curve. The progress is logarithmic. Every time the volume doubles, the time per unit drops to 90 percent of the time per unit at half the volume. Suppose we wish to purchase 800 units of a highly labor-intensive, expensive product which will be produced by a group of workers over a two-year period. The 100th unit has been produced at a labor time of 1,000 hours. With a 90 percent learning curve, the labor time for the 200th unit would drop to 900 hours and the 400th unit to 90 percent of 900 hours. Table 9–1 shows the figures.[6]

---

[5]Also called the *time reduction curve* or *manufacturing progress curve*. When used to analyze overall management efficiency and effectiveness changes in a business strategy context, the term *improvement curve* is used also.

[6]The figures in Table 9–1 use the cumulative average curve technique. As the quantity doubles, the rate of learning is constant. This is known as the *Boeing Curve*. An alternative approach, which produces a unit curve, is referred to as the *Wright Curve*. Further exposition of the two approaches, which produce somewhat different results, is presented in Charles H. Adams, "The Improvement Curve Technique," Section 1.13 in the *Guide to Purchasing* (New York: The National Association of Purchasing Management, 1980).

TABLE 9–1   90 Percent Learning Curve Example

Production Unit	Labor Hours per Unit
100	1,000
200	900
400	810
800	729

These figures may be plotted on rectangular coordinates as shown in Figure 9–1. Using logarithmic coordinates, this curve is a straight line, as shown in Figure 9–2.

It is important to recognize that the choice of learning curve, be it 95, 90, 85, or 80 percent or any other figure, is not an exact science. Normally, fairly simple tasks, like putting parts into a box, tend to have a learning curve close to 95 percent. Medium complexity tasks often have learning curve rates between 80 percent and 90 percent, while highly complex tasks tend to be in the 70 percent to 80 percent range.

Learning Curves May Be Adjusted

The new product situation can be compared to other situations where the same or similar circumstances were present. It can be established afterward what really happened and what the actual curve was. It also is possible to wait for some preliminary production data, which can then be used to plot the curve because, theoretically, only two points are required to fix the curve's location (using log-log paper). Thus, for new products and relatively short runs, actual production information may be requested on the first significant run and renegotiation requested on the basis of actual data if uncertainty exists as to which learning curve is appropriate.

The learning curve or improvement function implies that improvement never stops, no matter how large the volume becomes. The potential of the learning curve in supply management has not yet been fully explored. It is a powerful concept and of great use to the buyer. Progressive discounts, shortened lead times, and better value can be planned and obtained through its use. In the last decade, the learning curve has been used along with target pricing to set progressively lower price targets for future deliveries.

Total Cost of Ownership

TCO Defined

The purchaser should estimate the total cost of ownership (TCO) before selecting a supplier. Broadly defined, total cost of ownership includes all relevant costs, such as purchasing administration, follow-up, expediting, inbound transportation, inspection and testing, rework, storage, scrap, warranty, service, downtime, customer returns, and lost sales. The acquisition price plus these in-house costs is the total cost of ownership. A total cost

FIGURE 9–1

90 Percent Learning Curve Plotted on Standard Graph Paper

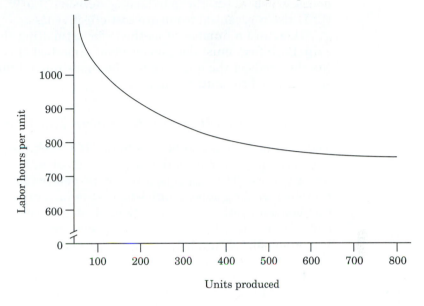

FIGURE 9–2

90 Percent Learning Curve Plotted on Log-Log Paper

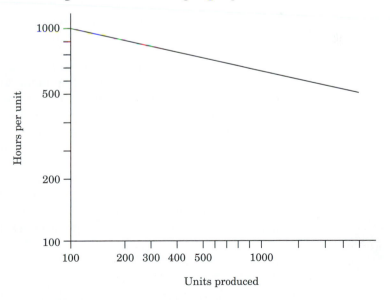

approach requires the cooperation of engineering, quality, manufacturing, and purchasing to coordinate requirements such as specifications and tolerances which affect the purchasing decision. Early supplier involvement (ESI) also is essential to ensure cost-effectiveness.

There are a number of methods for estimating the total cost of ownership. Each firm must develop or adopt a method of cost modeling that best fits the needs of the organization. Methods range from simple checklists to sophisticated computer programs.

Total Cost Modeling and Reducing Total Cost of Ownership

The concept of total cost of ownership (TCO) acknowledges that acquisition price is merely one part of the costs associated with owning a good or procuring a service. TCO models attempt to determine all the cost elements, thereby revealing opportunities for cost reduction or cost avoidance for each cost element, rather than merely analyzing or comparing prices. The difficulty lies in identifying and tracking these cost elements and using the information appropriately to compare different suppliers. (See also Life Cycle Costing in Chapter 16.)

Analyzing Cost Elements   In close buyer-supplier relationships, the seller may willingly share cost data with the buyer. In other situations, the buyer or sourcing team may have to develop its own cost model to prepare for negotiations. There are many approaches to cost modeling, from very informal ones to highly sophisticated, complex computer models. One way of analyzing cost elements is demonstrated by a model that refers to three cost components: (1) pre-transaction, (2) transaction, and (3) post-transaction (Figure 9–3).[7] The acquisition price is broken down into the individual cost elements from which the price is derived. Each of these cost elements then can be analyzed by the buyer for areas of reduction or avoidance. Cost elements are both tangible and intangible, meaning that many are difficult to estimate.

The notion that an attempt should be made to identify and analyze all costs of ownership drives many of the purchasing strategies discussed in this book. For example, longer-term, closer buyer-supplier relationships, partnering arrangements and alliances, early supplier and purchaser involvement; all can facilitate total cost modeling, improve negotiations and decision making, and result in increased competitiveness for the firm.

Sources of Cost Reduction   In a study of buyer-supplier partnering pairs, Hendrick and Ellram reported that the main sources of reduction in total cost of ownership were (1) long-term purchase agreements, (2) joint cost-reduction programs, (3) early supplier involvement in design, and (4) commitments to purchase

---

[7]Lisa Ellram, "Total Cost of Ownership: Elements and Implementation," *International Journal of Purchasing and Materials Management,* Winter 1993, p. 7.

FIGURE 9–3

Major Categories for the Components of Total Cost of Ownership

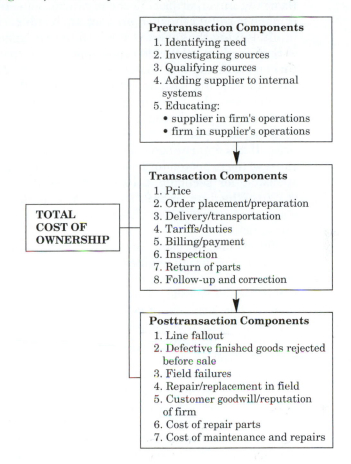

suppliers' capacity.[8] Buyers reported that these reductions came primarily from providing suppliers with (1) technical support, including quality methods; (2) training; (3) asset sharing or other financial support; and (4) special technology.[9]

Target Pricing

Target Pricing Defined

Target pricing is experiencing growing use in North America. Target pricing focuses the attention of everyone in the organization on designing costs out of products rather than on eliminating costs after production has begun.

---

[8]Thomas Hendrick and Lisa Ellram, *Strategic Supplier Partnering: An International Study* (Tempe, AZ: Center for Advanced Purchasing Studies, 1993), p. 29.
[9]Ibid.

Example

This concept is a logical extension of the quality movement which forwarded the perspective that it makes sense to build something right the first time. Basically, in target pricing the organization establishes the price at which it plans to sell its finished product, then subtracts out its normal operating profit, leaving the target cost which the organization seeks. The target cost is then further subdivided into appropriate cost sectors such as manufacturing, overhead, and materials and services. Purchasing becomes responsible for working with suppliers to achieve the materials and services target. For example, if the end product is a manufactured item that will be sold for $200, and purchased goods represent 60 percent of each dollar in sales revenue, then purchasing would be responsible for $120 of the $200 selling price. If it is determined that a 10 percent reduction in price is desirable because of the expected impact on sales revenue, then purchasing would be responsible for securing a 10 percent reduction in its portion of the costs ($120) of the item, or $12. This means purchased materials, on a unit basis, should not exceed $108. This becomes the target materials cost in the pricing structure.

Cost Reductions Due to Target Pricing

Target pricing results in companywide cost reductions, in (1) design to cost, on the part of design engineering; (2) manufacture to cost, on the part of production; and (3) purchase to cost, on the part of purchasing. From the purchasing and supply management standpoint, target pricing can benefit purchasing by providing a means of documenting specific price reductions needed from suppliers, demonstrating purchasing's contribution to the pricing goals of the firm, and documenting purchasing's contribution on a product-by-product basis. To be effective, target pricing works best when the customer has some clout in the supply chain; when there is some loyalty between buyer and seller, as in a partnering arrangement or alliance; and when the supplier also stands to benefit from the cost reductions.

The cost reductions on the part of the supplier conceivably can come from several areas—the supplier can seek reductions in overhead expenses and/or general and selling and administrative expenses; the supplier can improve efficiencies in labor as measured by the learning curve; or the supplier can seek labor and material cost reductions. This last option requires the supplier to pass down these techniques to *its* suppliers in the supply chain. Overall, target pricing provides purchasing with (1) a measurable target for purchasing performance, (2) a yardstick for measuring cost reductions, and (3) a means of measuring the supplier's efficiency. As with all cost analysis tools, the expected benefits from the target costing process must exceed the costs associated with conducting the analysis.

Elements of Successful Target Pricing

Target pricing cannot occur in a vacuum. To be successful, the effort requires cross-functional team efforts, early supplier and early purchasing involvement, concurrent engineering, and value engineering. In a CAPS study, *The Role of Supply Management in Target Costing,* the companies participating in the study reported that they used target costing to increase competitiveness, increase cooperation with suppliers and get earlier supplier involvement, and to improve cost management.[10]

Activity-Based Costing

ABC Translates Indirect Costs into Direct Costs

Traditional cost accounting introduces distortions into product costing because of the way it allocates overhead on the basis of direct labor. In the past, when labor costs often were the largest cost category, this allocation made sense. However, as the cost of materials has eclipsed labor costs as the single largest cost factor, accountants have looked for other ways to allocate overhead.[11] Basically, activity-based costing (ABC) tries to turn indirect costs into direct costs by tracking the cost drivers behind indirect costs. One of the biggest hurdles in ABC is the cost of tracking indirect costs and translating them into direct costs, compared with the benefits of being able to assign these costs to specific products more accurately. In ABC, manufacturing overhead is divided into costs that change in response to unit-level activities (in proportion to the number of units produced), batch-level activities (in proportion to the number of batches produced), and product-level activities (that benefit all units of a product). The remainder are true fixed costs and are allocated the same way as traditional cost accounting.

Chrysler Example of Activity Based Costing

Chrysler Corporation began implementing ABC in 1991 and claims to have generated hundreds of millions of dollars in benefits by simplifying product designs and eliminating unproductive, inefficient, or redundant activities.[12] Chrysler has gone beyond a piecemeal use of ABC and developed activity-based management. Setting up an ABC system is a huge task because it is more complex and detailed than traditional cost accounting and requires many more statistical measures to assign the overhead costs.

It is easy for those trying to apply the ABC concept to collect too much detail and be unable to make much sense out of it. Even so, it is a powerful tool and one that has many implications for supply management.

Uses of Activity Based Costing

Buyers can use activity-based costing as a tool to reduce supplier costs by eliminating nonvalue-adding activities, reducing activity occurrences, and reducing the cost driver rate. To accomplish these goals, buyers must collect data from suppliers on activities (specific tasks), cost drivers (a metric to measure activity), cost driver rates (rate at which cost is incurred), and units of cost driver (the amount of activity). Buyers then can determine which activities

---

[10]Lisa M. Ellram, *The Role of Supply Management in Target Costing* (Tempe, AZ: Center for Advanced Purchasing Studies, January 1999).

[11]This section is drawn largely from John C. Lere and Jayant V. Saraph, "Activity-Based Costing for Purchasing Managers' Cost and Pricing Determinations," *International Journal of Purchasing and Materials Management,* Fall 1995, pp. 25–31.

[12]Joseph A. Ness and Thomas G. Cucuzza, "Tapping the Full Potential of ABC," *Harvard Business Review,* July–August 1995, p. 131.

add value and should occur, and which do not add value and should be eliminated. Even if an activity is deemed value-adding, it may be possible to reduce the number of times the activity occurs, thereby reducing cost. For example, receiving inspection may be rated as nonvalue-adding and targeted for elimination, or it may be deemed value-adding but the number of receipts requiring inspection may be reduced, thereby reducing costs. Lastly, the cost of the activity itself may be targeted as an area for improvements in efficiency through value analysis and system redesign.

Negotiation Strategy and Practice

As the status of the supply function in well-managed companies has increased in importance, a more professional attitude has developed in the people responsible for the operation of the function. As the professional competence of the personnel has increased, greater use has been made of the more sophisticated tools available to the business decision-making executive. Negotiation is a prime example of this developing professionalism.

Situations Where Negotiation May Be Valuable

The discussion of some of the elements and considerations that affect the price of an item makes it obvious that negotiation can be a valuable technique to use in reaching an agreement with a supplier on the many variables affecting a specific price. This is not to say that all buying-selling transactions require the use of negotiations. Nor is the intention to indicate that negotiation is used only in determining price. Reaching a clear understanding of time schedules for deliveries, factors affecting quality, and methods of packaging may require negotiations of equal or greater importance than those applying to price.

A list of some of the various kinds of purchasing situations in which the use of negotiations should prove valuable follows:

1. Any written contract covering price, specifications, terms of delivery, and quality standards.

2. The purchase of items made to the buyer's specifications. Special importance should be attached to "first buys," because thorough exploration of the needs of the buyer and the supplier often will result in a better product at a lower price.

3. When changes are made in drawings or specifications after a purchase order has been issued.

4. When quotations have been solicited from responsible bidders and no acceptable bids have been received.

5. When problems of tooling or packaging occur.

6. When changing economic or market conditions require changes in quantities or prices.

7. When problems of termination of a contract involve disposal of facilities, materials, or tooling.

FIGURE 9–4

Model of the Negotiation Process

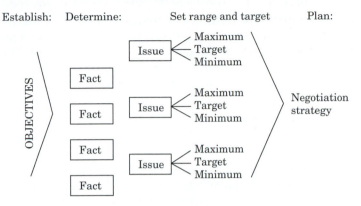

8. When there are problems of accepting any of the various elements entering into cost-type contracts.

9. When problems arise under the various type of contracts used in defense and governmental contracting.

Framework for Planning and Preparing for Negotiation

Basic Steps in Developing a Negotiation Strategy

Success in negotiation largely is a function of the quality and amount of planning that has been done. Figure 9–4 presents a model of the negotiation process. The basic steps in developing a strategy for negotiation are:[13]

Objectives

1. Develop the specific objectives (outcomes) desired from the negotiation. This is done by gathering relevant information; generating, analyzing, evaluating, and selecting alternatives.

Data

2. Gather pertinent data. Here is where cost analysis comes into play.

Facts

3. Determine the facts of the situation. A fact is defined as an item of information about which agreement is expected. For example, if the supplier's cost breakdown states that the direct labor rate is $20.10 per hour, and you agree, that is a fact.

Issues

4. Determine the issues. An issue is something over which disagreement is expected. The purpose of negotiation is to resolve issues so that a mutually satisfactory contract can be signed. For example, if the supplier

---

[13]For a more detailed discussion of the preparation and planning for negotiation see Michiel R. Leenders and Anna E. Flynn, *Value-Driven Purchasing: Managing the Key Steps in the Acquisition Process* (Burr Ridge, IL: Irwin Professional Publishing, 1995), Chapter 6, "Negotiation."

claims the manufacturing burden rate is 300 percent of direct labor costs, but your analysis indicates a 240 percent burden rate is realistic, this becomes an issue to be settled through negotiation.

Positions of Strength

5. Analyze the positions of strength of both (or all) parties. For example, what is the supplier's capacity, backlog, and profitability? How confident is the supplier of getting the contract? Is there any time urgency? The process of analyzing strengths helps the negotiator establish negotiation points, avoid setting unrealistic expectations, and may reveal ideas for strategies. The negotiator (or team) should be able to generate a list of 12 to 24 points for either side through a brainstorming process.

Gap Analysis on Range of Acceptable Results

6. Set the buyer's position on each issue, and estimate the seller's position on each issue based on your research. What data will be used to support the buyer's position? What data might support the seller's position? Two questions should be asked after analyzing positions of strength: (1) "Whose position is stronger?" and (2) "Which points give each side the most strength?" The answer to the first question should help determine how realistic the objectives are, and if they need to be changed or clarified. The answer to the second question tells the negotiator what his or her key points will be in the negotiation, and what to expect from the other side. If done well, this information allows the negotiator to prepare counterarguments. By estimating the range of acceptable results for both buyer and seller, the negotiator can determine (1) if there is a zone of overlap, meaning negotiation is feasible and likely to result in an agreement; or (2) if there is a gap between the objectives of the parties (see Figure 9–5). If there is a gap, the negotiator must determine if it can be closed, and if not, does negotiation even make sense in this particular situation?

Strategy

7. Plan the negotiation strategy. Which issues should be discussed first? Where is the buyer willing to compromise? Who will make up the negotiation team (it frequently is composed of someone from both engineering and quality control, headed by the buyer)? Establishing a range and a target for each objective sets reasonable objectives which the negotiator feels can be achieved. The tactics used in the actual negotiation may mean starting out at a more extreme position than the negotiator truly believes is achievable. The decision about tactics should be based on the negotiator's understanding of the situation and the parties involved in the negotiation. If the goal of negotiation is performance, then the *way* negotiation is conducted is important because it affects the intention to perform. If the tactics used leave the other party feeling negative toward the negotiator or the results, there may be little commitment to the agreement or to solving any problems that might arise during the life of the contract.

Review

8. Brief all persons on the team who are going to participate in the negotiations.

FIGURE 9–5

The Zone of Negotiation

1. The seller and purchaser overlap.

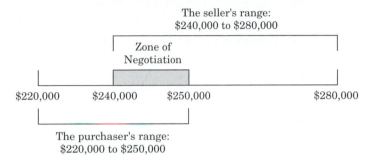

2. The seller and purchaser do not overlap.

Source: Michiel R. Leenders and Anna E. Flynn, *Value-Driven Purchasing: Managing the Key Steps in the Acquisition Process* (Burr Ridge, IL: Irwin Professional Publishing, 1995), p. 145

Rehearse   9. Conduct a dress rehearsal for the people who are going to participate in the negotiations.

Conduct   10. Conduct the actual negotiations with an impersonal calmness.

Ground Rules for Successful Negotiation

Groundrules Before the Negotiation

While negotiation skill is more of an art than a science (although cost analysis techniques will provide the buyer a sound technical basis for setting the buying organization's position on cost and price issues and planning and executing a strategy), the experience of many organizations and purchasing managers has resulted in some general negotiation ground rules. If the buyer is not following each of these ground rules, it is likely that, from a buying point of view, negotiation outcomes probably could be improved. These ground rules are broken down into three time phases—before, during, and after the negotiation sessions:

 I. Before the Session:

 A. Preparation

 1. Establish possible sources.

 2. Analyze the supplier's position.

3. Make a facilities survey.

4. Make a financial analysis of the supplier.

5. Analyze the supplier's proposal.

6. Organize the negotiation team.

7. Get a clear understanding of the work statement.

8. Determine negotiation objectives.

9. Prepare alternative action courses.

10. Know your own authority.

11. Provide adequate conference facilities.

12. Set up the meeting room in advance.

B. Basic Ideas

1. Be prepared to compromise.

2. You will have to "sell" your position.

3. Keep a poker face.

4. Don't ever underestimate the seller.

5. Never let your guard down.

6. Take your time and do the job right.

7. Alcohol and negotiation don't mix.

8. Be reasonable; don't push too far.

9. Regardless of your offer, the seller will want more.

10. Nervousness on your part will be interpreted as a sign of weakness.

Groundrules During the Negotiation

II. During the session:

A. Size Up the Seller

1. Watch for roving eyeballs—and your opponent can read upside down.

2. Spot their leader—who really can make concessions?

3. If they're hesitant to discuss an issue, it shows vulnerability.

4. If the seller has no data on a key issue, it shows vulnerability.

5. Be intense, concentrate; look the other party right in the eye and listen to what he or she has to say.

B. Strategy

1. Take command—sit at the head of the table.

2. Know names and pronunciation of supplier personnel.

3. Establish extent of supplier representatives' authority.

4. Assess supplier's minimum position.

   5. Talk positively.

   6. Phrase your questions to encourage a positive answer.

   7. Compromise on minor points when advantageous.

   8. If you can compromise early in the session, you set the stage for the supplier to reciprocate.

   9. Start with the easy issues first.

   10. Avoid taking on an either-or position. The supplier may get up and leave.

   11. Never give anything away.

   12. Don't go beyond your mental and physical endurance.

C. Tactics

   1. Don't reveal maximum position.

   2. Don't argue without reason.

   3. Don't lose your cool.

   4. Don't commit beyond your authority.

   5. Remember, the supplier has to "win" too.

   6. Don't interrupt; it is disrespectful and may "turn the other party off."

   7. The best reply to a totally unacceptable offer is complete silence.

   8. Don't go off on tangents—keep the discussion on track—time is valuable.

D. Resolving Negotiation Deadlocks

   1. Go on to another position.

   2. "I see your position—now try to understand mine."

   3. "You suggest a solution."

   4. "We've come too far to get bogged down now."

III. After the Session:

Groundrules After the Negotiation

   1. Make sure all items are covered in the final agreement.

   2. Know how and when to terminate a session.

   3. Keep complete notes on all points of agreement—both parties should initial or sign.

   4. Analyze what happened and why.

   All negotiation has an economic as well as a psychological dimension. It is important to satisfy both of these dimensions to achieve a win-win result. The trends towards teaming, single sourcing, partnering, and empowerment reinforce the need for supply personnel to be superior negotiators, both with suppliers and with others in their own organization. Actually, negotiations inside one's own organization to obtain cooperation and support for supply initiatives may be more challenging than those with suppliers.

Forward Buying and Commodities

Forward Buying Defined

Forward buying is the commitment of purchases in anticipation of future requirements beyond current lead times. Thus, an organization may buy ahead because of anticipated shortages, strikes, or price increases. As the time between procurement commitment and actual use of the requirement grows, uncertainties also increase. One common uncertainty is whether the actual need will be realized. A second concern is with price. How can the purchaser ascertain that the price currently committed is reasonable compared to the actual price that would have been paid had the forward buy not been made?

Examples of Commodities

Commodities represent a special class of purchases frequently associated with forward buying. Almost all organizations purchase commodities in a variety of processed forms. For example, an electrical equipment manufacturer may buy a substantial amount of wire, the cost of which is significantly affected by the price of copper. Many organizations buy commodities for further processing or for resale. For them, the way they buy and the prices they pay for commodities may be the single most important factor in success. Cash prices for selected commodities are reported daily in *The Wall Street Journal* and many other sources, in hard copy or electronic form.

Forward Buying versus Speculation

All forward buying involves some risk. In ordinary forward buying, purchases largely are confined to actually known requirements or to carefully estimated requirements for a limited period of time in advance. The essential controlling factor is need. Even when the organization uses order points and order quantities, the amount to be bought may be increased or decreased in accordance both with probable use and with the price trend, rather than automatically reordering a given amount. Temporarily, no order may be placed at all.

Forward Commitments Ensure Supply

This may be true even where purchases have to be made many months in advance, as in the case of seasonal products, such as wheat, or those that must be obtained abroad, such as cocoa or coffee. Obviously, the price risk increases as the lead time grows longer, but the basic reason for these forward commitments is assurance of supply to meet requirements and, only secondarily, price.

Speculation seeks to take advantage of price movements, with need for supply as a secondary concern. At times of rising prices, commitments for

Speculative Buying Defined	quantities beyond anticipated needs would be called speculation. At times of falling prices, speculation would consist of withholding purchases or reducing quantities purchased below the safety limits, and risking stockouts as well as rush orders at high prices, if the anticipated price decline did not materialize.

At best, any speculation, in the accepted meaning of the term, is a risky business, but speculation with other people's money has been cataloged as a crime. It is purchasing's responsibility to provide for the known needs to the best advantage possible at the time, and to keep the investment in unused materials at the lowest point consistent with safety of operation.

Speculation versus Gambling

Gambling Defined	Just where the line of distinction between speculation and gambling is to be drawn is a matter of individual judgment. There are certain practices, however, that can only be classified as gambling. If a person undertakes a venture in which there is an unknown chance to win, it is clear that venture is not speculation. If a purchaser tries to guess what the market trend is likely to be for some commodity with which he or she has had no experience and practically no knowledge, he or she is a gambler. Others in the same category are those who, regardless of their experience with a particular commodity, lack adequate data on which to forecast probable price movements.
Distinctions Between Forward Buying, Speculation, and Gambling	The distinction between ordinary forward buying, speculative purchasing, and gambling should be reasonably clear. It is important to note that the three policies are quite different. The first policy is, in most cases, unavoidable. The second is debatable. If an organization deliberately undertakes a policy of speculative buying, it is adopting a policy which it may feel is profitable but which cannot be harmonized with the purpose for which it is organized. Gambling is never to be condoned.

Organizing for Forward Buying

Risk Management Is a Key Issue in Commodity Buying	The organization for determination and execution of policy with regard to long-term commitments on commodities whose prices fluctuate varies widely depending on the organization's size, the extent to which it desires to speculate, and the percentage of total cost represented by those volatile commodities. Risk management is a key issue in commodity acquisition. In some instances, the top executive exercises complete control, based almost wholly on personal judgment. In other cases, although the top executive assumes direct responsibility, an informal committee provides assistance.

Some organizations designate a person other than the supply manager, whose sole responsibility is over speculative materials and who reports directly to top management. In a large number of firms the supply manager controls the inventory of such commodities. In a few companies almost complete reliance for policy execution is placed in the hands of an outside agency that specializes in speculative commodities.

The soundest practice for most organizations would appear to be to place responsibility for policy in the hands of a committee consisting of the top executive or general manager, an economist, a risk manager, and the supply manager. Actual execution of the broad policy as laid down should rest with the purchasing department.

Control of Forward Buying

Example of Controls on Speculative Buying

Safeguards should be set up to ensure that the administration of a speculation will be kept within proper bounds. The following checks set up by one leather company are given merely as an illustration: (1) Speculative buying must be confined to those hides which are used in the production either of several different leathers or of the leathers for which there is a stable demand. (2) Daily conferences are held among the president, treasurer, sales manager, and hide buyer. (3) Orders for future delivery of leather are varied in some measure in accordance with the company's need for protection on hide holdings. Because the leather buyer is willing to place orders for future delivery of leather when prices are satisfactory, this company follows the practice of using unfilled orders as a partial hedge of its hide holdings. In general, the policy is to have approximately 50 percent of the total hides the company owns covered by sales contracts for future production of leather. (4) A further check is provided by an operating budget which controls the physical volume of hides rather than the financial expenditures, and which is brought up for reconsideration whenever it is felt necessary. (5) There is a final check which consists of the use of adequate and reliable information, statistical and otherwise, as a basis for judging price and market trends.

This particular company does not follow the practice of hedging on an organized commodity exchange as a means of avoiding undue risk, though many companies do. Nor does this company use any of the special accounting procedures, such as last-in, first-out, or reproduction-cost-of-sales, in connection with its forward purchases.

These various control devices, regarded as a unit rather than as unrelated checks, should prove effective. They are obviously not foolproof, nor do they ensure absolutely against the dangers inherent in buying well in advance. However, flexibility in the administration of any policy is essential, and, for this one company at least, the procedure outlined combines reasonable protection with such flexibility.

In organizations requiring large quantities of commodities whose prices fluctuate widely, the risks involved in buying ahead may under some circumstances be substantially minimized through the use of the commodity exchanges.

The Commodity Exchanges

Prime Function of a Commodity Exchange

The prime function of an organized commodity exchange is to furnish an established marketplace where the forces of supply and demand may operate freely as buyers and sellers carry on their trading. An exchange that has facilities for both cash and futures trading can also be used for hedging operations. The rules governing the operation of an exchange are concerned primarily with procedures for the orderly handling of the transactions negotiated on the exchange, providing, among other things, terms and time of payment, time of delivery, grades of products traded, and methods of settling disputes.

Conditions for a Successful Exchange

In general, the purposes of a commodity exchange will be served best if the following conditions are present:

1. The products traded are capable of reasonably accurate grading.
2. There is a large enough number of sellers and buyers and a large enough volume of business so that no one buyer or seller can significantly influence the market.

In order for a commodity exchange to be useful for hedging operations, the following conditions should also be present:

1. Trading in "futures"—the buying or selling of the commodity for delivery at a specified future date.
2. A fairly close correlation between "basis" and other grades.
3. A reasonable but not necessarily consistent correlation between "spot" and "future" prices.

All of these conditions usually are present on the major grain and cotton exchanges, and in varying degrees on the minor exchanges, such as those on which hides, silk, metals, rubber, coffee, and sugar are traded. Financial futures also permit a firm to hedge against interest rate fluctuations, which are one of the strongest factors affecting exchange rate fluctuations.[14]

Sources of Commodity Information

Probably the most easily accessed source of information about futures and options prices is the commodities section carried Monday through Friday in *The Wall Street Journal*. It reports prices from several of the exchanges, including the Chicago Board of Trade; Chicago Mercantile Exchange; Coffee, Sugar and Cocoa Exchange, New York; COMEX, Division of the New York Mercantile Exchange; New York Cotton Exchange; International Petroleum Exchange; Kansas City Board of Trade; London International Financial Futures Exchange; Minneapolis Grain Exchange; New York Mercantile Exchange; Singapore International Monetary Exchange, Ltd.; Sydney Futures Exchange; and Winnipeg Commodity Exchange.

---

[14]Martin Mayer, "Suddenly It's Chicago: In Trading Pits Once Dominated by Pork Bellies and Wheat, Financial Futures Have Been Setting World Prices," *New York Times Magazine*, March 27, 1988, p. 23.

Commodities Typically Traded on an Exchange

The commodities traded on the exchanges vary; if the volume is not large enough, a given commodity will drop off the exchange either temporarily or permanently. However, the following agricultural items, metals, petroleum products, and currencies normally are among those listed on any given day: corn, oats, soybeans, soybean oil, wheat, canola, cattle, hogs, pork bellies, cocoa, coffee, sugar, cotton, orange juice, copper, gold, platinum, silver, crude oil, heating oil, gasoline, natural gas, Japanese yen, Deutsche mark, Canadian dollar, British pound, Swiss franc, Australian dollar, and Mexican peso.

In most cases, the prices quoted on the exchanges and the record of transactions completed furnish some clue, at least, to the current market price and to the extent of the trading in those commodities. They offer an opportunity, some to a greater extent than others, of protecting the buyer against basic price risks through hedging.

Limitations of the Exchanges

Grading Often Inaccurate

There are limitations to these exchanges as a source of physical supply for the buyer. In spite of a reasonable attempt to define the market grades, the grading often is not sufficiently accurate for manufacturing purposes. The cotton requirements of a textile manufacturer are likely to be so exacting that even the comparatively narrow limits of any specific exchange grade are too broad. Moreover, the rules of the exchange are such that the actual deliveries of cotton do not have to be of a specific grade but may be of any grade above or below basic cotton, provided, of course, that the essential financial adjustment is made. This also holds true for wheat. Millers who sell patented, blended flours must have specific types and grades of wheat, which normally are purchased by use of a sample.

Difficulty in Meeting Actual Physical Commodity Requirements

There are other reasons why these exchanges are not satisfactory for the buyer endeavoring to meet actual physical commodity requirements. On some of the exchanges, no spot market exists. On others there is a lack of confidence in the validity of the prices quoted. Crude rubber, for example, is purchased primarily by tire manufacturers, a small group of very large buyers. On the hide exchange, on the other hand, a majority of hides sold are byproducts of the packing industry, offered by a limited number of sellers. An increase or a decrease in the price of hides, however, does not have the same effect on supply that such changes might have on some other commodities.

It is not asserted that these sellers use their position to manipulate the market artificially any more than it is asserted that the buyers of rubber manipulate the market to their advantage. In these two cases, however, the prices quoted might not properly reflect supply and demand conditions.

Hedging

The advantage of the commodity exchanges to a manufacturer is that they provide an opportunity to offset transactions, and thus to protect, to some extent, against price and exchange risks. This commonly is done by *hedging*.

Hedging Defined

A hedging contract involves a simultaneous purchase and sale in two different markets, which are assumed to operate so that a loss in one will be offset by an equal gain in the other. Normally this is done by a purchase and sale of the same amount of the same commodity simultaneously in the spot and futures markets.

Hedging can occur only when trading in futures is possible. A simple example of hedging to illustrate the above statement follows:

In the Cash Market	*In the Futures Market*
On September 1:	
Processor buys	Processor sells
5,000 bushels of wheat shipped from country elevator at $4 per bushel (delivered Chicago)	5,000 bushels of December wheat futures at $4.10 per bushel
On October 20:	
Processor sells	Processor buys
flour based on wheat equivalent of 5,000 bushels priced at $3.85 per bushel (delivered at Chicago)	5,000 bushels of December wheat futures at $3.95 per bushel
Loss of 15¢ per bushel	Gain of 15¢ per bushel

Hedging Is a Form of Insurance

In the foregoing example it is assumed that the cash or spot price and the futures price maintained a direct correlation, but this is not always the case. Thus, there may be some gain or loss from a hedging operation when the spread between the spot price and the futures price does not remain constant. *Hedging can be looked on as a form of insurance, and like insurance, it is seldom possible to obtain 100 percent protection against all loss, except at prohibitive costs.* As the time between the spot and future declines, the premium or discount on the future declines toward zero (which it reaches when spot = future). On seasonal commodities, this decline in price differential usually begins six to eight months in advance. Under certain circumstances, this phenomenon can make "risk-free" speculation possible. For example, when the speculator has access to a large amount of money, at least three times the value of the contract, and when a six- to eight-month future premium exceeds the sum of contract carrying cost and inventory and commission cost, the "speculator" can buy spot and short the future with a precalculated profit. Volume on the exchange should be heavy for this kind of operation.

While there are other variations of the techniques used in hedging, the one simple example is sufficient for the present discussion of forward and speculative buying.

Successful hedging on an exchange requires skill and experience and capital resources. This suggests certain limitations imposed on small organizations. It also explains why organizations using large amounts of a certain

Requirements for Succcessful Hedging

commodity often own seats on the exchange that deals in that commodity. A representative of the firm may then be constantly on the watch for advantageous opportunities for placing, withdrawing, or switching hedges between months and can translate this judgment into action immediately. To be successful, the actual procedure of hedging calls for the close observation of accumulating stocks of the commodity, the consequent widening or narrowing of the spreads between prices quoted on futures contracts, and the resulting opportunities for advance opening and closing of trades. These factors are constantly shifting on the exchanges. The skill of the hedger is reflected in the ability to recognize and grasp these momentary opportunities.

Obstacles to Hedging

Hedging may not always be helpful or advantageous to the purchaser. One obstacle to a wider use of the exchanges is the lack of understanding by potential users as to when and how to use them. Another limitation is the vacuum effect when one of the relatively few large commodity brokers goes bankrupt, pulling some clients along.

Moreover, most brokers have not shown extensive interest in the industrial market. Most brokers probably will admit that they can barely afford to service a straight hedger because they may have to send out six monthly position statements and four or more margin calls for a single round turn commission, while their faithful "traders" will often maintain a substantial cash account and net them several round turn commissions per month with a minimum of bookkeeping.

Many managers still view futures trading with suspicion and tend to blame past mistakes on the system rather than managerial errors of judgment. The large variations in commodity prices in recent years may well have sensitized a number of managers to the opportunities in futures trading, where before there seemed little need to be involved.

Sources of Information Regarding Price Trends

On what is the buyer's judgment as to price trends based? Roughly speaking, there are three general sources of information, all subject to marked limitations with respect to their value and dependability. Most research firms and publications have online services as well as hard-copy publications.

Specialized Forecasting Agencies

One source of information consists of the services of specialized forecasting agencies, such as Moody's Investors Service.

Data in the Public Domain

The second includes a wide variety of governmental and other published data. These include the *Federal Reserve Bulletin,* the *Survey of Current Business, Business Week, Barron's,* and *The Wall Street Journal.* Trade magazines also are helpful in particular industries and are typified by such publications as *Iron Age* and *Chemical Marketing Reporter.* Probably the most-watched indicator of industrial purchase prices is the producer price index (PPI) compiled and released monthly by the Bureau of Labor Statistics. It previously was called the wholesale price index (WPI). The PPI measures prices charged by producers for some 3,000 industrial commodities, including plastics, hardware, electronics, paper, and metals. A companion measure, also produced monthly by the Bureau of Labor Statistics, is the consumer price index (CPI). The CPI is based on the prices charged by producers of goods and services sold to final consumers (households).

The third comprises the highly unscientific—but nevertheless valuable, if properly weighted—information derived from sales representatives, other buyers, and others with whom the buyer comes in daily contact.

ISM Report on Business

Two of the more valuable sources of information are the ISM (formerly NAPM) Manufacturing *Report on Business* (ROB) and the non-manufacturing ROB released monthly by the Institute for Supply Management. The national Business Survey Committee of NAPM provides a useful service by presenting a composite reading by purchasing managers from more than 300 organizations across the United States on prices, inventory levels, lead times, new orders, production, and employment. Information is presented on specific commodity changes as well as summary commodity reports by the various ISM commodity committees.

Questions for Review and Discussion

1. What is the significance of the Sherman Antitrust and the Robinson-Patman acts to the industrial buyer?
2. What advantages does the competitive bid process have as a method of price determination?
3. What are cash discounts, quantity discounts, trade discounts, and cumulative discounts? Should the buyer attempt to use these discounts? How?
4. When, and how, is negotiation used, and what can be negotiated?
5. What is a learning curve and how can it be used?
6. How is supplier cost related to supplier price?
7. What are the various ways by which prices are determined?
8. What methods can the buyer use to establish price for (1) sensitive commodities, (2) special items, (3) standard production items, and (4) items of small value?
9. Distinguish between direct and indirect costs. How can the buyer analyze these costs?
10. What can the buyer do if he or she suspects collusion on the part of suppliers?
11. Why might a buyer wish to hedge a commodity purchase? How would the buyer do that?
12. Does hedging remove all risk?

13. What is the difference between forward buying, speculation, and gambling? In what situation would a buyer use each technique?
14. What is activity-based costing (ABC) and how can the buyer use ABC to reduce costs?
15. What is total cost of ownership (TCO) and how is it determined?

References

Burt, David N., Warren E. Norquist, and Jimmy Anklesaria, *Zero-Base Pricing: Achieving World Class Competitiveness Through Reduced All-In-Costs,* Chicago, IL: Probus Publishing Company, 1990.

Cooper, Robin and Regine Slagmulder, *Target Costing and Value Engineering,* Portland, OR: Productivity Press, and Montvale, NJ: The IMA Foundation for Applied Research Inc., 1997.

Ellram, Lisa, "Total Cost of Ownership: Elements and Implementation," *International Journal of Purchasing and Materials Management,* Fall 1993.

Ellram, Lisa M., *Total Cost Modeling in Purchasing,* Tempe, AZ: Center for Advanced Purchasing Studies, 1994.

Fisher, Roger and Scott Brown, *Getting Together: Building Relationships as We Negotiate,* New York: Penguin Books, 1989.

Fisher, Roger and Danny Ertel, *Getting Ready to Negotiate: The Getting to Yes Workbook,* New York: Penguin Books, 1995.

Fisher, Roger, William Ury, and Bruce Patton. *Getting To Yes: Negotiating Agreement Without Giving In,* New York: Penguin Books, 1991.

Hendrick, Thomas and Lisa Ellram, *Strategic Supplier Partnering: An International Study,* Tempe, AZ: Center for Advanced Purchasing Studies, 1993.

Lere, John C. and Jayant V. Saraph, "Activity-Based Costing for Purchasing Managers' Cost and Pricing Determinations," *International Journal of Purchasing and Materials Management,* Fall 1995.

Monczka, Robert M. and Robert J. Trent, *Purchasing and Sourcing Strategy: Trends and Implications,* Tempe, AZ: Center for Advanced Purchasing Studies, 1995.

Newman, Richard G. and John M. McKeller, "Target Pricing—A Challenge for Purchasing." *International Journal of Purchasing and Materials Management,* Summer 1995.

Ness, Joseph A. and Thomas G. Cucuzza, "Tapping the Full Potential of ABC," *Harvard Business Review,* July–August 1995.

Perdue, Barbara C, "Material Cost Sensitivity: Some Consequences and Antecedents," *International Journal of Purchasing and Materials Management,* Summer 1992.

Sakurai, Michiharu, *Integrated Cost Management: A Companywide Prescription for Higher Profits and Lower Costs,* Portland, OR: Productivity Press, 1996.

Shank, John K. and Vijay Govindarajan, *Strategic Cost Management: The New Tool for Competitive Advantage,* New York: The Free Press, 1993.

Teplitz, Charles J., *The Learning Curve Deskbook: A Reference Guide to Theory, Calculations, and Applications.* New York: Quorum Books, 1991.

Ury, William, *Getting Past No: Negotiating Your Way From Confrontation to Cooperation,* New York: Bantam Books, 1993.

CASE 9–1
GLOBAL HEAT EXCHANGERS INC.

Deirdre Collins, buyer-expediter for Global Heat Exchangers Inc. (GHE), was faced with an important purchasing decision. A large new client had just signed for a substantial order, and production was scheduled to begin in a couple of days. Unfortunately, the original pricing of the project was now being threatened because a GHE supplier had just raised its prices considerably.

Company Information. Global Heat Exchangers Inc. (GHE) was established in 1920 and had since established a strong reputation as a leading designer and manufacturer of a wide range of specialized heat transfer equipment. Their refined manufacturing process had enabled GHE's heat exchange systems to find applications in a wide variety of industries, including pulp and paper, power generation, electrical transmission and distribution, and other process-related industries. Some of these systems were known to last more than 20 years, so long-lasting relationships in the industry were normal.

GHE had operated as a distinct entity under various ownerships during its evolution and maintained a leadership position in the industry. In 1991, GHE was acquired by Zest Industries, and became a member of the Zest Heat Transfer Group. Zest was a large privately held corporation in the United States with more than 12,000 employees.

GHE's facility was divided into two principal areas: (1) the manufacturing facility, and (2) the office building. The manufacturing building consisted of fabrication, machine shop, assembly, testing, and research and development areas, totaling approximately 94,000 square feet with 80 employees. The office building consisted of sales, purchasing, engineering, estimating group, accounting, and management, totaling approximately 9,000 square feet with 60 employees.

GHE's renowned international reputation was supported by various sales offices across North America as well as foreign offices in Australia, China, Pakistan, Sweden, and the United Kingdom. Some of the more recent large international projects included hydroelectric installations in India, electric transmission systems in Europe, giant water-pumping systems in California, and several waste-to-energy facilities in the Far East.

The Purchasing Department. Deirdre was a 10-year veteran of GHE. She worked with Charlie Bond in the purchasing department and they were each responsible for the procurement of different parts. They each worked very closely with managers in the engineering and estimation departments. Deirdre believed that "communication" was the key to the successful coordination of these groups,

I am always in contact with the people in engineering and estimation because we want to make sure that the system we design at GHE is of the highest quality but still reasonably priced. This takes a great deal of coordination amongst ourselves so that the operation runs smoothly.

Deirdre also commented on the importance of her position and the effect on profits,

The money I can save is free-and-clear profit. Purchasing is very critical to the bottom line and every penny counts towards the estimate.

The Estimating Process. The complexity of the purchasing decision depended on whether an order was for a standard or custom heat exchange system. A standard unit usually required only one motor and a simple design and could be ordered from GHE's catalogue. The price was relatively low (approximately $5,400 for an average standard system) and thus stock was either readily available or could easily be replenished.

An order for a custom unit, on the other hand, entailed a complex estimation process. Custom units were much larger and at least 20 times more expensive than standard units. They required several motors and were often designed and manufactured with specific materials in mind. Before a large custom order was filled, GHE policy required that an estimate be sent back to the prospective client for approval.

An estimate request typically arrived through the sales department and the specs were then forwarded to the estimation group. The estimation group worked very closely with the engineering department so that the design of the system would match the specs from the client. Once the design was completed, the estimation group worked with the purchasing department to come up with the formal estimate. The estimate was then passed on to sales, who forwarded it to the client for sign-off.

GHE estimates were typically valid for only 30 days, after which they were void and had to be renegotiated. This constraint was the industry standard and many of Deirdre's suppliers offered GHE similar terms. Deirdre often felt that GHE's turnaround time was quick and that usually the client was the one to slow down the transaction.

We work closely with each other to make sure that the process is fast so we can keep business moving. However, one shouldn't forget that our clients have their own sales, estimation, engineering, and purchasing departments as well so it takes time for orders to get through their whole system and we sometimes end up not hearing from them for a while.

The Japanese Account. On March 1, GHE's sales manager, head engineer, and president returned from Tokyo with an estimate request for a custom heat exchange system for a large Japanese power-generating plant. The prospective order was lucrative and the expected contribution from the sale was projected to be substantial. The president, a recently assigned executive from Zest Industries, was extremely excited about the potential new business, given its exposure to Far Eastern markets, and reiterated the importance of this deal with all key personnel at GHE, including Deirdre.

Over the next week, members of the sales, engineering, and estimation departments worked earnestly on the estimate and forwarded the final requisition of parts to Deirdre. Deirdre had little difficulty in sourcing the estimates for the required materials from her long-standing suppliers and submitted the information back to the group. The proposed heat exchange system required dozens of customized motors and tubes as well as the use of a specialized titanium alloy which would prove to be very expensive, amounting to 50 percent of overall cost. An appropriate margin was added to the final cost estimate and the contract was sent back to Tokyo within the week, priced at $1.2 million.

3:13 P.M. on April 17. At 3:13 P.M. on April 17, Deirdre had just returned from a long lunch party that was thrown by the president to celebrate the Japanese acceptance of GHE's estimate that had been received the previous day. The whole company was excited about the order and the potential new business that this client would bring in the future, and all seemed bright at GHE. Deirdre sat down in her office and read the fax (see Exhibit 1).

She gasped at the contents of the announcement and reread it to make sure. Titania's price increase would result in a substantial underestimate of the cost of the original Japanese order and might well result in a loss to GHE. She shook her head in disbelief and wondered what her next move should be.

EXHIBIT 1   Fax to: Deirdre Collins

TITANIA LTD.

FAX SENT: April 17th

ATTENTION: Deirdre Collins
Buyer–Expeditor, Global Heat Exchangers Inc.

Deirdre:

I wanted to personally notify you of our recently published price changes that we are advertising in our new catalogue (your copy is in the mail and should arrive in your office shortly).

As you will notice, there was a substantial increase in our Titanium sheet metal units of nearly 25%. Given your request for a materials estimate on this particular item dated March 3rd, I thought you should be aware of the change. I understand that your old request was for a substantial amount of volume. I am sorry about the price increase (it was out of my control) and I hope it does not affect your future business with us. I eagerly anticipate continuing our long-standing relationship.

Sincerely yours,

Charles Pappas

Charles Pappas
National Sales Director
Titania Ltd.

CASE 9–2
MASTECH INC.

Robert Fisk, purchasing manager for MasTech Inc. of Detroit, Michigan, was preparing for a meeting the following day with the plant general manager, Andrew Ross. MasTech, a Tier 1 supplier for the auto industry, was under tremendous cost pressures from its customers, and Robert had to recommend whether the company should change its steel supplier for an important product.

Company Background. MasTech Inc. was a division of Omron Corporation, a large North American automotive parts manufacturer with annual sales of $10 billion. Omron's customers included General Motors, Ford and DaimlerChrysler as well as several Japanese and European automakers. It employed 50,000 people, working in 170 plants throughout North America, Europe and Asia. Omron used a decentralized philosophy, and each plant was evaluated as a profit center.

MasTech supplied a variety of stamped-metal components to automotive assembly plants in Michigan, and its annual sales were $280 million. Each plant had its own purchasing department responsible for all direct and indirect materials purchases.

Robert Fisk had been the purchasing manager for MasTech for the last 10 years. Working under Robert's direct supervision was a senior materials buyer, a materials buyer, and an expeditor. Robert paid personal attention to steel contracts because steel accounted for approximately 60 percent of total costs.

The Ford Cross-Member Contract. Suppliers in the automotive industry provided engineering and technical support to their customers during product development. Once in production, suppliers were expected to provide defect-free products with JIT delivery. Furthermore, the automakers specified annual cost reductions that typically ranged from 3 to 5 percent.

Four years previously, MasTech had won the bid to produce a cross-member part for the frame of a new Ford truck model that went into production two years later. The contract specified annual cost reductions of 3 percent over the life of the contract.

The cross-member required a total of 130,000 tons of steel annually, which was purchased from a major mill, Uxbridge Steel (Uxbridge). MasTech, which used Uxbridge as a supplier for several components, negotiated a price of $30 per hundredweight, FOB MasTech.[1] As was standard practice in the industry, Uxbridge used Vaughan Steel Processing (Vaughan) to do all its secondary processing: pickling, slitting, and edge trimming. The steel was shipped to MasTech directly after processing at Vaughan.

MasTech's steel suppliers were required to make deliveries according to a fixed schedule, sometimes as frequently as every 4 to 8 hours. If deliveries were not made according to the schedule, MasTech could face machine down-time and risk delaying shipments to customers. Robert estimated that it cost MasTech $1,500/hour per line to be idle, while costs of idling a car assembly plant were about $300,000 per hour.

Supply Problems. Robert Fisk was concerned about Vaughan's delivery performance. Since production started on the cross-member, Vaughan had been able to supply only 75 percent of MasTech's requirements and Robert had been forced to turn to alternate sourcing, incurring a 10 percent price premium. Robert commented, "Vaughan won't carry the inventory I think they should, and as a result they miss a lot of our deliveries."

Demand for steel had been strong the past two years, but indications were that the market was be-

ginning to weaken. Consequently, Robert asked Colgon Steel to quote on MasTech's cross-member requirements. Colgon had not been profitable in recent years and was anxious to secure additional volume. Robert received a quote of $24.75 per hundredweight for unprocessed steel, FOB Ashgrove Steel Processing (Ashgrove).

Ashgrove indicated that it would charge MasTech $4.75 per hundredweight for processing and delivery. Although MasTech had never used Ashgrove for its steel processing requirements, the company did have a good reputation. Ashgrove was a relatively small processor, but the president indicated that they would add another line just for MasTech's business.

Alternatives Available to Robert. Robert indicated to Uxbridge that he was market testing the steel for the Ford cross-member and asked his supplier to revisit their pricing. As a result, Uxbridge agreed to drop the price of the finished product to $29.75 per hundredweight and offered to sell unprocessed steel at $24.75 per hundredweight FOB Ashgrove.

Andrew Ross was expecting a large part of the contractual 3 percent price reduction to come from a reduction in steel costs. In advance of his meeting with Andrew, Robert needed to decide what action he should take and to identify the savings he expected would accrue to MasTech.

CASE 9–3
CHEVRON CORPORATION: THE PC SELECTION TEAM (ABRIDGED)

Jean Wolcott, alliance manager, Chevron Information Technology Company, was preparing for the second meeting of the Desktop Life Cycle Management Team, scheduled for Friday, April 25 at the San Ramon, California, office complex. It had been decided during the first team meeting, held the previous day, that the Chevron Supplier Quality Improvement Process (CSQIP) framework should be followed to select a supplier for desktop computers. The meeting on Friday would focus on assessing

---

[1] hundredweight = price per 100 pounds

factors that might influence the total costs of operating desktop computers at Chevron Corporation. It was now April 23, and Jean wanted to make her own assessment of total cost factors in advance of the session two days hence.

Chevron Corporation. Chevron Corporation was a publicly held, worldwide petroleum and chemical company headquartered in San Francisco, California. One of the world's largest integrated petroleum companies, Chevron operated in more than 90 countries and employed approximately 34,000 people.

Ken Derr, Chairman and CEO of Chevron, strongly believed that decentralization and empowerment should be the philosophical base for a major reorganization at Chevron. Thus, four major operating companies (OpCos) were identified: a U.S. upstream company called Chevron Production Company (CPDN); a U.S. downstream company called Chevron Products Company (CPDS); all of Chevron's non-North American upstream activities were organized under Chevron Overseas Petroleum Inc. (COPI); and Chevron Chemicals Company (CCC), which remained essentially unchanged. Each OpCo was expected to operate within Chevron's framework of corporate values, policies, and financial guidelines, but had considerable autonomy for the development and execution of business plans that had to be approved at the Chevron corporate level.

Chevron Information Technology Company (CITC), headquartered in Chevron Park, San Ramon, California, provided information technology support to Chevron locations worldwide. As part of a previous corporate reorganization, some IT responsibilities, such as control over network architecture, hardware and software, had been distributed to the OpCos. Consequently, each OpCo had its own information technology group, which meant that CITC's involvement with individual business units varied substantially. Furthermore, a common standard for information technology did not exist within the company currently. Dave Clementz, president of CITC, described the situation:

Chevron found itself with a conglomeration of hundreds of different personal computers and software programs. The variety of configurations, life cycles, and service contracts posed serious usage and maintenance issues

for the company. Our network was not providing us the service capabilities that we needed and was becoming increasingly expensive to maintain. For example, because we did not have a standard software program, even simple activities, such as opening documents, could be a problem.

Last year, a consensus began to develop that we needed to assess our distributed IT philosophy. As a result, we formed a broad-based group from the various business units to examine Chevron's IT strategy. It became known as the 'Vision Study'. One of its important recommendations was the creation of a universal, high-performance computer network worldwide. Our Global Information Link Project, which we called the 'GIL' Project, was our means of accomplishing this objective.

The Gil Project. The GIL Project started in March. Its main objective was to establish a flexible and reliable IT infrastructure by standardizing all aspects of the network and computing environment at Chevron Corporation worldwide. GIL would connect more than 30,000 desks across more than 700 worksites in more than 90 countries. Ed Miller was named GIL project manager, responsible for coordinating the project teams set up to make recommendations concerning each of the major areas of Chevron's IT infrastructure, such as operating systems, servers, software, telecommunications and desktop systems. Ed would also be responsible for overseeing GIL implementation.

Tom Bell was the team leader responsible for recommending the desktop computer system that Chevron would adopt as part of the GIL Project. The members of the Desktop Life Cycle Management Team were Marjorie Ferrer and Pete Sandoval, from Chevron Production Company; Mike Jochimson and Joe Panto, from CITC; Faith Bovard, from finance; Shelli Peacock, from Chevron Petroleum Technology; and Jean Wolcott, from purchasing.

The Desktop Life Cycle Management Team was a critical component of the GIL Project, as described by Tom Bell:

Our team's involvement was considered critical to the GIL Project on two dimensions.

First, the desktop standard impacted several of the other GIL activities. The other GIL teams needed to know which hardware standard had been approved before they could complete their assignments. You might say that we were on the critical path.

The second aspect was financial. It was expected that the IT investments associated with the GIL Project would represent an initial investment of approximately $150 million. We anticipated that the desktop hardware portion would make up about $90 million. Spending this kind of money meant that we would need approval from the Board of Directors.

Tom Bell made the follow observations regarding the involvement of Ed Miller:

Ed was the ideal selection for the position of GIL project manager. He had a high energy level and was focused on the project objectives, but Ed also had an ability use his relaxed style to keep things in perspective for those around him. Ed also insisted on empowering the team leaders. He was involved in key decisions but relied heavily on the judgement of the project teams.

The Chevron Production Company IT Standard. Chevron Production Company (CPDN) was responsible for Chevron's North American upstream operations, consisting of exploration and production facilities. CPDN conducted a study two years ago that resulted in the establishment of a desktop standard with a personal computer (PC) and laptop from Global Technology Company (GTC). Last year, CPDN replaced all of its desktop machines and leased approximately $20 million worth of GTC equipment. Tom Bell commented on the CPDN experience:

Management at CPDN recognized the benefits of standardization early. They went through a detailed study and settled on a laptop and a PC from Global Technology Company. Tricon Inc. was selected as the reseller, responsible for delivering the equipment, installation, asset disposal, and warranty service. The selection of GTC did not come as surprise. They are one of the world's largest computer technology companies with total revenues of about $60 billion, and Tricon is one of their largest distributors and a global technology services company. We wanted to leverage the experience of CPDN regarding desktop systems and made sure they were involved on our team.

Outcome of the First Team Meeting. The Chevron Desktop Life Cycle Management Team held its first meeting on April 22. During that meeting Tom Bell reviewed the team objectives and schedule.

The team's first objective was to evaluate appropriate desktop supply alternatives and make a recommendation concerning appropriate cost-effective desktop standards for both PCs and laptops. This recommendation would include the selection of a supplier or suppliers for desktop systems. Chevron currently had approximately 25,000 PCs and 5,000 laptops in use in its worldwide operations. Four manufacturers supplied approximately 90 percent of the computers currently in use at Chevron: GTC, Saba Computer Company, Vytec Inc., and Cassin Technologies. Saba was a global manufacturer and developer of computer equipment and systems, networking products, printers, scanners, and support and maintenance services. Its head office was located in San Diego, California, and the company had annual revenues of $40 billion. Vytec, with its head office in San Antonio, Texas, was a low-cost manufacturer of computer hardware and had annual revenues of approximately $25 billion. Cassin, with annual revenues of $10 billion, sold all of its computers directly to end consumers, bypassing the industry's traditional distribution network. Cassin's head office was in Houston, Texas.

The second team objective dealt with timing of the project. It was important that the team complete its assignment before June 20. Any delays beyond this date would affect other GIL project teams.

Jean Wolcott was asked to lead the next meeting scheduled for April 4, when the entire team would use CSQIP to evaluate its supply options.

CSQIP. The basic premise behind CSQIP was that Chevron would gain competitive advantage by forming mutually beneficial alliances with world-class suppliers, characterized by shared business objectives, strategies to accomplish those objectives, a system of metrics for measuring progress, and ongoing teamwork and communication between customer and supplier. CSQIP supplier alliances were reserved for goods and services that offered the greatest potential for cost savings, typically high-expenditure, high-complexity materials and services. It could be applied to either an existing supply relationship or to a new purchase decision. CSQIP had been successfully applied to a number of products and services, such as line pipe, control valves, trucking, lubricants, copiers and underwater services. The Alliance Improvement Teams had produced average savings of 8 to 10 percent, and as much as 25 percent of the contract value in the services arena. Currently, Chevron was expected to spend $2.6 billion under its alliance program.

Total cost of ownership was a primary driver of the CSQIP process, based on the belief that poor quality increased costs. Consequently, while price was recognized as important, it was regarded as only one element of the supply relationship. Under the CSQIP process, total cost of ownership was described as all direct and indirect costs incurred over the life of a material or service, such as engineering, inventory, installation and testing, operations and maintenance, and retirement or disposal.

Chevron had a number of alliance managers trained in the CSQIP procedure. These individuals provided direct assistance, CSQIP training, and expertise within departments or OpCos.

The CSQIP Steps. CSQIP involved a number of steps, which could be divided into two phases: supplier selection and process improvement. Each step in the process involved specific activities. See Exhibit 1 for an outline of the CSQIP steps and Exhibit 2 for main issues addressed during the supplier selection phase.

Preparing for the Next Team Meeting. Although the team did not have much time to complete its assignment, Jean knew that its recommendations would be scrutinized thoroughly. The review process would involve three stages. First, the team's recommendations would be presented to CITC management for review and approval. An executive group, the Outsourcing Guidance Review Team, responsible for technology policy within Chevron, would also have to review the proposal. This committee included Dave Clementz; Don Paul, vice president technology and environmental affairs; Marty Klitten, CFO; and Ron Kiskis, corporate vice president. Finally, given the size of the expenditure, the team's recommenda-

EXHIBIT 1 CSQIP Steps

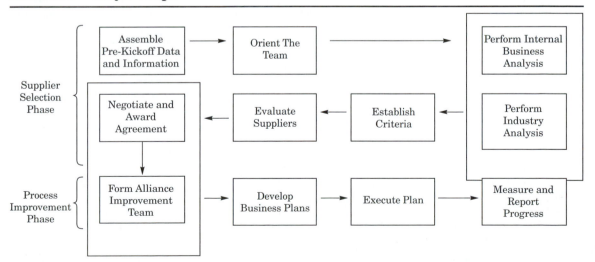

Exhibit 2   CSQIP Process Activities

Assemble Pre-Kickoff Data and Information and Orient the Team

Assemble data	• Collect information relating to the anticipated purchase, such as existing volumes, suppliers, outstanding contracts
Orient the team	• Define project scope and team authority
	• Establish what the project has been designed to accomplish and why it is important
	• Establish project objectives, including costs and financial benefits
	• Determine project timing and schedule

Perform Internal Business Analysis

Develop initial supplier selection criteria	• Brainstorming exercise to develop initial list of criteria for supplier selection
Evaluate total cost of ownership drivers	• Collect data from internal and external sources that provide information regarding total cost of ownership
	• Brainstorming exercise to explore total cost factors
	• Refine supplier selection criteria

Perform Industry Analysis

Evaluate industry structure	• Evaluate structure of the supply chain in the industry, including manufacturers, wholesalers, and distributors
	• Determine which companies are leaders within their industry segments
	• Develop an initial supplier list

Establish Criteria

Establish supplier evaluation criteria	• Finalize criteria to be used in the evaluation of potential suppliers

---

Evaluate suppliers

Create questionnaire and assign points	• Develop detailed questionnaire to be completed by potential suppliers
	• Assign weights to each question
Develop supplier list	• Finalize supplier list based on industry assessment and supplier evaluation criteria
Evaluate responses	• "Score" supplier responses and rank suppliers
Create shortlist of suppliers	• Create shortlist of suppliers for on-site visits
Prepare for on-site visits	• Identify new questions or requirements for clarification of information
	• Prepare agenda for meeting(s)

tions had to be formally adopted by the Chevron Board of Directors.

Jean had asked to lead the meeting on April 25, during which time the team would concentrate on the internal business analysis step in the CSQIP framework and create a list of factors that might affect the total cost of ownership of operating desktop computers at Chevron. During this session, each member of the team would be expected to help create a list of factors contributing to the total cost of ownership as part of a brainstorming exercise. Jean and the team would then use this information to help develop criteria for evaluating potential suppliers.

In order to be fully prepared for the meeting herself and because she had never tried to apply the total cost of ownership concept to the acquisition of computers, Jean decided to think through on her own what cost factors might apply to desktop PCs and laptops.

CASE 9–4
PRICE FORECASTING EXERCISE*

You and ____ other members of the class have been asked to forecast the price of a commodity on ____. So that your organization may take the most advantageous procurement action possible, your organization needs $5 million worth of this commodity for delivery between ____ and ____. The amount—$5 million worth—is based on the spot price of this commodity on ____. Your report must address the following four questions:

Question 1. What is the current ____ spot price of this commodity, based on what quotation? What is the specification of the commodity, and what is the minimum amount of purchase required for the quoted price to hold? How much in weight or volume does $5 million represent?

Question 2. What is the current futures for ____?

*Your instructor will supply the missing information, dates, etc.

Question 3. What spot price do you forecast for this commodity on ____? Why?

Question 4. In view of your forecast, what recommendations would you make to the executive committee of your organization with regard to the purchase of this commodity? Would you advise buying now and taking delivery now, or later? Would you hedge? Would you delay purchase? Anything else? What savings do you forecast from your recommendation?

Qualifications

1) The commodity selected may not be a pegged price in the market in which you are purchasing. It must be a freely fluctuating price, and it must be traded on a recognized commodity exchange. Prices must be reported daily in an accessible news source.

2) Approval for a selected commodity must come from the instructor. No two teams may select the same commodity. Commodity selection is on a first-come, first-served basis.

3) Foreign exchange rates may be an important consideration in your decision.

4) This report has four parts:
   a) A written report (in at least two copies) to be handed in on ____ before 4:30 P.M.
   b) A five-minute class report to be presented orally during class on ____.
   c) A written evaluation report (in at least two copies) to be handed in before 4:30 p.m., ____, including the ____ actual spot price. The evaluation should compare a savings (loss) estimate in view of the recommended action for the weight calculated in the report.
   d) A one-minute report on ____ highlighting the evaluation.

5) Group names and commodity selections to be submitted no later than 4:30 P.M., ____.

Special Remarks

1) The amount of $5 million is in U.S. dollars. Exchange rates with foreign currencies have to be considered as part of this problem.

2) There is a commission charge for every commodity. Please determine what this is for your commodity and include it in your calculations.

3) In the case of purchase and storage ahead, the carrying cost is 2 percent per month.

4) If the market has a daily variation and quotes high and low closing for the day, please be consistent and use the same type of quotation throughout.

5) Use the same source (publication) for your future price and your spot price.

CASE 9–5
COMMODITY PURCHASING GAME

In this game you will have the chance to try your skill as a commodity purchaser. You will be using information similar in type to that available to Ms. Martin, the purchasing manager of a well-known chocolate bar corporation.

Because raw material accounts for 50 percent of the cost of producing a chocolate bar, the purchasers in the chocolate bar business have a great deal of responsibility on their shoulders.

Among other functions, Ms. Martin, at the beginning of each month, has to decide how many pounds of cocoa should be purchased during the coming weeks of that month. When doing this, she takes into account the expected need of the production department, the time of the year, the inventory on hand, the cost of short supply, the cost of carrying inventory, and, finally, the commodity market trends, more specifically, cocoa.

You will be able in this game to make similar decisions, although the game will be a simplified version of the actual situation. The most important features of this simplification are, first, it will not be possible for you to buy cocoa after the first day of the month (you are allowed to purchase cocoa only once a month—on the first day); and, second, it will not be possible for you to buy cocoa on the futures market.

Cocoa Need. Company sales, and industry sales in general, are very much influenced by seasonal factors. Because the chocolate has a tendency to melt in the warm months of the year, sales usually slow down during the summer months and rebuild very quickly in the fall when the manufacturers start their promotion again. For the last six years, July has been the slowest month for sales and September the biggest.

Because chocolate bars have a limited shelf life, and because it is company policy to supply freshly made chocolate bars to the retailers, it is company practice not to stockpile finished goods. Actually, chocolate bars sold in one month have to be produced in the same month.

In the last five years, the company's cocoa need has grown almost constantly. Cocoa requirements have increased 200 percent in this five-year period. Last year's cocoa purchases were 4.76 million pounds. An average of the cocoa requirements for the last three years, broken down per month, is shown in Exhibit 1. The curve shown is only the average of the experience of many years. In any given year, the monthly percentage of total need might vary $\mp$ 3 percentage points from what is given by the curve. For example, January's figure of 10 percent is really the midpoint of a possible low of 7 percent and a possible high of 13 percent.

From past experience, Ms. Martin knows that the production department uses approximately 60 percent of the total yearly cocoa purchases in the last six months of the year. And, moreover, 55 percent of this last six months' need is used in September and October.

Production scheduling is done on a weekly basis. Ms. Martin has no precise idea of what the actual total monthly production need for cocoa will be on the first day of that month, other than from her judgment of need level of prior periods and from consideration of the general shape of the need curve shown in Exhibit 1.

Raw Material. Cocoa, the basic raw material in chocolate, has an especially volatile price, and there is no way to hedge completely against the wide price swings. Chocolate comes from cocoa beans, a crop subject to wide production fluctuations with a stable and generally rising demand. Furthermore, it takes 7 years for new cocoa trees to come into production (15 years to reach full production), and drought and disease can sharply reduce supply in a matter of months or even weeks.

Using the company's expected sales and expenses for the year, Ms. Martin estimates that

EXHIBIT 1   Cocoa Need per Month by the Production Department

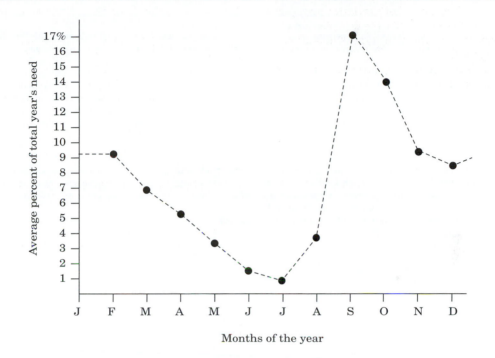

Months of the year

when she pays 48 cents a pound for cocoa, the contribution per pound purchased is 13 cents, and any increase in the price paid for cocoa has a direct reverse effect on the amount of contribution and vice versa. (If she pays 49 cents per pound, then the contribution would be one cent less or 12 cents, etc.)

In order to be as efficient as possible in her predictions of future cocoa prices, Ms. Martin keeps informed by means of trade journals; she follows the futures market closely and studies the past performance of cocoa prices.

As of October 1, Ms. Martin has assembled the information given in Exhibits 2, 3 and 4. Company policy does not allow her to carry an inventory of more than 1.2 million pounds of raw cocoa in her monthly ending inventory. The company is short of funds, and the president is not anxious to exceed borrowing limits set by the bank.

Costs Involved. In deciding on purchasing alternatives, Ms. Martin bears in mind several costs

which she knows to be fairly accurate. These costs are inventory costs and stock-out costs.

Inventory Costs. Storage cost for one pound of raw material is 0.4 cents per month. This amount takes into account interest on tied-up capital, insurance, deterioration, and direct handling expense. Ms. Martin knows that over the period of a season, inventory carrying charges can reasonably be calculated on the basis of inventory on hand at the end of each month.

Stockout Costs: Ms. Martin also considers stock-out costs. A stock-out cost occurs whenever the production demand for raw cocoa in a particular month is greater than the available raw cocoa in inventory. For example, if 50,000 pounds of raw cocoa are on hand at the beginning of the month, 50,000 pounds are purchased, and the need during the month totals 110,000 pounds, then a stock-out of 10,000 pounds occurs. The company then has to

Exhibit 2   Size of Upcoming Crops Hold Key to Cocoa Prices (October 1)

Prices of cocoa beans have risen 8 percent since September 22. The increase follows a roller-coaster ride which took the market from a long-term low in July of last year to a 39-month peak in mid-July of this year, then down again by some 21 percent.

Harvesting of the main crop in Ghana, the world's largest cocoa producer, reportedly has been delayed by adverse weather. In addition, recent rains may have reduced yields in several African-producing areas. Black pod disease reportedly has hit the Brazilian crop, and Russia has told Ghana it wants early deliveries of the 100,000 long tons of cocoa pledged for this season and of cocoa on which Accra defaulted last season. Ghana, in turn, has requested an extension of one month or more for deliveries on sales contracts with the United States and Europe that were originally scheduled for the current quarter.

Future Boost

Renewed buying interest by large manufacturers, coupled with trade and speculative purchases, helped boost cocoa futures. However, the extent to which supplies tighten in the next month or two will depend greatly on the size of invisible stocks and of future government purchases from African growers, who have been given an incentive through purchase price increases by the Cocoa Marketing Boards.

The current New York spot prices of Accra (Ghanaian) cocoa beans, at 24 cents per pound compares with quotes of 44.50 cents on September 22, 33.50 cents a year ago, and a peak 56.50 cents on July 14 of the current year. During the 10-week price slump, the open interest in New York cocoa futures shrank from a record 38,054 contracts (30,000 pounds each) on August 10 to fewer than 28,700 contracts; it now aggregates 29,500 contracts.

On the New York Cocoa Exchange, the December future currently is selling at around 45.04 cents, up from 40.44 cents on December 22. The March option is quoted at around 46.22 cents, against 41.84 cents on September 22. The May future is selling at 47.08 cents. The distant December option is at 49.44 cents.

British Bean Experts

According to London's Gill and Duffus, Ltd., unfavorable weather held this year's world cocoa bean crop to 1,214,000 long tons, 20 percent below a year earlier. In the face of this dip, relatively attractive prices and rising incomes are expected to push the current year's world cocoa bean grindings (not to be confused with actual consumption) to a record 1,414,000 long tons. This is 83,000 long tons (6.2 percent) above that of last year.

Allowing 1 percent for loss in weight, output seems to be lagging anticipated grindings by a record 212,000 long tons. This being the case, the October 1 world carry-over of cocoa beans, which is estimated at around 366,000 long tons, is barely a three-month supply. Nine years ago, a similar drop to a three-month supply saw prices average 68 cents, far above the current market.

On the eve of the coming season, the trade lacks accurate information on the size of the major new African crops. During recent months, African governments have sold ahead a large portion of the prospective new main crop at prices well above those of a year ago. Ghana's advance sales are placed above 275,000 long tons, some 100,000 more than last year, at prices ranging between 46 cents and 52 cents a pound.

Prior to the recent reports of adverse weather, the trade generally estimated the coming season's world cocoa output at around 1,300,000 long tons, some 60,000 to 86,000 tons above last season. This includes this year's prospective main and mid crops in Ghana of between 435,000 and 475,000 long tons versus 410,000 tons last year, and a record 572,000 long tons two years ago. Guess estimates for Nigeria range between 200,000 and 210,000 tons, against 182,000 last season, and a record 294,000 tons two years ago, but may fail to account fully for losses due to the country's tribal unrest. Output from the Ivory Coast is tentatively forecast at between 120,000 and 150,000 tons, up from 112,000 tons last season, and close to its record of 145,000 tons.

Bad weather and pod rot, a fungus that causes seed to rot, have caused the experts to drop their estimates on the Brazilian crop to 130,000 or 135,000 long tons, down from 158,000 tons of last season. Recent reports indicate that the crops in other Latin American countries also will lag last season's levels, which may drop next season's yields for our Southern neighbors some 60,000 to 75,000 tons below the 283,000 tons of last year. Adding everything together, the coming season's cocoa bean harvest is likely to range between 1,250,000 and 1,350,000 long tons, which would be a good deal smaller than the current year's anticipated world cocoa bean grindings.

How closely output matches next year's consumption is the key to the cocoa market. Bulls on cocoa believe that prices have not been high enough to discourage the steady rise in usage. They attribute the July to September slump mainly to forecasts of increased crops, tight money, and the large open interest which invited volatile prices.

EXHIBIT 3   Cocoa Spot Price and Cocoa Futures Market (October 1)

	Futures Market
December	45.04
March	46.22
May	47.08
July	47.84
September	48.62
December (next year)	49.44

Spot Price: 48.0 cents per pound.

EXHIBIT 4   Past Performance of Cocoa on the Commodity Market

Past Performance of Cocoa on the Commodity Market

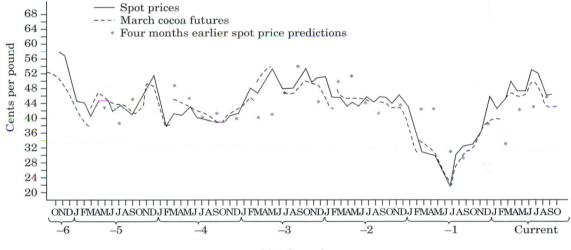

place rush orders for raw cocoa and, consequently, is forced to pay a cent per pound premium.

Ms. Martin's Commission. The president of the company was convinced that incentives for executives were important. Therefore, part of Ms. Martin's salary was based on her performance as a cocoa purchaser. She receives a 5 percent commission on the monthly net contribution to profits.

Net monthly contribution = Monthly contribution less monthly stock-out costs (or monthly inventory carrying costs)

Closing Inventory Target. At the end of the game, each group is expected to have a closing inventory of 200,000 pounds of raw cocoa. Every group who fails to reach this 200,000 pound target will be penalized in the following way.

1. For every pound in excess of the aforementioned target:

   As in every other month, the company will have to pay an inventory carrying cost, and, moreover, there will be an extra charge of 6.0 cents per pound over the 200,000 pound target.

EXHIBIT 5 Result Form

	Stock on hand at start of month in lbs. = ending inventory of previous month	Purchases in lbs.	Total available for production in lbs. (3 = 1 + 2)	Production requirements in lbs.	Ending inventory in lbs. (5 = 3 + 4) Cannot be less than 0 or greater than 1,200,000 lbs. Penalty for any excess of $2,000 in commission	Stock-out in lbs. (6 = 4 + 3 if greater than 0)	Stock out costs (7 = 6 × $.06)	Inventory carrying costs (8 = 5 × $.004)	Contribution per lb. purchased	Total monthly contribution (10 = 2 × 9)	Total monthly costs (11 = 7 + 8)	Net monthly contribution (12 = 10 − 11)	Monthly commission on contribution (13 = 5% × 12)	Cumulative commission (14 = 13 + 14) previous month
	1	2	3	4	5	6	7	8	9	10	11	12	13	14
August	50M	350M	400M	450M	0	50M	$3,000	0	7.0¢	$14,500	$3,000	$21,500	$1075	($1075)
September	0	1,100M	1,100M	900M	200M	0	0	$800	12.8¢	$140,800	$800	$140,000	$7,000	($8,075)
October	200M													
November														
December														
January														
February														
March														
April														
May														
June														
July														
August														
September														

2. For every pound short in relation to the aforementioned target:

The company will have to pay 6 cents per pound and will have to buy sufficient cocoa at the September 1 spot price to bring the inventory level to 200,000 pounds.

How to Play the Game. In the actual conduct of this game, teams will be used to make the purchasing decisions normally made by Ms. Martin. On the first day of each month, each team will decide on the quantity of cocoa to be purchased. This decision will be made by the team by whatever means it chooses. Thus, a prediction from a plot of past month's performance might be used by some teams, a pure guess by others. In making the decision, teams will want to consider both the possibilities of future needs and the inventories now on hand as well as their forecast of cocoa spot prices behavior.

After each team has made its purchasing decision for the coming month, the instructor will announce the next month's price and actual consumption during the past month. Given this information, teams can calculate, using Exhibit 5, all of the necessary costs and, finally, the "net commission of the purchaser." They can then decide how much cocoa, if any, to purchase for the next month.

The object of the game is to increase as much as possible the purchaser's cumulative commission over 12 months. This means that teams will have to decide whether it would be cheaper in the long run to incur some inventory or stockout costs, depending on their predictions of the cocoa price behavior on the commodity market. At the end of each month, every team's results will be shown on the screen in front of the class and, at the end of the twelfth month, the class will discuss each team's method of predicting sales and cocoa prices. Teams will probably find it advantageous to split the work of making sales estimates, calculating costs and profit, and estimating the next period cocoa spot price.

Summary of Important Points to Remember When Playing the Game

1. Purchases can be made only on the first day of the month.

2. You cannot buy cocoa on the futures market.

3. It is a company practice to purchase cocoa on the first day of each month.

4. It is not possible to carry an inventory of more than 1.2 million pounds of raw cocoa. Penalty for excess of $2,000 in commission and excess stock will be returned to the vendor with a 6 cent penalty per pound on top of the $2,000 penalty.

5. At a purchase price of 48 cents per pound, the cocoa will bring a contribution of 13 cents. This contribution is directly related to the purchased price. (A 1-cent increase in the cost results in a 1-cent decrease in the contribution, and vice versa.)

6. There is an inventory carrying cost and a stockout cost which are directly deducted from the contribution amount to give the net contribution.

7. There is a closing inventory target of 200,000 pounds.

Result Form Used. To make the keeping of results easier for each team, a form has been distributed (see Exhibit 5). The exact steps in using this form are shown on the form itself.

Example. Each team member should carefully trace the proceedings as outlined in the following example to understand all of the steps involved in playing and recording the game.

Ms. Martin has already used the "Result Form" to record the operating results of the two months prior to October. On August 1, Ms. Martin had to decide how many pounds of cocoa should be purchased. Knowing the spot price on August 1 was 54 cents a pound, she thought, after consulting the trade journals and studying the futures market, that the prices would go down; therefore, she decided to purchase cocoa to supply the need of the current month only. She then consulted the production need curve and came to the conclusion that the need of that month would be approximately 300,000 pounds. Knowing that she had 50,000 pounds of cocoa in inventory, and wanting to keep a safe margin, she purchased 350,000 pounds of cocoa at the price of 54 cents per pound. She then entered the following figures on the "Result Form."

Column (1) = 50,000 pounds (from column (5) previous month)	Column (6) = 50,000 pounds
	Column (7) = $3,000
Column (2) = 350,000 pounds	Column (8) = $0
	Column (9) = $0.07
Column (3) = 400,000 pounds	Column (10) = $24,500
	Column (11) = $ 3,000
Column (4) = 450,000 pounds	Column (12) = $ 21,500
	Column (13) = $ 1,075
Column (5) = 0 pounds	Column (14) = $ 1,075

At the end of the month of August, Ms. Martin received from the production department the exact figure of the month's requirements, 450,000 pounds. Because there were only 400,000 pounds of cocoa in inventory, the company had to make a last-minute order to another supplier of cocoa at a premium of $0.06/lb. With this information, Ms. Martin could now calculate her net commission according to the company's norms. She entered the following figures on the "Result Form."

Start of the Game. The game proper starts on October 1. At the beginning of the game there are 200,000 pounds of cocoa on hand. It is now up to each team at this time to decide on the coming year's purchases and, thus, start playing the game. We will assume that the cumulative commission of $8,075 to the end of September has been paid to Ms. Martin and that each team will start again from zero. Please use Exhibit 6 as the sample for your group's reporting form, which should be handed in to the instructor each period.

EXHIBIT 6 Report Form

Decision Report	*Result Report*
Month 1 .... Group #	Last month's results net commission $ ....
Purchases .... pounds of cocoa	Cumulative commission to date $ ....

10 PURCHASING LOGISTICS SERVICES

Chapter Outline

Key Questions for the Purchasing Decision Maker

SHOULD WE
- Designate method of shipment and carrier, or let the supplier do it?
- Use FOB origin or FOB destination terms, or some other designation?
- Outsource some or all of the logistics function to a third party?

HOW CAN WE
- Develop an effective logistics strategy?
- Document loss or damage claims more effectively?
- Ensure that we attain the optimum mix of reliability, costs, and service from transportation and logistics service providers?

Logistics Defined

Purchased goods must be transported from the point they are grown, mined, or manufactured to the place needed, with inventories held at a minimum amount, to ensure production and customer service. The management of inventory in motion and at rest is referred to as logistics. Logistics is defined by the Council of Logistics Management as "that part of the supply chain that plans, implements, and controls the efficient, effective flow and storage of goods, services, and related information from the point of origin to the point of consumption in order to meet customers' requirements."[1] Logistics **Three Categories of Logistics Costs** costs can be divided into three categories—inventory carrying costs, administrative costs, and transportation—with transportation accounting for the bulk of the costs. The emphasis on reducing costs and cycle time throughout supply chains highlights the importance of inventory velocity and increases the need for competitive transportation and other logistics services as an alternative to maintaining costly inventories. Advances in information management systems, coupled with the speed of Internet communications, has greatly enabled the flow of real time information and the reduction of inventory throughout supply chains.

The purchase of logistics services demands a high degree of skill and knowledge if the costs of movement are to be minimized while at the same time meeting service needs. Due to the complexity of the logistics industry, the multitude of rules and regulations, and the significantly larger number of alternatives available as a result of deregulation, getting the best value for an organization's logistics dollar involves much more than simply "getting the best rate."

Total Business Logistics Costs

The total business logistics costs in the United States in 1999 was estimated at 9.9 percent of gross domestic product (GDP), or about $921 billion in a $9.26 trillion economy. These costs were divided into $332 billion in inventory carrying costs, $554 billion in transportation, and $35 billion

---

[1]Council of Logistics Management (CLM), *Definition of Logistics, www.clm1.org.*

in administration.[2] Logistics costs as a percentage of GDP generally have declined over the past two decades, dropping from 15.7 percent in 1980 to 11.4 percent in 1990 and to 9.9 percent in 1999.[3]

Inventory Carrying Costs and Administrative Costs. Inventory carrying costs are those costs associated with holding goods in storage, including interest charges, warehousing, obsolescence, deterioration, labor costs, insurance, and taxes. In the *11th annual State of Logistics Report,* Delaney credited the Internet and trends in business-to-business e-commerce with improving the visibility of inventory in motion.[4] As a share of GDP, inventory carrying costs have been falling in both the United States and Canada since 1982 from about 2.5 percent to about 1.1 percent. A larger share of inventories is held by wholesalers and retailers than manufacturers. Warehousing services are increasingly important in providing value-added services such as assembling kits, bar coding, labeling, and providing fulfillment services for e-commerce companies.

Transportation Costs. Transportation costs have remained stable at about 6 percent of the U.S. GDP and are currently about 4 percent of the Canadian GDP. Keeping these costs stable may be difficult if fuel costs rise and there are labor shortages. For 1999, the total transportation costs were broken down into the following amounts by type of freight as:

	United States[5]		Canada[6]	
	Dollar Volume (in billions)	Percentage	Dollar Volume (in billions)	Percentage
Highway	$450	81	$12.5	46
Railroads	36	6	4.5	16
Water	22	4	2.4	9
Pipelines	9	2	N/A	N/A
Air	26	5	4.3	16
Freight forwarders	6	1	3.6	13
Shipper related costs	5	1	N/A	N/A
Total	$554 billion	100%	$27.3 billion	100%

---

[2]Data from R. V. Delaney, Cass Information Systems, *11th Annual State of Logistics Report* (St. Louis, MO: 1999) and Eno Transportation Foundation, *Transportation in America,* Annual Report 1999, found in *Logistics Management and Distribution 2000 Annual Report,* July 2000, pp. 45–46.

[3]R. V. Delaney, Cass Information Systems, *11th Annual State of Logistics Report,* St. Louis, MO: 1999.

[4]Ibid.

[5]Data from R. V. Delaney, Cass Information Systems, *11th Annual State of Logistics Report* (St. Louis, MO: 1999) and Eno Transportation Foundation, *Transportation in America,* Annual Report 1999, found in *Logistics Management and Distribution 2000 Annual Report,* July 2000, pp. 45–46.

[6]Transport Canada, *Transportation and the Canadian Economy, Contribution of Transportation to the Economy, Commercial Transportation, www.tc.gc.ca,* February 22, 2001.

In Canada, rail and water carriers lost market share over the last 20 years, but with the rapid growth of intermodal transportation due to a strong economy, recovery of world commodity prices, and the railroads' investments in equipment, facilities, and technology, rail is experiencing a comeback.[7] Trucking has also remained strong due to trade expansion and regional economic growth across Canada.[8] Truck and rail combined accounted for 62 percent of Canada's transportation costs in 1999.

Transport Costs May Be a Large Share of Total Cost of Ownership

A large share (about half) of the total transportation cost is for movement of goods from the supplier's facility to the point where the industrial buyer needs them. Depending on the type of goods being moved, transportation may account for as much as 40 percent of the total cost of the item, particularly if it is of relatively low value and bulky, such as construction materials. But in the case of very-high-value, low-weight and bulk electronics goods, transport costs may be less than 1 percent of total purchase costs. It is not unusual in many firms to find that an average of 10 percent of their purchase expenditures go for incoming transportation costs. While target savings vary from firm to firm, many have found that only a modest effort to manage incoming transportation services more efficiently will result in substantial savings, often 10 to 15 percent of the freight bill.

Multiple Objectives when Buying Transportation Services

If minimization of costs were the only objective in buying transportation services, the task would be easy. However, the transportation buyer must look not only at cost but also at service provided. For example, items are purchased to meet a production schedule, and the available modes of transport require different amounts of transport time. If items are shipped by a method requiring a long shipment time, inventory may be exhausted and a plant or process shut down before the items arrive. Also, reliability may differ substantially among various transportation companies; service levels, lost shipments, and damage may vary greatly between two different carriers. The buyer should use the same skill and attention in selecting carriers as used in selecting other suppliers. The effects of transportation deregulation have made the carrier selection and pricing decision far more important today.

In addition, JIT purchasing systems (Chapter 6), global sourcing (Chapter 14), and outsourcing (Chapter 8) make logistics decisions more crucial. With JIT, deliveries must be on time, with no damage to the items in transit, because minimal inventories are maintained. Inventory cost savings should offset additional transportation costs. With global sourcing, extended lead times and distances place additional pressure on the transport decision-maker. The option to outsource some or all of the logistics function also adds complexity to the analysis of options and the management of inventory at rest and in motion.

---

[7] Ibid, and Ken Mark, "Railroads Steam Ahead," *Materials Management & Distribution,* July 1999, *www.mmdonline.com,* February 22, 2001.

[8] Transport Canada.

Trends in Transportation Buying

With the continued trend toward more deregulation of the transportation industry and the development of intermodal service, the focus for the transport buyer has shifted from mode of transport to breadth of service, information systems, timeliness (reliability and speed), and rates. Breadth refers to the ability of a carrier to handle multiple parts of the logistics process, including transportation, warehousing, inventory management, and shipper-carrier relationships. Outsourcing, or using third-party logistics service (3PL) providers, is increasingly considered by shippers as their organizations downsize, focus on core competencies, and seek partnerships or alliances with key suppliers. Because of the importance of speed—both in terms of providing reliable, consistent, on-time service, and moving goods through the system quickly—shippers are seeking core carriers with whom they can develop closer relationships to reduce cycle time. The development of information systems and the application of e-commerce tools to both inbound and outbound transportation also contribute to timeliness and breadth of service. Shippers are demanding improved communications and information systems to facilitate tracking and expediting orders. Because delays in the supply chain may lead to higher inventory levels and increase total cost, the whole logistics process is viewed as an area where cost avoidance and cost reductions will reap bottom-line rewards.

Organization for Logistics Decisions

In the *Survey of Career Patterns 2000* conducted by the Ohio State University Logistics Research Group, it was reported that organizations incorporate logistics into their corporate structure in one of four ways: (1) as part of each corporate division, (2) as a separate logistics division, (3) as a centralized logistics staff, or (4) as a combination of divisional and centralized activities. Surveys from the last several years indicate that the combined organizational form is most widely used. From 1997 to 2000, survey respondents reported more *director* job titles and fewer *manager* titles, with the number of vice presidents staying about the same. Fifty-two percent reported being housed in a logistics department, and a growing number (18 percent) work within a supply chain management department.[9]

Size of Organization Impacts How Decisions Are Made

Due to the large number of dollars involved in the movement of goods into and out of an organization and the potential effect on profits, large firms have a separate logistics services department with specialists in areas such as selection of carriers and routing, determination of freight classification and rates, tracing shipments, and handling claims in the case of loss or damage to goods during shipment. In the very large firm, the logistics function may be specialized even further, based on the purpose of ship-

---

[9]Ohio State University Logistics Research Group, *Survey of Career Patterns 2000,* *www.clm1.org.,* February 23, 2001.

ment. For example, an automobile producer may have three separate departments, one concerned with incoming materials shipments, one making the decisions on in-plant and interplant materials movement, and the third concerned with the shipment of finished goods through the distribution channels to customers. In an organization operating under the materials management concept, the transportation or logistics manager may have responsibility for all types of materials movement. This person must recognize that storage, handling, and shipping of raw materials and finished goods does not add value to the product. Instead, it is a key cost element in the operation of the firm and should be managed to minimize costs, within the parameters of needed service.

In the medium-sized and smaller organization, the number of logistics decisions may not be large enough to warrant a full-time logistics specialist. Here the transport decisions are handled by the buyer or purchasing manager. This means that the buyer must have enough knowledge to make decisions on preferred free on board (FOB) terms, classification of freight, selection of carriers and routing, determination of freight rates, preparation of necessary documentation, expediting and tracing of freight shipments, filing and settling claims for loss or damage in transit, and payment procedures for transport services received. This person must make these decisions in light of their impact on other areas such as inventory levels, carrying costs, and the use of capital.

Third-Party Logistics Service Providers

3PL Defined

Third-party providers are firms that act as intermediaries between trading partners, for example, shippers and carriers. Third-party logistics (3PL) service providers include freight bill auditors, site selection consultants, carriers, and transportation intermediaries who may or may not own any assets. A quick Internet search for *third-party logistics providers* will result in a long list of companies offering a wide range of services. The use of 3PLs is referred to as outsourcing or contracting out (See Chapter 8 for a discussion of outsourcing).

Use of Third Party Logistics Is Growing

According to Delaney, 3PL services originated in the 1930s, but government regulation stymied growth. With deregulation beginning in the late 1970s and the shakeout in surface transportation, it was not until the 1990s that 3PLs gained ground. Delaney estimated that 3PLs managed $50 billion of logistics expenditures in 2000.[10] The services that 3PLs may provide include all trucking and warehousing services, express, courier, and freight forwarding, dedicated human resources, and customized systems and communications. The growth of intermodal (joint shipping modes such as rail and truck) encourages the development of a seamless

---

[10]Robert Delaney, *A Six Month Update of the 11th Annual "State of Logistics Report©,"* Cass Information Systems, January 22, 2001, p. 2.

web of steps in the transportation and logistics process. Many companies are developing a relationship with a core carrier(s) and having the core carrier place staff on-site (sometimes referred to as co-location or JIT II®) to manage the day-to-day logistics decisions. The continuing development of computer information systems, electronic data interchange (EDI), and other electronic commerce linkages allow the carrier's on-site personnel to track and expedite the shipper's goods.

Purchasing's Involvement in Transportation

Purchasing's Involvement in Logistics Decisions is Growing

The involvement of the purchasing department in transportation decisions is significant and growing as a result of the added alternatives opened up by deregulation. A 1995 study by the Center for Advanced Purchasing Studies found that in 305 large organizations, inbound traffic reported to purchasing in 51 percent of the firms, which was up from the 40 percent that had reported to purchasing seven years earlier (1988). In the case of the outbound traffic function, it reported to purchasing in 39 percent of the firms in 1995, which also was up from the 31 percent that reported to purchasing in 1988.[11] These results were in line with those of a 1991 study of 678 U.S. organizations in 29 industry groups in which it was found that in 90 percent of the firms, purchasing personnel were involved in inbound transportation activities.[12]

Trend Toward Greater Deregulation

Regulatory Reform. For about 90 years, from 1887 to 1977, the U.S. transportation industry was closely regulated under laws passed by Congress and regulations promulgated by various federal and state regulatory agencies. These laws generally were passed to ensure that transport services were available in all geographic areas and without discrimination. Since the late 1970s, a significant amount of regulation of the transportation industry has been removed in the United States. In Canada, the deregulation trend started in 1986, and the Canada Transportation Act (CTA) of 1996 is under review to assess if the CTA provides Canadians with an efficient, effective, flexible, and affordable transportation system. Transportation between and among the United States, Canada, and Mexico has been, and will continue to be, affected by the gradual implementation of the North American Free Trade Agreement (NAFTA).

Three Categories of Regulatory Reform

Changes brought about by regulatory reform can be put into three categories: (1) shipper-carrier relationships, (2) the carrier marketplace, and (3) the importance and impact of logistics decisions on the total supply chain or network. Shipper-carrier relationships: companies reducing their carrier base and forming closer relationships, including partnerships, between buy-

---

[11]Harold E. Fearon and Michiel R. Leenders, *Purchasing's Organizational Roles and Responsibilities* (Tempe, AZ: Center for Advanced Purchasing Studies, 1995), p. 19.

[12]Julie J. Gentry, *Purchasing's Involvement in Transportation Decision Making* (Tempe, AZ: Center for Advanced Purchasing Studies/National Association of Purchasing Management, 1991), p. 6.

ers and carriers; more innovative rates and services, electronic data interchange and electronic commerce, and globally aligned supply chains. The carrier marketplace: deep price discounting from new entrants; large numbers of entries and exits of carriers; competition from third-party logistics (3PL) providers; substitution of trucking for airfreight where possible; expansion of intermodal services. The importance and impact of logistics decisions: increasing importance of inbound transportation decisions; greater involvement of purchasing in logistics decision making; closer relationships between purchasing and traffic/transportation/logistics departments. The bottom line is that this new, largely deregulated transportation environment provides a substantially larger number of alternatives for the buyer.

Four Major Issues Face Decision-Makers

In the early twenty-first century, logistics decision-makers face a number of major issues related to congestion, mergers and antitrust immunity, liability, and safety regulations.

Disparate Stakeholders Difficult to Appease

Congestion. In the transportation industry, congestion, congestion, congestion sums up many of the concerns of shippers, carriers, and the general public. Resolving the concerns of these disparate stakeholders is no easy task for legislative bodies. Dealing with an aging air traffic control system; antiquated infrastructure (roads, bridges, tunnels, ports); citizens concerned about noise, traffic, and safety while also demanding low-cost goods and services from business and industry all make for interesting legislative wrangling. Stiffer environmental regulations in all three NAFTA nations as well as internationally put additional cost pressures on logistics decision-makers. (See Chapter 11 on Investment Recovery for a further discussion of environmental initiatives.)

Mergers and Antitrust Concerns. Currently, both ocean shipping and railroads are immune to antitrust laws. In March 2000, when the Canadian National and the Burlington Northern Sante Fe railroads announced plans to merge, the U.S. Surface Transportation Board (STB) declared a 15-month moratorium on rail mergers to assess the effect this might have. The Canadian government's Competition Bureau is also assessing the proposed merger's potential effects. If approved, this merger would essentially result in two dominant transcontinental railroads. Since the Staggers Rail Act was passed in 1980, there has been a steady consolidation in the rail industry, with severe service disruptions following several of the more recent mergers.

Consolidation in Rail Cause for Concern

The STB is considering "not only the direct impacts of that combination (the BNSF and CN proposed merger), but also evidence of the cumulative impacts and crossover effects that would likely occur as other railroads developed strategic responses in reaction to the proposed new system."[13] On February

---

[13]Testimony of Linda J. Morgan, Chairman of the Surface Transportation Board, before the Senate Committee on Appropriations, Subcommittee on Transportation, September 12, 2000. *www.stb.dot.gov.*

15, 2001, Canadian National Railway submitted a supplemental document to the STB regarding a NAFTA (North American Free Trade Agreement) arbitration decision concerning cross-border investments. This arbitration found that the United States was not in compliance with NAFTA when it blocked Mexican investment in trucking companies operating in the United States. It will be interesting to see how the proposed merger plays out considering the U.S.- and Canadian-government interest as well as the added wrinkle of an international trade agreement. Of equal interest is the U.S. foot-dragging on implementation of a NAFTA provision concerning Mexico-U.S. cross-border trucking operations.

Another area of concern to U.S. shippers is the five-year extension of antitrust immunity granted to motor carrier rate bureaus and the rate classification system. This primarily affects small shippers who are charged rate bureau classification rates on less-than-truckload (LTL) shipments. Large shippers negotiate discounts off class rates of as much as 70 percent. This extension was passed by Congress despite the stated intention of the Surface Transportation Board to not renew the antitrust exemption unless class rates were brought in line with market-driven rates.[14]

Cargo Liability Concerns. The growth of intermodal shipments and global business activities has made the process of determining liability a difficult task. This leads to unnecessary delays and drives costs into the process. The European Commission has set up a group of legal experts to attempt to simplify cargo liability regulations and develop a uniform, internationally accepted code. One suggestion from the EC groups is to assign responsibility to the contracting intermodal carrier. In the United States this issue has also been the subject of legal and legislative discussion, but also without any final decision. Efforts to update the U. S. Carriage of Goods at Sea Act (COGSA) to provide a single cargo-liability system were under way in 2000. This issue was slated for further discussion at the third EU-USA Forum on Freight Intermodalism scheduled for 2001. Meanwhile, shippers, carriers, and insurance providers are left to untangle things whenever loss or theft occurs.

Safety Regulations. Trucking is the dominant means of transporting goods in the United States and Canada. This probably comes as no surprise to anyone who has traveled on any major freeway system in either country. In the United States, pending rules and regulations about truck sizes and weights, and hours-of-service rules for drivers could add greatly to motor carriers' cost of doing business.

The U.S. Department of Transportation (DOT) has proposed *hours-of-service rules* about how long drivers can sit behind the wheel each day and each week. Shippers and carriers are worried that these new rules would re-

Liability Concerns are an International Issue

Proposed Hours-of-Service Rules for Truckers

---

[14]William J. Augello, "Congress' Christmas 'Present' to Shippers," *Logistics Management & Distribution Report,* February 29, 2000.

duce driver productivity, require them to redraw networks and distribution patterns, and force them to hire more drivers at a time when drivers are in short supply to start with.[15] Robert Delaney, a vice president of Cass Information Systems, estimates that the costs of these new rules could amount to $50 billion over three years. He also estimates that the resultant delays in shipping could lead to businesses carrying another $100 million in inventory and incurring another $25 million in inventory carrying costs over three years.[16] The U. S. DOT has considered imposing these work rules out of concern for highway safety and in an effort to reduce highway accidents and fatalities. On average, there are 14 deaths and 350 injuries every day of the year from truck-related crashes.[17] The annual comprehensive cost of crashes involving large trucks (gross vehicle weight rating of more than 10,000 pounds) has been estimated at more than $30 billion.[18]

Debate Over Truck Size and Weight Limits

Another area that has major cost implications for the trucking industry is *truck size and weight limits.* Driven by high fuel costs and driver shortages, truckers are looking for ways to minimize costs. Their thinking is that if the maximum weight for trucks with a sixth axle is raised from 80,000 pounds to 97,000, they will need fewer drivers and less fuel overall. Public interests groups have safety concerns about this proposal. In December 1999, the Federal Highway Administration announced a study, required by Congress in the Transportation Equity Act for the Twenty-First Century, to examine the economic, safety, and infrastructure impacts of truck weight standards on specialized hauling vehicles.

Structure of U.S. Transportation Agencies

Three Major Independent Bodies in the DOT

Department of Transportation (DOT).   The DOT, established by Congress in 1966 as an arm of the executive branch of the government, is headed by a secretary, who has cabinet status. It has responsibility for safety, systems, technology, and mass transit development. The intent of Congress was "to concentrate and allocate federal resources in order to attain an integrated national transportation system, to identify significant transportation problems, to provide executive leadership in transportation, and to provide policy guidance . . ."[19] The DOT and three major independent bodies, the

---

[15]Peter Bradley, "Motor Carriers: Half Full or Half Empty," *Logistics Management & Distribution Report,* July 2000, p. 57.

[16]Ibid.

[17]Frank N. Wilner, "Possible to Probably," *Traffic World,* August 9, 1999.

[18]Jing-Shiarn, Wang, Ronald R. Knipling, and Lawrence J. Blincoe, "The Dimensions of Motor Vehicle Crash Risk," *Journal of Transportation and Statistics,* May 1999. Found in *The Large Truck Crash Picture,* prepared by the Office of Data Analysis & Information Systems, the Federal Motor Carrier Safety Administration, and the U. S. Department of Transportation, August, 2000, *www.dot.gov.*

[19]Grant M. Davis, *The Department of Transportation* (Lexington, MA: Heath Lexington Books, 1970), p. 2.

Maritime Administration (MARAD), the Surface Transportation Board (STB), and the Federal Motor Carrier Safety Adminstration (FMCSA), administer the nation's commercial transportation industries.

MARAD Oversees Water-borne Commerce

The Maritime Administration (MARAD) "facilitates the efficient and secure movement of people and cargo in domestic and international water-borne commerce . . ."[20] Its goals are to assure national security, enhance the competitiveness of the U.S. shipyard industry, improve intermodal transportation system perfomance by applying technology and innovation, and increase the U.S. maritime industry's participation in foreign and domestic trade.

STB Facilitates Surface Transportation

Surface Transportation Board. Virtually all federal oversight of domestic barge and truck operators was eliminated with the closeout of the Interstate Commerce Commission, and the STB took over. The mission of the STB is "to facilitate commerce by providing an effective forum for efficient dispute resolution and facilitation of appropriate market-based business transactions."[21] Commercial freight issues that come before the board include railroad rate and service issues, rail restructuring transactions (mergers, line sales, line construction, and line abandonment) and rail-related labor matters; certain trucking and ocean shipping rate matters; and certain pipeline matters not regulated by the Federal Energy Regulatory Commission.

FMCSA Works to Prevent Commercial Vehicle Fatalities and Injuries

The Federal Motor Carrier Safety Administration (FMCSA), formerly a part of the Federal Highway Administration, was established within the Department of Transportation in January 2000 to prevent commercial motor vehicle-related fatalities and injuries. FMCSA focuses on strong enforcement of safety regulations, targeting of high-risk carriers and commercial motor vehicle drivers, improving safety information systems and commercial motor vehicle technologies, strengthening motor vehicle equipment and operating standards, and increasing safety awareness.

Structure of Canadian Transportation Agencies

Four Groups within Transport Canada

Transport Canada. Transport Canada is the department in the federal government responsible for developing and administering policies, regulations, and services for the best possible transportation system (commercial and freight) for Canada. Four groups, the Policy Group, the Safety and Security Group, the Programs and Divestiture Group, and the Support Group, work within Transport Canada at the headquarters in Ottawa.

---

[20]Department of Transportation, Maritime Administration, *www.marad.dot.gov.*
[21]The Surface Transportation Board, Who's Who and What Does it Do?, *www.stb.dot.gov.*

The Policy Group sets departmental strategic policy, and policies related to trade and rail, highways, motor carrier and air transportation; and assesses overall transportation system performance.

The Safety and Security Group is responsible for developing and enforcing regulations for marine, rail safety, transport of dangerous goods, motor carrier safety and vehicle emissions.

The Programs and Divestiture Group is responsible for the transfer of ports, harbours, and airports to communities; the oversight and lease management of divested properties; the operation of state-owned properties; and environmental, technical, and real property management.

The Support Group, which includes Corporate Services, Communications, and Departmental General Counsel, provides overall support to carry out the work of Transport Canada. In addition, Transport Canada has five regional offices and numerous local centers.

The TSB Advances Transport Safety

Transportation Safety Board (TSB).   The TSB was created by the Canadian Transportation Investigation and Safety Board Act of 1989 to provide a legal framework for advancing safety in marine, rail, pipeline, and aviation.

Transportation Industry Segments

Air Cargo Deregulated

Air Cargo Industry.   Deregulation of the air cargo industry gave carriers the right to serve additional markets, revise schedules, adjust rates, and set tariffs at any level they wish. It also allowed air cargo carriers to own a motor carrier and to apply for an all-cargo certificate, regardless of prior experience.

Trends in Air Passenger Industry

Air Passenger Industry.   The law deregulating the air passenger traffic industry was passed in 1978 (Public Law 95–504, the Airline Deregulation Act). It led to the elimination of restrictions on pricing and routes, began the elimination of the Civil Aeronautics Board (CAB), and allowed totally free entry into and exit from the airline business. The result was a world of competition from new, low-cost entrants. We have seen, and will probably continue to see, consolidation of the major airlines. Dallas-based Southwest Airlines, the eighth largest airline in the United States, has been consistently profitable through a strategy of low-cost, no-frills service and narrow-body planes. Other airlines are now imitating Southwest. There is a move toward narrow-body aircraft, shorter turnaround time on the ground, and point-to-point service. These changes impact the passenger airlines' ability to provide cargo service. Narrow bodies mean freight must be handled in bulk rather than containers; there is less space for cargo; and there is less ground time to transfer freight. The result is higher handling costs and increased risk of delay and damage. Consider what this has meant for the U.S. Postal Service, which relies on commercial carriers to move mail and cargo, versus a company like Federal Express that owns its own airplanes.

Motor Freight Industry.   Trucking has undergone many changes since passage of the Motor Carrier Act of 1980. In the short term, the buyer has realized major benefits through a wider variety of price/service options and greater competition in pricing. There are more trucks and trucking firms competing for the same freight, but there is not enough freight for everyone to be profitable. Within 10 years of passage of the Motor Carrier Act of 1980, the number of carriers had more than doubled. The shakeout in the trucking industry continues into the early twenty-first century with bankruptcies and the consolidation of carriers. For example, as of 1991 only 10 of the 60 largest less-than-truckload (LTL) carriers from 1968 were still in business.[22]

The Shakeout in Trucking Continues

Purpose of Regulatory Reform

It was the intent of Congress in passing the Motor Carrier Act that this ambitious law would conserve energy and provide more cost-effective service to benefit the buyer. The law eliminated rules requiring carriers to take circuitous routes or to stop at intermediate points; it allowed trucks to make pickups and deliveries at intermediate stops along their routes; it allowed greater ease of entry into the industry and required less documentation for certification. The ICC granted a certificate to anyone who supplied a useful service, unless it found that the service would be inconsistent with present or future public convenience. The "Declaration of National Transportation Policy" was amended to state that the goal is "to promote competitive and efficient motor transportation" and "to allow a variety of quality and price options to meet the changing market demands and diverse requirements of the shipping public."

Problems Since Partial Deregulation

The Negotiated Rates Act of 1994 (NRA94) sought to remedy some of the problems created by the partial deregulation of motor carriers under the Motor Carrier Act of 1980. After 1980, carriers and shippers were allowed to negotiate rates, which then were to be filed with the ICC. In the rush of entrants into the trucking industry after deregulation in 1980, many carriers failed to file the lower negotiated rates with the ICC. As carrier bankruptcies increased, shippers were being held to claims of undercharges because the lower negotiated rates had not been filed with the ICC. The Supreme Court held in *Maislin Industries* v. *Primary Steel* that filed rates were paramount and allowed bankruptcy trustees to collect for undercharges as far back as five years. The Negotiated Rates Act and the Trucking Industry Regulatory Reform Act (TIRRA) of 1994 provided some relief for shippers by allowing for negotiated rates and establishing claims procedures for undercharges. The NRA also requires that a written agreement must be in place, separate from the bill of lading receipt, signifying that a legal agreement exists for a long-term relationship between a shipper and carrier for a series of shipments. Without a properly prepared contract, the ICC could find the contract invalid, resulting in undercharge claims.

---

[22]Frank Reagan, "How LTL Carriers Set Rates," *Inbound Logistics,* January 1991, p. 22.

Mergers Have Reduced the Number of Rail Freight Carriers

Railroad Industry.   The Staggers Rail Act of 1980 was intended to enable the railroads to compete more fully with one another and with trucks and barge lines. It allowed faster rate changes; intermodal transport (rail and truck, for example); the ability to enter into long-term rate and service contracts with shippers; expedited abandonment and merger procedures; and deregulated piggyback service. Since the Staggers Act, mergers have reduced the number of major rail-freight carriers from 13 in 1978 to 7 major railroads and 2 regionals in the United States, and 2 major railroads in Canada in 2000. The 1995 merger of Burlington Northern and Santa Fe Railway (BNSF) created the largest rail system in the United States, with 31,000 miles of track crossing the West, Midwest, and South. In May 2000, BNSF and the Norfolk Southern Railway Company announced nonstop transcontinental intermodal service between the West Coast, the Southwest, and the Southeastern United States. In late 1999, BNSF and Canadian National Railway announced plans to merge. This action led both the Canadian Competition Bureau and the U.S. Surface Transportation Board to put things on hold until analysis is done on the impact of having only two dominant transcontinental railroads.

Impact on Service Levels

The consolidation of railroads has had a negative impact on service quality levels, with shippers reporting an on-time performance of 70 percent or less in 2000.[23] Service disruptions affected shippers and carriers in 1997 when Union Pacific absorbed Southern Pacific and in 2000 when Norfolk Southern and CSX Transportation divided up Conrail. Successfully integrating disparate systems has proven to be a major challenge for the rail industry and is a key driver in the holdup of the BNSF and CN merger. For example, Norfolk Southern's income from rail operations dropped 32 percent in 2000 as it struggled to absorb part of the Conrail system.[24] Despite spending tens of millions of dollars on integration, resulting service problems led many shippers to switch to motor carriers. In addition to consolidation woes, the rail industry faces rising costs from union wage increases and high fuel costs.

FOB Terms and Incoterms

FOB and FAS Defined

The term FOB stands for *free on board,* meaning that goods are delivered to a specified point with all transport charges paid. The specific responsibilities of the seller and buyer in the United States under the terms FOB and FAS, *free alongside ship,* are covered in Article 2-319 of the *Uniform Commercial Code.* There are several variations in FOB terms, as Figure 10–1 shows. Articles 2-320 to 2-324, address other delivery terms. Shipping terms and the

---

[23]Peter Bradley, "Railroads: Merger Debate Continues," *Logistics Management & Distribution Report,* July 2000, p. 66.
[24]Ibid., p. 64.

FIGURE 10–1

FOB Terms and Responsibilities

FOB Term	Payment of Freight Charges	Bears Freight Charges	Owns Goods in Transit	Files Claims (if any)	Explanation
FOB origin, or FOB freight collect	Buyer	Buyer	Buyer	Buyer	Title and control of goods passes to buyer when carrier signs for goods at point of origin
FOB origin, freight prepaid	Seller	Seller	Buyer	Buyer	
FOB origin, freight prepaid and charged back	Seller	Buyer	Buyer	Buyer	Seller pays freight charges and adds to invoice
FOB destination, freight collect	Buyer	Buyer	Seller	Seller	Title remains with seller until goods are delivered
FOB destination, freight prepaid	Seller	Seller	Seller	Seller	
FOB destination, freight prepaid and charged back	Seller	Buyer	Seller	Seller	Seller pays freight charges and adds to invoice
FOB destination, freight collect and allowed	Buyer	Seller	Seller	Seller	Buyer pays freight charges and deducts from seller's invoice

responsibilities of buyer and seller in international contracts are covered by Incoterms (see Chapter 14), which were first originated in 1936 by the International Chamber of Commerce (ICC) and continue to be updated by the ICC. Already recognized as the international standard by custom authorities and courts in all the main trading nations, Incoterms gained greater prominence when in July 2000 the United Nations Commission on International Trade Law recommended worldwide use of them in international trade transactions.[25]

FOB Point Determines Four Things

The selection of the FOB point is important to the purchaser, for it determines four things:

1. Who pays the carrier.
2. When legal title to goods being shipped passes to the buyer.
3. Who is responsible for preparing and pursuing claims with the carrier in the event goods are lost or damaged during shipment.
4. Who routes the freight.

---

[25]Press release from the International Chamber of Commerce, *UN Body Commends Incoterms 2000*, July 19, 2000.

The claim that FOB destination is always preferable because the seller pays the transportation charges is incorrect. While the seller may pay the transportation charges, in the final analysis the charges are borne by the buyer, because transportation costs will be included in the delivered price charged by the supplier. In effect, if the buyer lets the supplier make the transportation decisions, then the buyer is allowing the supplier to spend the buyer's money.

Variation in FOB Terms

In purchases from international suppliers, FOB is an Incoterm meaning Free On Board (Named Port of Shipment), and the seller passes title to the goods to the buyer when the goods are passed over the rail of the ship. The ocean carrier typically does not provide any insurance on goods in transit; therefore, it is important when goods are bought FOB origin for the buyer to ensure that adequate insurance coverage is provided. The two marine freight terms commonly used are *CFR* and *CIF. CFR, cost and freight,* is similar to FOB origin, with freight charges paid by the seller. However, under CFR the buyer assumes all risk and should provide for insurance. *CIF, cost, insurance, and freight,* means that the seller will pay the freight charges and provide appropriate insurance coverage. This is similar to FOB destination, freight prepaid. In some instances, the buyer may wish to obtain equalization of freight charges with the nearest shipping point of the seller, or some competitive shipping point. In that case, the following clause can be used: "Freight charges to be equalized with those applicable from seller's shipping point producing lowest transportation cost to buyer's destination."

Freight Classification

Proper classification of freight shipments is of primary importance in the purchase of transportation services. Shippers are responsible for knowing the specific description of the merchandise being moved, and this classification determines the applicable tariff, or freight rate. For example, the gauge of steel being shipped determines the appropriate freight classification; if the wrong classification is indicated, it literally can make a difference of thousands of dollars in freight charges on a large shipment. These commodity word descriptions must be used in shipping orders and bills of lading and must conform to those in the applicable tariff, including packing specifications, where different rates are provided for the same article according to the manner in which it is packed for shipment. Failure to use the correct classification description will result in the carrier assessing an incorrect rate and possibly result in a charge that the shipper is fraudulently classifying shipments to get unwarranted low rates.

Incorrect Classifications May Result in Additional Charges

Four Characteristics of Classifications

Classifications for rate-making purposes are driven by four main characteristics: *density,* weight per cubic foot; *stowability,* excessive weight or length, stackable, and freight configuration; *handling,* special equipment, and extra personnel; and *liability,* value per pound, and risk of damage or pilferage.[26] The transportation buyer should be especially concerned with the classification of the freight for which he or she is contracting for transport. Appeals for a rate reduction to a National Classification Committee Classification Panel must indicate the similarities between your product and the industrywide average of products in that class.

Uniform Classification System

The Uniform Freight Classification for railroads and the National Motor Freight Classification (NMFC) provide a uniform classification system that can be updated as needed. Class rates are the freight rates that apply to all the goods or commodities grouped under that general class heading. Most articles are shipped under a "class rating," which is the normal freight classification, which then determines the applicable freight rate. Many raw materials move under "commodity rates," which normally are lower than class rates. Since deregulation, most rates are established or changed through negotiations between shippers and carriers.

Selection of Mode and Carrier

Normally, the buyer will wish to specify how purchased items are to be shipped; this is the buyer's legal right if the purchase has been made under any of the FOB origin terms. If the purchaser has received superior past service from a particular carrier, it then becomes the preferable means of shipment.

Buyers Normally Want to Specify Carrier

As one would expect, buyers are most concerned that the supplier (carrier) meet its delivery promises (deliver on schedule) and provide the movement service without damaging the goods. On the other hand, if the buyer has relatively little expertise in the traffic area and the supplier has a skilled logistics department, it might be wise to rely on the supplier's judgment in carrier selection and routing. Also, in a time of shortage of transport equipment (railroad cars, trucks, or drivers), the supplier may have better information about the local situation and what arrangements will get the best results. And, if the item to be shipped has special dimensional characteristics, requiring special rail cars, the supplier may be in a better position to know what's available and the clearances needed for proper shipment.

Inherent Advantages of Different Transport Modes

Each form of common carrier transportation—for example, rail, truck, air, and inland water—has its own distinct advantages for shippers in respect to speed, available capacity, flexibility, and cost. By the same token, each mode has inherent disadvantages. For example, comparing air with truck transport, air

---

[26]Ray Bohman, "Is the Classification on Your Products Outdated?" *Logistics Management & Distribution Report,* July 1999.

has the advantage in terms of speed; truck transport can accommodate greater volume and has lower rates and greater flexibility in terms of delivery points. The astute buyer must recognize such advantages/limitations and arrive at the best overall balance, considering the needs of the organization.

Mode of Transport

Selecting Mode of Transport is First Step

The first step is to determine the mode of transport—rail, truck, air, or water—which will best meet the transport requirement. Within each surface transportation mode, regulated carriers are further defined as Class I, II, or III based upon annual operating revenues. Revenue thresholds are: Class I: motor carriers of property, $5 million; railroads, $50 million; and motor carriers of passengers, $3 million; Class II: motor carriers of property, $1–$5 million; railroads, $10 million–$50 million; and motor carriers of passengers, under $3 million; and Class III: motor carriers of property, $1 million; and railroads, $10 million.

Most studies show that service reliability (on-time performance) is the primary consideration when selecting a mode of transportation.[27]

Freight Terminals

Four Types of Terminals

Four types of terminals are in common use: (1) pickup and delivery, (2) breakbulk, (3) relay, and (4) interlining. The person who selects motor carriers and routes needs to be familiar with the various types of carriers and systems for movement in order to choose the best combination(s).

Motor Carriers

Three Categories of Motor Carriers

Motor carriers can be divided into several categories: (1) less-than-truckload (LTL), (2) truckload (TL), and (3) small parcel, ground. The trucking industry in general is facing a number of cost pressures already discussed in this chapter. These are brought on by driver recruitment and retention problems, possible hours-of-service rules that restrict driver work time, rising insurance and interest costs, rising fuel costs, and overcapacity problems in the event of an economic downturn.

Less-than-Truckload (LTL) Carriers.   In the late 1990s and early twenty-first century, service options were plentiful and rates were competitive. Overlapping services of regional and national LTL carriers increased competition and helped shippers. On the other hand, shippers' use of premium ground services instead of airfreight and the trend toward smaller, more frequent shipments helped LTL carriers and small-parcel carriers.

---

[27]Julie J. Gentry, *Purchasing's Involvement,* op. cit., p. 7; and Peter Bradley "Railroads: Merger Debate Continues," *Logistics Management & Distribution Report,* July 2000, p. 66.

Truckload (TL) Carriers.   Truckload carriers provide an empty trailer and the shipper fills it with goods. There is no classification, and the charge simply is based on miles and service. Shippers are developing the concept of the core carrier as they rationalize or reduce their supply base of carriers, and TL contract carriers are pursuing their substitution for private fleets as companies seek to improve efficiencies through outsourcing. TL carriers want to provide the inbound and outbound over-the-road movement for a particular company, but some also are offering a full-service logistics package (warehousing, inventory management, audit and payment, EDI, and MIS systems integration).

The interstate trucking deregulation will reduce the need for some inventory and warehouses put in place earlier because of regulation. Contract logistics and time-based competition opportunities will increase for TL carriers. The North American Free Trade Act (NAFTA) also opens the possibility of transborder operations, and carriers are working out cooperative arrangements to capitalize on NAFTA. Another piece of the TL market is the movement of goods within the United States that are part of a larger international movement of goods.

Problem of Driver Recruitment and Retention

One area of concern for long-haul operators is the persistent driver recruitment and retention problem that has resulted in idle equipment (for example, an $80,000 asset sitting in the yard for lack of a driver) and difficulty in meeting delivery promises. This puts pressure on operators to increase wages and benefits for drivers and to find ways to make the job more attractive for drivers who spend weeks at a time on the road.

Rail Carriers and Intermodal Shipments

Following partial deregulation of the railroads in 1980, rates dropped, and productivity, profitability, and service quality improved as a result of a huge decrease in the work force, shedding of unprofitable lines, and improvements in fuel efficiency and plant and equipment. However, the mergers and acquisitions in the rail industry in the 1990s resulted in huge service disruptions that sent many shippers back to the trucking sector.

Intermodal Defined

Intermodal business—the movement of goods in trailers or containers via rail coupled with at least one other transport mode, such as truck or air—has increased due in large part to increased reliability from technological and operational improvements. To be competitive with other shipping modes, the railroads have developed special equipment and services. Piggyback service—where truck trailers are loaded on special rail cars for long-distance shipment—and containerization—where specially designed containers are loaded, delivered by rail or truck to a wharf, hoisted on board a ship, and then offloaded onto rail or truck carriers for shipments to their final destination—are examples of innovations in shipping methods. Since piggyback service was completely deregulated in 1980, attractive arrangements often are possible, and growth in piggybacking has been substantial.

The 1994 Teamsters union contract allows LTL carriers to double the amount of intermodal business they do with the railways. Although growth has been tempered by equipment shortages and clogged yards, the prospects are excellent for continued growth in this area.

However, railroads still suffer from an image of long transit times and poor service. Shippers question whether rail can meet time-definite and flexibility requirements. Computers and state-of-the-art technology boost efficiency in equipment transfers, and dead time in yards is down. AC-traction locomotives require fewer costly power units and increase speed and reliability. Double-stack and even triple-stack trains are used for high-density freight, and road railers, equipped with both rail wheels and truck tires, are finding a niche.

Air Carriers

Integrated Carriers Dominate U.S. Domestic Air Freight

Changes in the air cargo industry include more integrated carriers serving both the package express markets and heavy air cargo; passenger airlines, often allied with forwarders, competing for cargo; rapidly expanding international markets; and further consolidation of airfreight forwarders.[28] In 1994, integrated carriers (truck-air) like UPS and Federal Express controlled 60 percent of the tonnage and 77 percent of the revenue of the U.S. domestic airfreight market, up from 55.5 percent of tonnage in 1993.[29] Scheduled passenger airlines have been unable to capture much of the domestic airfreight market due to trends toward narrow-body aircraft, quick turnaround at airports, tightening capacity, and globalization of many carriers and privatization of foreign carriers. In the international airfreight market, scheduled passenger carriers in partnership with airfreight forwarders are still in demand since they offer the expertise of the forwarder and a cost advantage compared to foreign cargo carriers.

Time-Definite and Time-Deferred Services Defined

Integrated carriers also have been able to meet the growing demand for time-definite and deferred services. Time-definite means getting the goods where they need to be when the shipper wants them there, but it does not necessarily mean overnight. Deferred services refers to the use of ground transportation for airfreight products in situations where integrated carriers like UPS, Roadway, and Landair offer faster, reliable transportation. Growth in deferred services grew by 23 percent in 1994 compared to a 13 percent growth in overnight services.[30] Shippers are able to generate the savings of JIT inventory management without relying on overnight services due to carrier improvements in efficiency.

---

[28]Toby B. Gooley, "Air Carriers: The Urge to Merge," *Logistics Management and Distribution Report,* July 2000, p. 73.

[29]Colography Group, "Losing Control at High Altitude," *Distribution,* July 1995, p. 69.

[30]Marcia Jedd, "Losing Control at High Altitude," *Distribution,* July 1995, p. 62.

Expedited Transportation

**Expedited
Transportation
Defined**

Expedited transportation refers to any shipment that requires pickup service and includes a specific delivery guarantee. In the United States this is typically less than five days. Although shipments may move via domestic air, ground parcel, less-than-truckload, or air-export services, in 1999 about 95 percent of the cargo was shipped domestic ground parcel (51.4 percent) and domestic air (43.7 percent).[31]

Small-Shipment Services

**Growth of
Express
Markets Is
Exploding**

Under deregulation, competition for small-shipment services (now defined as 150 lbs. or less) has become intense. Buyers now can use some of the standard purchasing techniques, such as systems contracts, aggressive negotiation, multiple sourcing, quotation analysis, target pricing, and vendor evaluation, to get better purchasing arrangements with carriers. Traditional airfreight growth has slowed to 6 percent a year, while the growth of express markets is about 25 to 40 percent a year. Competition is intense among express carriers as they move to cross over into the heavy-lift air cargo market. The emerging integrated carriers, those with their own aircraft like Federal Express, are capturing a larger share of the market. Volume discounts, bar code tracking systems, and ground networks are the distinguishing factors.[32]

Same-Day Service

**Same-Day
Service
Growing**

Another growth area is same-day service, which is being developed by express carriers such as Seattle-based Airborne Express' subsidiary, Sky Courier, and Irvine, California-based Burlington Air Express' international next-flight-out service. The same-day niche is growing rapidly and expanding into the international market. The entrance of UPS and Federal Express into the same-day service sector will increase visibility and market size. The users of same-day service range from the entertainment, advertising, and legal industries to manufacturers. The same-day service is used when the cost of not having a critical part or document is greater than the amount (sometimes as low as $159) spent on same-day service.[33]

---

[31]The Colography Group's U.S. Expedited Cargo Market Projections for CY2000 found in "It's the Highway Not the Skyway," by James Aaron Cooke, *Logistics Management and Distribution Report,* October 1, 2000.

[32]Peter Bradley, "Rapid Transition Marks the Industry," op. cit., pp. 71–73.

[33]Tony Dollar, "The Faster Mode Gets Faster," *Distribution,* July 1995, p. 70.

Forwarders and Brokers

Competition Among Forwarders is Intense

Airfreight forwarders are marketing and operations organizations that move air cargo. They may own (although most do not) or lease aircraft or buy dedicated space on scheduled carriers. Consolidation of air forwarders is occurring as shippers demand linkages between their supply and distribution channels and worldwide transportation networks. Successful airfreight forwarders offer warehousing, freight forwarding, and customs clearance services. Integrated carriers are making forays into the air forwarders' market domestically, but most integrated carriers still concede to the expertise of forwarders in the international market. As the passenger carriers' share of the cargo business decreases, the competition among forwarders intensifies.

Surface (domestic) freight forwarders consolidate small shipments into rail cars and piggyback trailers and operate large fleets of trucks for pickup and delivery. Many are also brokers. Freight brokers find loads for carriers or trucks for shippers. Foreign freight forwarders operate internationally. Custom house brokers collect duties, clear shipments, and provide information for importers. Nonvessel-owning common carriers (NVOCCs) provide the less-than-container-load (LCL) equivalent of LTL motor carriers and are most competitive in consolidating small shipments into a container and delivering it.

Ocean Carriers and Ports

Example of a Shippers' Association

The Ocean Shipping Reform Act of 1998 continued the trend of deregulation in ocean shipping by allowing shippers to negotiate rates and services with individual carriers across multiple trade lanes and to form buying consortia of unaffiliated shippers, consolidators, and freight forwarders. Since the act went into effect, a number of innovations have been seen in the ocean shipping industry, including the formation of shippers' associations, the beginnings of contract logistics services, and online auctions. For example, DuPont Global Logistics joined forces with BDP International, a freight forwarder, to form a shippers' association for small shippers to consolidate volume. Maersk-Sealand and APL have both developed contract logistics subsidiaries with international operations. Other ocean carriers, either in isolation or in partnership with an existing third-party logistics service provider, are also developing contract logistics capabilities. Online

Online Auctions Used Successfully

auctions have been used to speed up the RFP process by allowing shippers to post an RFP electronically and then compare bids and make a selection in hours rather than days. The electronic bid system has worked well for smaller and midsized shippers, freight forwarders looking for rates and service for their clients, and those with spot shipments and/or shipments to unfamiliar destinations. As with other online auction applications, shippers and carriers are sorting out when auctions are effective and when long-term relationships and direct negotiations are more advantageous. Technology will continue to be used to cut transaction costs and increase information availability; more mergers are likely; and changing fuel and operating costs will continue to impact rates.[34]

Vessel-Sharing Agreements Signal Carrier Consolidation

Vessel-sharing agreements (VSAs) have brought cooperation among ocean carriers on the inland side and may lead to joint purchases of container ships and sharing inland terminals and space on double-stack trains. The VSAs signal the growing dominance of a few carriers and fewer service options for shippers. In the United States, the consolidation of carriers has resulted in a consolidation of service calls at ports. Superports must be able to accommodate larger container ships and have the operational space to handle the growing number of containers. Because new facilities in the United States are usually built with public monies, it is difficult in tough fiscal times to fund the facilities improvements. Environmental issues preventing or slowing dredging to make ports viable also has hindered port growth in the United States.

Factors Determining Choice of Carrier

Carrier Selection. After determining the mode of transport, a decision must be made on a specific carrier and the specific routing of the shipment. The 1991 CAPS study found that the most influential factor in determining choice of carrier is on-time deliveries (25 percent of total possible ranking points); followed by rates (18 percent); geographic coverage, and time in transit (each 10 percent); shipment tracing, and care in handling (each 6 percent); financial condition of carrier (5 percent); door-to-door deliveries (4 percent); through routing, type of equipment, and convenient schedules (each 3 percent); handling of claims (2 percent); and insurance coverage, shipment consolidation, EDI capabilities, consolidating/breaking capabilities, and other factors (each at 1 percent).[35] This information should be part of the purchase order. The buyer then may wish to keep track of the freight movement to ensure that it is going as planned.

Because more carriers are available since deregulation, the buyer now can use a variety of transportation directories, similar to the standard supplier selection directories, to develop an initial list of alternatives. For ex-

Transportation Directories

ample, the *Inbound Traffic Guide* contained in the *Thomas Register of American Manufacturers* is an annual directory of approximately 500 pages that simplifies the identification of firms in the transportation area: air express/expedited package services; airlines, domestic and international; bulk transfer facilities; customs house brokers; export packing services; freight consolidation; freight forwarding; freight forwarding, foreign; inland water transportation; ocean carriers; ports; public warehouses; railroads; shippers' associations; software; special equipment carriers; transportation brokers; and trucking.[36] A similar directory is published by Chilton in its *Distribu-*

---

[34]Toby B. Gooley, "Ocean Shipping: Surprises Dead Ahead," *Logistics Management & Distribution Report,* pp. 79–83.

[35]Julie J. Gentry, *Purchasing's Involvement,* op. cit., p. 7.

[36]*1996 Inbound Traffic Guide,* Vol. 30 of *Thomas Register of American Manufacturers,* 86th ed. (New York: Thomas Publishing Co., 1996).

tion magazine, listing motor carriers, ocean carriers, airport facilities, North American ports, airfreight and small package express services, rail services, and commercial warehousing.[37] *Purchasing* magazine also publishes an annual *Purchasing Transportation Sourcing Guide.*[38]

Factors Influencing Mode, Carrier and Routing

The factors to be considered when selecting mode of shipment, carrier, and routing include the following:

Required Delivery Time May Drive Mode Selection

Required Delivery Time.   The required date for material receipt may make the selection of mode of shipment quite simple. If two-day delivery from a distant point is needed, the only viable alternative probably is air shipment. If more time is available, other modes can be considered. Most carriers can supply estimates of normal delivery times, and the purchaser also can rely on past experience with particular modes and carriers. Time-definite services are in demand as organizations focus on time-based competition and JIT inventory management systems.

Dimensions of Service

Reliability and Service Quality.   While two carriers may offer freight service between the same points, their reliability and dependability may differ greatly. One carrier may: (1) be more attentive to customer needs; (2) be more dependable in living up to its commitments; (3) incur less damage, overall, to merchandise shipped; and (4) in general be the best freight supplier. The buyer's past experience is the best indicator of service quality.

Available Services.   If the item to be shipped is large and bulky, a particular mode of transportation may be required. Special container requirements may indicate only certain carriers who have the unique equipment to handle the job. As the demand for third-party logistics services grows, shippers want services like warehousing and inventory management in addition to transportation services. Managing the links in the supply chain means more sophisticated carriers.

Type of Item Being Shipped.   Bulk liquids, for example, may indicate railroad tank car, barge, or pipeline. Also, the safety requirements for hazardous materials may make certain carriers and routings impractical or illegal.

Shipment Size.   Items of small size and bulk can be moved by the U.S. Postal Service, and companies such as Federal Express and United Parcel Service, or airfreight forwarders. Larger shipments probably can be moved more economically by rail or truck.

---

[37]*Distribution,* July 1995 and later issues.
[38]"Purchasing's Transportation Sourcing Guide 1995," *Purchasing,* (Newton, MA).

Possibility of Damage.   Certain items, such as fine china or electronics equipment, by their nature have a high risk of damage in shipment. In this case, the buyer may select a mode and carrier by which the shipment can come straight through to its destination, with no transfers at distribution points to another carrier. It is part of the buyer's responsibility to ensure that the packaging of goods is appropriate for both the contents and mode of transport.

Cost of the Transport Service.   The buyer should select the mode, carrier, and routing that will provide for the safe movement of goods, within the required time, at the lowest total transport cost. This requires a thorough knowledge of freight classifications and tariffs. Also, the buyer may make certain trade-offs in purchasing transportation, just as trade-offs are made in selecting suppliers for other purchases.

Carrier Financial Situation.   If any volume of freight is moved, some damages will be incurred, resulting in claims against the carrier. Should the carrier get into financial difficulty, or even become insolvent, collection on claims becomes a problem. Therefore, the buyer should avoid those carriers who are on the margin financially. While in an era of deregulation there are many new entrants in the transportation industry, there also are many exits, and the number of bankruptcies—combined with changes in the laws and regulations governing transportation—may cause shippers to get hit with undercharge bills years after the service was provided.

Handling of Claims.   Inevitably, some damage claims will arise in the shipment of quantities of merchandise. Prompt and efficient investigation and settlement of claims is another key factor in carrier selection.

Carrier Rating Systems.   Also, because now the buyer is not "locked in" to only certain carriers but can elect to change carriers or split business among competing carriers, it is important, at least for those 20 percent of the carriers with which the firm does 80 percent of its transport volume, that some formal system for rating carrier performance be developed and used. An example of a simple form developed by one company to assist plants and the corporate office to evaluate their experiences with each carrier is shown in Figure 10–2.

Private or Leased Carrier Defined

Private or Leased Carriers.   One alternative to using a common carrier might be to use private or leased equipment. A private carrier or a leased carrier does not offer service to the general public. Many companies have elected to contract for exclusive use of equipment; and some have established their own trucking fleet through use of either company-owned or leased tractors and vans.

FIGURE 10–2

Carrier Rating Form

Carrier name: _____ Date: _____

Business allocation decision (circle one)

	Decline	Status quo	Growth

Areas rated:

1. Branch/plant

    a. Tracing, expediting (0-5): responds quickly, accurately.

    b. Pickup and delivery service (0-10): reliable, on schedule, customer service-oriented.

    c. Loss and damage (0-5): incidence, reconciles discrepancies quickly, good controls.

    d. Transit time reliability (0-10): service performance, customer satisfaction.

    e. Equipment condition (0-10): in proper repair, placards available.

    f. Special service and innovativeness (0-10): provides trailer spotting when requested, trailer pools, provides special pickups and deliveries.

2. Corporate

    a. Billing (0-5): accuracy, submits original freight bills.

    b. Financial (0-15): quick, debt/worth, operating ratios, trends, mergers, ownership.

    c. Service (0-10): interface tracing, expediting, general carrier cooperation.

    d. Claims ratio (0-10): payment or claim resolution history, loss and damage control program.

    e. Data inquiry (0-15): automated systems, agreeable interface.

    f. Innovativeness (0-5): industry leader, new ideas, distribution-oriented.

    g. Pricing (0-5): willingness to negotiate, independent action, alerts shipper.

Advantages and Disadvantages of Leasing

Leasing gives the firm much greater flexibility in scheduling freight services. It can be economically advantageous, but unless the equipment can be fully utilized through planned back-hauls of either semifinished or finished goods, it may turn out to be more costly than use of the common carrier system. Also, it is important that the firm recognize and provide adequate protection against the very substantial dollar liability that may result in the case of an accident.

Under deregulation, the use of private or leased vehicles is a much more viable alternative and is a type of make-or-buy decision. The regulations covering use of private or leased equipment have been relaxed to permit firms with wholly owned subsidiaries to engage in intercorporate hauling and to back-haul product, which may provide the volume needed to make this alternative economically worthwhile.

Freight Rates

Classification Drives Freight Rates

The charges for freight movement are determined by the classification of the item transported and the appropriate rate tariff. The tariffs of common carriers are publicly available to any interested party, although they are voluminous and difficult to read and interpret except by someone skilled in rate analysis. With deregulation, rate changes occur more frequently, and many carriers have their own, separate tariffs.

The basic charge is determined by the class rate, although lower commodity rates can be arranged for some items. Additional variations are available, provided the shipper is knowledgeable and innovative enough to obtain them.

Quantity Breaks. As with other purchases, carriers (suppliers) offer lower rates if the quantity of an individual shipment is large enough. Both rail and motor carriers offer discounts for full carload (CL) or truckload (TL) shipments. These will be substantially less per pound than less-than-carload (LCL) or less-than-truckload (LTL) quantities. If the shipper can consolidate smaller shipments to the same destination, a lower rate may be available (called a *pool car*). In some instances, shippers may band together through a shippers' association to get pool car transport rates.

Unit Train Defined

The unit train is another innovation by which the shipper gets a quantity discount. By special arrangement with a railroad, a utility company, for example, is provided one or more complete trains, consisting of 100-plus coal cars, that run shuttle between the coal mine and the utility's place of use. This speeds up the movement, and the materials are moved at an advantageous commodity rate. Also, under the Staggers Rail Act of 1980, shippers now can enter into long-term price and service contracts directly with a railroad.

Types of Rate Discounts

Under the pricing flexibility granted by the Motor Carrier Act of 1980, four basic types of rate discounts have developed; the buyer in some instances can take advantage of one or more of them and possibly enjoy substantial savings. They are:

1. *Aggregate Tender Rates.* This provides a discount if the shipper will group multiple small shipments for pickup or delivery at one point.

2. *Flat Percentage Discount.* This provides a discount to the shipper if a specified total minimum weight of less-than-truckload shipments is moved per month. This encourages the shipper to group volume with one carrier.

3. *Increased Volume-Increased Discount Percentage.* Discount (sometimes, even as high as 50 percent) is applied if a firm increases its volume of LTL shipments by a certain amount over the previous month's volume.

4. ***Specific Origin and Destination Points.*** This provides a specified discount if volume from a specified point to a specified delivery point reaches a given level.

Released Rates. The common carrier assumes liability for the full value of the goods shipped, unless damage occurs due to acts of God; shipper negligence; acts of public authority, such as governmental seizure of goods; or the inherent nature of the goods, such as self-igniting chemicals. However, the shipper may negotiate a released rate, which is a lower than normal rate, if it is willing to accept a lower than full liability for damage on the part of the carrier. The shipper must assess the relationship between the lower rate and the risk of damage. It may decide to carry a separate insurance policy to protect against the increased risk of damage.

Documentation in Freight Shipments

Bill of Lading Defined

The bill of lading (B/L) is the key document in the movement of goods. The bill has been standardized and carriers are responsible for issuing a proper bill, although in practice it normally is prepared by the shipper. The original copy of the B/L describes the shipment and is a receipt by the carrier for the goods. Signed by both the shipper's and carrier's agents, it is proof that shipment was made and is evidence of ownership. It is a contract and fixes carrier liability; normally it will be kept by the party who has title to goods in transit, for it must be provided to support any damage claims. Copy 2, the Shipping Order, is retained by the carrier and is used as shipping instructions and as a basis for billing. As with most other documentation, electronic versions and online systems management is common in many organizations.

Variations on the Bill of Lading

There are several variations on the B/L:

1. *Uniform Straight Bill of Lading:* This is the complete B/L and contains the complete contract terms and conditions.

2. *Straight Bill of Lading—Short Form:* Contains those provisions uniform to both motor and rail. Short bills are not furnished by carriers but instead are pre-printed by shippers.

3. *Unit Bill of Lading:* This is prepared in four copies; the extra copy is the railroad's way-bill. This way-bill moves with the shipment and may be of assistance in expediting freight movement.

4. *Uniform Order Bill of Lading:* Printed on yellow paper (the other B/Ls must be on white paper), this also is called a sight draft bill of lading. It is a negotiable instrument and must be surrendered to the carrier at destination before goods can be obtained. Its primary use is to prevent delivery until payment is made for the goods. To obtain

payment, the shipper must provide a sight draft, along with the original copy of the B/L, to its bank; when the draft clears, the bank gives the B/L to the shipper, who then can obtain delivery of the merchandise.

Each shipment must have a bill of lading, which is the contract, spelling out the legal liabilities of all parties. No changes to the original B/L can be made unless approved by the carrier's agent in writing on the B/L.

Other important documents are the AirBill for air shipments, the commercial invoice, the export declaration, the certificate of origin (NAFTA), the packing list, and the import entry summary.

Expediting and Tracing Shipments

Expediting Defined

As with the normal purchase of goods and services, expediting means applying pressure to the carrier in an attempt to encourage faster than normal delivery service. The carrier often can and will provide faster service to assist the shipper in meeting an emergency requirement, provided such requests are made sparingly. Expediting should be done through the carrier's general agent and, if at all possible, the carrier should be notified of the need for speed as far in advance of the shipment as possible.

Tracing Defined

Tracing is similar to follow-up, for it attempts to determine the status (location) of items that have been shipped but have not yet been received, and thus are somewhere within the transportation system. Tracing also is done through the carrier's agent, although the shipper may work right along with the carrier's agent in attempting to locate the shipment. If tracing locates a shipment and indicates it will not be delivered by the required date, then expediting is needed.

Impact of EDI and E-Commerce

Getting results in tracing is a function of the kinds of movement records maintained by the carrier and the type of information available to the person doing the tracing. As electronic data interchange (EDI) and e-commerce tools become more widely implemented, tracing will be done faster and more accurately. EDI standards have been established for the transportation industry, and EDI is used to varying degrees by the major rail carriers. Other tracing tools include "800" phone-line tracing systems, and fax reports from carriers.

For example, in attempting to trace a CL rail shipment, the tracer should have (1) date material shipped, (2) description of material, (3) car number, (4) carrier, (5) origin, (6) destination, and (7) route. While the ease with which various shipments can be traced will vary among carriers and various modes of transportation and may change from time to time as carriers and modes change their policies and record-keeping systems, the current traceability is:

CL rail: If one has the car initial and number, date of shipment, and routing, the railroad can locate a car quickly. Most have computerized locator systems.

LCL rail: Ability to locate a given shipment varies greatly among carriers. Some maintain detailed records; others maintain minimum records, making tracing almost impossible.

TL motor: If the shipper has the trailer number, most carriers can quickly tell the approximate current location because it is kept track of through a series of movement points.

LTL motor: Normally, motor carriers can give complete and accurate information because they account for LTL shipments as they move through the various checkpoints.

Air shipment: Information on exact location normally can be obtained with little difficulty.

Parcel Post: No records are maintained; tracing is impossible.

Small package express shipments: Shipment status can be supplied quickly and accurately.

Freight forwarders: Because they use the service of common carriers, it is possible to trace these shipments in the same way that other shipments can be traced.

Water carriers: Shipment can be located easily because material is receipted for when put aboard and it normally doesn't change carriers.

Loss or Damage Claims

Liability Depends on Service and Terms

The carrier's liability varies depending on the service provided and the contractual terms between the shipper and the carrier. To collect on proper claims, the owner of the merchandise must file properly supported claims. If the merchandise is being shipped under any of the FOB origin terms, the buyer will have to pursue the claim. If the shipment is FOB destination, the supplier must process the claim, but because the merchandise is in the buyer's hands, the buyer will have to supply much of the information to support the claim. The DOT estimated that of the $7 trillion worth of goods shipped in 1999 to, from, or within, the United States, about 2 to 5 percent were affected by damage or theft.[39] Although seemingly small, any increase directly impacts the bottom line. LTL carriers are responding to claims faster, with 78 percent of claims settled in 30 days or less.

---

[39]Richard Biter, Deputy Director, U.S. Department of Transportation, Office of Intermodalism, *www.dot.gov,* April 17, 2001.

The Bill of Lading provides: ". . . Claims must be filed in writing with the receiving or delivering carrier, or carrier issuing this bill of lading; or carrier on whose line the loss, damage, injury, or delay occurred, within nine months after delivery of the property or, in case of failure to make delivery, then within nine months after a reasonable time for delivery has elapsed; and suits shall be instituted against any carrier only within two years and one day from the day when notice in writing is given by the carrier to the claimant that the carrier has disallowed the claim . . ." Under this provision, carriers generally have established nine months as the claim filing period, and two years and one day for the filing of court suits in the case of disallowed claims.

Documentation of Evident Damage Advisable

Unconcealed Loss or Damage. When it is evident on delivery that loss or damage has occurred, this must be noted on the carrier's delivery receipt and signed by the carrier's delivering agent. If this is not done, the carrier may maintain that it received a "clear receipt" and not admit any liability. It is a good idea for the receiving department to have an instant camera available, take one or more photos of the damaged items, and have them signed by the carrier's representative. Then, the local freight agent should be notified and an inspection report requested. This telephone request should be followed up in writing.

If it can be proven that the loss or damage occurred while the goods were in the carrier's possession, and if the cost of the damage can be established, prompt carrier payment should be expected. However, with the entry into the market of many new motor carriers, and an increasing number of bankruptcies, some shippers have had difficulty in collecting amounts due them. This points up the need on the buyer's part to do a careful job of financial analysis in selecting motor carriers.

Concealed Loss or Damage. Merchandise found short or damaged only after the container is opened is known as *concealed loss or damage.* The unpacking should be discontinued, photos taken, and the carrier's local agent should be requested to inspect the items and prepare an inspection report.

Difficult to Determine Point at which Damage Occurred

Concealed loss or damage claims often are difficult to collect because it is hard to determine whether the loss or damage took place while the shipment was in the carrier's possession or whether it occurred before the shipment was delivered to the carrier.

The time limit to file a claim with a carrier varies with the different modes of transportation and with different carriers. Because it changes from time to time, it is advisable to clarify this point in discussions with the supplier.

Payment of Freight Bills

All common carrier freight bills must be paid within a set number of days. Current regulations require common carrier rail bills to be paid within five days, and common carrier motor bills within 15 days of receipt, although payment terms may be negotiated with the carrier. Obviously, if the supplier pays the bills and includes them in its invoice for goods submitted to the buyer, the buyer may not be paying the charges for, say, 30 to 60 days, depending on the payment arrangements covered by the purchase order. If a maximum payment period were not specified and standardized, some large shippers, by virtue of their volume, might insist on very long payment terms, which would discriminate against the smaller shippers.

Filing Overcharge Claims

If, due to the short payment terms, the shipper pays an overcharge as a result of (1) an error in classification, (2) an error in rate charged, (3) an error in weight, (4) duplicate payment of the same freight bill, or (5) calculation error(s), with rail, truck, and small-package carriers there is a limited period to file an overcharge claim with the carrier. If the claim is substantiated by evidence, there should be no problem in recovering from the carrier, assuming the carrier is not in financial difficulty. By the same token, the carrier has the same period to bill shippers for any undercharges. Procedures for filing loss or damage and overcharge claims for air shipments vary with individual airlines.

Demurrage

Demurrage Defined

Demurrage charges often are incurred by shippers or receivers of merchandise. This simply is a daily penalty charge for a rail car or a motor van that is tied up beyond the normal time for loading or unloading. Typically, the period before which the "clock" begins to run on the demurrage penalties starts from 7 A.M. of the first regular working day by which the carrier has spotted the car or van ready for unloading. The free period on the loading of outbound rail cars is 24 hours; for the unloading of inbound cars it is 48 hours. For motor carrier vans, the free period is much shorter. These times are subject to change.

If demurrage were not charged, some firms would use the carrier's equipment as a free storage facility. The daily demurrage rate becomes progressively higher the longer the car or trailer is tied up, until it gets almost prohibitive. A shipper can enter into an averaging agreement with a carrier, whereby cars or vans unloaded one day early may be used to offset cars that are unloaded a day late. In an averaging agreement, settlement is made monthly. If the shipper owes the carrier, payment must be made; if the carrier owes the shipper, no payment is made, but instead the net car balance starts at zero in the new month. The purchasing department should be aware of the normal number of rail cars or vans that can be unloaded each day and attempt to schedule shipments in so that they do not "back up" and result in payment of demurrage penalties.

Freight Audits. Because of the complex regulations under which carriers operate, and the increased number of alternatives available under deregulation, a careful audit of paid freight bills often will uncover instances of overpayment to the carrier. Savings from freight bill audits may range from 5 percent to 20 percent of the charges depending on the commodity shipped.[40]

Use of Freight Audit Consultant

In the larger firm, in-house freight bill audit capability often is available. In the smaller firm, the use of an outside freight audit consultant, referred to as a *traffic consultant* or *rate shark,* should be used. The rate shark will examine all paid freight bills in an attempt to spot overpayment due to wrong classification, wrong rate, duplicate payment, or calculation errors. When overpayments are found, the rate shark will process a claim with the carrier. The agreement with the shipper typically is that the rate shark retains 50 percent of the dollars recovered, although occasionally the outside auditor will work for a smaller percentage. Due to the complexity of the freight purchase area, even a company with a sophisticated, well-trained traffic staff probably pays some overcharges, and with the advice of an outside auditor could generate substantial recoveries. And with the rate shark, if nothing is recovered no payment is made.

A pre-payment audit should be performed to make corrections before making payment, and a post-payment audit will protect the shipper within the confines of the three-year moratorium. Carriers (and bankruptcy trustees) also perform carrier audits to determine if any undercharges occurred. Carriers also have a limited time to adjust the bills and collect payment for undercharges.

Developing a Logistics Strategy

Tools and Techniques for Strategy Development

The changes in the regulatory environment of transportation, advances in information management systems, and the growing concern with managing both upstream (suppliers) and downstream (end customers) in supply networks have brought rapid and continuous change to logistics management. The same principles of effective purchasing and supply management can and should be applied to logistics services. Development of a logistics strategy should include:

Value analysis of alternatives: A service requirement value analysis may turn up totally adequate, lower-cost transport arrangements.

Price analysis: Rates vary substantially and decisions should be made only after consideration of all possibilities. Competitive quotes should be obtained. Negotiation of big-ticket transportation now is possible.

Consolidate freight, where possible: Volume discounts may reduce transport costs substantially. Systems contracts and blanket orders may be advantageous. If JIT purchasing is in use or being

---

[40]Jack Englehart, "Freight Bill Auditing: Saving Your Company $$$," *NAPM Insights,* January 1994, p. 5.

implemented, consolidation of several JIT suppliers may be cost-effective.

Analyze and evaluate suppliers: Carrier selection and evaluation systems can provide data needed for better decision making. Four areas to evaluate are (1) financial, (2) management, (3) technical/strategic, and (4) relational, or overall corporate relationship between carrier and shipper.[41]

Reassess the possibilities of using different transport modes: This would include using private trucking and intermodal transportation, such as piggybacking. The savings often are substantial.

Develop closer relationship with selected carriers: Data that enable better planning of transport requirements should be shared to take advantage of the specialized knowledge of both buyer and carrier. A reduced carrier base and partnerships or logistics alliances might be considered.

Cost analysis / reductions: Long-term contracts; partnerships; third-party involvement; freight consolidation; demurrage; packaging; and service, quality, and delivery requirements offer opportunities for cost reductions.

Outsourcing, third-party logistics, contracting out: As organizations downsize, focus on core competencies, and face time-based competition, the decision to contract with a company or several companies to provide complete logistics services should be considered.

Safety considerations: Safety issues may be related to downward pressure on driver's income since deregulation, and to shipper demands that may result in shippers and carriers agreeing to unrealistic, legally unattainable delivery schedules. These pressures may lead to drivers falsifying log books to conceal violations of hours worked and miles driven, and to accidents involving commercial vehicles. Avoidance of safety problems should be a key element in the strategy.

Environmental factors: Growing concerns over clean air and water, the transport of hazardous materials, and fuel/energy consumption also must be taken into account.

A New Era for Transportation
A summary of the changes in transportation that have occurred recently, and the opportunities they provide, was well stated by the manager of transportation services at Asea Brown Boveri (ABB): "The Surface Transportation Board and the Department of Transportation (DOT) have replaced the ICC. While they will retain some of the previous responsibilities of the ICC, many of the ICC requirements and regulations are gone. Transportation finally is

---

[41]Joseph Cavinato, "How To Evaluate a New Supplier," *Distribution*, May 1989, pp. 54–56.

falling into the realm of commercial contracting rather than regulated tariffs. Transportation issues will be resolved under common law in the courts
rather than under the ICC. With the ICC Termination Act, we truly have a
new era of transportation pricing, contracting, and liability. Hopefully it will
open many new opportunities for shippers in all industries."[42]

Questions for Review and Discussion

1. How has transportation deregulation affected the purchase of logistics services?
2. What factors should be considered in selecting a mode of transportation? A carrier?
3. How do firms organize to handle the logistics function?
4. Why might an organization decide to outsource all or some of its logistics activities to a third party?
5. What types of transportation damage might occur, and how should each be handled?
6. Why is classification so important in buying transportation services?
7. What is the use and significance of the bill of lading?
8. What does FOB mean? What variations are there in FOB terms?
9. Why should a buyer audit payments for freight purchases?
10. What strategies should be developed to effectively manage the logistics function?
11. How would logistics decisions be affected by a JIT purchasing arrangement?
12. Under what circumstances might a buyer prefer each of the following carriers: TL, LTL, air, water, rail, intermodal?

References

Ballou, Ronald H. *Business Logistics Management,* 4th edition, Upper Saddle River, NJ: Prentice-Hall, 1999.

Bowersox, Donald J. "The Strategic Benefits of Logistics Alliances." *Harvard Business Review,* July–August 1990.

---

[42]From a March 14, 1996, letter to one of the authors from John Arbeiter, Manager of Transportation Services, Purchasing and Transportation, ABB Business Services, Windsor, CT.

Federal Motor Carrier Safety Administration, *2010 Strategy and Performance Planning, www.spp.fmcsa.dot.gov.*

Gentry, Julie J. *Role of Carriers in Buyer/Supplier Strategic Alliances.* Tempe, AZ: Center for Advanced Purchasing Studies/National Association of Purchasing Management, 1995.

Gentry, Julie J. *Purchasing's Involvement in Transportation Decision Making.* Tempe, AZ: Center for Advanced Purchasing Studies/National Association of Purchasing Management, 1991.

Incoterms 2000. New York: International Chamber of Commerce (ICC) Publishing Inc., 2000.

Johnson, James C., Donald F. Woods, Daniel L. Wardlow, and Paul R. Murphy, Jr. *Contemporary Logistics,* 7th edition, Upper Saddle River, NJ: Prentice-Hall, 1999.

Lambert, Douglas M., James R. Stock, and Lisa M. Ellram. *Fundamentals of Logistics Management,* Burr Ridge, IL: Irwin/McGraw-Hill, 1998.

LaLonde, Bernard J. and Terrance Pohlen. *Survey of Career Patterns 2000.* The Ohio State University Logistics Research Group, 2000, www.clm1.org.

U.S. Department of Transportation, Bureau of Transportation Statistics; U.S. Department of Commerce, Census Bureau; Statistics Canada; Transport Canada; Instituto Mexicano del Transporte; Instituto Nacional de Estadistica, Geografia e Informatica; and Secretaria de Communicaciones y Transportes. *North American Transportation Figures,* BTS00-05, Washington, D.C., 2000.

Ramburg, Jan. *ICC Guide to Incoterms 2000.* New York: International Chamber of Commerce (ICC) Publishing Inc., 2000.

Stock, James R. and Douglas M. Lambert. *Strategic Logistics Management,* 4th edition, Burr Ridge, IL: Irwin/McGraw-Hill, 2001.

World Class Logistics: The Challenge of Managing Continuous Change. Prepared by Michigan State University for the Council of Logistics Management, Oak Brook, IL: Publications Department, 1995.

CASE 10–1
GREAT WESTERN BANK

The Great Western Bank of San Diego placed an order for 12 special-purpose accounting machines with the Data-Max Corporation of Cincinnati, Ohio. Great Western and Data-Max agreed to a firm-fixed price of $9,500 per unit, FOB the shipping point (Cincinnati). In the purchase order, the bank's purchasing agent designated a particular carrier (Yellow Freight) and Data-Max returned a signed acknowledgement copy without change in any of the terms and conditions.

On completion of the 12 units three months later, Data-Max shipped them via a different common carrier than Yellow Freight. At the time of shipment, an invoice was mailed to Great Western. To take advantage of the 2 percent cash discount, Great Western paid the invoice immediately, as was its custom. The machines had not yet arrived.

Unfortunately, as the truck was passing through Illinois, the driver lost control; the vehicle was involved in an accident, and the truck and contents were destroyed. The 12 machines were a total loss.

The buyer, on contacting Data-Max relative to the loss, was told: "Look, we sold these machines to you F.O.B. Cincinnati, and title passed at the time they were loaded on the carrier. That's the law." At this point, the buyer pointed out that Data-Max had not shipped via the carrier specified on the purchase order. To this Data-Max replied: "Sure, that's true. But we saved you money by shipping via a less expensive transportation method. [This was, in fact, true.] Furthermore, you acknowledged and accepted our action by paying our invoice, for the invoice clearly stated the date and method of shipment. It is your responsibility to work out any adjustment for the loss directly with the truck line."

CASE 10–2
GEO PRODUCTS

In early April, Sharon Lee, supervisor of purchasing and transportation at Geo Products (Geo) in Georgia, had to decide on the future transportation needs of the company. Increased sales would place significant demands on the company's resources, including transportation. As a result, Sharon had been asked by the plant manager to develop a suitable transportation strategy by April 15.

Industry. Geo manufactured kitchen and bathroom cabinets and mirrors. Geo competed in the upper end of the market, manufacturing high-quality products. Based on current sales forecasts, management expected Geo to double its output over the next 12 months.

Most of the big players in the industry had a linear relationship between transportation expenses and revenue. It was estimated that an average relationship would be 20:1 and varied depending on the distance the product was shipped.

Company Background. Geo was a subsidiary of Star Corporation (Star). Star, a financial holding company, had two manufacturing operations in Canada and four in the United States. The Georgia plant was intended to meet market demand in the southeastern states.

Georgia plant operations ordered supplies and services based on confirmed customer orders and promised delivery dates. The plant produced approximately 30,000 units last year.

Approximately nine years prior, the Georgia plant had an exclusive third-party contract with a transportation company that provided on-site support. However, at that time, the company was faced with intense competitive pressures and looked for other, more cost-effective alternatives. As a result, Geo negotiated with Eastern Leasing Company (Eastern) to lease two trucks and to provide transportation services through a separate trucking services company (TSC). Under the arrangement with Eastern, Geo contacted TSC when shipments required delivery. Although only two trucks were officially leased by Geo, TSC was flexible in providing more trucks and drivers when necessary.

Transportation Activities. Regular weekly deliveries were made to customers in the southern states. The routes for each truck were specified, with one customer typically being visited once per week. Occasionally, two visits per week were necessary when extra orders were placed and all units could not be filled in the first shipment.

Payment to TSC was made on a per mile basis, whereas Geo's customers were charged $11 per unit for delivery, regardless of the size and number of units delivered or ordered. Payment to the leasing company was $1/mile whether the trailer was full or half-empty. Last year, Geo spent approximately $200,000 on TSC fees and paid approximately $160,000 to Eastern as part of the lease arrangement.

When the quantity to be delivered was not large enough for a whole trailer or delivery dates did not fit with the pre-planned route, Geo would hire the services of other common carrier truck lines. In these situations, Geo was charged on the basis of weight or square footage. These shipments took longer for delivery because common carriers typically made a number of stops for other companies also sharing the trailer before reaching Geo's final destination. Last year, Geo spent about $80,000 on LTL loads.

The Transportation Decision. Because of the forecast increase for the coming 12 months, Sharon was concerned that the company might not be able to meet the future market requirements with the existing two trucks. She felt that a number of possible alternatives existed. First, she could continue with the current approach and use common carriers to handle the additional volume. A second alternative was to lease an additional truck from Eastern. Finally, she could restructure the existing arrangement and negotiate a contract with a carrier to provide on-site service.

Sharon knew she had to develop a plan to support the projected growth at the Georgia plant for the April 15 meeting with the plant manager.

CASE 10–3
SPECIALTY BREWERS

In April, Al Mayfair, national purchasing manager, Brewing Materials, had eight weeks to reach a decision about a recent proposal from one of Specialty's hops suppliers. The supplier had offered to do all the processing and storage of this vital ingredient. This would change the current system under which six different hops growers processed and shipped a year's supply of hops at a time to each of Specialty's 12 breweries.

Specialty Brewers. Specialty Brewers operated 12 plants in different regions of the United States. It had grown largely by acquiring small breweries which had loyal local followings in smaller markets.

Hops Procurement. Under the present arrangement, hops were purchased from six of the dozen suppliers located in the state of Washington, in the northwest United States. These growers harvested the crop, processed it to make it ready for brewing, and packaged it in 20 kg containers. Twenty of these containers were then loaded on pallets and trucked to Specialty's 12 breweries across the states. Full truckloads (46 pallets/truck) were shipped whenever possible to take advantage of freight rates that were considerably lower than LTL (less-than-truckload).

Specialty contracted for a year's supply of hops at a time, and the entire year's supply was shipped by the suppliers to the breweries when processing was complete. Because the breweries each had different production capacities, their requirements for hops varied. Their freight costs also varied because of differing distances from the point of origin (Exhibit 1).

The present arrangement had several benefits for Specialty. The first was the transportation savings made possible by shipping only full truckloads of hops, instead of shipping by the pallet. The second benefit was security of supply. Clearly, with a full year's inventory of hops on the premises, breweries need not worry about a production interruption caused by a lack of hops.

Finally, Al felt that diversifying the supply of hops among six producers had benefits for Specialty, because their bargaining power with each individual grower was greater than it would have been if they relied on just a single source.

The Proposal. In what Al felt was a bid for market dominance by the leading Washington hops grower, the following proposal had been put to Specialty by International Hops Supply (IHS):

- IHS would purchase hops—on Specialty's behalf and subject to a prearranged contract—from the other Washington growers, sufficient to supply the needs of all their breweries.

- IHS would do the processing and packaging, and would store the hops on its premises under appropriate cold-storage conditions.

- On instructions from Specialty Breweries, LTL quantities (in one-pallet increments) would be shipped to the breweries. Specialty would be invoiced for hops only after they were shipped.

IHS would make the decisions about which growers would supply the raw hops, but the transportation logistics for the deliveries would be handled by the individual breweries. While Specialty would still be free to contract with other suppliers under this arrangement, Al anticipated that this would happen in emergencies only, and that substantial price

EXHIBIT 1   Breweries, Freight Rates, and Hops Requirements

	Required Pallets	Total Freight $	Old Average Freight / Pallet	New Average Freight / Pallet
Eugene (Oregon)*	85	1336	16	44
Boise (Idaho)	75	2778	37	44
Billings (Montana)	75	3336	44	88
Cheyenne (Wyoming)	20	2085	104	123
Omaha (Nebraska)	63	5235	83	167
Dayton (Ohio)	155	12356	80	229
Columbus (Ohio)*	50	4005	80	229
Cleveland (Ohio)*	153	12192	80	229
Albany (New York)*	308	23352	76	273
Jacksonville (Florida)	8	2392	299	299
Tampa (Florida)	23	4655	202	308
Fort Lauderdale (Florida)	24	5667	236	352
Totals	1039	79389		

* These breweries required off-site storage for 30% of their total annual hops requirements. Cost for this was $6.00 per month, plus a one-time charge of $4 per pallet.

Note: Specialty head office assessed a 12%/annum charge on working capital.

premiums would apply to purchasing small quantities of hops on a spot basis.

The proposal seemed attractive to Al for several reasons. First, it would eliminate outside storage costs for the breweries. They currently had on-site cold storage facilities for a percentage (in some cases all) of their annual hops needs, but in several cases they had to pay third parties to store hops in excess of their own holding capacity (Exhibit 1).

The second benefit had to do with Al's other responsibilities. Looking after transportation and other supply logistics each year occupied a significant portion of his time, during a period when Al was swamped with other duties. Letting the breweries and IHS handle the majority of the details would enable Al to give more attention to matters that had greater monetary significance for Specialty.

Finally, IHS had a history of good relations with Specialty, and Al considered them a reliable and competent supplier.

The Decision. Al needed to make a decision on this matter quickly, but because of the vital importance of hops to the brewing process, he could not afford to put the supply of hops to the breweries at risk. Possible transportation delays were one concern; because accepting the proposal would mean more frequent, smaller shipments, the risk of a shipment being held up would be increased. If there were insufficient hops inventory on hand, production at that brewery would be shut down until the hops arrived.

A second concern had to do with the adjustments required in operating practices at the breweries. Each brewery had a raw materials coordinator who currently did not devote much attention to the hops inventory because large supplies were usually on hand. Al was aware of the potential for human error under conditions of change, and he wondered if the brewery-based personnel would make the modifications in their operating practices necessary to ensure that hops stockouts did not occur.

Third, Al knew that the financial aspects of the proposal were impossible to ignore. To be competitive with the very large-scale U.S. breweries would take every cost-saving innovation that Specialty could devise.

Al broke his decision criteria down this way, in no particular order of priority:

1. Make hops available to each brewery at the lowest possible total cost.

2. Ensure that the possibility of stockouts at the breweries is minimized.

3. Maintain the long-run stability of supplier relationships to prevent bargaining power imbalances that might lead to unreasonable price fluctuations.

4. Manage his own time in such a way that his personal value-added to Specialty is at a maximum.

He now needed to compare the cost of the proposal with the cost of the current supply system. He could assume that the hops usage rates at the breweries were level throughout the year and use the expected average price of $7.25/kg for hops to calculate the cost of the present system. Storage costs, whether on-site or off-site, were calculated based on the maximum volume of hops stored for the entire length of time that any storage was needed. The full storage facility, including cooling system operation, had to be maintained regardless

of the actual amount of hops in it at a given point in time.

The proposed change would price hops at $7.25/kg, plus a financing charge of 1 percent added to the prevailing New York prime interest rate. In addition, IHS would assess a storage fee of $4 per month per pallet for those hops not yet shipped. Order quantities and frequencies could be based on an economic order quantity (EOQ) computation, broken down by brewery because their freight costs were all different. Al was not sure what order cost was appropriate to reflect the cost of long-distance telephone calls to trucking firms, and the cost of sending confirmatory documentation to IHS.

After determining the costs, Al knew he also needed to think about the other implications of his decision. There were aspects of this matter that were difficult to quantify. His proposal, due in eight weeks, had to take into consideration the possible long-term effects of each alternative on supply security and supplier relations; his boss would need a well-reasoned argument supporting one side or the other.

11 INVESTMENT RECOVERY

Chapter Outline

Key Questions for the Purchasing Decision Maker

SHOULD WE
- Use an online auction as a means of disposing of scrap, surplus, and excess?
- Centralize responsibility for investment recovery?
- Attempt to use scrap, surplus, and excess materials in-house?

HOW CAN WE
- Improve the return from the investment recovery process?
- Reduce the quantities of materials and equipment to be disposed of?
- Make business decisions that are financially superior and environmentally sound?

Managers are concerned with the effective, efficient, and profitable recovery and disposal of scrap, surplus, obsolete, and waste materials generated within the firm. In recent years, disposal problems have become more complex and important as companies have become larger, more diversified in product lines, more global in operations, and more decentralized in management. The focus on the entire supply chain means that managers must look for return loops to recapture their initial materials investment through remanufacturing, repair, reconfiguration, and recycling. Added to this is the need to develop and use new methods for avoiding the generation of solid waste products in the first place and better means of disposing of other wastes that are discharged into the air and waterways, causing pollution. Cleaning up pollution is expensive and so avoiding the purchase, use, emission, or disposition of hazardous materials is the basis of a sound environmental management approach. This approach also puts purchasing in a critical position within the organization.

Integrated Waste Management System

The need for environmentally protective waste management and the need to reduce the amount of waste generated have led to development of the concept of an integrated waste management system. This plan calls for source reduction (eliminating unnecessary discards before they enter the waste stream), recycling (returning a product to commerce), resource recovery (burning trash and recovering energy), and landfills (providing the final disposal option for materials that cannot be reclaimed).

While this chapter analyzes and discusses the supply department's role in environmental management systems, the alert supply executive must also keep abreast of new technology concerned with avoiding and eliminating causes of pollution. Materials no longer can be selected and used without considering their eco-efficiency, i.e., improving material utilization per unit of production, their recyclability, and their potential for generating hazardous

Salvage is Big Business

waste. The salvage of all types of materials in U.S. industry is big business. The American scrap recycling industry's products are worth at least $20 billion a year. In 1999 in the United States alone, scrap recyclers handled approximately 120 million tons of recyclables destined for domestic use and overseas markets. This tonnage included approximately:

- 60 million tons of scrap iron and steel
- 47 million tons of scrap paper and paper board
- 5.1 million tons of scrap aluminum
- 1.7 million tons of scrap copper
- 1.1 million tons of scrap stainless steel
- 1.4 million tons of scrap lead
- 248,000 tons of scrap zinc
- 2.3 million tons of scrap glass or cullet (beverage containers only)
- 745 million pounds of scrap PET plastic bottles
- 734 million pounds of scrap HDPE plastic bottles[1]

Not only does the proper sale of scrap, surplus, and waste result in additional income for the seller, it also prevents pollution and serves to conserve raw material resources and energy. For example, every ton of iron and steel scrap recycled saves one-and-one-half tons of iron ore, one ton of coke, and one-half ton of limestone, plus the energy required to convert the raw materials into virgin product. This scrap is collected for beneficial reuse, conserving impressive amounts of energy and natural resources in the recycling process. For example, according to the Environmental Protection Agency (EPA), recycled aluminum saves the nation 95 percent of the energy that would have been needed to make new aluminum from ore. Recycled iron and steel result in energy savings of 74 percent; recycled copper, 85 percent; recycled paper, 64 percent; and recycled plastic, more than 80 percent.

Energy Savings Through Recycling

An increasingly complex and stringent set of federal and state regulations has been enacted over the last 25 years to protect the environment. This has complicated the scrap recovery process and increased the potential liability risks for both the generators and processors of scrap. For example, with metal-working turnings, oil and chemical residues present a risk; plated, coated, or painted scrap may contain cadmium, lead, or zinc; pipe, insulated or coated wire, and cable often have asbestos, lead, or chemical residues; and closed containers present a risk of explosions and chemical residues. The purchasing department must be aware of these risks, as they affect its ability to profitably dispose of scrap and surplus.

---

[1]Institute of Scrap Recycling Industries (ISRI), Mission and Goals, *www.isri.org*, April 20, 2001.

U.S. Environmental Initiatives

Why are environmental issues of concern to U.S. supply managers? For one thing, the people of the United States consume approximately 25 percent of the world's resources despite representing only 5 percent of the world's population. Both business and government leaders should consider the impact of these numbers.

Four pieces of federal legislation impact the sourcing and scrap disposal market and procedures used:

1. Resource Conservation and Recovery Act (RCRA), passed in 1976. This was the cornerstone hazardous waste control law, although it was not implemented by the Environmental Protection Agency (EPA) until 1980. The RCRA identifies which industrial wastes are corrosive, toxic, ignitable, or chemically reactive. The EPA has promulgated regulations prescribing how these potentially dangerous items are to be treated, disposed of, or stored. In some instances RCRA permits are needed. The law assigns "cradle-to-grave" responsibility to hazardous waste generators.

"Cradle to Grave" Responsibility Assigned

Impact on Purchasers: Purchasers contracting for waste disposal may want to (1) ensure that a disposal supplier is competent and reputable and has an EPA permit, (2) require the supplier to warrant that employees are trained in handling the specific waste, and (3) insist on the right to inspect the facility and the EPA permit.

2. Toxic Substances Control Act (TSCA), passed in 1976. This act established a master database, the Toxic Substances Control Act Inventory List (TSCAIL) of every chemical approved for use in the United States. The act regulates procedures used in the manufacture, use, and distribution of chemicals. Included are polychlorinated biphenyls (PCBs), which the 1979 EPA regulations specify must be disposed of in chemical waste landfills.

Procedures are Regulated for Chemical Industry

Impact on Purchasers: Requires suppliers to warrant that any chemical or chemical mixture they provide is listed by the EPA.

3. Comprehensive Environmental Response, Compensation, and Liability Act (CERCLA), passed in 1980, including Superfund Amendments, and the Reauthorization Act of 1986. This is known as SARA or Superfund, for it gives the EPA authority to order the cleanup of solid waste sites and to recover the costs, if necessary, from those responsible for the pollution damage. Figure 11–1 lists the accomplishments of Superfund from 1993 to 1999. This potential liability has made it more costly or impractical to process certain types of scrap and will reduce the amounts of secondary (reprocessed) materials available. Some states have passed tougher cleanup laws that require companies that own or sell industrial property to foot the cleanup bill on properties on which pollution of

Superfund Cleanup and Cost Recovery

FIGURE 11–1

Superfund Accomplishments 1993 versus 2000

	January 1993	September 2000
Cleanup construction completed	155	700
Sites deleted from the National Priorities List (NPL)	40	217
Remedial cleanup construction under way, completed, or deleted from the NPL	42%	76%
Final cleanup plans approved	600	1,200
Removal actions taken at hazardous waste sites to reduce the threat to public health and the environment	3,200	6,300
Proposed, final, and completed NPL sites	1,280	1,510

Superfund Facts — The Program at Work, U.S. Environmental Protection Agency, *www.epa.gov/epahome*, November 15, 2000.

the site through improper disposal of hazardous waste has caused health risks to the community.

Impact on Purchasers: Purchasers must track the amount and type of chemicals that enter and leave the plant and consult the Material Safety Data Sheets (MSDS) discussed later in this chapter.

4. Clean Air Act Amendments (CAA) of 1990. Required the reduction of emissions of more than 189 specific chemicals identified by the EPA as toxic. Major polluting plants are required to install the "best available technology" to reduce emissions by 90 percent. The law also mandates the phaseout of ozone-depleting chemicals such as CFCs, HCHCs, and halons, and the reduction of vehicle emissions of carbon dioxide, hydrocarbons, and other pollutants by 90 percent.

Emission Reductions Mandated

Impact on Purchasers: Purchasers can choose environmentally friendly products, establish criteria for supplier selection that limit purchases from suppliers that sell damaging products, and be alert to alternatives, substitutes, or new technology that may help their companies meet the goals of the Clean Air Act.

Definition of "Environmentally Preferable"

Environmentally Preferable Purchasing Program. The Environmentally Preferable Purchasing Program is a federal agency-wide program to encourage and assist executive agencies in purchasing decisions. Executive Order 13101 defines environmentally preferable as ". . . products or services that have a lesser or reduced effect on human health and the environment when compared with competing products or services that serve the same purpose." Environmentally preferable purchasing is defined as "incorporating key environmental factors with traditional price and performance considerations in purchasing decisions."[2] The EPA has developed the Environ-

---

[2]Environmentally Preferable Purchasing, Office of Pollution Prevention and Toxics, United States Environmental Protection Agency, *www.epa.gov/opptintr/epp.*

mentally Preferable Purchasing (EPP) database of environmental attribute information for products ranging from appliances to vehicles. The database also includes contract language that has been used by others to obtain products and services considered by the EPA to be environmentally preferable. Although this program was developed for federal agency procurement, commercial purchasers also will find the information useful.

Voluntary Compliance Programs. Business and government typically have had an adversarial relationship because of the belief that environmental responsibility was inconsistent with the profit motive. As more people come to believe that it makes economic sense to practice environmentally sound operations, business and government may be able to work together for common goals. The EPA is attempting to develop a more comprehensive program designed to hold down the costs of environmental continuous improvement. The goals are to develop an industry-by-industry approach, coordinate rule making, simplify recordkeeping and reporting requirements, permit streamlining, and review enforcement/compliance objectives. Toward those goals, the EPA has developed a wide range of voluntary compliance programs listed in Figure 11–2. Detailed information on these and other EPA programs is available on the EPA Web site, *www.epa.gov.* Of particular interest to supply managers is the Environmental Accounting Project, which provides accounting tools and techniques for incorporating environmental, health, and safety costs and benefits into business decision-making.[3]

Cost Control of Environmental Initiatives

Supply Chain Management and Environmental Performance. The emphasis on managing a network of supply chain partners leads to a number of cost reduction opportunities in areas that may have been previously neglected by management. Environmental, safety, and health is one such area. Some of the ways in which cost reduction efforts have also resulted in improvements in environmental performance are:

Examples of Improvements in Environmental Performance

- Reducing the obsolescence and waste of maintenance, repair, and operating (MRO) supplies through better materials and inventory management.
- Substantially reducing the costs from scrap and materials losses.
- Lowering the training, handling, and other expenses for hazardous materials.
- Increasing revenues by converting wastes to byproducts.
- Reducing the use of hazardous materials through more timely and accurate materials tracking and reporting systems.
- Decreasing the use and waste of chemicals, solvents, and paints through chemical service partnerships.

---

[3]EPA, Enhancing Supply Chain Performance with Environmental Cost Information, EPA 742-R-99-002, April 2000, p. 7.

FIGURE 11–2

The EPA's Voluntary Compliance Programs

Climate Wise - a voluntary government-industry partnership designed to help businesses turn energy efficiency and environmental performance into a corporate asset.

Commonsense Initiative - a new approach for the EPA in creating policies and environmental management solutions that relate to industry sectors.

Design for the Environment - a voluntary program designed to help businesses incorporate environmental considerations into the design and redesign of products, processes, and technical and management systems.

Electronic Commerce/Electronic Data Interchange (EC/EDI) - a program working to introduce electronic reporting for all major environmental compliance programs, both for reports submitted directly to the EPA and for those submitted to state or local agencies under delegated programs.

Environmental Accounting Project - voluntary program to encourage and motivate businesses to understand the full spectrum of their environmental costs and integrate these costs into decision making.

Environmental Leadership Program - a program designed to recognize and provide incentives to facilities willing to develop and demonstrate accountability for compliance with existing laws.

National Environmental Performance Track Program - Designed to recognize and encourage top environmental performers: those who go beyond compliance with regulatory requirements to attain levels of environmental performance and management that benefit people, communities, and the environment.

Sector Facility Indexing Project - a pilot program that provides comprehensive information on the environmental performance of hundreds of facilities in five major industries.

Sustainable Industry Project - a program designed to explore, design, and promote industry sector-based approaches to environmental protection.

WasteWise - a voluntary program that targets the reduction of municipal solid waste; waste that would otherwise end up in a trash dumpster.

- Recovering valuable materials and assets with efficient materials recovery programs.[4]

Environmental managerial accounting can be used to track and report the costs of activities normally assigned to overhead, including waste disposal, training expenses, environmental permitting fees, and other environmental costs. By applying activity-based costing techniques, an organization can track costs back to the responsible products and processes, analyze the cost drivers, and explore alternative cost-reduction opportunities.[5]

Ashland Specialty Chemical Company Example

For example,[6] Ashland Specialty Chemical Company developed an activity-based costing model that included 32 environmental, health and safety (EH&S) activities that normally occur at manufacturing sites. Appropriate personnel were interviewed to identify potentially significant EH&S costs and a priority ranking was established. Employees then estimated the number of hours they spent on these activities and identified relevant associated costs, either facility or corporate, such as materials and supplies and

---

[4]Ibid, p. 7–8.
[5]Ibid, p. 8.
[6]Ibid, pp. 40–50.

outside contractor or consulting fees. Further data collection and analysis done by a cross-functional team resulted in the application of Pareto analysis (See Chapters 3 and 5) which identified the opportunities (20 percent) that would yield 80 percent of the potential improvements. One outcome of the study was the team's recommendation to change the plant's waste water and byproduct neutralization process from a highly labor-intensive process to largely an automated one.

Andersen Corporation Example

At Andersen Corporation, the largest manufacturer of wood windows and patio doors in North America, the Corporate Pollution Prevention Team worked to reduce emissions from the painting process. Suppliers were asked to develop new paints that eliminated TRI chemicals (specific toxic chemicals) and worked as well, or better, than the original chemistry. Andersen committed to working closely with suppliers and promised a substantial portion of its paint purchases to successful suppliers. After a three-year development period, some suppliers were able to provide new paints, thereby enabling Andersen to greatly reduce its TRI waste stream.[7]

Canadian Environmental Initiatives

The *Auditor General Act* of 1995 added the environment to the three Es of economy, efficiency, and effectiveness for which the Auditor General conducts value-for-money audits.[8] This act required 24 federal departments and agencies to prepare a sustainable development strategy for tabling in Parliament every three years, and created within the Auditor General's office the position of Commissioner of the Environment and Sustainable Development. Sustainable development is defined as "development that meets the needs of the present without compromising the ability of future generations to meet their own needs."[9] Sustainable development may be achieved by many actions, including:

Sustainable Development Defined

- The integration of the environment and the economy.
- Protecting the health of Canadians.
- Protecting ecosystems.
- Meeting international obligations.
- Promoting equity.
- An integrated approach to planning and making decisions that takes into account the environmental and natural resource costs of different economic options and the economic costs of different environmental and natural resource options.

---

[7]Ibid, p. 36.

[8]"The Commissioner's Mandate," Commissioner of the Environment and Sustainable Development, *www.oag-bvg.gc.ca.*

[9]"Appendix A - Auditor General Act," *www.oag-bvg.gc.ca*, February 21, 2001.

- Preventing pollution.
- Respect for nature and the needs of future generations.[10]

Transport Canada Example

For example, Transport Canada's Sustainable Development goal is a transportation system that provides affordable access to freight and passenger services and does so in an environmentally sound and equitable manner. The department's Sustainable Development Strategy for 2001–2003 addresses the following seven challenges:

1. Improving education and awareness of sustainable transportation.
2. Developing tools for better decisions.
3. Promoting adoption of sustainable transportation technology.
4. Improving environmental management for Transport Canada's operations and lands.
5. Reducing air emissions.
6. Reducing pollution of water.
7. Promoting efficient transportation.[11]

International Environmental Initiatives

Importance of Environmental Issues to Business

A survey of 100 of Europe's leading business analysts and decision-makers from France, Germany and the United Kingdom revealed that corporate social and environmental responsibility has moved from an option to a mandate for chief executive officers. "On almost every front, business is being pressed to assume responsibilities it has not always been prepared to face," said Robert Davies, chief executive of the Business Leaders Forum. "Corporate (social and environmental) responsibility is on the mainstream agenda for public companies concerned about customers, employees, and communities. The case for responsible business starts with demonstrating it is possible for companies to create value for both society and shareholders," Davies added. "Indeed, leading companies are beginning to recognize that these are mutually reinforcing objectives."

The survey's key findings are:

- 66 percent of business opinion leaders "agree strongly" that corporate responsibility will be important in their assessment of companies.
- 64 percent "agree strongly" that corporate responsibility will affect their own decisions.
- 42 percent "agree strongly" that corporate responsibility will affect share price.

---

[10]Ibid, Article 21.1.

[11]Transport Canada, "Sustainability," *www.tc.gc.ca/envaffairs/english/sustain.htm.*

- The most important environmental issues cited by survey participants are air and water pollution, waste and recycling, and climate change.[12]

ISO 14000 Environmental Standards. ISO 14000, similar to ISO 9000 in management principles, focuses on environmental issues. One is not a prerequisite for the other. ISO 14000 standards were introduced in 1996, and approximately 21,500 companies worldwide had been certified as of November 2000, including 1,130 U.S. locations and 521 Canadian locations.[13]

Elements of an Environmental Management System

ISO 14000 standards describe the basic elements of an effective environmental management system (EMS) and do not replace federal, state, and provincial environmental laws and regulations. The standards include creating a corporate environmental policy, setting objectives and targets, implementing a plan to achieve the objectives and targets, performance measurement and corrective action, and continuous improvement. ISO 14000 standards are process, not performance, focused. They describe how a company can implement an EMS and achieve its objectives and targets.[14]

Two Categories of Standards

The ISO 14000 series consists of standards related to EMS (ISO 14001 and ISO 14004) and standards related to environmental management tools, such as environmental auditing, environmental performance evaluation, environmental labeling, and life-cycle assessment. These standards are divided into the two general categories shown in Figure 11–3. The EMS standards provide the framework for the management systems, and the life-cycle assessment standards focus on evaluation and analysis of products and processes.[15]

Reasons for Supply Managers Interest in ISO 14000

There are several reasons why supply managers should be concerned with the ISO 14000 standards. In the long-run, firms with EMS should provide lower costs and offer fewer problems to their customers. From a total cost perspective, firms that control waste and conserve energy as part of an EMS are not only being environmentally responsible, they also should be more efficient. They also have less risk of exposing their customers to legal liabilities associated with violation of state and federal environmental legislation, such as the Superfund Act. Furthermore, purchasers should avoid dealing with firms that may provoke a strong negative reaction because of poor environmental performance. (Chapter 12 covers the legal aspects of purchasing.)

---

[12]*Environmental Network News,* "Big Business Puts Environment in its Big Picture," Tuesday, June 27, 2000.

[13]ISO World, *www.ecology.or.jp/isoworld/english/analyl14k.htm,* February 2001.

[14]Tom Tibor and Ira Feldman, *ISO 14000: A Guide to New Environmental Management Standards* (Burr Ridge, IL: Irwin Professional Publishing, 1996).

[15]Steve Melnyk et al., *ISO 14000: Assessing Its Impact on Corporate Effectiveness and Efficiency* (Tempe, AZ: Center for Advanced Purchasing Studies, 1999).

FIGURE 11–3

ISO 14000 Framework

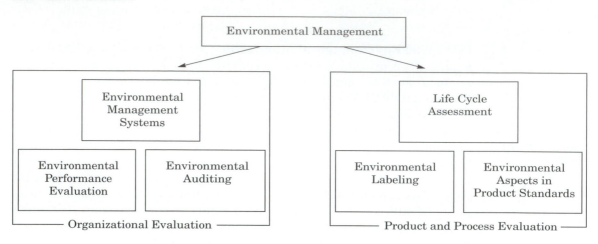

Source: Steve Melnyk et al., ISO 14000: Assessing Its Impact on Corporate Effectiveness and Efficiency (Tempe, AZ: Center for Advanced Purchasing Studies, 1999).

ABB Example of ISO 14000 Implementation

For example, ABB is a global technology company serving customers in power transmission and distribution; automation; oil, gas and petrochemicals; building technologies; and financial services; with about 165,000 employees in more than 100 countries. More than 97 percent of its sites worldwide have implemented ISO 14001 as their Environmental Management System. Additionally, ABB is moving forward with the development of Environmental Product Declarations (EPDs) for its major product lines. As of February 2001, four EPDs had been certified to comply with ISO 14025 and 14040-43, 15 more were ready for certification, and another 10 were in the development process.[16]

Benefits of Effective Disposal

Reasons for Limited Interest in Investment Recovery

It is surprising that more attention has not been given by organizations to the whole problem of investment recovery and disposal. There are several reasons. One of the most important is that *scrap* suggests something that has no value and the junk man can take away—in other words, something a company is willing to sell if it can get anything for it, but, if not, it is willing even to pay somebody to haul away. Another reason is that many concerns are not large enough to maintain investment recovery departments because the amounts of scrap and surplus they generate do not appear great

---

[16]ABB News ISO 14001, *www.abb.com.,* February 25, 2001.

enough to warrant particular attention. However, the potential benefits of effective investment recovery programs to organizations are numerous and include recovery of raw material costs, cost reduction and avoidance, improved company image, compliance with government regulations, and resource conservation.[17]

Scrap is often a potential source of profit, and therefore, the most obvious contribution of properly managed disposal activities is cost recovery. For example, Signetics Company, an electronics firm, claims to have generated more than $1 million in annual bottom-line income over 14 years by reclaiming and recycling precious metals, other metals, and solder.[18]

Costs Rising at Land-Fills

Directing residuals to landfills is an expensive disposal option. Tolling costs at landfills often exceed $100 per ton in some regions and are continuing to escalate.[19] Associated costs, such as handling and transportation, make using landfills even more expensive. Firms can reduce their costs or avoid cost increases by examining ways to reduce or reuse their scrap materials.

Disposition costs are often ignored by managers who prefer to concentrate on more traditional cost areas, such as direct labor and raw material costs. In situations where firms produce a high volume of scrap, regular examination of plant investment recovery activities can lead to cost-reduction initiatives. Managers should examine scrap handling processes, segregation activities, logistics costs, and fees charged by dealers, brokers, and processors.

Ford Reevaluated Disposal Practices

Ford is an example of an organization that has recently reevaluated its disposal practices by negotiating scrap management contracts with eight companies to manage its industrial scrap metal at its North American operations. Instead of selecting bids from more than 100 brokers and processors each month as under the previous system, current suppliers have been awarded one-year contracts. These eight processors will be involved in evaluating opportunities at Ford plants to reduce disposal costs, concentrating on the areas of processing and transportation.[20]

The "Greening" of Business

Governments, shareholders, and consumers are pressuring firms to develop and implement policies that protect the natural environment. This process has been referred to as the "greening" of business.[21] Most industrialized countries are setting aggressive recycling targets for their industries.

---

[17]P. Fraser Johnson, "Ferrous Scrap Disposition Strategies: An Analytical Model of Residual Disposal," unpublished doctoral dissertation, The University of Western Ontario, September 1995.

[18]Terry Sullivan, "Scrap: Victim of Benign Neglect," *Electronic Buyers News,* September 25, 1989, p. 16.

[19]"How to Throw Things Away," *The Economist,* April 13, 1991, p. 17.

[20]Michael Marley, *American Metal Market,* Thursday, September 20, 1995, vol. 103, no. 181, p. 1.

[21]Noah Walley and Bradley Whitehead, "It's Not Easy Being Green," *Harvard Business Review,* May-June 1994, p. 46.

Such pressures have been particularly strong in Europe, where Germany has passed ambitious legislation that imposes responsibility for recycling consumer waste on manufacturers.[22] Purchasing managers can make a contribution by identifying materials suitable for recycling or reuse, examining alternative and innovative disposal options, and securing raw materials which maximize production yields.

Categories of Material for Disposal

Reasons Why Material Becomes Disposable

No matter how well a company is managed, some excess, waste, scrap, surplus, and obsolete material will develop. Every organization tries, of course, to keep such material to a minimum. But try as it may, this never will be wholly successful. The existence of this class of material is the result of a wide variety of causes, among which are over-optimism in the sales forecast; changes in design and specifications; errors in estimating usage; inevitable losses in processing; careless use of material by factory personnel; and over-buying resulting from attempts to avoid the threat of rising prices or to secure quantity discounts on large purchases.

We are not presently concerned with the methods by which excess, waste, scrap, or obsolete material may be kept at a minimum; these already have been discussed in connection with proper inventory and stores control, standardization, quality determination, and forward buying. The immediate problem has to do with the disposition of these materials when they do appear. We first need to distinguish among the six categories of material for disposal.

Excess or Surplus Materials

Surplus Materials Result From Inaccuracies in Quantity Decisions

Excess (or surplus) material is that stock which is in excess of a reasonable requirement of the organization. It arises because of errors in the amount bought or because anticipated production did not materialize. Such material may be handled in various ways. In some cases it can be stored until required, particularly if the material is of a nonperishable character, if storage costs are not excessive, and if there is a reasonable expectation that the material will be required in the future. Occasionally it may be substituted for more active material. Or, if the company operates a number of plants, it may be possible to transfer the excess to another plant. There are times, however, when these conditions do not exist and when prompt sale is desirable. The chances for change in the style or design may be so great as to diminish considerably the probability that this particular material may be required. Or, it may be perishable. Factory requirements may be such as to postpone the

---

[22]Frances Cairncross, "How Europe's Companies Reposition to Recycle," *Harvard Business Review,* March–April 1992, p. 34.

demand for large amounts of this material so far into the future that the most economical action is to dispose of it and repurchase at a later date.

Many companies set some rough rule of thumb by which to determine when a stock item is to be classified as surplus. Thus, according to one manufacturing organization:

Defining Excess Material

> Generally speaking, the question of excess material should be decided on a six-month basis. Customarily, the excess would be that amount of material on hand which represents more than a six-months' supply. There are exceptions, however. Some material deteriorates so rapidly that any quantity on hand greater than two or three months' supply should be treated as excess material. In other cases, where it takes six months or longer to buy new material, more lengthy supply periods are frequently essential.

This rule suggests that all material should be grouped into rough classifications, and normal requirement and supply periods established for each. Mere classification in itself is not sufficient. As with all classes of material, systematic, physical stock-taking, continuous review of inventory records, and occasional cleanup campaigns also are necessary.

Another source of excess material usually appears on the completion of a construction project. The company just referred to covers this situation as follows:

> All new material for a specific property on order and not used on the project in question constitutes an inventory and must be treated as such. As soon as the work is completed, all new, unused material should be transferred immediately to the custody of the stores department.

Provision also is made for the proper accounting of used material created or resulting from demolition work carried on in conjunction with construction projects.

In the case of one large manufacturing company, if the sales department has definitely obligated the company to make a certain quantity of an item, or has set up a sales budget for that quantity subsequently accepted by the management, and later finds itself unable to dispose of its quota, the losses sustained on the excess material are charged to that particular item or sales classification. The same practice is followed if the sales department, by virtue of recommending a change in design, creates an excess of material.

Obsolete Material or Equipment

Obsolete material differs from excess stock in that whereas the latter presumably could be consumed at some future date, the former is unlikely ever to be used inside the organization which purchased it. For example, typewriter ribbons in a stock room become obsolete when the machines they fit are replaced by word processing equipment. Material becomes obsolete as a result of a change in the production process or when some better material is substituted for that originally used.

**Obsolete is a
Relative Term**

Once material has been declared obsolete, it is wise to dispose of it for the best price that can be obtained.

Although material or equipment may be obsolete to one user, this need not mean that it is obsolete to others. An airline may decide to discontinue using a certain type of airplane. This action makes not only the plane but also the repair and maintenance parts inventory obsolete. But both may have substantial value to other airlines or users of planes.

Rejected End Products

Because of the uncertainties of the production process, or because of complex end-product quality specifications, a certain percentage of completed products may be rejected by outgoing quality control as unsatisfactory. In some instances these finished products can be repaired or re-worked to bring them up to standard, but in other instances it is not economic to do so. The semiconductor industry is a good example; because of the technological complexities of the process, the "yield" on a particular production line may be such that only 70 percent of the finished devices measure up to end-product specifications.

**Ways of
Handling
Rejected End
Products**

The rejected products may then be sold to users who do not require the normal quality in purchased items. These might be classified as factory seconds. One problem is that if the end product is identified with a name or trademark, unscrupulous buyers may then turn around and remarket the item as one which measures up to the stated quality requirements for the original item. To avoid this, the sales contract may include a statement that "the buyer agrees and warrants that the product will not be resold in its present form or for its original usage application." If the seller does not feel this contract clause provides adequate protection, then the firm may find it necessary to destroy the rejected items (as is done in the pharmaceutical industry), remove the distinguishing mark or identification, or melt the product down to recover any valuable metal content. Signetics Company destroys excess inventory and outdated ICs and recovers precious metals on-premises to prevent substandard parts entering the gray market.[23]

Scrap Material

Scrap Defined

Scrap material differs from excess or obsolete stock because it cannot properly be classified as new or unused. Scrap is a term which may be applied to material or equipment that is no longer serviceable and has been discarded. It includes such items as worn machinery and old tools. In such cases, scrap arises because the company is replacing old machines with others that are more modern and more productive. A concern buying new machines, tools,

---

[23]Sullivan, "Scrap: Victim of Benign Neglect," op. cit., p. 16.

and other equipment normally maintains a depreciation charge intended to cover the original cost of such items, so that the value of a machine has been written off by the time it finally is discarded. Such a depreciation charge normally covers an obsolescence factor as well as ordinary wear and tear. Actually, however, a discarded or scrapped machine may still have a value for some other manufacturer in the same type of business or in some other industry. It consequently may be disposed of at a price that will show a profit in many instances. This replacement of old or obsolete machines by others capable of greater production at the same or lower cost provides a real profit-making opportunity.

Scrap Can Take Many Forms

Another form of scrap is represented by the many byproducts of the production process, such as fly from cotton spinning, warp ends from weaving, and ferrous and nonferrous metal scrap from boring, planing, and stamping machines; flash metal from the foundry process; or paper cuttings from the binding process, as when this book was bound. Start-up adjustment scrap is frequently significant, and in industries like papermaking, paper converting, printing, and polyethylene pellet manufacturing, it is one major reason for a significant price increase for small custom orders. The faster and the more automated the equipment, the higher the start-up scrap will be as a percentage of the total material used in small orders. Commonly, items of this class, which are a normal part of the production process, are considered a form of scrap; such material frequently may be salvaged. In the metal industries, the importance of scrap in this form has a definite bearing on costs and prices. For instance, a selection from among forgings, stampings, or castings may depend on the waste weight. The waste weight to be removed in finishing plus labor costs of removing it may make a higher-priced article the better value. In turning brass parts, the cost of the material (brass rod) may be greater than the price of the finished parts because the recovered brass scrap is such an important element in the cost. Indeed, scrap is so valuable as an element in cost that it is not unusual for the purchase contract on nonferrous metals to include a price at which the scrap will be repurchased by the supplier.

Two Categories of Scrap Metal

Scrap metals normally are separated into ferrous and nonferrous categories. Ferrous includes those products conceived from iron and generally are attracted by the scrap man's geiger counter (an ordinary magnet). The ferrous group consists of scrap steel, cast iron, white iron, and so on. The nonferrous group includes four broad families: (1) red metals, which are copper based, (2) white metals, which are aluminum, tin, lead, or zinc based, (3) nickel alloys, and (4) precious metals—for example, gold, silver, and palladium—known as exotics.

Recycling Scrap is Big Business

There are some 1,500 scrap dealers and brokers in the United States who buy, broker, and/or process scrap commodities, including metals, paper, plastics, glass, rubber, and textiles. The dealer or broker acts as an intermediary between the seller (normally the purchasing department) and the final buyer (such as a steel mill). These scrap buyers and suppliers of equipment and services to the scrap industry are represented by the Institute of Scrap Recycling Industries (ISRI), a trade association that has developed detailed, extensive specifications governing the grading and shipping of ferrous and nonferrous scrap materials, glass cullet, paper stock, and plastic scrap.[24] The ISRI Scrap Specifications Circular 1998 is available on the ISRI Web site, *www.isri.org.*

Waste

Waste Has No Current Economic Value

Waste is material or supplies that has been changed during the production process and which through carelessness, faulty production methods, poor handling, or other causes has been spoiled, broken, or otherwise rendered unfit for further use or reclamation. There is a form of waste not due to obsolescence and yet not a result of carelessness or poor handling. Waste, for example, may occur by the fact that the material is not up to specifications because of faulty machinery or breakdowns, or because of unforeseen chemical action. In some instances, waste can be defined simply as the residue of materials that results from the normal manufacturing process and which has no economic (resale) value. An example is the smoke produced by burning fuel or in the smelting process, or the cutting oil that has become so badly contaminated as a result of the normal manufacturing process that it cannot be reclaimed. However, what is waste today and has no current economic value may change tomorrow. For example, years ago the natural gas produced in crude oil production was waste and was flared off in the oil fields because it had no sales value; today it has substantial economic value.

Hazardous Waste

Three Stages of Dealing with Hazardous Waste

Hazardous waste is defined by the Superfund Act as toxic, ignitable, corrosive, or dangerously reactive substances. The United States produces about 212 million tons of hazardous waste a year. Efforts to deal with the problem have gone through three stages. In stage 1, the focus was on highly visible sources of pollution, for example, smoke stacks. In stage 2, the focus was on less visible, uncontrolled hazardous waste sites, e.g., buried waste. In stage 3, the focus is on limiting production of hazardous waste, recycling, and source reduction. Because of purchasing's role in the acquisition of materials and the disposal of waste, purchasers should consider the total cost of hazardous waste for the company. These costs include direct cleanup costs, disposal costs (rapidly rising due to a landfill shortage), administrative and legal costs, and new plant and equipment costs (to reduce waste and deal with contaminated plants).

---

[24]The Institute of Scrap Recycling Industries, 1325 G Street, N.W. Suite 1000, Washington, D.C. 20005, is a national association of firms that are predominantly processors and brokers of scrap. The Institute publishes several reports on the scrap industry and provides much data. ISRI also offers an arbitration service to its members, *www.isri.com.*

The Institute of Scrap Recycling Industries proposes the following action plan, which undoubtedly would involve purchasing:[25]

Action Plan for Hazardous Waste Management

Phase I: Develop an inventory of products containing toxic heavy metals.

Phase II: Consider how best to handle the hazardous materials that have the potential to contaminate currently nonhazardous waste.

Phase III: Define how best to encourage the future substitution of nonhazardous materials for the hazardous materials used now and previously used.

Phase IV: Consider how best to deal with those materials that pose long-term hazardous waste threats and for which no substitutes appear economically feasible.

Purchasing's Role

Purchasers play a key role in transferring information required by the Hazard Communication Standard (HCS) or "right-to-know" law developed by the Occupational, Safety and Health Administration (OSHA). Material Safety Data Sheets (MSDS) provide the information necessary to recognize potential health hazards to employees and the community at large. The purchaser should request an MSDS from the manufacturer or supplier, perform a hazard evaluation considering the need for the chemical against the potential hazard to employees and the community, and, if necessary, develop sourcing and usage alternatives. The MSDS should be kept on file.

Packaging and Movement of Hazardous Waste

Laws and regulations for hazardous materials also cover packaging and movement of hazardous materials. Title 49 of the Code of Federal Regulations (CFR), based upon the recommendations of the United Nations Committee of Experts on the Transport of Dangerous Goods, divides hazardous materials by degree of danger into three "packing groups." Packing Group I, the highest degree of hazard, includes the most highly corrosive materials; Packing Group II, medium danger goods; Packing Group III, lowest hazard of regulated materials. Steps are outlined for packaging, filling, and closure.

Differences of opinion may exist as to the exact definitions of scrap, excess, and waste. From the standpoint of the purchasing manager who has to dispose of the material, these differences are secondary. The objective is to realize as large a return as possible from the safe disposal of these items.

Responsibility for Material Disposal

The question of who bears the responsibility for the management of material disposal in an organization has more than one answer. In large companies where substantial amounts of scrap, obsolete, surplus, and waste materials

---

[25]The Institute of Scrap Iron and Steel Inc., "Dealing with Potential Hazardous Waste and Potentially Non-Recyclable Materials," op. cit., p. 18.

are generated, a separate department may be justified. The manager of such a department may report to the general manager or the production manager. In some companies there is, within the manufacturing department, a separate investment recovery, salvage, or "utilization" division to pass on questions about possible reclamation. Indeed, the place of the "investment recovery" division is well-established among many larger firms. This division is primarily a manufacturing rather than a sales division and is concerned with such duties as the development of salvage processes; the actual reclamation of waste, scrap, or excess material; and the reduction of the volume of such material. Most companies depend on the purchasing department to handle disposal sales.

A study of purchasing organizational relationships, conducted in 1995 by the Center for Advanced Purchasing Studies, covered the practices of 302 major organizations in the United States and Canada. That study found that purchasing was responsible for scrap/surplus disposal/inventory recovery in 63 percent of the firms.[26] The 1999 CAPS *Performance Benchmarks for Investment Recovery*[27] found that the ratio of total gross revenue to operating expense was 20, giving a benefit-to-cost ratio of 20 to 1. The average benefit provided by each investment recovery employee was $1,733,690. Internal transfers as a percentage of total transactions was 44.7 percent. Third-party sales transactions as a percentage of total transactions was 65.2 percent.

Reasons Purchasing May Be Responsible for Investment Recovery

Some very legitimate reasons for assigning disposal of materials to the purchasing/materials management function include: (1) knowledge of price trends; (2) contact with salespeople is a good source of information as to possible users of the material; (3) familiarity with the company's own needs may suggest possible uses for, and transfer of, the material within the organization; and (4) unless a specific department is established within the firm to handle this function, purchasing is probably the only logical choice.

In conglomerate and highly diversified and decentralized types of organizations, there is a great need for the coordination of salvage disposal if the best possible results are to be obtained. Where a corporate purchasing department is included in the home-office organization structure, even if only in a consulting relationship with the various divisions of the company, available information and records and established channels of communication should help to ensure that salvage materials generated in any part of the company are considered for use in all parts of the company before being offered for sale.

Turnkey Environmental Contracting is Feasible for Some

Because the social and financial stakes are high and because of the complexity of laws and regulations, turnkey environmental contracting is a possible option for small- to medium-sized waste generators with needs that are

---

[26]Harold E. Fearon and Michiel R. Leenders, *Purchasing's Organizational Roles and Responsibilities* (Tempe, AZ: Center for Advanced Purchasing Studies, 1995), p. 20.

[27]*Performance Benchmarks for Investment Recovery,* Tempe: Center for Advanced Purchasing Studies, 1999 (1997 data).

too diverse or too small to be handled directly by treatment, storage, or disposal facilities.

The general conclusion is that, except in the cases of companies with separate salvage or investment recovery departments, management has found the purchasing department, because of its knowledge of materials, markets, prices, and possible uses, in a better position than other departments of the company to salvage what can be used and to dispose of what cannot.

Keys to Profitable Disposal

Obviously, the optimum solution would be not to generate materials that need disposal. While this is not totally possible, every effort should be made, through good planning and taking advantage of modern technology, to minimize the quantity of material generated.

Compare Options to Achieve Greatest Gain

The disposition of all kinds of scrap and surplus materials always should be handled to reduce the net loss to the lowest possible figure or, if possible, achieve the highest potential gain. The first thought, therefore, should be to balance against each other the net returns obtained from each of several methods of disposition. Thus, excess material frequently can be transferred from one plant to another of the same company. Such a procedure involves little outlay except for packing, handling, and shipping. At other times, by reprocessing or reconditioning, material can be salvaged for use within the plant. Such cases clearly involve a somewhat larger outlay, and there may be some question as to whether, once the material has been so treated, its value, either for the purpose originally intended or for some substitute use, is great enough to warrant the expense.

Because the decision whether to undertake the reclamation of any particular lot of material is essentially one of production costs and of the resultant quality, it should be—and commonly is—made by the production or engineering departments instead of by purchasing or the scrap department. The most the purchasing manager can do is to suggest that this treatment be considered before the material is disposed of in other ways.

Disposal Channels

There are several possible means of material disposal. In general, the options are, in order of maximum return to the selling company:

Use Elsewhere within the Firm on an "As Is" Basis. An attempt should be made to use the material "as is," or with modification, for a purpose other than that for which it was purchased; for example, substitution for similar grades and nearby sizes, and shearing or stripping sheet metals to obtain narrower widths. In the case of a multidivision operation, periodically each division should circulate to all other divisions a list of scrap/surplus/obsolete material and equipment; arrangements then may be made for interplant transfer of some of the items. In some organizations with an Enterprise Resource Planning (ERP) system (See Chapter 4), a national and even global database has been developed for individuals from the same organization to post and purchase spares, obsolete materials, and excess supplies from one another more efficiently and cost-effectively than in the past.

Hewlett-Packard Reuse and Recycling Program

Hewlett-Packard developed a reuse and recycling program called Alternate Sourcing to transform retired, excess products and parts into useful service parts through disassembly and refurbishment.[28] Unusable material is sent to lower-level, noncompetitive recovery channels. In the United States, Alternate Sourcing receives more than 250 metric tons per month of retired assets, excess inventory, and manufacturing fallout from Hewlett-Packard and other companies. Thirty percent of the material has internal service utility and is reused, 70 percent has no internal utility in its existing form, but 85 percent of the total can be recycled, and less than 15 percent goes to landfill. Hewlett-Packard's goal is zero percent to landfill within five years.

Reclaim for Use within the Plant. For example, can the material be reclaimed or modified for use by welding? Welding has become a very important factor in disposing of materials to advantage. Defective and spoiled castings and fabricated metal parts can be reclaimed at little expense; short ends of bar stock and pipe can be welded into working lengths; and worn or broken jigs, fixtures, and machine parts can be built up or patched. Furthermore, castings and fabricated metal parts can be reduced in size by either the arc or acetylene cutting process. Or perhaps a steel washer(s) could be stamped out of a piece of scrap (referred to as off-fall) that is a normal output of the production process. Precious metal scrap often is shipped to a precious metal refiner, who processes it back into its original form and returns it for use as a raw material, charging the purchasing department a tolling charge for its services.

As a result of the materials shortages of the early 1970s, the environmental movement of the 1980s, and new recycling processes of the 1990s, many firms have become interested in the possibilities of recycling materials, such as paper, copper, zinc, tin, aluminum cans, and precious metals. In addition to economic advantages, this may provide a partial solution to some of our environmental problems. For example, since 1990, Hewlett-Packard has diverted more than 18 million pounds of material from landfills by recycling every toner cartridge received through its HP Planet Partners™ LaserJet Toner Cartridge Recycling Program into raw materials for use in the manufacture of everyday products.[29] One of the problems faced by pur-

Recapturing Materials at Hewlett-Packard

---

[28]Kathy Stuesser and Landon J. Napoleon, "A High-Tech Quest to Reduce Landfill," *NAPM Insights,* February 1994, p. 62.

[29]Insert in Hewlett-Packard LaserJet Toner Cartridge box, February 19, 2001.

chasers is the tendency to coat, bond, or blend materials in such a way that they become nonrecyclable in the future.

The opportunities for recycling, and thereby reducing the waste stream, extend beyond municipal recycling systems and include programs that "close the loop" by collecting the material, turning it into cost-competitive, high-quality, recycled content products and selling them back to the purchaser. By forming a partnership with grocery store chains like Giant Foods, Rubbermaid Commercial Products (RCP) in Winchester, Virginia, collects stretch pallet plastic wrap from the groceries and recycles it for use in manufacturing products. The partnership provides a consistent source of large quantities of clean, recycled plastic.[30]

Sell to Another Firm for Use on an "As Is" Basis. Can any other manufacturer use the material either "as is," or with economical modification? It should be noted that sales can often be made direct to other users who may be able to use a disposal item in lieu of a raw material they currently are buying. Or, one firm's surplus or obsolete equipment may solve another firm's equipment requirements nicely. A good example of this is the market that has existed for years for DC-9 aircraft, which are obsolete for one air carrier and are bought for use by supplemental or commuter airlines. In some cases, and particularly prevalent in public agencies, surplus or obsolete equipment and vehicles are sold at public auction. Some companies permit employees to buy, as part of their employee relations program, used equipment or surplus materials at pre-set prices. If this is done, adequate controls should be established to ensure that the return to the firm is at a reasonable level.

Return to Supplier. Can it be returned to the manufacturer or supplier from whom it was purchased, either for cash or for credit on other later purchases? A great deal of steel scrap is sold by large-quantity purchasers directly back to the mills, who use it as a raw material in the steel production process. Normally, the firm using this disposal avenue must be a large consumer. In the case of surplus (new) inventory items, the original supplier may be willing to allow full credit on returned items.

Sale through a Broker. Brokers can handle the sale of scrap. Their role is to bring buyer and seller together, for which they take a commission. Much metal scrap is disposed of through this channel. Brokers also exist to handle the purchase and sale of obsolete, surplus, used, and rebuilt equipment and typically specialize by either industry—for example, bakery—or type of equipment—for example, computers. This medium often is used by the selling organization and may present interesting alternatives for the buyer in the equipment acquisition process.

For example, iSolve.com is an online marketplace for buyers and sellers of new and like-new inventory, excess capacity, idle assets, and real estate.

---

[30]Harold Leibovitz, "Cost-Effective Systems for Recycling Plastics," *NAPM Insights,* March 1994, p. 43.

Online Market-places Available

Listings are provided in a wide range of key vertical markets, offer a transaction-based commerce site with full functionality to negotiate and close business, and deliver merchant services to ensure successful transactions.[31] The Inter-Continental Metal Exchange (IME) is a free, worldwide information exchange for those companies and individuals who buy/sell/trade.[32]

Four Reasons the Return From Sale to Local Scrap Dealer May Be Low

Sale to a Local Scrap or Surplus Dealer. All communities of any size will have one or more scrap dealers. The return from sale through this channel likely will be low, for four reasons:

1. There may be only one dealer, a noncompetitive, sole buying source.
2. The dealer assumes the risk of investment, holding, and attempting to find a buyer. The profit margin for assuming this risk may be quite high.
3. Extra movement and handling, which is costly, is involved.
4. The seller usually doesn't become an expert in the scrap market, due to the relatively small volumes involved; the scrap or surplus dealer is an expert. However, the industrial scrap merchant may provide several valuable services, for example, recommendations on handling, sorting, and processing methods; supply collection containers; and provide pickup of materials.

Non-Profit Clearing-houses Distribute Donations

Donate, Discard, or Destroy the Material or Item. In some instances a firm may decide to donate used equipment to an educational or charitable organization, taking a tax deduction. Because the tax aspects of such contributions are complex, the advice of tax counsel should be obtained as part of the decision process. A number of nonprofit clearinghouses distribute goods to schools and charities. Among these organizations are the National Association for the Exchange of Industrial Resources (NAEIR), the Industrial Materials Exchange (IMEX), and the Gifts-in-Kind Clearinghouse. Share the Technology Computer Recycling (*www.sharetechnology.org*) offers a searchable database which connects donors and recipient nonprofit organizations. The National Recycling Coalition (*www.nrc-recycle.org*) maintains a database of U.S. recyclers. The Parents, Educators & Publishers (PEP) Directory of Computer Recycling Programs (*www.mircoweb.com/pepsite/ Recycle/recycle_index.html*) lists agencies that facilitate donations of used computer hardware to schools and community groups in the United States, Canada, the United Kingdom, Africa, Australia, India, Jamaica, and Bahrain. Apple Computer's Systems Remarketing Group refurbishes returned computers, printers, and other peripherals and distributes the equipment through a number of channels including donations to schools, nonprofit agencies, and other organizations.[33]

---

[31]*www.isolve.com,* April 20, 2001.
[32]*www.metalworld.com/exchange,* April 20, 2001.
[33]Leibovitz.

**Discarding is
a Last Resort**

If no buyer or user can be found for the item, the firm may have to destroy or bury the item. This can be quite costly because of the landfill shortage in the United States and the liability posed by environmental hazards. Caution should be taken to protect the environment and to ensure that disposal methods for dangerous materials do not create a safety hazard to the public. The Investment Recovery Association, an international nonprofit trade association of firms with established investment recovery programs, provides assistance in disposing of recyclable products, capital assets, and surplus materials.

Disposal Procedures

When selling scrap and surplus materials, adequate procedures must be established that will protect the company from loss due to slipshod methods, dishonest employees, and irregular practices on the part of the purchaser. These procedures must cover a broad range of activities, including segregation and storage, weighing and measuring, delivery, negotiation, supplier selection, and payment.

Contamination of scrap with foreign materials will often significantly reduce its recovery value. If two types of scrap, for example, steel and copper scrap, are mixed, the return per pound on sale likely will be less than the lowest-priced scrap, because any buyer must go to the expense of separating the scrap before processing. Consequently, scrap should be segregated, prepared, and analyzed systematically during the various stages of the production process in order to protect its value.

**Scrap Must
Be Segregated
to Realize
Greatest Gain**

Scrap can be segregated by type, alloy, grade, size, and weight, and should be done at the point where the scrap is generated. This requires proper planning and organization of segregation activities, which includes providing instructions to employees at collection points. Training programs can also be used to help company employees identify and separate scrap materials. Plants, not the dealers or the processors, should control the collection and classification of scrap materials, and company personnel should be familiar with the grades of scrap produced. Periodic studies should be conducted to evaluate the most effective methods of disposing of scrap in light of changing volumes and different mixes of scrap grades.

Adequate controls should be in place for accurate reporting and payment. All sales should be approved by a department head, and cash sales should be handled through the cashier and never by the individual whose duty it is to negotiate the sale. All delivery of byproducts sold should be accomplished through the issuing of an order form, and a sufficient number of copies should be made to provide a complete record for all departments involved in the transaction. The shipping department should determine the weight and count, and this information should be sent directly to the billing department without going through the hands of those who negotiated the sale.

The department responsible for the performance of this function should maintain a list of reputable dealers in the particular line of material or equipment to be disposed of and should periodically review this list. At frequent intervals, the proper plant official should be instructed to clean up the stock and report on the weights and quantities of the different items or classes of items ready for disposal.

Selecting a Scrap Dealer

A common procedure is to send out invitations to four or five dealers to call and inspect the lots and quote their prices FOB factory yard. Such transactions usually are subject to the accepted bidder's check of weights and quantities and are paid for in cash before removal. Not infrequently, acceptable and dependable purchasers with whom satisfactory connections have already been established are relied on as desirable purchasers, and no bids are called for from others. Technology tools are increasingly applied to investment recovery programs, as demonstrated by a 1999 benchmarking study conducted by the Center for Advanced Purchasing Studies.

Web-Based Investment Recovery

In the CAPS study, fifty-four percent of surveyed companies used the Internet as a marketing tool and 45 percent used the company intranet. The Internet pages received an average of 28 inquiries per month and the intranet an average of 41 inquiries per month. Of Investment Recovery departments whose role it was to locate and purchase used machinery and equipment, an average of $209,000 was bought via a Web search. The average external sales via Internet was $1,049,333; the average Internal transfers via intranet was $822,631; the average percent of total sales via Internet was 21.8 percent; the average percent of total sales via intranet was 23.5 percent. The average annual cost of maintaining Web activities was $7,471. Sixty-eight percent of companies maintained their Internet pages internally, and 32 percent maintained them by subscription service. One hundred percent of companies maintained their intranet pages internally. Clearly the Internet and a company's intranet can be used to facilitate the investment recovery process.

If a firm generates large amounts of scrap materials consistently, the bidders may be asked to bid on the purchase of this scrap over a time period of six months to a year. It is generally advisable to rebid or renegotiate such contracts at least annually to encourage competition. However, when establishing contract duration, plants need to consider the associated transaction costs. Not only are there administrative costs of soliciting bids, other costs need to be taken into account, such as possible production interruptions as equipment provided by the old processor is replaced by the new processor. Plants often negotiate long-term agreements with their processors in order to encourage investment in equipment viewed as beneficial by plant management.

Use of Escalator Clauses in Agreements

Often the disposal agreement will have an escalator clause in it, tying the price to changes in the overall market, as reported in a specifically designated issue, such as the first Tuesday of each month of the *American Metal Market*. The market prices of many grades of scrap materials can vary widely over a relatively short time period, which is the reason for the use of escalator clauses. For example, over a one-year period, the price of scrap steel, No. 1, heavy metal composite, increased from $130.50 per gross ton to $141.75 (8.6 percent); No. 1 heavy copper, Chicago, rose from $0.87 to $1.04 (19.5 percent); and segregated low-copper aluminum clips, Chicago, went from 45.5 cents to 58.5 cents (28.6 percent).[34] Scrap prices are just as volatile on the downside during certain time periods.

The contract for sale of scrap items should include price and how determined, quantities involved (all or a percentage), time of delivery, FOB point, cancellation privileges, how weights are determined, and payment terms. For reporting purposes, revenues associated with the scrap disposal activities should be credited to separate accounts, as opposed to netting them against a purchase or expense account. The practice of netting scrap revenues against raw material costs may be justified for statement presentation purposes, but such revenue should be itemized on management statements and budgets.

Investment Recovery Examples

Most items can be disposed of profitably by use of imagination, creative thinking, and problem-solving. Recent research on the importance of environmental considerations in strategic purchasing and supply chain management indicates that avoidance of violations is still the primary focus.[35] Yet many organizations are coming up with creative and cost-effective ways to handle investment recovery challenges.

UPS. For example, United Parcel Service (UPS) joined with The Alliance for Environmental Innovation, a joint initiative of the Environmental Defense Fund (EDF) and The Pew Charitable Trusts, to ensure that UPS met performance specifications, costs targets, and required standards. As a result of the alliance project,

Results of UPS Initiative

- UPS nearly doubled the amount of post-consumer recycled material in the UPS box and is using at least 80 percent post-consumer recycled material in the Express Letter,
- Reduced waste and pollution from production of all shipping materials by an average of 13 percent, and
- Projected a savings of more than $1 million annually by cutting energy costs and reducing the amount of material used.[36]

---

[34]*American Metal Market,* Thursday, September 14, 1995, Vol. 103, no. 177, p. 12.

[35]Joseph R. Carter, and Ram Narasimhan, *Environmental Supply Chain Management* (Tempe, AZ: Center for Advanced Purchasing Studies, 1998).

[36]Lori A. Sisk and Roberta J. Duffy, "At the Drawing Board," *Purchasing Today,* May 1999, p.p. 63–64.

Personal Computer (PC) Recycling.[37] A huge investment recovery challenge faces every nation as its inhabitants use more and more electronic devices in their work and home life. Consider the case of personal computers. A typical PC is 40 percent steel, 30–40 percent plastic, 10 percent aluminum, and 10 percent other metals, including copper, gold, silver, cadmium, and platinum, plus glass and lead for the monitor. A computer purchased today will be obsolete within three years, and that life span is shrinking. In 1999, the U.S.-based National Recycling Coalition conducted a survey of electronic recycling efforts. It found that in 1998, 20 million computers were taken out of service and only 2.3 million were recycled. Between 2000 and 2007, it is projected that 500 million PCs will become obsolete. What becomes of all those old computers and all those valuable resources?

Number of Obsolete PCs Sky-rocketing

The most desirable option is to find a use for PCs in their current condition. Obsolete is a relative term. If a PC is no more than five years old and in good condition, there may be plenty of organizations and people for whom your obsolete PC would represent leading-edge technology. The first task would be to research opportunities to either sell or donate an organization's old PCs. There are also organizations like the Computer Recycling Center, a nonprofit organization in Santa Clara, California, that refurbish computers and provide them to people who would not otherwise have access to the technology.

First Option: Sell or Donate

The second option is to recapture the valuable materials in the various components. This can be done in a number of ways. Computer manufacturers often have extensive recycling programs. For example, Hewlett-Packard recycles 3.5 million pounds of electronic equipment a month in its own recycling plant. IBM's IntelliStation E Pro Computer has eight major parts made from 100 percent recycled plastic, and the cover of its RS/6000 server contains 25 percent recycled plastic.

Second Option: Recapture Materials

Recycling companies take apart the machines either by hand or with shredders and then separate the materials. Figure 11–4 shows what can become of the recaptured materials.

Selecting the Right Disposal Partner

Challenge in Selecting a Disposal Partner

Selection of the appropriate firm to handle waste and scrap removal can be a challenging, yet critical, task. First, most scrap materials can be sold. However, purchasing managers are used to buying, not selling, materials. Second, hazardous materials must be properly disposed of; failure to do so can result in substantial fines and cleanup costs. This requires an understanding of regulatory issues surrounding residual disposition. Third, disposal methods

---

[37]This example was drawn from the following articles by Heidi Schuessler, *Breaking Down All Those Computers: Glass Over Here, Plastic There* and *Recycling Efforts Take Off at Last, The New York Times* on the Web, November 23, 2000.

FIGURE 11–4

Materials Recaptured from a Computer

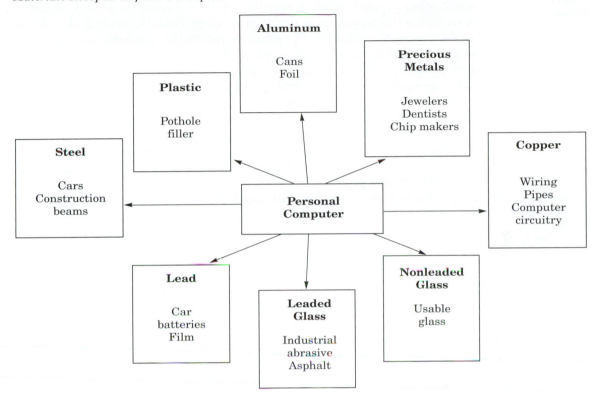

have implications for the general manufacturing operation. Decisions, such as segregation, impact a plant's processing operations and influence its cost structure. Consequently, traditional purchasing precepts do not always apply when selecting a firm to handle disposal activities.

In most situations, plants must rely on support from scrap dealers to help manage elements of their disposal activities. As a result of the costs associated with regulatory noncompliance, generators of scrap and waste must be aware of what happens to the material after it leaves the company premises. Consequently, only approved processors, dealers, or brokers should be used, with qualification based on a range of possible criteria: secondary processing and waste treatment capabilities and capacity; size and capacity of truck fleet; ability to provide dependable service; problem-solving capabilities; ability to provide destruction of scrap products in order to avoid entry into the market; and financial stability. Assessing the financial stability of the dealer, broker, or processor often requires obtaining a list of credit references or obtaining a credit report from an organization such as Dun & Bradstreet.

Volume Influences Disposal Choices

    The volume of scrap or waste material has a significant influence on how companies choose to manage their disposal activities. Plants with high volumes often support disposal activities with dedicated staff and employ a greater level of resources in the disposition process. Depending on volume, logistics systems also differ. For example, plants that generate a high volume of a particular grade of scrap may find it cost-effective to utilize rail transportation or specialized highway trailers. Plants producing lower volumes may use smaller, less traditional forms of transportation.

    Every effort should be made to obtain maximum competition from sources available to buy scrap or surplus material. Unfortunately, the number of potential users and buyers of scrap in a particular area may be small, resulting in noncompetitive disposal situations. Purchasing should actively attempt to find new buyers and encourage then to compete in terms of price paid and services provided.

Organizational Performance Impacted by Investment Recovery

    Investment recovery involves supplier management issues, which have implications for the overall performance of the firm. Measuring total costs of disposition is useful as a means of identifying a range of opportunities to work with disposal partners with the objective of improving activities. For example, in a cooperative relationship, joint problem-solving efforts can be utilized by the plant and scrap investment buyer as a response to changing issues. Make-or-buy decision criteria can be applied to determine the appropriate mix of activities for the plant; these activities should be reevaluated regularly to adapt to changing situations.

Questions for Review and Discussion

1. Why is investment recovery often a responsibility of the purchasing department?

2. How can the firm obtain maximum return from disposal of unneeded items?

3. What specific procedures should purchasing use to dispose of unneeded items?

4. What are the channels used in disposing of items? What are the advantages of each?

5. What is the difference between surplus material, obsolete material, rejects, scrap, waste, and hazardous waste?

6. What are the four categories of nonferrous scrap metals? Give an example of an item in each category. What formal specifications are available for use in buying and selling these metals?

7. How do environmental concerns affect the disposal of scrap, surplus, and obsolete materials?

8. How can the Internet be used to facilitate investment recovery programs?

References

Bloom, Gordon F. and Michael S. Scott Morton. "Hazardous Waste Is Every Manager's Problem." *Sloan Management Review,* Summer 1991.

Cairncross, Frances. "How Europe's Companies Reposition to Recycle." *Harvard Business Review* 70, no. 2 (March–April 1992).

Carter, Craig R. and Marianne M. Jennings, *Purchasing's Contribution to the Socially Responsible Management of the Supply Chain,* Tempe, AZ: Center for Advanced Purchasing Studies, 2000.

Carter, Joseph R. and Ram Narasimhan, *Environmental Supply Chain Management,* Tempe, AZ: Center for Advanced Purchasing Studies, 1998.

The Economist. "How to Throw Things Away," April 13, 1991.

The Environmental Protection Agency (EPA). *The Lean and Green Supply Chain: A Practical Guide for Materials Managers and Supply Chain Managers to Reduce Costs and Improve Environmental Performance.* EPA742-R-99-003, February 2000, *www.epa.gov.*

The Environmental Protection Agency (EPA). *Enhancing Supply Chain Performance with Environmental Cost Information: Examples from Commonwealth Edison, Andersen Corporation, and Ashland Chemical.* EPA 742-R-99-002, April 2000, *www.epa.gov.*

European Computer Manufacturing Organisation (ECMA)

Johnson, P. Fraser. "Ferrous Scrap Disposition Strategies: An Analytical Model of Residual Disposal." Unpublished doctoral dissertation, The University of Western Ontario, September 1995.

Melnyk, Steven, Roger Calantone, Rob Handfield, R. L. Tummala, Gyula Vastag, Timothy Hinds, Robert Sroufe, Frank Montabon, and Sime Curkovic, *ISO 14000: Assessing Its Impact on Corporate Effectiveness and Efficiency,* Tempe, AZ: Center for Advanced Purchasing Studies, 1999.

Performance Benchmarks for Investment Recovery. Tempe, AZ: Center for Advanced Purchasing Studies, 1999 (1997 data).

Swedish IT-Companies Organisation (SITO) (*www.sito.se*), provides documents and guidelines describing environmental attributes of electronic equipment.

Walley, Noah and Bradley Whitehead. "It's Not Easy Being Green." *Harvard Business Review* 72, no. 3 (May–June 1994).

CASE 11–1
NOVA STAMPING COMPANY

Sandra Glassford, purchasing manager at Nova Stamping Company, Detroit plant, was working in her office in June when the plant manager, Jim Armstrong, walked in and announced, "Head office just gave us approval for the two new 800-ton presses. I want you to give some consideration as to how we should handle disposing of the old equipment."

Nova Stamping Company. Nova Stamping Company ("Nova") manufactured metal stampings and assemblies for the North American automotive industry. The Detroit plant had sales of $35 million and employed 155 people. The plant was one of three manufacturing facilities operated by the company; the other two were located in Canada. The company's customers included General Motors, Ford, Chrysler, and several Japan–based automotive companies.

Nova transformed flat rolled steel into structural components, which were shipped to automobile assembly plants on a JIT basis. The manufacturing process at Nova involved the use of tools, set up in stamping presses, that "stamped" steel sheets into finished parts. Depending on their size, presses were able to accommodate either multiple or single dies. Typically, presses supported a number of different dies, and setups occurred at least once per shift. Nova often used welding equipment to assemble its stampings into larger components.

Equipment Disposal Issue. Although the basic manufacturing process in the automotive stamping industry had not changed dramatically over several years, new presses were being equipped with features such as automatic transfer devices and PLC controllers which improved their productivity, efficiency, and uptime. Nova was systematically upgrading its equipment in response to competitive pressures in the industry. Such investments were usually coordinated with the introduction of new products in order to match the manufacturing capabilities of its presses with its products.

The Detroit plant had recently been awarded a large contract from Ford, which required the replacement of several old, smaller stamping presses and support equipment with two new machines with a capacity of 800 tons. The machines that would be replaced by the two new presses are listed in Exhibit 1 on the next page.

All of the equipment identified as obsolete was expected to remain in production until the two new presses were delivered in approximately eight months. In conversation with Alex Brown, the plant maintenance supervisor, Sandra understood that several of the machines needed an overhaul if they were to remain in production beyond the following year. Other machines were at the end of their useful lives, and therefore, not worth repairing.

The Equipment Disposal Issue. Sandra understood that management would expect her to identify the most beneficial disposal option for the obsolete equipment. However, because she had almost no experience with equipment disposal, she wondered how to proceed and what criteria should be used to assess the various options. How much was the equipment worth and who should she call to get prices? Were there any legal considerations of which she should be aware? Who should be responsible for removing the equipment from Nova's plant?

Installation of the new equipment was important to the successful launch of the new Ford business. Sandra wanted to make sure that she addressed each of the relevant issues associated with the disposal of the obsolete equipment in order to avoid complications.

CASE 11–2
ORNEX

On June 3 Greg Saunders, materials manager at Ornex, a parts manufacturer in Detroit, Michigan, heard the company had not been awarded a large new contract it had expected from its main automotive customer. Greg had ordered a substantial shipment of customized metal powder in anticipation of this contract, and now he wondered how to dispose of the raw material on hand.

Exhibit 1   Obsolete Equipment

Machine	Specifications	Machine	Specifications
Press #20	70 ton capacity 18" × 30" bed acquired: 1973	Press #19	300 ton capacity 48" × 96" bed acquired: 1961
Press #5	75 ton capacity 30" × 48" bed acquired: 1960	Press #39	135 ton capacity 48" × 60" bed acquired: 1968
Press #41	110 ton capacity 36" × 48" bed acquired: 1968	Press # 15	135 ton capacity 40" × 54" bed acquired: 1968
Press # 4	200 ton capacity 34" × 58" bed acquired: 1973	Press # 14	165 ton capacity 48" × 96" bed acquired: 1960
Welder #121 & Welder #122	75 KVA capacity 12" throat acquired: 1972	Press # 23	70 ton capacity 23" × 34" bed acquired: 1960
Press # 7	115 ton capacity 33" × 67" bed acquired: 1962	Press # 26	165 ton capacity 48" × 84" bed acquired: 1964
Press # 8	165 ton capacity 30" × 60" bed acquired: 1964	Press # 9	150 ton capacity 30" × 50" bed acquired: 1971

Ornex. Ornex, an automotive parts manufacturer, had been supplying North American automobile companies for four decades. Some of the products manufactured included transmission gears, hubs, and crank shafts. The plant employed approximately 150 people, and Ornex manufactured 12 different automotive parts.

Ornex's mission was: "to produce world-class competitive products that exceed our customers' expectations in quality, cost, and delivery through people, teamwork, and technology."

Raw Materials Purchasing. Ornex obtained metal powders from two major sources: 60 percent of its requirements came from FE Metal Powders Inc. based in Quebec, and the remainder from Simpsons Powders Inc. based in the United States. Both of these suppliers performed rigorous tests on their metal powders, and Greg considered these two companies to have the highest quality raw materials in the industry.

Because of the high demand for metal powders, delivery schedules varied depending on the type of product requested by Ornex. Delivery normally took 10 weeks for standard products and up to 16 weeks for special formulations of metal powders. Thus, long lead times required extensive inventory planning. Moreover, occasionally raw material had to be ordered prior to confirmation of a customer contract.

The metal powder suppliers recognized the difficulties with material planning and offered most parts manufacturers a consignment period of 60 – 120 days. The consignment clause meant that Ornex only paid for powder it used. Thus, if a metal powder had been purchased for a major job prior to the acceptance of a bid, and if that job was awarded to a competitor, the powder could be returned as long as it was unused and had been purchased in the last two to four months. However, consignment did not apply to any type of customized order.

The New Contract. In July of the previous year, Ornex had submitted a bid to manufacture "races," a new type of transmission part for its primary automotive customer. If the bid were accepted, production would have to begin the following March. Due to the long raw material lead time, Greg placed an initial order for the customized raw iron powder in early November. FE Metal Powders was selected to provide 400,000 pounds of powder at a cost of $0.60 per pound. After the 16-week waiting period, the 400,000 pounds would be delivered in monthly shipments of 100,000 pounds each.

By March however, Greg still has not received contract confirmation. The iron powder began to accumulate in inventory, but Greg was not concerned because the plant had adequate space. However, on June 3 the automobile company awarded the bid to a competing automotive supplier. Greg immediately requested the cancellation of all remaining deliveries. FE Metal Powders agreed to cease all shipments, but at this late date Ornex had already acquired 300,000 pounds of customized raw iron. This inventory had been purchased on credit. The supplier would be demanding payment by the end of the month.

The Current Situation. Greg wondered what his best option was with respect to the 300,000 pounds of metal powder already in Ornex's inventory. He could see at least two options. First, Ornex could return the inventory. FE Metal Powders understood the nature of this/or the company's dilemma and verbally agreed to take back the inventory. FE Metal Powders would act as a selling agent and try to resell the inventory to another parts manufacturer. Ornex would be required to pay a commission of $0.20 per pound. This would protect FE Metal Powder from future loss if it could not resell the customized powder. Even though this would mean a loss for Ornex, this alternative was worth considering.

If the customized powder could not be used within one-and-a-half years, or if the seal on the package were broken, the powder could develop rust. If rust balls developed, this would burden the company with further costs for screening out the rust if the powder was to be used.

Greg also was considering keeping the inventory on hand. Greg anticipated that 100,000 pounds of the customized powder could be used in the near future. However, the remaining stock probably would not be completely cleared out for another 18 months. Greg knew that inventory carrying costs at Ornex were usually calculated at 2 percent per month of the value of the inventory. There was adequate space to hold the powder in the current facilities, but the real concern was rusting of the unused powder. Greg knew that the longer the packages remained sitting in inventory, the greater the probability that the packages could be broken. He also recognized that if this alternative was chosen, a payment schedule for the powder would have to be negotiated with FE Metal Powders.

12 LEGAL ASPECTS OF PURCHASING

Chapter Outline

Key Questions for the Purchasing Decision Maker

SHOULD WE

- Put all purchase agreements in writing?
- Inspect goods before payment?
- Insert a commercial arbitration clause in large-dollar purchase agreements?

HOW CAN WE

- Protect against price fluctuations in long-term contracts?
- Minimize our own personal liability for purchase actions?
- Avoid legal disputes with suppliers?

The competent professional purchaser does not require the training of a lawyer but should understand the basic principles of commercial law. Such understanding should enable recognition of problems and situations that require professional legal counsel and also provide the knowledge to avoid legal pitfalls in day-to-day operations.

Seldom will either buyer or seller resort to the courts to enforce a purchase contract or assess financial damages. In those infrequent situations where formal legal action is the last resort, the legal costs can be high and the outcome uncertain. *The competent purchaser wishes to avoid such situations* **Legal Action Is** *and will take legal action only as a last resort.* A knowledge of the law of con-
a Last Resort tracts will help the purchaser avoid such legal involvement and position the organization to successfully pursue, or defend itself against, such lawsuits.

Legal Authority of the Purchasing Officer

What is the purchasing officer's legal status? Briefly, he or she has the authority to attend to the business of purchasing in accordance with the instructions given by his or her employer. These instructions usually are broad in character. There should be, and in all progressive organizations there is, a clear understanding as to what the purchasing officer is expected to do. This normally is covered by a job description (see Figures 2-1 and 2-2 for sample job descriptions). Attention already has been called to the necessity for a clear understanding of duties simply as a matter of good business policy. The reasons for this clear understanding, important as they are from other points of view, are strengthened by the fact that the law assumes an agreement between the agent and the employer as to the scope of the authority. Presum-
Scope of ably, the purchasing officer performs these assigned duties to the full extent
Authority of his or her capacity. In other words, the purchasing officer has a right to ex-
Defined pect from the employer a clear understanding as to his/her duties and re-

sponsibilities; the purchasing officer, in turn, is expected to perform these duties in a loyal, honest, and careful manner. So long as he or she does this, the obligations to the employer, from a legal point of view, are fulfilled. In agreeing to render service to an employer, there is no implied agreement that no errors will be made, for some errors are incidental to all vocations.

Buyer Must Use Due Care

By special stipulation, the purchasing manager may even assume responsibility to the principal for the risks from honest error, but such arrangements are rare. Nevertheless, when a person accepts an appointment to serve as an agent for the principal, the implication exists that the person possesses the necessary skill to carry on the work. In some cases, a very high degree of skill is demanded and accepting an appointment under such circumstances implies the necessary skill. There are, of course, many possible modifications of this general statement. The purchasing officer becomes liable to the employer when damage occurs through active fault or through negligence. Many difficulties arise in attempting to define what negligence is, although in general it may be said to constitute an "omission of due care under given circumstances."

The buyer also has an obligation to keep his or her employer informed about specific actions taken to perform the purchasing function and to report resultant outcomes from these actions. In addition, records must be kept and an accounting made for any funds or property handled. If the purchaser does not fulfill these obligations, his or her employer may sue for damages.

Apparent Scope of Authority Defined

Because the purchasing officer is acting as an agent for the company he or she represents, it follows that the officer is in a position to bind the company within limits. Actually, of course, the power of an agent to bind the principal may greatly exceed the right to do so. This right is confined by the limits assigned, that is, in accordance with the actual authorization; power to bind the principal, however, is defined by the *apparent* scope of authority, which in the case of most purchasing officers is rather broad. Unauthorized purchasers, for example, an engineer who agrees to buy something from a salesperson, acquires apparent authority as soon as the company ratifies the purchase by receiving and making payment. The engineer now has indefinite apparent authority to buy similar products from the same supplier for similar dollar amounts. Each time the company ratifies an unauthorized purchase a valid contract is created and apparent authority is created. Procurement card programs, which give limited authority to nonpurchasers, set spending limits, and designate what can and cannot be purchased, are an effective and legal means of giving limited authority to persons outside the purchasing department, thus allowing purchasing professionals to focus on more critical goods and service.

Furthermore, to avoid personal liability, it must be made clear to the person with whom the buyer deals that the buyer is acting as an agent. In fact, the law requires even more if buyers are not to be held personally liable; not only must they indicate that they are acting as agents, but also the person with whom they are dealing must agree to hold the principal responsible, even though the latter is at the moment unknown.

Implied Authority Defined

The actual authority delegated to an agent is not limited to those acts which, by words, the agent is expressly and directly authorized to perform. Every actual authorization, whether general or special, includes by implication all such authority as is necessary, usual, and proper to carry through to completion the main authority conferred. The extent of the agent's implied authority must be determined from the nature of the business to be transacted. These powers will be broad in the case of one acting as a general agent or manager. It is the duty of the third party dealing with the agent to ascertain the scope of the agent's authority. Statements of the agent as to the extent of powers cannot be relied on by the third party. Any limitation on the agent's power which is known to the third party is binding on the third party.

Personal Liability of the Purchasing Officer

Five Conditions Governing Personal Liability

Purchasing officers may be held personally liable under certain conditions when signing contracts. These conditions include: (1) making a false statement concerning authority *with intent to deceive,* or when the misrepresentation has the natural and probable consequence of misleading; (2) performing a damaging act without authority, even though believing they have such authority; (3) performing an act that is itself illegal, even on authority from the employer; (4) willfully performing an act that results in damage to anyone; and (5) performing damaging acts outside the scope of their authority, even though the act is performed with the intention of rendering the employer a valuable service. In each of these cases, the supplier ordinarily has no recourse to the company employing the agent because no valid contract existed between the seller and the purchasing firm. Because such a contract does not exist, the only recourse the supplier commonly has is to the agent personally.

Should the question arise as to who may be sued on contracts made within the apparent scope of the agent's authority but beyond the actual scope, because of the fact that there were limitations on the latter unknown to the seller, it may still follow that the principal can be held liable. Under these circumstances, the agent probably is in the wrong and is, of course, answerable to the principal. Buyers may also be answerable to the seller on the ground of deceit, or the charge that they are the real contracting parties, or for breach of the warranty that they were authorized to make the precise contract they attempted to make for the principal.

Moreover, suits have been brought by sellers against purchasing managers when it was discovered that the latter's principal was for some reason unable to pay the account. For example, such conditions have arisen when (1) the employer became insolvent or bankrupt; (2) the employer endeavored to avoid the legal obligations to accept and pay for merchandise purchased by the purchasing manager; or (3) the employer became involved in litigation with the seller, whose lawyers decided that the contract price could be readily collected personally from the purchasing manager.

Although a purchasing officer should never attempt to perform the duties of a competent lawyer, the alert buyer and purchasing manager should keep informed about court decisions and changes in laws that affect his or her actions. Purchasing trade publications normally report court decisions and major changes in laws that impact the performance of the buying function.

As previously stated, purchasing officers are personally liable for the commission of any illegal act, and this liability holds even though they are unconscious of the illegality of the act and though it is done under the direction of the employer. A buyer is not likely to commit an illegal act consciously; but under the stress of severe competition, in an effort to secure as favorable terms as possible for his or her company, the buyer may run afoul of the law **Antitrust Laws** unintentionally. It is well to remember that the antitrust acts apply to buy-**Also Apply to** ers as much as to sellers. The U.S. Supreme Court has held that these acts **Buyers** are applicable to all attempts to restrain trade, even though the restraint is exercised on those not engaged in the same line of business and is based on purchasing activities rather than selling activities—provided that the net result of the act is to restrain competition.[1] (See Chapter 9 for a discussion of antitrust legislation.)

The Purchase Order Contract

Uniform Many federal, state, and local statutes govern purchasing practice, but the **Commercial** Uniform Commercial Code (UCC) covers most of the transactions involving **Code Covers** the purchase and sale of goods. The UCC does not cover the purchase of ser-**Sale of Goods** vices or combined contracts of goods and services if services constitute more than 50 percent of the contract. In these situations, common law applies. Common law is established by cases decided in U.S. courts. Purchasers may want to include separate terms relating to the goods portion of the contract so that the UCC applies to that portion of the contract. (See Chapter 17 for a discussion of purchasing of services.) The UCC resulted from the joint efforts of the American Law Institute and the National Conference of Commissioners on Uniform State Laws. Since the first publication of the Uniform Commercial Code in 1952, it has undergone numerous revisions and refinements, with the latest edition coming in 2000.[2] All states except Louisiana have enacted the code into law.

Article 2, Uniform Commercial Code - *Sales,* governs purchase/sale transactions and applies to transactions by *merchants,* defined as "a person who deals in goods of the kind, or otherwise by his occupation holds himself out as

---

[1]Christopher L. Chaney, "Steering Clear of Legal Issues Takes Diligence," *Electronic Buyers' News,* December 4, 1995, p. 74.

[2]The American Law Institute and National Conference of Commissioners on Uniform State Laws, *Uniform Commercial Code, 2000 Official Text* (Philadelphia, PA: The American Law Institute, 2000).

having knowledge or skill peculiar to the practices or goods involved in the transaction, or to whom such knowledge or skill may be attributed by his employment of an agent or broker or other intermediary who by his occupation holds himself out as having such knowledge or skill."[3] In Article 2, a buyer is defined as a person who buys or contracts to buy goods, and a seller is a person who sells or contracts to sell goods. These changes are addressed in the appropriate sections of this chapter.

Article 2 of the UCC Governs Commercial Sales

When Does the UCC Not Apply

The UCC applies only to legal situations arising in the United States (and then only to 49 of the states—not to Louisiana. Because Louisiana has a legal system based on the Napoleonic Code, there would be no need to adopt the UCC, which clarifies and updates English common law). If the buyer feels that legal problems may arise in dealing with a supplier outside the United States, the purchase contract then should specify under which country's laws the dispute would be adjudicated. If both countries have adopted the United Nations Convention on Contracts for the International Sale of Goods (CISG), the CISG will apply *unless* both parties agree to something else. Canada, for example, does not have a standardized set of commercial laws for the entire country; each province has developed its own set of laws dealing with property and civil rights within its boundaries, and there are major differences between the laws of some provinces.

Four Factors of a Valid Contract

A valid contract is based on four factors:

1. Competent parties—either principals or qualified agents.
2. Legal subject matter or purpose.
3. An offer and an acceptance.
4. Consideration (bargained-for exchange).

Level of Detail in Terms and Conditions Varies

The purchase order generally is regarded as containing the buyer's offer and becomes a legal contract when accepted by the supplier. Many purchase order forms have a copy that includes provision for acknowledgment or acceptance. There has never been universal agreement on how detailed the terms and conditions that are printed on the purchase order should be. Some companies' forms use the reverse side to spell out the complete terms and conditions that apply to any transaction. Some companies may include a separate printed sheet detailing terms and conditions applying to that specific order. Other companies provide only for the very basic items necessary for a valid offer and depend on the provisions of the UCC for proper legal coverage. The purchasing officer should rely on the legal counsel responsible for handling legal matters for the company in determining the policy to be followed.

Buyer or Seller May Make an Offer

An *offer* can be equally valid if made by a seller, either in writing or verbally. Such an offer becomes a legal contract when accepted by the buyer. Regardless of whether an offer is made by the buyer or the seller, it can be modified or revoked before it is accepted. However, an offer in writing that

---

[3]Ibid., 2-104.

includes an assurance that the price will remain firm for a specified period may not be revoked prior to the expiration of that period. Under the UCC, if a seller makes a firm offer to sell, it generally must be held open for a "reasonable" time period. This reasonable time period generally has been held to be three months, unless a shorter period is stated by the seller at the time the offer was made.[4]

The courts generally have held that advertisements and price lists do not constitute legal offers unless specifically directed to the buyer, or unless an order placed on the basis of the advertisement or price list is specifically accepted by the supplier.

Acceptance of Orders

Because the purchase order form or the sales contract is intended to include all the essential conditions surrounding the transaction, it is customary to include in the agreement a statement such as, "Acceptance of this order implies the acceptance of conditions contained thereon." The purpose of such a provision is to make all the conditions legally binding on the seller and to avoid cases in which the seller advances the defense that he or she was not aware of certain conditions. Statements similar to that indicated are found in practically all purchase agreements to give warning that there are conditions attached, either on the front or on the reverse side of the contract.

Having placed an order with a supplier, the purchasing officer wishes to ensure that the order has been accepted. To obtain such assurance, it is customary to insist on a definite supplier acknowledgment, usually in written form. It is not uncommon to incorporate, as a part of the contract, a clause requiring that the acceptance be made in a particular manner, in which case a form is enclosed with the order, and the purchase order contains a clause which stipulates: "This order must be acknowledged on the enclosed form."

The question may arise as to when an offer either of sale or of purchase has been accepted. As a matter of law, the person making an offer may demand, as one of the conditions, that acceptance be indicated in a specific manner. Ordinarily, however, when an offer is made, the offeror either expressly or by implication requires the offeree to send the answer by mail, facsimile, or other electronic transmittal. When the answer is duly posted, faxed, or electronically transmitted, the acceptance is communicated and the contract is completed from the moment the letter is mailed, the telegram is sent, or the fax or the electronic document complete with a digital signature is transmitted. Any reasonable manner of acceptance is satisfactory, unless the offeror makes it quite clear that acceptance must be made in a particular manner. Acceptance may be "in any manner and by any medium reasonable in the circumstances."[5] This allows for the use of new communication media.

Acceptance Can Take Several Forms

[4]Ibid., 2-205.
[5]Ibid, 2-206.

The increased use of facsimiles (fax), electronic data interchange (EDI), and the advent of Web-based purchasing systems to send bids, purchase orders, and contracts requires buyers and sellers to agree on procedures and terms and conditions to prevent disputes that might end up in court. The National Conference of Commissioners on Uniform State Laws and the American Law Institute developed and proposed a body of law related to electronic commerce. Instead of including this in the rules in the UCC, the committee recommended that state legislatures decide whether or not they wish to adopt the proposals as state law.[6] The U.S. Congress, as well as many other government bodies around the world, passed legislation making digital signatures legal.

Digital Signatures Legal in Many Nations

Sometimes the supplier may use an acknowledgment form of its own, which may conflict with some of the conditions stated in the purchase order. Often in such situations, a careful comparison is not made of *all* conditions stated in the offer with *all* conditions stated in the acceptance. If litigation subsequently occurs between buyer and seller, application of the UCC may resolve the question:

The UCC Is Used to Determine Contract Validity

(1) A definite and reasonable expression of acceptance or a written confirmation which is sent within a reasonable time operates as an acceptance, even though it states terms additional to or different from those offered or agreed upon, unless acceptance is expressly made conditional on assent to the additional or different terms.

(2) The additional terms are to be construed as proposals for addition to the contract. Between merchants, such terms become part of the contract unless:

  a. the offer expressly limits acceptance to the terms of the offer;

  b. they materially alter it; or

  c. notification of objection to them has already been given or is given within a reasonable time after notice of them is received.

(3) Conduct by both parties that recognizes the existence of a contract is sufficient to establish a contract for sale, although the writings of the parties do not otherwise establish a contract. In such case, the terms of the particular contract consist of those terms on which the writings of the parties agree, together with any supplementary terms incorporated under any other provisions of this Act.[7]

A clause that would materially alter the contract and result in surprise or hardship if incorporated without express awareness by the other party is, for example, one that negates standard warranties which usually apply, or one that requires quantity guarantees where the usage of the trade allows

---

[6]Helen M. Pohlig, "Keeping Pace with the Times," *Purchasing Today,* July 1999, p. 24.
[7]UCC, 2-207.

greater quantity leeways. If the additional or different terms do not materially alter the deal, then they will be incorporated into the contract, unless the other party objects to them within a reasonable time. Thus, if the buyer does not wish to get into a dispute as to whether the seller's acceptance materially alters any of the provisions of the original offer, on the face of the purchase order (PO) should be placed a statement that "Absolutely no deviations from the terms and conditions as contained in this offer will be permitted."

Purchases Made Orally

Purchase of Goods Must Be in Writing if $500 or More

Most professional buyers have occasion to place orders over the telephone or orally in person. However, the UCC specifies that:

1. Normally there must be some written notation if the price of the order for the sale of goods is $500 or more.

2. If the seller supplies a memorandum that is not in accordance with the buyer's understanding of the oral order, he or she must give a notice of objection to the supplier within 10 days of receipt of the memorandum to preserve his or her legal rights.[8]

When an alleged oral agreement is partially performed, for example, one of ten lots is delivered and then the purchaser cancels, the partial performance can validate the contract, but only for the amount already accepted. An exception to this falls under the doctrine of promissory estoppal which says if one party "relied to its detriment" on the promises made by the other party, the entire contract may be validated. Some type of writing is needed to demonstrate that a contract exists, but performance, partial or complete, removes the requirement for writing either for the partial or complete fulfillment of the contract. Both the buyer and seller may rely on the doctrine of promissory estoppal, which is an exception to the statute of frauds.[9]

To safeguard against misunderstandings when in a conversation with a supplier, say "this is not an order" if you are seeking information only; instruct your suppliers not to begin work without authorization; and document all changes made after the purchase order has been issued.

Authority of Suppliers' Representatives

Another important consideration relates to the authority of the salesperson representing a company with which the purchasing officer is transacting business. Subject to the many exceptions arising out of varying circumstances, the courts have consistently held that although an employer is bound by all

---

[8]Ibid., 2-201.

[9]William A. Hancock, "Partial Performance in Oral Agreements," *NAPM Insights,* August 1990, p. 8.

A Salesperson May or May Not Have Authority to Conclude a Contract

the acts of an agent acting within the scope of the employment, a salesperson's ordinary authority is simply to solicit orders and to send them to his or her employer for ratification and acceptance. It therefore behooves the purchasing officer to know definitely whether or not a salesperson has the authority to conclude a contract without referring it to the company which he or she represents.

Even if a supplier does not authorize its salesperson to enter into binding contracts, and although the company may do nothing to lead others to believe that its representative has such power, yet if the salesperson does enter into a contract with a buyer, that contract is likely to be held valid unless the seller notifies the buyer within a reasonable time that the salesperson has exceeded his or her authority. In other words, a contract results because the conduct of the seller is interpreted as acceptance. If the purchasing officer wishes assurance that the salesperson does have authority to sign the contract for the supplier, it is a simple matter to request a letter, signed by an officer of the supplier firm, specifying that the salesperson has the authority of a sales agent.

False statements on the part of the seller or its representative regarding the character of the merchandise being purchased cause the contract to become voidable at the option of the other party. It is true that this "undoubted right" to rely on sellers' statements is at best a highly qualified right, the value of which depends on the circumstances surrounding the transaction. However, aside from any legal question which is involved under ordinary circumstances, the seller is likely to be sufficiently jealous of its reputation and goodwill to make substantial concessions.

Inspection

Right to Inspect Goods Before Acceptance

One important right of the buyer is that of inspecting the goods before acceptance. The purpose of this rule is to give the buyer an opportunity to determine whether or not the goods tendered comply with the contract description. It is well established that buyers who inspect goods *before* entering into a contract of sale are put on guard and are expected to use their own judgment with respect to quality, quantity, and other characteristics of the merchandise. The UCC states that "when the buyer before entering into the contract has examined the goods or the sample or model as fully as he desired, or has refused to examine the goods, there is no implied warranty with regard to defects which an examination ought in the circumstances to have revealed to him."[10]

Where a purchaser accepts merchandise after inspection, either as to quality or quantity, the buyer ordinarily is prevented from raising an issue with respect to these points. Also, a seller cannot be held responsible for the

---

[10]UCC, 2-316 (3).

Inspection and Payment Terms May Impact the Seller's Liability

failure of equipment to perform the work which the buyer expected of it, if the latter merely provides material specifications without indicating to the seller the purpose to which the equipment or goods are to be put. In some purchase contracts, payment may be required before the buyer has had an opportunity to inspect the goods; for example, payment may be made before the seller actually ships the goods. Payment in this case does not constitute an acceptance of the goods or impair the buyer's right to inspect or any of the buyer's remedies on breach of contract.[11] In a JIT or ship-to-stock arrangement where goods are not inspected, the buyer needs to specify in the written contract a time-frame for notification of defects because the UCC does not cover these situations completely.

The courts generally have held that if a purchaser is not sufficiently experienced to be able to judge adequately the goods inspected, or if he or she relies on a fraudulent statement made by a seller and purchases in consequence of that fraudulent statement, the buyer then may rescind the contract or hold the seller liable for damages.

Cancellation of Orders and Breach of Contract

Once a contract is made, it is expected that both parties will adhere to the agreement. Occasionally one or the other seeks to cancel the contract after it has been made. Ordinarily this is a more serious problem for the seller than it is for the buyer, although occasionally a seller may wish to avoid complying with the terms of an agreement, in which event it may refuse to manufacture the goods or delay the delivery beyond the period stipulated in the agreement. The rights of the purchaser under these circumstances depend on the conditions surrounding the transaction. The seller is likely to be able, without liability, to delay delivering purchased goods when the buyer orders a change in the original agreement that may delay the seller in making delivery.

Collecting Damages for Failure of Delivery

If the seller fails to make delivery by the agreed time, the purchaser may without obligation refuse to accept delivery at a later date. However, the attempt to secure what the buyer might consider reasonable damages resulting from a breached sales contract is likely to be difficult, because the courts experience a good deal of trouble in laying down rules for the guidance of the jury in estimating the amount of damages justly allowed a buyer who sustains financial losses resulting from a seller's failure to fulfill a contract of sale. If there is a general rule, it is that the damages allowable to a purchaser if a seller fails to deliver goods according to contract are measured by the difference between the original contract price and the market value of the merchandise at the time when the buyer learned of the breach of contract and at

---

[11]UCC, 2-512.

the place where the goods should have been delivered, together with any incidental and consequential damages provided in Section 2-715.[12]

The seller is sometimes confronted by an attempted cancellation on the part of the buyer. It is not unusual, therefore, to find in the sales contract the following clause: "This contract is not subject to cancellation." As a matter of fact, the inclusion of such a clause has little practical effect, unless it is intended merely to indicate to the purchaser that if he or she attempts to cancel, a suit for breach of contract may be expected.

Market Conditions Influence Available Options

However, in a very strong seller's market, where the breach of contract by the seller is related to failure to deliver on a promised date or even to abide by the agreed price, the practical alternatives open to the buyer are almost nil. The latter still wants the goods and may be unable to acquire them from any other supplier on time or at any better price. Much the same restriction, in fact, exists even where the contract provides for the option of cancellation by the buyer. The purchaser wants goods, not damages or the right to cancel. If the chances of getting them as promptly from any other supplier are slight, the buyer is likely to do the best he or she can with the original supplier, provided, of course, that bad faith as to either price or delivery is not involved.

Warranties

Over time, the rules governing warranty arrangements between buyer and seller have advanced from *caveat emptor* (let the buyer beware) to the legal provisions of the UCC, which recognize four types of warranties:

Four Types of Warranties

1. Express warranty.
2. Implied warranty of merchantability.
3. Implied warranty of fitness for a particular purpose.
4. Warranty of title.[13]

Express

Essentially, express warranties include promises, specifications, samples, and descriptions pertaining to the goods that are the subject of the negotiation.

Merchantability

Implied warranty of merchantability has to do with the merchantable quality of goods, and the applicable UCC statutes have developed out of mercantile practices. Accepted trade standards of quality, fitness for the intended uses, and conformance to promises or specified facts made on the container or label are all used as measures of marketable quality.

Fitness for Particular Purpose

Implied warranty of fitness for a purpose usually results from a buyer's request for material or equipment to meet a particular need or accomplish a

---

[12]UCC, 2-713.
[13]UCC, 2-312, 2-313, 2-314, and 2-315.

specific purpose. The UCC provides that "where the seller at the time of contracting has reason to know any particular purpose for which the goods are required, and that the buyer is relying on the seller's skill or judgment to select or furnish suitable goods, there is . . . an implied warranty that the goods shall be fit for such purpose."[14] If the buyer provides detailed specifications for the item requested, the seller is relieved of any warranty of fitness for particular purpose.

Title

Warranty of title ensures that there are no liens against the title to the goods, and the goods are free from patent or copyright infringement.

Exclusions to Warranties

Under the UCC, suppliers may still write disclaimers or exclusions to warranties.[15] To exclude express warranties, suppliers may include a clause stating that "no express warranties have been made by the supplier except those specifically stated in this contract." To exclude implied warranties, suppliers must put the disclaimer in writing in a conspicuous place. Typical language is, "No implied warranties of merchantability or fitness for a particular purpose accompany this sale." A general disclaimer may be made by labeling the sale "as is" or "with all faults." Also, if the buyer examines the goods before the sale, the buyer is bound by all defects found and those the buyer should have found.[16]

Acceptance and Rejection of Goods

Forms of Acceptance

The acceptance of goods is an assent by the buyer to become the owner of the goods tendered by the seller. No unusual formalities are necessary to indicate that the buyer has accepted the goods. Any words or acts that indicate the buyer's intention to become the owner of the goods are sufficient. If the buyer keeps the goods and exercises rights of ownership over them, acceptance has taken place, even though the buyer may have expressly stated that the goods are rejected. If the goods tendered do not comply with the sales contract, the buyer is under no duty to accept them; but if the buyer does accept the goods, he or she does not thereby waive the right to damages for the seller's breach of contract. If the buyer accepts goods that do not comply with the sales contract, the seller must be notified of the breach within a reasonable time. What is a "reasonable time" is determined by normal commercial standards.[17] Recent legal rulings indicate that if the buyer tells the supplier about a problem, and even if the supplier tries to fix the problem but the buyer fails to specifically give notice "of breach," the supplier may have room for legal negotiating.[18] In the event the seller delivers goods or the tender of

---

[14]UCC, 2-315.
[15]UCC, 2-316.
[16]Gaylord A. Jentz, J.D., "Exclusion of Warranties," *NAPM Insights,* July 1991, p. 8.
[17]UCC, 2-607.
[18]William A. Hancock, "The UCC Notice Requirement," *NAPM Insights,* October 1990, p. 8.

Buyer's Three Options at Time of Delivery

delivery fails in any way to conform to the contract, the buyer has the option to (1) reject the whole shipment, (2) accept the whole shipment, or (3) accept part of the shipment and reject the balance. Rejection, of course, must be within a reasonable time after delivery and the seller must be notified promptly. The buyer must hold the goods, using reasonable care, until the seller has had sufficient time to remove them.[19] The question of whether to reject goods delivered under a particular order may arise from various causes and may be dealt with in a variety of ways. For instance, the goods may be late, may have been delivered in the wrong amount, or may fail to meet the specifications. The important thing to keep in mind is that the purchaser wants the goods. A lawsuit, therefore, is not desirable, even though the buyer may be granted any one of the commonly recognized judicial remedies for breach of contract, such as money damages or insistence on performance. Aside from the fact that it is goods the buyer wants, legal action is uncertain and often costly; it may take a great deal of time; and it may cause the loss of a good supplier.

Possible Adjustments in Case of Breach

The purchasing officer, therefore, usually seeks other means of adjustment. Several courses are open. The first question is the seriousness of the breach. If not too serious, a simple warning to the supplier may be quite adequate. If somewhat more stringent action is called for and if the goods received are usable for some purpose, even though not quite up to specifications, a price adjustment frequently can be worked out to the mutual satisfaction of the buyer and the seller. Sometimes the goods, though not usable in the form received, may be re-processed or otherwise made usable by the supplier, or by the purchaser at the supplier's expense. If the goods are component parts, they may be replaced by the supplier. If equipment is involved, or even processed material that is incapable of being efficiently used in its present form, the supplier may correct the defects at the user's plant. Or, as a last resort, the goods may be rejected and shipped back to the supplier, usually at the supplier's expense.

In some cases, purchasers use a full-payment check to settle a dispute. In this case the purchaser sends a check for what he or she believes covers the goods, less the cost of the defect, and writes the words "Payment in Full" to indicate that this is a settlement. The supplier, under the UCC, can cash the check and write "under protest" or "without prejudice" to protect its rights to try to collect the balance due. The courts recently have ruled that there is an offer and acceptance, hence a valid contract, if the check and notice were sent to a specific person who knowingly cashes the check. If, however, the check were merely sent to accounts receivable or some other routine processing area of the supplier's company, there would not be a real acceptance, and the supplier would still have rights to try to collect or settle the balance with the buyer.

[19]UCC, 2-601 and 2-602.

Protection against Price Fluctuations

Two Forms of Cancellation

Cancellations can be the direct result of action by the buyer. They arise in two ways, the first of which is not recommended. It comes about because the buyer, if compelled to live up to the agreement, would lose money. Conditions may have changed or sales may have fallen off. Therefore, the buyer no longer wants the goods. The market price may have dropped and the buyer could now buy the goods for less money. Faced with these conditions, the buyer seeks some form of relief. He or she becomes extremely watchful of deliveries and rejects goods that arrive even a day late. Inspection is tightened, and failure to meet any detail in the specifications is seized on as an excuse for rejection. Such methods should never be followed by a good purchasing officer.

The second form of cancellation may arise in a perfectly legal and ethical manner, through evoking a clause—occasionally inserted in purchase contracts—that seeks to guarantee against price decline. In purchasing goods subject to price fluctuations, it is in the interest of the buyer to be protected against unreasonable price changes. Occasionally, a long-term contract is drawn up that leaves the determination of the exact price open until deliveries are called for. To meet these conditions, a clause such as the following may be incorporated in purchase contracts:

Means of Price Determination Clause

Seller warrants that the prices stated herein are as low as any net prices now given by you to any customer for like materials, and seller agrees that if at any time during the life of this order seller quotes or sells at lower prices similar materials under similar conditions, such lower prices shall be substituted for the prices stated herein.

These stipulations against price decline are not confined to purchase agreements; under some circumstances the buyer may receive price reductions on the seller's initiative. An example of this type of clause is the following:

Price Reduction Clause

Should the purchaser at the time of any delivery, on account of this contract, be offered a lower price on goods of equal quality and in like quantity by a reputable manufacturer, it will furnish the seller satisfactory proof of same, in which event the seller will either supply such shipment at the lower price or permit the buyer to purchase such quantity elsewhere, and the quantity so purchased elsewhere will be deducted from the total quantity of this contract. Should the seller reduce its prices during the terms of this contract, the buyer shall receive the benefit of such lower prices.

Such clauses are legally enforceable and frequently work to the buyer's advantage. However, the administrative problems in seeing to it that these clauses are lived up to are substantial. The moral effect doubtlessly is greater than the legal.

Title to Purchased Goods

The professional buyer should have a clear understanding of when the title of goods passes from the seller to the buyer. Normally, there will be an agreement on the FOB (free on board) point, and the buyer receives title at that point (see

FOB Designation Determines When Title Transfers

Chapter 10 for domestic transactions, and Chapter 14 for international transactions). Sections 2-319 and 2-320 of the UCC cover the legal obligations under the various shipping terms (FOB, FAS, CIF, and C&F). On capital goods it is particularly important for tax and depreciation reasons to establish title before the tax-year ends.

If the buyer specifies a particular carrier for transportation of goods, the seller is responsible for following the buyer's instructions, which are part of the contractual agreement, subject to any substitution necessary because of the failure of the specified carrier to provide adequate transportation services. Of course, the seller must promptly notify the buyer of any substitutions made. If the buyer elects not to specify a particular carrier, the seller then may choose any reasonable carrier, routing, and other arrangements. Whether or not the shipment is at the buyer's expense, as determined by the FOB term used, the seller must see to any arrangements reasonable in the circumstances, such as refrigeration, watering of livestock, protection against cold, and selection of specialized cars.

Conditional Sales Contract

In some instances, the buyer is given possession of the goods prior to the passing of a legal title. This is known as a *conditional sales contract* and the full title passes to the buyer only when final payment is made. This procedure permits a buyer to obtain needed material or equipment now and to pay at some future time.

Uniform Computer Information Transaction Act

E-Commerce and the Law. In the 2000 revision of the UCC, the committee decided not to include a new section of Article 2 to deal with e-commerce. They did, however, propose a body of law, the Uniform Computer Information Transaction Act (UCITA), related to e-commerce, which a number of states have since adopted.

The Uniform Computer Information Transaction Act (UCITA)

UCITA Adapts Existing Contract Law to the Digital Marketplace

In 1993, the drafters of the UCC began an open review process to develop Article 2B, UCC-Sales, to include software and information transactions. It was later decided that a separate set of provisions, now known as the Uniform Computer Information Transaction Act (UCITA), should be developed based on the software licensing model. UCITA was approved by the National Council of Commissioners on Uniform State Laws (NCCUSL) in July 2000, and is now up for adoption by the legislatures of each of the 50 states. UCITA is a commercial code that would provide uniform rules and standards for electronic contracting that are based on existing principles of contract law adapted to the digital marketplace. UCITA was designed to recognize that technology is changing rapidly and that a flexible legal framework is essential. It is expected that UCITA, if adopted by the states, will reduce litigation while supporting continued growth of the computer information industry and expansion of electronic commerce.[20]

---

[20]Micalyn S. Harris, "Is UCITA Worthy of Active Support?" *The Metropolitan Corporate Counsel 40,* October 1999, found at *www.2bguide.com/legart.html.*

Uniform Electronic Transactions Act (UETA)

UETA Validates Use of Electronic Records and Signatures

Another body of legislation, the Uniform Electronic Transactions Act (UETA), was approved and recommended for enactment by the National Conference of Commissioners on Uniform State Laws in July 1999. UETA validates the use of electronic records and electronic signatures. As of December 2000, 22 state legislatures have adopted it and 7 others are considering it. The Federal E-Sign Act (discussed later in this chapter) allows a state to preempt the act if it has enacted UETA. UETA and the E-Sign Act (Public Law No. 106-229) bear many similarities, and in some situations the language of UETA was borrowed by the authors of the E-Sign bill. However, there are differences. UETA is more comprehensive than E-Sign and addresses some topics differently. UETA contains provisions for the following issues that are not dealt with in the E-Sign Act:

- *Attribution.* An electronic record or signature is attributed to a person if it was an act of that person.
- *Effect of other State Law.* UETA recognizes that an electronic signature is just as effective, valid, and enforceable as paper. However, questions of authority, forgery, and contract formation are determined by other state law.
- *Effect of Party Agreement.* The parties to the contract are free to enter into agreements concerning their use of electronic media.
- *Send and Receive.* UETA ties the determination of when an electronic record is sent or received to the communications systems used by the parties to the contract.
- *Effect of Change or Error.* E-Sign does not contain provisions for dealing with mistakes in electronic communications, while UETA does contain such provisions for breaches in security procedures and mistakes made by an individual dealing with an electronic agent. Unless otherwise specified, the rules of mistake apply.
- *Admissability.* UETA specifies that electronic records cannot be excluded as evidence solely because they are in electronic format.[21]

Electronic Signatures

Digital Signature Defined

One of the critical issues in e-commerce transactions has been the legality of electronic or digital signatures for contractual purposes. The term digital signature is used generically here to mean electronic authentication of documents. The governments of many countries as well as the United Nations Commission on International Trade Law (UNCITRAL) and the European Union have focused on the legal aspects of e-commerce.[22] The telecommuni-

---

[21]Patricia Brumfield Fry, "A Preliminary Analysis of Federal and State Electronic Commerce Laws," UETA Online, *www.uetaonline.com/docs.*

[22]McBride, Baker & Coles, "E-Commerce Spotlight," *www.mbc.com/ecommerce/recent_updates.asp.*

cations ministers of the 15 member nations of the European Union (EU) passed the Electronic Signature Act, which grants digital signatures the same legal status as written ones. It must be approved by each EU government before going into effect. Canada Bill C-6, The Personal Information Protection and Electronic Documents Act, was enacted October 26, 1999, and several provinces including Saskatchewan, Manitoba, and British Columbia have enacted provincial legislation related to various aspects of e-commerce. Legislation is also pending in Yukon, Nova Scotia, Quebec, and Ontario. The Uniform Law Conference of Canada has proposed a draft of a Uniform Electronic Commerce Act.

Japan enacted the Japanese Law Concerning Electronic Signatures and Certification Services on May 24, 2000. In 1998, the United States and Japan issued a Joint Statement on Electronic Commerce which recognized that electronic commerce will be "an engine of economic growth in the twenty-first century. . . . and e-commerce will enhance the standard of living of citizens in the United States and Japan as well as the rest of the globe." The joint statement went on to say, "The Governments of the United States and Japan recognize the importance of working together to promote global electronic commerce." Four general principles were endorsed:

Four Principles of US-Japan Joint Statement

1. The private sector should lead in the development of e-commerce and in establishing business practices.

2. Both governments should avoid imposing unnecessary regulations or restrictions on e-commerce.

3. Governments should encourage effective self-regulation through codes of conduct, model contracts, guidelines, and enforcement mechanisms developed by the private sector.

4. Cooperation and harmonization among all countries, from all regions of the world and all levels of development, will assist in the construction of a seamless environment for electronic commerce.[23]

US E-Sign Law

In the United States a number of states have passed legislation on electronic signatures, but the passage of the Electronic Signatures in Global and National Commerce Act (Public Law No. 106–229) in June 2000 was an attempt to develop uniform rules across the country. The E-Sign bill was introduced to regulate interstate commerce by electronic means by permitting and encouraging the continued expansion of electronic commerce through the operation of free market forces, and for other purposes. This statute, which went into effect October 1, 2000, grants online legal or financial agreements signed with a digital signature or chain of electronic code equivalent legal status with handwritten signatures and paper documents. It includes

---

[23]*Joint Statement on Electronic Commerce by U.S. and Japan,* found on Web site of McBride, Baker & Coles, *www.mbc.com/ecommerce.*

electronic record-keeping provisions effective March 1, 2001. The E-Sign statute specifies that:

1. No one is obligated to use or accept electronic records or signatures.
2. If a notice must be provided to a consumer in writing, an electronic version is permissable only if the consumer has consented to accepting an electronic version and demonstrated that he can access the information electronically.
3. A state may preempt the act only if it has adopted the Uniform Electronic Transactions Act or by passing a law that is technologically neutral.

The important features of the U.S. law are (1) technology-neutral standards which prevent governments from legislating a specific type of technology, and (2) party autonomy or the right of businesses to "freedom of contract" in determining the terms and conditions specified in a transaction. Technology-neutral means that parties entering into electronic contracts can choose the system they want to use to validate an online agreement.

Congress also adopted the *Federal Information Policy Act of 2000* to provide for the coordination of federal information policy through the establishment of a Federal Chief Information Officer and an Office of Information Policy in the executive office of the president, and to otherwise strengthen federal information resources management. A key task is to develop and implement procedures for the use and acceptance of electronic signatures by agencies.

Act Recognizes Special Circumstances of Small Business

The Electronic Commerce Enhancement Act of 2001

On February 14, 2001, the Electronic Commerce Enhancement Act of 2001 (H.R. 524) was referred to the Committee on Commerce, Science, and Transportation. This act, a bipartisan consensus (meaning it was supported by both the Republicans and the Democrats), was reintroduced out of recognition that while large corporations move their business transactions online, small and medium-sized businesses face challenges in implementing electronic commerce activities. For the prosperity of the economy, small companies in the supply chain must go online as well. Also noted by Congress was the fact that these small companies lack the necessary information to make informed decisions on choosing e-commerce products and services.

H.R. 524 will attempt to promote electronic commerce in small to medium-sized companies by identifying the challenges they face and then establish programs to assist them in overcoming these obstacles. These programs include the electronic linkage of manufacturers, assemblers, and suppliers that will enable them to exchange product, manufacturing, and other business data within the supply chain. By allowing the National Institute of Standards and Technology to assist small and medium-sized businesses to successfully integrate electronic commerce, Congress will attempt to promote effective standards for helping these businesses prosper in our economy.

Antitrust and E-Marketplaces

Reasons for Antitrust Concerns

As discussed in Chapter 4, a business-to-business e-marketplace is an Internet exchange where goods are traded. Both the Federal Trade Commission (FTC) and the U.S. Department of Justice have raised questions about the potential for price-fixing and collusion. Two different types of e-marketplaces exist. The first type, the ones run by a neutral third party in which buyers pool their requirements for specific items, such as office supplies, are not under scrutiny. The second type, industry sites owned and operated by competitors, who together represent more than 50 percent of an industry market share, raise antitrust concerns. Three activities cause the concern: (1) the potential for sharing information among competitors that may allow for price increase or the development of a monopoly; (2) the danger of one buyer or a consortium of buyers acting as one to coerce a supplier to accept a price lower than what would occur in a competitive market; and (3) suppliers may not be in a position to freely decide not to participate.[24]

Supporters of industry e-marketplaces argue that firewalls can be used to protect against competitors sharing information. Such e-marketplaces also are compared to Internet shopping malls where direct competitors colocate and share expenses for things like security. Well-crafted B2B operating rules may be enough to eliminate concerns, and traditional antitrust analysis is feasible.

Patents and Product Liability

Patent Defined

Patents are granted by the U.S. Patent Office (or a similar agency in other countries) to provide the inventor/developer the sole rights of making, using, and selling the item in question—and denying others the right to also do so, unless the inventor decides to sell the patent rights. Unless otherwise agreed between buyer and seller, if a supplier regularly deals in a particular line of goods, that supplier implicitly warrants that the goods delivered do not infringe against the patent rights of any third party. However, when the buyer

Avoid Patent Infringement

orders goods to be assembled, prepared, or manufactured to his or her own specifications, and if this results in an infringement of a patent or trademark, then the buyer may be liable to legal action. There is, under such circumstances, a tacit representation on the part of the buyer that the seller will be safe in manufacturing according to the specifications, and the buyer then is obliged to indemnify the seller for any loss suffered.[25] If a charge of patent infringement is made against the buyer, he or she must notify the supplier promptly so that the charge can be defended, or settlement made,

---

[24]*Antitrust: B2B e-Marketplaces,* American Bar Association Committee on Cyberspace Law, Legislative Reporters, found on *www.abanet.org/buslaw/cyber/legislation/anti.html.*

[25]UCC, 2-312 (3).

in a timely manner. Also, if a seller attempts to include a patent disclaimer clause in the sales contract, the buyer should be extremely cautious in accepting such a clause, because there may be costly litigation if patent infringement has occurred.

An even-more-delicate matter may arise when a buyer requests a supplier to manufacture an item, to the buyer's specifications, that includes a new idea, process, or product that has not yet been awarded patent protection. This often happens in the high-technology industries. The buyer does not want to lose the right to the new development and possible subsequent financial rewards. The buyer's purchase contract should address this matter with an appropriate protection clause, formulated with the advice of legal counsel.

Recent Developments in Patent Law

Two recent developments in patent law are of interest to supply managers.[26] One, the danger of infringing broadly worded patents, such as those related to e-commerce technology, has decreased dramatically as a result of a recent ruling by a federal appeals court. Two, under a new rule enacted by the U.S. Patent and Trademark Office (USPTO), proprietary information contained in patent applications will now be made public 18 months after the application is filed. Also under this new rule, if an organization believes a patent application to be too broad, the organization may submit written materials to USPTO in an attempt to persuade it not to issue a patent.

Product safety and product liability considerations have become much more important over the last two decades, due to increased government regulations and judicial interpretations of the existing laws. This has magnified the involvement and responsibility of purchasing managers, as firms attempt to reduce the financial threat arising from product liability problems.

Strict Liability

The *strict liability* concept is based on the idea that manufacturers warrant that their products are not unreasonably hazardous, but if they are, the manufacturer is responsible to persons injured through use of the product. Under strict liability, the burden of proof was on the injured party to prove that the product was defective, that the defect was present when the product left the manufacturer, and that the defect did cause the injury. The law focused on showing that there was a design defect, and the plaintiff (injured party) had to prove fault on the part of the manufacturer.

Absolute Liability

Since the 1960s, the trend has been toward application of the concept of *absolute liability* on the part of the manufacturer or seller for all accidents involving the use of its products. The courts have begun to hold that the manufacturer or seller is responsible to the consuming public when it markets a product causing personal injury, and that the financial burden of accidental injury is the responsibility of the manufacturer and is considered to be a cost of production. The plaintiff (injured party) does not even have to prove that the product was unreasonably dangerous. The key issue is

---

[26]Timothy Baumann, "New Developments in Patent Law," *Purchasing Today*, April 2001, p. 26.

whether the manufacturer should have expected misuse or abnormal use by the consumer; if so, the manufacturer is liable. Since this interpretation, a large number of damage awards have gone against producers and sellers.

Purchasing's Role in Product Liability

The purchasing department now must take a more active role in confirming that potentially hazardous purchased items incorporated into an end product or service are properly inspected to make sure they are not defective. This requires a close working relationship with other departments of the firm, such as design, engineering, quality control, manufacturing, and marketing, to ensure that the organization is not being unreasonably exposed to product liability lawsuits. The increased application of strict liability tests and the lack of federal product liability laws means that an organization may assume greater liability based on the actions of the purchaser. Hence, purchasing managers must ensure defect-free materials and components capable of performing a full range of applications and uses, in compliance with relevant standards, tests, and criteria for product safety.

Commercial Arbitration

Regardless of the type of contract, disputes will arise sooner or later. These disagreements are annoying, but, for reasons that have been given, it usually is not advantageous to go to court over them. In the majority of cases they are settled by some compromise. Occasions do arise when such compromises cannot be effected. To meet these situations and yet to avoid the necessity of resorting to a court of law, arbitration clauses frequently are included in commercial contracts. These provide that an impartial arbitrator, or panel of arbitrators, will listen to the evidence and then render a judgment, which both parties have agreed in advance to accept without appeal. This is much less costly and time-consuming than court action.

Arbitration Clauses

However, merely because the contract includes a provision calling for arbitration, the purchasing officer may not be as fully covered as many have believed. There are prepared arbitration clauses that are valid, irrevocable, and enforceable under the arbitration laws[27] of certain states, notably: New York, New Jersey, Pennsylvania, Massachusetts, California, Louisiana, Connecticut, Rhode Island, New Hampshire, Arizona, Oregon, Ohio, and Wisconsin. For matters under jurisdiction of the federal courts, there is the Federal Arbitration Law. Even in states which do not have such laws, it is possible to demand arbitration if provision is made for the necessary procedure in the contract, and if there is a statute making *future* disputes the subject of binding arbitration agreements.

The use of arbitration clauses in contracts is a reasonable measure of protection against costly litigation. To ensure this protection, the following

---

[27]*The Code of Arbitration Practice and Procedure* of the American Arbitration Association contains full information on the arbitration laws of the various states.

queries should be made with reference to arbitration clauses which are to be incorporated in commercial agreements:

Ground Rules for Arbitration Clauses

1. Is your clause in proper form under the appropriate arbitration laws? Unless properly drawn, it may not be legally valid, irrevocable, and enforceable.

2. Does your clause fully express the will of the parties or is it ambiguous? If it is uncertain in its terms, the time and expense involved in determining the scope of the clause and the powers of the arbitrators under it may destroy its value or increase costs.

3. Does your clause ensure the appointment of impartial arbitrators? If a person serving as arbitrator is an agent, advocate, relative, or representative of a party, or has a personal interest in the matter being arbitrated, the award rendered may be vacated by the court on the ground of evident corruption or partiality on the part of an arbitrator.

4. Does your clause provide adequately, by reference to the rules of an association or otherwise, for a method of naming arbitrators, thus safeguarding against deadlocks or defaults in the proceedings? If not, the actual hearing of the dispute may be unduly delayed, and the practical value of the arbitration may be defeated.

Questions for Review and Discussion

1. Under what conditions is it realistic for a buyer to cancel a contract? For a seller to cancel a contract?

2. Does a supplier have to accept a PO exactly as offered by the buyer to create a legally binding contract? Explain.

3. How much knowledge of the legal aspects of purchasing should a buyer have?

4. What is commercial arbitration? When and how should it be used?

5. Does a salesperson have basically the same legal authority as a buyer? If not, how do they differ?

6. What are the legal rights of the buyer if goods delivered by a supplier do not measure up to the specifications?

7. Under what conditions might purchasing agents be held personally liable for contracts they enter into?

8. Is an oral contract legally enforceable? Under what conditions?

9. What authority does a purchasing agent have to make decisions that are binding on the principal? What responsibility do purchasing agents have for the consequences of their decisions?

10. What actions can the purchasing agent take to protect patent rights and avoid legal action for patent infringement?
11. How will the trends in product liability affect purchasing decisions in the future?
12. What legal issues would you want to consider before setting up an e-procurement system in a company?

References

King, Donald B. and James J. Ritterskamp Jr. *Purchasing Manager's Desk Book of Purchasing Law,* 3rd ed. Englewood Cliffs, NJ: Prentice Hall, 1997.

National Association of Purchasing Management, *NAPM Supply Management Series: Contract Development and Management Guide.*

Smedinghoff, Thomas J. (Edt), Andrew R. Basile Jr., and Geoffrey Gilbert. *Online Law: The SPA's Legal Guide to Doing Business on the Internet.* Chicago: Addison-Wesley, 1996.

Uniform Commercial Code, 1994 Official Text. Philadelphia, PA: American Law Institute and National Conference of Commissioners on Uniform State Laws, West Publishing Company, 1995.

Wydick, Richard C. *Plain English for Lawyers.* 4th edition, Carolina Academic Press, 1998.

CASE 12–1
BRASSCO

On March 2, Harry Jones, materials manager of Brassco, received a letter from a supplier who was refusing Harry's request to terminate Brassco's linen laundering contract. Jones firmly believed that the contract contained an exit clause that could be executed with proper notice, but his supplier had a different interpretation.

Brassco Purchases. With 280 employees and $100 million in sales annually, Brassco manufactured copper fittings for a variety of industrial users. As materials manager, Harry Jones was re-sponsible for purchases of about $70 million, of which about 60 percent were for raw materials.

Laundering. Recently the state government had launched a new environmental initiative to reduce landfill waste by 50 percent over a five-year period. The government indicated that one method of achieving this goal would be through an aggressive application of 'The 3Rs' of reducing, reusing, and recycling, and that regular company audits would be performed in accordance with the regulation. In keeping with this mandate, Brassco attempted to reduce its daily waste production by, among other initiatives, replacing many of its disposable paper products with reusable linen equivalents.

Harry Jones observed that the excessive use of paper towels in the plant was creating significant waste each day. By replacing these towels with their linen counterparts, he was able to make progress toward the environmental goal. However, as a result of the change, he required a laundering service to maintain the program.

Currently, Brassco had a rental and laundering contract with Riddirt for floor mats, uniforms, protective garments, and gloves, which amounted to about $40,000 annually. Harry decided to ask Riddirt to quote on the new contract, but he also asked several other commercial launderers to quote on both the new linen towel contract and the existing Brassco laundering requirements. Harry believed that administration and coordination effort could be reduced if all of Brassco's laundering needs were single sourced.

The Bids. To Harry's surprise, only one company, Able Cleaners, was able to quote on the towel contract, while several companies, including Able, quoted on the remaining cleaning needs of Brassco. (See Exhibit 1.)

Unfortunately, Able Cleaners was not the lowest overall bidder because a combination of two suppliers resulted in a lower overall dollar cost to Brassco. What was even more surprising for Harry was that Riddirt's current contract price of $40,000 for floor mats and clothing was about 30 percent higher than the lowest alternate option.

Termination of Riddirt Contract. Consequently, Harry decided to terminate the Riddirt agreement. On review of the Riddirt contract he had on file, Harry noted that Clause 5 regarding the term of the rental service agreement stated:

The Agreement shall be in force for period of five years from the date hereof, and thereafter for an equal period, unless terminated by written notice by either party prior to sixty days before the contract expiration date.

On March 1, he, therefore, sent a fax to Riddirt, stating:

Please accept this fax as written notification to terminate our existing agreement effective May 20 . . .

A Difference of Opinion

Early the following morning, Harry received a response from Riddirt indicating they were unwilling to accept Brassco's request for termination. In their opinion, it was in clear violation of the signed contract. They explained that Brassco was locked in for a minimum five-year term, which would not expire for another two years. Further, Riddirt believed that the contract clearly outlined that unless Brassco provided notice 60 days prior to the contract end date, the service agreement would automatically be renewed for a subsequent five-year term.

Harry was frustrated and uncertain how to proceed. He knew that contract law was complex. However, in his evaluation of the contract, which had been negotiated prior to his arrival at Brassco, he understood that he could terminate his obligation to Riddirt any time prior to the last 60 days of the five-year term. He was also frustrated by the automatic rollover clause, as he wondered what would have resulted if the bidding process had never happened and his attention hadn't been drawn to the contract's details.

EXHIBIT 1   Selected Quotes for Brassco Laundering

	New Linen Towel Service	Existing Uniform Rental and Cleaning
Able Cleaners	$40,500	$38,000
Cleano	no bid	32,200
Wilkens	no bid	30,100
Riddirt	no bid	40,000[*]

[*]not a re-bid, current contract price

13 RESEARCH AND MEASUREMENT

Chapter Outline

Key Questions for the Purchasing Decision Maker

SHOULD WE

- Recognize purchasing research as a formal activity?
- Benchmark our purchasing processes?
- Develop a consistent, formal system for evaluating purchasing performance?

HOW CAN WE

- Measure purchasing performance effectively?
- Benchmark our own departmental performance?
- Prepare more accurate budgets?

In a rapidly changing environment such as we have experienced recently, innovation and improvements in productivity can best be managed if we look at what might be possible, develop comprehensive plans, evaluate accomplishments and shortfalls, and report outcomes. This chapter covers purchasing research, budgets, performance measurement, and reports to senior management. It considers the need for supply managers to evaluate and report on their performance and the requirements senior management places on the purchasing function for reports and information.

Purchasing Research

Four Major Areas of Research

Purchasing research is the systematic collection, classification, and analysis of data as the basis for better purchasing decisions. Figure 13–1 shows some of the data (information) that might be required for effective buying decisions. The studies conducted in purchasing research include projects under the major research headings of:

1. Purchased materials, products, or services (value analysis).
2. Commodities.
3. Suppliers.
4. Purchasing processes.

Considerable attention has been given to a similar activity in the counterpart function of marketing research. Marketing research generally is well accepted in all medium- to large-sized firms as a necessary ingredient in decision making, and it has produced significant results for those firms that practice marketing research systematically.

FIGURE 13–1

Ingredients of Effective Buying

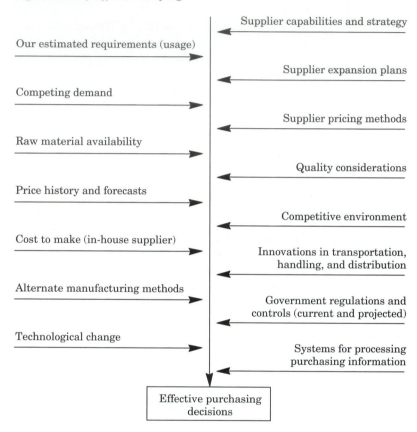

Purchasing research, if approached in an organized manner, also has the potential for generating major improvements in purchasing decision making, although it has been overlooked by many firms in the past.

Organization for Purchasing Research

Three Ways to Conduct Purchasing Research

A firm could conduct purchasing research in one of three ways: (1) the assignment of full-time personnel to the task, (2) the use of regularly assigned buying and administrative personnel to conduct purchasing research as a secondary assignment, or (3) the use of cross-functional teams to bring an expanded knowledge base to the research process.

Full-Time Researchers

As with its counterpart function, marketing research, there are persuasive arguments for the assignment of full-time personnel to perform the purchasing research task. These positions typically are titled purchase analyst, cost management specialist, value analyst, or commodity specialist. (See Figure 13–2 for an example of a job description for a supply cost man-

FIGURE 13–2

Deere and Company Job Description for Supply Cost Management Specialist

Job Title:	Supply Cost Management Specialist
Department:	Supply Management
Supervises:	None, may facilitate/lead team activities
Job Function:	Enabling the design and procurement processes to obtain the best value from the supply base.

Primary Duties:

1. Develop cost models and tables for direct materials to be used for:

   — evaluating cost competitiveness of product designs

   — creating product target costs on a part-by-part basis

   — creating supplier target costs to enable fact-based negotiations

   — highlighting potential cost reduction areas

2. Utilize cost management techniques to give accurate and timely cost evaluations of designs on a part-by-part basis.

3. Support Strategic Sourcing in meeting or exceeding product cost goals for direct material.

4. Support Strategic Sourcing in all aspects of cost reduction activities including:

   — utilizing cost management techniques to determine potential areas for cost reduction

   — tracking, forecasting, and budgeting for cost reduction of Order Fulfillment Process (OFP) cost activities

   — facilitating the JD CROP (John Deere Cost Reduction Opportunities Process) at the Unit level

   — participating or facilitating the Compare and Share process with Strategic Sourcing and the Value Improvement process

5. Participate or lead Enterprise-level cost management activities such as cost modeling or training

agement specialist at Deere and Company). The division of the supply function into operational and strategic elements, coupled with downsizing and flattening of the organization, has led to an increased use of cross-functional sourcing teams, or strategy-oriented commodity managers who do the research and planning but don't actually do the buying.

Dedicated Staff with Specialized Skills. A thorough job of collecting and analyzing data requires blocks of time, and in many purchasing departments the buyers do not have this time. They are fully occupied finding workable solutions to immediate problems. Furthermore, many areas of purchasing research (for example, economic studies and analysis of business processes) require in-depth knowledge of research techniques. These research techniques call for a level of skill not possessed by the typical buyer, primarily because research skill is not one of the criteria used in selecting persons for buying positions.

The purchase researcher often must take a broad view of the overall effects of purchasing decisions on operating results. The buyer, on the other hand, may be so engrossed in his or her own responsibility area that the big picture goes unrecognized.

Decision Making. In the final analysis, purchasing decisions are made by the buyer or administrator; the purchase researcher merely presents data and advises. In some instances, conflict may develop between the researcher and the decision maker; thus the recommendations of the researcher may not receive fair consideration and the value of the efforts will be negated.

Cross-Functional Teams

Based on the argument that the buyer is the most familiar with the goods and services acquired, one model is placing responsibility for purchasing research with the buyer. One possibility—somewhat of a compromise between using a full-time purchase analyst and spreading out research responsibility to individual buyers—is the formation of cross-functional teams to pursue various projects. Such teams have various titles such as sourcing team, commodity management team, or value analysis team. (See Chapter 2 for more information concerning cross-functional teams and organizational issues.)

Five Conditions for Successful Teams

The difficulty with the team approach is that it is hard to pinpoint responsibility for results when it is diffused over a number of individuals. However, the team approach can work satisfactorily, provided that (1) team members are carefully selected to ensure that each really has something to contribute; (2) the team has strong leadership (from a functional point of view, it probably should be someone from the supply area); (3) a specific set of objectives and expectations of results is formulated and communicated to each member and the team as a whole; (4) each team member's normal job responsibilities are rearranged to give that person the time and the resources necessary to ensure results; and (5) performance evaluation and reward systems foster team participation and overall team performance. If any of these five conditions is not present, less than optimum outcomes are almost certain.

Identifying Opportunities

Because the types of data that bear on a major purchasing decision are numerous and because many different items are bought, the number of possible purchase research projects is almost infinite. However, even if a company has full-time purchase analysts, it has limited resources and must use some method of deciding which purchase-research projects should have top priority.

Following is a list of criteria that are used by firms in deciding where they will direct their research effort. This is not intended to be in priority order (although by far the most used is the "top dollar" criterion).

Criteria Used to Allocate Research Dollars

1. *Value of product or service.* Top dollar (current or projected).

2. *Product profitability.* Red dollar (unprofitable end product).

3. *Price/cost characteristics.* Infrequent price changes, frequent or seasonal price fluctuations, end-product cost not competitive, raw materials costs rising at a greater rate than selling price of product.

4. *Availability.* Limited number of suppliers, new suppliers adding to available supply, possibility of international sourcing, possibility of in-house manufacture or outsourcing.

5. *Quality.* Have had quality or specification problem.

6. *Data flows.* Information for decisions often inaccurate, late, or unavailable; cost of data is excessive.

Research on Purchased Materials, Products, or Services (Value Analysis)

While the research topics in this area are principally concerned with the specific products being purchased, the ways in which these requirements are acquired should also be scrutinized. Most of them fall under the generally understood category of *value analysis,* which historically is the area of purchasing research that first received attention, publicity, and acceptance.[1] Value analysis (VA) originally was developed by Lawrence D. Miles of the General Electric purchasing organization. The technique received wide acceptance in U.S. industry, and it has been exported to Japan, where it is cited as a cornerstone of Japan's cost-effective manufacturing system. Japan even gives the Miles Award to those firms making the most effective use of value analysis. Although initially used as a purchasing tool, value analysis is now applied to anything that costs money and can benefit from improvement.

---

[1]The best, most comprehensive treatment of value analysis is by Lawrence D. Miles, *Techniques of Value Analysis and Engineering,* 2nd edition (New York, NY: McGraw-Hill, 1972).

**Function
Compared to
Cost**

Value analysis compares the *function* performed by a purchased item with the *cost,* in an attempt to find a lower cost alternative. The first step in value analysis is selecting a part, material, or service to analyze, then forming a cross-functional value analysis team (often including a supplier), and then defining the function of the item or service in a verb and noun combination. For example, if the can that holds a soft drink is selected for value analysis, its function might be defined as "holds liquid." This approach encourages creative thinking and keeps the value analysis team from locking onto the existing solution, an aluminum can, as the only solution. Value analysis is a systematic approach that should become an ongoing part of the supply management process.

**Ford Value
Analysis
Center**

Many discrete goods manufacturers, such as consumer electronics and automotive companies, use value analysis. For example, Ford has been using value analysis for many years and has set up its Value Analysis Center in Livonia, Michigan. Ford conducts three-day workshops at the center with cross-functional teams made up of Ford design and release engineers, an assembly process expert, the installation engineer at the plant, the supplier's engineer, a Ford purchaser, a Ford cost estimator, and a finance estimator from the supplier. Larry Denton, director of the Ford Value Analysis Center, describes the process as follows: "You have the part on the table and you have a competitor's part, tear-down boards, and a team of about 10 people with a professional facilitator to go through and brainstorm ideas on how to lower cost. We use the value equation $V = F/C$ (value = function over cost)." The objective is to either enhance the function of the part while keeping cost constant, or reduce the cost and maintain the same function.[2]

**Value Analysis
Compared
to Value
Engineering**

Because purchasing decisions often are made under a good deal of time pressure, and because technology and manufacturing methods change fairly rapidly, in many instances a higher priced item is purchased than is necessary. Some people make the distinction that *value analysis* is done on purchased items used in the ongoing production process, while *value engineering* looks at cost savings possibilities in the design stage, where items are being specified, and before production purchases actually are made. Obviously, value engineering at the design stage to arrive at the lowest-cost material specification and design that will adequately perform the function is the most efficient way to do the job, but unfortunately this analysis, due to time pressures, often is not done.

Moreover, after a product has been on the market for a while, greater certainty about demand, new technological options, or suppliers may become available and prices of key materials or components may have changed.

---

[2]Anonymous, "Ford Stresses Value Analysis to Lower Cost," *Purchasing,* March 7, 1996, pp. 54–55.

Therefore, a careful value analysis after the original design may reveal surprising opportunities for value improvement, even if the original design had been carefully value engineered. Value analysis techniques are equally applicable to services and can be applied to purchasing processes and e-commerce activities.

Therefore, value analysis presents a fruitful area for purchase cost-reduction. Detailed information on various aspects of the item to be purchased will enable a more intelligent choice from alternatives, thus providing better utilization of the purchasing dollar. Included as research topics are:

Value Analysis Topics

Investment Recovery.   Analysis of disposal methods (including recycling), channels, and techniques to isolate those that will provide greatest net return to the firm.

Lease or Buy.   Collection of data on the advantages and disadvantages of each alternative so that the most attractive decision can be identified.

Make or Buy and Continue Making or Outsource.   Comparison of economic and managerial outcomes from each alternative in order to make an informed choice.

Packaging.   Investigation of processes and materials to determine the lowest cost method of meeting requirements.

Specification.   Analysis of current specs to be sure they outline the required level of performance, and do not result in the purchase of unneeded attributes or unnecessarily high levels of performance, and enable competitive purchasing.

Standardization.   Review of uses to which specific products are put, and consideration of the possibility of using one item to fill the needs for which multiple items currently are purchased.

Substitution.   Analysis of the technical and economic ramifications of using a different item than the one presently purchased.

Supplier Switching.   Consideration of specialty suppliers who may be capable of providing improved value.

Value Analysis Approach

The standard approach to value analysis, which encompasses most of the topics listed earlier, is to pose and provide detailed answers to a series of questions about the item currently being bought. Figure 13–3 details this approach and lists the standard value analysis questions.

FIGURE 13–3

The Value Analysis Approach: Comparison of Function with Cost

I.   How to get started in Value Analysis: VA is a valuable operation in many companies. It is a means of reducing costs without impairing product quality.

II. Select a relatively high-cost or high-volume purchased item to value analyze. This can be a component, material, or service. Select an item you believe is costing more than it should.

III. Find out completely how the item is used and what is expected of it—its *function*.

IV. Ask questions:
1. Does its use contribute value?
2. Is its cost proportionate to its usefulness?
3. Can basic and secondary functions be separated?
4. Have functional requirements changed over time?
5. Does it need all its features?
6. Is there anything better for the intended use?
7. Are the original specs realistic under today's conditions?
8. Can the item be eliminated?
9. If the item is not standard, can a standard item be used?
10. If it is a standard item, does it completely fit your application or is it a misfit?
11. Does the item have greater capacity than required?
12. Is there a similar item in inventory that could be used?
13. Can the weight be reduced?
14. Have new materials or designs been developed that would alter performance of the product?
15. Are closer tolerances specified than are necessary?
16. Is unnecessary machining performed on the item?
17. Are unnecessary fine finishes specified?
18. Is commercial quality specified?
19. Can you make the item cheaper yourself?
20. If you are making it now, can you buy it for less?
21. Is the item properly classified for shipping purposes?
22. Can cost of packaging be reduced?
23. Are your suppliers being asked by you for suggestions to reduce cost?
24. Do material, reasonable labor, overhead, and profit total its cost?
25. Will another dependable supplier provide it for less?
26. Is anyone buying it for less?

V.   Following the initial analysis:
1. Where practical, get samples of the proposed item(s).
2. Select the best possibilities and propose changes.

VI. Follow-up: Were the expected benefits realized?

VII. Outcome: *A thorough study is almost certain to uncover many potential savings!*

Target Costing

Combining Value Analysis and Target Costing

Target costing is an approach where the estimated price of a product or service is provided to the supplier with the objective of reaching specific cost objectives. Target prices can be set for new or existing products or services. Effective target-costing processes require establishing detailed cost breakdowns and value analysis to determine how function of the product or service can be achieved while simultaneously achieving the targeted cost.

Firms that use target costing with their suppliers often use cross-functional teams consisting of engineers, purchasing staff, and cost analysts, with representatives from both the purchaser and the supplier.

Target Costing at Honda of America

Honda of America credits target costing as one of the major contributing factors to its profit turnaround in the mid-1990s. Purchased components from suppliers represent between 70 and 80 percent of Honda's cost of sales. The target costing process at Honda begins at the design phase, using cost models developed by R&D and procurement staff, and the target costs are used to evaluate supplier costs to determine their accuracy. The Honda sales group sets the selling prices for new models, and based on the estimated profit margin, target costs are set for each of the parts that make up the automobile. Individual target costs are set before design drawings are authorized. In effect, the target costs represent the budget for the new vehicle.[3]

Commodity Studies

Reasons for Studying Commodities

Commodity studies are directed at providing predictions, or answers to questions, about the short- and long-term future purchasing environment for a major purchased commodity or item. Such information should provide the basis for making sound decisions and presenting purchasing management and top management with relatively complete information concerning future supply and price of these items.

Typically, the focus of such research is on items that represent a major amount of purchase dollars, but it could be done on items of smaller dollar magnitude that are thought to be in critically short supply. Major raw materials, such as steel, copper, or zinc, normally would be studied, but manufactured items, such as motors or semiconductors, also might be researched. This area probably is the most sophisticated in terms of difficulty and skills needed to do a good job.

Major Areas of Analysis in a Commodity Study

A comprehensive commodity study should include analyses of these major areas: (1) current and future status of our company as a buyer; (2) production process alternatives; (3) uses of the item; (4) demand; (5) supply; (6) price; and (7) strategy to reduce cost and/or ensure supply. Figure 13–4 provides a set of guidelines that might be used to conduct a commodity study.

Some companies do very sophisticated commodity research, resulting in a well-documented strategic purchase plan. While a planning horizon of 5 to 10 years is the norm, some firms make a 15-year rolling forecast that is updated each year. If a firm makes a 15-year strategic marketing plan, it makes sense to couple this with a strategic supply forecast and plan, for in the long-term the acquisition of an adequate supply of critical materials may be the crucial determinant in the organization's success in meeting its market goals. Firms need to make realistic estimates of price trends so they can plan their strategy of adjusting material inputs to counter this trend. Also, the

---

[3]Lisa Ellram, *The Role of Supply Management in Target Costing* (Tempe, AZ: Center for Advanced Purchasing Studies, 1999).

FIGURE 13–4

Commodity Study Guidelines

The information resulting from a commodity study should:

1. Provide a basis for making sound procurement decisions.
2. Present purchasing management and top management with information concerning future supply and price of purchased items.

The completed commodity study should provide data and/or answers for each of the following points or questions. (The investigation should not be limited to these items; depending on the particular commodity under consideration, additional items may be very pertinent, and some of the listed items may not be important.)

   I.   *Current and Future Status:* includes a description of the commodity, its current usage and forecast of future requirements, suppliers, price, terms, annual expenditures, mode of transport, and current contracts.

  II.   *Production Process:* includes how the item is made, the materials used, the supply/price status of these materials, the labor required, the current and future labor situation, alternative production processes, and the possibility of making the item, that is, costs, time factor, and problems.

 III.   *Uses of the Item:* includes primary use(s), secondary use(s), possible substitutes, and the economics of substitution.

 IV.   *Demand:* includes the firm's current and future requirements, inventory status, sources of forecast information and lead times, and competing demand—current and projected—by industry, by end-product use, and by individual firm.

  V.   *Supply:* includes current producers—location, reliability, quality, labor situation, capacity, distribution channels, and strengths and weaknesses of each supplier; total (aggregate) supply situation—current and projected—and external factors—import issues, government regulations, technological change forecast, political and ecological trends/problems.

 VI.   *Price:* includes economic structure of producing industry, price history and future forecast, factors determining price, cost to produce and deliver, tariff and import regulations, effects of quality and business cycle changes on price, estimated profit margins of each supplier, price objectives of suppliers, potential rock-bottom price, price variance among user industries.

 VII.   *Strategy to Reduce Cost and/or Assure Supply:* considering forecast supply, usage, price, profitability, strengths and weaknesses of suppliers, and our position in the market, what is our plan to lower cost, what is your plan to assure supply? Make the item in-house, short-term contract, long-term contract, acquire or develop a producer, find a substitute, import, hedging, value-engineering/analysis, negotiate volume commitments with suppliers?

VIII.   *Appendix:* includes general information, for example, specifications, quality requirements and methods, freight rates and transportation costs, storage and handling, raw materials reserve; and statistics, e.g., price, production, and purchase trends.

---

availability of supply for many items is questionable due to dependence on international supply sources, whose stability may be doubtful because of international politics and depletion of reserves.

Supplier Research

While the two research areas discussed earlier, value analysis and commodity studies, were directed primarily at the item being purchased, research in this category has its principal emphasis on the source of the purchase. In short, the previous two areas were the *what;* this one concerns *from whom.* Obviously, the more knowledge a buyer has about present and potential suppliers, their method of operation and market position, the better is his or her ability to select or create adequate, appropriate supply sources and to prepare for and successfully conduct supplier negotiations. Supply-base reduction or rationalization and the implementation of electronic purchasing processes allow many firms to free up supply managers to focus their efforts on key suppliers.

There are 10 specific topic areas in this category:

Analysis of Financial Capacity. Investigation of the financial health of present or potential suppliers helps assess the risk of the supplier's running into financial trouble and its effects on the buying firm. While this type of analysis often is done within the financial department of a firm, in some cases it has been pulled into purchasing and made a responsibility of purchasing research to ensure that it is done with requisite thoroughness, considering the potential dollar value of the risk involved. For example, several purchasers of computer software and hardware from substantial manufacturers have been surprised suddenly to find that their supplier "has gone bankrupt" in the computer business. (See the Don Willit Associates case at the end of Chapter 15.) With proper analysis, such a situation could have been anticipated well in advance.

Analysis of Production Facilities. Collection of data on the supplier's physical facilities emphasizes capacities and limitations.

Finding New Supply Source. It is worthwhile to search to uncover new suppliers for a purchase need. Research and long-range planning may lead to reverse marketing where the buying firm persuades a supplier to develop the ability to meet the buyer's needs now and in the future.

Supplier Cost Analysis. Understanding suppliers' costs is a very effective negotiation tool and important information used for managing supply chain costs effectively. It provides information concerning what is a fair price and an evaluation of whether the most efficient processes are being used. Estimates of supplier costs can be developed for both products and services and should include: direct material, direct labor, engineering, tooling, plant/facilities overhead, general and administrative expense, logistics/distribution costs, and profit. These data can provide the basis for establishing target prices in negotiation planning.

Supplier cost analysis has become a common research area, probably because it produces very large and immediate savings. Much cooperation between purchasing and the firm's industrial engineering personnel is needed to produce maximum results. Many firms have developed computer models that estimate costs for key purchased products and services based on standard assumptions about cost factors (for example, material prices and direct labor rates). Buyers then have immediate cost analysis capability. In some industries, such as the automotive sector where long lead times for tooling and product development may require awarding business prior to negotiating final pricing, supplier cost analysis is an important aspect of the activities of the commodity sourcing team.

Single Sourcing. Analyzing the supplier's management capabilities is essential before negotiating a complete contractual agreement in which all contingencies are anticipated. The buyer may gain significant advantages from volume leverage. However, the potential costs from supply interruption caused by problems in the single-source supplier's plant or in the transportation system can be great. Developing closer relationships with single sources can reduce the risks somewhat by binding the futures of the two organizations together in a way that encourages cooperation, trust, and commitment to the success of both firms. By forming a partnering arrangement or strategic alliance with a single source, both organizations can focus on joint problem solving, process improvements, and increased profitability.

Supplier-Purchased Material Quality Assurance. It is useful to develop a system with suppliers that will reach agreement on quality standards, arrive at quality yields, determine training needs of supplier production and quality personnel, establish a system for mutual tracking of quality performance, and determine needed corrective action.

Supplier Attitude Survey. A systematic survey of suppliers' attitudes towards the buying firm and its purchasing practices can identify how the buyer/seller relationship could be improved. This information can be used in reviewing and modifying purchasing organization and policy.

Supplier Performance Evaluation. Collection and analysis of performance data is the basis for determining how good a job is being done by a given supplier so that decisions on sources for rebuys can be made more intelligently and present suppliers can be advised where improvement is needed. In partnering arrangements or alliances, the performance of the supplier is assessed regularly in an effort to reveal opportunities for process improvements, cycle-time reduction, cost reductions, and quality and service improvements.

Supplier Sales Strategy. A better understanding of a supplier's objectives and the means it is using to achieve these goals allows the buyer to anticipate the supplier's actions and design a purchasing strategy to provide for the continued supply of needed items at lowest total cost.

Countertrade. Foreign customers may require countertrade. Many countries have clauses in government supply contracts requiring local content, usually specified as a percentage or as a fixed dollar-value amount. This essentially is a barter agreement, and in some companies supply analysts are responsible for gathering and analyzing the data that form the basis for such agreements. (See Chapter 14 for a detailed discussion of Countertrade.)

Purchasing Processes

**Areas of
Interest in
Purchasing
Processes
Research**
Adequate knowledge about items to be purchased and the supplier from whom the purchase might be made, while important in attaining maximum value from the purchasing dollar, does not ensure that the purchasing transaction will be handled in the most efficient manner. Equally important is how the purchase is made. Efficient administrative procedures not only will reduce the expense of departmental operations but also will facilitate wise decisions on items purchased and their source. Research topics concerning purchasing processes are directed at improving administration of the purchasing system, ensuring speed and cost-effectiveness by eliminating unnecessary steps, and automating where possible through Internet and intranet applications. Specific topic areas usually researched include the following: supplier selection and sourcing, purchase ordering systems, supplier assessment, accounts payable, internal approval processes, early supplier involvement and selection, inventory control, and e-commerce.

Assessing Purchase Research Results

Supply managers who use purchasing/supply management research are satisfied that it has paid off for their firms. Those with organized purchase research efforts feel it would be impossible for purchasing to continue making the current level of contribution to corporate success and profits without an aggressive program. Purchasing research has arrived on the corporate scene, but most managers contend that its potential really has been only partially tapped.

**Purchasing
Research
Contributes
Substantially**
Purchasing research can contribute substantially to the ability of the purchasing department to cope successfully with future material uncertainties and the demands for greater purchasing effectiveness.

Planning

**The Annual
Sales Forecast
Starts the
Planning
Process**
The actual supply planning process starts with information derived from the annual sales forecast, production forecast, and general economic forecast. The sales forecast will provide a total measure of the requirements of materials, products, and services to be acquired by purchasing; production forecasts will provide information on the location at which the materials, products, and services will be required; and the economic forecast will provide information useful in estimating general trends for prices, wages, and other costs.

In most organizations, less than 20 percent of the number of line items purchased account for more than 80 percent of the dollars spent. In breaking down the broad forecast into specific plans, the next step is to make price and supply availability forecasts for each of the major requirements.

**Buying Policy
is Linked to
Forecasts**

The estimates of material consumption are broken down into monthly and quarterly time periods. These quantities are checked against inventory control data that take into account lead times and safety stocks. These estimates then are related to the price trend and availability forecasts for the material under consideration and a buying plan is developed. If the forecasts predict ample supplies of the material and a possible weakening in prices, a probable buying policy will be to reduce inventories to the lowest level that is economically feasible. On the other hand, if the forecasts predict a short supply and increasing price trend, prudence indicates a buying policy that will ensure adequate stocks are on hand or are covered by contract, and the possibility of forward buying is considered.

The procedure outlined earlier is used for raw materials, component parts, and services. In forecasting trends that will affect the availability and price of component parts, consideration has to be given to the conditions expected to be present for the period being forecasted in the industries in which the parts' suppliers operate.

Major requirements can be classified into related product groups. The pattern of analysis followed in forecasting for the major items can be used for the related product groups.

**Buying Policy
Flows to
Individual
Buyers**

After the monthly and quarterly unit quantities and estimated dollar costs for each item or related product group are tabulated and modifications are made as a result of developing a buying plan, individual buyers make an analysis of the items for which they are responsible. Further modifications in prices may be made because of the objectives that they have established to guide their activities for the period of the forecast.

Special projects, such as the construction of new facilities or planning for the manufacture of new major products not previously produced, may create uncertainty as to the time periods when new equipment or products will be needed, making planning difficult.

Purchasing Budgets

The supply budgeting process should start with a review of purchasing goals and objectives, followed by a forecast of action and resource needs to meet the goals, and then the development of a budget.

**Four
Purchasing
Budgets Must
Be Developed**

Four separate budgets are commonly developed:

**The Materials
Budget
Reflects
Expected
Expenditures
for Materials
Purchases**

Materials (Operations) Purchase Budget. The materials or operations budgeting process begins with an estimate of expected operations, based on sales forecasts and plans, which can be used to derive the total dollar budget for material purchases. Investments in materials can be substantial; meanwhile, shortages can lead to expensive stock-outs. The primary advantage of going through the materials budget planning process is that it identifies cash flow commitments and isolates problems well in advance of their occurrence. Sensitivity analysis can provide management with an opportunity to explore and/or develop other alternatives. Typically the materials purchase budget has a planning horizon of one year or less, except in the case of high-dollar, complex, long production-cycle products, such as aircraft or power plants where a multiyear budget is needed.

The MRO Budget May Be Calculated Using Past Ratios

MRO Budget. The MRO budget covers a purchase plan, typically for a 12-month period, for all the maintenance, repair, and operating supplies that will be needed. Because the number of individual line items likely will be so large that it is not feasible to budget for each one, this purchase plan normally is arrived at by the use of past ratios, for example, MRO cost, adjusted by anticipated changes in inventory and general price levels.

The Capital Budget Covers Projected Equipment Purchases

Capital Budget. The capital expenditure plan often has a several-year horizon, based on the firm's strategic plan for product lines, market shares, and new ventures. Based on production needs, obsolescence of present equipment, equipment replacement needs, and expansion plans, decisions can be made on projected capital purchases. In making the capital budget, such things as supplier lead times (which may be quite long), cost of money, anticipated price escalation, and the need for progress payments to equipment suppliers must be considered.

The Administrative Budget Includes All Expenses for Staffing and Running the Purchasing Department

Administrative Budget. The annual administrative budget, based on anticipated operating workloads, should be prepared for all of the expenses incurred in the operation of the purchasing function. Such expenses include salaries and wages; space costs, including heat and electricity; equipment costs; information technology charges; travel and entertainment expense; educational expenditures for personnel who attend seminars and professional meetings; postage, telephone, and fax charges; office supplies; subscriptions to trade publications; and additions to the purchasing library. If a budget were in effect for the previous fiscal period, a comparison between budget and actual expenditures should be made to reconcile any substantial differences. Expenditures should be compared with budget estimates on a monthly basis to control operating expenses and detect problem areas promptly. After reviewing the department's operating expense history, a budget should be prepared for the next fiscal period including provisions for salary increases, personnel additions or deletions, and estimates of all other expenses as anticipated by the requirements of the purchasing plan. The final budget then should be coordinated with the total budget for the organization.

Performance Measurement and Operations Reports

In a highly competitive environment, only the efficient and effective survive, and organizations that are successful over time recognize the need for continuous improvement of their operations. Performance measurement provides a continuing base for evaluating progress. Purchasing operations reports communicate key performance measures to purchasing managers and senior management to evaluate the performance of the supply function, providing comparisons between current period operations with similar figures over previous periods and with budgeted or forecasted performance levels. Consequently, establishing appropriate performance measures helps focus management attention and company resources on key areas and forms the basis of communication and management control.

Why Is Appraisal Needed?

Benefits of Performance Appraisal

The benefits from a careful appraisal of purchasing/supply department performance are many: (1) It focuses attention on the priority areas, making it more likely that objectives will be realized; (2) it provides data for taking corrective action, if needed, to improve performance; (3) by isolating problem areas, it should help to develop better relationships with other functional areas; (4) it spotlights the training needs of personnel; (5) the possible need for additional resources, for example, personnel or computer support, is documented; (6) it provides the information to keep top management informed of purchasing progress; (7) those people performing at a better-than-normal level can be identified and rewarded, which should improve motivation in the organization.

Appraisals May Lead to Improvements to the Bottom Line

An increasing number of managers recognize that a properly organized supply function, staffed by competent employees, is capable of significant contributions. Periodic appraisals of the performance of the function may lead to savings, which flow directly to profit. The supply function has many opportunities to create or add value to the firm's products and services through its internal interactions and external involvement. The focus on value means a shift in emphasis from cost savings and efficiency to the creation of value. Specific goals must be established for purchasing/supply performance, and these goals and objectives must be reflected in the performance measurement systems and reward structures of the firm. The amount of effort and persistence of the individual is influenced by goals and objectives, and performance measures provide guidelines for decision making, and behavioral- or outcomes-based feedback can enhance performance.

Problems in Appraisal

It is one thing to recognize the need for performance appraisal and quite a different situation to develop meaningful methods for measuring performance.

Need for Clearly Defined Objectives

Research in organization theory and human behavior in organizations has produced greater understanding of how to organize for effective results. We have learned about the importance of clearly defining the purpose and the objectives or goals we expect a function and the employees in that function to achieve. A major problem in many organizations has been the lack of clearly defined objectives for the purchasing department and its personnel. Unless it can be determined what is to be evaluated, the question of how to make an evaluation has little meaning.

Objectives

**Objectives
Should Flow
from the
Organization's
Strategic Plan
to the
Function and
then to the
Individual**

The chief purchasing executive has the basic responsibility for determining general objectives for the function and the coordination of such objectives with the strategic objectives of the company as a whole. Once the overall objectives or targets are outlined, they are provided to subordinates, not as a directive but as general guidelines for those who have decision-making authority to use in establishing the objectives that will govern their activities for some period of time. When properly administered, the individual's objectives act as a motivating force to give direction to work and, subsequently, a basis for appraising performance. The more responsibility the individual exercises in establishing and implementing objectives, the greater the opportunity for the motivation of that employee and the individual's satisfaction that comes from a sense of accomplishment and achievement.

Budgets and Standard Costs

**Variances
Between
Budget and
Actual are One
Means of
Evaluation**

One of the key evaluation tools used in most organizations is the budgetary process. If the materials purchase, MRO, capital, and purchasing administrative budgets are carefully prepared, based on realistic assumptions about the future, they do provide a reasonable standard against which actual expenditures can be compared. If significant variances between budget (standard) and actual have occurred, in the absence of documented evidence that the assumptions on which the budget was based have changed, then a judgment can be made that performance was either superior or less than satisfactory, depending on whether the variance was positive or negative.

**Purchasing
Should Be
Involved in
Setting
Standard Costs**

Standard costs also are used in many organizations to evaluate the purchasing department's pricing performance. Standard costs should be set based on anticipations of future overall market price movements; to do this with any degree of realism, purchasing must have a major input in setting such price/cost standards. If the standards are set solely by cost accounting, based almost completely on historical cost performance, then they lose much of their utility as a standard for judging performance. But if realistic standards, taking into account overall economic/market trends, are set, then they do provide a practical and useful type of standard for measuring purchasing's price effectiveness.

Procedures Used in Evaluation

**Two
Evaluation
Approaches**

Two approaches can be taken in evaluating the performance of the purchasing function:

1. The continuing evaluation that compares the operating results with the plan, budget, and objectives established for the department and personnel.
2. Audit conducted by someone outside the department or the company.

Areas of Appraisal

Working cooperatively with the chief purchasing executive and staff, internal or external auditors can help make objective appraisals in areas such as:

1. Workload allocations.
2. Purchasing department relationships with other departments, and problem areas.
3. Relationships with suppliers—their attitudes toward the organization and toward the buyers.
4. Adherence to policies and procedures as detailed in policy statements and manuals.

Operations Reports

Chapter 3 explored many of the information flows that directly affect the decision-making activities of purchasing personnel. These information flows can be broadly classified as originating from the interface relationships with other functional areas within the firm and contacts with the outside worldwide marketplace. When the materials plan and the budget are submitted to top company management executives for approval, they provide the basic reports about expected activity for the forecast period. The accuracy of the projected plans and strategies is checked when reports on the actual performance of the supply function are made.

Emphasis on what information should be reported will vary with the type of industry. Many purchasing executives limit their reports to a tabulation of the figures showing:

Three Elements of Purchase Reports

1. Total dollar volume of purchases.
2. Total dollars spent for department operating expenses.
3. Total number of purchase orders issued.

Some Simple Comparisons May Be Made

In some instances these figures are related to each other by calculating average figures and percentages to show:

1. Average dollar cost of the purchase orders written as:

$$\frac{\text{dollar cost of operating the department}}{\text{number of POs written}}$$

2. Operating costs as a percentage of total dollar volume of purchases.
3. Operating costs as a percentage of total dollar volume of sales.

Comparing the above figures and ratios with similar figures for previous time periods provides some perspective on what is happening in the purchasing function. However, these reports are of little use in providing a basis for evaluation of how effectively the purchasing function is providing the materials and equipment needed at the lowest net cost, considering quality, service, and the needs of the user. Note that the lowest price is not necessarily the lowest net cost.

Computerized management information systems are capable of providing information promptly and in a form that facilitates analysis of most purchasing activities. However, what to report, the frequency of reporting, and how to report are decisions that require careful analysis.

In general, purchasing operating reports which are prepared on a regular basis—monthly, quarterly, semiannually, or annually—can be classified under the following headings and include:

Market, Economic, and Price Analysis

1. Market and economic conditions and price performance.

   a. Price trends and changes for the major materials and commodities purchased. Comparisons with (1) standard costs where such accounting methods are used, (2) quoted market prices, and/or (3) target costs, as determined by cost analysis.[4]

   b. Changes in demand-supply conditions for the major items purchased. Effects of labor strikes or threatened strikes.

   c. Lead time expectations for major items.

Inventory Analysis

2. Inventory investment changes.

   a. Dollar investment in inventories, classified by major commodity and materials groups.

   b. Days' or months' supply, and on order, for major commodity and materials groups.

   c. Ratio of inventory-dollar investment to sales-dollar volume.

   d. Rates of inventory turnover for major items.

Analysis of Purchasing's Effectiveness

3. Purchasing operations and effectiveness.

   a. Cost reductions resulting from purchase research and value analysis studies.

   b. Quality rejection rates for major items.

   c. Percentage of on-time deliveries.

   d. Number of out-of-stock situations which caused interruption of scheduled production.

   e. Number of change orders issued, classified by cause.

   f. Number of requisitions received and processed.

   g. Number of purchase orders issued.

   h. Employee workload and productivity.

   i. Transportation costs.

---

[4]One useful means of evaluating the reasonableness of prices actually paid is to compare actual price to an index of market prices. This can provide a good reading on whether the trend of purchasing's prices paid performance is better or worse than that being experienced by the overall market.

<table>
<tr><td>

Analysis on Administrative and Financial Activities

</td><td>

4. Operations affecting administration and financial activities.

   a. Comparison of actual departmental operating costs to budget.

   b. Cash discounts earned and cash discounts lost.

   c. Commitments to purchase, classified by types of formal contracts and by purchase orders, aged by expected delivery dates.

   d. Changes in cash discounts allowed by suppliers.

</td></tr>
</table>

Types of Performance Measurement Systems

Four Types of Measurement Systems

Performance measures—for example, quality, delivery and cost—focus the buyer's attention on particular criteria and the impact of the decisions made by the buyer. Four types of performance measurement systems can be used: (1) an efficiency-oriented system; (2) an effectiveness-oriented system, (3) a multiple-objectives system, and (4) a naive system.[5]

Material Cost Reductions, Operating Costs, and Order Processing Time Measure Efficiency

Efficiency-Oriented Performance Measurement System. The traditional approach to measuring purchasing performance is the efficiency system, which emphasizes cost and departmental operating efficiency. Performance measures are purchased material cost-reductions, operating costs, and order processing time. As discussed in Chapter 1, purchasing makes a direct contribution to the bottom line of the firm because of the profit leverage effect of purchasing. In firms where efficiency measures are used to assess performance, one would expect to find specific objectives related to efficiency. For example, a buyer may have a stated goal of reducing the price of a particular item by 5 percent this year.

Direct and Indirect Contributions to Profit Are Measured to Determine Effectiveness

Effectiveness-Oriented Performance Measurement System. The effectiveness-oriented system evaluates contribution to profit, quality of supplier relations, and levels of customer satisfaction. In efficiency systems, the focus is on reductions in purchased materials prices. In effectiveness systems, both the direct and indirect contributions of supply to profit are measured. The benefit may come from reductions in operating costs or materials costs, enhancements in the performance of others (quality improvements in materials that lead to fewer defects and more satisfied end customers), shorter lead times, and/or increased sales due to increased value in the eyes of the end customer.

Measuring Supplier Relations

    Measures of supplier relations require looking at the relationship from both sides. Measures of supplier performance include the traditional aspects of quality, delivery, and cost, but also more qualitative dimensions such as

---

[5]Ellen J. Dumond, "Performance Measurement and Decision Making in a Purchasing Environment," *International Journal of Purchasing and Materials Management,* Spring 1991, pp. 22–23; and Ellen J. Dumond, "Moving Toward Value-Based Purchasing," *International Journal of Purchasing and Materials Management,* Spring 1994, pp. 5–8.

communication and cooperation. The quality of the service provided to the supplier by the buying organization also is measured.

Measuring End-Customer Satisfaction

Using end-customer satisfaction as a measure of the effectiveness of purchasing makes a lot of sense because the actions of purchasing affect customer satisfaction. In reality, this measure is difficult to operationalize. If the buyer makes a decision that results in improved quality of the end product, it may positively affect customer satisfaction. Conversely, if purchasing focuses on buying at the lowest price, the reliability or quality of the end product may be low and customer satisfaction may decrease.

Objectives May Conflict in Multiple-Objectives Systems

Multiple-Objectives Performance Measurement System. The multiple-objectives system considers both efficiency and effectiveness measures. One of the problems with multiple-objectives systems is that the objectives often conflict with each other. For example, cost of purchases may be rated highly due to the buyer's focus on attaining items at the lowest cost, but this price buying may result in negative ratings on contribution to profit because of poor-quality purchased materials and high defect rates, which lead to reduced customer satisfaction. A system composed of multiple measures is a good idea, but it must be carefully constructed to avoid conflict.

Goals and Measurement Criteria Lacking in Naive Systems

Naive Performance Measurement System. In the naive system no goals or criteria are provided; buyers simply are told that an appraisal will be made of their performance. Unfortunately, far too many firms operate in this manner. Without specific objectives, performance measures, and feedback, the buyer is unlikely to perform at his or her maximum capacity.

Purchasing Performance Measurement[6]

The old adage, "If you don't measure it, you can't manage it," still applies today. While most managers acknowledge the importance of performance measurement and evaluation systems, many firms have had trouble devising appropriate measurement and evaluation tools. These problems include:[7]

Problems in Developing Measurement Tools

1. There are no industrywide standards of functional performance.

2. A lack of management information systems (MIS) support.

3. Differences in the scope and sophistication of purchasing/supply, even within the same firm (operational versus strategic roles).

4. No agreement on what constitutes purchasing effectiveness.

5. An historical focus on functional goals without linkages to the corporate goal-setting process.

---

[6]This section is drawn from Harold E. Fearon and William A. Bales, *Measures of Purchasing Effectiveness* (Tempe, AZ: Center for Advanced Purchasing Studies, 1997).

[7]Robert M. Monczka and Robert J. Trent, *Purchasing and Sourcing Strategy: Trends and Implications* (Tempe, AZ: Center for Advanced Purchasing Studies, 1995).

As a result of the strong interest in this area, various studies throughout the 1980s and 1990s have analyzed the evaluation criteria used to measure purchasing performance, including ongoing research by the Center for Advanced Purchasing Studies (CAPS) investigating measurement systems in supply organizations.

CEOs Rank Top Five Needed Measures

The CAPS research has examined measurement needs from the perspective of both the CEO and the chief purchasing officer (CPO). When the CEOs of North America's largest manufacturing and service firms were asked to rank the most-needed measures for purchasing, the top five rated measures were: quality of purchased items, key supplier problems that could affect supply, supplier delivery performance, internal customer satisfaction, and purchased inventory dollars.

The CAPS research also developed a 90-item list of purchasing measures, grouped into six categories: developing supplier base, cost-effectiveness, systems utilization, organization, managing supplier base, and overall performance evaluation. CPOs from 285 large U.S. and Canadian manufacturing firms were asked to rate each of the 90 measures in terms of value and actual use. The three highest-rated measures, based on assessed value were:

Top Three Measures in Terms of Value

1. Use of leverage through combining volumes.
2. Accurate, timely, and efficient data collection.
3. Price negotiations resulting in savings.

Top Three Measures in Terms of Use

However, in terms of actual usage, the three highest-rated measures were:

1. Price negotiations resulting in savings.
2. Department budget versus actual expenditure.
3. Past delivery performance.

Calculating the Measurement Assessment and Reality (MAR) Score

To reconcile the use of a particular measure versus how valuable the CPOs considered it, the researchers created a rating system called "MAR," which stands for measurement assessment and reality. It is calculated by dividing the actual usage percentage into 100 and multiplying that product by the assessment average (from 1, most useful, to 5, least useful), or:

$$\frac{100}{\text{Usage \%}} \times \text{assessment average} = \text{MAR}$$

Interpreting a MAR Score

Thus, if a given measure were used by 100 percent of the firms in a study and all firms strongly agreed on the usefulness of the measure, it would be:

$$\frac{100}{100} \times 1 = \text{MAR of 1}$$

Therefore, the lower the MAR score, the stronger the combination of perceived value of the measure and its actual use by the firms in the study.

Table 13-1 shows the 20 purchasing measures with the highest MAR scores, arranged by the six measurement categories used in the study.

TABLE 13-1   Top 20 Purchasing Measurements, Based on Measurement Assessment and Reality (MAR), Out of 90 Possible Measures

Developing Supplier Base (7)

MAR*	Rank†	
1.93	3	Past delivery performance
2.10	5	Require suppliers to have creditable quality programs and stress continuous improvement
2.31	7	Use of continuous improvement programs
2.43	11	Major suppliers are certified
2.49	13	Commitment of suppliers to long-term aggressive price goals
2.64	15	Financial/managerial/labor health of suppliers
2.76	18	Support and interest of suppliers in long-term contracts (3 or more years)

Cost-Effectiveness (4)

1.78	1	Price negotiations resulting in savings
1.86	2	Use of leverage through combining volumes
2.36	10	Incoming and/or outgoing freight costs
2.47	12	Use of formal commodity strategies

Systems Utilization (4)

2.35	9	Use of PCs and workstations
2.58	14	Accurate, timely, and efficient data collection
2.71	17	Complete linkage between user departments (internal customers), purchasing, and accounts payable/finance
2.77	19	Use of EDI (Electronic Data Interchange)

Organization (2)

2.22	6	Department budget vs. actual expenditures
2.32	8	Use of benchmarking for continuous improvement

Managing Supplier Base (2)

1.99	4	Monitoring of delivery performance
2.67	16	Number of suppliers critical to organization's supply base

Overall Performance Evaluation (1)

2.78	20	Evaluation of overall performance by the person to whom purchasing reports

*MAR calculated by assessment of value (1 to 5), times 100, divided by actual usage.
†Rank out of 90 measures.

Five Measures with Highest Combined Value and Use

The five purchasing measures which had the highest value assessment *and* use (MAR) by CPOs in major firms were: (1) price negotiations resulting in savings (MAR of 1.78), (2) use of leverage through combining volumes (1.86), (3) past delivery performance (1.93), (4) monitoring of delivery performance (1.99), and (5) require suppliers to have creditable quality programs and stress continuous improvement (2.10). These five measures with the highest combination of assessment *and* use all are in the areas one typically would consider to be purchasing's emphasis: price, delivery, and quality.

Poorest Rated Measures

While not shown in Table 13-1, the poorest-rated of the 90 rated measures (tied for last place) were the number of supplier satisfaction surveys this year versus goal, and purchasing dollars moved from outsourcing to insourcing (both with an MAR of 16.94).

Guidelines for Establishing a Measurement System

Each organization has its own unique needs, and measures must be tailored to fit the situation. However, there are 12 guidelines that managers should follow when establishing a measurement system:

1. Measures need to be designed for use at a point in time.
2. Each organization has specific measurement needs at a given point in time.
3. Measures should address financial results, supplier performance, computer systems, and internal practices and policies.
4. Measures must change frequently.
5. Trend analysis often is useful.
6. Measures should not be overdone or underutilized.
7. Measures are only tools.
8. Benchmarking is a source of new ideas and measures.
9. Senior management must see value in the measures used.
10. Measures can show the effectiveness of purchasing and identify areas needing improvement.
11. Ensure the credibility of measures.
12. Continuous improvement in purchasing depends on measurement.

If the purchasing function really is to make a strategic contribution to the competitiveness of the organization, it must focus on quality, cost, customer service, and cycle time. In the view of many purchasing professionals, purchasing's main emphasis must be on creating a competitive supply base, which "develops suppliers' resources to achieve competitive advantages and attains most-favored-customer status with respect to suppliers' technology, cost, and capacity availability."[8] To do this requires:

---

[8]Anne Millen, "How Effective is Purchasing?", *Purchasing,* October 25, 1990, p. 58.

Guidelines for Creating a Competitive Supply Base

1. A change in emphasis from efficiency measures, such as the cost to issue a purchase order, to strategic issues, such as early supplier involvement in product design and development.

2. A movement from supplier relationships that are adversarial to ones that are cooperative and complementary—the partnership approach.

3. Selection of suppliers based on their quality control processes instead of incoming inspection acceptance/rejection numbers.

4. Streamlining the supplier base to emphasize concentrating business with only the best and most reliable suppliers.

5. Emphasis on continuous process improvement (CPI) in the supplier base *and* the purchasing function.

Appraising Team Performance

Rewards Must Be Linked to Team Performance

The increasing use of cross-functional sourcing teams has left many organizations struggling to develop performance appraisal and reward systems that foster team participation. Finding the right balance between evaluating individual performance and team performance is a difficult task. According to Monczka and Trent, in their study of cross-functional sourcing teams, nearly 60 percent of the participating firms reported that team members did not receive any evaluation or recognition for team participation, and when team members were evaluated it was usually done by the individual's immediate manager.[9] The lack of linkage between team performance and the firm's reward system (salary increases, promotions, bonuses) may discourage participation in teams. Monczka and Trent found that the level of commitment to team activities was related to the extent of the connection between rewards and team performance or individual contribution, the extent to which the individual's performance evaluation was based on team participation and/or performance, and the extent to which team performance actually affected the evaluation.[10] If there are rewards for team participation, members will make the effort.

Combining Team-Based and Individual Evaluations

How to Evaluate Team Performance. A combination of individual and team evaluations and rewards is needed in an effective evaluation system. In North America this is a major cultural shift from rugged individualism to the efforts and output of the whole team. Evaluation of individual contributions only may discourage team participation, and evaluation of overall team performance only may also discourage the individual. The goal should be to move toward a team-based evaluation, or a combination of individual and team evaluations.

---

[9] Robert M. Monczka and Robert J. Trent, *Cross-Functional Sourcing Team Effectiveness* (Tempe, AZ: Center for Advanced Purchasing Studies, 1995).

[10] Ibid, pp. 45–46.

Three Options for Evaluating Team Performance

Who Should Evaluate Team Performance? Evaluating team performance can be tricky. Three options are possible. (1) The immediate manager of each team member evaluates the individual. The weakness of this model is that the managers may not be involved in the team in any detailed fashion, and so he or she is evaluating from a distance. Also, different managers may evaluate similar performance differently. The lack of consistency in evaluating members of the same team may result in lessened commitment and lowered morale of the team members. (2) Team members evaluate each other. This ensures that those closest to the team activities perform the evaluations. However, the team members may not be very objective in evaluating the overall team performance. (3) A joint evaluation process is used. The team members evaluate each other (including the team leader); the team leader evaluates each member; and an external manager evaluates overall team performance or output.

Evaluation and Reward Systems Drive Behavior

Effective team performance, like effective individual performance, is more likely to occur if specific goals and objectives are established and if evaluation and reward systems foster team participation and performance.

Purchasing Performance Benchmarking

Internal Comparisons Valid, But Limited in Value

The evaluation, or measurement, of purchasing performance has always been a vexing problem for purchasing professionals. Traditionally, firms have concentrated on analyzing their own internal trends, by comparing their current purchasing performance with their own past performance, to determine improvement. Although this certainly is a valid form of performance measurement, it does not tell the firm how its performance compares to that of its competitors. In today's globally competitive business environment, this approach ignores what your competitors are doing.

Industry standards for *overall* firm performance (such as profit, sales, and return on assets) in an industry long have been available through the use of published financial reports. But performance numbers for the purchasing function have not been available, due to the sensitive nature of the data. Many firms have not been anxious to make public to their competitors how or what they are doing, for obvious competitive reasons.

Benchmarking Defined

Key Question in Benchmarking

To remedy this lack of data, starting in late 1989 the Center for Advanced Purchasing Studies (CAPS) began to collect data from firms to develop purchasing benchmarks, standards for measuring quality or value. In general, benchmarking is a process that allows a company to evaluate it work methods, processes, services levels, or products against meaningful standards. In a purchasing context, benchmarking permits companies to answer the question, "How are we doing compared to other firms?" by providing averages and ranges for measures of purchasing performance. This should lead a company toward those changes needed for developing industry-best practices and, in turn, superior performance.

An extension of purchasing performance benchmarking is purchasing process benchmarking. While performance benchmarking measures *what* results organizations have achieved in their purchasing/supply activities,

Process Benchmarking Compared to Performance Benchmarking

process benchmarking attempts to determine *how* an organization achieves results in purchasing and supply. A firm may send a team into another firm in an attempt to identify the best practices of the firm being benchmarked. This must be done with great care, for no two organizations are identical; direct comparisons are difficult to make. Also, in process benchmarking one wants to determine the practices used by those firms getting superior results. But unless a careful performance benchmarking study has been done, it is difficult to identify the superior performers.

CAPS Benchmarking Studies

The CAPS benchmarking data give purchasing professionals the reference point they need to evaluate their own firm's performance. Since CAPS is an independent, not-for-profit research organization, it can collect these data from firms because of its impartial third-party status. On any one benchmark, CAPS provides, based on performance data from the largest 10 to 20 firms in a given industry, only the average and the range. Individual firms and their specific numbers are never identified. Please see the Red Sea Corporation case at the end of this chapter for the CAPS summary of the Purchasing Performance Benchmarks for the U.S. Food Manufacturing Industry.

CAPS has established 21 standard benchmarks:[11]

1. Purchase dollars as a percentage of sales dollars
2. Purchasing operating expense dollars as a percentage of sales dollars
3. Purchasing operating expense dollars as a percentage of purchase dollars (cost to spend a dollar)
4. Purchasing employees as a percentage of company employees
5. Sales dollars per purchasing employee
6. Purchase dollars per purchasing employee
7. Purchase dollars per professional purchasing employee
8. Percentage of total purchase dollars influenced/assisted by purchasing
9. Percentage change in total purchase dollars influenced/assisted by purchasing
10. Percentage of cost reduction savings as a percentage of total purchase dollars generated by purchasing
11. Average annual spend on training for the purchasing function
12. Percentage change in the number of active suppliers accounting for 80 percent of purchase dollars
13. Percentage of total purchase dollars spent with minority-owned suppliers

---

[11] Center for Advanced Purchasing Studies, *www.capsresearch.org/standard,* February 2001.

14. Percentage of total purchase dollars spent with woman-owned suppliers

15. Percentage of total purchase dollars spent with small business suppliers

16. Percentage of total purchase dollars spent through EDI

17. Percentage of total purchase dollars spent through e-markets

18. Percentage of total purchase dollars spent through reverse auctions

19. Percentage of total purchase dollars spent via strategic alliances

20. Percentage of total purchase dollars spent through consortia

21. Percentage of total purchase dollars transactions processed via procurement cards

CAPS Benchmarking Studies Available on Web Site

As of early 2001, CAPS had benchmarking reports available for: aerospace/defense contracting, automotive, banking, beverage, cable telecommunications, carbon steel, chemical, computer and telecommunications equipment, DOE contractors, engineering and construction, electrical equipment, food manufacturing, higher education, investment recovery, life insurance, machinery, mining, municipal governments, paper, personal care products, petroleum, pharmaceutical, semiconductor, ship building, state and county governments, telecommunications services, textiles/apparel, transportation, and utilities. Several of these industries have been benchmarked a number of times to identify performance trends.

Questions for Review and Discussion

1. How does value analysis differ from value engineering? What are the steps in performing value analysis on a purchased item?

2. What are the various subject areas of purchasing research? Which area do you think would be most productive in *(a)* the short run, and *(b)* the long run?

3. In what ways might a firm organize to do purchasing research? What are the advantages and disadvantages of each? Which would you recommend in a *(a)* small organization, *(b)* medium-sized organization, and *(c)* large organization?

4. On which basis would an organization decide where to direct its purchasing research efforts?

5. What questions would be asked in making a commodity study; where would you obtain the information?

6. What is the difference between a purchasing plan and a purchasing budget? In which areas should a purchasing budget be prepared? How would these budgets be established?

7. Why isn't there a standard system for evaluating purchasing performance that could be used by all types of firms and not-for-profit organizations? How difficult would it be to develop such a standard system?

8. What kinds of information on purchasing performance should be maintained in the purchasing department? How can this information be used?

9. What are the key measures of purchasing performance? What will the purchasing manager learn from each?

10. Are standard costs and budgets useful in the appraisal process? Under what conditions?

11. Why would an organization want to "benchmark" its purchasing function? How would it do this?

12. What is the difference between purchasing performance benchmarking and purchasing process benchmarking?

References

Anonymous, "Ford Stresses Value Analysis to Lower Cost," *Purchasing,* March 7, 1996, pp. 54–55.

Black, Dennis E., "Measuring Relative Productivity and Staffing Levels in a Federal Procurement Office," *International Journal of Purchasing and Materials Management,* Summer 1995, pp. 44–50.

Center for Advanced Purchasing Studies, *www.capsresearch.org/standard,* February 2001.

Dumond, Ellen J., "Performance Measurement and Decision Making in a Purchasing Environment," *International Journal of Purchasing and Materials Management,* Spring 1991, pp. 22–23.

Dumond, Ellen J., "Moving Toward Value-Based Purchasing," *International Journal of Purchasing and Materials Management,* Spring 1994, pp. 5–8.

Ellram, Lisa, *The Role of Supply Management in Target Costing,* Tempe, AZ: Center for Advanced Purchasing Studies, 1999.

Fearon, Harold E. and William A. Bales, *Measures of Purchasing Effectiveness,* Tempe, AZ: Center for Advanced Purchasing Studies, 1997.

Hartly, Janet L., "Collaborative Value Analysis: Experiences from the Automotive Industry," *The Journal of Supply Chain Management,* Fall 2000, pp. 27–32.

Miles, Lawrence D., *Techniques of Value Analysis and Engineering,* 2nd edition, New York, NY: McGraw-Hill, 1972.

Millen, Anne, "How Effective is Purchasing?" *Purchasing,* October 25, 1990, p. 58.

Monczka, Robert M. and Robert J. Trent, *Purchasing and Sourcing Strategy: Trends and Implications,* Tempe, AZ: Center for Advanced Purchasing Studies, 1995.

Monczka, Robert M. and Robert J. Trent, *Cross-Functional Sourcing Team Effectiveness,* Tempe, AZ: Center for Advanced Purchasing Studies, 1995.

Morgan, Jim, "Benchmarking Is Not An Instant Hit," *Purchasing,* May 23, 1996, pp. 42–44.

Case 13-1
Red Sea Corporation

Earl Jones, vice president of purchasing at the Red Sea Corporation, had just received the most recent CAPS (Center for Advanced Purchasing Studies) Purchasing Performance Benchmarks for the U.S. Food Manufacturing Industry. Red Sea had not been one of the firms which provided the data for this study.

Red Sea Corporation's annual sales volume was close to the average sales reported for the sample group and was part of the food manufacturing industry with a wide range of canned, frozen, and packaged consumer goods.

Earl Jones carefully read the summary provided in the CAPS report. He knew that some of these benchmarks covered areas in which Red Sea has its own performance measures, while others were quite different.

Further explanations of each benchmark and how they were calculated were shown on the following pages in the report. Before worrying about these details, however, Earl was anxious to consider the larger picture first.

Earl Jones wondered of what use the CAPS data might be for his organization. Before requesting one of the analysts in the purchasing research group to determine what Red Sea's equivalent benchmark figures would be, Earl Jones wanted to be sure this exercise would be beneficial. If Red Sea's figures were close to industry average, what would this indicate? Similarly, what if significant differences existed, either high or low? Earl decided he should examine each of the benchmarks closely with these thoughts in mind.

Case 13-2
Chemical Treatment Company (CTC) Ltd.

Stephen Wagner, owner and president of CTC Ltd., was considering the construction of an onsite laboratory to perform chemical waste analysis currently contracted out to independent labs.

Company Background. The Chemical Treatment Company Ltd. was one of several small waste management firms specializing in the processing and disposal of chemical waste from about 300 local industrial clients. The company had grown steadily over the years with client fees now totaling about $3.5 million. CTC currently employed 17 people.

The Chemical Treatment Industry. The process of chemical waste disposal began with a sales call to a potential or existing client in order to gather a sample of the company's waste. The sample was then analyzed by a laboratory to determine its chemical content and, based on the results, was assigned a price per load by the general manager. Prices did not vary significantly throughout the industry and clients tended to stay with the same treatment company, unless they were dissatisfied with the level of service received. First-time customers would normally seek a company with a reputation for service and reliability. Once the price was agreed upon, the waste was transported to on-site storage receptacles where chemicals were allowed to settle for 3 to 4 weeks by a process called phase separation. A second sample may be taken upon receipt of the load and sent to the lab in order to match specifications with the original sample. If the load did not match, the treatment company had the option of issuing a surcharge, rejecting the load, or accepting it with the gamble of receiving a lower margin on disposal.

Based on the new specifications of the waste, a set charge for dumping was arranged with a disposal site. The chemicals were then bulked and batched according to their density and type and transported to the disposal site. If the specifications of the load received did not match the specifications agreed upon earlier, the disposal site could levy a surcharge of up to 50 percent of the original price, or reject the load outright. Given the high cost of transport, waste management firms would generally pay the surcharge.

CTC's Current Operations. CTC Ltd. currently did not have its own laboratory and therefore contracted out waste analysis to independent labs for a fee of approximately $50/test. Because sample analysis generally took four weeks and a charge was negotiated before this time, CTC did not take second samples. Also, CTC did not have the storage capacity to hold chemical waste this length of time. As a result, CTC was being surcharged on approximately 7 percent of its loads by the disposal site. Last year, surcharges totaling $52,500 were applied to 100 loads. With disposal fees normally amounting to $2,500 per load, Mr. Wagner was concerned about his company's ability to monitor the loads received by clients and the subsequent loss of or reduction in margins at the disposal site. It was also suspected that disposal sites would levy charges regardless of the load specifications because CTC could not monitor outgoing shipments.

The On-Site Laboratory. In order to eliminate surcharges levied against CTC, Mr. Wagner was considering the construction of an on-site testing facility. Samples could then be taken upon receipt of the shipment and before the processed waste was shipped out, in addition to the initial sales call test. The lab would have the capacity to perform 8,000 tests per year, with results available for any particular test in two days. During the past year CTC contracted out 2,520 lab tests. Costs for this facility are outlined in Exhibit 1.

Other Considerations. With the increased concerns regarding environmental issues, clients were becoming more and more interested in the disposal of their waste products. Because the lab would have to meet government regulations with regard to safety and accuracy, it was felt that having an on-site testing facility would improve the reputation and legitimacy of the company. Also, waste analysis could be significantly expedited, thereby eliminating the long lag time for price quotes. Finally, there was potential for future revenue generation by selling laboratory services to other interested firms.

With the increase in surcharge fees rising steadily, Mr. Wagner knew that a decision would have to be made quickly. In order for the laboratory to be completed during this year, construction would need to begin soon and equipment would have to be ordered by the end of the week.

EXHIBIT 1   Projected Laboratory Costs

Item	Cost
Equipment[1]	$160,000
Portable[1]	35,000
Lab technicians (2) @ $22,000 each	44,000/yr.
Chemists (2) @ $25,000 each	50,000/yr.
Furniture[1]	10,000
Supplies[2] (glassware, chemicals, etc.)	2,000/mo.
Utilities	500/mo.
Insurance	500/mo.

[1]Depreciated using the straight-line method over five years.

[2]Based on estimated requirements assuming the same number of loads as in the past year.

14 GLOBAL SUPPLY MANAGEMENT

Chapter Outline

Key Questions for the Purchasing Decision Maker

SHOULD WE
- Be more aggressive in sourcing globally?
- Play a more active role in initiating countertrade deals?
- Buy directly from the supplier or through an intermediary?

HOW CAN WE
- Locate international suppliers?
- Organize to do global purchasing most effectively?
- Overcome the potential problems faced in purchasing from international suppliers?

Opportunities and Challenges of Globalization

Since the end of World War II, many different events and forces have set in motion developments aimed at relaxing the barriers to, and expanding, world trade. In attempting to seize opportunities in the new global marketplace, companies are deploying their organizations on a global scale. For supply managers, globalization represents both opportunities and challenges. It presents the opportunity to deliver improved value to end customers by developing world-class supply relationships in terms of cost, quality, delivery, and performance. Global buying represents an important opportunity for astute purchasing managers and, for many companies, it is a competitive necessity. Meanwhile, managing international supply networks presents a number of challenges in areas such as source identification and evaluation, international logistics, communications and information systems, and risk management.

Managing a global supply network requires a unique set of skills and capabilities compared to managing domestic suppliers only. This chapter describes the opportunities and issues associated with global procurement with the objective of preparing supply professionals for the challenges of managing global supply networks.

Globalization of World Trade

International Agreements Foster Free Trade

In the efforts to rebuild the economies of Western Europe and Japan after World War II's massive destruction, international agreements included provisions for encouraging trade between the free nations. In 1960 the United States, Canada, and the countries of Western Europe (later joined by Japan, Australia, and New Zealand) created the Organization for Economic Cooperation and Development (OECD) to enable closer cooperation on economic problems. And in 1967 the Kennedy Round—the sixth postwar round of multilateral trade negotiations held under the General Agreement on Tariffs and Trade (GATT)—was completed. In this round, the United States, Canada, the European Economic Community, Japan, and other major trading powers agreed to deep cuts in their tariffs on manufactured goods. The revised GATT of 1980 provided for additional gradual tariff reductions, and in 1982 the member nations again endorsed the principle of free trade and pledged not to impose any new trade restrictions.

Formation of the European Union

The European Union, the disintegration of the USSR, the reunification of Germany, the North American Free Trade Agreement (NAFTA), and the abolition of apartheid in South Africa created challenging opportunities for the global economy in the 1980s and 1990s. In 1992, the European Union (EU), consisting of 15 nations, created a single market without internal borders for goods and services. On January 1, 1999, the "euro" was officially introduced, beginning the transition to a new single currency for 11 of the member countries in the EU. Although the national currencies of the euro block countries did not disappear, the "no compulsion, no prohibition" rule stipulated that the timetable for completing the transition period was July 1, 2002. The move to the euro will affect a number of business activities, such as accounting procedures, billing, legal contracts, pricing, and information systems. However, the common currency promises to allow for easier price comparisons and lower foreign currency transaction costs.[1]

Formation of World Trade Organization (WTO)

Following the Uruguay Round of trade negotiations, the World Trade Organization (WTO) was formed on January 1, 1995. It replaced GATT, which had been in existence since 1947, as the international organization overseeing the multilateral trading system. The WTO has more than 130 member countries, which account for more than 90 percent of world trade.

---

[1]Robert K. Larson and Ajay Adhikari, "The Euro: Ready or Not, Its Here!" *The Ohio CPA Journal,* January–March 2000, pp. 8–12.

Its overriding objective is to help trade flow smoothly, freely, fairly, and predictably. The WTO accomplishes this objective by administering trade agreements, acting as a forum for trade negotiations, settling trade disputes, reviewing national trade policies, assisting developing countries in trade policy issues, and cooperating with other international organizations. While GATT dealt mainly with trade in goods, WTO also has new agreements on trade in services and intellectual property rights.[2]

The Importance of Global Purchasing

Growth of Global Sourcing

Several factors are focusing attention on the international sourcing alternative, not the least of which is that the world has grown a good deal smaller, figuratively, in the last 50 years, with the increased speed of transportation and communication. The Internet is expected to accelerate the trend to global purchasing, making it easier for source selection and reducing communication problems. A survey by *Purchasing Magazine* found that 63 percent of the purchasing organizations surveyed said their firms sourced some goods offshore. Eighty percent of those that buy globally said that they increased offshore purchases over the previous five years, and 64 percent expected to see a corresponding increase in the coming five years.[3]

Global Trade in Goods and Services

The total value of world merchandise exports in 1999 was $5.47 trillion. However, international trade is not restricted to goods alone. World commercial services exports in 1999, such as transportation, construction, communications, computer and information, insurance, and financial services, was $1.35 trillion.[4] The World Trade Organization estimated that total trade in 1997 was 14 times the level of 1950.[5]

U.S. Imports

The Stubborn U.S. Trade Deficit

In 1971 the United States imported more dollar value of merchandise than it exported for the first time since 1888. This trade deficit was due in part to rising prices for U.S. manufacturers, and increased international competition in fields the United States once had dominated. The deficits that occurred in the 1970s and 1980s (1971, 1972, 1974, 1976, and each year thereafter) were due in large part to the sharp increases in the price of imported petroleum products, which quadrupled in 1974 and doubled in 1979 and 1980.[6] While U.S. exports grew in the 1990s, the rate of growth has not been enough to shrink the trade deficit.

---

[2]World Trade Organization, *www.wto.org,* January 2001.
[3]Anonymous, "Global Sourcing to Grow — But Slowly," *Purchasing,* May 18, 2000. pp. 24–28.
[4]World Trade Organization, *International Trade Statistics 2000,* 2000.
[5]World Trade Organization, *The WTO in Brief, www.wto.org,* January 2001.
[6]U.S. Department of Commerce, International Economic Indicators, May 1995.

TABLE 14-1   **U.S. Imports and Exports and Merchandise Trade Balance 1950–1999**[7]

Year	Imports ($ Millions)	Exports ($ Millions)	Surplus or (Deficit) ($ Millions)
1950	$ 8,984	$ 10,282	$ 1,298
1960	15,075	20,612	5,537
1970	39,756	42,590	2,834
1980	256,984	220,786	(36,198)
1990	495,300	393,600	(101,700)
1995	743,543	584,742	(158,801)
1996	795,289	625,075	(170,214)
1997	869,704	689,182	(180,522)
1998	911,896	682,138	(229,758)
1999	1,024,618	695,797	(328,821)

[7] 1950 through 1980: *1985 International Trade Statistics Yearbook,* vol. 1, *Trade by Country,* (New York, NY: United Nations, 1987). 1990: *Economic Indicators,* May 1995, (Washington, DC: U.S. Government Printing Office). 1995–1996: *U.S. Census Bureau, Statistical Abstract of the United States: 1999* (119th edition), Washington, DC, 1999. 1997–1999: U.S. Census Bureau, *www.census.gov,* report FT900 (99) (CB-00-94), January 2001.

TABLE 14-2   **U.S. Imports and Exports by Country, 1999**[8]

Country	Imports ($ Millions)	Percent of Total Imports	Exports ($ Millions)
Canada	$ 198,711	19.4	$ 166,600
Japan	130,864	12.8	57,466
Mexico	109,720	10.7	86,909
China	81,788	8.0	13,111
Germany	55,228	5.4	26,800
United Kingdom	39,237	3.8	38,407
Taiwan	35,204	3.4	19,131
South Korea	31,179	3.0	22,958
France	25,708	2.5	18,877
Italy	22,357	2.2	10,091

[8] U.S. Census Bureau, *www.census.gov,* report FT900 (99) (CB-00-94), January 2001.

U.S. imports climbed over the $1 trillion level for the first time in history in 1999 (see Table 14-1). With exports of $696 billion in that same year, the U.S. trade deficit also hit a record level, standing at $329 billion for 1999. Table 14-2 shows that the leading sources of imported goods and commodities were Canada, Japan, Mexico, China and Germany. In the case of Japan, there were more than twice as many imports, mostly imported motor vehicles and components, than exports.

Types of Commodities Imported into the U.S.

The breakdown of types of commodities imported into the United States in 1999 is shown in Table 14-3. Vehicle imports — cars, trucks, vans, and their parts — were the largest import category in 1999, at $140 billion. In that same year, vehicle exports were only $54 billion. The United States also

TABLE 14-3   U.S. Imports by Selected Commodities, 1999[9]

Commodity	$ Millions	Percent
Agriculture Commodities	36,681	3.7
Televisions, VCRs, etc.	50,936	5.1
Clothing	56,412	5.7
Chemicals	63,825	6.4
Mineral Fuels	75,803	7.6
ADP Equipment, Office Machinery	84,430	8.5
Electrical Machinery	88,620	8.9
Machinery	91,396	9.2
Vehicles	145,927	14.7
Other Manufactured Goods	300,467	30.2

[9]U.S. Census Bureau, *www.census.gov,* report FT900 (99) (CB-00-94), January 2001.

imported $91 billion in machinery (general industrial, metal working, power generation, and specialized industrial), $89 billion in electrical machinery, and $84 billion in office machines and automated data processing equipment. The United States relies on a number of commodity imports. Mineral fuel imports were $76 billion and agricultural commodities were $37 billion in 1999. The other manufactured goods category includes a number of imported products such as furniture, footwear, iron and steel products, and scientific instruments.

Reasons for Global Purchasing

The reasons for sourcing abroad are many and vary with the specific commodity needed. However, the underlying, summary reason for using an international supplier is that better value is perceived to be available from that source than from a domestic supplier.

While the specific factor that makes the international buy look attractive will vary from commodity to commodity (technological know-how can shift from one country to another over time, the ability and willingness to control quality can change, and from time to time a stronger U.S. dollar makes the price of offshore goods more attractive), there are 10 specific reasons that may cause an offshore supplier to be selected as the preferred source.

Price

Competitive pressures have grown more intense over the past 10 years. This has caused North American firms to seek out and evaluate alternatives for reducing costs, and reductions in tariffs have helped make global sourcing an attractive alternative.

Lower Overall Cost Key Reason to Buy Internationally

Most studies show that the ability of an offshore supplier to deliver product in the United States or Canada at a lower overall cost than domestic suppliers is a key reason to buy internationally. Says one director of purchasing, "GATT is very positive from a cost-saving point. With the drop in import duties on our international supplies from approximately 7 percent to 0 percent, the organization has saved $200,000 in the past year."[10] Another purchasing manager said, "Our experience has been such that once the domestic suppliers become aware that you are sourcing internationally, they tend to reevaluate their cost structures to become more competitive."[11] A director of global purchasing and world trade said, "Eventually, we will end up with a borderless world, with low-cost areas supplying high-cost areas. Everyone will have access to the same markets. Local, smaller organizations will be able to compete with larger ones."[12] In short, cost/competitive pressures make global sourcing a necessity for survival for many firms.

Reasons for Lower Costs

While it may seem surprising that an offshore supplier can produce and ship an item several thousand miles at lower cost, there are several reasons why this may be the case for a specific commodity:

1. The ***labor costs*** in the producing country may be substantially lower than in North America. Certainly this has been the case for many of the producers in the Far East and is a key reason why many U.S. firms have set up manufacturing facilities there. Companies chase low labor costs and move facilities to those countries with the most attractive wage rates. Many companies that moved to South Korea, Hong Kong, Singapore, or Taiwan have now moved to Malaysia, Indonesia, Thailand, People's Republic of China, or the Philippines. A recent study found that average wage rates in Mexico were approximately 7 percent of average wage costs in the United States and approximately 9 percent of average wage costs in Canada.[13] When evaluating labor costs, factors such as productivity and quality must also be taken into account.

Companies Chase Low Labor Costs

2. The ***exchange rate*** may favor buying offshore. When the U.S. dollar gets progressively stronger, as was the case in the late 1990s, it effectively reduces the selling price of products bought from international suppliers. A weakened dollar makes imports more expensive and less attractive.

Favorable Exchange Rate

3. The ***equipment and processes*** used by the international supplier may be more efficient than those used by domestic suppliers. This may be because their equipment is newer or because they have been putting a greater share of their gross domestic product into capital

Efficiency

[10, 11]Brad Minnick, "GATT's Here: Now What," *NAPM Insights,* May 1995, p. 63.

[12]Cherish Karoway, "Going Global: Purchasers Take the Plunge," *NAPM Insights,* July 1995, p. 46.

[13]Robi Bendorf, "Pay Attention to Labor Rates," *Purchasing Today,* August 1999, p. 14.

investment. A good example of this is the steel industry in the Far East.

4. The international supplier may be concentrating on certain ***products and pricing*** export products at particularly attractive levels to gain volume. While there are many attempts to prevent dumping practices, control of this is complex and has never been particularly effective. Keep in mind that some countries and regions have developed infrastructures and supply networks that support the efficient production of certain goods. For example, integrated circuits, computers, and computer parts in Malaysia; jewelry in Italy; clothes and shoes in China; and wire and cable assemblies in Mexico.

Government/Marketing Pressures

North American firms produce many goods that are sold (exported) around the world. The United States exported $696 billion in 1999, up from $16 billion in 1953; Canada exported $327 billion (Canadian dollar value) in 1999, compared to $4 billion in 1953.[14] It makes sense to consider the alternatives of buying from suppliers in customer countries; also many multinational firms accept that they have a social responsibility to buy product from suppliers in nations in which they operate plants, as a means of developing those nations. Additionally, many nations insist as a condition of sale of a major product — for example, aircraft — to their country that the seller agree to buy a specified value of goods in that country. These types of arrangements are called offset agreements, covered in more detail later in this chapter.

Quality

While the quality level of the international sources generally is no higher than from domestic suppliers, on some items it is more consistent—for example, steel pipe for the petroleum industry. This is due to several factors, such as newer, better capital equipment; better quality control systems; and the offshore supplier's success in motivating its work force to accept responsibility for doing it right the first time (the zero defects concept). Also, some North American firms buy internationally to round out their product line, with domestic suppliers furnishing "top-of-the-line" items and international suppliers filling in some of the "low-end" holes.

Unavailability of Items Domestically

Certain raw materials—for example, coca and coffee, chrome, and palladium—are available only from certain international sources. And as the comparative

---

[14]1993 *International Trade Statistics Yearbook,* vol. 1, *Trade by Country* (New York, NY: United Nations, 1995). U.S. Census Bureau, *www.census.gov,* report FT900 (99) (CB-00-94), January 2001. Statistics Canada, *www.statcan.ca,* January 2001.

Shifting Comparative Economic Advantage

economic advantage shifts, some manufactured products—for example, certain office equipment such as desktop computer printers, and video equipment—also primarily are available only from international producers. Consequently, for many organizations, global purchasing has become a necessity.

Faster Delivery and Continuity of Supply

Local Inventory Speeds Delivery

Because of limited domestic capacity, in some instances the international supplier can deliver faster than the domestic supplier. The international supplier may even maintain an inventory of products in North America, available for immediate shipment.

Better Technical Service

Superior Distribution Network

If the international supplier has a well-organized distribution network in North America, better supply of parts, warranty service, and technical advice may be available than from domestic suppliers.

Technology

Specialization

Increasingly, as domestic and overseas firms specialize, technological know-how in specific lines varies. Particularly in the case of capital equipment, such as for the primary metals industry (steel and aluminum), international suppliers may be more advanced, technologically, than their North American counterparts.

Marketing Tool

To sell domestically made products in certain other countries, it may be necessary to agree to purchase specified dollar amounts from suppliers in those countries.

Tie-in with Offshore Subsidiaries

Support for Local Economy

Many North American firms operate manufacturing, distribution, or natural resource-based companies in other countries. A conscious decision may be made, particularly in the case of developing countries, to support the local economy by purchasing there for export to North America.

Competitive Clout

Competition tends to pressure the domestic supplier to become more efficient, to the long-term benefit of both that supplier and the buyer. Purchasers use imports or the threat of imports as a lever to pressure concessions from domestic suppliers. One steel buyer reflected that she "would not be getting current $50/ton-and-higher discounts were it not for the import situation."

Potential Problem Areas

**Seventeen
Potential
Problem Areas**

While it is not possible in this chapter to give a complete discussion of all the potential problem areas faced in international buying and the methods for minimizing the impact of each, the major ones can be highlighted. The same principles of effective purchasing discussed throughout this book apply to international purchasing, but some unique problems arise when dealing across country boundaries. Seventeen potential problem areas will be highlighted. The astute buyer will recognize that he or she must consider the total cost of ownership, and not just the initial purchase price, when evaluating an international source.

Source Location and Evaluation

**Expense of
Source
Evaluation**

The key to effective purchasing is, of course, selecting responsive and responsible suppliers. This is sometimes difficult to do, because obtaining relevant evaluation data is both expensive and time-consuming. The problem is intensified when the potential suppliers are located far away. However, the methods of obtaining data on international suppliers essentially are the same as for domestic suppliers (discussed in Chapter 7). In addition to the background data obtained (discussed later in this chapter under "Information Sources"), certainly the best method of obtaining detailed data is an on-site supplier visit. Because a visit to a supplier(s) in another country is expensive and time-consuming, it must be planned in great detail. If the dollars and risk involved are great, the on-site visit is a necessity. Firms doing a great deal of international buying will make frequent visits to overseas sources; for example, in a firm buying millions of dollars worth of video electronics equipment, the responsible purchasing manager may spend 20 to 30 percent of his or her time in the Far East visiting and negotiating with potential or actual suppliers.

There are alternatives to personal on-site visits. A survey by *Purchasing Magazine* found a growing use of consultants and local third-party purchasing organizations.[15] The Internet has made information on potential sources more readily available, and e-mail represents a cost-effective method of communication.

Lead/Delivery Time

**Areas
Requiring
Additional
Lead Times**

Improvements in transportation and communications have reduced the lead time for international purchases. However, there are several areas where the buyer should anticipate additional lead time:

---

[15]Anonymous, "Global Sourcing to Grow — But Slowly," *Purchasing,* May 18, 2000. pp. 24–28.

1. Establishing credit for first-time international buyers often involves obtaining a letter of credit, which may take several weeks.

2. Even with improvements in transportation, the buyer may still experience delays, particularly with inland carriers in the foreign country.

3. Delays in U.S. and Canadian customs are also possible. Proper documentation and customs bonds help expedite shipments through customs. The customs bond allows goods to be released after inspection and lets the buyer pay duties later.

4. The time goods are in port also depends on the number of ships in line for unloading. Also, unloading usually takes place only during regular business hours.[16]

Selecting the mode of transport is an important decision in international sourcing because of long supply lines and greater risk of loss or damage. High-value, low-weight electronics items may move by airfreight, and delivery time may be almost as short as from domestic suppliers. But if the purchased item is costly to transport, it should move by ocean shipment, and the lead time may be several months. This means that for high-bulk, high-weight, low-value commodities, such as steel, the buying firm must do a much longer-range planning job (which is possible in most firms) and must notify the offshore supplier promptly of any schedule changes. Also, the selection of the transportation carrier must be done with great care. To compensate for transport uncertainty, the buyer may insist that the supplier maintain a safety stock inventory in North America. Some type of performance bond also might be required.

Growth in Online Information Systems

The lead time necessary to source offshore is also shortening because of the new information systems. Software now allows importers to view importing as a process of "one giant flow of information."[17] Fully integrated import control software packages enable international operations, customs brokers, and carriers to transmit import information into the buying organization's database. Tasks that can be managed on such a system include creating detailed item listings and purchase orders, handling letters of credit, tracking and tracing shipments, generating customs information, and handling invoice payments.[18] Customs brokers can use the system to speed up customs clearances by storing and collecting information, performing customs processes, and depositing customs entries. Air and ocean carriers also can access the system to deposit shipment information and bills of lading the day they are issued.

---

[16]Larry H. Lawhon, "A Beginner's Guide to International Lead Times," NAPM Insights, July 1995, p. 24.

[17]Tony Dollar, "Import Logistics," *Distribution,* April 1995, p. 44.

[18]Tony Dollar, "Import Logistics," *Distribution,* April 1995, p. 46.

3M Benefits from Electronic Import Control System

3M estimates that, in its first year, its import control system saved the company $1 million to $2 million, increased the import department's productivity, and received the U.S. Customs Service's support. After implementation of the duty drawback feature, additional savings were $600,000 to $800,000. The greatest savings came from reducing in-transit inventory.[19]

Expediting

Because of distance, expediting an offshore firm's production/shipment is more difficult. This places a premium on knowing a supplier's personnel and ensuring that they are responsive. Some firms also arrange to have an expediter on contract in the offshore country or to use personnel from a company-owned subsidiary closer to the supplier to assist with expediting problems.

Political and Labor Problems

Depending on the country in which the supplier is located, the risk of supply interruption due to governmental problems—for example, change in government or labor strikes—may be quite high. The buyer must assess the risk and, if it is high, the buyer must establish some system to monitor these concerns so that warning signs of impending problems are flashed in time to devise an alternative solution.

Hidden Costs

When comparing an offshore with a domestic source, it is easy to ignore some of the costs in the offshore purchase. The buyer must compare total landed cost before opting for an international supplier. The following checklist of cost factors is recommended:[20]

Checklist of Cost Factors

- Price in U.S. dollars.
- Commissions to customs brokers.
- Terms of payment costs and finance charges: letter of credit fee, translation costs, exchange rate differentials.
- Foreign taxes imposed.
- Extra inventory, plus inventory carrying costs.
- Extra labor, documentation.
- Obsolescence, deterioration, spoilage, taxes, losses to damage or theft, longer delivery time-frames, administrative costs, business travel.

---

[19]Tony Dollar, "Import Logistics," *Distribution,* April 1995, p. 47.

[20]Victor Pooler, *Global Purchasing: Reaching for the World* (New York, NY: Van Nostrand Reinhold, 1992).

- Packing, marking, and container costs.
- Fees for consultants or inspectors.
- Marine insurance premium.
- Customs documentation charges.
- Import tariffs.
- Transportation costs, including: from manufacturer to port, ocean freight, from port to company plant, freight forwarder's charges, port handling charges, warehouse costs.

Currency Fluctuations

Buyers Must Forecast Exchange Rate Movement

Should payment be made in the buyer's currency or that of the country in which the purchase is made? If payment is to be made in a short period of time, there may be less of a problem. However, if payment is not due for several months or if the supply relationship lasts for a long time, the exchange rates could change appreciably, making the price substantially higher or lower than at the time the agreement was originally signed. Since 1973, most significant world exchange rates have floated freely, and sometimes changed rather rapidly, due to economic, political, and psychological factors. This means that the buyer, when contracting, also must make a forecast of how the exchange rates likely will move between now and the time of payment. In addition, certain countries from time to time impose restrictions and controls on the use of their currency. This requires that the buyer have a good source of financial advice. Probably the most conservative approach is to price in U.S. dollars, for the buyer then knows exactly what the cost will be, but this denies the advantage of a lower price if the dollar increases in exchange value between the time the contract is written and the time when payment is made. Various approaches are possible, such as pricing in the supplier's currency with a contractual limit to the amount of exchange rate fluctuation permitted, up or down. Or, the really knowledgeable buyer may protect against an unfavorable rate change by dealing in foreign currency options (trading in currency options began in 1983). Close cooperation with finance is required to assure the corporation manages all of its currency inflows and outflows effectively.

Payment Methods

The method of payment often differs substantially in international buying than in domestic buying. In some instances, the international supplier may insist on cash with the order or before shipment. Suppliers with whom the buyer has established a long-term relationship may be willing to ship on open account. But the seller may insist that title to goods does not pass until payment is made. The instrument used in this case is a bill of exchange

Bill of Exchange Defined

(draft) which the seller draws on the buyer and to which it attaches the shipping document before handing it to its bank for collection. The bank, in turn, sends the documents to a bank in the buyer's country, together with instructions covering when the documents are to be released to the buyer—normally at time of presentation—a sight draft. Or the supplier may insist on a letter of credit, which is drawn by the buyer's bank at the buyer's request, and guarantees that the bank will pay the agreed-on amount when all prescribed conditions, such as satisfactory delivery, have been completed.

Letter of Credit Defined

Quality

It is extremely important that there be a clear understanding between buyer and seller of the quality specifications. Misunderstandings can be quite costly, due to the distances involved. Also, there could be a problem in interpretation due to use of the metric system if the buyer's company is not used to working in metrics. In addition, it is important that both buyer and seller agree on what quality control/acceptance procedures are to be used.

Warranties and Claims

In the event of rejection for quality reasons, what are the responsibilities of both parties? Due to distances, return and replacement of items is complex and time-consuming. Are there provisions for the buyer reworking the items? Who pays for rework, and how are the rework costs calculated? Obviously, these areas should be agreed to in advance of the purchase.

Tariffs and Duties

A tariff is a schedule of duties (charges) imposed on the value of the good imported (or, in some cases, exported) into a country. While, theoretically, the world is moving to eliminate tariffs through the various World Trade Organization agreements, they still exist. The buyer must know which tariff schedule(s) applies and how the duties are computed. Additionally, the contract should make it clear who pays the duty—buyer or seller. A Certificate of Origin, issued by a proper authority in the exporting country, is the document used to certify the origin of materials or labor in the manufacture of the item. It is used to obtain preferential tariff rates, when available. In 1991 the United States adopted the Harmonized Tariff Schedule to provide a uniform, updated international coding system for goods moving in international trade.

Cost of Noncompliance

　　The cost of noncompliance with import regulations can be staggering. In a case where containers are marked with incorrect country of origin, the costs can include delayed receipt of goods, charges for freight forwarders or attorneys to get the goods released from customs, remarking, storage, and time to fix the problem. For more serious offenses, fines may apply, legal action may be required, and seizure, and possibly forfeiture, of goods may occur.

Paperwork Costs

Global purchasing requires additional documentation, mainly for duty and customs, logistics activities, payment and financial transactions. Even with developments such as electronic funds transfers and Internet-based communications systems, the paperwork costs in international buying pose a major problem. Besides being frustrating, it can be a drag on the speed of operations.

Legal Problems

If potential legal problems are a risk in domestic buying, they are several times greater in international buying. If delivery time is critical, a penalty or liquidated-damages clause tied to late delivery may be advisable. Also, a performance bond may be required; or, a bank guaranty providing for payment in case of specified nonperformance may be substituted for the performance bond. Litigation is time-consuming and expensive, therefore, agreements to settle international trade disputes by international arbitration are becoming increasingly common.

CISG Defined The United Nations Convention on Contracts for the International Sale of Goods (CISG) went into effect January 1, 1988. CISG applies only to the sale of goods and does not apply to consumer goods and services. As of 1999, 50 countries, including Canada, Mexico, and the United States, had adopted the CISG. The goal of the CISG was to create a uniform international law for the sale of goods. There are several key differences between the Uniform Commercial Code (UCC) and the CISG, and purchasers should be aware of them. These are:

Differences between the UCC and the CISG

1. Under the UCC, the terms of a contract may vary in the acceptance from the proposed contract and a contract still may exist. Under the CISG, however, no contract is created if the terms of acceptance differ from the proposed terms.

2. Under the UCC, the statute of frauds requires a written agreement if the value of the goods exceeds $500. Under the CISG there is no dollar limit.

3. Under the UCC, there are implicit warranties, such as warranty of merchantability, and a warranty of fitness for purpose. Under the CISG, there are additional warranties.

Purchasers should consider carefully the laws under which an international contract is governed. If trading with a company in a country where CISG has been adopted, the CISG governs the contract and the buyer should understand the differences between CISG and the UCC. CISG allows the parties to "opt out" and agree on other relevant law to govern the contract.

**What Body of
Law Applies**

However, unless another body of law specifically is stated and agreed upon, the CISG will apply automatically if both nations have adopted the CISG. Likewise, if the other party is from a country that has not adopted CISG, for instance Japan, and wants to have its domestic law apply, the U.S. purchaser may try to get agreement on using the CISG.

Other laws affecting international transactions are the Exxon-Florio Amendment to the Omnibus Trade Competitiveness Act of 1988 (reenacted 1991), the International Traffic-in-Arms Regulations (ITAR), antiboycott legislation, and the Foreign Corrupt Practices Act.

Logistics and Transportation

**Integrated
Logistics
Defined**

Logistics presents some of the biggest problems for buyers involved in international sourcing. The trend toward integrated logistics on the domestic side is mirrored by a similar move in global purchasing. Integrated logistics refers to the coordination of all the logistics functions—the selection of modes of transportation and carriers, inventory management policies, customer service levels, and order management policies. Logistics companies that provide a wider base of services, thereby allowing firms to coordinate logistics functions, should enable more cost-effective and competitive international sourcing.

Many firms outsource their logistics activities to third-party logistics providers. Deregulation and globalization have resulted in a series of mergers and alliances in the third-party logistics industry, as service providers attempt to provide a global presence for their major customers. A survey of the CEOs of 22 the largest third-party logistics companies in the United States found that all but 2 of the companies had expanded their operations outside the United States, with most attention given to Asia and Europe.[21]

**Most Popular
Services**

In a 1995 survey of 98 international freight forwarders, Murphy and Daley found that international freight forwarders (IFFs) are becoming increasingly diversified, offering, on average, 21 of 23 listed functions.[22] The most popular services include payment of freight charges, tracing and expediting shipments, making routing recommendations, issuing export declarations, and preparing certificates of origin. Traditionally, IFFs arranged for water shipments and air-freight forwarders arranged for air shipments. While IFFs still generate more of their revenue from water (68 percent) than air (32 percent) shipments, the number of IFFs arranging only water transport is decreasing. Further evidence of an integrated logistics approach is the diversity of services generating revenues for IFFs. Only 20 percent of respon-

---

[21]Robert C. Lieb and Hugh L. Randall, "1997 CEO Perspectives on the Current Status and Future Prospects of the Third-Party Logistics Industry in the United States," *Transportation Journal,* vol. 38, no. 3, 1999, pp. 28–42.

[22]Paul R. Murphy and James M. Daley, "International Freight Forwarders: Current Activities and Operational Issues," International Journal of Purchasing and Materials Management, Vol. 31, No. 3 (1995), pp. 22–26.

dents generate all their revenue from forwarding activities. Customs broker (CB) services and nonvessel-operating common carrier (NVOCC) services are the other two logistical intermediary services typically offered. The growth of one-stop service providers is likely to continue and appears to be in congruence with intermodalism (for example, air-sea, rather than all air) and outsourcing.

Incoterms

The shipping terms and responsibilities are more complex in international sourcing than in domestic transportation. The International Chamber of Commerce has created Incoterms (International Commercial Terms) as a uniform set of rules to clarify the costs, risks, and obligations of buyers and sellers in an international commercial transaction. Almost any foreign purchase or sale contains a reference to Incoterms. These rules were first published in 1936 and are modified periodically. The most current version is Incoterms 2000.[23]

The 13 Incoterms have been grouped into four different categories:[24]

Group E—Departure

1. EXW: Ex Works (*named place*). The seller/exporter makes the goods available at his or her premises and the buyer assumes all costs and risks from seller's plant. This arrangement places the greatest responsibly on the buyer. The seller does not clear the goods for export and does not load the goods for transport.

Group F—Main carriage unpaid

2. FAS: Free Alongside Ship (*named port of shipment*). The seller clears the goods for export and places them alongside the vessel for loading. The buyer takes possession at the dock of the port of export.

3. FCA: Free Carrier (*named place*). The seller clears the goods for export and delivers them to the carrier specified by the buyer at the named location, where the buyer takes possession. The "named place" is domestic to the seller and the carrier can be a shipping line, an airline, a trucking firm, a railway, or an individual or firm that undertakes to procure carriage by any of these methods of transport, including intermodal, such as an international freight forwarder.

4. FOB: Free on Board (*named port of shipment*). The seller clears the goods for export and is responsible for the costs and risks of delivering the goods past the rail at the named port of export. Title passes once the goods are passed over the ship's rail. FOB is used only for

---

[23]Edward G. Hinkelman, *Dictionary of International Trade,* 4th edition (Novato, CA: World Trade Press, 2000).

[24]Ibid.

ocean or inland waterway transport. It should not be confused with the conventional North American term "F.O.B."

Group C—Main carriage paid by seller

5. CFR: Cost and Freight (*named port of destination*). The seller is responsible for clearing the goods for export, delivering the goods past the ship's rails at the port of shipment, and paying the costs to transport the goods to the named port of destination. The buyer assumes responsibility for risk of loss or damage and additional transportation costs once the goods pass the ship's rail at the port of shipment.

6. CIF: Cost, Insurance, and Freight (*named port of destination*). The seller clears the goods for export, is responsible for delivering the goods past the rail at the port of shipment, pays the costs associated with transport of the goods to the port of destination, and procures and pays for marine insurance in the buyer's name for the shipment. The buyer assumes responsibility for risk of loss or damage as well as any additional transportation costs.

7. CIP: Carriage and Insurance Paid (*named port of destination*). The seller clears the goods for export, delivers them to the carrier, and is responsible for paying for carriage and insurance to the named port of destination. The seller is also responsible for unloading, customs clearance for import, and duties. Once the goods are delivered to the carrier, the buyer is responsible for all additional costs.

8. CPT: Carriage Paid To (*named port of destination*). The seller clears the goods for export and delivers them to the carrier and is responsible for paying carriage to the named port of destination. The seller also is responsible for the costs of unloading, customs clearance for import, and duties. The buyer is responsible for all additional costs, such as procuring and paying for insurance coverage.

Group D—Arrival

9. DAF: Delivered at Frontier (*named place*). The seller clears the goods for export and is responsible for making them available to the buyer at the named place. The buyer is responsible for procuring insurance, unloading, and customs clearance for import. Frontier can include the frontier at export.

10. DDP: Delivered Duty Paid (*named place of destination*). The seller clears the goods for export and is responsible for making them available to the buyer at the named place of destination, including customs clearance for import. Therefore, the seller assumes all responsibilities for all costs associated with transportation to the named place of destination, including duties and other costs payable upon import. The buyer is responsible for unloading.

11. DDU: Delivered Duty Unpaid (*named place of destination*). The seller clears the goods for export and is responsible for making them available to the buyer at the named place of destination. This term is used when the named place of destination is other than the seaport or airport. The buyer is responsible for customs clearance for import, duties, transportation costs to the final destination, and any other costs.

12. DEQ: Delivered Ex Quay (*named port of destination*). The seller clears the goods for export and is responsible for making them available to the buyer on the quay (wharf) at the named port of destination. The buyer is responsible for import clearance, duties, and other costs upon import, as well as transport to the final destination.

13. DES: Delivered Ex Ship (*named port of destination*). The seller clears the goods for export and is responsible for making them available to the buyer on board the ship at the named port of destination. The seller is responsible for unloading and clearing the goods for import.

Certain Incoterms apply to only sea transport: FAS, FOB, CFR, CIF, DES, and DEO. EXW, FCA, CPT, CIP, DAF, DDU, and DDP apply to all modes of transport including intermodal. It is possible, and in some cases desirable, to agree to add wording to the Incoterms that specifies buyer, seller, and carrier responsibilities. For example, agreeing to DDP terms obligates the seller to pay for import duties, but using the term "DDP VAT Unpaid" means that the seller is not responsible for paying Value Added Taxes.[25]

Limitations of Incoterms

Incoterms do not (1) apply to contracts for services; (2) define contractual rights and obligations other than for delivery; (3) specify details of the transfer, transport, and delivery of the goods; (4) determine how title of the goods will be transferred; (5) protect either party from risk of loss; (6) cover the goods before or after delivery; and (7) define the remedies for breach of contract.[26]

In addition, packaging and insurance decisions in international purchasing are much more complex than in domestic buying. Although it is the responsibility of the seller to provide packaging, it is important that the buyer and seller agree on arrangements for packaging in the contract. Although many Incoterms do not obligate either the buyer or the seller to procure insurance, both parties should recognize the risks and make arrangements for suitable coverage.

---

[25]Ibid.
[26]Ibid.

Language

Words mean different things in different cultures. An American word (legitimate or slang) may have a different connotation in the United Kingdom or in South Africa (both English-speaking countries). Consider then the difficulties of communicating with someone who doesn't speak English, when everything must go through a translator and the North American buyer doesn't even know what connotations the words used by the translator have. Because of these language difficulties, some firms insist that the purchasing manager who is going to have repeated dealings with non-English speaking suppliers be multilingual or take a crash language course prior to discussions with foreign suppliers. The buyer still will have to use an interpreter, but the buyer will be a bit more comfortable in the discussion situation.

Communications

North American purchasers are used to instant communication when dealing with their domestic supply network partners. E-mail, phone, and fax all help make communication fast, inexpensive, and reliable. However, global purchasing can involve problems with communication. These relate to time zone differences and problems with the communication network itself. When dealing with suppliers in areas such as Asia, purchasers cannot simply pick up the phone and talk with their supplier any time of the day or night. Because of the time differences, some communication must be done in the evening or early hours of the morning. Furthermore, long-distance telephone calls add to the costs of global purchasing. Poor reliability of communication networks in some regions of the world also may create difficulties.

Cultural and Social Customs

Even in various parts of North America, business customs vary from area to area, for example, Boston or New York City compared with Houston or Birmingham. Certainly business/social customs vary even more widely in other countries. Good purchasers do not focus only on the economic transaction, but also on the non-economic needs of their supply network partners. Furthermore, problems caused by cultural misunderstandings can lead to higher supply chain costs. Therefore, purchasers need to have cross-cultural skills and must adjust to their suppliers' customs if they are to be effective in communicating and negotiating with suppliers.

Guidelines for Doing Business Cross-Culturally

In general the following guidelines should be followed:[27]

1. Even if English is spoken, speak slowly, use more communication graphics, and avoid the use of metaphors and jargon.

2. Bring an interpreter to all but the most informal meetings. Allow extra time to educate interpreters on issues.

---

[27]Dick Locke, *Global Supply Management,* (New York, NY: McGraw-Hill, 1996).

3. Document in writing the main conclusions and decisions.

4. Learn about the country's history and taboos.

5. Do not use first names unless invited to do so.

6. Get cultural advice from professionals or your own company employees, not from supplier representatives in the United States.

7. Expect negotiations to last longer with some cultures as the supplier learns to accept you and your company as a customer.

Examples of World Regional Differences

Some examples of world regional differences are:

Asia: In Asia the ordering of names—given and surname—varies from country to country. Ask and get the name right. Err on the side of formality; avoid first names.

Middle East: An Arab businessman may interrupt a meeting repeatedly to talk to others who wander in and out. This is not considered rude; rather, it reflects the communal style of doing business.

Latin America: Names are often a combination of the mother's and the father's, with the father's name used in conversation. Latin Americans have less need for personal space than most Americans. A Latin American associate will stand nose to nose when talking to you to establish intensity and intimacy.

Europe: Europeans are more formal than Americans, and so do not use first names unless invited to. Formal business attire is common in many countries.

Ethics

Foreign Corrupt Practices Act Defined

Because of perceived problems involving U.S. firms dealing with foreign customers or suppliers, Congress passed the Foreign Corrupt Practices Act (FCPA) in 1977. Basically, this law prohibits U.S. firms from providing or offering payments to officials of foreign governments to obtain special advantages. The FCPA distinguishes between transaction bribes and "variance" or "outright" purchase bribes. The FCPA does allow transaction bribes or facilitating payments ("grease") to persuade foreign officials to perform their normal duties, such as getting a phone installed or processing papers. The types of actions that might trigger an investigation into outright or variable bribes are payments of large commissions, payments to individuals who do not render substantial services, and payments made in cash and labeled miscellaneous. Because this type of environment is one in which the North American purchasing professional may have little experience, it is essential that he or she become familiar with the FCPA, the Omnibus Trade Act of 1988, and individual country customs.[28]

---

[28]Glenn A. Pitman and James P. Sanford, "The Foreign Corrupt Practices Act Revisited: Attempting to Regulate Ethical Bribes' in Global Business," *International Journal of Purchasing and Materials Management,* vol. 30, no. 3, 1994, p. 16.

Information Sources for Locating and Evaluating International Suppliers

In international sourcing the task of locating potential suppliers is more difficult than in domestic source selection. However, with some variation, similar types of information sources are available to the buyer, as follows:

U.S. Department of Commerce

1. The U.S. Department of Commerce can supply current lists of names and addresses of foreign suppliers, by general types of products produced. The district offices, located in most major U.S. cities, can be helpful in obtaining this information.

Chambers of Commerce

2. The chambers of commerce located in major cities in the United States and around the world will help U.S. buyers locate sources.

International Chamber of Commerce

3. The International Chamber of Commerce has contacts through its country branches around the world and will supply leads to possible sources.[29]

Embassies

4. Almost all countries of the world maintain an embassy in Washington, D.C. The major industrial nations (and many of the lesser-developed countries) maintain a trade consulate in the United States (typically in Washington, D.C., but many also have an office in other major cities, such as New York, Miami, New Orleans, Chicago, San Francisco, or Los Angeles). If requested, they will supply names of suppliers and often much background information, for their role is to promote exports from their country.

Purchasing Professionals

5. Typically, the purchasing department of a company with experience in international buying is willing to share that information with other buyers, providing they are not direct competitors. The local associations of the National Association of Purchasing Management (NAPM) and the Purchasing Management Association of Canada (PMAC) often can facilitate such an information exchange.

Suppliers

6. Current domestic suppliers often are in a position to supply information and leads on noncompetitive suppliers.

Importers and Brokers

7. Importers and foreign trade brokers make it their business to keep abreast of developments in the supply base of the countries with which they deal, and they can give the buyer a great deal of useful information.

Banks

8. Almost all the major banks have an international trade department. In addition to supplying information on currency, payment, documentation procedures, and governmental approval procedures, this department can assist in locating potential sources.

---

[29]The address is International Chamber of Commerce, 38 Cours Albert 1er, 75008 Paris, France; *www.iccwbo.org;* tel. 33 1 49 53 28 28; fax: 33 1 49 53 28 59; e-mail: webmaster@iccwbo.org.

Supplier Directories

9. Every major industrial country has at least one supplier locator directory, similar to the commonly used *Thomas Register of American Manufacturers*. For example, *Kelly's Directory* publishes supplier locator directories for the United Kingdom as well as many of the countries in Europe, Africa, and Asia.[30] The foreign trade consulate or embassy of any nation will refer you to the appropriate directory, for that is probably what they use when asked to provide a list of potential suppliers.

Associations

10. The International Federation of Purchasing and Materials Management (IFPMM), made up of member nation associations, maintains a list of correspondents in many foreign countries.[31] These are buyers and purchasing managers who have agreed to supply to buyers in other nations information on suppliers in their own countries.

Dun and Bradstreet

11. Dun & Bradstreet has offices in many countries and can supply a D&B report on many firms.

12. The Internet can be used to gain access to Web sites for companies and government organizations. For example, Kelly's Web site provides a search engine for locating OEMs, component, and consumable suppliers. Most large and medium-sized companies have

Web Sites

Web sites that describe their main products and services. Governments have extensive Web sites that provide information about everything for trade statistics to assistance for importing and exporting goods and services.

With the availability of these information sources, locating international suppliers is no real problem. The evaluation of a specific supplier's capabilities is a bit more difficult. Two key sources of evaluation information are the shared experiences of other purchasing people, which usually can be obtained simply by asking, and the supplier visit, which was discussed earlier in this chapter. If a supplier visit is not made, the buyer should at least ask the potential supplier for information such as (1) list of present and past North American customers; (2) payment procedures required; (3) banking reference; (4) facilities list; (5) memberships in quality, specification-setting associations; and (6) basic business information, such as length of time in business, sales and assets, product lines, and ownership.

---

[30]The address is Kelly's Directories, Windsor Court, East Grinstead House, East Grindstead, West Sussex, RH19 1XA, England; *www.kellys.reedinfo.co.uk;* tel. 342 335852; e-mail: kellys.mktg@reedinfo.co.uk.

[31]The address of the IFPMM Secretariat is Rockhgasse 6 P.O. Box 131, A-1014 Vienna, Austria; *http://members.eunet.at/ifpmm;* tel. 43 (1) 533 86 38 78; fax: 43 (1) 533 86 36 79; e-mail: secretariat@ifpmm.co.at.

Global Sourcing Organizations

Structuring for Global Purchasing

The structure of a global purchasing organization is influenced by the location of the key suppliers and company operations, and the overall corporate organizational structure. Companies with a decentralized organization structure give business unit purchasing staff responsibility for international purchasing. In a centralized or hybrid structure, global supply activities can be coordinated through several organizational models. One approach is to create regional purchasing offices, such as the approach taken by Unisys. The global supply organization at Unisys has a chief purchasing officer for each of its four regions — the United States; Europe, Middle East and Africa; Asia and the Pacific; and Latin America and the Caribbean — each reporting to the corporate vice president of global procurement. Furthermore, the structure in each region was identical. The vice president of global procurement believed that some procurement activities, such as customer sales support, process management, and supplies and services, required close geographic proximity. However, commodity management represented one area where geographic location was not always important. While it was necessary to negotiate local and regional supply agreements for many commodities, responsibility was divided between the European and U.S. commodity purchasing organizations for its global suppliers. Discussions between the corporate vice president of global procurement and the commodity management directors for the United States and Europe led to consensus regarding lead responsibility for global commodities. Such decisions were based on supplier location, previous experience of the U.S. and European purchasing staff with the commodities in question, and staff availability.[32]

Regional Purchasing Offices: Unisys Example

Global Commodity Management Organizations

THOMSON multimedia Example

Another approach is the creation of a global commodity management organization. This approach makes sense when there are a large number of common requirements across facilities or business units, and the supply base is not always located in the same geographic area as the buying company's operations. The global commodity managers are responsible for identifying world-class suppliers for important raw materials and services common to the company's global operations. Meanwhile, local supply managers are allowed to focus on identifying capable local suppliers for materials and services unique to their operation. Such was the case at THOMSON multimedia, which had its main operations in North America and Europe but relied heavily on suppliers in Asia. Given the large number of common requirements and suppliers, along with the geographical spread of manufacturing and laboratory facilities, the vice president of worldwide sourcing deemed it essential to increase the staffing of global commodity management. Therefore, the number of global commodity coordinators was

---

[32]Michiel R. Leenders, and P. Fraser Johnson, *Major Changes in Supply Chain Responsibilities* (Tempe, AZ: Center for Advanced Purchasing Studies, 2001).

increased from just one to 10 persons, each assigned worldwide responsibility for a specific group of common requirements. A major challenge for each global commodity coordinator was the appropriate melding of local and regional concerns and interests with global ones.[33] (See Figure 2-5.)

International Purchasing Offices

A third approach to global sourcing is the creation of international purchasing offices (IPOs). International purchasing offices can be focused on the basis of commodities, such as important raw materials, or on the basis of projects, such as large capital projects. Typically, IPOs are used when the company does not have a presence in the same geographic region where important suppliers are located. The logic of establishing IPOs is that the local presence of supply personnel can provide access to better suppliers and lower total costs. IPOs facilitate activities such as local sourcing and review, supplier development, materials management, quality control, and payment, and can employ local personnel thoroughly familiar with the language, culture, and way of doing business in that country or geographic area.

Intermediaries

Should purchases be made direct from the supplier or through an intermediary? This depends on factors such as how much specialized international buying knowledge is available in the purchasing department and the volume and frequency of sourcing expected. Many firms use intermediaries for some or all of their global purchasing. The following list describes some of the options available.

Import Brokers and Agents

For a fee (usually a percentage of purchase value—and it can be as high as 25 percent), the broker or agent will assist in locating suppliers and handling required paperwork. In most situations, title passes directly to the buying organization. The buyer, of course, must make sure the fee is reasonable with regard to the services performed.

Import Merchant

The import merchant makes a contract with the buyer and then buys the product in its name from the foreign supplier, takes title, delivers to the place agreed on with the buyer, and then bills the buyer for the agreed-on price. Obviously, the buyer pays a fee (buried in the price paid) for the buying services provided.

---

[33]Ibid.

Seller's Subsidiary

Purchasing from the North American subsidiary of a foreign supplier is a common approach. The subsidiaries provide the benefits of location (right time zone), conduct business in English, and accept payments in U.S. dollars. They also might provide credit terms. The subsidiary can make it easy to buy from its parent company's remote facilities, but remember, they are not the manufacturer, which may add costs and make communication difficult.

Sales Representatives

Some companies hire sales agents to represent them in various regions of the world. Typically, sales representatives handle low volume/value contracts and are paid a commission by the supplier, which is included in the price of the goods.

Trading Company

A trading company is typically a large firm that normally handles a wide spectrum of products from one or a limited number of countries. Trading companies are used extensively by Japanese firms to move products into North America. The advantages to the buyer of using a trading company are (1) convenience; (2) efficiency; (3) often lower costs, due to volume; (4) reduced lead times, because it often maintains inventory in North America; and (5) greater assurance of the product meeting quality specifications, because the trading company inspects in the producing country before shipment. But, as with any supplier, the buyer should check out the trading company carefully.

Countertrade

Countertrade Defined

Countertrade is a fancy term for a barter agreement, but with some new twists. Barter has been around for years and takes place when payment between buyer and seller is made by the exchange of goods rather than cash. U.S. firms, in times of shortage, often swap merchandise; for example, a utility trades fuel oil to another utility in exchange for copper cable, as a matter of expediency. However, the complexities of international trade, particularly with developing countries, have brought some new variations, with purchasing right in the middle of the action. There are five principal variations, which are explained more fully in the Center for Advanced Purchasing Studies 1991 study, *Countertrade: Purchasing's Perceptions and Involvement.*[34]

---

[34]Laura B. Forker, *Countertrade: Purchasing's Perceptions and Involvement* (Tempe, AZ: Center for Advanced Purchasing Studies, 1991).

Barter/Swaps

Barter involves the exchange of goods instead of cash. Typically, barter takes place when a country, which is short of hard currency, agrees to exchange its product for another country's product, such as Chinese tungsten for stainless steel. This normally is a rather clean transaction, for the firms (countries) are exchanging equivalent dollar values. If goods of the same kind, for example, agricultural items or chemicals, are exchanged to save transportation costs, the arrangement is called a swap.

In a mixed barter, the seller ships product of a certain value—for example, motors—and agrees to take payment in a combination of cash and product—for example, wheat. It then is up to purchasing to resell the product for cash or to barter it to someone else. A commodity that changes hands twice is referred to as a *two-corner trade*. If it changes hands three times, it is a *three-corner deal*. Purchasing often gets involved in situations where working out the particular barters or swaps is both difficult and time-consuming.

Offset Arrangements

Offsets are distinguished by the condition that one part of countertrade be used to purchase government and/or military-related exports. Under these agreements, in order to make the sale, the selling company agrees to purchase a given percentage of the sales price in the customer country. The negotiation usually starts at 50 percent and then goes up or down from there. Whatever the figure agreed to, it then is up to purchasing to figure out how it can spend the specified amount for worthwhile goods or products. In some instances, the goods purchased later are resold, putting the purchasing department largely in the role of a trading company. Such resale occurs when purchasing cannot locate a supplier of suitable, needed merchandise in the customer country and simply makes a purchase of goods (that hopefully later will be salable) to complete the deal. Even if specific deals are unprofitable, firms engaging in countertrade usually are looking for long-term, meaningful, and mutually advantageous relationships with the other country.

When other countries buy North American-produced merchandise, they often push hard for offsets to gain access to technology, to get U.S. dollars, to increase employment, and/or to help maintain political stability by protecting jobs and domestic producers.

Counterpurchase

Counterpurchase agreements require the initial exporter to buy (or to find a buyer for) a specified value of goods (often stated as a percentage of the value of the original export) from the original importer during a specified time period.

Buyback/Compensation

In buyback agreements, the selling firm agrees to set up a producing plant in the buying country or to sell the country capital equipment and/or technology. The original seller then agrees to buy back a specified amount of what is produced by the plant, equipment, or technology. Buyback agreements can span 10 or more years.

Switch Trade

In switch trades, a third party applies its "credits" to a bilateral clearing arrangement. The credits are used to buy goods and/or services from the company or country in deficit. Usually a broker or trading house handles the switch.

Reasons to Use Countertrade

Countertrade is used in situations where a country has a shortage of foreign exchange or a shortage of credit to finance its desired trade flows, wishes to diversify its foreign exchange earnings, or is encouraging the development of the domestic economy by promoting labor-intensive exports. The number of countries participating in countertrade has increased from just 15 in 1972 to an estimated 140 countries, including many of the United States' main trading partners, such as Canada, the United Kingdom, and China.[35] Although the U.S. government generally views countertrade as contrary to an open free-trading system, it does not oppose participation by U.S. companies in countertrade transactions.[36]

The exact value of international countertrade transactions is not known — secrecy surrounding the transactions prevents the government from collecting this data.[37] However, studies have estimated the total value of countertrade at 15 to 30 percent of all world trade.[38]

Supply's Role in Managing Countertrade Arrangements

While countertrade traditionally was very common in the sale by U.S. firms of armament to foreign nations, its use has been extended into civilian government procurement projects, such as the sale of civilian aircraft, telecommunications, and technology systems. In the competitive global marketplace the ability to meet countertrade requirements in a cost-effective manner represents a competitive advantage. Supply has a legitimate role in managing countertrade arrangements, and those responsible for negotiating arrangements with customers that involve countertrade should involve supply personnel early in the process in order to provide opportunities for feed-

---

[35]John Stevens, "Global Purchasing and the Rise of Countertrade," *Purchasing and Supply Management,* September 1995, p. 28.

[36]Pompiliu Verzariu, *The Evolution of International Barter, Countertrade and Offset Practices: A Survey of the 1970s through the 1990s,* U.S. Department of Commerce, International Trade Administration, Office of Finance, March 2000.

[37]Ibid.

[38]Laura B. Forker, "Countertrade's Impact on the Supply Function," *International Journal of Purchasing and Materials Management,* Fall 1995, pp. 37–45.

back concerning cost implications, the status of the countertrade market, sourcing information, and the availability of suppliers and opportunities for barter.

In a 1995 study of 72 firms engaging in countertrade, Pearson and Forker discovered that purchasing usually is not involved in the decision to engage in countertrade, and purchasing is consulted in the preliminary negotiations only if it is held in high esteem by executive management. Purchasing's contribution comes after the decision has been made, at the stage where potential counterpurchases are being evaluated. Given the risks of countertrade—the possibility of poor quality goods and services, the development of unprofitable deals, and the acceptance of goods and services that do not match marketing channels — the purchasing function should be able to contribute more in the proposal evaluation stage.[39]

Guidelines for Engaging in Countertrade

While in many instances countertrade arrangements may present very complex problems to the selling firm's purchasing department in discharging the countertrade obligations, they may provide the opportunity to develop lower cost sources of supply in the world marketplace. However, because it has become a "way of life" for many purchasing professionals, several guidelines are suggested:

(1) Decide whether countertrade is a viable alternative. If a company does not have the organization to do the international sourcing required, it should refuse to participate. (2) Build the cost of countertrade into the selling price. (3) Know the country—its government, politics, regulations. (4) Know the products involved, and what's available. (5) Know the countertrade negotiation process—offset percentage, penalties, and time period.[40]

American Countertrade Association

The American Countertrade Association (ACA) is a group whose members include key U.S. manufacturers, exporters, and international trade financiers involved in selling and investing in a variety of industries, including electronics, commodities, telecommunications, power generation, defense, and aeronautics. The purpose of the ACA is to provide a forum to educate and network for the purpose of creating new ways to facilitate trade flows and investments into countries that either have difficulties externalizing hard currency or imposing certain countertrade purchase or offset obligations on vendors. The ACA has more than 100 U.S.-based members.[41]

---

[39]John N. Pearson and Laura B. Forker, "International Countertrade: Has Purchasing's Role Really Changed?" *International Journal of Purchasing and Materials Management,* vol. 31, no. 4, Fall 1995, p. 42.

[40]David B. Yoffie, "Profiting from Countertrade," *Harvard Business Review,* May–June 1984, pp. 8–16.

[41]The address for the ACA is 818 Connecticut Ave, NW, 12th Floor, Washington, DC 20006; tel: (202) 887-9011; fax: (202) 872-8324; e-mail aca@countertrade.org; *www.countertrade.org.*

Foreign Trade Zones

Foreign Trade Zone Defined

A *foreign trade zone (FTZ)* is defined as "special commercial and industrial areas in or near ports of entry where foreign and domestic merchandise, including raw materials, components, and finished goods, may be brought in without being subject to payment of customs duties. Merchandise brought into these zones may be stored, sold, exhibited, repacked, assembled, sorted, graded, cleaned, or otherwise manipulated prior to reexport or entry into the national customs territory. U.S. FTZs are restricted-access sites in or near ports of entry, which are licensed by the Foreign Trade Zone Board and operated under the supervision of the U.S. Customs Service. Zones are operated under public utility principles to create and maintain employment by encouraging operations in the United States that might otherwise have been carried on abroad."[42, 43]

The Foreign Trade Zones Act was passed in 1934 and has been amended periodically. It is codified in the United States Codes as Title 19, Sections 81a through 81u. Initially, FTZs were used primarily as custom-bonded warehouses, but the 1950 Boggs Amendment permitted manufacture and exhibition in the FTZ. As a consequence of the continuing foreign trade deficits, Congress amended the FTZ Act in 1980 to permit the base price of duty computation to exclude labor, overhead, and gain (profit).

Two Categories of FTZs

There are two categories of FTZs, general purpose zones and subzones. General purpose zones handle merchandise for many companies and are typically sponsored by a public agency or corporation, like a port authority. Subzones are special purpose zones, usually located at manufacturing plants. Subzones are usually preexisting manufacturing sites that operate under the guarantee of a local general purpose site. There are no legal differences in the types of activities that can be undertaken at zones or subzones. According to government data, subzones accounted for approximately 85 percent of the $157 billion in activity in U.S. FTZs in 1998. In 1998 there were 145 FTZs, with 204 facilities using subzone status in 1998.[44]

Major Functions in FTZs

Each FTZ differs in character depending upon the functions performed in serving the pattern of trade peculiar to that trading area. The major functions that may be conducted within a zone are:

Manufacturing. Manufacturing involving foreign goods can be carried on in the zone area. International goods can be mixed with domestic goods and, when imported, duties are payable only on that part of the product consisting of offshore goods. This activity offers an excellent opportunity for use

---

[42]Edward G. Hinkelman, *Dictionary of International Trade,* 4th edition (Novato, CA: World Trade Press, 2000).

[43]Information concerning U.S. foreign trade zones can be obtained from the Foreign Trade Zones Board, Department of Commerce, Washington D.C. 20230; tel. (202) 482-2862; fax. (202) 482-0002; *http://ia.ita.doc.gov/ftzpage.*

[44]William Daley and Robert Rubin, *60th Annual Report of the Foreign Trade Zones Board to the Congress of the United States for fiscal year ended 1998,* U.S. Department of Commerce, 1999.

of foreign trade zones. In some circumstances the final assembled product may qualify for reduced duties, or might have no duties imposed if it has more than 50 percent U.S. content of labor or components. Such merchandise can be classified as "American made" for purposes of export under NAFTA. Besides reduced duties, there is a saving on interest, because duty payments are not due until the merchandise leaves the FTZ and enters the United States.

Transshipment. Goods may be stored, repacked, assembled, or otherwise manipulated while awaiting shipment to another port, without the payment of duty or posting a bond.

Storage. Part or all of the goods may be stored at a zone indefinitely. This is especially important for goods being held for new import quotas or until demand and price increase.

Manipulation. Imported goods may be manipulated, or combined with domestic goods, and then either imported or reexported. Duty is paid only on imported merchandise.

Refunding of Duties, Taxes, and Drawbacks. When imported merchandise that has passed through customs is returned to the zone, the owner immediately may obtain a 99 percent drawback of duties paid. Likewise, when products are transferred from bonded warehouses to foreign trade zones, the bond is canceled and all obligations in regard to duty payment and time limitations are terminated. Also, exporters of domestic goods subject to internal revenue taxes receive a tax refund as soon as such products move into a foreign trade zone.

Exhibition and Display. Users of a zone may exhibit and display their wares to customers without bond or duty payments. They can quote firm prices (because they can determine definite duty and tax rates in advance) and provide immediate delivery. Duty and taxes are applicable only to those goods that enter customs territory.

BMW Example

When BMW announced its decision to build a $1.2 billion automotive assembly facility in South Carolina, it applied for FTZ subzone status. As an FTZ subzone, BMW has received several benefits. It defers duty payments on imported vehicles and components until the vehicles actually enter the United States; because two-thirds of the plant's production is exported, BMW avoids paying U.S. duties on component parts used on vehicles that are exported; and component parts from overseas suppliers are delivered directly to the assembly facility, supporting JIT delivery arrangements.[45]

If the purchasing executive has large overseas suppliers or is contemplating importing substantial amounts of dutiable products, savings can be realized on duties or drawbacks, and on the cost of shipping both imported materials to plants in the hinterland and manufactured products back to the same port for export. The functions actually performed in any zone, in the

---

[45]Beth M. Schwartz, "FTZ Success," *Transportation and Distribution,* vol. 40, no. 7, July 1999, p. 40.

last analysis, depend on the inherent nature of the trading and commercial community and demands made by users of zone facilities.

Main Reason for Using an FTZ

The principal reason for using an FTZ is to avoid, postpone, or reduce duties on imported goods, making imported goods more competitive in the U.S. marketplace and creating economic benefits for the local community through job creation. The potential disadvantages of the FTZ are (1) the additional labor costs and operating and handling costs associated with its use and (2) the uncertainty of its long-term use due to changes in foreign trade agreements that are reducing and eliminating import duties.

Foreign Trade Zones Compared with Bonded Warehouses

Bonded Warehouse Defined

A bonded warehouse is "a warehouse owned by persons approved by the Treasury Department, and under bond or guarantee for the strict observance of the revenue laws of the United States; utilized for storing goods until duties are paid or goods are otherwise properly released."[46] The purpose of bonded warehousing is to exempt the importer from paying duty on foreign commerce that will be reexported or to delay payment of duties until the owner moves the merchandise into the host country. Goods can be stored for three years.[47] At the end of the period, if duty has not been paid, the government sells the goods at public auction.

All merchandise exported from bonded warehouses must be shipped in the original package unless special permission has been received from the collector of customs. Any manufacturing must be conducted under strict supervision and the resulting items must be reexported.

Maquiladoras

Maquiladoras are Examples of the FTZ Concept

Mexico's maquiladoras are examples of the foreign trade zone concept or industrial parks. Non-Mexicans can own the maquila, or plant, in the maquiladora in order to take advantage of low Mexican labor costs. Parts and supplies enter Mexico duty free, and products exported to the United States are taxed only on the value added in Mexico. There are nearly 4,000 maquiladora facilities currently operating along the U.S. — Mexican border, employing more than 1 million people, a source of $40 billion in Mexican exports.[48]

With NAFTA eliminating North American trade barriers, the future of the maquiladora operations has been called into question. However, in the meantime, maquiladora operations are a critical and successful dimension of Mexico's economy.

---

[46]Edward G. Hinkelman, *Dictionary of International Trade,* 4th edition (Novato, CA: World Trade Press, 2000).

[47]Extensions may be granted on application.

[48]Lara L. Sowinski, "Maquiladora's: Pending Changes on the Horizon," *World Trade,* September 2000, pp. 88–92.

TIBs and Duty Drawbacks

TIBs Apply to Imports That Will Be Reexported Later

A temporary importation bond (TIB) permits certain classes of merchandise to be imported into the United States. These are articles not for sale, such as samples, or articles for sale on approval. A bond is required, usually for an amount equal to twice the estimated duty. While there is a fee for the TIB, the net effect is that no duty is paid on the merchandise, provided it is reexported. The TIB is valid for one year, with two one-year extensions possible. However, if the goods are not exported on time, the penalty can be twice the normal duty, which is why the TIB must be for twice the normal duty.

Duty Drawbacks Permit Refunds on Certain Duties

Duty drawback permits a refund of duties paid on imported materials that are exported later. The buyer enters into a duty drawback contract with the U.S. government, imports the material for manufacture, and pays the normal duty. If the final manufactured or processed product is exported within five years of import, duty drawback can be obtained. There are three main types of duty drawback: direct identification drawback, substitution drawback, and rejected merchandise drawback. Provisions for duty refunds differ slightly under each type.[49]

North American Free Trade Agreement

The U.S.—Canada Free Trade Agreement (FTA) went into effect on January 1, 1989. On January 1, 1994, the North American Free Trade Agreement (NAFTA), to be phased in over a 15-year period, took effect for the United States, Canada, and Mexico. The end result of NAFTA will be the elimination or reduction of tariffs and the reduction of nontariff barriers to trade among the three member countries. By 1999, almost all of the $365 billion in merchandise traded between Canada and the United States was duty free, while about two-thirds of the $195 billion in Mexico-U.S. trade was duty free. (See Table 14-2.)

NAFTA Eliminates or Reduces Tariffs Among Member Countries

Rules of Origin

Tariffs are being phased out gradually. Until they are totally eliminated, buyers must adhere to NAFTA's complicated rules of origin. Goods that are wholly produced in the United States, Canada, or Mexico are classified as "originating goods" and are eligible for preferential reduced tariff rates. Other goods are taxed as if they were from any other country.[50] Filling out and filing the certificate of origin is a major problem for many importers because of inconsistent and product-specific rules and documentation. Purchasers can file an annual blanket certificate if they anticipate buying the same goods more than once a year.[51]

---

[49]Edward G. Hinkelman, *Dictionary of International Trade,* 4th edition (Novato, CA: World Trade Press, 2000).

[50]Philip Yale Simmons, "Beware of NAFTA's *Rules of Origin,'* " *NAPM Insights,* July 1994, p. 25.

[51]Peter S. Brown, "What's New about Sourcing in Canada," NAPM Insights, September 1994, p. 6.

Possibility of a Free Trade Area of the Americas

In 1991, Argentina, Brazil, Paraguay, and Uruguay created a customs union called Mercosur. Chile and Bolivia became associate members in 1996 and 1997 respectively.

At the Summit of the Americas in 1994, 34 nations from the Western Hemisphere committed themselves to the creation of a free trade area of the Americas by the year 2005.[52] Working groups are discussing, drafting, and revising recommendations related to each of the 23 summit goals.

The United States began negotiations with Chile in 1999 on a trade pact that could ultimately lead to a hemispherewide agreement. The most likely scenario would be an expansion of NAFTA to include Chile and possibly certain other members of Mercosur.

Purchasers wishing to trade internationally have to stay informed about world trade developments and agreements so as to exploit new opportunities and avoid supply problems.

Questions for Review and Discussion

1. What are the factors/forces that have caused the increase in international trade? What growth will occur in the next 10 years?
2. Why have North American firms become actively involved in global purchasing?
3. What do firms see as the principal advantages to be gained when they buy globally?
4. How can the buying firm minimize the problem areas connected with global buying? Which do you feel are most serious?
5. How can the buyer best get a list of potential international sources? Evaluate potential suppliers?
6. Discuss the pros and cons of buying direct versus using some form of middleman.
7. What are the forms of countertrade, and what problems do they cause for the buyer? How can the buyer help make countertrade work?
8. How can the buyer make effective use of foreign trade zones?
9. What advantages are there for purchasers as a result of the North American Free Trade Agreement (NAFTA)? What is a certificate of origin? Why does the buyer need to be concerned with this?
10. What are Incoterms? What factors should be considered when selecting an Incoterm?

---

[52]G. Philip Hughes, "One Year after the Summit of the Americas," *The Wall Street Journal,* December 29, 1995, p. A7.

References

Anonymous, "Global Sourcing to Grow — But Slowly," *Purchasing,* May 18, 2000. pp. 24–28.

Bendorf, Robi, "Pay Attention to Labor Rates," *Purchasing Today,* August 1999, p. 14.

Brown, Peter S., "What's New about Sourcing in Canada," *NAPM Insights,* September 1994, p. 6.

Dollar, Tony, "Import Logistics," *Distribution,* April 1995, p. 44.

Forker, Laura B., *Countertrade: Purchasing's Perceptions and Involvement,* Tempe, AZ: Center for Advanced Purchasing Studies, 1991.

Forker, Laura B., "Countertrade's Impact on the Supply Function," *International Journal of Purchasing and Materials Management,* Fall 1995, pp. 37–45.

Hinkelman, Edward G., *Dictionary of International Trade,* 4th edition, Novato, CA: World Trade Press, 2000.

Hughes, G. Philip, "One Year after the Summit of the Americas," *The Wall Street Journal,* December 29, 1995, p. A7.

Karoway, Cherish, "Going Global: Purchasers Take the Plunge," *NAPM Insights,* July 1995, p. 46.

Larson, Robert K. and Ajay Adhikari, "The Euro: Ready or Not, Its Here!" *The Ohio CPA Journal,* January–March 2000, pp. 8–12.

Lawhon, Larry H., "A Beginner's Guide to International Leadtimes," *NAPM Insights,* July 1995, p. 24.

Lieb, Robert C. and Hugh L. Randall, "1997 CEO Perspectives on the Current Status and Future Prospects of the Third-Party Logistics Industry in the United States," *Transportation Journal,* vol. 38, no. 3, 1999, pp. 28–42.

Leenders, Michiel R. and P. Fraser Johnson, *Major Changes in Supply Chain Responsibilities,* Tempe AZ: Center for Advanced Purchasing Studies, 2001.

Locke, Dick, *Global Supply Management,* New York, NY: McGraw-Hill, 1996.

Minnick, Brad, "GATT's Here: Now What," *NAPM Insights,* May 1995, p. 63.

Pitman, Glenn A. and James P. Sanford, "The Foreign Corrupt Practices Act Revisited: Attempting to Regulate 'Ethical Bribes' in Global Business," *International Journal of Purchasing and Materials Management,* vol. 30, no. 3, 1994, p. 16.

Pearson, John N. and Laura B. Forker, "International Countertrade: Has Purchasing's Role Really Changed?" *International Journal of Purchasing and Materials Management,* vol. 31, no. 4, Fall 1995, p. 42.

Pooler, Victor, *Global Purchasing: Reaching for the World,* New York, NY: Van Nostrand Reinhold, 1992.

Schwartz, Beth M., "FTZ Success," *Transportation and Distribution,* vol. 40, no. 7, July 1999, p. 40.

Simmons, Philip Yale, "Beware of NAFTA's Rules of Origin, *NAPM Insights,* July 1994, p. 25.

Sowinski, Lara L., "Maquiladora's: Pending Changes on the Horizon," *World Trade,* September 2000, pp. 88–92.

Stevens, John, "Global Purchasing and the Rise and Rise of Countertrade," *Purchasing and Supply Management,* September 1995, p. 28.

U.S. Census Bureau, *www.census.gov,* Report FT900 (99) (CB-00-94), January 2001.

U.S. Department of Commerce, International Economic Indicators, May 1995.

Verzariu, Pompiliu, *The Evolution of International Barter, Countertrade and Offset Practices: A Survey of the 1970s through the 1990s,* U.S. Department of Commerce, International Trade Administration, Office of Finance, March 2000.

World Trade Organization, *www.wto.org,* January 2001.

World Trade Organization, *International Trade Statistics 2000,* 2000.

World Trade Organization, *The WTO in Brief, www.wto.org,* January 2001.

Yoffie, David B., "Profiting from Countertrade," *Harvard Business Review,* May–June 1984, pp. 8–16.

CASE 14-1
GLOBAL PHARMACEUTICALS LTD.

Ian Grant was the Purchasing Agent for the Animal Health Group of Global Pharmaceuticals Ltd. in London, Ontario. In January, he was planning the transfer of production of eight products from the plant in Germany to the London facility. He wondered how he should manage the purchasing transition, particularly the supply of raw materials and packaging for these products.

Global Pharmaceuticals Ltd. Background. Founded in 1849, Global Pharmaceuticals Ltd. (GPL) was headquartered in New York and had established a worldwide reputation for excellence and innovation. The company employed more than 40,000 persons in 55 countries, and the products were sold in more than 150 nations. Last year, net sales were US $8 billion and net income exceeded US $1 billion, the highest level in company history.

The company was organized into three segments: Health Care, Animal Health, and Consumer Health Care. The Health Care Group marketed prescription drugs, medical implant products and medical devices. This group accounted for 87 percent of company sales. The Animal Health Group produced vaccines and other medicines for dogs, cats, livestock, and poultry. Animal Health's sales were approximately 8 percent of the total. The smallest division, the Consumer Health Care Group (5 percent of total sales), produced over-the-counter products such as suntan lotion, mouthwash, and shaving cream.

The company recently focused on its strategic mission of "discovering, developing, and bringing to market health-care products in an effective manner that fulfill unmet medical needs." A number of operations that either did not meet the company's goals or were not related to health care had therefore been recently sold or closed. A number of businesses that complemented GPL's strategy had also been acquired or were in the negotiation stage.

Animal Health Group. The Animal Health Group faced major changes. By the end of January, GPL would have acquired Jones Clarke Animal Health (JCAH), which would push GPL to the number one position in the world in animal health products. GPL had traditionally held the leading position in medicines for large animals, plus a strong presence in Latin America and Japan. JCAH, on the other hand, had leading product lines in companion animal products in North America and in vaccines worldwide, plus superior organizational strength in Europe and Australia. It was planned that the combination of these firms would lead to the creation of a single, integrated unit that would place GPL in a position to satisfy the Animal Health Group vision: "We will be The Driving Force in the animal health industry." Production sites for the joint company of JCAH and GPL numbered 36 in 30 different countries and there were 7 research sites.

Supplier Approval Process. In order to manufacture animal health products, GPL required a number of items, such as chemical compounds, syringes, bottles, boxes, and labels. Most of these items were subject to stringent regulatory requirements (content, measurement scale, language, dosage) that varied by country. At the London, Ontario plant, the purchasing department was responsible for sourcing more than 1,100 raw material and packaging items worth in excess of $11 million (Canadian) per annum. All items had to be purchased from an authorized supplier of GPL. To become an Approved Supplier, the candidate had to pass a series of tests that could take up to one year to complete. The approximate procedure follows:

1. A copy of the Standard Operating Procedures for the product had to be provided, and these procedures should be accepted by GPL.

2. A Certificate of Analysis of a lot also should be provided, and this certificate had to match the Standard Operating Procedures.

3. Three samples from three different lots should be provided, along with the Certificates of Analysis for each lot.

4. The samples would be chemically tested by GPL, and the results had to match the Certificates provided and be acceptable to GPL.

5. The results would be analysed and approval had to be received from the following areas: Product Development, Quality Control and Manufacturing.

6. A small, pilot batch would be run at the GPL plant using the supplies, and the results would then be tested.

7. After the supplier had successfully passed steps 1 to 6 above, then supply would begin. The first three lots were to be fully tested by GPL, and, if accepted, then the supplier would become an Approved Supplier of GPL subject to periodic lot testing.

German Plant Closure. It was announced in October last year that its only plant in Germany would close by December of this year. The products produced there would be transferred to the London, Ontario, plant on a phased basis, starting in June and commencing full production a year later. It was planned that the German plant would increase production sufficiently to provide enough inventory to satisfy demand until the London plant could provide adequate supply. The addition of these eight products (See Exhibit 1) to the London portfolio would increase production at that plant by 30 percent. Capacity was not an issue.

By January it was apparent that the German plant would not be able to increase production for sufficient inventory to last the phase-in period due

EXHIBIT 1   **Global Pharmaceuticals Ltd., Animal Health Products to be Transferred from Germany to London, ON**

Product Name	No. of Formulations	Sizes	No. of Label Languages
Tetratex (injection)	1	1	8
Vetracil (tablets)	2	2	9
Baxotil (Suspension)	1	2	3
Baxotil (Paste for dogs)	1	2	13
Baxotil (Paste for cats)	1	2	13
Federex (Paste)	1	1	1
Vitopax (1% paste)	1	1	2
Vitopax (10% paste)	1	2	2

to low productivity rates and morale. Also, the German government would not allow the plant to run on overtime hours. It was clear that the transition to London would have to be achieved even earlier than planned to avoid stock-outs.

The approved suppliers for the German plant consisted of both large and small operations that were located all over Europe. A sample of some of the suppliers were:

Name: E. Merk
Location: Karlsruhe, Germany
Size: Approx. 400 employees
Product: Chemicals

Name: R. Knof
Location: Karlsruhe, Germany
Size: Family operation, 3 employees
Product: Printing of barrel of syringes

Name: Union Plastics
Location: St. Didier-En-Valley, France
Size: 100 employees
Product: Syringe barrels and plungers for syringes

Name: Loffler
Location: Freyung, Germany
Size: 410 employees
Product: Syringe barrels and plungers for syringes

As Ian Grant contemplated his moves over the next six months, he wondered how he could ensure that the London plant had all the necessary supplies for production in an efficient and timely manner.

CASE 14-2
MARATHON OIL COMPANY INTERNATIONAL

In October, R. J. Engel (Bob), procurement supervisor for the Worldwide Exploration and Production Division of Marathon Oil Company in Houston, Texas, as a member of the purchasing managerial team faced the following decision: What should his input as procurement supervisor for the Worldwide Exploration and Production Division be on the issue concerning the location of the new International Purchasing Office (IPO) for the new Sakhalin Island project, and what factors should influence the decision?

General Company Background. Marathon Oil Company was a fully integrated energy company with worldwide operations in exploration, production, refining, and sales of petroleum-based products. Geographically, the company was organized in five major regions in the United States and four international regions. Managers compared or benchmarked the company with the top 10 integrated oil companies of the world. The company was about 100 years old and had undergone major downsizing and reorganization in the past three years. The employee base was reduced by about 25 percent.

Marathon had successful operations in the North Sea of the United Kingdom. The Brae complex in the North Sea comprised four fields. Marathon also had operations in Ireland, Egypt, Indonesia, and Tunisia. Most of the international operations were joint ventures or consortia with several partners involved in each field.

Marathon and a partner pioneered the export of liquefied natural gas (LNG) from Alaska to Japan in 1969. The partnership designed and operated two liquefied natural gas (LNG) ships. In 1994, the two original ships were replaced with bigger ships. Each new vessel had a capacity of 87,500 cubic meters of LNG.

Marathon was the operator for a five-company international consortium seeking the rights to develop two worldclass oil fields offshore of Sakhalin Island in Far Eastern Russia. It was estimated that the two fields contained total recoverable reserves of 750 million barrels of liquid hydrocarbons and 14 trillion cubic feet of natural gas. The Sakhalin Island project was an exciting new international project for Marathon. When opened, this new project would operate under some of the most severe climatic conditions in the world. Two test wells had been drilled in this project and the results were prolific. Marathon and its four consortium partners applied to the parliament of the Confederation of Independent States (CIS) for rights to develop the two Sakhalin fields. The consortium included Marathon from Houston, Shell of Holland, McDermott from Houston, and Mitsui and Mitsubishi from Japan. In addition to return on investment, each of the partners had different project roles and interests. Marathon was the site operator and lead in engineering, construction, and field operations. Shell, with other interests in Russia, was an investor and involved in engineering. McDermott was to build the platforms. Mitsui was to build the gas liquefaction plant in the Sakhalins and transport the LNG to Japan. Mitsubishi was primarily in the partnership to finance the Japanese interests. The consortium had invested $100 million in engineering and project planning and expected the total project costs to be in the range of $11 billion.

Corporate Purchasing. In the most recent reorganization of corporate purchasing, particular emphasis was placed on inventory management, purchasing of commodities, and the level of centralization and delegation of purchasing authority. Bob Engel joined the company as procurement supervisor for Worldwide Exploration and Production Division during its reorganization. Marathon purchasing was both centralized and decentralized.

About 35 percent of all buys for the regions were controlled from corporate purchasing in Houston. Decentralized purchases were primarily for equipment or commodities tied to the local areas and incidentals associated with a particular site or facility.

Marathon had one IPO in Aberdeen, Scotland. It supported the North Sea operations and was colocated with the engineering and other site management operations.

Even though the company had many blanket orders in effect, the company initiated about 2.5 million to 3 million transactions per year. Much of this activity was to buy more than $12 million in maintenance, repair, and operations items (MRO) for the many sites and facilities. Ninety percent of the transactions accounted for only about 10 percent of the value of purchased goods and services.

Marathon Oil Company recently commenced using procurement (p-cards). By October, Marathon had 442 p-cards in the hands of 303 cardholders. Some cardholders had multiple cards to satisfy cost distribution procedures between consortium members on a site. Purchasing had also initiated a very successful reverse EDI program in several domestic regions. Reverse EDI meant that the supplier input the product order and cost data into the system after receiving a telephone order from a field site or facility. The EDI system created the record and led to payment by Electronic Funds Transfer (EFT). The EDI process included an automatic audit system and error range that corrected price and total cost down or up if errors or over-billing were discovered. The EDI system utilized a value-added network (third party) to connect the company and the selected suppliers.

The Sakhalin Island Project. Marathon wanted to establish an IPO to support the development phase of the Sakhalin project. The location of the International Purchasing Office for the new Sakhalin Island project was of concern to Bob Engel. This area would ultimately be responsible for materials and service support to the Sakhalin fields as the fields developed and were placed in operation. Although the approval date of the rights request by the CIS government was uncertain, approval could come any day. Marathon needed to be ready to execute its plans for the IPO for the Sakhalin project on very short notice.

The Sakhalin Island area was primitive. Marathon engineers would have to develop and build a port and roads and expand the airfield and the entire infrastructure necessary to support the oil fields. The construction season averaged only about three to four months each year because of the extreme climatic conditions. Engineers estimated that it might take up to three years to mobilize the resources and get the project established. Marathon had about 200 people currently assigned to the project. Once a platform was established, drilling and oil field operations would be year-round because most operations would be weath-ered inside the platform. Engineers had determined that all of the equipment and nearly all of the supplies needed to establish and maintain the Sakhalin fields would have to be brought in from outside the Sakhalin Islands.

London, Houston, or Tokyo were considered possible locations for the IPO. Bob Engel and others in the purchasing team knew that three of the five consortium companies had offices in London. Two of the companies were major entities from Japan. Satisfactory telephone, fax, and computer communication could be established by Marathon from the Sakhalin site to London, Houston, or Tokyo.

Bob Engel and the managerial team knew they had to have the IPO plan ready, and location of the IPO was one of the major questions for the plan. What factors were important in this decision and where should they plan to locate the IPO?

15   PUBLIC PURCHASING

Chapter Outline

Key Questions for the Purchasing Decision Maker

SHOULD WE
- Operate as though we are different from private industry?
- Use the bid process to determine suppliers and prices?
- Show favoritism to local, small, minority- and women-owned suppliers?

HOW CAN WE
- Incorporate commercial practices while still upholding our special responsibilities to taxpayers?
- Deal with outside pressures from our constituents?
- Increase our "clout" with suppliers?

Any coverage of supply management should give due attention to the unique problems of purchasing by public agencies (federal, state, provincial, county, municipal, public school systems, public libraries, public hospitals, public colleges and universities, and various governmental commissions). In the United States, the federal government is the single largest consumer of goods and services in the country, spending more than $200 billion annually on goods and services and another $240 billion indirectly through grant disbursements.[1] The funds spent by public supply managers deserve the same serious attention as dollars spent by industrial purchasers, as the source of these funds is the taxpayer. If public funds are spent effectively and efficiently, benefits will accrue to all those people who pay for, and obtain the benefits from, the services provided by government.

If the total, annual tax-supported budget of a given governmental unit is $2 billion, purchased supplies, materials, services, and construction probably account for approximately $500 million, which is much less than the purchase/sales ratio of the typical industrial firm, because government operations are very labor intensive. But, if an overall 10 percent reduction in supply costs could be effected through better management of the supply function, that would result in a savings to taxpayers of some $50 million—a significant amount, to say the least. This translates into a higher level of service, lower tax rates, or some combination of both. The public is interested in greater governmental efficiency and is mandating this through the ballot box. Efficient and effective government supply management can play a major role in making government responsive to the needs of the people.

---

[1]Environmentally Preferable Purchasing, U.S. Environmental Protection Agency, *www.epa.gov/opptintr/epp,* February 17, 2001.

During the 1990s a number of procurement reform initiatives were undertaken in the United States. In 1993, Former Vice President Al Gore's report resulting from the National Performance Review (NPR), *From Red Tape to Results: Creating a Government that Works Better & Costs Less,* outlined steps for streamlining government operations to make government "work better and cost less"—at an estimated savings of $108 billion over a five-year period. Procurement reform represented 21 percent ($22.5 billion) of the projected total savings.[2] The 1995 and 1996 Congressional debates concerning the need to balance the federal budget in the next seven years showed the continuing interest of the public in more cost-effective government. By 2001, the work had moved from developing new laws and rules to actually implementing procurement reform in far-flung contracting offices and changing the behavior and thinking of government contract officers. Reflective of this new approach to government contracting are the comments of Deidre Lee, head of the Office of Federal Procurement Policy (OFPP) at the Office of Management and Budget.

Procurement Reform a Big Part of Streamlining Government

"What we are saying to contracts people is that you no longer can just wait and say: 'Tell me when you need something.' You've got to understand the agency's mission, understand your agency's plan, read the budget, know what your agency's going to do. Then from that, work with your technical community and say: 'OK, it looks like we're going to need X in the next year.' You've got to be involved upfront in planning so that you're involved in the business strategy. Otherwise, you only end up solving part of the problem and you have a less than ideal business relationship. Under the old structure, a lot of people thought their value was in issuing contracts, and they'd get a little bit concerned when a contract didn't have their agency's name at the top. That's not our mission. Our mission is to get the result, and the result is not a contract written; it is a service or product delivered. We've got to move people along this continuum so that not only are they involved earlier, but they're willing and able and free to use multiple types of contracts, not just traditional methods."[3]

Government Is Big Business

The figures in Table 15–1 show the magnitude of government spending. Government purchases, in total, increased by 142 percent from 1975 to 1985, but only 46 percent from 1985 to 1995, due in large part to decreases in defense spending and efforts to reduce other government spending. The increase from 1975 to 1985 in federal government purchases (187 percent) was greater than that of state and local purchases (116 percent), due largely to stepped-up expenditures for national defense. Department of Defense (DOD) expenditures amounted to approximately 80 percent of the total federal government purchases of goods and services in the late 1980s, but only about 64 percent in

---

[2]Cherish Karoway, "Simplifying Government Procurement," *NAPM Insights,* September 1994, p. 61.

[3]Anne Laurent, "Making Reform Stick," *Government Executive Magazine,* August 30, 1999, *www.govexec.com,* February 21, 2001.

TABLE 15–1   **Government Purchases of Goods and Services, 1933 to 2000 ($ billions)**

	Purchases		
	Federal	*State and Local*	*Total*
1933	2.0	6.0	8.0
1941	16.9	7.9	24.8
1950	18.4	19.5	37.9
1970	96.2	123.3	219.5
1985	353.9	464.7	818.6
1990	424.0	674.1	1098.1
1995	439.2	694.7	1133.9
1996	445.3	726.5	1171.8
1997	456.9	766.5	1223.3
1998	453.7	808.4	1262.1
1999	470.8	855.0	1325.7

Source: *Federal Reserve, www.federalreserve.gov.* February 27, 2001.

the mid-1990s.[4] The increase from 1985 to 1995 in federal government purchases (22 percent) was less than that of state and local purchases (64 percent) as responsibility for many categories of expenditures shifted from the federal to the state and local levels, and defense spending continued to be cut. From 1995 to 1999, federal purchases increased 7 percent while state and local went up 23 percent. Government purchasing is big business, deserving major attention from government administrators!

Government Buying and Industrial Buying Basically the Same

The most important message of this chapter is that government buying *basically does not differ* from industrial purchasing. The same concepts of good supply management discussed in this text are applicable and should be followed to obtain maximum value for public dollars spent. The objectives of governmental supply are basically the same as for industrial supply and include: (1) assuring of continuity of supply to meet the service needs; (2) avoiding duplication and waste through standardization; (3) maintenaning and improving quality standards in goods and services purchased; (4) developing a cooperative environment between supply and the agencies and departments served; (5) obtaining maximum savings through innovative supply and application of value analysis techniques; (6) administering the supply function with internal efficiency; and (7) purchasing at the lowest life cycle cost, consistent with quality, performance, and delivery requirements (or as the military puts it, "obtain the most bang for the buck").

The major focus of this chapter will be to point out those areas, or practices, of governmental acquisition that may differ, at least in part, from those

---

[4]*Federal Reserve Bulletin,* July 1995, p. A29.

of industrial supply. The differences largely are a matter of degree, often caused by the specific legislation and statutes under which public supply operates, and are not in direct conflict with industry practice. The public supply manager, alert to these variations, will attempt to turn them into opportunities to maximize the value obtained. In conclusion, the history, specific organization, and practices of purchasing for the federal government, and for state and local government, are discussed.

Characteristics of Public Purchasing

Source of Authority

The authority of the public buyer is established by law, regulation, or statute, such as federal and state constitutions and laws and municipal ordinances. The public buyer must observe the appropriate legal structure under which purchasing operates; ultimate responsibility is to some legislative body and the voters who elect that body. The industrial buyer, on the other hand, is responsible to an administrative superior and, ultimately, to the owner(s) of the firm.

Changes Are Difficult to Make in Public Purchasing
When questions of authority or the interpretation of the legal requirements arise, they are referred to the legal officer of the governmental agency (ultimately the attorney general's office in the case of federal or state purchasing, or the county or city attorney). This relationship is synonymous with that of the legal counsel of a private firm. If legislative changes are needed to permit the public buyer to do a more effective buying job, the cooperation of the agency's legal advisor should be sought. While changing the law is difficult and may take a long time to accomplish, the public buyer continually must assess the situation and press for needed modifications. An example of one such change (legal authority to use blank check purchase orders) is discussed later in this chapter.

Responsible and Responsive Bidder Defined
Governmental purchasing law requires that the contract be awarded to the lowest "responsible" and "responsive" bidder. A *responsible* bidder is a supplier deemed fully capable and willing to perform the work; a *responsive* bidder is one who has submitted a bid that conforms to the invitation for bid. While this sounds reasonable for both private- and public-sector purchasers, the difference is that the public buyer has less room for judgment or flexibility when dealing with suppliers whose ability to perform is marginal. The need to justify and document all actions and decisions limits the buyer. Evaluation criteria may be narrow and very specific and have several legal constraints, leaving little room for value judgments. Part of the aim of procurement reform is to place the focus on finding the "best value" provider for goods and services. In this case, price is only one part of best value and is weighed in conjunction with other criteria such as technical competencies. According to Lee, head of the Office of Federal Procurement

Policy, "best value" is "the logical combination of the best technical solution and the best price in the appropriate measure for the product or service being purchased."[5]

Budgetary Restrictions/Limitations

The Budgeting Process May Be Time-Consuming

The use of budgets for planning and control is well known to buyers in both private industry and government. As with any plan, when the environment or assumptions under which the budget was made change, the plan (budget) should be revised. Often the final budget for purchases is approved by a legislative body on a line-item basis, and changes in the budget for each line item must be approved by that legislative body in advance of expenditure. Obtaining such approval may be a very time-consuming process, due to the series of steps and public hearings required.

As a result, if the needed funds are not already in the budget, the public buyer may find it impossible to take advantage of spot buys of larger quantities of materials at particularly advantageous prices. In the private firm, funds normally can be made available in a very short time if the purchasing department can present a convincing case for spending those funds. This puts a real premium in public buying on the long-term planning and budgeting needed to anticipate requirements and opportunities; this planning often must be done at least 18 months in advance. Additionally, good management is necessary to ensure that last-minute, often unwise purchases are not made just to obligate funds by an end-of-the-year budget expiration date.

Outside Pressures

A Strong Business Case for a Public Purchasing Decision is Critical

The public buyer realizes that the money spent comes from the taxpayer, and these taxpayers may become very vocal in their attempts to influence how this money is spent and with which suppliers. It is not unusual for a given supplier firm to attempt to influence, through the political process, the placement of major dollar purchase contracts. In a sense, this is a type of reciprocity, with the taxpaying supplier firm feeling that because it is providing the tax dollars from which public purchases are made, it should be selected as the supplier from which government buys needed goods and services. It is the rare public buyer who does not, from time to time, receive a telephone call that starts, "You know, our firm pays a substantial amount of taxes, and we feel that we should receive better treatment [be able to sell more] from governmental purchasing."

When the industrial buyer receives such a request, it can be countered by the response that "the supplier selected must be able to give us, in our judgment, the best ultimate value for dollars spent." However, the public buyer knows that such a statement may not satisfy the caller, and that pub-

---

[5]Ibid.

lic purchasing may have to supply facts and figures to back up its decision to buy from a particular supplier.

Supply Base Constant or Growing

In the private sector the trend is toward a smaller supply base, but the 1999 Center for Advanced Purchasing Studies benchmarking studies found that the majority of state and local governments reported that their supplier base had remained constant over the last year,[6] and municipal governments had increased their number of active suppliers by 2.4 percent.[7] The CAPS *Cross Industry Comparison of Standard Benchmarks* in 28 industries found there was a 4.1 percent average decrease in the number of active suppliers, while in state and county governments there was a 3.3 percent increase, and in municipal governments, a 2.4 percent increase.[8]

Non-purchasing People Make Many Purchasing Decisions

A large portion of the expenditures of public funds is handled by people outside the purchasing or supply function. A 1995 CAPS study, *Purchasing of Nontraditional Goods and Services,* found that in government, the purchasing department spent 49 percent of the total purchase dollars, and the finance, communications, and human relations departments spent 29 percent.[9] Purchasing tends to be more involved in the purchase of goods than services, and the CAPS study found that 62 percent of the government purchase dollars spent were for services and only 38 percent were for goods; it is no surprise that nonpurchasing people are making many buying decisions. The question is, are these people making sound purchasing decisions, and would there be a benefit from involving the supply department in these nontraditional areas?

Public Purchasers Buying More Services

One of the many changes in private and public sector purchasing is the increasing involvement of purchasing departments in buying services. The 2000 *Cross Industry Comparison* reported that state and county purchasing departments spent 64 percent of the dollars for services, and municipal purchasing spent 65 percent.[10] As a result of this increased involvement, it was also found that purchasing was responsible for 79 percent of the total purchase dollars, and 72 percent in municipal governments.[11]

Greater Support of Public Service Programs

In the last decade, there has been much interest on the part of the public in providing increased government support to certain special-interest segments of society. Certain minority member segments are assumed to have been the

---

[6]Center for Advanced Purchasing Studies, *Purchasing Performance Benchmarks for State and County Governments 1999, www.capsresearch.org.,* February 21, 2001.

[7]Center for Advanced Purchasing Studies, *Purchasing Performance Benchmarks for Municipal Governments 1999, www.capsresearch.org.,* February 21, 2001.

[8]Center for Advanced Purchasing Studies, *Cross Industry Comparison of Standard Benchmarks, Spring 2000, www.capsresearch.org.,* March 4, 2001.

[9]Harold E. Fearon and William A. Bales, *Purchasing of Nontraditional Goods and Services* (Tempe, AZ: Center for Advanced Purchasing Studies, 1995), pp. 19 and 39.

[10]Ibid.

[11]Ibid.

MWBE Programs

victims of past unfair, discriminatory actions. The general public has deemed that, in the interest of equity, these special-interest segments should receive special consideration in future actions. Through the legislative process, laws have been passed to encourage the redress of these past injustices, and purchasing is one natural area through which funds can be channeled to these special-interest segments. Examples are programs to favor small business firms in the award of purchase contracts, or the support of minority-owned suppliers through special consideration in evaluating supplier capability and the placement of purchases.[12] Some government entities have enacted set-aside programs or price preference programs, requiring that a certain percentage of business be given to targeted groups. These programs often are called Minority/Women Business Enterprise (M/WBE) Programs.

While the long-term benefits to society may be worthwhile, in the short term, the governmental buyer may have to use a mix of suppliers that meets the public's social demands but results in higher prices paid for items received. For example, a decision may be made that a specific percentage of total government purchasing dollars will be spent with minority-owned supplier firms. To meet that goal, a much greater amount of administrative time may be required to find and qualify suppliers, and some purchases may be made from suppliers that will not give maximum value for the purchase dollar. The public purchaser should make sure that the extra short-run costs from such actions are identified and agreed to by the legislative or administrative body setting such goals.

Impact of Streamlining Efforts on Small and Minority Businesses Debatable

Trade groups representing small and minority-owned businesses believe that efforts to streamline government procurement, particularly the National Performance Review (NPR), threaten to dilute or eliminate legislation that awards contracts to small and minority businesses. NPR goals of best-value considerations, simplified procedures, and an electronic marketplace may favor large businesses. Conflicting data and reports have emerged from various federal and public agencies. For example, a study conducted by the U.S. General Accounting Office (GAO), "Small Business: Trends in Federal Procurement in the 1990s," reported that the share of federal dollars awarded to small businesses under new kinds of contracts, especially multiple-award contracts in which agencies are allowed to purchase indefinite amounts of goods and services, increased by one-third from fiscal 1994 to fiscal 1999.[13] The study also found that the overall share of federal procurement dollars going to *small businesses for all types* of contracts had declined from about 25 percent in the mid-1990s to 23 percent in 1998 and 1999. The GAO study did not include governmentwide acquisition contracts which have been blamed for small businesses' declining share of federal procurement dollars.

---

[12]Robert W. Menestrina, CPCM, "Ready! Fire! Aim! The DOD Five Percent Minority Purchase Goal: Reflections on a Misdirected Program," *National Contract Management Journal* 24, Issue 1, (1991), pp. 47–55.

Perceived Absence of Interest Costs

Opportunity Costs of Funds Invested in Inventory

One of the principal considerations in the industrial firm in determining inventory levels is the interest or opportunity cost of money tied up in inventory. It is often argued that governmental agencies need not consider money costs in their decisions, because the funds are tax dollars that came into the governmental coffers at a specific date. This is spurious reasoning, for (1) government agencies today typically labor under a burden, large or small, of financial indebtedness, either short or long term, and interest cost is a very real cost of operation; and (2) when governmental funds are tied up in purchased inventories, these funds are not available for employment in other productive uses. This effectively means that there is an opportunity cost of funds invested in inventory. The public supply manager may have to take special care to persuade other governmental administrators that inventory investment is expensive, and this cost should be considered in making acquisition/inventory decisions.

Little Formal Inspection

Most industrial firms have a quality control or inspection department that handles decisions on both outgoing, finished products and incoming raw materials or supplies. However, many governmental agencies (with the military as a notable exception) do not have any specialized inspection personnel. Yet, incoming inspection is needed in the case of many of the items bought.

Steps to Ensure Conformance to Specifications

Steps must be taken to ensure that items delivered by suppliers do meet the purchase specifications. Depending on the specific item being bought: (1) the user can be advised to check delivered items immediately and report any quality variance; (2) the supplier may be asked to supply notarized copies of inspection reports which show the specific tests conducted and the raw test data which resulted and formed the basis for a decision to ship the items; (3) the buyer may send materials, or samples, out to an independent testing laboratory; (4) the buyer may employ someone to come into the organization to inspect purchased items, for example, the U.S. Department of Agriculture will inspect meat and produce items in most areas for a reasonable charge; (5) the buyer may decide to perform certain simple tests on selected items; or (6) a separate incoming quality control department can be established within the public agency, if a persuasive case can be made that this is needed to ensure that fair value is received for dollars spent.

Lack of Traffic Expertise

Most industrial firms of any size have a traffic specialist or group who handles both inbound and outbound shipments. However, it is rare for public

---

[13]Jason Peckenpaugh, "Report Finds Procurement Reforms Don't Hurt Small Businesses," *GovExec.com,* January 31, 2001, *www.govexec.com/ sailyfed,* February 20, 2001.

FOB Destination and Its Consequences

supply departments to have a traffic expert or access to such an individual. Yet, materials movement often accounts for a significant part of the total cost of items bought and has increased in importance due to the widened alternatives resulting from transport deregulation (see Chapter 10). As a result of this lack of expertise, the public buyer often specifies FOB destination as the shipping basis, which may not be the most economical, because the buyer loses control over traffic decisions.

A trained traffic person might make a major contribution in such areas as classification and routing of shipments, selection of carriers, determination of freight charges, and filing damage claims, generating savings that would be several times the salary received plus overhead. Transportation is one of the areas where many public purchasers are taking a look at outsourcing or contracting out with third-party logistics service companies.

Time Required to Modify the Organization

The Change Process May Be Lengthy

Changes in the organization structure of public supply—for example, the adding or deleting of positions, the changing of reporting relationships, or the redefinition of position duties and responsibilities—often take much longer to accomplish than would be required in an industrial firm. Frequently such changes require a public hearing and normally an investigation by someone from the personnel division. Also, the final approval may require action by some legislative body, such as a state legislature or a city council, and this may require several months. In one sense, this provides stability to public purchasing; on the other hand, the time required may be so long that managers get discouraged and don't bother pressing for needed change.

Salary Levels

Government Salaries versus Industry Salaries

It is easier to make salary-level adjustments in the private sector than in the public sector. However, contrary to popular opinion, the salary levels of public buyers, at least at the lower to medium job assignment levels, are equal to those in industrial purchasing. Thus, the public supply department is normally not at any salary disadvantage in recruiting personnel and should be able to attract good people. But at the top levels, government pays salaries that are far below those of industrial firms. A vice president of purchasing for a large industrial firm may be paid an annual salary of over $200,000 and stock options, while it is unusual for the director or chief procurement officer in a public purchasing department to make more than $75,000. Some of the heads of state purchasing departments are paid a salary in the $40,000 to $55,000 range, which is low relative to the responsibilities of the job. Hopefully, the legislative bodies who set public purchasing salaries now are beginning to recognize the need to pay more realistic salaries to attract and retain top-quality managers.

Lack of Confidentiality

The "Fishbowl" The public buyer lives in a "fishbowl." All information on prices submitted by suppliers, and the price finally paid, must be made available to any taxpayer requesting it. Any special arrangements between the buyer and the successful supplier, and the final purchase contract, are public knowledge. Because suppliers realize that all data are available to competitors, they naturally are hesitant to offer the public buyer any special deals in an attempt to gain business, for this would become known quickly and would be demanded immediately by all other customers as well. The net effect is that the public buyer probably will pay, on the average, higher prices than paid by the buyer in the private firm.

Admittedly, there is an advantage in the buyer being able to compare prices with those that others are paying, and this is perfectly legal in public buying, for the buyer is free to talk and exchange supplier information and prices paid with other public buyers. This ensures that one public buyer will not be paying a higher price than that paid by other agencies. Yet, in the final analysis, this practice operates to the long-term disadvantage of the public buyer, for no supplier will be anxious to give a public buyer a particularly attractive price knowing it will be divulged to a number of other public buyers, who will demand equal treatment.

Lack of Confidentiality Greatest Obstacle to Good Public Purchasing This lack of confidentiality creates the greatest obstacle to good purchasing by public agencies. It is an understandable requirement, because the funds are obtained from the collective taxpayer who has a right to know how and why tax dollars are spent. Yet, it puts the public buyer at a real disadvantage. Value judgments are difficult to make due to the intense scrutiny of public purchasers' decisions.

Importance of Specifications

Specifications Are the Basis of the Bid Process Because a very large part of public acquisition is based on the bidding process, it is vital that specifications for needed items be clear and accurate and written to ensure that several suppliers can compete for the business. These specifications take the form of written descriptions, blueprints, drawings, performance requirements, industry standards, or commercial designation (trade or brand name). Unless all potential bidders can be furnished a complete and usable set of specifications, the bidding process will be imperfect and will not produce the competition necessary to provide best value. In addition, if a bidder can show that the specifications were not uniform, or were subject to varying interpretations, there is a good chance that legal action can be brought to overturn the purchasing department's contract award, resulting in lengthy and costly delays in contract performance.

The development of good, clean specifications requires considerable time and effort, and some governmental procurement agencies have full-time personnel who work on the preparation and refinement of specifications. Considerable communication between the purchasing agency and the user is necessary to develop clear specifications, and the advantages of standardization between user agencies can be significant.

Government Specifications Available to Private Industry

The public or private buyer can take advantage of the specification work done by governmental agencies at the local, county, state, or federal level. The federal government, through the General Services Administration (GSA), has developed a multitude of specifications for use in federal purchasing, and these are readily available to anyone wishing to use them. The *Index of Federal Specifications, Standards and Commercial Item Descriptions*[14] lists the available specifications three ways: (1) alphabetically, (2) numerically, and (3) by federal supply class (FSC). Each specification or standard is described briefly and the price at which the item can be purchased from the GSA is shown. A similar *Department of Defense Index of Specifications and Standards* lists the unclassified military specifications used by the Defense Department; it is a consolidation of separate indices formerly published by the individual military agencies. It can be purchased from the Superintendent of Documents.

While the work done in preparing these specifications can be of much use to other public buyers, it should be noted that some of them are more cumbersome than needed. The General Accounting Office has been particularly critical and has advocated using simpler, commercial-type specifications where practical.

Acquisition Procedures

Dollar Thresholds

The mandate that the public sector seek maximum competition dictates the procedures used in public buying and distinguishes these procedures from those used in private procurement. The procedure used to purchase a needed good or service is often determined by established dollar thresholds. These categories are:[15]

1. Small-Dollar Purchases for items below the threshold for competitive bids or quotes.

2. Request for Quotations (RFQ) for items below the threshold for issuing a formal bid solicitation, but high enough to require competitive quotations.

3. Invitation for Bids (IFB) for items above the threshold to issue formal bid solicitation, normally for a product or contractual (nonprofessional) service.

---

[14]The *Index* can be purchased from the General Services Administration, Federal Supply Service Bureau, Specifications Section (3FBP-W), Suite 8100, 470 L'Enfant Plaza SW, Washington DC 20407. It is also available at GSA regional offices.

[15]Ron C. Gauthier, "Purchasing in the Fishbowl," op. cit., pp. 21–22.

4. Request for Proposal (RFP) for professional services or high-tech needs when formal bid solicitations are required.

5. Emergency Purchases for unplanned needs to protect public health, life, or property.

6. Sole-Source Purchases for high-tech or mechanical needs where compatibility is required, or to purchase a unique item or service.

7. Negotiated Acquisition, usually part of an RFP or sole-source purchase, or to acquire exempted services such as utilities, power, or landfills.

Emphasis on the Bid Process

Price Is Heavily Weighted in Bid Process

Public statutes normally provide that the award of purchase contracts should be made on the basis of open, competitive bidding. This provision is supposed to ensure that all qualified suppliers, who are taxpayers or who employ personnel who are taxpayers, have an equal opportunity to compete for the sale of products or services needed in the operation of government. Because the bids received are open to public inspection, it would be difficult for the public buyer to show favoritism to any one supplier. However, this system tends to put a heavy weight on price as the basis for supplier selection, for it might be difficult for the buyer to defend selecting a supplier whose price is higher than that of the low bidder. Ideally, the buyer might choose to buy from someone other than the low bidder due to anticipated superior performance factors, but this may be difficult to quantify and thus difficult to defend.

Competitive bidding is time-consuming and requires administrative paperwork; for this reason, statutes often will specify that informal bids may be used as the basis of awarding purchase orders for requirements under a certain dollar amount, for example, $1,000. Also, in the case of items available from a sole source, purchase decisions may be made on the basis of formal negotiation; however, the sole-source supplier situation should be avoided if at all possible, for this is a difficult situation and also costly, in terms of purchasing administrative expense.

When informal quotations are used to buy requirements of relatively low value, all essential steps of formal bidding should be used, except that only a limited number of bids will be solicited, and this will be done by telephone requests. The buyer needs accurate records of the suppliers requested to give a phone quote and the reason(s) why a particular supplier was selected, in the event that the decision is challenged later. Chapter 9 contains sections on the use of quotations and negotiation as methods of price determination.

Use of Bid Lists. On the purchase of items that probably will require repeated purchase actions, a master bid list is compiled. This requires the buyer to specify the characteristics that should be present in any qualified supplier firm, such as size (which relates to ability to provide the needed

Process for Repeat Purchases

quantities), financial stability, quality control procedures, finished goods inventory levels (which may determine how quickly items can be obtained), warranty policy, spare parts availability, accessibility of maintenance/repair personnel, and transportation facilities. Then, the purchasing department will conduct whatever type of supplier survey or investigation is required to ensure that a given supplier can meet the minimum level of each important characteristic. If a given supplier is checked out and found to be unsatisfactory, this information should be communicated directly to that supplier so the supplier will know the types of changes necessary if it is to compete for future business.

Blackballing or Redlining Defined

Deletions from the bid list will be made in the case of suppliers who receive purchase awards and then do not perform according to the terms of the purchase agreement. This often is referred to as *blackballing* or *redlining* the supplier, and it is a perfectly legitimate practice, providing the decision to drop a supplier from the bid list can be substantiated with facts and figures from the purchasing department's supplier performance evaluation system. Obviously, a supplier being dropped from the bid list for cause should be notified of this action and the specific reasons for the action. One reason for deletion may be the unwillingness of a supplier to submit any bids over an extended period of time for specific requirements. If this is not done, the bid list may become too large and unwieldy, resulting in unneeded costs from sending out bid requests that will not be productive.

The public buyer generally must be willing to consider any supplier who requests to be put on the bid list, after, of course, an investigation of the supplier has been made. However, the competent public buyer should be equally as aggressive as the private industry buyer in ferreting out new supply sources.

As part of the bidder qualification process, some type of supplier information form is used. However, even though this is a good initial starting point for the selection of qualified suppliers, it will not contain enough information for a complete evaluation, and the public buyer probably will need to make an on-site supplier visit.

Publicly Announcing Requests for Bids

Advertising. The bid list, if properly developed and maintained, should provide a large enough group of qualified suppliers to enable the public buyer to obtain competition in the bid process. However, many public purchasing agencies, as a matter of normal operating policy or because it specifically is required by statute or regulation, also advertise upcoming purchase needs in the local newspaper, in the legal paper (normally a weekly), or electronically on the Internet. The advertisement may simply state that if any given supplier firm wishes to receive a request for bid for a particular requirement, it should contact the purchasing department or download the information from the Web site. The buyer then must determine whether the firm asking to bid meets the minimum supplier qualifications.

Advertising is simply a means of publicly announcing that a purchase will be made. In most instances, it will not produce any new suppliers, but it ensures that purchasing is not conducted under any veil of secrecy.

Competitive Bid Procedures Establish Equal Opportunity for Bidders

Bid Procedures. In a formal bid system, the bidder typically will be sent (1) a complete list of specifications that the item being supplied must meet (in complicated procurements, the specification package may consist of several pages—several hundred pages, in some instances—and may detail the kinds of quality control procedures the buyer [and supplier] will use to ensure that the goods delivered do, in fact, meet specifications); (2) a list of instructions to the bidder, spelling out how, when, where, and in what form bids must be submitted; (3) general and special legal conditions that must be met by the successful bidder; and (4) a bid form on which the supplier will submit price, discounts, and other required information.

The bidder typically must submit any bid on or before a specified date and hour, as for example, 1 P.M. on March 15. No bids will be accepted after the bid closing; late bids are returned, unopened, to the bidder. No changes normally are permitted after the formal bid is received, although some agencies do permit the substitution of a new bid for the original, unopened bid, provided it is received before the bid opening date. The place where the bid must be delivered, usually the purchasing department, should be specified, and many public purchasing agencies use a locked container to maintain all sealed bids until the date and hour of the bid opening.

While these bid procedures may appear rather complicated, they do establish an environment in which all qualified suppliers have an equal opportunity.

Use of Bid Bonds. Often the bid package requires that any bidder submit a performance bond at the time of the bid. In some states this is a legal requirement, particularly in the case of purchased items or construction contracts for large dollar amounts. As an alternative, some public purchasing agencies require that the bid be accompanied by a certified check or money order in a fixed percentage amount of the bid. In the event the bidder selected does not agree to sign the final purchase contract award, or does not perform according to the terms of the bid, this amount is retained by the purchasing agency as liquidated damages for nonperformance. Obviously, the bid bond or bid deposit is an attempt to discourage irresponsible bidders from competing. In high-risk situations the extra cost of the bid bond, which in some way will be passed back as an extra cost to the buyer, is warranted; in the purchase of standard, stock items available from several sources, the use of a bond is questionable.

Three Types of Bonds

Technically, there are three general types of bonds available. The bidder purchases each, for a dollar premium, from an insurance company, thus effectively transferring some of the risk to the insurance carrier:

1. The *bid (or surety) bond* guarantees that if the order is awarded to a specific bidder, it will accept the purchase contract. If the supplier refuses, the extra costs to the buyer of going to an alternative source are borne by the insurer.

2. The *performance bond* guarantees that the work will be done according to specifications and in the time specified. If the buyer has to go

to another supplier for rework or to get the order completed, purchasing is indemnified for these extra costs.

3. The *payment bond* protects the buyer against liens which might be granted to the suppliers of material and labor to the bidder, in the event the bidder does not make proper payment to its suppliers.

Generally, the added security provided by these bonds offsets the cost added to the contract. However, in a multiple-year contract or one with high initial costs, the purchaser may want to break the performance bond into periods or stages of completion to avoid having the surety write the bond too high and increase the cost of the contract too much.

**Bids Are
Publicly
Opened**

Bid Opening and Evaluation. At the hour and date specified in the bid instructions, the buyer will open all bids and record the bids on some type of a bidder spreadsheet. In some agencies, the buyer must call out the supplier name and bid, and a clerk records the information, checks the actual bid form for the amount, and then certifies that the information on the spreadsheet is correct. Usually, any citizen who wishes can attend the bid opening and examine any of the bids. Often suppliers who have submitted bids, or ones who have chosen not to bid but who wish to see the bids of other suppliers, will attend the opening. After the bids are recorded, the original bids should be retained for later inspection by any interested party for a specified time period (often 12 months).

The buyer then must make a selection of the successful bidder, based on the bid which will give the greatest value. Obviously, if all the specifications and conditions are met by a qualified supplier, the lowest bid will be selected. Otherwise, the bid process is destroyed. If someone other than the low bidder is selected, the buyer documents the decision very carefully, for it may be formally challenged later on in the courts.

In some public agencies, a purchase award cannot be made unless at least some minimum number of bids (often three) has been received. If the minimum number is not received, the requirement must be rebid, or the buyer must be able to justify that the nature of the requirement is such that it is impossible to obtain bids from any more suppliers.

Bid Errors. If the successful, low bidder notifies the buyer after the bid has been submitted, but before the award of the purchase order has been made, that an error has been made, the buyer normally will permit the bid to be withdrawn. However, the buyer makes some permanent note of this, because it reflects on the responsibility of the bidder.

**Resolving
Problems After
the Order Has
Been Awarded**

A much-more-serious problem arises if the bidder, claiming a bid error, attempts to withdraw the bid *after* it has been awarded the order as the successful bidder. Of course, the use of a bid bond in the bid process is an attempt to protect the buyer if such a problem arises. If the bid bond were not used, the buyer must weigh the probability of having severe problems involving court action to force performance or collect damages against the problems and costs of now going to the closest other successful bidder (who now may not be interested) or going through the bid process again. Legal counsel is normally sought, but if the mistake were mechanical in nature, that is, the figures were added up incorrectly, the courts probably will side with the supplier. However, if it were an error in judgment, for example, the supplier misjudged the rate of escalation in material prices and used this figure in making the bid, then the courts generally will not permit relief to the supplier. Also, for the supplier to gain relief in the courts, the supplier must be able to show that once the error was discovered, the buying agency was notified promptly.

Obviously, if the buyer receives a bid which common sense and knowledge of the market indicates is unrealistic, the bid should be rechecked and the bidder requested to reaffirm that it is a bona fide bid. In the long run, such action likely will be cheaper for the buying agency than if a long and involved legal action ensues, with an uncertain outcome.

Action if Collusion Suspected

Bid Awards. As stated earlier, if two or more responsible bidders offer to meet the specifications and conditions, the low-price bidder is selected. If other than the low bidder is selected, the buyer must be prepared to justify the decision with additional information. If identical low bids are received, and the buyer has no evidence or indication of any collusion or other bid irregularities, then a public "flip of the coin" is a satisfactory means of resolving the deadlock. If the buyer suspects collusion, all bids should be rejected and the requirement rebid. Additionally, this should be reported to the appropriate legal counsel, for example, the state attorney general or federal Justice Department, for investigation and action.

The public buyer has no obligation to notify unsuccessful bidders of the award because the bid opening was a public event and the bid and award documents are retained in the purchasing department and may be viewed, on request, by any interested individual. Courtesy suggests, however, that if an unsuccessful supplier makes a telephone or letter request for information, that information be provided promptly and the requestor invited to come in and examine the file.

Difficulty in Recognizing Past Performance

It is often difficult in public procurement to recognize the past performance of a supplier, particularly if it has been excellent. A simple example will suffice. In a particular school district, Anderson Cleaning did an outstanding job of providing cleaning and maintenance service for school buildings. Anderson lost its multimillion dollar contract to another supplier which had bid about $1,000 lower. The performance of this second bidder was highly unsatisfactory and caused many complaints. Under the existing procurement bylaws, it was not possible to recognize Anderson's superior performance.

Similarly the cost of switching from one supplier to another was assumed to be nil. In the private sector, a well-performing incumbent supplier will benefit from the user's and purchaser's judgment that a switch may not be justified because the price savings is unlikely to equal the switching or higher life-cycle costs. For example, in 1999 the U.S. Air Force was criticized for its use of a private sector past-performance survey in determining which firms to invite to bid on several large blanket purchase agreement (BPAs). Although backed by the Office of Federal Procurement Policy (OFPP), the Air Force changed its procedures to include an opportunity for vendors to comment on past performance ratings.[16]

Trends in Public Purchasing

Procurement reform in public purchasing is occurring at all levels—federal, state/provincial, and local (counties and municipalities). In a 1999 study, *Purchasing Performance Benchmarks for State and County Governments,* conducted by the Center for Advanced Purchasing Studies (CAPS), two similarities between public and private procurement emerged: (1) using automated purchasing systems to process transactions and track purchasing activities (84.6 percent), and (2) multiple-year contracts (100 percent).[17] Similar innovations are being implemented on the federal government side. Three evident trends are centralization, privatization, and the adaptation of commercial business practices to public purchasing.

Delegation and Centralization Must be Balanced

Centralization. Whether the pendulum swings toward centralized or decentralized purchasing depends in part on the economy. Budget deficits are often a driving force in moves to dismantle centralized purchasing in the public sector. The National Institute of Governmental Purchasing adopted a resolution in 1989 to emphasize the benefits of centralized purchasing in terms of economies of scale and consistency. The goal to balance delegation and centralization is the same for the public sector as it is for the private sector. In the CAPS benchmarking study on state and local government purchasing, 35 percent of the respondents reported utilizing some form of centralized purchasing. The breakdown was: (1) centralized, in which all or almost all purchasing/contracting is done through one centralized organization or location for the entire organization (35 percent); (2) centralized/decentralized, in which some purchasing/contracting is centralized, but purchasing is also decentralized at major operating divisions or locations (37.5 percent); and (3) virtual centralization, in which there is a centralized contracting process with decentralized execution (22.5 percent), and

---

[16]Laurent.

[17]Center for Advanced Purchasing Studies, *Purchasing Performance Benchmarks for State/Country Governments 1999, www.capsresearch.org,* February 27, 2001.

(4) decentralized (5 percent).[18] In a similar study of municipal governments, 61.1 percent reported utilizing a centralized/decentralized purchasing organization and 38.9 percent a centralized organization.

Privatization Defined

Privatization or Outsourcing. There is a growing trend in public (and private) purchasing to buy services and goods rather than make them in-house. Strictly speaking, privatization refers to the government getting out of a business altogether and turning it over to private enterprise. Much of what is occurring is really contracting out or outsourcing, rather than stepping out of the loop. Initially driven by political interests, many people are now looking at outsourcing as a way to reduce costs, gain shorter implementation times, and produce better-quality services.

Often the threat of privatization is enough to encourage productivity improvements in in-house operations. In 1995, the city of Los Angeles got promises of 25 percent productivity improvements over a three-year period after threatening to privatize the city's sanitation department.[19] Many analysts of government recommend privatizing rather than working to improve the in-house operation. Others question whether a public entity that cannot manage a service well will have the knowledge and expertise to negotiate a cost-effective contract. With low-cost financing and no need for profits, public entities should have a built-in cost advantage. However, tighter budgets and demands for improved service levels lead many in the public sector to look to the private sector for efficient and cost-effective solutions. For example, the National Solid Waste Management Association encourages local governments to privatize solid waste collection, disposal, and processing operations because private haulers typically use smaller, more efficient pickup crews, have lower absenteeism, have higher productivity because they serve more households per hour, and less downtime because they buy standardized trucks with larger capacity and maintain the vehicles on a regular schedule.[20]

Obstacles and Opportunities

Commercial Practices. Procurement reforms in the 1990s led to the adoption and adaptation of many commercial practices to public purchasing. These include payment processes, contract types, electronic procurement, and investment recovery programs.

Government Purchasing Cards. In 1998, the General Services Administration initiated the GSA SmartPay program. Five leading-edge credit card services were awarded contracts to provide federal agencies a new way to pay for commercial goods and services as well as travel and fleet-related expenses. The GSA SmartPay contracts, effective from November 30, 1998, through November 29, 2003, have five one-year options to renew. The program was

---

[18]Ibid.

[19]Jeff Bailey, "Garbage Budget: How Can Government Save Money? Consider the L.A. Motor Pool," *The Wall Street Journal,* July 6, 1995, p. 1.

[20]*Industry Issues: Privatization,* National Solid Waste Management Association (NSWMA), *www.envasns.org/nswma/,* February 20, 2001.

adopted to: (1) provide flexibility, (2) improve payment processes, (3) stream-line the purchasing process, (4) allow agencies to receive performance-based refunds, (5) streamline financial operations and accurately allocate costs, and (6) provide choice of card services.[21] Procurement cards are also used at the state, county, and municipal levels.

Contract Types.   At all levels of government purchasing, different contract vehicles are being explored for use. The main concern is to ensure that the type of contracts used do not impede the government's ability to achieve its other goals of fairness and equity to all sizes and types of suppliers. For government purchasers, the social concerns of government cannot be ignored.

Electronic procurement.   As a result of the 1994 Federal Acquisition Streamlining Act, most federal agencies developed electronic procurement systems through which they post requests for proposals (RFPs) and receive bids. The electronic posting system (*www.eps.gov*), a joint venture of several agencies, allows contractors to see RFPs from a variety of government agen-cies. One of the concerns with using e-commerce in public purchasing is the impact on small businesses' ability to do business with government agencies. The Small Business Adminstration's (SBA) office of advocacy reports that only about 1.4 percent of small businesses use the Internet to buy and sell goods and services, and most do not have e-commerce capability due to pro-hibitive upfront costs and doubts that the investment will yield a return.[22]

Environmental and Investment Recovery Programs.   Concern with the mountains of waste generated in the United States has led to a number of government initiatives related to environmental management systems and investment recovery. For example, Executive Order 12999 (1996) stream-lined the transfer of excess and surplus federal computer equipment to our nation's classrooms. This initiative tackles both the recycling issue and con-cern with the state of the nation's public education system. The Environ-mental Protection Agency has also initiated a program, the Environmentally Preferable Purchasing Program, a federalwide program to encourage and as-sist executive agencies in purchasing decisions (discussed in detail later in this chapter). (See also Chapter 11, Investment Recovery.)

Federal Government Purchasing

There are some specific peculiarities in federal government purchasing, apart from those differences between public and private purchasing dis-

---

[21]GSA SmartPay, *www.gsa.gov,* February 21, 2001.

[22]Katy Saldarini, Small Businesses Missing Out on Federal E-commerce Efforts, *GovExec.com,* April 13, 2000, *www.govexec.com/dailyfed.,* February 20, 2001.

cussed earlier. While space does not permit an in-depth review of these items, a brief discussion is in order.

History

Congress passed a law in 1792 which gave the Treasury and War departments the authority and responsibility to make purchases for the government. Over the intervening years, federal legislation has been extended to require, in certain instances, such things as public bid openings and bid bonds and has established extensive rules and procedures for military purchases.

Purpose of Office of Federal Procurement Policy

In 1974 the Office of Federal Procurement Policy (OFPP) was set up to coordinate and improve the efficiency of government purchasing. This agency received much criticism for its failure to address major policy issues in federal purchasing, dealing instead with primarily procedural matters. The OFPP sponsored the preparation of the Federal Acquisition Regulations (FAR) which guide all federal government purchases. The Federal Acquisition Institute (FAI) was established in 1976 for the purpose of developing the knowledge and skills of federal procurement personnel through a program of determining training needs and then encouraging and/or providing seminars, courses, or other opportunities to meet these defined needs. The Federal Acquisition Reform Act was introduced in the U.S. Senate on January 15, 1979.

Intentions Behind Federal Acquisition Act

The intent of this act was to establish that federal procurement actions should rely primarily on the private sector to (1) best meet public needs at lowest total cost; (2) substitute the incentives of competition for regulatory controls; (3) encourage innovation; (4) expand the supply base; (5) provide opportunities to minority-owned firms; (6) initiate large-scale production only after adequate operational testing; (7) allow contractors to make a profit commensurate with opportunities in other, comparable markets; and (8) promote effective competition by giving the government buyer concept, design, performance, price, total cost, service, and delivery alternatives.[23]

Competition Is Goal of CICA

Probably the most significant piece of procurement legislation enacted by Congress in the 1980s was the Competition in Contracting Act of 1984 (CICA). The intent of CICA was to promote full and open competition where all responsible offerers are allowed to compete. It eliminates some of the requirements for formal advertising; requires more procurement planning and research; encourages greater use of commercial, as opposed to specially made, products; and fosters the use of performance specifications. The overall effectiveness of CICA is questionable because by requiring additional bureaucratic procedures it has increased the amount of time and effort needed to issue a government contract.[24]

---

[23]"Federal Acquisition Reform Act" introduced in the Senate of the United States, 96th Congress, 1st Session, on January 15, 1979, Section 2.

[24]Stanley N. Sherman, *Government Procurement Management,* 3rd ed. (Gaithersburg, MD: Wordcrafters Publications, 1991), p. 121.

Procurement Reform Bill of 1994

Another procurement reform bill was passed by Congress in 1994, and it:

- Simplifies the recordkeeping contractors must do on contracts under $100,000.
- Frees purchases of $2,500 or less from small business set-asides and competitive bidding.
- Raises from $25,000 to $40,000 the upper limit of awards that can be made by simplified procurement procedures.
- Broadens and simplifies procedures for buying commercial, "off-the-shelf" items.[25]

Key Pieces of Purchasing Legislation in the 1990s

In the 1990s, three key pieces of legislation were passed, (1) the Federal Acquisition Streamlining Act of 1994 (FASA),[26] (2) the Clinger-Cohen Act of 1996[27], and (3) the Small Business Reauthorization Act of 1997. FASA codified the ability of agencies to enter into task- or delivery-order contracts with multiple firms for the same or similar products, known as *multiple award contracts* (MAC). These contracts provide for the purchase of an indefinite quantity, within stated limits, of supplies and services during a fixed period. Deliveries or performance of tasks are scheduled by placing orders with the contractor. The Clinger-Cohen Act of 1996 provided for the use of multiagency contracts and what are known as *governmentwide acquisition contracts* (GWAC), in which one agency may pay an administrative fee to use contracts for information technology products and services operated by another agency. The Small Business Reauthorization Act of 1997 increased the small-business contracting goal from not less than 20 percent to 23 percent. Other changes include the reduction in overall federal procurement expenditures and, less directly, the downsizing of the acquisition work force, which may have contributed to the use of streamlined procurement practices.[28] The total amount of goods and services that the government purchased declined by about 7 percent from an inflation-adjusted $224 billion in fiscal year 1993 to $209 billion in fiscal year 1999. From 1990 to 1998, the federal acquisition work force was reduced from 165,739 to 128,649, or about a 22 percent reduction.[29]

Small Business Favoritism

Federal legislation in 1953 established the Small Business Administration (SBA) to provide aid, counsel, and assistance to small firms. In general, a

---

[25]"Procurement Reform Bill Finally Passes," *Purchasing,* October 6, 1994, p. 19.

[26]P. L. 103–355, October 13, 1994.

[27]Enacted as Divisons D and E of the National Defense Authorization Act for Fiscal Year 1996 (pp. L. 104–106, Feb. 10, 1996).

[28] U.S. General Accounting Office Report to Congressional Requesters, *Small Business: Trends in Federal Procurement in the 1990s,* pp. 4–5.

[29]Ibid, p. 10.

small business is defined as one that is independently owned and operated, is not dominant in its field, and has dollar receipts below a certain number, depending on the particular industry. The SBA operates a Prime Contracts Program, which provides that on federal contracts above a certain dollar amount, a percentage of the contract is set aside for small business firms. The SBA and the buying agency then attempt to find and assist small firms in qualifying for and obtaining the amount of purchases set aside.

In 1961, Congress passed Public Law 87–305, which provides that "a fair proportion" of purchases of items from public funds be awarded to small businesses. If a large firm obtains a government contract over a certain amount, it must make a "best effort" to locate and place orders with small subcontractors for a specific percentage amount of the total contract. This may result in paying premium prices to small firms and increasing the administrative expense of purchasing. Congress justified this action by arguing that small business must be supported if it is to survive.

On June 2, 1999, the Office of Management and Budget (OMB) announced that 10 federal agencies with the largest procurement budgets can ignore small business set-aside rules in certain industries.[30] According to the Office of Federal Procurement Policy (OFPP), full competition between small and large suppliers will bring the lowest cost to the buying agency. Although set-asides can be ignored, the agencies must audit their contract awards and demonstrate that they still are awarding a set amount of business to small businesses. This program, known as the small business competitiveness program, was designed to demonstrate if small businesses can compete effectively in certain industries without federal set-asides, and if targeted objectives and management techniques can expand opportunities for small businesses.[31]

**Possible
Impact of
Government-
wide Contracts
on Small
Businesses**

Governmentwide acquisition contracts (GWACs) may be harmful to small businesses because they involve multiyear commitments, include multiple products or services, and require large geographic service coverage. A study by the SBA reported that more than 60 percent of federal prime contract dollars in fiscal 1998 were spent by agency procurement centers which, on average, awarded only 6.3 percent of contract dollars to small firms.[32] The Small Business Reauthorization Act of 1997 may help small businesses operate in the new climate by including rules that allow small businesses to band together to bid for GWACs. Individual agencies also are finding ways to promote small business contracting through outreach programs. For example, the Department of Commerce has created a multiple award contract designed only for small, disadvantaged and women-owned businesses,[33] and the Department of

---

[30]*The Federal Register,* June 2, 1999, Volume 64, Number 105, pp. 29693–29702.
[31]Ibid.
[32]Katy Saldarini, "Report: Procurement Reform Hurts Small Businesses," *GovExec.com,* June 9, 1999, *www.govexec.com/dailyfed,* February 20, 2001.
[33]Ibid.

Energy has established a number of outreach programs including a mentor-protégé program and new policies and procedures designed to increase the participation of small, minority-owned businesses.[34] (See Chapter 7 for a discussion of sourcing from small and disadvantaged businesses.)

Labor Surplus Area Favoritism

The Department of Labor classifies certain cities or areas as ones which have an unusually high unemployment rate or an unusually high number of hardcore disadvantaged persons. Certain government purchasing requirements then are set aside for placement of a given percentage of the total buy with firms in those areas. A small business in a labor surplus area is in a particularly advantageous position to compete for these purchases, although the net effect may be that the government (taxpayer) pays a premium price for purchased requirements.

Buy American Act

Congress passed the Buy American Act ostensibly to make sure that the United States maintains its production capability in several "essential" areas, even though foreign firms are able to produce more efficiently and thus undersell domestic firms on requirements for delivery in the United States. It provides that on certain government requirements the purchase order will be awarded to the domestic firm, provided that its price is not over a given percentage amount (normally 6 percent, or 12 percent if it is a labor surplus area) higher than that offered by the foreign supplier.

Environmentally Preferable Purchasing

Environmentally Preferable Defined

All federal procurement officials are required by Executive Order 13101 and Federal Acquisition Regulation (FAR) to assess and give preference to those products and services that are environmentally preferable.[35] The Environmentally Preferable Purchasing Program is a federal governmentwide program to encourage and assist executive agencies in purchasing decisions. Executive Order 13101 defines environmentally preferable as ". . . products or services that have a lesser or reduced effect on human health and the environment when compared with competing products or services that serve the same purpose." Environmentally preferable purchasing is then defined as "incorporating key environmental factors with traditional price and performance considerations in purchasing decisions."[36] The EPA has developed

---

[34]Patricia Guadalupe, "New DOE Contracts," *Hispanic Business,* July/August 2000, p. 22.
[35]Ibid.
[36]Environmentally Preferable Purchasing, Office of Pollution Prevention and Toxics, United States Environmental Protection Agency, *www.epa.gov/opptintr/epp.*

the Environmentally Preferable Purchasing (EPP) database of environmental attribute information for products ranging from appliances to vehicles. The database also includes contract language that has been used by others to obtain products and services considered by the EPA to be environmentally preferable. (See Chapter 11, Investment Recovery, for further discussion of environmental management as it relates to supply management.)

General Services Administration (GSA)

As a result of a governmental committee (the Hoover Commission) report in 1949, Congress passed Public Law 152, the Federal Property and Administrative Services Act of 1949. The General Services Administration (GSA) was set up under that act. GSA is responsible for all federal purchasing, except that done by Department of Defense (DOD), the National Aeronautics and Space Administration (NASA), and the Energy Research and Development Agency (ERDA). In fact, these agencies, as well as certain state, county, and local agencies, also can buy against GSA contracts. GSA is organized under a central office in Washington, D.C., and 10 regional offices. It sets standards for government purchases, buys and stores for later use (primarily through the Federal Supply Service, which is responsible for supplying common-use, commercial-type items to federal agencies), and issues long-term contracts at set prices. When an agency needs an item, it simply cites the appropriate GSA contract. In some instances, GSA actually operates retail-type stores, where any federal purchaser can go to obtain things such as office supplies and equipment. It also operates the GSA Interagency Motor Pool System. The GSA is the government's biggest e-commerce success with *GSAAdvantage.gov,* which lists more than a million items and sold more than $100 million of goods to government buyers in 1999.[37]

The GSA is Responsible for Most Federal Purchasing

GSA buying is, without question, big business. Efforts are under way to transform the GSA into an organization responsible for policy and oversight, and to place greater reliance on the private sector. The intention is to sell or privatize GSA's business units and transfer remaining service functions to the agencies. The goal in creating the proposed Office of Policy and Oversight is to increase accountability for results, encourage innovation, and enhance governmentwide planning, while ensuring responsible asset management.[38]

Military Purchasing

Following the experience of World War II, and after several studies to review past experience, Congress passed the Armed Services Procurement Act of 1947 (Title 10 of the U.S. Code) which provides the authority for today's purchasing

---

[37]Bob Tedeschi, "Making Uncle Sam a Big Web Buyer," *The New York Times on the Web,* *www.nytimes.com,* August 7, 2000.

[38]Budet of the U.S. Government, 1996, p. 883.

actions by the Department of Defense. In addition, it permits the use of negotiated procurements under certain conditions; it prohibits the use of cost-plus-profit-as-a-percentage-of-cost type contracts; and it establishes the policies under which purchasing for the Armed Forces is to be conducted. To meet the intent of the Armed Services Procurement Act, the Department of Defense originally adopted the Armed Services Procurement Regulations (ASPR) as the "bible" for military procurement personnel. Adoption of the Federal Acquisition Regulations (FAR) largely has superseded both the ASPR and the Defense Acquisition Regulations (DAR).

Four Types of Contracts

There are four types of contracts in common use by military buyers:

Firm-Fixed-Price (FFP) Contract. The price set is not subject to change, under any circumstances. This is the preferable type of contract, but if the delivery date is some months or years away and if there is substantial chance of price escalation, a supplier may feel that there is far too much risk of loss to agree to sell under an FFP contract.

Price Not Subject to Change

Cost-Plus-Fixed-Fee (CPFF) Contract. In situations where it would be unreasonable to expect a supplier to agree to sell at a firm fixed price, the CPFF contract can be used. This situation might occur if the item is experimental and the specifications are not firm, or if costs in the future cannot be predicted. The buyer agrees to reimburse the supplier for all reasonable costs incurred (under a set of definite policies under which "reasonable" is to be determined) in doing the job or producing the required item, plus a specified dollar amount of profit. A maximum amount may be specified for the cost. This contract type is far superior to the old "cost-plus-percentage" type, which encouraged the supplier to run the costs up as high as possible to increase the base on which the profit is figured. While the supplier bears little risk under the CPFF, because costs will be reimbursed, the supplier's profit percentage declines as the costs increase, giving some incentive to the supplier to control costs.

CPFF Contracts Are Used When Costs Are Unpredictable

Cost-No-Fee (CNF) Contract. If the buyer can argue persuasively that there will be enough subsidiary benefits to the supplier from doing a particular job, then the supplier may be willing to do it provided only the costs are reimbursed. For example, the supplier may be willing to do the research and produce some new product if only the costs are returned, because doing the job may give the supplier some new technological or product knowledge, which then may be used to make large profits in some commercial market.

Supplier Benefits in Other Ways

Cost-Plus-Incentive-Fee (CPIF) Contract. In this type of contract, both buyer and seller agree on a target cost figure, a fixed fee, and a formula under which any cost over- or underruns are to be shared. For example, assume the agreed-on target cost is $100,000, the fixed fee is $10,000, and the incentive sharing formula is 50/50. If actual costs are $120,000, the $20,000 cost overrun would be shared equally between buyer and seller, based on the

CPIF Contracts Encourage Efficiencies

50/50 sharing formula, and the seller's profit would be reduced by $10,000, or to zero in this example. On the other hand, if total costs are only $90,000, then the seller's share of the $10,000 cost underrun would be $5,000. Total profit then would be $10,000 + $5,000, or $15,000. This type of contract has the effect of motivating the supplier to be as efficient as possible, because the benefits of greater efficiency (or the penalties of inefficiency) accrue in part, based on the sharing formula, to the supplier.

McDonnell Douglas Example

With annual military expenditures comprising close to 65 percent of the total federal expenditure bill, it is obvious that very large dollar amounts can be saved or lost by the military's purchasing decision makers. For example, McDonnell Douglas Corporation was awarded a $6.6 billion defense contract to develop the C-17 cargo plane and to build the first six production aircraft. By August 1991, McDonnell Douglas was one year behind schedule and cost overruns were estimated to be between $1.4 billion and $2.6 billion.[39] Although the C-17s perform well, Congress then negotiated a separate offer initiated from Boeing to replace some of the C-17 orders with 747 jumbo jets in an effort to reduce costs. In early 1995, the Air Force estimated that the C-17s "should cost" an average $210 to $220 million. The threat of competition from Boeing has led McDonnell Douglas to offer as much as a 40 percent cut in price on the C-17s.[40]

Reforms in Military Purchasing

Increasing attention is being given to searching out and correcting inefficient purchasing practices, as the aggregate purchase dollars are so large. Since the president's 1983 task force on cost control issued its recommendations on inefficiencies in spare parts procurement and the work done by defense suppliers, reforms have been instituted. Some of these reforms are:

1. A requirement that replenishment spare parts be acquired in economic order quantities whenever possible.

2. An emphasis of buyers on competition and cost savings in personnel evaluations.

3. A review of the availability and cost of each item and the history of the item.

4. Establishment of a competition advocate for each agency. The advocate shall promote the use of competitive methods of procurement.[41]

---

[39]Rick Wartzman, "McDonnell Douglas Seen Exceeding Cap on C-17 Cost," *The Wall Street Journal,* August 26, 1991, p. A3

[40]Jeff Cole, "McDonnell Douglas Offers to Cut Price of C-17 Military Planes by Up to 40%," *The Wall Street Journal,* August 1, 1995, p. 1.

[41]Curtis R. Cook, "Spare Parts Procurement within the Department of Defense: Separating Fact from Fiction," *National Contract Management Journal* 23, Issue 2, (1990), p. 10.

The consequences of these reforms have been a dramatic *increase* in administrative lead times and a *decrease* in prices.[42] However, the public still perceives military procurement as marked by incompetency and unethical behavior. An example of the type of regulation that warrants this perception is one requiring contractors to bring a stenographer with three sharpened No. 2 pencils to technical reviews—even if the note taker has a laptop![43]

Efforts to Make Military Purchasing More Cost Effective

The military is very sensitive to such criticism and is taking steps to make its purchasing practices more cost-effective. For example, the Department of Defense is now making wider use of putting suppliers on its "blacklist" if they are convicted of fraud or bribery or for repeated failure to perform properly on contracts received, thus denying them the opportunity of selling to the military. The Secretary of Defense has ordered sweeping changes in its $13 billion yearly parts purchase to develop greater competition among suppliers, identify overpriced items, and demand refunds from their manufacturers. DOD audits have recovered more than $2.8 billion from contractors who either overcharged for spare parts or received unreasonably high profits on spare parts contracts.[44] Also, the military buyer must attempt to obtain the rights to technical data and equipment designs when he or she contracts with a supplier so it will be easier to obtain competition on later buys. According to the Secretary of Defense, the procurement changes which are being phased in are "turning the present system upside down." Key to this new system is that DOD will buy under commercial standards rather than specialized military specifications. In addition to phasing out the old "mil specs," much greater use will be made of performance specifications.[45]

United States Postal Service (USPS)

The largest governmental purchasing organization, after the DOD and GSA, is the United States Postal Service (USPS). The USPS is a quasi-governmental organization, operating under an 11-member Board of Governors. It is self-supporting through the sale of its services. Purchases amount to about $5 billion of goods and services annually. Key purchased items are supplies, services, and equipment; facilities (including design, construction, and related services) and real estate; and mail transportation services of all kinds.

Under the Postal Reorganization Act of 1970, USPS is permitted to establish its own procurement rules and regulations, operating like a private business. It is exempt from many of the laws, regulations, and executive orders pertaining to federal procurement, such as the Competition in Con-

---

[42]Ibid.

[43]"Forget the No. 2 Pencils," *Business Week,* July 31, 1995, p. 49.

[44]Ibid, p. 48.

[45]Thomas E. Ricks, "Pentagon, in Streamlining Effort, Plans to Revamp Its Purchasing Procedures," *The Wall Street Journal,* June 30, 1994, p. A12.

tracting Act and its policy of "full and open competition." For many years, USPS did not take advantage of the procurement flexibility allowed by the Postal Reorganization Act. Instead, it operated under the *Postal Contracting Manual,* issued in 1972, which was based on Department of Defense procurement policies.[46] In 1988 the USPS issued a new *USPS Procurement Manual* designed to take advantage of the best of both public and private procurement practices. In 1997 the *USPS Purchasing Manual* was released.[47] The Postal Service's purchasing philosophy is built on four guiding principles:

1. We make our requirements known to the marketplace.
2. We tell suppliers how we will evaluate proposals.
3. We award contracts on the basis of best value for our purchasing dollars.
4. We promote economic development in the community we serve by providing access to small, minority-, and women-owned businesses.[48]

As a quasi-governmental organization, the USPS purchasing and materials section tries to combine private-sector innovations and efficiencies with public-sector focus on fairness and accountability of a public agency.

Structure of USPS Purchasing Procedures

The vice president of the USPS purchasing and materials department operates with a headquarters and 10 purchasing and materials service centers and several facilities services offices. At headquarters, purchasing is commodity-based with three organizations: headquarters, major facilities, and national transportation purchases. Small dollar-value purchases (local buys) are typically made by local post offices around the country. For purchases over $10,000, "adequate competition" is sought to ensure that enough qualified suppliers participate to ensure the right quality and quantity at a fair and reasonable price. Opportunities are advertised in Business Opportunity Bulletins (*http://www.usps.purchasing.com*), as well as locally, on the Internet, and in the *Commerce Business Daily* (CBD) and the *Journal of Commerce*. The Supplier Automated Database (SADI — *http://www.purchasing.gov/sadi*) is a register of suppliers that is used as a sourcing tool by buyers. Proposals are evaluated on the basis of best value, not exclusively on lowest price.

The growing development of alternative communication methods, such as fax, electronic data interchange, Internet, phone, video, express package delivery, and private delivery services, make it essential that the USPS

---

[46]General Accounting Office, *Procurement Reform: New Concepts Being Cautiously Applied at the Postal Service* (Washington, D.C.: GAO), August 1991, pp. 1–2.

[47]*USPS Purchasing Manual* (Washington, D.C.: United States Postal Service), January 1997, *www.usps.com*.

[48]"Let's Do Business: Letter to Suppliers," *www.new.usps.com*.

operates effectively and efficiently, if it is to compete. The purchasing and materials department has to play a major role in accomplishing this.

State and Local Government Purchasing

While purchasing done by state, county, municipal, and other public agencies tends to follow all the basic guidelines of public purchasing, some of the unique aspects should be commented on briefly.

History

Centralized and Hybrid Purchasing Structures Prevalent in State and Local Governments

The state of Oklahoma was first, in 1910, to establish centralized purchasing. With that start, in the 1920s, along with budget reform, many additional states adopted central purchasing. As of 1994, all the states, with the exception of Mississippi, have adopted central purchasing.[49] However, in many states there is not total centralization of purchasing, for many state agencies often handle their purchasing separately from the central purchasing office. One good example of this is the state universities, which often do all the purchasing needed by their institutions. They can use advantageous, existing state contracts. Of the 35 municipal governments participating in the 1999 CAPS *Purchasing Performance Benchmarks for Municipal Governments,* 7 (38.9 percent) operate in a centralized purchasing structure, 11 (61.1 percent) are in centralized/decentralized structures, and none used a completely decentralized purchasing structure.[50] For state and county governments, 15 (37.5 percent) operated in a centralized/decentralized structure, 14 (35 percent) used a centralized one, 9 (22.5 percent) used virtual centralization, and 2 (5 percent) used a decentralized structure.[51]

Participation in GSA Contracts

Those political subdivisions (cities, counties, and states) which are the recipients of some type of federal grant or funding are eligible to use the GSA contracts. In some instances this will allow the agency to buy items at a lower price and with substantially lower administrative cost. Certainly the public buyer should at least check out the GSA prices before making a decision.

---

[49]"Table 1: Centralization of Procurement Authority," in *State and Local Government Purchasing,* 4th ed. (Lexington, KY: National Association of State Procurement Officers [NASPO], 1994).

[50]*Purchasing Performance Benchmarks for Municipal Governments* (Tempe, AZ: Center for Advanced Purchasing Studies, 1999) *www.capsresearch.org.*

[51]*Purchasing Performance Benchmarks for State/County Governments* (Tempe, AZ: Center for Advanced Purchasing Studies, 1999), *www.capsresearch.org.*

Prison-Made Goods

Some states require that if one of the state's penal institutions produces items that also are required in the operation of state government, that penal institution must be given absolute preference in purchasing. The items produced might include foodstuffs, shoes, work clothing, and license plates. The public purchasing officer should know what kinds of items are available from the penal institutions and should communicate to the prison administrators the quality requirements which goods must meet.

Cooperative Purchasing

In the last decade or so, the cooperative purchasing approach has received much attention, interest, and use in public purchasing. Basically, it is a system whereby two or more public, or not-for-profit, purchasing departments pool their requirements so that they can talk with suppliers about substantially larger purchase quantities than would be required by any one buyer. It has been used successfully by local government units, public school districts, and hospitals, and it has its primary advantage for the smaller purchasing unit. The savings from purchasing consortiums can be significant.

Premier, Inc. Example of Cooperative Purchasing

For example, three of the largest U.S. hospital cooperatives formed Premier Inc. Premier negotiates contracts with manufacturers on behalf of 1,757 hospitals with combined annual revenues of $89 billion. Premier has already negotiated savings of 25 – 30 percent in some instances.[52]

Two Types of Cooperative Purchasing

Two basic variations are used in cooperative purchasing: (1) joint buying, where two or more purchasing departments agree to pool their requirements for a particular item and let one of the purchasing departments commit the total purchase quantity to a specific supplier at a specific price, and (2) a formal, contractual arrangement where several individual purchasing departments agree to establish and fund a separate cooperative buying agency, typically called a consortium, and to use the purchasing services of that agency. For example, several hospitals in a particular area could agree to pool their requirements for basic items and then hire a full-time buyer (manager) of a cooperative hospital purchasing agency. The administrative costs of the cooperative agency would be shared by all hospital members on some basis, such as size of hospital or total purchase dollars spent through the cooperative group. Such cooperative agencies exist in the health-care field in several states, and many universities are affiliated with the cooperative buying arm of the National Association of Educational Buyers, Inc.[53]

Advantages and Disadvantages of Cooperative Buying

Some of the advantages of cooperative buying are: (1) lower prices; (2) improved quality, through improved testing and supplier selection; (3) reduced

---

[52]Ron Stodghill II, "Attack of the Health-Care Colossus," *Business Week,* May 20, 1996, p. 40.

[53]National Association of Educational Buyers, Inc. (NAEB), 450 Wireless Blvd., Hauppauge, NY 11788.

administrative cost; (4) standardization; (5) better records; and (6) greater competition. Among the problems cited as arising from cooperative buying are: (1) inferior products; (2) longer lead times; (3) limited items available; (4) more paperwork; and (5) inability of small suppliers to compete, due to larger quantities required.

Local-Bidder Preference Laws

Rationale for Local-Bidder Preference Laws

In many governmental jurisdictions, the applicable law or statute states that, all other things being equal, local bidders must be granted a certain percentage price preference in bidding against nonlocal suppliers. For example, if a local supplier submits a bid that is not over a given percent, for example, 5 percent, higher than nonlocal suppliers, then the local supplier must be awarded the purchase order, assuming all other factors are equal. This is a form of protectionism similar to that of the Buy American Act. The argument for this is that local suppliers have employees in the local area, and the award of orders to local suppliers provides support for the local economy.

Opposition to Local Preference Laws

This practice is opposed by most purchasing professionals as being noncompetitive, which means that higher prices are paid for purchases than are necessary. It negates the advantages of economic specialization, and local suppliers, knowing that such a preference is to be applied, will have a tendency to submit a bid that is higher than they otherwise would offer. If one believes in totally fair, open competition, then all suppliers, regardless of location, should be permitted to compete solely on the basis of their ability to provide maximum value for the public funds expended. The National Association of State Purchasing Officials has gone on record as strongly opposing local-preference laws.

Examples of Innovations in Public Purchasing

Innovations in Government Purchasing

The prevailing attitude of business people and the general public is that government purchasing systems and procedures are far less efficient and bound by substantially more "red tape" than the general practices of private industry. While that may be so, it need not be. Sound purchasing management applied to the governmental purchasing/materials management process can result in cost-saving innovations. For example, the department of materials management of Maricopa County, Arizona (the largest county in the state in terms of both population and industry base, encompassing the metropolitan Phoenix area) instituted a blank check (check with purchase order) system as a means of reducing the administrative payment cost and the aggravation of supplier back orders. Because the Arizona Revised Statutes (ARS) under which governmental units operate prohibited payment of public funds until materials or services actually were received, the legislature had to be persuaded to modify the appropriate ARS to permit use of this innovative system. With this legislative modification, the blank check buying system could be used by many public purchasing units. More recently, Arizona State University adopted a Procurement Card Program to simplify the purchasing process and reduce cycle time.

TABLE 15–2   Government Purchases of Goods and Services, 1933 to 2000 ($ billions)

	State/Local Governments % Using Purchasing Innovation	Municipal Governments % Using Purchasing Innovation
Small order system for independent purchases by departments	80.0	89.5
Percent of purchase dollars spent through small order system	17.6	11.5
Percent of transactions processed through small order system	42.4	55.7
Procurement credit cards	63.2	
Automated purchasing systems	84.6	94.7
Have a Web site	NA	89.5
Use the Internet for:		
Sourcing	NA	88.9
Communication with peers	NA	94.7
Communication with suppliers	NA	89.5
Research	NA	100.0
Distribution of supplier information	NA	50.0
Electronic document exchange to:		
register bidders	NA	52.9
notify about solicitations	NA	73.7
distribute solicitations	NA	42.1
accept solicitations	NA	15.8
invoice/receive payment	NA	10.5
make award	NA	10.5
Minority/Women Business Enterprise (M/WBE) program:	NA	64.7
outreach program	NA	84.6
price preference program	NA	37.5
set-aside program	NA	44.4
Multiple-year contracts	100	NA
Cooperative purchasing	87.5	NA
Internal customer satisfaction surveys	84.4	NA
External (supplier) satisfaction surveys	34.4	NA
Cost reduction targets	37.5	NA
Cycle-time reduction	34.4	NA
Price reduction targets	28.1	NA
Supply base reduction targets	0.0	NA

NA: data not available

The 1999 *Purchasing Performance Benchmarks for Municipal Governments* and for *State and County Governments* indicated the usage of purchasing innovations shown in Figure 15–2.

Longer Term Contracts

Public supply has traditionally operated on an annual contract basis. This has normally been tied to the annual budgeting process and/or the argument that it is improper to commit future funds not part of the current budget or the current mandate of the elected representatives. Limiting contracts for requirements that clearly extend well past a 12-month period to one year will not only increase the amount of work for supply managers, but also decrease the chances of obtaining better value by extending the length of the contract. It is encouraging to see that the use of multiple-year contracts is increasing in the public sector in recognition of value opportunities formerly foregone.

Use of Automated Systems

There is an increasing trend to use automated systems in public supply to provide greater responsiveness to user needs, to decrease procuring costs, and to obtain superior value. Some of the more interesting applications have been the use of electronic bid boards and the Internet to provide easy supplier access and greater geographical coverage.

Model Procurement Code

Starting in the late 1960s, a committee of the American Bar Association began discussing the need for a model procurement code for state and local purchasing activities. A code was needed for two reasons: first, the substantial amounts of money spent on state and local purchasing; and second, because the federal government supplies funds to state and local governments, the spending of these funds should comply with sound purchasing practices.[54] After going through several public hearings and drafts, the code was adopted in 1979 and revised in 1999. The underlying purposes and policies of this code are:

Purposes of the Model Procurement Code

a. to simplify, clarify, and modernize the law governing procurement by this [State];

b. to permit the continued development of procurement policies and practices;

c. to make as consistent as possible the procurement laws among the various jurisdictions;

---

[54]Wayne A. Casper, "The Public Procurement Code: What It Can Do," *NAPM Insights,* January 1994, pp. 38–40.

d. to provide for increased public confidence in the procedures followed in public procurement;

e. to ensure the fair and equitable treatment of all persons who deal with the procurement system of this [State];

f. to provide increased economy in [State] procurement activities and to maximize to the fullest extent practicable the purchasing value of public funds of the [State];

g. to foster effective broad-based competition within the free enterprise system;

h. to provide safeguards for the maintenance of a procurement system of quality and integrity, and

i. to obtain in a cost-effective and responsive manner the materials, services, and construction required by [State] agencies in order for those agencies to better serve this [State's] businesses and residents.[55]

The code itself is a 75-page document, divided into 12 parts or Articles, as follows:

Article 1: General provisions.

Article 2: Procurement organization.

Article 3: Source selection and contract formation.

Article 4: Specifications.

Article 5: Procurement of infrastructure facilities and services.

Article 6: Modification and termination of contracts for supplies and services.

Article 7: Cost principles.

Article 8: Supply management.

Article 9: Legal and contractual remedies.

Article 10: Intergovernmental relations.

Article 11: Assistance to small and disadvantaged businesses; federal assistance on contract procurement requirements.

Article 12: Ethics in public contracting.[56]

While certain of the individual sections and the wording of principles and policies therein are open to criticism and modification, the overall code has been helpful in assisting governmental units at all levels to improve their purchasing policies, procedures, and systems. Because the code was to provide a statute outlining the fundamentals of sound purchasing, the American

---

[55]*The Model Procurement Code for State and Local Governments,* (Washington, D. C.: American Bar Association, February 1999), *www.abanet.org.*

[56]Ibid.

Bar Association later presented a set of recommended, comprehensive, and integrated regulations that a governmental unit could use to implement the code. This 265-page document, published in 1980, gives the language which could be used in developing a comprehensive policy manual governing a public purchasing operation.[57]

As a follow-up to the full code, the American Bar Association approved and published in August 1982 a model procurement ordinance for use by smaller units of local government. This 26-page document generally is a condensation of the full code, with essentially the same articles, except that Articles 7, 8, 10, and 11 were not developed in condensed form.[58]

Results of Model Procurement Code-Based Legislation

The results of the model procurement code-based legislation include: (1) changes to competitive bid requirements that allow the purchaser more leeway in analyzing the capabilities of suppliers and room to award to other than the low bidder, (2) the creation of competitive sealed proposals allowing for negotiations and revisions of proposals, (3) suspension and disbarment of suppliers under certain circumstances, and (4) administrative procedures for resolving bid protests and claims.[59] As a result of the implementation of model procurement code-based legislation, a body of case law is developing which can be used along with the code in legal disputes.

Health-Care Purchasing

Many of the nation's 5,117 hospitals and 1,624 clinics are operated by the public sector (federal, state, county, city, and quasi-public not-for-profit corporations). In 1998, national health-care expenditures were $1.15 trillion. Health-care costs in the United States grew in double digits for 25 years but slowed in the 1990s. During the 1980s, costs increased at an annual rate of 11 percent on average, but in 1998 they were up by less than 6 percent from 1997.[60]

Purchasing Impacts the ROA of Health-Care Organizations

Approximately 20 percent of a hospital's revenue goes toward the purchase of consumables (medical supplies, linens, food, and so on) and construction and equipment. A hospital's efficiency and return-on-assets is directly affected by how the purchasing function is performed. Efficiencies are available when any hospital recognizes it must manage materials instead of merely issuing purchase orders.

---

[57]The Model Procurement Code for State and Local Governments: Recommended Regulations (Washington, D. C.: American Bar Association, August 1980).

[58]*The Model Procurement Ordinance for Local Governments* (Washington, D.C.: American Bar Association, August 1982).

[59]Ibid., p. 40.

[60]"Health United States, 2000." Department of Health and Human Services, Centers for Disease Control and Prevention, and National Center for Health Statistics.

Diagnosis-Related Groups (DRGs) Provide an Incentive to Manage Costs

Because of the rapid rise of health-care costs—in 1982 they increased 11.9 percent while the consumer price index rose less than 4 percent—it became clear that at that rate the Medicare Hospital Insurance Trust Fund would be depleted by 1990. Congress then instituted health-cost-containment procedures as part of the Tax Equity and Fiscal Responsibility Act (TEFRA) passed in 1982. Under TEFRA, illnesses are classified into more than 400 so-called diagnosis-related groups (DRGs), and hospitals are reimbursed for Medicare patients at amounts based on the average cost of the specific DRG in each of nine regions of the country. If a given hospital's costs for a particular procedure, such as a simple appendectomy, are greater than the average cost for that DRG in its area, it will lose money, for its actual costs will be only partially reimbursed. The DRG-based payment system has been adopted for reimbursements by state agencies and private businesses. Thus a real incentive for holding down costs has been applied. The DRG system encourages efficiency, and purchasing is one of the key areas where potentially large cost savings can be made.

Example of E-Marketplace

Purchasing cost savings are being sought through application of e-commerce tools.[61] For example, *Marketplace@Novation* is an Internet health-care marketplace run by Novation, a combination of the supply programs of VHA and UHC. Novation manages more than $15 billion in annual purchases for more than 2,100 members of VHA and UHC, as well as 5,300 organizations that buy supplies through HealthCare Purchasing Partners International LLC, another Irving, Texas-based GPO that is owned by VHA and UHC. The technology side of the e-marketplace is being provided by Neoforma, a company that builds and operates Internet marketplaces for health-care trading partners.

To date, 69 manufacturers and distributors have agreed to participate in Marketplace@Novation, representing in total more than $5 billion in annual contract and non-contract sales to VHA and UHC members. In addition, 344 hospitals, representing more than $8.6 billion in annual supply purchases, have chosen to use Marketplace@Novation as their supply chain solution. Each hospital has committed to transacting a minimum of 50 percent of its annual supply purchases through Marketplace@Novation within 18 months. To date, Neoforma has connected 114 hospitals to Marketplace@Novation and has an additional 78 hospitals in active implementation.

As with other B2B marketplaces, it remains to be seen if buyers and sellers of medical products will accept Neoforma's business model of providing an online marketplace for the purchase and sale of medical products; and if Neoforma can manage its growth and related technological challenges while also successfully managing its changing relationships with its partners, suppliers, and strategic customers.

---

[61]*Business Wire: Health Wire,* February 28, 2001.

Questions for Review and Discussion

1. Which commercial practices would you recommend for adoption by public purchasing to make it more effective? Why? If adopted, would these practices compromise any of the goals of government purchasing?

2. Are there any differences between federal purchasing and state and local purchasing? Discuss.

3. How do the objectives of public purchasing differ from those of industrial buying?

4. Discuss the advantages and problems arising from local bidder preference laws in state and local purchasing.

5. What are performance bonds, and why are they used?

6. How does the bid process in public buying differ from that used in industrial buying?

7. What are the major differences between public buying and industrial buying? Which would be easier to do?

8. Under what circumstances should each of the four common military contract types be used?

9. Considering the magnitude and complexity of military purchasing, can it ever really be efficient and cost-effective? What changes should be made in current practices?

10. How can industrial buyers use federal government purchase specifications?

11. Does the Buy American Act promote efficient purchasing? Justify the continuation or repeal of the act.

12. Are there any major differences between purchasing for a health-care organization and a manufacturing firm? What changes would be required?

References

Best Practices for Collecting and Using Current and Past Performance Information. Office of Federal Procurement Policy, Office of Management and Budget, Executive Office of the President, May 2000, *www.arnet.gov/Library/OFPP/Best Practices/pastperformanceguide.htm.*

Carey, John. "Attention Pentagon Shoppers." *Business Week,* May 27, 1996.

Center for Advanced Purchasing Studies, *Purchasing Performance Benchmarks for Municipal Governments,* 1999.

Center for Advanced Purchasing Studies, *Purchasing Performance Benchmarks for State/County Governments,* 1999.

Cook, Curtis R. "Spare Parts Procurement within the Department of Defense: Separating Fact from Fiction." *National Contract Management Journal* 23, Issue 2, 1990.

Crossan, Merhel. *The Procurers: Assessing Canada's #1 Market.* Toronto, Ontario: McGraw-Hill Ryerson, 1991.

Fearon, Harold E. and William A. Bales. *Purchasing of Nontraditional Goods and Services.* Tempe, AZ: Center for Advanced Purchasing Studies, 1995.

The Model Procurement Code for State and Local Governments. Washington, D.C.: American Bar Association, February 1999.

The Model Procurement Code for State and Local Governments: Recommended Regulations. Washington, D.C.: American Bar Association, August 1980.

The Model Procurement Ordinance for Local Governments. Washington, D.C.: American Bar Association, August 1982.

Small Business Trends in Federal Procurement in the 1990s. United States General Accounting Office Report to Congressional Requesters, January 2001.

State and Local Government Purchasing Principles & Practices, 5th ed. Lexington, Ky.: National Association of State Procurement Officers, 1997.

Survey of State and Local Government Purchasing Practices, 5th ed. Revised. Lexington, Ky.: National Association of State Procurement Officers, 1999.

CASE 15-1
CITY OF ROXBOROUGH

On April 14, after the annual bids for sodium hypochlorite were opened, Mr. Joel Graham, assistant director; Purchasing and Supply, for the city of Roxborough, realized that the two lowest bids had been submitted by two different persons of the Ryerson Company.

The city of Roxborough provided social services like recycling, snow removal, roads, garbage disposal, and pollution and water control to the residents of Roxborough, a municipality of about 300,000 people. The city's financial reputation was reasonably strong. Its current borrowing rate for 10-year bonds was 7.5 percent per annum.

Purchasing and Supply Division. The mission of the Purchasing and Supply Division (PSD) was to support the end users with the expertise as to quality, price, and time for a particular good or service. PSD had purchasing, bidding, disposal, and warehousing authority for the city of Roxborough and reported directly to the Finance Department.

The Director of PSD, Mr. James Jardine, managed the entire operation. Mr. Graham was one of two assistant directors and he was responsible for pollution control and special projects. He also managed the clerical staff and the inventory warehouse staff, bought major services, and was responsible for the stores function.

The Bidding Process. The end users provided PSD with specifications for their requirements. The end users and the PSD jointly decided on the potential suppliers of a particular product and a bidders list was made. For requirements below $56,000, a short-cycle 10-day process could be applied in which quotations or requests for proposals were sought. The city of Roxborough's managers were required to invite bids for any equipment or product purchases in excess of $56,000. The potential suppliers were sent an Invitation to Bid. This bid included:

1. The Form of Bid [required if bidders were interested in supplying the product(s)].
2. Bid Information regarding closing date and time (normally every Wednesday at noon) and opening of the bids (normally five minutes after the bids were closed).
3. The Specification Requirements.
4. The Terms and Conditions of the Contract.
5. An Agreement.

Exhibit 1 provides an excerpt of some relevant city by-laws governing purchasing.

The director of PSD normally opened the bids and a clerk recorded the bids on a Bid Summary Sheet. The opening of bids was a public event normally attended by suppliers who had submitted bids. During the days following the bid opening, the PSD made a bid evaluation. The selection of the successful bidder was based on several criteria, the most important being conformance to specifications and conditions. If all of the specifications and conditions were met, the lowest bid was normally selected and the contract awarded. If other than the lowest bidder were selected, the director documented the decision very carefully as protection against any future challenge in the courts. If identical low bids were received from different companies, the contract was either split or the current supplier was awarded the contract. Legal counsel was normally sought if any errors were made in the bidding process.

The Sodium Hypochlorite Bid. The need for the sodium hypochlorite had been established as part of the water treatment, sewage, and odor control chemicals. Mr. Graham was the PSD contact person for these contracts. This was the first time that there was a combined bid for the same chemicals requested by three different end users: Engineering Sewage, Parks and Recreation, and Water Works. Previously, purchasing for the three departments had been decentralized. The combined expenditure for all the water, sewage, and odor control chemicals totaled $500,000.

The annual requirement for sodium hypochlorite was 132,000 liters, with little seasonal variation and monthly delivery. Three companies had submitted four bids. The sales manager and sales representative of the Ryerson Company each had submitted independently, a first for the city of Roxborough. Exhibit 2 shows the Bid Summary.

EXHIBIT 1   City of Roxborough—Excerpts from the Purchasing Bylaws

Conditions Applicable to All Bids

The following conditions with respect to the condition of bid documents apply to all sealed bids:

a. Bids received by the City Clerk's Department later than the specified closing time shall be returned unopened to the bidder.

b. A bidder who has already submitted a bid may submit a further bid at any time up to the official closing time. The last bid received shall supercede and invalidate all bids previously submitted by that bidder.

c. A bidder may withdraw his or her bid at any time up to official closing time by letter bearing his or her signature and seal as in his or her bid submitted to the City Clerk.

d. The City reserves the right to accept or reject any bid.

EXHIBIT 2 (CASE 15-1)   City of Roxborough—The Bidding Process

	Ryerson Company	*James Corp.*	*J.O.N.*
	Bid (1) **Bid (2)**		
Specifications Sodium hypochlorite 12% Trade (Na OC1) Minimum available chlorine 12% (w/v basis) Maximum free caustic soda 0.8% by weight 132,000 liters	(1) Specifications met (2) Specifications met	Specifications met	Specifications met
Credit Terms	(1) Net 30 days (2) Net 30 days	2/10 net 30	Net 30 days
Price per liter $ **(tax included)**	(1) 0.1710 (2) 0.1760	0.1770	$\leq$ 6819 lit loads = 0.1803 $\geq$ 6820 lit loads = 0.1771

Bid 1 in the Ryerson Company was submitted by the sales manager. The second bid was submitted by the sales representative one day later but still before the bid deadline.

When the director of PSD opened the bids, he asked "How could this have happened?" Mr. Graham knew he had to investigate the situation immediately and decide on the next step. As he was returning to his office, he thought about some of the alternatives. Should he notify Ryerson, and whom should he notify in the company? Should he call the Legal Department for advice? Was the bidding process destroyed? Would an investigation be necessary if Ryerson did not submit the lowest bids? What would have happened if the second Ryerson bid were lower than the first?

On going over the bid invitation records, Mr. Graham's investigation showed that Ryerson appeared twice on the bidding list. He knew that his time was limited since he had only a couple of days in which to recommend an award to the council.

Disputes. In cases of dispute as to whether or not a product or service bid or delivered meets the condition in the accepted bid, the decision of the director of Purchasing & Supply of the corporation shall be final and binding on all parties.

CASE 15-2
DON WILLIT ASSOCIATES

Don Willit was retained as a consultant to help select suppliers and implement a computer systems reengineering project for a major East Coast city. It was the third and final phase of a project that required him to work with a 20-member Administrative Computer Steering Committee (ACSC) appointed by the city's Chief Administrator specifically to oversee the computer systems updating. After a number of delays, the ACSC had finally agreed that, despite a number of concerns, Supplier C was the most appropriate supplier by a wide margin. It was decided that Mr. Willit should write a formal recommendation to city council explaining the choice of the ACSC before the formal presentation to the elected officials was made. Mr. Willit had just finished the first draft of the formal recommendation when he heard that Supplier C had announced a loss for the year which reduced its equity by nearly half.

Background. Mr. Willit had originally been retained by the city a year earlier when more than 1,000 personal computers were about to be installed throughout the municipal offices. While updating its PCs, the city council had expressed a desire to gain as much uniformity as was practical in the data processing equipment. The selection criteria for the PC replacement program had been fairly straightforward. The new hardware had to be equal to or better than the equipment being replaced in terms of hardware quality and performance. The equipment and its accompanying software package also had to be compatible with and able to communicate with the existing office automation software, which included a particular word processing package used by more than 900 professional and clerical workers in the city.

In studying bids submitted by four major suppliers, it had become apparent that only one (Supplier C) had a software package that was totally compatible with the city's current needs. Don had heard rumors about Supplier C having some serious financial problems, and he was somewhat surprised when this supplier offered to supply one authorized copy of the required word processing software package free of charge to the city with each PC purchased. The bids from Suppliers A, B, and D were price competitive with each other and with Supplier C except for the required software package. Suppliers A, B, and D were each passing along a charge of $400 per unit for the necessary software—a charge which they would be obliged to pay Supplier C (who was the developer of the package) if they were awarded the contract.

The inclusion of the free software packages caused the city to contract with Supplier C for the purchase of personal computers. The savings was so significant, approximately 15 percent of the life cycle cost of the total project, that the selection of one of the other suppliers would have been very difficult to rationalize.

Shortly after the replacement of the PCs, the city issued a request for proposals for an updated communications network. A number of different suppliers submitted proposals, and the most appropriate in terms of capability and price was tendered by Johnston Corp. Although the choice of Johnston had been tentatively made, the ACSC hoped that the signing of a contract could be post-poned until a supplier for the new corporate computer system had also been selected. The intent was to avoid compatibility problems.

Corporate Computer System Selection. It had been estimated that the corporate administrative information system and computer complex would represent an expenditure of approximately $3 million for hardware and software on top of the nearly $5 million already allocated for the new PCs and communications network. The corporate system expenditure would consist of about $2 million for a bank of three large mini-computers, plus about $1 million for software and training. The corporate system had to be capable of supporting transaction processing from more than 1,000 PC clients and their various communication needs. The applications software that would accompany the new corporate system would require about 20 major applications. The basic primary requirements would include a Financial Information System (FIS), Human Relations (Personnel) Information System (HRIS), Ratepayer Information System (RIS), and Office Information System (OIS).

Once again, although it was not new technology, Supplier C's applications software was judged to be significantly superior to that of the other three suppliers. On a 10-point scale rating system devised by Mr. Willit and the ACSC, Supplier C's applications software earned a grade of 9.2 versus a grade of 4.6 for Suppliers B and D and a grade of 3.6 for Supplier A. Further, Supplier C was the least expensive solution of the four bidders on a five-year life cycle basis. It was agreed that Mr. Willit would write a formal recommendation to contract with Supplier C for the corporate computer system and applications software, and that copies of his proposal would be distributed to the city councilors at the special meeting where the recommendations were to be formally presented.

Mr. Willit decided to write the first draft of the proposal to present to the ACSC for further input before finalizing the recommendations for the city council. Just as he finished the first draft, he learned that Supplier C had announced a loss of nearly $750 million on sales of about $1.9 billion. While he considered this news by itself to be very bad, he was even more concerned to learn that the loss dropped Supplier C's equity in half to just below $1 billion. It appeared that another year of similar losses could potentially bankrupt Supplier C unless a successful merger could be arranged. The news left Mr. Willit wondering whether he should carry on with the current proposal and add a note of explanation about Supplier C, or ask the ACSC to reopen the bidding process for new proposals with the hope of finding a more suitable supplier.

CASE 15-3
TRICITY

On November 20, Elaine Carter, manager of Purchasing and Supply for TriCity, got off the phone frustrated. According to the fleet manager from Environmental Services, an out-of-stock wiper blade had idled an expensive snow-removal truck. Elaine was concerned that the new integrated procurement system was affecting her department's service. How many other orders were not being processed by the new system? She knew that the situation required immediate attention and sat down to think of possible solutions.

TriCity. TriCity, a Midwestern city of about 330,000, was responsible for an area of 41,110 acres. The city's responsibilities ranged from police services to the management of parks and recreation facilities. The organization of the city's departments is provided in Exhibit 1. Environmental Services represented the highest budget allocation due to the nature of its activities.

Annual budgets defined capital works, money set aside for specific projects like new road construction, and operational expenditures, for daily expense needs. Every department was allocated a certain amount of capital works and operational budget yearly. At the end of the year, any unused capital works budget was withdrawn from the departments, whereas unused operational budget was carried forward to the next year.

The city was accountable to the tax-paying public for its expenditures. It was the responsibility of the city's government to ensure efficient and appropriate use of funds.

The Purchasing and Supply Department. Purchasing and Supply was part of the Finance and Administration department of TriCity. It provided purchasing to all departments of the city, excluding the police department. It also provided warehousing services for supplies that were part of the regular materials inventory, such as stationery and maintenance equipment. Essentially, every service within the city departments was a customer of the Purchasing and Supply office. Its mission statement was:

> Obtaining the right goods and services when needed at the right price through a fair and competitive process.

The Ordering Process. Individual departments initiated the process to purchase goods and services. The request was sent to Purchasing and Supply who filled the order from the warehouse, or initiated the process of purchasing from third-party suppliers. Supplier selection was restricted to lowest-cost bidder and specifications set by the requesting department. Purchasing and Supply tracked orders to ensure delivery occurred within an acceptable time-frame. Supplier payments were coordinated by the office, too.

The warehouse stocked items that had been purchased in bulk and that were part of operational expenditure. Customers could request an order from inventory, and the Purchasing and Supply staff would ready the items for pickup. It was the responsibility of the end users to ensure that items they used regularly were in stock. Purchasing and Supply would reorder based on request only.

If the order was not in inventory, the office initiated one of the following processes:

Bid	For orders of over $58,000
Formal Quote	For orders between $15,000 - $58,000
Informal Quote	For orders below $15,000

The format of supplier selection followed a similar process in all cases (lowest bid for customer-defined specifications). Level of approval authority defined which order process would be used.

Integrated Procurement. A new computer system had been implemented in Purchasing and Supply a month ago. Still in the early stages of implementation, Elaine was faced with several challenges that the new system brought to her department.

Because integrated procurement, as the system was called, was not customized, it limited online ordering to 10 major customers only and relegated the rest to a manual system to order their supplies. The previous system had allowed all customers online ordering capabilities. The new system provided limited order management information to the customers placing the orders, reducing information on their budget balances. Internally, Elaine found that her staff disliked the data entry requirements of the new system. Whereas the old system allowed for manual input within one screen, the new system required seven screens of input. Most of the staff personnel had been in the department for more than 10 years and were used to the previous system. In their opinion the new system appeared to increase the staff workload, with a lower level of service to the end users.

Integrated procurement was a finance-based system. Because it was not customized to the Purchasing and Supply department, several ordering processes needed revision. For example, for those departments who no longer had online ordering capabilities, faxed requisitions required manual follow-up. Order status checks required telephone contact with the order customer. With resource restrictions ever prevalent in the public sector, Elaine was not sure how to provide adequate staff to handle the increased workload.

However, Elaine also knew that the long-term advantages of the new system were potentially great. The new system integrated previously stand-alone systems. Purchasing, accounts, warehousing and payroll were some of the main modules of the new system. Integrating these systems allowed superior management control–supplier payments and customer orders could be tracked better, reports on staff productivity were available for the first time, and back orders were filled automatically through the warehouse. Moreover, integrated procurement allowed supplier performance appraisal on a continuous basis. These tools could ul-timately help Elaine improve the efficiency of the entire buying process. The new system also provided the initial step towards Internet-enabled business.

Impact of Change. Many of Elaine's customers had not been happy with the new system implemented in her office. They felt they had lost control over some critical parts of the ordering process.

Service issues with major projects could also result in the involvement of elected representatives at City Hall in the process. It was not uncommon for elected representatives to ask about purchasing issues with projects in which they had a particular interest. Therefore, any changes that appeared detrimental to these interests were not looked upon favorably.

Coupled with the external pressures, Elaine had also faced resistance from her staff. During the training on the new system, her staff had voiced concerns about the lower productivity levels. After launch date, new issues arose daily. Elaine had thought the old system could be abandoned soon after the launch of integrated procurement but she was not sure now.

The Wiper Blade Stock-Out Problem. Elaine reviewed the wiper blade stock-out problem. An order entered by the fleet division of Environmental Services, one of the customers who had online access, for a wiper blade had failed to transmit through the new system properly. Because the warehouse had not received a request for the blade, it was not reordered. The fleet manager was claiming that the snow-removal truck that had required the blade could not be used because the blade was out of stock, costing the department idle time.

Elaine wondered what could have caused the order not to be processed. Was it human error in data entry– this *was* a new system? Or were there technical glitches involved? Either way, Elaine had to solve the immediate problem for the fleet department. However, she also was concerned about similar problems arising with other orders. What could she do to prevent this from happening again? What safety measures should she implement?

EXHIBIT 1 Purchasing and Supply's Customers

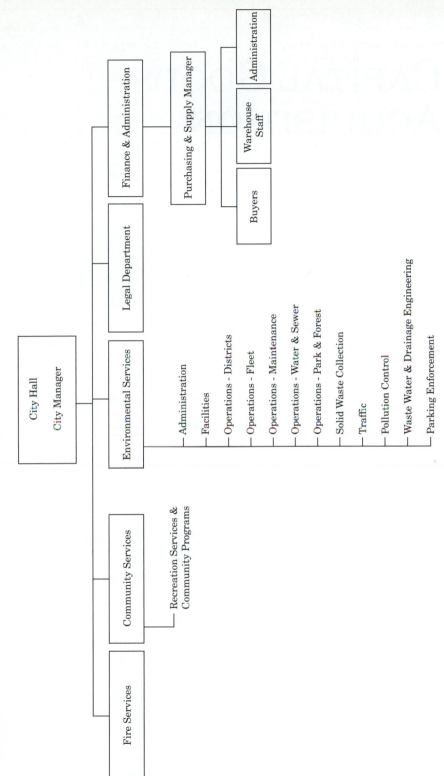

City Hall
City Manager

- Fire Services
- Community Services
  - Recreation Services & Community Programs
- Environmental Services
  - Administration
  - Facilities
  - Operations - Districts
  - Operations - Fleet
  - Operations - Maintenance
  - Operations - Water & Sewer
  - Operations - Park & Forest
  - Solid Waste Collection
  - Traffic
  - Pollution Control
  - Waste Water & Drainage Engineering
  - Parking Enforcement
- Legal Department
- Finance & Administration
  - Purchasing & Supply Manager
    - Buyers
    - Warehouse Staff
    - Administration

C H A P T E R

16 Capital Goods Acquisition

Chapter Outline

Key Questions for the Purchasing Decision Maker

SHOULD WE
- Buy or lease new equipment?
- Buy used equipment?
- Change the way we buy construction?

HOW CAN WE
- Dispose of replaced or obsolete equipment?
- Improve the development of new equipment?
- Distinguish between routine and strategic capital acquisition?

The acquisition of capital goods may represent a key strategic move for an organization that could affect its competitive advantage for years to come. On the other hand, it could be a routine matter of no great consequence. However, capital goods combining equipment and construction represent some unique acquisition challenges.

New Equipment—New Technology

Intel: Move toward Performance-Based Contracting

Competitive advantage stems from product or service differentiation or low-cost production. New technology frequently permits an organization to gain competitive advantage on both grounds—different products and services at significantly lower cost. New technology is, therefore, of significant strategic interest to most organizations. And new technology almost always implies new equipment and new processes. It is this strategic dimension of new equipment acquisition that has traditionally been overlooked by purchasing. Intellectual property rights, speed of acquisition, installation and debugging, continuing supplier support for operational performances and upgrades, and development of the next generation of technological advances become prime matters of corporate concern. For example, in the semiconductor industry, capital equipment purchases normally represent the largest single percentage category of all purchase dollars. At Intel, the goal is to tie capital equipment purchasing and equipment service to performance-based contracting. Thus, the supplier gets paid for up-time and quality output. The more the running time exceeds agreed-to output goals, the greater the rewards for the supplier. Future plans are driven by the need for continuous improvement in cost per wafer and number of wafers per year per machine. Only a few key supplier partners are included in Intel's longer range technology road maps planning process—looking five years out. Total cost of ownership, not just the cost of the equipment itself, drives future technology decisions. Obviously, the corporate team approach is required to manage this process, and exceptionally capable individuals need to represent supply on the corporate team. Not all equipment purchased is as advanced as that described above. There are some basic considerations to procuring new equipment that are ever present.

New Equipment Acquisition

Two Classifications of Equipment

A useful classification of equipment is the division into multipurpose and single purpose. Multipurpose equipment may have a variety of uses, may be used in many industries, tends to have longer technological life, and may have considerable salvage value. Forklift trucks and standard lathes are typical examples. Single-purpose equipment is designed to do one or several operations well, substantially better than a multipurpose piece of equipment could. On the other hand, its specificity limits its potential use, and its usefulness is closely tied to the need for operations it performs. Such special equipment is often limited to one industry and may even be limited to one customer. The purchaser's specifications are important, requiring extensive consultation between the technical personnel of both buyer and supplier. The salvage value of special equipment may be low, with the drawback that the need for the tasks may disappear before the equipment is physically worn out.

Minor or accessory equipment is normally used in an auxiliary capacity and tends to be of much lower dollar value. Its cost may not even be capitalized, and much of it tends to be standardized. Small power packs and motors are typical examples.

Special Problems of Equipment Buying

Equipment procurement raises special problems:

High Risk

1. The purchase of the equipment may be of such strategic importance to the organization that factors like secrecy and ability to be first in the marketplace with output from the equipment become prime driving factors. The risk associated with failure, technological or otherwise, may also be very high. Supplier selection decisions under these circumstances are key corporate strategic decisions.

Large Dollars

2. The buying of equipment usually requires that substantial amounts of money be expended for a single purchase. Sometimes the sum is so large as to call for a special form of financing, such as a bond issue, leasing, or payment on an installment plan.

Infrequent Purchase

3. Because of their comparatively long life, equipment items are likely to be bought less frequently than other types of purchases.

Total Cost Difficult to Calculate

4. The final cost of equipment is more difficult to determine with exactness than, for example, the final cost of raw materials. The initial cost of equipment is but a part of the total cost, which involves a whole series of estimates, such as the effects of idle time, of obsoles-

cence, of maintenance and repair, of displaced labor, and even of direct operation factors. Some of these items may never be known exactly, even after experience with the particular piece of equipment in question. Moreover, many of the costs, such as insurance, interest, obsolescence, and depreciation, continue even when the equipment is not in actual use. The income to be derived is also problematical, and, thus, even when it is possible to compute approximate costs, it is often difficult to determine how soon they will be offset by revenues. These comments are particularly applicable to nonproduction equipment, such as cranes and hoists.

Timing of Purchase

5. The demand for equipment more than the demand for any other type of industrial good is a derived demand. Pricewise, the best time at which to buy is, therefore, particularly hard to determine. Only when the need and the justification for the equipment have been established is there a possibility that its actual purchase may be delayed or hastened by price considerations. Because equipment is not commonly bought until needed, it is seldom bought during periods of business recession, although prices for equipment normally are low at such times and many good arguments can be advanced for buying then. Aside from absence of immediate need, manufacturers in periods of slack business tend to watch their assets carefully. Also, labor may be cheaper during recessions, and there is less incentive to substitute machinery for labor. The reverse conditions prevail in times of prosperity.

Environmental Issues

6. The purchase of equipment frequently involves problems concerning its environmental impact and the wisest method of disposition of the displaced item. Not only may the future disposal of the equipment itself be an environmental issue, but the materials the equipment processes and needs for its operation and maintenance may also have a significant environmental impact. (See Chapter 11, Investment Recovery.)

Tax Considerations

7. Tax considerations such as depreciation allowances may significantly affect the delivery and transfer of ownership dates.

Technology Forecasting

8. Technology forecasting plays a role in purchasing new equipment. How long before this equipment will be obsolete? Can it be modified subsequently? What kind of technology is likely to replace it? Should we buy now or later? Can we live with the old equipment a bit longer? The rate of technological obsolescence of equipment is a particularly thorny problem. Equipment, like components, is experiencing shorter life cycles. New technologies, such as stereolithography (SLA) and laminated object manufacturing (LOM), permit rapid prototyping. Purchasers can specify changes desirable in current equipment and expect rapid modification as well as rapid development of new models. Thus the risk of technological obsolescence is increasing.

**Length of
Start-up
Period**

9. Equipment, particularly major installations, may require a significant period of start-up, during which extra purchasing support may have to be provided to deal with all kinds of emergencies. The equipment choice may well commit the organization to a series of other decisions of a permanent nature, such as the type of product to be manufactured, allocation of space, the method of its production, and the cost of operation.

**Integration
with
Established
Processes**

10. It is necessary to analyze not only the particular equipment in question but also such elements as plant layout, kind of power used, types of machines used for other operations, and the like. In short, the proposed installation must be looked on as an integral part of an established process; and its coordination with the existing facilities must be obtained, even though extensive changes may be required to effect economical production.

**Eight Reasons
to Purchase
Equipment**

Equipment purchases involve, in part, engineering and production considerations and, in part, factors largely outside the scope of these functions. From the former standpoint, there are eight commonly recognized reasons for purchase: (1) capacity, (2) economy in operation and maintenance, (3) increased productivity, (4) better quality, (5) dependability in use, (6) savings in time or labor costs, (7) durability, and (8) safety, pollution, and emergency protection. Beyond these engineering questions are those which only the marketing, purchasing, or financial departments, or general management itself, can answer. Is this a key strategic commitment? Are style changes or other modifications in the present product essential or even desirable? Is the market static, contracting, or expanding? Does the company have the funds with which to buy the machine which theoretically is most desirable, or is it necessary, for financial reasons, to be satisfied with something that is perhaps less efficient but of a lower initial cost? What should be done in a case in which the particular equipment most desirable from an engineering standpoint is obtainable only from a manufacturer who is not thoroughly trustworthy or perhaps is on the verge of bankruptcy? Should we be the first or the last purchaser of this equipment? Such questions are quite as important in the final decision as are the more purely engineering ones. For this reason it is sound practice to form a team including representatives from engineering, using departments, finance, marketing, and supply to work jointly on major equipment acquisitions.

In some organizations the volume of equipment purchases is so great that a special person or team of employees in supply is assigned the equipment acquisition task exclusively. The title of equipment buyer is a common one in such instances, as is manager of equipment purchases.

Importance of Cost Factors

**Key Questions
Related to Cost**

Once the need for new equipment has been determined, one of the first questions to be considered is that of cost. Is the equipment intended for replacement only or to provide additional capacity? What is the installed cost of the equipment? What will start-up costs be? Will its installation create problems with plant layout? What will be the maintenance and repair costs, and who will provide repair parts and at what cost? Are accessories required, and if so, what will their costs be? What will be the operating costs, including power and labor? What is the number of machine-hours the equipment will be used? Can the user make the machine or must it be bought outside? At what rate is the machine to be depreciated? What financing costs are involved? If, as is usually the case, the equipment is for production, what is the present cost of producing the product compared with obtaining the item from an outside supplier and of producing the unit with the new equipment?

Life Cycle Costing or Total Cost of Ownership

LCC and TCO Defined

The U.S Department of Defense has strongly encouraged the use of life cycle costing (LCC) as a decision approach to capital investments. In industry the term *total cost of ownership* (TCO) conveys the same meaning. The philosophy behind LCC is relatively simple. The total cost of a piece of equipment goes well beyond the purchase price or even its installed cost. What is really of interest is the total cost of performing the intended function over the lifetime of the task or the piece of equipment. Thus, an initial low purchase price may mask a higher operating cost, perhaps occasioned by higher maintenance and down-time costs, more skilled labor, greater material waste, more energy use, or higher waste-processing charges. Because the low bid would favor a low initial machine cost, an unfair advantage may accrue to the supplier with possibly the highest life-cycle-cost equipment. It is the inclusion of every conceivable cost pertaining to the decision that makes the LCC concept easier to grasp theoretically than to practice in real life. As many of the costs are future ones, possibly even 10 to 15 years hence and of a highly uncertain nature, criticisms of the exactness of LCC are well founded. Fortunately, computer programs are available varying from simple accounting programs, which compute costs from project life cycles, to Monte Carlo simulation of the equipment from conception to disposal. The computer allows for testing of sensitivity, and, when necessary, inputs can be changed readily.

The normal emphasis, particularly in governmental acquisition, on the low bid finds, therefore, a serious and preferable alternative in LCC. The experience with LCC has shown in a surprising number of instances that the initial purchase price of equipment may be a relatively low percentage of LCC. For example, computers, if purchased, seldom account for more than 50 percent, and most industrial equipment falls into the 20 to 60 percentage range of LCC.

In one total-cost-of-ownership study for a multimillion dollar piece of equipment, 139 different cost elements were identified for the computer simulation of the process.

Engineering Service

Most sellers of major equipment maintain an intimate and continuing interest in their equipment after it is sold and installed. Two major questions are involved in providing engineering service: Why is the service given and accepted, and what is the cost of such service?

Compensating the Seller for Engineering Services

Presale Service. Technical sales service is provided by a supplier to a potential or actual purchaser of equipment to determine the design and specifications of the equipment believed best suited to the particular requirements of the buyer and also to ensure that, once bought, the equipment functions properly. It is nearly always related to the "individualized buying problem of particular users." There is, however, another side to this question of sales service. For one thing, the prospective buyer may ask for and receive a great deal of presale service and advice without a real intention of buying or knowing full well that the firm providing the service will under no circumstances receive an order. Not only is such a procedure unethical, but the buyer who pursues it will sooner or later find the organization's reputation for fair dealing has suffered seriously. The problem of engineering service is really twofold, with both phases, however, involving cost. The first phase relates to the method followed by the seller in charging for presale service. Such service is clearly a matter of sales promotion, and when no subsequent sale results or when the profit on the sale is insufficient to cover the cost of the service fully, some other means of recovery must be found. One suggestion for meeting this particular problem is that a specific charge, either a flat fee or one computed on the basis of actual cost, be made for presale engineering service, with the recipient of the service paying this charge whether or not a purchase is made subsequently.

Postsale Service. Often equipment is sold with a production guarantee, an additional reason for supervising both the installation and the operation of the equipment. Even after this initial period, the seller may provide for regular inspection to ensure the proper operation of the machine. The prime abuse of postsale services arises from those firms that insist on furnishing and charging for it whether or not the buyer feels a need for it.

Selection of the Source

Factors Influencing Supplier Selection

Selection of the proper source requires careful consideration in any purchase of major equipment. In the purchase of raw materials and supplies, quick and reliable delivery and the availability of a continuous supply are important reasons for choosing a particular supplier. These characteristics are often not so important in equipment purchases. The reliability of the seller and a reasonable price are, of course, important, regardless of what is being bought. But, as contrasted with raw materials, what may be called cooperation in selecting the right type of equipment, proper installation, common interests in efficient operation—in short, a long-continuing interest in the product after it is sold—becomes very important. So, too, does the availability of repair parts and of repair services throughout the entire life of the machine. Satisfactory past relationships with the equipment supplier weigh heavily in the placing of future orders. The interest of operations, engineering, or technical personnel in capital equipment is such that they usually have a strong supplier preference. For large companies, manufacturing equipment in their own shops has always been an alternative. Some even have subsidiaries specializing in equipment design and manufacture. Where secret processes give a manufacturer a competitive edge, such in-house manufacture is almost essential. In JIT, as identified in Chapter 5, one of the capabilities a JIT adopter is supposed to have is in-house modification of equipment. This is often related to setup time reduction and small-run capability enhancement. In-house equipment design and modification capability clearly is a major asset in assessing supplier technological proficiency.

Design and R&D Considerations

Key Questions to Determine Allocation of R&D Costs

Where a customer may require new equipment currently not available on the market, the question of development and design needs to be addressed. In cases where the purchaser has such a unique application that the equipment is clearly usable only by the one purchaser, the cost of development and design can properly be charged to the one customer. Many defense applications fall into this category. A more-complex issue arises when potential benefits might arise to the supplier in terms of additional expertise transferable to other products or services or similar equipment salable to other customers. Who should pay for development and design under these circumstances? What benefits should accrue to the purchaser of the first piece of equipment of the new generation? Should both purchaser and supplier share in the development and design costs and both benefit from future sales to others in the form of patents, royalties, or percentage fees? Furthermore, there are two standard issues in any new equipment product: (1) Who will pay for development and design and how, and (2) how will the risk of failure be shared between buyer and supplier? Practices will vary between industries and circumstances. There may be interesting opportunities for purchasers who are capable of assuming the development cost and technological risk factors to reap future rewards from their entrepreneurial role.

Legal Questions

Attention should also be directed to the legal questions that arise in connection with equipment buying. The danger of liability for patent infringement constitutes one problem. The extent of liability for accidents to employees is another. Again, equipment sales contracts and purchase agreements are often long and involved, offering many opportunities for legal controversies. Various forms of insurance coverage are used and are often subject to varying interpretations. Any purchased machine must comply fully with the

Long-Term Liability Issues Must Be Addressed

safety regulations of the state, province, or country in which it is to be operated, and these safety regulations vary greatly in different locations. Federal government OSHA (Occupational Safety and Health Act) requirements have to be followed. The question of consequential damages is a particularly touchy one. Should the seller of a key piece of equipment be responsible for the loss of sales and contribution when the machine fails because of a design or fabrication error? Such losses may be huge for the buyer. In one company, gross revenues of $1 million per day were lost for six months because of the failure of a new piece of equipment costing $800,000! Many equipment acquisitions need careful scrutiny and interpretation by qualified legal counsel.

Special Budgeting Procedures

When the financial budget is set up, it is customary to make provisions for two types of capital expenditures. The first type covers probable expenditures which, although properly chargeable to some capital account, are still too small to be brought directly to the attention of the finance committee or controller. Customarily, some limit is fixed, such as $2,000 to $10,000. The second type includes expenditures for larger amounts. Inclusion in the budget normally constitutes neither an authorization to spend that amount of money nor an approval of any specific equipment acquisition. This authorization must be obtained subsequently from the executives concerned, and their specific approval is given only after they have examined carefully a preliminary analysis of the project. A formal appropriation request is called for, giving a detailed description of what is to be bought, estimates of the costs involved, the savings likely to result, the causes which have created the need, the effect of the purchase on the organization as a whole, and whatever other information those initiating the request feel is pertinent. In light of these facts, together with the data regarding other financial requirements of the company and its financial position, a decision is made as to the wisdom of authorizing the particular expenditure under consideration.

The Capital Budgeting Process

Disposition of Obsolete or Replaced Equipment

What to do with old or replaced equipment is an interesting question. One procedure is to trade in the old machine on the new, with the supplier making an allowance and assuming the burden of disposal. Barring other considerations, the decision of whether to trade in or not is largely dependent on which will result in the lowest net cost to the purchaser. Since trade-ins are a form of price concession, they may not accurately reflect current market values of the old equipment. In some industries, old equipment may be in perfect operating condition and its disposal may well create unwanted competition. At other times, it may represent a health or environmental hazard, or contain special secret features. Destruction may be a reasonable solution in all these instances.

Options for Disposition Must Be Carefully Analyzed

In large organizations, equipment displaced in one area may be of use in another within the same organization. It is normal practice for purchasing departments to circulate lists or maintain an online database of items available within the organization before searching for other disposal alternatives. Some companies with intranets (see Chapter 4) have developed an online database so that all business units can post and acquire useable equipment more easily. If a company has global operations, then what has become obsolete equipment for one location may be seen as the latest technology in another. If the equipment can be transported and set up cost-effectively, this may be preferable to buying new equipment. Transfer pricing is usually based on book value, and the transportation charges are assumed by the receiving unit or department. Another option is to sell the old equipment to a used equipment dealer. It may be possible to find a direct buyer or to sell the old machine as scrap. Some of these procedures are discussed indirectly in Chapter 11, "Investment Recovery." As in all other situations involving disposal, environmental considerations will impact the disposal method chosen. Disassembly of equipment may be required for proper recycling.

Procurement of Used Equipment

In our discussion of equipment purchases thus far, it has been assumed that the buyer was acquiring new equipment. An alternative is the purchase of used equipment, which raises special issues. In general, the same rules of evaluation apply as in the case of new equipment. One important difference, however, may be that, ordinarily, manufacturers' services and guarantees do not apply to such purchases. The value of these intangibles is difficult to determine. Many buyers would say that they are more important with used equipment than with new, and that their value may be greater than any differential in price.

Developments in Fleet Management

Fleet management of vehicles requires special attention to the decision of when to replace a vehicle with another. Interesting developments in fleet management include the purchase of vehicles from automobile rental companies (with still relatively low mileage, but a significant amount of new car depreciation knocked off), the use of leasing companies or third-party logistics providers, and driver purchase options.

Reasons for Buying Used Equipment

Some of the reasons for the purchase of used equipment are:

1. When price is important, either because the differential between new and used is great or the buyer's funds are scarce.
2. For use in a pilot or experimental plant.
3. For use with a special or temporary order over which the entire cost will be amortized.

4. Where the machine will be idle a substantial amount of time.

5. For use of apprentices.

6. For maintenance departments (not production).

7. For faster delivery when time is essential.

8. When a used machine can be easily modernized for relatively little or is already the latest model.

Sales Contract Terms

Used equipment may be offered with different contract terms:

1. The equipment may be available "as is," and perhaps "where is." A sale "as is" means that the contract carries essentially "no warranty, guarantee, or representation of any kind, expressed or implied, as to the condition of the item offered for sale." "Where is," of course, is self-explanatory.

2. The equipment may be sold with certain specific guarantees, preferably expressed in writing. This practice is found more generally among used equipment dealers, though they sometimes may offer equipment "as is."

3. Finally, the equipment may be sold "guaranteed and rebuilt." The equipment is invoiced as such; it has been tested; and it carries a binding guarantee of satisfactory performance for not less than 30 days from the date of shipment.

There are various channels through which used equipment is bought and sold. These include the manufacturer who accepted the used equipment as a trade-in, direct sale to user, brokers, auctions, and dealers.

Leasing Equipment

Many manufacturers of capital equipment lease as well as sell their equipment. Those who advocate leasing point out that leasing involves payments for the use of the assets rather than for the privilege of owning the asset. Short-term rentals are a special form of lease with which everyone is familiar. Short-term rentals make a lot of sense when limited use of the equipment is foreseen and the capital and/or maintenance cost of the equipment is significant. Often an operator can be obtained along with the piece of equipment rented. The construction industry is a good example where extensive use is made of short-term rentals. Most lease contracts can be drawn to include an "option to buy" after some stated period. It is important for anyone considering the lease of capital equipment to be sure that the Internal Revenue regulations are understood. Canadian and American government interpretation is similar. The Internal Revenue Service's position on ascertaining the tax status of leases is relevant:

Conditions Determining Sale Rather Than Lease

In the absence of compelling factors of contrary implication, the parties will be considered as having intended a purchase and sale rather than a rental, if one or more of the following conditions are covered in the agreement:

1. Portions of periodic payments are specifically applicable to any equity to be acquired by the lessees.
2. The lessees will acquire title on payment of a stated amount of rentals.
3. The total amount which the lessee is required to pay for a relatively short period constitutes an inordinately large proportion of the total sum required to be paid to secure transfer of title.
4. The agreed rental payments exceed the current fair-rental values.
5. The property may be acquired under a purchase option which is nominal in relation to the value of the property at the time when the option may be exercised, as determined at the time of entering into the original agreement, or which is a relatively small amount when compared with the total payments which are required to be made.
6. Some portion of periodic payments is specifically designated as interest or is otherwise recognizable as the equivalent of interest.

Unless the lease rental payments can be treated as an expense item for income tax purposes, some of the possible advantages of the equipment lease plan may not be realized.

In the past, some large manufacturers of machines and equipment employing advanced technology preferred to follow a policy of leasing rather than selling their equipment. Government antitrust actions have aimed at giving the user the right to determine whether to lease or purchase. The leasing may be done by the manufacturers of the equipment, by distributors, or by companies organized for the specific purpose of leasing equipment. At times, as in the construction industry, an owner of equipment who has no immediate use for it may lease or rent it to other concerns that may have temporary immediate need for it. An interesting phenomenon with leasing occurs in large organizations, including public agencies. Because lease costs are normally charged to operating instead of capital budgets, department heads may try to acquire equipment through the back door by leasing when the capital budget does not permit purchase. This can easily lead to abuse and some very high rental costs. In one government agency, the rental of recording equipment over a six-month period equaled the purchase cost. Buyers need to be aware of this practice and on the lookout for costly subterfuges involving leasing.

Abuse of Leasing

Advantages and Disadvantages of Leasing

The advantages of leasing may be listed as follows:

Advantages of Leasing

1. Lease rentals are expenses for income tax purposes.
2. Small initial outlay (may actually cost less).
3. Availability of expert service.
4. Risk of obsolescence reduced.
5. Adaptability to special jobs and seasonal business.
6. Test period provided before purchase.
7. Burden of investment shifted to supplier.

For example, automobile fleet managers frequently prefer leasing when their fleet is spread across the country and when the leasing company has greater purchasing clout and better disposal ability. There are certain equally clear disadvantages, however:

Disadvantages of Leasing

1. Final cost may be high.
2. Surveillance by lessor entailed.
3. Less freedom of control and use.

Many leases need to be watched with care because they are one-sided in their terms, placing virtually all the risks on the lessee. For instance, what are the arrangements for replacing equipment when it is obsolete or no longer serviceable? Is the lessee free to buy supplies anywhere, such as paper for copying machines? Are the actual charges what they appear to be? Are there onerous limitations on either the maximum or the minimum output or other such operational factors as the number of hours per day or number of shifts the equipment may be used or on using attachments? What limitations, if any, are there to the uses to which the equipment may be put?

Types of Leases

Financial Lease

The two main types of leases are the financial and the operational lease. The financial lease may be of the full payout or partial payout variety. In the full payout form, the lessee pays the full purchase price of the equipment plus interest and, if applicable, maintenance, service, record-keeping, and insurance charges on a regular payment plan. In the partial payout plan, there is a residual value to the equipment at the end of the lease term and the lessee pays for the difference between original cost and residual value plus interest and charges. The financial lease cost is made up of the lessor's fee, the interest rate, and the depreciation rate of the equipment. The lessor's fee depends on the services offered and may be as low as 0.25 percent of the gross for straight financing without other services. The interest rate will depend both on the cost of money to the lessor and the credit rating of the lessee. The depreciation normally varies with the type of equipment and its use.

**Operational
Lease**

The operational lease is in its basic form noncancellable, has a fixed term which is substantially less than the life of the equipment, and a fixed financial commitment which is substantially less than the purchase price of the equipment. Service is the key factor in the operational lease, with the lessor assuming full responsibility for maintenance, obsolescence, insurance, taxes, purchase, and resale of equipment, and so on. The charges for these services must be evaluated by the lessee against other alternatives which may be open.

Categories of Leasing Companies

Careful analysis of how the lessor will profit from the leasing arrangement is vital in obtaining a satisfactory price. Because most leasing companies have standard procedures for calculating leases but are seldom willing to disclose these procedures or the vital figures behind them, it behooves the buyer to search carefully before signing. As lessors are more likely to disclose competitors' procedures and figures than their own, the search need not be seen as an impossible task. There are four major structures of leasing relationships, each with its special implications (see Figure 16-1).

**Lessor Buys,
Finances, and
Services
Equipment**

The Full-Service Lessor. Full-service lessors are most common in the automotive, office equipment, and industrial equipment fields. The lessor performs all services, purchases the equipment to the buyer's specifications, and has its own source of financing. This type of lessor generally obtains discounts or rebates from the equipment manufacturers, which are not disclosed to the lessee. Profits also are obtained on the maintenance and service charges which are included in the lease rate. Care should be taken on long-term leases that contain an escalation provision to allow such escalation only on that portion of the lease on which costs might rise.

**Lessor
Finances
Lease, But
Does Not Buy
or Service
Equipment**

The Finance Lease Company. This type of lessor does not purchase or maintain the equipment, so that the lessee deals directly with the equipment manufacturer. The lessor frequently has access to funds at close to prime rate and is able to make its profit by lending above this. Occasionally, if a relatively short lease is involved, the lessor may wish to profit from the resale value of the equipment and may offer unusually low lending rates. A profitable lessor may benefit from the investment tax credits and depreciation, which to a less-profitable lessee may be meaningless. When a lessee has already reached the limits on its investment tax credits because of large capital expenditures but the lessor is not yet at the limit, leasing may similarly benefit both.

**Reasons OEM
Will Lease
Equipment**

Captive Leasing. The prime purpose of captive leasing is to encourage the sale and use of the parent's equipment. There are several reasons why the original equipment manufacturer (OEM) may choose to lease rather than to sell:

1. To secure either wider distribution or a higher margin.
2. To reduce the credit risk.

FIGURE 16-1

Four Leasing Structural Relationships

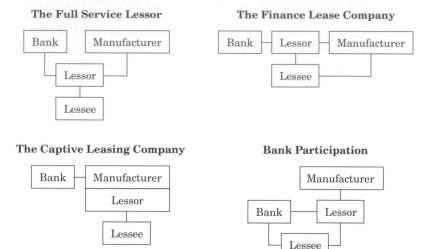

3. To sell a full line or to increase the volume of sales of supplies.

4. To control the secondhand market.

5. To stabilize the company's growth through securing distribution in times of recession when sales, especially of new as contrasted with used equipment, are difficult to make.

6. To control servicing.

7. To protect a patent position.

Obviously, a transfer price for the equipment holds between the parent and the lessor. Sometimes a lessor will quote a 2 percent sales-tax figure on the rental value, when in reality the lessor may be charged only with a use tax which applies to only 50 percent of the rental value. A lessee might expect to gain at least a 1 percent benefit from negotiation here.

Banks Only Provide Financing

Bank Participation. There are advantages to bank participation in cases where the lessee has a good credit rating. The bank may be willing to finance part of the lease at rates slightly over prime because it is a low-risk and low-nuisance lease. The lessor looks after the purchasing, servicing, and disposal of the equipment, relieving the bank of tasks it normally has little expertise in.

Lessor Evaluation

Quite aside from any weighing of the specific advantages and disadvantages and beyond the actual terms of the lease, any prospective lessee of equipment needs to exercise the utmost care in passing judgment on the lessor. Is the lessor:

1. Reasonable and fair in dealing with customers?
2. Devoting as much attention and money to research as alleged?
3. Strong financially?
4. If a sole source, prone to be arbitrary in the periodic adjustment of rental and other fees?

The Acquisition of Construction

Construction represents a special class of capital goods. In the first place, land or space needs to be available for construction. Therefore, the question may arise of real estate acquisition with all of the attendant issues of office or plant location involving deeds, access, zoning restrictions, taxes, and availability of services such as water, electricity, telephone, and disposal. Other issues may involve distance from customers, suppliers, and labor and transportation access and costs. Obviously, many of these issues are properly the domain of other functions in the organization. In organizations in a rapid expansion mode, such as fast-food chains, or those with substantial land holdings, a separate real estate or facility management department may manage all real estate acquisition and maintenance. In the construction of buildings for offices, production, warehouses, stores, restaurants, maintenance, hotels, education, or research, the intended use of the facility will be the prime concern in its design. It is possible for larger organizations to maintain an in-house architectural and structural, plumbing, air conditioning, and electrical engineering staff. Even in these organizations, the possibility of make or buy exists. A core group of specialists on staff may be augmented with outside consulting assistance when demand peaks occur or special expertise is required. If building needs to be done in a large variety of locations, possibly domestic and foreign, local expertise familiar with climatic conditions, building codes, and construction contractors may be absolutely necessary. It is normal in many construction projects that the cost of the design is a relatively small portion of the total project cost, possibly in the 7 to 12 percent range. Yet, the design itself will be a major determinant of final project cost. Therefore, it is important to examine the question of design acquisition or design management by a set of criteria going well beyond the cost of the design phase itself.

Possibility of Outsourcing Design and Engineering

The Traditional Approach to Construction and Pitfalls

In the traditional construction sequence of project concept, capital request, design, construction bids, contractor selection, and construction, many high-cost pitfalls exist. Changes during the construction phase are almost invariably expensive and time-consuming. The capital approval process is often lengthy and by the time capital is approved, the amount of time available for design, bids, and construction is tight. Rushing through these phases becomes costly and prone to mistakes. The original cost estimate may not be realistic because all details of the design were not yet known, market conditions for construction or labor may have changed, or the project itself may have evolved into a different concept. If construction bids received exceed the original capital request approved, the uncomfortable decision needs to be made whether to start cost cutting or to engage in a lengthy, and possibly futile, attempt to get approval for more funds. The intent here is not to paint all construction as a messy and problem-filled area. To the contrary, the existence of all of these possible pitfalls suggests that there is plenty of room for improvement and problem avoidance by sound project management. And, because many of the costs and problems center on the need for outside consultants and contractors, proper supply management is a vital component of successful construction.

Proper Supply Management Can Add Value

Different Approaches to Construction Acquisition

It is not surprising that a number of approaches have evolved to address the key problem areas in construction. Most attempt to ensure proper quality, delivery on time, and cost control. Clearly, even if the traditional approach is followed in all the phases of construction, selection of the right consultants and architects, the right contractors and subtrades, with proper coordination and appropriate lead times for all activities, will increase the chances of success.

E-construction Example

E-construction is the application of Internet tools to the construction project management process. Online tools allow easier, faster, and less costly coordination of numerous separate teams over the life of a project. Centralized communication is the key feature of these e-commerce sites. Large contractors such as Turner Corporation and Bechtel already are using e-tools to communicate with partners and subcontractors, buy materials, and bid for jobs.[1] However, e-commerce has not been widely adopted by second- and third-tier suppliers (less than $100 million in revenue) in the construction industry. In these businesses, communication is still done largely by fax, voice mail, and overnight shipping, resulting in a huge loss in potential savings. Forrester Research projects that only about 11 percent of total construction spending will be conducted online by 2004.[2]

E-commerce Providers Enable Faster Communication

An e-commerce provider such as Cephren or Bidcom charges an upfront fee and a monthly maintenance fee. In return, the entire construction team is linked with passwords enabling differing levels of access to information and services related to their project. Through Web collaboration, the most-

---

[1] Bob Tedeschi, "Internet Reshapes the Construction Industry," *The New York Times on the Web,* February 21, 2000, *www.nytime.com/library.*
[2] Ibid.

current blueprints and work schedules can be posted, e-mail notifications sent to appropriate parties, and a virtual paper trail is created of who viewed what and when, thereby providing a compendium of evidence. Architectural drawings can be viewed online and printed from the user's computer whenever changes are made rather than waiting for them to be commercially printed, packaged, and shipped. After the job is completed, equipment manuals and building specifications can be stored on disks or cartridges.

Project Management Tools Essential to Success

Project management techniques like Program Evaluation Review Technique (PERT) and Critical Path Method (CPM) can assist greatly. By focusing on the activities on or close to the critical path, they permit proper analysis and planning as well as monitoring. Obviously, purchase lead times for various phases are absolutely critical. The availability of a contingency fund to deal with unexpected problems as they arise also will assist in preventing the project from going off schedule. Incentive clauses or bonuses for early or on-time completion and penalty clauses for lateness may also assist in ensuring on-time completion. In public procurement, the use of bid bonds and performance bonds is intended to ensure contractor commitment and performance.

Prime Contractor— Inhouse or Outsourced

Some interesting options exist in construction which do not follow the traditional process. For example, one key issue deals with the question of who is the prime contractor. It is possible to perform this task in-house or to assign responsibility outside. For those organizations without in-house expertise, this question should not even arise. Another possibility is to go to a

Turnkey Project

turnkey project. The purchaser will specify requirements, probably as a set of performance specifications, and a large contractor or a consulting firm will look after all subsequent phases. This clearly places responsibility for quality, delivery, cost, and performance with one party and allows this party to find its own solutions to specific design or construction challenges. Another option is the request for proposal (RFP) route, rather than having an archi-

RFP Route

tect or design engineer produce a specific design. This approach allows the contractors to suggest building materials and a construction design and methodology particularly suited to their own strengths and circumstances. RFPs may also be posted online, bids received electronically, and awards posted after the selection has been made.

The request for quote (RFQ) or request for proposal (RFP) needs to include the unique features of the construction services purchase. These include:[3]

Drawings. Include if necessary.

Work Changes. Identify when and how changes are determined and accepted, and include a requirement for itemized labor and material charges with percentage material markup caps.

---

[3]Richard E. Lohmann, "More Than Just Bricks and Mortar," *Purchasing Today,* November 1998, p. 51.

Acceptance Criteria. Clearly identify when acceptance has been made.

Modifications. Acknowledge receipt of modifications to avoid trouble later on. Consider including a document for submitting quotations or proposals for modifications.

Evaluation Criteria. Clearly identify the decision criteria for selection, for example, costs, completion date and time-frame before project can begin, work schedule, potential subcontractors, expertise of supplier's staff, conformance to buyer's terms and conditions, and past history.

Payment Process. Establish the process using referenced American Institute of Architects (AIA) documents.

Insurance and Bonds. Establish performance and payment requirements (including figures and reference to AIA documents).

Termination Criteria. Establish termination criteria including violation of contract requirements (also covering federal and state laws).

Project Schedules. Require the submission of proposed project schedules prior to execution of any work, and specifications for any products or materials to be installed. Schedules should include the number of days before project can begin, and the number of days for completion.

Site Inspection/Walk-through. Require information if applicable.

Subcontractors. Require a list.

Liquidated Damages. Include in the event of project delays.

Pricing Options. List acceptable pricing options.

Statement of Work. Clearly define the supplier's responsibility. (See Chapter 17, Services Purchasing, for more information on writing a statement of work).

Application of Value Engineering Techniques

It is possible and desirable to use value analysis/value engineering techniques during the concept and design steps to ensure that the best-value option evolves. Another option is to select a contractor during the concept stage and use the contractor to design and build to a specific performance, cost, and delivery target. Dramatic savings in time and cost may be possible if the right contractor is selected early on. The new building of the Rotterdam School of Management at Erasmus University was completed in less than half the conventional time and less than half the conventional construction cost using this approach. The contractor chosen had just completed a large apartment block project and was able to use the same construction forms and crews and similar materials on the new school building.

On-Site Considerations in Construction

During the construction phase, if it is to be carried out on space owned and operated by the buying organization, special contract provisions may need to deal with issues like identification and security; hours of access to the site; noise, dress, and safety regulations; access to food service; recreational, office, production, and other facilities; deliveries; conduct; and cleanliness.

Purchasing Involvement in Construction

In many organizations, construction is largely left to the engineering department, and purchasing may or may not send out the request for bids. Meaningful purchasing department involvement will require that the buying staff have special construction expertise. Moreover, as in all other types of acquisition, early purchasing involvement in the project is absolutely necessary if value analysis, request for proposal, and other innovative supply options should be explored. Because many other functions aside from purchasing and engineering should be involved early in construction planning, the idea of using a task force or project team approach is highly appealing. It is appropriate that the supply function be included on such a team.

Questions for Review and Discussion

1. Could equipment purchasing be strategic?
2. How can a reasonable value be placed on engineering service supplied by a potential supplier of equipment?
3. What are some typical problems encountered in the acquisition of construction?
4. How might e-commerce tools be used to reduce, eliminate, or contain construction costs?
5. What could be the advantages of buying on a turnkey basis?
6. How might one dispose of a capital good?
7. Why would anyone prefer to buy instead of lease?
8. Why is capital goods acquisition different from the purchase of raw materials?
9. What are the problems of using total cost of ownership or life-cycle costing?
10. What are the advantages of using a full-service lessor?

References

McConville, John G. *1996 International Construction Costs and Reference Data Yearbook,* John Wiley & Sons, 1996.

Knod, Edward M. and Richard Schonberger. *Operations Management.* Homewood, IL: Irwin/McGraw-Hill, 2001.

Zuehlke, Barb. "To Beat the Competition . . . Companies Need to Get Products to Market Faster than Ever." *OEM Off Highway,* March 1995.

CASE 16-1
MARK APPLETON

In early February, Mark Appleton, senior contracts buyer for Browne and Coulter Engineering (BCE), found himself at odds with Sheila Forker, project engineer, on a small construction project. Mark believed it should be given to the low bidder, but Sheila did not agree.

BCE was a large engineering firm specializing in large, heavy custom-equipment manufacture. It was necessary for one of the current projects in the plant to construct a small testing laboratory with some unusually tight specifications on its sound-proofing.

Sheila Forker had asked Mark to request bids for the laboratory's construction and had sent along, as was customary, a list of recommended contractors. On looking over the four contractors engineering recommended, Mark believed BCE would not have much success with them. He, therefore, requested from Sheila Forker, the project engineer, permission to add two more names to the list: Andrews Construction and Moore Brothers.

When the six bids were received, only one of the four contractors engineering had recommended came in with what Mark believed to be a meaningful bid. Foster Construction bid $572,000. The other three companies recommended by Sheila had bids over $650,000, while Moore Brothers bid $604,000 and Andrews Construction bid $404,000. When Mark sent to Sheila his recommendation to go with Andrews, she refused it on the ground that BCE had no experience with Andrews and a "high level of comfort" with Foster. Because Foster had been on engineering's original list of recommended contractors, Sheila insisted this was the logical choice. Given the project's tight deadline Mark knew he had to resolve this issue quickly.

CASE 16-2
CASSON CONSTRUCTION

On May 20, Robert Casson, vice president of Casson Construction, a general contractor in Portland, Oregon, was considering the performance of the precast concrete subcontractor on a $1.9 million dollar, tightly scheduled, high-profile library renovation. He had just finished writing a letter to Langford Precast advising them of their breach of contract. Robert now wondered what action he should take to ensure the successful completion of the project.

Casson Construction. Robert Casson for the last two years had been in partnership with his father in the medium-sized general contracting firm, Casson Construction. Currently, the firm had contracts ranging from $100,000 to $5 million dollars under way in a variety of commercial, residential, industrial and institutional buildings. The firm was known in the local area for quality construction and teamwork. Robert's father described his objective on the library project as "to manage the project to create a partnership between the university, the design consultants, and the contractor in order to produce a building which everyone can look at with pride." He believed that in order for the team members to work together over the course of a project, everyone had to "bend a bit to accomplish something, not trying to point out a weakness and not taking advantage of someone's weakness." He hoped that his sons would continue to manage the business with this philosophy in mind when they took over the firm.

The Competitive Bid System. General contractors bid on new projects in competition with other contracting firms. A general contractor obtained working drawings for a new building from the architect or a local construction association, obtained prices from the various trades required to complete the project (steel, masonry, precast concrete, etc.), and submitted a price for constructing the building to the university. Universities frequently prequalified general contractors to ensure that the contractors who submitted bids had sufficient experience to carry out the work. Once the bids were submitted, the university would select the low bidder, ensure that the bid was in order, and award the firm the project. Occasionally, universities would not prequalify the contractors to open up the field of competition for new entrants on smaller projects.

The Library Renovation Project. The local university decided not to prequalify the general contractors prior to calling for the submission of bids for the renovation and addition to its Family Law Library. Casson Construction was eager to submit a bid on the project because the job was an opportunity for the firm to take on a large project for a substantial client with the prospect of significant future business.

When the bids were opened on November 10, Robert Casson knew that his firm's bid of $1,886,000 was low by $87,000 in relation to the next lowest bidder's bid. The contract would be a "nosebleed" for his firm and would have to be carefully managed to avoid incurring any additional time on the site that would eat up the firm's slim profit margin.

The Precast Subcontract. The work contained in the precast subcontract was divided into two categories, precast parking bumpers and architectural precast concrete. The precast parking bumpers were simple in shape and required a low level of finish. The architectural precast, which formed the surrounds for the windows and was incorporated in horizontal bands on the exterior walls of the building, was highly detailed and required several different sections of different lengths and profiles as well as a high degree of finish. During the bid period of the project, Casson Construction requested prices from two local precast concrete suppliers. Of the two, Langford Precast submitted the lower bid and was carried by Casson Construction in their bid price. Once Casson Construction had been

awarded the contract by the university, they issued a purchase order on December 4 to Langford Precast. Casson Construction had worked with Langford on other, less complicated jobs and, although they had had a few scheduling problems with Langford, both firms had managed to get the job done.

Project Management. The general contractor was responsible for the overall control of a project, from initial bid to completion, and employed the subcontractors for the specific trades. The individual subtrades on a typical project included everything from site services to the installation of washroom accessories. Casson Construction included a 4 percent fee on the value of subcontractors' work in its bid price for the management and coordination of subcontractors' work. As Project Manager for the library renovation, Robert Casson scheduled the work of the different subtrades on site and coordinated each subcontractor's work with the other trades.

Project Schedule. The university had dictated in the terms of the contract that the renovation project had to be substantially completed on August 6. Robert knew that the university was serious about the deadline because alternative space could not be arranged if the project was late and the faculty depended on the library to do research. If the project was late, the best that Robert Casson could hope for was that the university would charge his firm $1,000/day minimum for the use of alternative lecture halls. The worst-case scenario was that the university would never again consider a bid from his firm. No monetary value could be ascribed to the loss of the firm's reputation for on-time delivery.

Litigation in the Industry. In considering how to handle this situation, Robert could not help himself from thinking about a period of litigation he had just come through. Robert had been in court for 1½ weeks the previous month for a case which took place a year earlier on a townhouse project. Robert had taken over the project from another project manager and had opted to throw an excavation subcontractor off the job for breach of contract. The case cost Casson Construction $15,000 before it went to court and $25,000 in court. In the end, the judge ruled that Casson Construction should have nursed the subcontractor along through the job and then back-charged the firm for the delay at the end of the contract.

Langford Precast. Robert knew that as of May 20, Langford Precast had very little invested in the library project. Robert could not confirm exactly how much of the architectural precast had been produced in Langford's plant and was concerned that Langford would simply walk off the job if given the opportunity. If Langford abandoned the project, Robert knew it would take him at least five or six more weeks and cost a minimum of $20,000 to get another precast supplier on site. The original order was already five weeks late.

As Robert considered his options for managing Langford Precast and completing the project on time, he knew that there were four perspectives he had to consider—his firm's, Langford Precast's, the university's, and the legal eyes that would judge the case on the documentation provided in court if the problem could not be resolved now.

Robert had just finished writing a letter to Art Langford, president of Langford Precast, expressing his serious concerns. (See Exhibit 1). Although he hoped his letter would spur Langford on to complete the project, he wondered what action to take in case Langford failed to meet its commitment.

EXHIBIT 1   Letter Dated May 20, from Robert Casson to Mr. Art Langford, President, Langford Precast.

CASSON CONSTRUCTION

May 20

"Registered Mail"
"Copy Hand-Delivered"

Dear Art:

Re: Family Law Library Project

Purchase Order No. 310-6

We have advised your office several times on the importance of meeting the contract schedule.
The project must be substantially complete by August 6.

You were advised by us that your precast was expected to arrive as per our construction schedule during the first two (2) weeks of April.

During a meeting on March 2, you advised both the Architect and me that meeting the schedule date would not be a problem.

You also advised at the aforementioned meeting that the following items, required by the contract documents, would be complied with immediately.

1. Resubmittal of your shop drawings conforming to the Architect's comments made on your initial "revise and resubmit" shop drawing submittal.

2. Submittal of a color and texture sample by March 8.
   Actual color and texture sample was submitted to the Architect on this site May 6.

3. Submittal of actual precast shapes by March 15.
   One precast shape was submitted for approval May 6.

In addition, you have indicated verbally to us that your planned production time, for the entire order, is approximately twelve (12) working days.

Well, it is now May 20, and you have not yet delivered a single piece of precast.

We have attempted to be understanding in this situation. We have ignored the several outstanding telephone messages left by both my superintendent and myself. We have offered site dimensions. We have rescheduled other site work around your late delivery.

As of late, you verbally advised me that you would ship May 14. Then you advised me May 17. Then you advised my superintendent May 18. This type of scheduling inconsistency is a nuisance, however, your order is already a minimum five (5) weeks late.

As in the past, we feel it necessary to advise you that your failure to deliver your product is delaying the installation of the stone veneer. The lack of the stone veneer installation is delaying the overall production schedule of the project.

If the project is not substantially complete by August 6, the University will incur costs and will very likely seek to legally recover these costs.

The delay of the project completion will at the very least damage our reputation with this Client. More than likely, the delay will result in litigation between ourselves and the University.

We will have no choice but to litigate with any subtrade or supplier who has substantially delayed the project schedule in order to recover our damages.

Surely, you can appreciate the magnitude of the situation. Our potential losses would far exceed the entire value of your contract.

Please deliver your precast order immediately.

Yours truly,

Robert Casson

17 SERVICES PURCHASING

Chapter Outline

Key Questions for the Purchasing Decision Maker

SHOULD WE
- Improve the way we evaluate service suppliers?
- Be concerned with the service purchases that are not handled by the purchasing department?
- Have closer involvement with service requisitioners?

HOW CAN WE
- Improve our service make-or-buy decisions?
- Change our service quality assurance?
- Get better value for our service dollar?
- Work more effectively with the user of the service?

Services

The effective acquisition of services represents a significant challenge. Thus far, in this text, the prime focus has been on the acquisition of products, raw materials, purchased parts, equipment, and MRO items. Normally, in these purchases it is recognized that service is a factor in evaluating the best buy. Service in this context includes, but is not limited to, installation; training of the purchasers, operators, or staff; technical advice; maintenance; provision of backup capacity or people; trouble-shooting; documentation; quality control assistance; inspection; translation; and so on. Almost invariably, however, the product emphasis is primary and the service dimension secondary in the overall purchase decision. One notable exception, of course, has been the purchase of transportation, a common service purchase covered in Chapter 10.

Services which may have to be acquired by any organization are extremely diverse. For example, a brief and far-from-complete listing might include:

Examples of Services

Advertising	Courier services
Architectural	Customs brokerage
Auditing	Data processing
Banking	Demolition
Cafeteria/catering	Engineering design
Computer programming	Environmental cleanup
Construction	Hazardous waste disposal
Consulting	Health benefit plans
Contract packaging	Household/office moves

Information systems	Research & development
Inspections	Sales promotion
Insurance	Security
Interior decorating/space planning	Signage
Janitorial	Snow removal
Landscaping/lawn service	Space/storage rental
Legal	Telephone
Mail services	Temporary help
Maintenance	Training
Medical	Transport of goods
Payroll	Trash removal/disposal
Photography	Travel (air, hotel, auto rental)
Property management	Utilities (electric, gas, water)
Records management	Vending
Recruiting/outplacement	Workers' compensation
Reproduction/copying	insurance

This chapter provides a framework for dealing with the acquisition of services in the traditional context as well as those situations where the acquisition of a service is primary. This chapter focuses on understanding services better, followed by a discussion of the acquisition process used for services.

How Significant Are the Dollars Spent for Services?

Tracking Service Purchase Dollars Is Difficult

A Center for Advanced Purchasing Studies (CAPS) research project completed in 1995 focused on the breakdown in the firm of the dollars spent for goods compared to the dollars spent for services, and how the dollars paid out to service suppliers could be spent more effectively.[1] The average expenditure of the 116 large organizations in the study for the total of all categories of the 20 goods and 69 services was $1.21 billion and probably was understated due to the difficulty some organizations have in tracking purchase dollars.

Over half (54 percent) of the purchase dollars were spent for services, not for goods. This was true for the total number of organizations as well as for the organizations in both the service and governmental sectors. But in the manufacturing sector, as one might expect, the dollars spent for goods were larger than for services. Table 17-1 shows the numbers, highlighting the significance of the services purchasing decisions.[2]

---

[1] Harold E. Fearon and William A. Bales, *Purchasing of Nontraditional Goods and Services* (Tempe, AZ: Center for Advanced Purchasing Studies, 1995); p. 73.

[2] Ibid., p. 8.

TABLE 17-1   Goods versus Services Spend

	Percent of Total Purchase Dollars Spent for:	
	Goods	*Services*
Total of 116 Organizations	46	54
59 manufacturing firms	61	39
23 service firms	19	81
34 governmental organizations	38	62

Purchasing Department Involvement

Of the 54 percent of the total purchase dollars which the CAPS study showed were spent for services, the 10 largest categories of service purchase items (percent of *total purchase* dollars and percent of *total service purchase* dollars) and the percent of these purchases that are handled by the purchasing department are shown in Table 17-2.[3] Of these services purchases, utilities account for 4.8 percent of the total dollars spent by the organization (only 26 percent of these dollars are handled by purchasing); insurance accounts for 4.4 percent of the total, but only 6 percent by the purchasing department; sales/promotion is 3.9 percent of the total, with 48 percent handled by the purchasing department; health benefit plans is 3.3 percent of total, with only 5 percent handled by the purchasing department; and travel: air tickets accounts for 3.1 percent of total spend, with the purchasing department handling only 12 percent of those purchases.

Magnitude of Dollars Spent on Services

Two surprises are evident from an analysis of the data in Table 17-2. First is the sheer magnitude of the dollars spent for purchased services. In total, an organization spends more for services than for goods. Just the 10 service categories listed account for almost a third (31.4 percent) of the total dollars spent for purchases. Obviously, a reduction of even 5 percent in overall prices paid to buy these 10 services would have a *major* impact on an organization's profitability. Second is the surprisingly low involvement of the purchasing department in the buying of services. Overall, it handles only 27 percent of the service dollars spent. In only one category (consultants—55 percent) is the purchasing department handling half-or-more of the dollars spent. There are three explanations for this: (1) The complexity of specifying service needs and analyzing potential service providers means that the user has greater expertise than the purchasing department. (2) The buying of services involves more of a personal relationship between the service supplier and user. Goods purchasing, on the other hand, is based more on a business relationship between the goods supplier and the purchasing department. (3) Many services in the past have been available only in a governmentally-regulated environment, in which the price and

Low Purchasing Involvement in Services Purchasing

[3]Ibid., p. 21.

TABLE 17-2   **Dollars Spent for Purchase of Services, as Percent of Total Purchase Dollars, and Percent of Total Service Dollars; Percent of Service Purchase Dollars Handled by Purchasing Department**

Total Service Purchase Dollars and Top 10 Categories	Percent of Total Purchase Dollars	Percent of Total Service Purchase Dollars	Percent of Dollars Spent by Purchasing Department
Total services	54.0	100.0	27
Utilities	4.8	9.0	26
Insurance	4.4	8.2	6
Sales/Promotion	3.9	7.2	48
Health benefit plans	3.3	6.1	5
Travel: air tickets	3.1	5.8	12
Construction	2.6	4.9	42
Consultants	2.6	4.8	55
Transport of goods	2.5	4.7	33
Banking	2.2	4.2	0
Copying	2.0	3.6	19

service-delivery requirements were essentially the same from all suppliers. Or, in some instances, there was only one source available. The utility, insurance, health delivery, airline passenger, and freight movement industries are examples where regulated monopolies were common and little competition existed. In short, it probably didn't make much difference who the supplier was (and the firm may not have had any choice), and the price was not negotiable.

Opportunities For Cost Reduction

This situation has changed substantially, starting in the 1980s. The philosophy of deregulation caused many of the governmentally-protected monopolies to be disbanded, and firms in the utility, freight movement, air passenger travel, and health-care industries now have to compete for business. Price and service aspects are negotiable. The purchasing department, with its knowledge of the purchasing process, is now assuming a larger role in the purchase decisions on the acquisition of services. And it is having success in buying such services ". . . from airplane tickets and telephones to computer classes . . . the leverage in trimming [such costs] is enormous." Companies are discovering in services ". . . a lost, lush continent for cost reduction."[4]

What Makes Services Different?

Inability to Store

One of the most-commonly-mentioned special attributes of services deals with the inability to store services. This attribute arises because many ser-

---

[4]Shawn Tully, "Purchasing's New Muscle," *Fortune,* February 20, 1995, p. 76.

vices are processes (which may or may not be associated with a product). This implies that timing of the delivery has to coincide with the purchaser's specific needs and that the consequences of improper timing may be very serious and costly. Suppliers, trying to service a variety of customers, need to ensure that sufficient capacity is available to satisfy the needs of all.

Difficult to Assess Quality

The inability to store many services also creates quality assurance difficulties. It may not be possible to inspect a service before its delivery. And, by the time of delivery, it may be too late to do anything about it. Anyone who has ever suffered through a boring speaker or a bad airline flight will attest to that.

Intangible Nature

The specification and measurement of quality in a service may present significant difficulties. Frequently, services have both a tangible and an intangible component. In writing about the hospitality industry, Dr. William Martin identified the procedural and the convivial sides of hospitality services.[5] The procedural side deals with the ways in which customers' product needs are effectively and efficiently met. The convivial side deals with what the customer expects in addition to satisfactory food and drink. In his words,

Restaurant Example

> It deals with the need to be liked, the need to be respected, the need for social interaction, the need to feel important, the need to be relaxed, comfortable, and pampered, and the need to enjoy the company of other people in a welcoming environment.[6]

From the restaurant's perspective, conviviality is provided when the service crew shows a genuine personal interest in customers. Such interest is displayed when service personnel are friendly, courteous, and enthusiastic; when they show they appreciate their customers' patronage; when they are knowledgeable about the products they are selling; when they use sales techniques tactfully and effectively; and when they strive to meet each customer's unique expectations for quality service. In short, conviviality means that service personnel have people skills.

Of course, judgment is a third component of the mix. It allows personnel to deal with unusual events and special requests, and it gives them the overall ability to adjust to the circumstances as they arise.

A Framework for Analyzing Services

It is important to recognize that not all services are the same. The variation between services may affect the acquisition perspective. From an acquisition point of view, the following should be considered: value, repetitiveness, tangibility, direction, production, nature of demand, nature of delivery, degree of customization, and the skills required for producing the service. Each of these will be discussed in turn.

---

[5]William B. Martin, *Quality Service: The Restaurant Manager's Bible* (Ithaca, N.Y.: Cornell University, School of Hotel Administration, 1986).
[6]Ibid., p. 33.

Goal: Attain Best Value

It is useful to recognize that, ultimately, the goal of effective acquisition of services is to obtain best value. In this sense there is no difference between the acquisition of services and goods. And the best buy in services represents the appropriate trade-off between quality, delivery, quantity, cost, continuity, flexibility, and other relevant factors. Determination of the need and the ability to assess what should be considered best value in any particular service present the real challenges in the acquisition process.

Value of the Service

Applying ABC Analysis to Service Purchases

One very broad cut at services would be to classify them as high, medium, or low value. This could be done in the typical ABC/Pareto analysis. Obviously, from an economic value perspective, greater acquisition attention should be spent on the high-value services. Value in this context is probably best expressed as a combination of money spent on this service in one shot, or over a specific time period, such as a year. It also should be recognized that some services may require a very careful acquisition process because of the potential impact they could have on the whole organization. For example, the improper removal of asbestos from a building may make the whole building unusable. A consultant to assist in the long-term strategic planning of the organization may have a very significant, long-term impact.

Degree of Repetitiveness

Inhouse or Outsourced Buying Expertise

For the acquisition of repetitive services, it may be possible to develop an acquisition system and specialized expertise within the organization. For example, it would be appropriate to have specialized buying expertise in the acquisition of maintenance and security services. On the other hand, for unique service requirements, special assistance may have to be sought outside of the organization, and the acquisition may be handled on a project basis.

Degree of Tangibility

By definition, every service tends to have an intangible dimension, such as the conviviality dimension in the hospitality industry. Even so, some services can be seen as more tangible than others. For example, an architect will produce a drawing or a design which can be examined by others and which ultimately will result in a physical structure. Although the structural features of the physical representation of the design can be examined, the aesthetic features of the design are much more difficult to evaluate and subject to a wide variety of responses. On the other hand, the advice from a consultant on a new marketing strategy may be almost totally intangible.

Establishing Standards is Difficult

The development of standards in any contract for services is obviously difficult. Sometimes it is possible to get around this by using expressions of satisfaction or dissatisfaction by various users or experts as a substitute. For example, how many complaints are received about the cleanliness of the building? Or, how many experts believe the software program to be acceptable? It should be recognized that the selection of experts or evaluators in itself represents a statistical quality problem. Some people may be more eager than others to express their opinions, and their views may not be representative of the whole group. Relying solely on complaints may give a biased response.

One way to deal with the acquisition of intangible services is to substitute qualifications for the people or equipment providing the service. For example, the number of personnel in the organization who have appropriate training in the particular discipline, and the capability of the various pieces of equipment, can be specified ahead of time. Similarly, it may be possible to poll a number of clients of the organization to determine their satisfaction with the particular supplier. Unfortunately, many segments of the service sector are plagued by high personnel turnover, and the addition or loss of a few key people can make a significant difference in any one firm. Nevertheless, many important services, such as professional services, either are not plagued by turnover or are such that turnover is planned for, such as in food and janitorial services.

Direction of the Service

Service for People or Buildings and Equipment

Another aspect of service deals with whether or not it is directed at people. For example, food services are for people; maintenance services may be for buildings or equipment. When services are directed at people, it is important to recognize the special needs of the persons who will be most affected by the service. The ultimate user likely will play a major role in both the specification of the service and the assessment of whether satisfactory quality has, in fact, been delivered. If services directed at people have an important intangible component, assessment may require a period of exposure of both supplier personnel and purchaser personnel to each other to determine compatibility. In baby-sitting, for example, is it the parents or the children, or both, who determine the selection?

Production of the Service

Services Produced by Equipment

Services can be produced by people or equipment, or a combination of both. Services of low labor intensity may have a high capital or asset component. Typical examples would include real estate and equipment rentals, computer processing, transportation, and communication services as well as custom processing of a machine-intensive nature. In the specification stage, understanding the underlying technology or asset base is important. During the acquisition stage, potential suppliers can be assessed on the basis of their asset capacity and availability as well as the state of their technology. The delivery of this kind of service is more likely at the location of the supplier's premises or of its equipment, although hookup may be directly to the purchaser's site. Quality monitoring and evaluation may be process oriented, with emphasis on the performance of the underlying capital asset.

Services Produced by People

Services with high labor intensity include activities like hand harvesting, installation and maintenance, education, health support, and security, as well as the full range of professional activities like consulting, engineering, accounting, medical, and architectural services. Here the quality of the "people component" is the primary concern.

Services involving largely lower- to medium-skilled people may focus more on cost minimization and efficiency. Services requiring highly skilled individuals may require the purchaser to distinguish between levels of professional skill and may require extensive ongoing communication between requisitioner and purchaser through all phases of the acquisition process.

Nature of the Demand

Continuous, Periodic, and Discrete Services

The demand for a particular service may be continuous, periodic, or discrete. The typical example of a continuous service may be insurance, or a 24-hour, around-the-clock security service. A discrete or one-shot service may be the acquisition of an interior decorator to suggest a new color scheme for an office complex. The continuous service may provide the opportunity to monitor progress and make alterations as information about the quality of service becomes evident. For discrete services, the monitoring capability may have to be shifted to the various stages in the delivery production, if this is possible. The real problem here may be that by the time the service is delivered, it is too late to make significant changes. Periodic service may be regular, such as once a week or once a month, as with regular inspections, or it may vary with need, as in repair services.

Nature of Service Delivery

Service Delivery on Buyer's Premises

The nature and place of service delivery may have significant acquisition repercussions. For example, if the delivery of the service occurs on the premises of the purchaser, the contract agreement may have to address a number of provisions. For example, in construction or installation services, questions of security, access, nature of dress, hours of work, applicability of various codes for health and safety, what working days and hours are applicable, and what equipment and materials are to be provided by whom are all issues that need to be addressed as part of the contract.

Service Delivery on Supplier's Premises

On the other hand, when the service is provided on the supplier's premises or elsewhere, many of these concerns may not arise, provided the service is not directed at personnel of the purchaser.

Degree of Customization

It makes a substantial difference whether a service is standard or is customized specifically for the purchaser. Generally speaking, the less the con-

Standard Services are Easier to Specify

sumer contact, the more standard the service becomes, and, probably, the less the importance of intangibles. Specification of these kinds of services probably is easier because of the standardization and the common nature of the purchase. With many purchasers in the market, standard specifications probably are available. If there are many suppliers, it may be possible to use competitive bidding techniques, expect quantity discounts, and use a standard type of supplier evaluation.

With highly customized services, the specification process may become more difficult and the options more difficult to understand. The involvement of the end consumers in this specification process then becomes more important. The possibility of trade-offs in various make-or-buy suboptions needs to be explored before final specifications are agreed to. The acquisition process itself may be less definite, because various suppliers may offer substantially different options. Evaluation of supplier performance may have to recognize the purchaser's share of responsibility for quality at the point of delivery.

Skills Required for the Service

Cost/Benefit Analysis of Skills

The production of a service may require a full range of skills, from unskilled on the one extreme to highly skilled on the other. In services requiring relatively unskilled labor, such as grass cutting and other simple maintenance tasks, price emphasis is likely to be high and ease of entry into (and exit from) the service also may be high. On the other extreme, the acquisition of highly skilled services may focus far more on qualifications of the skilled persons, concern over the specific persons who will be performing the service, and recommendations from other skilled persons and users. Frequently, in highly professional services the cost of the professional service may be relatively low compared to the benefit expected. For example, a good design may increase sales substantially; a good architect may be able to design a low-cost, but effective structure; and a good consulting recommendation may turn a whole organization around. It often is difficult to deal with this trade-off between the estimated cost for the job versus the estimated benefits.

The Acquisition Process for Services

Four Areas of Service Acquisition

Thus far, the discussion has centered primarily on understanding the nature of the service to be acquired. Now, the acquisition process used for services is discussed to highlight several unique dimensions. Four areas of the acquisition process are covered: (1) need recognition and specification; (2) analysis of supply alternatives, including sourcing, pricing, and options; (3) the purchase agreement, including special provisions; and (4) contract administration, including follow-up, quality control, payment, records, and supplier management and evaluation.

Need Recognition and Specification

Those in purchasing must ask some very basic questions regarding any service. Typical questions include: Why is this service necessary? What is important about this service? What represents good value? How is quality defined for the service? How is the service produced? How do we know we received what we expected?

The SOW is the Basis of the Contract

Developing the Statement of Work (SOW). The statement of work (SOW) is the document that describes the needs of the internal customer, communicates those needs to the supplier, and ultimately becomes the basis of the service contract. The user(s), the buyer, and a key supplier(s) may be involved in its development. Unwritten user expectations will either not be met or end up as an issue during the contract negotiations rather than being part of the proposals prepared by potential sources. The SOW also provides the buyer with a basis for assessing the supply market to determine the feasibility of a supplier meeting the user's requirements within the established parameters (price, time-frame, quality, etc.). A sample statement of work for a janitorial service is shown in Figure 17-1.

The characteristics of the particular service to be acquired can be checked against those discussed earlier in this chapter to establish priority and areas of concern. The need for user involvement in need recognition and definition is high in many services because of the user-supplier interface, so common in most services, and the importance of nontangible factors. Careful documentation of need requirements, including the necessity for nontangibles, is the foundation on which a sound acquisition approach is based. Sound documentation will facilitate supplier search and selection, contract

FIGURE 17-1

Sample statement of work for a janitorial service:[7]

- Description of premises to be cleaned (including space maps if necessary).
- Specific description of services to be provided (for example, uncarpeted floors shall be wet-mopped, dried, and spray buffed; all wax marks shall be removed from baseboards).
- Frequency of services (nightly, weekly, monthly, quarterly) outlined by area (for example, lobby, kitchen areas, elevators).
- Specification of any materials to be used (such as cleaning agents or polishes) and how they are to be obtained.
- Reports or other required periodic documentation.
- Insurance requirements (for example, automobile liability, commercial general liability, workers' compensation) and liability.

[7]Michelle B. Knepper and Mark K. Lindsey, "Clean up Your Act," *Purchasing Today,* March 1999, p. 47.

content and administration, and quality control. Where possible, measurable attributes or actions which are part of the service need to be identified and quantified. Also, if the service can be broken down into chronological stages, it will be useful to detail progress due dates or milestones. For example, for an employee morale survey, the supplier's due dates might be:

Progress Due Dates

Overall Research Design—February 1,

Questionnaire Design—April 1,

Questionnaire Administration—June 1, and

Survey Results Report—September 1.

It is important to recognize that the accompanying commitments for the purchasing organization need to be agreed to, for example:

Overall Research Design Review—January 15,

Questionnaire Approval—March 15,

Employees Available for Questionnaire Administration—April 1 to June 1, and

Preliminary Results Report Review—August 15.

In many services, the need recognition and definition require a dual definition. It is necessary to document exactly what it is that the supplier will provide, and also what the purchaser will do to help the supplier perform as required. Value analysis techniques can and should be applied to service need definition. Early involvement of purchasing with users during need recognition and definition is essential in the appropriate search for value.

Analysis of Supply Alternatives

In the acquisition of services, the analysis of supply alternatives includes sourcing, pricing, and source options, as well as make or buy.

Service Suppliers Are Often Small

Sourcing. In sourcing, it is useful to recognize that many service organizations are relatively small. Therefore, many of the characteristics of small suppliers are likely to be considerations in dealing with service organizations. If the service supplier is small, there also is a high likelihood that it will be a local source.

In sourcing, references from other users are particularly useful and should be checked carefully. A typical parallel in consumer buying is the value of a word-of-mouth reference in selecting a restaurant. A typical checklist for rating potential consultants might include factors like: reputation, relevant experience, integrity, size, fees, availability, quality and background of personnel, timetable for the work, consulting approach, capability to train and communicate, and even personal chemistry. Each factor would have to be weighted and each consultant rated accordingly.

Pricing. Pricing in services may be fixed or variable, by the job or by the hour, day, or week. Prices may be obtained by competitive bid if the size of the contract warrants it; enough competitors are available; and adequate, specific, consistent specifications can be prepared.

Negotiation is another common method for establishing prices and may be the only option in sole-source situations. In services, purchasing clout does count and it can be used effectively by the knowledgeable purchaser. Understanding the cost structure of the service will be helpful in revealing negotiation opportunities.

Estimating Time Required May Be Difficult

In some situations it may be difficult to estimate the total time required for a given service task, and with professional services it is not unusual to give estimates of professional time required without committing to a specific figure. Most purchasers probably would prefer such contracts to have a "not to exceed limit." Some professionals, such as architects, may quote their fee based on a percentage of the total job cost. But from a purchasing standpoint, this removes the incentive for the architect to seek the best value for the total job.

Other terms and conditions. Besides price, service agreements may also include clauses on confidentiality, discounts, warranties, limitations of liability, and indemnification as well as anything specific or unique to that purchase.

For example, when contracting for consulting services, the contract might include a warranty clause, an independent contractor clause, a work product clause, and a non-disclosure clause.[8]

Warranty Clause. Depending on the clarity of functional requirements and the availability of objective criteria for assessing performance, the buyer may be able to negotiate a warranty for the consultant's work. If the work is unacceptable, the clause may require the consultant to redo it at no additional charge until it is acceptable. If the functional requirements are vague, it will be more difficult to find a consultant who will agree to this clause.

Independent Contractor Clause. To protect the buying organization, it is important to meet the IRS requirements for hiring an independent contractor and to include a clause stating that the contractor is independent and therefore responsible for filing his or her own taxes.

Work Product Clause. This clause will assign the ownership of the work product to the buying organization. While large consulting firms may not be willing to agree to this, many smaller consulting firms will. Even if ownership does not pass to the buying organization, the contract should require documentation of the work product to avoid future problems.

---

[8]Sara L. Vinas, "When You Want Renoir Instead of Picasso," *Consulting Services Guide — Supplement to Purchasing Today,* August 1999, p. 5.

Non-Disclosure Clause.   The contractor should be contractually obligated to keep the buying organization's information confidential. Consultants sell their services to many companies, some of whom may be competitors, and this clause can provide a remedy short of going to court.

RFPs Allow for Supplier Ingenuity

Source Options. Requests for proposal (RFP) are also common in a variety of services where the purchaser believes that supplier ingenuity or skill may reveal options not apparent to the purchaser. Proper briefing of potential bidders is still required so that every supplier fully and correctly understands the need to be fulfilled. The difficulty for purchasers with widely varying proposals is one of assessing which is superior. Moreover, the preparation of such a proposal may be expensive and may have to be paid for by the purchaser to ensure proper competition and proposal quality.

Trend Toward Outsourcing

Make or Buy in Services. Almost invariably, the question of make or buy is an important one in the acquisition of services. There appears to be a current trend to subcontracting out services traditionally performed in-house. Typical examples are security, food service, and maintenance, but also legal, engineering, software development, training, and other professional services traditionally performed in-house. Moreover, particularly with services, the option of partially making or partially buying may be present. For example, in auditing, the preparation of schedules can be left to the inside accountants, or to the outside auditors. An interior decorator may specify colors and furnishings but leave the purchasing to the procurement department and the painting and installation to the internal maintenance staff. On the other hand, the whole task could be purchased on a turnkey basis. The disassembly, repair, cleaning, and reassembly of equipment might be performed in-house, whereas regrinding or recalibration of key parts might be done outside.

A study by Arthur Andersen and the Economist Intelligence Unit, based on interviews with 50 global organizations and a survey of 303 senior executives in North America and Europe, concluded that corporate outsourcing would continue and grow. It characterized outsourcing "as a competitive tool, rather than just a simple means of cost control." Key findings were that 85 percent of the survey group outsource all, or at least part, of one business function and:

Business Functions Outsourced

- Legal work is outsourced by 59 percent of the firms, followed by shipping (41 percent), computer information systems (36 percent), and production-manufacturing (31 percent).

- 26 percent outsource at least one financial function. In whole or in part, 42 percent outsource pension management, followed by tax (40 percent), payroll (28 percent), and asset appraisal/valuation (24 percent).[9]

---

[9]"Growth in Outsourcing to Continue, Study Finds," *Investor's Business Daily,* December 28, 1995, p. A4.

An alert purchaser always should be on the lookout for opportunities to substitute low-cost, in-house work for high-cost, outside work. The reverse, of course, also holds true. If inside costs are high and outside costs are low and no other considerations are relevant, it provides much better value to have work done outside. Understanding the full nature of the service and how the various costs are built up for the service is, therefore, an important consideration in assessing the make-or-buy trade-off.

In or after periods of organizational downsizing it is not unusual to find firms who have let employees go or choose early retirement in a "rehire as a consultant" mode. This way valuable experience can still be accessed, but normally not on a full-time basis or for an extended period of time.

The Purchase Agreement

The purchase agreement for services usually is called a service contract or contract for services. It may be short or long term, a standard or custom document. A service level agreement (SLA) is the document that details the means, method, organization, and processes along with material requirements.

Service Contract Types Vary

Services lend themselves to a large variety of contract types, including fixed price, unit price, cost-plus-percentage-fee, cost-plus-fixed-fee, or incentive contracts. Many professional service providers try to use standard contracts agreed to by their professional association. Frequently, the associations even have guidelines as to appropriate fee structures and contracts for a particular kind of work. A purchaser never should feel compelled to accept these contracts as they are.

Most organizations over time develop contract language to suit their own needs and the specific service to be acquired. This tends to result in a wide range of different contracts, each with its own service-specific language. Thus, a security service contract will appear totally different from a contract for corporate maintenance, food service, or marketing consulting. Suppliers in each service area will be anxious to suggest the use of their own contracts. In the case of low-value services, using such a standard contract may be the simplest and least expensive solution.

Buyer-Service Provider Relationships. Buyer-supplier relationships are just as important with service providers as with sellers of goods. The large dollars spent on services and third-party providers directs attention to longer-term relationships. Buyers may decide to enter into long-term agreements, including partnering arrangements and alliances, with key service providers. Given the importance of people in the service quality equation, working toward more seamless relationships with service providers is a logical approach. Buyers cannot expect suppliers to share risks without also being willing to share rewards. It is important to develop ways to measure productivity gains along with bonus systems or other means of sharing these gains equitably. (See Chapter 8.)

Service Contract Administration

Service contract administration includes follow-up, quality control and supplier evaluation, payment, records, and other aspects of contract administration.

Follow-Up. Follow-up and expediting in services may require internal as well as supplier checking. Therefore, responsibility for follow-up with the supplier appropriately may be placed in the user department to help ensure user compliance with prior commitments and deadlines, while follow-up on internal commitments may become a joint responsibility for purchasing as well as the supplier. It is this commonly extensive user interface with supplier personnel during service delivery, and often before, that also affects other aspects of contract administration. For example, if a service is performed on site after-hours, security check-in sheets and access systems may be used to verify work patterns or area activity. Periodic site visits and a walk-through of the facility with the supplier's representative may lead to a better understanding of user needs. Some form of benchmarking against other providers may also be useful.

Quality Control and Supplier Evaluation. In highly tangible services, such as construction, quality control can be geared heavily toward the measurement of the tangible, in ways similar to standard quality assurance and control. Two aspects of service, the intangible and the noninventory, can create special quality measurement difficulties. The intangible dimension makes it more difficult to assess proper quality. All aspects of the ability of the actual service provider(s) (people) to consistently perform the service at the desired quality level are vital to the performance evaluation process. Were the supplier's personnel sufficiently courteous when dealing with the purchaser's employees? This may be measured by a survey, or by number of complaints received, but it is important to recognize that any standard, at best, will be imprecise.

Because the nature of many services prevents storage, delivery tends to be instantaneous. In other words, quality control will have to be performed while the service delivery is in progress, or afterward. And, it may be difficult to interrupt the process, even if simultaneous quality control is possible. Therefore, the quality risk in services may be relatively high compared to the purchase of products. In cases of quality failure, it may not be possible to return the services for a full refund.

Post-service evaluation is an essential component in effective service acquisition. The same checklist for consultants as used in sourcing, for example, can be used for post-service evaluation. At the very least, an informal evaluation should include two questions:

1. Did your problem or issue get resolved to your satisfaction?
2. Would you rehire this consultant in the future for another problem or issue?

Joint Responsibility of Internal User and Buyer

Quality Risk May Be High

Post-service Quality Evaluation

Additional questions regarding conformance to expectations of quality, timeliness, and cost are, of course, appropriate as well as feedback on the professionalism and service orientation of the consultant personnel.

Quality risk avoidance may be achieved by doing business with service suppliers found to be satisfactory in the past, by avoiding repeat business with suppliers who did not do a good job, by careful checking of suppliers beforehand with other users with similar needs, and careful pre-service delivery communication with the supplier and service users to ensure common understanding of requirements and expectations.

Five Dimensions of Service Quality

A formal service quality evaluation process developed by Parasuraman, Zeithaml, and Berry identifies five quality dimensions:

Reliability: ability to perform the promised service dependably and accurately

Responsiveness: willingness to help customers and provide prompt service

Assurance: knowledge and courtesy of employees and their ability to inspire trust and confidence

Empathy: caring, individualized attention the firm provides its customers

Tangibles: physical facilities, equipment, and appearance of personnel.[10]

The survey process measures the gap between service expectations along each dimension and the perceptions of actual service performance.

Payment Terms Vary

Payment. Payment for services may vary somewhat from payment for goods. Some services require prepayment, such as an eminent speaker; some immediately upon delivery, such as hospitality services; whereas others can be delayed. Small suppliers may find it difficult to offer extended payment terms, and early payment may be used as the inducement for price or other concessions sought by the purchaser. Progress payments are usual for large contracts spread over time, whereas regular payments are appropriate for ongoing services such as building maintenance or food service.

Records and Other Aspects of Contract Administration. As in all purchases, the need for proper records hardly needs to be reinforced for the acquisition of services. Part of the difficulty may be the feedback loop from user to purchasing and the retrievability of information regarding the service per-

---

[10]A. Parasuraman, V. A. Zeithaml, and L. L. Berry, "A Conceptual Model of Service Quality and Its Implications for the Future," *Journal of Marketing,* Fall 1985, pp. 41–50; and "SERVQUAL: A Multiple-Item Scale for Measuring Consumer Perceptions of Service Quality," *Journal of Retailing,* Spring 1988, pp. 12–40. These two references likely were the first presentations of this approach.

formed. Unless care is taken to preserve this information, it may be lost for future reference and consideration.

Changes to Service Contract Difficult

It is almost inevitable that contract administration for services will encounter the need for changes subsequent to contract signing. Delivery dates, the nature of the service, the quality of the service, the place for delivery, and other aspects may require change. What may seem like an innocuous change to the purchaser may be very difficult or expensive for the supplier. For example, a one-week delay in delivery may back the supplier into a serious capacity constraint. This is one reason why big weddings are always planned a long time in advance. The reverse also may happen. A supplier request for change may make life very difficult for the purchaser. Thus, mechanisms, as well as timely interaction between the appropriate representatives of supplier and buyer, need to be in place to deal with changes as necessary. Changes may be very costly and affect budget status and a host of other dimensions. Before changes are agreed to, both purchaser and seller need to assess the impact on their own organizations and the contract changes arising from them, including price. Obviously, if flexibility to change already is foreseen as important before contract signing, this should be addressed as part of the original need description. Then, in the search for a suitable supplier, flexibility becomes a key sourcing criterion, which later is written into the contract. According to Carolyn Gordon, contractor administrator with Anchorage Telephone Utility, sometimes you don't know until the contract administration period that you left something out of the SOW. In those situations, "You have to negotiate — not necessarily because [something is] not in the contract — but you negotiate putting it in the contract. Sometimes this happens. That's a reality. You can't cover everything. There are going to be changes. That's true with any professional or consulting contract."[11]

Changes Often Driven By Inadequate Description of Need

Getting Greater Supply Involvement

The opportunity to increase profits in an organization through more effective purchasing and supply management probably is greater in the acquisition of services than in goods. Why? A larger amount of money is spent for purchases of services (54 percent of the total purchase dollar) than for goods (46 percent), and the services purchases probably have not received the amount of attention in the past as the goods purchases decisions. Services purchases will receive greater attention today, as firms explore more fully all avenues to increasing profits and return on investment.

In most organizations the purchasing department has far less involvement in the buying of services than in purchasing goods. If the purchasing department were to get more involved (and services is a natural for team buying, consisting of user and purchasing department), the logical purchasing

---

[11]Derrick C. Schnebelt, "Putting It In the SOW," *NAPM Insights,* November 1, 1995, p. 39.

process it could bring to the team-buying decision process should result in substantial savings. Areas where large dollar savings are possible include advertising, banking, construction, consultants, copying, health benefit plans, insurance, sales promotion, space rental, temporary help, transport of goods, travel, utilities, and workers' compensation insurance.

Purchasing Can Add Value to Services Buying

In many organizations the effectiveness of services purchasing is not measured and probably could be improved substantially. The CEO in many organizations realizes that services purchases often are made without input from the purchasing department; he or she needs to evaluate whether this is the most effective way to handle it and, if not, make changes. "The 'purchasing buck' stops with the CEO. He or she must (1) set the right environment for effective spending, (2) insist that the accounting system identifies who spends money and how much, and (3) make sure the effectiveness of purchasing decisions is measured."[12] The ability of an organization to track the dollars spent on services and identify who (which department) makes the spending decision is probably the key to achieving the savings potential.

Process for Obtaining Results

Ten Steps to Greater Purchasing Involvement

Based on the experience of firms in which their purchasing departments successfully became involved in the buying of advertising; real estate; health benefits; PC/workstations, peripheral hardware, and support/service; and utilities, a 1995 Center for Advanced Purchasing Studies report suggested a 10-step process (or questions) for results:

1. Do the people now in the purchasing department have the skills needed for purchasing services?
2. Do they have the time? Can they make the time?
3. Obtain data on what services are bought, by whom, and the dollar amounts.
4. Take one area at a time.
5. Establish the team: the user(s), possibly finance and quality assurance, and supply.
6. Determine if the buying of the service, as now done, satisfies the user and represents effective spending.
7. The purchasing department should ensure that a logical purchasing process is used to make service purchasing decisions and arrive at the contract or agreement. The actual purchase order then can be handled (written) by the using department, but it is simply a release against the agreement.

---

[12]Harold E. Fearon and William A. Bales, *Purchasing of Nontraditional Goods and Services,* op. cit., p. 9.

8. All parties—user, supplier, and buyer—must agree on the specification.

9. If use of the logical purchasing process dictates that a change should be made in specification, supplier, price, terms, and so on, the purchasing department should make sure that the using department and senior management know what change(s) was made, and why.

10. If the purchase of a particular service currently is being done by some department other than purchasing, and it is being measured, and it is being done effectively, then leave it alone. As the saying goes, "If it ain't broke, don't fix it!"[13]

It is possible to make a matrix out of the various considerations in service acquisition. A simplified summary is provided in Table 17-3, highlighting the significant points in service nature and acquisition. Moreover, as in all other purchases, each service tends to have its own nomenclature, language, tradition, standard practices, technology, and so on, which need to be learned by the purchaser.

For those who look at the purchasing function as a service performed inside one's organization, it is possible to look at the other departments in the organization as the buyers of this service. How differently would the members of the purchasing department behave if their services actually were bought by the other departments? In a number of organizations, particularly large public and private organizations which operate on a decentralized, divisional basis, it is not at all uncommon to charge central purchasing services to specific divisional or departmental budgets. Neither is it unusual for those internal customers to complain about the size and nature of the charges incurred.

Team Buying in Services Purchasing

The purchase of services requires a tremendous amount of user or requisitioner input and cooperation. The idea of "team buying" of services is a natural. In fact, many users will question the usefulness of any procurement input at all, preferring to select their service providers on their own. Typical examples would include consulting services in the engineering, marketing, finance, data processing, personnel, and organizational strategy areas. Under those circumstances, the involvement of the purchasing department may be limited to a confirmation order.

E-commerce Applications to Service Buying

E-commerce tools are being used by a number of firms in the acquisition of services, such as buying temporary staffing services. These programs can be used to rein in maverick spending and compel users to follow a clearly defined purchasing process.

Rather than viewing services as an intraorganizational territorial battleground, purchasing should view its role as contributing to value received in cooperation with the service requesters. A thorough search of potential

---

[13]Ibid., p. 10.

TABLE 17-3 Summary of Service Characteristics and Acquisition Process Implications

Service Characteristic	Acquisition Process	Need Recognition, Description	Sourcing Alternatives, Pricing, Analysis	Agreement, Contract Provisions	Contract Administration Follow-up, Q.C., Payment, Records
Value					
	High	High attention	Careful Price sensitive Make or buy	Likely negotiated	High attention
	Low	Lesser attention	Low acquisition cost Local source	Standard if possible	Low attention
Repetitiveness					
	High	Develop standard	Test	Standard longer term	Standardize
	Low	Seek expert assistance	Seek expert assistance	Custom or one shot	Custom
Tangibility					
	High	Specs important	Pretest, samples	Similar to product purchase	Control for physical characteristics
	Low	References User involvement	Personalities important	Specified persons	User involvement high
Direction of					
	Equipment	Equipment familiarity	Equipment familiarity	Specified equipment performance	Control process quality
	People	User involvement high	User involvement high	People skills important	Control quality at user interface
Production by					
	Equipment	Specify equipment capability	Specify equipment capability Control for quality Worry about capacity	Specify equipment performance	Conditional on equipment use
	People	Specify people capability		Specify availability	User provides quality control

670

TABLE 17-3 Summary of Service Characteristics and Acquisition Process Implications (*continued*)

Service Characteristic	Acquisition Process	Need Recognition, Description	Sourcing Alternatives, Pricing, Analysis	Agreement, Contract Provisions	Contract Administration Follow-up, Q.C., Payment, Records
Demand	Continuous	Continuity	Reliability and continuity	Complete coverage	Control quality by sampling
	Discrete	Availability during need	Availability during need	Specify delivery	Control quality at delivery
Delivery	At purchaser	User interface important	User interface important	Access clauses	In-house quality control
	At seller	Good description	Location	Purchase access and progress reports	Concern over service completeness
Customization	High	User specification	Custom capability	Special contract	Quality control very specific and may withhold a large % of payment
	Low	Standard specs	Competitive bid	Standard contract	Standard quality control
Skills	High	User specification	Specify specific persons	Availability of individuals	Professional standards, regulations, user involvement
	Low	Standard specs	Competitive bidding	Standard contract	Minimize user hassle

service provider options may confirm that the requisitioner's original suggestion was the best, a considerable comfort to the requisitioner and confirmation for the organization that the best value is obtained. Services are growing rapidly in the economy as a whole. More and more purchasing departments find themselves involved in the purchase of services. Obviously, the well-prepared purchaser can make a significant contribution to the service user by applying sound purchasing theory and practice to the acquisition of services.

Questions for Review and Discussion

1. What contribution can supply make in the acquisition of services?
2. Why should it make any difference to the acquisition process whether a service is directed at people or equipment?
3. What are typical quality control difficulties in the acquisition of services?
4. What are some key differences between buying services and buying office supplies?
5. What is a good example of a service high in intangibles, and how would that affect the acquisition process?
6. How can one determine what represents good value in a service?
7. What are the contract administration implications in the acquisition of services?
8. Why are organizations buying more services outside?
9. Is make or buy a realistic option is the acquisition of services? Why and how?
10. How can cross-functional sourcing teams be used in the purchasing of services?

References

Consulting Services Guide — Supplement to Purchasing Today, August 1999.

Fearon, Harold E. and William A. Bales. *Purchasing of Nontraditional Goods and Services.* Tempe, AZ: Center for Advanced Purchasing Studies, 1995.

Graw, LeRoy H. and Deidre M. Maples. *Service Purchasing.* New York: Van Nostrand Reinholt, 1994.

Haywood-Farmer, John and Jean Nollet. *Services Plus Effective Service Management.* Boucheville, Quebec: G. Morin, 1991.

Parasuraman, A., V. A. Zeithaml, and L. L. Berry. "A Conceptual Model of Service Quality and Its Implications for the Future." *Journal of Marketing,* Fall 1985, pp. 41–50.

Parasuraman, A., V. A. Zeithaml, and L. L. Berry. "SERVQUAL: A Multiple-Item Scale for Measuring Consumer Perceptions of Service Quality." *Journal of Retailing,* Spring 1988, pp. 12–40.

CASE 17-1
ERICA CARSON

"We will do it for 10 percent less than what you are paying right now." Erica Carson, purchasing manager at Wesbank, a large Western financial institution, had agreed to meet with Art Evans, a sales representative from D. Killoran Inc., a printing supplier from which Wesbank currently was not buying anything. Art Evans' impromptu and unsolicited price quote concerned the printing and mailing of checks from Wesbank.

Wesbank, well known for its active promotional efforts to attract consumer deposits, provided standard personalized consumer checks free of charge. Despite the increasing popularity of Internet banking, the printing of free checks and mailing to customers cost Wesbank $8 million in the past year.

Erica Carson was purchasing manager in charge of all printing for Wesbank and reported directly to the vice president of supply.

It had been Erica's decision to split the printing and mailing of checks equally among two suppliers. During the last five years, both suppliers had provided quick and quality service, a vital concern of the bank. Almost all checks were mailed directly to the consumer's home or business address by the suppliers. Because of the importance of check printing, Erica had requested a special cost analysis study a year ago, with the cooperation of both suppliers. The conclusion of this study had been that both suppliers were receiving an adequate profit margin, were efficient and cost-conscious, and that the price structure was fair. Each supplier was on a two-year contract. One supplier's contract had been renewed eight months ago, the other's expired in another four months.

Erica believed that Killoran was underbidding to gain part of the check printing business. This in turn would give Killoran access to Wesbank's customers' names. Erica suspected that Killoran might then try to pursue these customers more actively than the current two suppliers to sell special "scenic checks" which customers paid for themselves.

CASE 17-2
TALBOT COUNTY SCHOOL BOARD

Introduction. Paul Travers, purchasing manager for the Talbot County School Board, was deciding on his next move. In February, the new owners of the company that serviced photocopiers in Talbot County's 30 schools notified Paul they would be increasing prices by over 50 percent. Paul knew school budgets had already been set and wondered what to do next.

Paul Travers. Paul had worked as the purchasing manager for the Talbot County School Board for 20 years. He was responsible for all of the purchasing requirements for the county's public schools. These purchases included items such as snow removal, window replacement, and servicing of photocopiers.

Budgets for all schools were typically set early in the year. Budgets were based on existing or new contracts for the services and appropriations that would be necessary for the school in a given year. School boards typically received their funding from municipal and state governments. Because of the funding cuts made at all levels of government, school boards were feeling pressure to cut costs wherever possible, and increasing expenditures once budgets were set was increasingly difficult.

Photocopiers in Talbot County's Schools. Each school in Talbot County had at least one photocopier. If the photocopier in a school broke down, it required immediate servicing, typically on the same day, as it was the only source the school had for making copies of office and class materials. Over the course of one year, Talbot County's schools collectively made approximately 8 million photocopies. These photocopiers had been purchased by the School Board five years ago and required servicing and toner replacement on a regular basis.

Sigma Servicing. Paul had dealt with Sigma Servicing, a photocopying service company, for the past six years. The school board never had a written contract with Sigma, but the company had held its prices at 0.9 cents per copy over the length of the relationship and had never indicated any displeasure with the arrangement. The cost per copy included the service charge and the charge for toner necessary over the course of the year, and was paid in advance by the school board.

Last November, Sigma was purchased by an individual who had been in the service business a number of years ago and decided to re-enter the market. Upon taking over the company, he began an examination of the existing service arrangements Sigma had with its customers. The new owner discovered that the business with the Talbot County School Board was actually operating at a loss and proceeded to inform Paul in February of his intention to raise prices and seek a new contractual agreement with the school board immediately. Otherwise, Sigma would withdraw its services.

The New Deal. The new owner of Sigma wanted to change the relationship so that service and toner charges would be applied separately to the School Board's photocopiers. The new total price would amount to 1.4 cents per copy, instead of the existing 0.9 cents per copy. Sigma also wanted any new deal to be retroactive to the beginning of the year, so it could recoup its losses.

Paul expected that the new price of 1.4 cents per copy was competitive with that of other companies. However, he requested that Sigma explore some alternative pricing options for the toner charge. As a result, Sigma undertook two studies: one in which generic toner was used instead of the brand the school board currently used, and another in which the toner was recycled with the use of a special container. The result of the first study showed that the yield from the generic toner was a disappointing 4,000 – 5,000 copies per bottle, indicating limited cost-savings opportunities. The second study indicated that the yield was 7,500 – 10,000 copies per bottle when the toner was recycled, resulting in a potential cost savings of about 0.2 cents per copy.

The Decision. Paul was frustrated by developments with Sigma. He had enjoyed a good relationship with the previous owner and was personally proud of the deal he had received during a time of budget cuts. Furthermore, he knew that the negotiations with the new owner would be drawn out and would require a great deal of time in his busy schedule. The negotiations also would be difficult in light of the fact that Sigma felt they had lost money on the previous arrangement, and that schools had already set their budgets for the year.

At this point Paul felt he had several available options. First, he could agree to pay the higher price to Sigma. He was concerned, however, about the budget implications of this alternative. Second, he could ask Sigma to use a recyclable toner, thereby avoiding a portion of the price increase. Third, Paul considered his possibilities of exploring relationships with other vendors.

Paul considered his options and wondered what he should do next. The issue of Sigma's request for a retroactive price increase effective the beginning of the year had to be taken into consideration when making his decision. He knew that he had to respond quickly as the schools required constant servicing and new toner for their photocopiers.

CASE 17-3
SCOPE REPAIRS

As manager of Clinical Engineering at Victoria Hospital in London, Ontario, Mark Greig was part of a team responsible for managing the hospital's medical technology. Mark knew something had to be done to improve the quality and cost of repairs being made to the hospital's flexible surgical scopes by outside firms. It was now early April, and Mark was eager to prepare for the monthly team meeting which was to take place on April 24.

Victoria Hospital. Victoria Hospital (VH) was one of the larger hospitals in Canada, with 667 beds and an annual budget of $250 million. The majority of this budget (81 percent) came from the Ministry of Health. The Ontario Health Insurance Plan (OHIP) was a major source of funds which contributed on a per service basis. VH, St. Joseph's Hospital (SJH), and University Hospital (UH) were the three largest hospitals in London. There was significant coordination between these hospitals, which were linked through the University of Western Ontario as "teaching hospitals." Although VH specialized in cardiology, pediatrics, and oncology, its services were extremely diverse, with specialists in most areas.

London's population was over 320,000, while Ontario's population of almost 9 million accounted for one-third of Canada's citizenry.

The Biomedical Engineering Department. The Biomedical Engineering Department (BED) was a team that focused on managing the hospital's medical technology. Services provided by BED included the purchase, maintenance, repair, and disposal of hospital equipment, and assisting departments in bringing new technology online. BED had an operating budget of approximately $1.5 million but was also responsible for managing VH's capital budget of approximately $2.3 million. Although most equipment repairs were covered by each individual department's budget, $35,000 of VH's capital budget was available for repairs costing over $1,000.

The BED team was directed by Steve Elder and was part of the Medical Operations Division of VH.

Other members of the team included Paul Howarth, Dennis Pickersgill, and Mark Greig. Paul, the equipment management coordinator, was responsible for the financial management of repair budgets and medical capital acquisitions. Dennis managed the technical concerns of the division as technical supervisor, and Mark was involved from an engineering perspective as manager of Clinical Engineering. Mark held a mechanical engineering degree and was an MBA graduate from the Ivey Business School.

Endoscopy. VH used flexible and rigid "endoscopes" in exploratory and minor corrective surgery. An endoscope was a device that could be inserted into the body to view areas such as the lungs, stomach, digestive tract, or major joints. Under most circumstances, the patient was awake during the operation. Most endoscopes were flexible and could be manipulated using angulation knobs, which controlled the vertical and horizontal movement of the device. Once inserted, a scope could perform various functions, such as suction and fluid exchange, and was particularly useful because of a video chip which allowed viewing of areas that would otherwise require major exploratory surgery. Endoscopy dealt with approximately 2,500 cases[1] in the past year.

Endoscopes were maintenance- and repair-intensive devices which involved extremely sensitive technology. The scopes were tested before and after every case. This rigorous process included cleaning, leak testing, measuring of angulation ranges, and video picture testing. Despite this careful maintenance, the scopes frequently broke down during surgery, which required aborting the operation and rescheduling the patient for the next day unless another scope could be made available. The scope requiring repair could be temporarily replaced by borrowing from SJH or UH (subject to availability) while the patient was put aside. The number of each type of scope that VH owned varied, but was as low as one or two scopes for some types.

Endoscopy purchased two or three new flexible scopes each year for a cost of approximately $20,000 each and spent an additional $20,000 to $30,000 per year on related equipment such as

---

[1]Case: Term used to refer to an individual patient.

video processors. The operating room (OR) also used some flexible and rigid scopes. Rigid scopes cost approximately $5,000 to $10,000 and were often replaced if they required a significant amount of repair. Total spending by the hospital last year on scope repairs including endoscopy, OR, and the general capital budget was approximately $60,000.

Original Equipment Manufacturers. There were three original equipment manufacturers (OEMs) in Ontario that sold endoscopes. VH and UH bought and serviced all of their scopes at Barton Surgical Ltd. (Barton), while SJH dealt with Weber Inc. (Weber). The third OEM, Bowe Technical (Bowe), was not used by any of the three teaching hospitals.

In choosing Barton as VH's scope supplier and servicer, VH's physicians were originally asked to decide which of the available scopes would be acceptable from a medical perspective. BED would then consider technical specifications and financial issues. VH had developed a long-lasting relationship with Barton and spent $150,000 on their products and services annually.

Because OEMs were the only companies that could provide the highly technical parts, they were the only option available for scope repairs, which usually took approximately two weeks. OEMs were extremely protective of their supply of parts. There was some concern among the health industry that OEMs were charging unreasonable prices for repairs. There was also the suspicion that occasionally unnecessary repairs were made. Historically, there was no way to verify estimates as even the process of removing the sealed casing on an endoscope required technical tools which were owned by the OEMs.

Out-of-Province Endoscope Repair. Recently, there had been other firms entering the endoscope repair industry in Canada and the United States. In mid-October last year, a representative from Larson Medical (Larson), based in Manitoba, introduced Larson to Paul Howarth and the Endoscopy department as a new player in the endoscope repair industry. The representative claimed that Larson could provide repair service for 20 to 80 percent cheaper than the OEMs, offered a 24-hour free estimate, three to five day turnaround, and stressed that they would "repair only what is broken and bill you accordingly."

In January of this year, a scope in need of repair was sent to Larson as a test case. The repair took approximately three weeks. After three weeks of use in which the scope was used 25 times, one of the angulation wires snapped. VH's intention at this point was to send the scope back to Larson for repair. Inadvertently, the scope was sent to Barton, the OEM. A few days later, a representative from Barton brought the scope to Mark Greig's office at VH. The sealed casing had been removed to expose the inside of the scope and Mark was shocked at what he saw. He could not believe that anyone would intentionally sabotage the scope nor could he believe that anyone could be so incompetent as to do such an unprofessional job (see Exhibit 1). The Barton representative explained that this was what could be expected when Barton scopes were repaired by third-party servicers.

BED's director, Steve Elder, who was going to Manitoba for other business, took the scope with him and visited Larson. They claimed no knowledge of the damage and would not let Steve talk to the repair person who was in charge of the repair. After some persistence, Steve was able to find the individual, who was clearly insulted and threatened to resign over Steve's suggestion that he was responsible for the damage. The scope was left with Larson and took over a month to repair— apparently due to difficulty in getting the necessary parts. When the scope finally returned, it was put back in use and an angulation wire snapped during the first case.

Mark was further confused by another strange event. A scope which had been sent to Barton only for repairs had been returned with an estimate for repairs which had resulted, Barton claimed, from a third party attempting to open the scope using improper tools.

In-House Repairs. VH repaired most of its equipment in-house. Due to the technical nature of the endoscopes and the difficulty of obtaining parts, all scope repairs were sent to outside firms. In November, last year, Steve Elder had attended a meeting of the Toronto Hospital's Consortium,

EXHIBIT 1   List of Items Damaged on the Repair of the Endoscope

February 3

1. Threaded attachment nut, used to seal the end of the body cover grip, was galled by attempted removal using improper tool.
2. Opening in forward body frame was damaged with the improper removal of an insert.
3. Upon damaging seal between main housing and body cover grip, glue was used to unsuccessfully attempt a seal.
4. Forward body trim nut to seal the forward body frame cover was also galled by attempting removal using improper tool.
5. The male threads on both the proximal and distal ends of the forward body frame were stripped.
6. An attempted remedy to correct the improper fit of body cover grip due to stripped threads was to add large quantities of silicone onto the "O" ring.
7. An edge on the UD guide plate was filed down approximately 2 mm for no apparent reason.
8. A brass angulation wire guide was removed, possibly because the threaded mounting holes were stripped.
9. In place of the two missing screws, two new holes were drilled and tapped to secure the UD guide plate.
10. Metal filings from the filed-down section were still found in the housing.
11. A spare screw was found floating in the housing when the housing was opened.
12. Angulation wires appear to have neither been replaced nor repaired.
13. The field service report and accompanying documentation from Larson do not indicate any difficulties in achieving a suitable repair.

which was a banded group of hospitals similar to the three major London hospitals. The consortium had been successful in combining purchasing initiatives and had moved their scope repairs in-house resulting in savings of 40 percent.

The BED team had been discussing a similar coordination between VH, UH, and SJH. Combined, the three hospitals spent approximately $240,000 on scope repairs annually. There were four possible levels of service for an in-house repair operation including preventive maintenance, screening before repair (estimates), minor repairs, and larger repairs. Historically, VH was involved in the preventative maintenance stage only. Mark estimated that 80 percent of repairs were in the first three stages only. He also realized that the fourth stage of repair would be impossible to move in-house for endoscopes due to a lack of technical knowledge. Recently, however, competitive pressure had made

Barton more responsive to assisting with the second and third stage.

If desired, the OEM would supply the parts for minor repair work and would give Mark a list of tools necessary, which would cost about $10,000. For an approximate cost of $2,000, Barton would also provide the training for the two technicians that would be necessary. These technicians would service the three hospitals' minor scope repairs and make estimates on major repairs. Each repair would take approximately three hours, which would significantly reduce the strain on Endoscopy while the scope was out of service.

Mark knew he had a lot of issues to tackle. The monthly department meeting, which would focus on endoscopes, was less than three weeks away. Specifically, Mark wanted to make some recommendations regarding the Barton/Larson situation and the in-house scope repair possibility.

18 STRATEGY IN PURCHASING AND SUPPLY MANAGEMENT

Key Questions for the Purchasing Decision Maker

SHOULD WE
- Develop a strategic plan for purchasing and supply management?
- Spend a major part of our time on strategic, rather than operational, issues?
- Integrate the purchasing/supply management process as a specific part of the organization's overall strategy?

HOW CAN WE
- Anticipate the changes we will face in the next 10 years?
- Obtain top management support for including supply as part of the organization's overall strategy?
- Generate the information needed to do strategic planning?

Key Question

Interest in strategic planning, its contribution to an organization's long-term success and survival, the tools for developing the strategic plan, and the sub-strategies available have drawn much attention over the past two decades. Certainly the purchasing and supply function, as a major decision area in the allocation of most organizations' resource stream, should be a "major player" in developing an overall strategy. The key question is: How can the purchasing function contribute *effectively* to organizational objectives and strategy? The accompanying question is: How can the organizational objectives and strategy properly reflect the contribution and opportunities offered in the supply arena?

Definition of Strategic Planning

There are many definitions of *strategic planning*. One of the pioneers in developing this approach, Peter F. Drucker, defines it as ". . . the continuous process of making present *entrepreneurial (risk taking) decisions* systematically and with the greatest knowledge of their futurity; organizing systematically the *efforts* needed to carry out these decisions; and measuring the results of the decisions against the expectations through *organized system-atic feedback.*"[1] He then states the key question in the strategic planning process as "*What do we have to do now* to obtain our objectives tomorrow?"[2]

Thus, a *strategy* is an *action plan* designed to achieve specific *long-term goals and objectives.* The strategy should concentrate on the *key factors necessary* for success and the *major actions* which should be taken now *to ensure the future.* It is the process of determining the relationship of the organization to its *environment,* establishing long-term *objectives,* and achieving the desired relationship(s) through efficient and effective *allocation of resources.*

Levels of Strategic Planning

Three Levels of Strategic Planning

To be successful, an organization must approach strategic planning on three levels:

1. *Corporate:* These are the decisions and plans that answer the questions of *What business are we in?* and *How will we allocate our resources among these businesses?* For example, is a railroad in the business of running trains? Or is its business the movement (creating time and space utility) of things and people?

2. *Unit:* These decisions mold the plans of a particular business unit, as necessary to contribute to the corporate strategy.

3. *Function:* These plans concern the "how" of each functional area's contribution to the business strategy and involve the allocation of internal resources.

Supply's Contribution to Business Strategy

Purchasing Can Contribute to Organizational Strategy

With the problems that have surfaced in the worldwide supply management arena over the past two decades (see Chapter 1), and the growing recognition by top management of the opportunities for attaining greater purchasing leverage over operating results, supply managers relatively recently have moved into the strategy area. A 1988 report by the Center for Advanced Purchasing Studies found that strategic planning is the top area in which purchasing has assumed an increased role or responsibility since 1980 (cited by 43 percent of the organizations).[3] Five additional CAPS studies done in

---

[1] Peter F. Drucker, *Management: Tasks, Responsibilities, Practices,* New York, NY: Harper & Row, 1974.
[2] Ibid.
[3] Harold E. Fearon, *Purchasing Organizational Relationships* (Tempe, AZ: Center for Advanced Purchasing Studies, 1988).

FIGURE 18-1

Supply Strategy Interpreted in Organizational Strategy

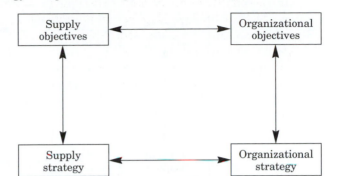

the 1990s reinforced the notion that linking supply strategy to corporate strategy is needed, but many firms do not yet have mechanisms in place to link the two.[4]

The key question, already mentioned, is how can purchasing contribute effectively to organizational objectives and strategies? The heart of this question lies in the term *effectively*. It connotes more than just a response to a directive from top management. It also implies inputs to the strategic planning process so that the units and/or the organizational objectives and strategies include supply opportunities and problems.

This is graphically shown in Figure 18-1 by the use of double arrows between supply objectives and strategy and organizational objectives and strategy.

A somewhat different look at supply strategy is given in Figure 18-2. This shows an effective supply strategy linking both current needs and current markets to future needs and future markets.

One of the significant obstacles to the development of an effective supply strategy lies in the difficulties inherent in translating organizational objectives into supply objectives.

---

[4]Harold E. Fearon and Michiel R. Leenders, *Purchasing's Organizational Roles and Responsibilities* (Tempe, AZ: Center for Advanced Purchasing Studies, 1995); Robert M. Monczka and Robert J. Trent, *Purchasing and Sourcing Strategy: Trends and Implications* (Tempe, AZ: Center for Advanced Purchasing Studies, 1995); Joseph R. Carter and Ram Narasimhan, *Purchasing and Supply Management: Future Directions and Trends* (Tempe, AZ: Center for Advanced Purchasing Studies, 1995); Phillip L. Carter, Joseph R. Carter, Robert M. Monczka, Thomas H. Slaight and Andrew J. Swan, *The Future of Purchasing and Supply: A Five- and Ten-Year Forecast* (Tempe, AZ: Centrer for Advanced Purchasing Studies, 1998); Ulli Arnold, Andrew Cox, Marion Debruyne, Jacques de Rijcke, Thomas Hendrick, Paul Iyongun, Jacques Liouville and Gyongyi Vorosmarty, *A Multi-Country Study of Strategic Topics in Purchasing and Supply Management* (Tempe, AZ: Center for Advanced Purchasing Studies, June 1999).

FIGURE 18-2

Supply Strategy Links Current and Future Markets to Current and Future Needs

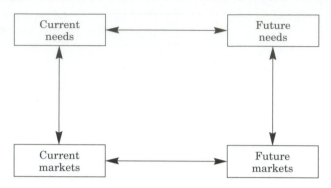

**Four
Categories of
Organizational
Objectives**

Normally, most organizational objectives can be summarized under four categories:

1. Survival
2. Growth
3. Financial
4. Environmental

Survival is the most basic need of any organization. Growth can be expressed in a variety of ways. For example, growth could be in size of organization in terms of number of employees or assets or number of operating units, or number of countries in which the organization operates, or in market share. Financial objectives could include: total size of budget, surplus or profit, total revenue, return on investment, return on assets, share price, or increases in each of these or any combination. Environmental objectives might include not only traditional environmental concerns like clean air, water, and earth, but also objectives such as the contribution to and fit with values and ideals of the organization's employees and customers, and the laws and aspirations of the countries in which the organization operates. The notion of good citizenship is embodied in this fourth objective.

Unfortunately, typical supply objectives normally are expressed in a totally different language such as: quality and function, delivery, quantity, price, terms and conditions, service, and so on. (See Figure 18-3.)

Major Challenges in Setting Supply Objectives and Strategies

**Interpreting
Objectives**

The first major challenge facing the purchasing and supply manager is the effective interpretation of corporate objectives and supply objectives. For ex-

FIGURE 18-3

Normal Organizational and Supply Objectives

Normal Organizational Objectives

1. Survival.
2. Growth.
3. Financial.
4. Environmental.

Normal Supply Objectives

1. Quality.
2. Quantity.
3. Delivery.
4. Price.
5. Service.

Choosing a Strategy

ample, given the organization's desire to expand rapidly, is supply assurance more important than obtaining "rock bottom" prices?

The second challenge deals with the choice of the appropriate action plan or strategy to achieve the desired objectives. For example, if supply assurance is vital, is it best accomplished by single or dual sourcing, or by making in-house? The U.S. Defense Department's supply planners face this issue. Because of the key role of electronics, does the United States need full chip-making capability domestically?

Integration

The third challenge deals with the identification and feedback of supply issues to be integrated into organizational objectives and strategies. For example, because any new technology can be accessed early through supply efforts, how can this be exploited?

The development of a supply strategy requires that the supply manager be in tune with the organization's key objectives and strategies and also be capable of recognizing and grasping opportunities. All three challenges require managerial and strategic skills of the highest order, and the difficulties in meeting these challenges should not be minimized. (See Figure 18-4.)

Social Issues and Trends

Supplier Diversity

During the 1970s and 1980s, interest grew rapidly in some of the areas that might be characterized as the social responsibility of firms. For example, during the Nixon administration, Executive Order 311625 was promulgated to encourage at the federal level minority business enterprises (MBEs), which in turn gave impetus to similar programs in the private sector. This has spawned programs such as Community Economic Development, Public Works Set-Asides, Small Business Administration (SBA) Guaranteed Loans, and MESBICS (Minority Entrepreneurial Small Business Investment Companies). The programs encourage business enterprise on the part of firms

FIGURE 18-4

Potential Business-Strategy Contribution Areas

---

1. Social issues and trends.
2. Government regulations and controls.
3. Financial planning with suppliers.
4. Product liability exposure.
5. Economic trends and environment.
6. Organizational changes.
7. Product or service line.
8. Competitive intelligence.
9. Technology.
10. E-commerce.
11. Investment.
12. Mergers/acquisitions/disinvestment.
13. Time-based competition.

---

and people who, for a variety of reasons, have not been able or permitted to compete effectively in the past. While most of the successes have been in the defense and auto industries, there has been some spill-over into other industries, for example, pharmaceuticals, petroleum, food manufacture, insurance, and banking. In the 1990s, efforts were made to dismantle many affirmative action-type programs.

Environmental Issues

Along with the MBE movement, attention has been directed at firms' responsibilities to protect the environment, which has culminated in various federal and state laws and regulations designed to ensure that the public's safety and use of air, water, and land are protected. Examples of the concerns are disposal of hazardous wastes, control of smoke and other pollutant emissions from manufacturing processes, flood control as a part of earth movement relating to subdivision construction, and reforestation after timber cuts.

Long-Term Benefits

These programs typically are costly to an organization in the short run, but the long-term benefits to the firm, in terms of public attitude and forestalling of potentially damaging, restrictive legislation, may far outweigh the costs. Purchasing's contribution in the strategy area is to pose questions, provide tentative solutions, and supply data, such as:

1. Is there a developing interest on the part of the general public and/or our publics? How potent is this interest? What are the ramifications to our long-term corporate development?

2. What are the direct and indirect costs to our firm from responding to these interests? What are the costs of not responding?

3. How can purchasing respond? What will it do to our short-term material costs? Long-term costs?

4. What risks—for example, supply disruptions or reduction in quality—are involved?

5. What objectives, short-term and long-term, should we set? How will we monitor progress toward these objectives?

Government Regulations and Controls

Adjusting to Government Actions

The firm must be conscious of impending governmental actions and forecast how these actions might impact the operation. Purchasing should monitor developing trends, forecast the outcomes and potential ramifications, and suggest ways the firm can adjust. If it can anticipate developments, it then can respond in a rational fashion.

The distressing incidents of product contamination in the food and pharmaceutical industry have resulted in a variety of governmental rules and regulations—for example, those of the Food and Drug Administration (FDA)—designed to protect the consuming public. These rules certainly will affect the purchase costs of packaging materials and equipment and the types of materials and equipment required. If purchasing is aware of new developments, technology, and suppliers of such packaging processes, it can understand and be part of a corporate team approach assisting top management in making the strategic decisions necessary to cope with these developments. It might result in product-line changes, such as tablets instead of capsules, or changes in the type of packaging used in presenting the product to the public.

Financial Planning with Suppliers

Varying Payment Terms

In most organizations, the dollar cash flow to suppliers is the largest or second largest outflow of funds (in labor-intensive firms, wage and fringe costs may be larger). Thus, the magnitude of purchase dollars has significant implications for the amount of working capital needed. If payment were extended to a 60-day rather than a 30-day basis, that would result in a one-time freeing up of working capital which then might be employed for other purposes. Suppliers would be participating in financing the purchasing firm's operation (a partnership arrangement, so to speak).

Supply might investigate the financial implications of stretching out payment arrangements and the feasibility of doing so. Obviously, any such arrangements could be made only with the cooperation of suppliers, and purchasing is in the best position to suggest and evaluate such possibilities. Similarly, an excess of cash might lead purchasing to explore quicker payment to obtain greater discounts. Clearly, any change in the cash discount terms would impact on both the buying and selling organizations' cash flow picture and overall profitability.

Product Liability Exposure

Product safety and product liability considerations have become much more important over the past two decades, due to changes in the liability environment and the ways judges and juries have interpreted the existing laws. Some of the court judgments have had an effect so severe that selling firms have been forced to declare financial bankruptcy; for example, the asbestos producers and sellers of products using asbestos. The concept of "absolute liability" basically says that the seller of a product has total liability to a user of its product if that user is injured, regardless of disclaimers made to the buyer at the time of sale. Because the purchasing department obtains materials and components from a multitude of suppliers, which then are incorporated into an end product, this requires a close working relationship between the buyer and the supplier, and the buyer's own design, engineering, quality assurance, manufacturing, and marketing departments. Purchasing must attempt to ensure that the organization is not being unreasonably exposed to potentially disastrous product liability lawsuits.

Absolute Liability

Supply's contribution to the business strategy is to ensure that risk is recognized and quantified, and reduced if possible. These considerations should be major inputs to the overall business strategy.

Economic Trends and Environment

Top management needs to be constantly aware of immediate and long-term structural shifts (changes) in the overall economic environment. If, for example, major changes in demand from sectors of business (nationally or internationally) are occurring or projected, this should be taken into account in formulating the overall corporate and/or business strategy.

Supply's Role as an Information Clearing-House

Supply can play a major role in identifying such trends and evaluating their long-term ramifications on the business. Because purchasing obtains a constant flow of information from a variety of external sources (see Figure 3-9 in Chapter 3) and is in almost daily contact with both primary and secondary suppliers, it can serve as a key conduit in obtaining, cataloging, and evaluating the long-term impact of these changes on the business.

Organizational Changes to Facilitate Long-Term Productivity and Efficiency

Purchasing's Role in Four Organizational Strategies

The traditional organization structures used to manage material flows may be revised from time-to-time to gain the communication and control necessary to facilitate greater productivity and efficiency. Purchasing should explore these possible changes and present the alternatives to top management. Such changes normally would impact substantially the relationship between purchasing and other organizational units; any decision to move to one of these different organizational arrangements would require an overall organization commitment to establish such modified relationships. Four possible changed organizational strategies in which supply would play a key role are:

1. *Materials Management.* In this organizational arrangement (see Chapter 1), all or most of the functions involved with the flow of materials into the organization would be arranged under one responsi-

ble manager, normally titled *materials manager.* The persons in charge of materials planning and scheduling, incoming transportation, purchasing, and materials inventory also play a key role.

2. *Project Management.* If key work projects or product lines can be segregated from other projects or products, the enhanced communication and coordination may favor setting up these operations as self-contained units, each with its own supply function. The use of cross-functional teams is one way to organize based on projects or products.

3. *Logistics-Management and Supply Chain Management.* In logistics, *all* the material flow functions, including the input functions (materials management) and the output functions (physical distribution management) might be included as part of an overall logistics organization. The resultant synergy may provide major advantages (see Chapter 2). The supply chain management concept represents an integration of information flows, extending from key suppliers and their suppliers' suppliers to end users.

4. *JIT Purchasing / Production.* This arrangement effectively couples the purchasing and production/operations functions together with the major suppliers, in effect vertically integrating the organization backward (in an operational sense). While it requires additional planning resources, the cost/production efficiencies may be substantially greater. Chapter 6 develops more fully the philosophy of this approach.

Product or Service Line

Examples of Strategic Changes in Lines of Business

Simply because an organization traditionally has produced and sold a particular product(s) or service(s) does not mean that it should continue in that mode. Examples of such strategic changes are U.S. Steel's (USX's) movement away from an almost total reliance on basic steel products and into the energy product line; General Electric's emphasis on financial services; and Westinghouse's major movement into the entertainment business with the acquisition of CBS.

The decision to add or drop a specific product line can be influenced by a myriad of factors, for example, profit margins, return on investment, consumer demand, competition from other firms, and purchased materials availability and cost. Supply should continually monitor supply market trends of major purchased raw materials, interpret these trends over the long run, and define the firm's options. Such long-term commodity forecasting normally is done as a part of the purchasing research effort (see Chapter 13, Research and Measurement).

Supply can make a major contribution to a firm's corporate and/or business strategy by continually keeping in touch with the supply market and

Ways Supply Can Contribute to Strategy

factoring in the effect of long-term trends on the firm's position and the cost of being in a particular product market. Changes in either long-term supply availability or cost of major raw materials might cause a firm to reevaluate its product-line strategy. For example, continued economic problems in the southern African countries which are major suppliers of metals such as chromite and cobalt might cause a firm to consider dropping end-product lines dependent on one or more of these raw materials or begin research efforts to develop suitable substitutes or other suppliers for these materials.

Competitive Intelligence

What Are Other Firms Doing?

To be successful in today's competitive world, the organization constantly must monitor industry trends and what other organizations are doing and planning to do. Is a key competitor planning to introduce a new product? For example, in the beverage industry, is a competitor going to market a new flavor? Is a competitor going to modify its existing product line? Is it introducing a packaging refinement? Is it withdrawing from a specific product line? The success of an organization is largely due to its ability to anticipate such competitive changes, rather than simply reacting. Similarly, on the public side, how effectively are governments in other parts of the country or world dealing with similar issues?

Because of its many contacts with suppliers' sales and technical personnel, purchasing often can get information that, when pieced together with information and data obtained by other company personnel, will provide advance warning of changes. Such information should be fed by purchasing into the firm's planning process on an organized basis.

Technology

Very few products or services are produced today in exactly the same manner as they were 10 years ago. In some industries, such as semiconductors, firms compete based as much on the technology they possess (the production process and the quality assurance system they use) as on the specific product produced. Staying in the forefront of technology development can give a firm a competitive edge that spells the difference between success and simply a marginal existence.

Purchasing's Three Contributions to Technology

Supply can contribute to technology in three primary ways:

1. By providing information to its own design/process/production people on developments in technology (obtained through its contacts with external information sources). This information can help mold the firm's own technology development.

2. By working with its own suppliers (early supplier involvement) to develop new technology that can be incorporated into the buying firm's operation. In some instances, specific suppliers can share the

financial risk in developing new technology. In some instances these costs are so large that it would not be feasible for the buying company to provide the total developmental resources on its own, as, for example, the development of a new jet engine to power a new commercial aircraft.

3. By assisting to "lock up" new, advantageous technology through exclusive agreements with suppliers. If this can be done, it may put the firm in a situation where it can produce products or services at lower total cost or with better overall quality performance than can be achieved by competitors.

E-Commerce

Incorporating E-Business Strategy into Organizational Strategy

Internet technology has changed the competitive landscape for many businesses. (See Chapter 4.) E-business applications provide opportunities for companies to change the way that they conduct business with their suppliers, customers, and employees. An e-business strategy requires companies to develop plans that move the organization from performing isolated tasks using the Web to a position where opportunities to use Internet technology are incorporated into the overall business strategy. This includes developing plans for reengineering business processes incorporating Internet technology, such as order fulfillment processes, product development, and production planning. While supply managers must be concerned with what to buy on the Web and how to buy using the Web, some of the important strategic questions facing executives include: Which exchanges should our company participate in? Should our company form a B2B exchange with our competitors? Should we demand that our suppliers conduct business with us online? What software should we be committing to?[5]

Investment Decisions

Any organization must continually monitor the rates of return it receives on its use of resources (investments). The cost of capital is constantly changing, and the attractiveness of various investments does not remain static.

Identify New Alternatives

While the supply area typically will not make the final decisions on where resources will be invested, it is in a position to make sure new alternatives are fed into the development of the organization's strategic plan. For example, the make-or-buy, lease-or-buy, and outsource alternatives may present some very cost-effective possibilities.

Supply is in a position to identify these strategic alternatives and to collect and classify much of the data needed to evaluate each alternative. The

---

[5]Richard Wise and David Morrison, "Beyond the Exchange: The Future of B2B," *Harvard Business Review,* November-December 2000, pp. 86–96.

Examples of Supply's Role in Strategic Decisions

make/lease/buy/outsource problem, and the role and methodology of purchasing in assessing alternatives, is discussed in Chapter 7, "Supplier Relations." Examples of these strategic decision problems, in which supply should play a key role, abound:

1. An organization could decide to lease much or all of its transportation equipment (autos, trucks, rail cars), thus freeing up the capital that otherwise would be tied up in that equipment.

2. A university might decide to use the services of an industrial caterer to operate its food service, rather than using its own personnel and equipment.

3. A steel producer has the alternative of buying, rather than making, steel slabs from a primary steel producer and then producing the finished steel products in its own facilities. This could result in a substantially changed cost posture for the steel producer and might allow equipment to be used for other purposes, or permit disinvestment, thus freeing up capital for other uses.

4. A consumer electronics firm might look at the possibility of sourcing out the complete television receiver, rather than buying the components and assembling the set.

Mergers/Acquisitions/Disinvestment

Vertical Integration and Disintegration

The overall possibilities from vertical integration or disintegration in the production of various products or services are many and have far-reaching consequences. For example, a producer of automobiles currently may buy radios from an outside supplier. A decision could be made to buy a radio producer, thus vertically integrating the production process. Further, the radio-producing plant could produce its own semiconductor devices, rather than buying them from a supplier. In the reverse direction, the auto producer now making its own radios might decide to sell off the radio producer and buy out (outsource) the radios.

Example: Mace Security International

A 1995 survey of 250 executives of midsized companies found that 25 percent plan to acquire one of their suppliers in the next few years as a way of increasing capacity and global competitiveness.[6] For example, when Mace Security International purchased a tear-gas supplier, it secured its supply of tear gas for its personal protection devices, but it also opened up the law enforcement markets that buy tear-gas grenades.[7] The focus on supply-base reduction and closer relationships with suppliers indicates that successful

---

[6]"Buy Suppliers, Not Just Supplies—That's the Strategy of More Manufacturers," *The Wall Street Journal,* January 4, 1996, p. A1.

[7]Ibid.

suppliers may become super-suppliers as they acquire smaller, regional suppliers or push them out of business.[8]

Make or Buy Example: Delphi Automotive

A critical question faced by virtually every company is how to protect its core competencies and the companion questions of what parts of the supply chain should our company control (make) and what should be purchased from our suppliers (buy). For example, the 1999 IPO of Delphi Automotive, formerly the automotive parts division of General Motors, sent a clear message that GM preferred to concentrate on automotive design and assembly, and control of its main components operations was less critical.[9] Such a disinvestment has important implications for the supply organization—once captive suppliers become independent companies, which affects price negotiations, how new business is awarded, and sharing of confidential information and technology.

Make or Buy Example: IBM

Maintaining a strategic view of supply chain design, including the make-or-buy decision, can have long-term strategic and financial implications. Fore example, IBM's decision to outsource key PC subsystems to Intel (microprocessors) and Microsoft (operating systems) had enormous consequences.[10]

Purchasing has the best overall viewpoint of the firm's suppliers' supply channels and the risks involved in supply movement. It is in a key position to feed this information into the organization's development of an overall strategy to cope with potential problems or opportunities.

Merger Example: BP and Amoco

Purchasing may also become a major element of merger plans. Some mergers and acquisitions are justified, in part, on the basis of purchasing savings. For example, the 1998 merger of oil giants BP and Amoco was expected to generate annual purchasing savings of $250 million over the following three years.[11]

Time-Based Competition

During the last decade, many organizations began to recognize the importance of time as a factor that could differentiate their products and services from those of their competitors. If price and quality essentially are the same, who can deliver fastest may be the factor on which buyers make their choice. The firm that can shorten its design-purchase-manufacture-delivery cycle time will increase its market share and have a better chance of survival.

Causes of Long Cycle Times

According to one study, some of the causes of longer-than-desired cycle times are "poorly engineered designs that cause delays in procurement and production; nonvalue-adding activities such as excessive inspection and

---

[8]Shawn Tully, "Purchasing's New Muscle," *Fortune*, February 20, 1995, p. 83.

[9]Delphi Automotive Systems, *www.delphiautomotive.com*, February 2001.

[10]Charles H. Fine, *Clock Speed* (Reading, MA: Perseus Books, 1998).

[11]"BP and Amoco Merger Plan Oils the Wheels for Purchasing Savings," *Supply Management*, August 20, 1998, p. 10.

approvals and rework; poor communication among functions (engineering, purchasing, production, quality, marketing); and the lack of synchronizing the flow of material, information, and decisions."[12]

Purchasing and supply should play a key role in spearheading efforts to reduce overall cycle time. It also should be able to make a realistic assessment of how successful its efforts at improved purchasing and supply chain management will be in compressing cycle times. With this information, senior management can better establish the firm's overall competitive strategies.

Risk Management

Supply Chain Risks

Every business decision involves risk, and supply is no exception. Almost invariably in financial instruments a higher rate of return is supposed to compensate the investor or lender for the higher risk exposure. Risks in the supply chain can be classified into two main categories: (1) the risk of interruption of the flow of goods or services, and (2) the risk that the cost of the goods or services will be higher than expected.

Both risks affect the bottom line of the purchasing organization and may occur simultaneously.

Supply Interruptions and Delays

Every purchaser fears the possibility that supply interruptions and delays will occur. Catastrophic events such as earthquakes, tornadoes, hurricanes, war, floods or fire may totally disable a vital supplier. Strikes may vary in length, and even short-term interruptions related to weather, accidents on key roads, or any other short-term factor affecting the supply and/or transport of requirements may affect a buying organization's capability to provide good customer service.

Factors Within the Purchaser's and Supplier's Control

A distinction can be drawn between factors beyond the purchaser's or supplier's control, such as weather, and those that deal directly with the supplier's capability of selecting its own suppliers, *managing internally, and its distribution* so as to prevent the potential of physical supply interruption. Careful supplier evaluation before committing to purchase can mitigate against the latter type of supply interruption. In situations of ongoing supply relationships, communication with key suppliers is essential.

Unfortunately, supply interruptions tend to increase costs. If last-minute substitutions need to be made, these are likely to be expensive. Idle labor and equipment, missed customer delivery promises, and scrambling all have increased costs associated with them.

---

[12]Thomas E. Hendrick, *Purchasing's Contributions to Time-Based Strategies* (Tempe, AZ: Center for Advanced Purchasing Studies, 1994).

Direct Increases in Cost

Quite different from supply interruptions are those risks directly associated with changes in the cost of the good or service purchased. A simple example comes from the commodity markets. Increases in the price of oil affect prices paid for fuel, energy, and those products or services that require oil as a key ingredient or raw material. A purchaser who has committed to a fixed price contract may find a competitor able to compete because commodity prices have dropped. Currency exchange rate changes and the threat of shortages or supply interruption also will affect prices, as will arbitrary supplier pricing decisions. Changes in taxation, tolls, fees, duties, and tariffs also will affect prices.

Given that both supply interruption and price/cost risks directly impact any organization's ability to meet its own goals and execute its strategies, supply chain risks—whether they are on the supply side, internal to the organization, or the customer side—need to be managed properly.

Managing Supply Risks

Managing supply risks requires (1) identification and classification of the risks, (2) impact assessment, and (3) a risk strategy.

Given that supply is becoming more and more global and supply networks more complex, risk identification is also becoming more difficult. The preceding discussion identifying supply interruption and price/cost changes as the two main categories has been highly simplified. Technology, social, political, and environmental factors have not even been mentioned yet. Technology has the potential of interrupting supply through the failure of systems and through obsolescing existing equipment, products, or services, or drastically changing the existing cost/price realities. A purchaser committed to a long-term fixed price contract for a particular requirement may find a competitor can gain a significant advantage through a technology-driven, lower-cost substitute. Environmental legislative changes can drastically offset a supplier's capability to deliver at the expected price or to deliver at all.

Because the well-informed supply manager is probably in the best position to identify the various supply risks his or her organization faces, such a risk identification should be a standard requirement of the job, including the probability of event occurrence.

Impact assessment requires the ability to assess the consequences of supply interruption and/or price/cost exposure. Correct impact assessment is likely to require the input of others in the organization, such as operations, marketing, accounting, and finance, to name just a few. Assessed potential impact from identified risk may be low, medium, or high.

Combining potential impact assessment with the probability of event exposure creates a table of risks with low probability and low impact on one extreme and high probability with high impact on the other.

**Managing
Supply Risks**

Obviously, high impact, high probability risks need to be addressed or, better yet, avoided, if at all possible.

Managing supply risks should be started at the supply level, but may escalate to the overall corporate level. Relatively simple actions such as avoiding high-risk suppliers or high-risk geographical locations, dual or triple sourcing, carrying safety stock, and using longer term and/or fixed or declining price contracts and protective contract clauses have been a standard part of the procurement arsenal for a long time. If most purchasers had their way, they would like to transfer all risk to their suppliers! However, the assumption of risk carries a price tag, and a supplier should be asked to shoulder the risk only if it is advantageous to both the supplier and purchaser to do so.

The Corporate Context

**Corporate Risk
Management**

Supply risk is only one of the various risks to which any organization is exposed. Traditionally, financial risks have been the responsibility of finance, property insurance part of real estate, and so on. The emergence of a corporate risk management group headed by a risk manager or chief risk officer (CRO), allows companies as a whole to assess their total risk exposure and seek the best ways of managing all risks. A supply manager's decision not to source in a politically unstable country because of his or her fear of supply interruption may also miss an opportunity to source at a highly advantageous price. A corporate perspective might show that the trade-off between a higher price elsewhere and the risk of non-supply favors the apparently riskier option. Mergers and acquisitions as well as insourcing and outsourcing represent phenomena full of opportunities and risks in which supply input is vital to effective corporate risk resolution. The decision as to how much risk any organization should be willing to bear and whether it should self-insure or seek third-party protection is well beyond the scope of this text. Nevertheless, it is clear that risk management is going to be an area of growing concern for supply managers.

Strategic Planning in Purchasing and Supply Management

Over the past 50 years, the purchasing function has evolved from a clerical-type activity to one in which professional managers perform the function in an asset management context. This change has stimulated the development of strategies to maximize performance.

**Profit-
Leverage and
Return on
Assets Effect**

In the 1960s, industry began to recognize the profit leverage of purchasing, the effect that supply performance has on return on assets (see Chapter 1), and that supply should be a profit-contributing function and not merely a routine order-placing activity. The 1970s provided some real shocks to the world business system—material shortages, the energy crisis, and rapid price escalation—and a realization that some of the old ways of doing business were outmoded and would not return. These events propelled purchasing into the limelight. In the 1990s, the focus on cost reduction, increased global competition, and the need to add value have drawn attention to purchasing and supplier relations. Purchasing must now look past the next requisition or the next quarter in the planning of key materials and ask the *what if* questions. Top management in many organizations has recognized the need to integrate long-run purchasing/materials planning into the overall corporate long-term strategic plan.

Competitive Position

Today, firms face the challenge of maintaining or regaining position in world competitive markets. The ability to relate effectively to outside environments—social, economic, political and legal, and technological (with its changing materials and processes)—to anticipate changes, to adjust to changes, and to capitalize on opportunity by formulating and executing strategic plans, is a major factor in generating future earnings and is critical to survival. Supply now must be forward-looking—it no longer is adequate simply to react to the current situation and problems. If purchasing is primarily in a reactive mode, doing only the urgent things, it will not address the really important issues. Instead, the energies of the people will be dissipated in dealing with immediate problems and "firefighting," which becomes largely a no-win situation.

The events of the decades of the 70s, 80s, and 90s have established the role of purchasing in strategic planning at the functional level (as well as the strategic business level).

Major Purchasing Functional Strategy Areas

Five Purchasing Substrategies

A strategy is an action plan designed to permit the achievement of selected goals and objectives. If well developed, the strategy will link the firm to the environment as part of the long-term planning process. An overall purchasing strategy is made up of substrategies, each of which is developed by using all available information in the formulation of a plan directed at the achievement of a *specific* purpose. All purchasing substrategies can be grouped together into five major categories:

1. *Assurance-of-Supply Strategies:* Designed to ensure that future supply needs are met, at least in terms of quality and quantity. Assurance-of-supply strategies must consider changes in both demand and supply. (Much of the work in purchasing research [see Chapter 13] is focused on providing the relevant information.)

2. *Cost-Reduction Strategies:* Designed to reduce the laid-down cost of what is acquired, or the total cost of acquisition and use—life cycle cost. With changes in the environment and technology, alternatives

may be available to reduce an organization's overall operating costs through changes in materials, sources, purchasing methods, and buyer-supplier relationships.

3. *Supply-Support Strategies:* Designed to maximize the likelihood that the considerable knowledge and capabilities of suppliers are available to the buying organization. For example, better communication systems (perhaps computerized) may be needed between buyer and seller to facilitate the timely notification of changes and to ensure that supplier inventory and production goals are consistent with the buying firm's needs. Buyer and seller also may need better relations for the communication needed to ensure higher quality and better design.

4. *Environmental-Change Strategies:* Designed to anticipate and recognize shifts in the total environment (economic, organizational, people, legal, governmental regulations and controls, and systems availability) so it can turn them to the long-term advantage of the buying organization.

5. *Competitive-Edge Strategies:* Designed to exploit market opportunities and organizational strengths to give the buying organization a significant competitive edge. In the public sector, the term *competitive edge* usually may be interpreted to mean strong performance in achieving program objectives.

Figure 18-5 is a conceptual flow diagram of the strategic purchasing planning process. It is important to recognize that the planning process normally focuses on *long-run opportunities* and not primarily on immediate problems.

Strategic Components

The number of specific strategic opportunities which might be addressed in formulating an overall supply strategy is limited only by the imagination of the supply manager. Any strategy chosen should include a determination of what, quality, how much, who, when, what price, where, how, and why. Each of these will be discussed further. (See Figure 18-6.)

What?

Probably the most fundamental question facing an organization under the "what" category is the issue of make or buy. Presumably, strong acquisition strengths would favor a buy strategy. (See Chapter 8).

Purchase of Finished Products on an "Our Own Label" Basis. While this is an unusual partnership strategy, in some instances a buying firm may decide to also distribute a purchased product, under its own name, to other

FIGURE 18-5

Strategic Purchasing Planning Process

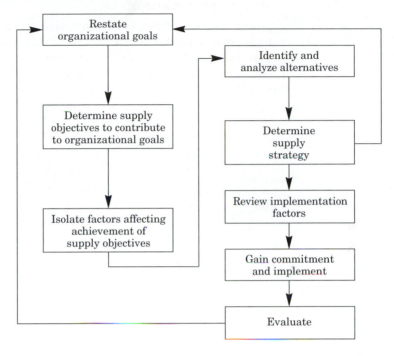

firms. This might be attractive because of the price that could be obtained due to the volume, and/or because of the buying firm's ability, due to its size, to support the product after sale. For example, a large purchaser of personal computers might enter into an arrangement with the supplier (manufacturer) to buy and market those same units under its own brand name. While this is not a typical strategy, it may have income-producing possibilities and could be considered by a purchasing department that is alert to innovative approaches.

Standard Versus Custom Goods and Services

Also included under the heading of what is to be acquired is the issue of whether the organization will acquire standard items and materials readily available in the market, as opposed to special, custom-specified requirements. Standard items may be readily acquired in the marketplace, but they may not afford the organization the competitive edge that special requirements might provide.

Quality?

Part of the what question deals with the quality of the items or services to be acquired. Chapter 5 addresses the various trade-offs possible under quality. The intent is to achieve continuous process improvement.

FIGURE 18-6

Supply Strategy Questions

1. What?
   Make or buy
   Standard versus special

2. Quality?
   Quality versus cost
   Supplier involvement

3. How Much?
   Large versus small quantities (inventory)

4. Who?
   Centralize or decentralize
   Quality of staff
   Top management involvement

5. When?
   Now versus later
   Forward buy

6. What Price?
   Premium
   Standard
   Lower
   Cost-based
   Market-based
   Lease/Make/Buy

7. Where?
   Local, regional
   Domestic, international
   Large versus small

Single versus multiple source
High versus low supplier turnover
Supplier relations
Supplier certification
Supplier ownership

8. How?
   Systems and procedures
   Computerization
   Negotiations
   Competitive bids
   Fixed bids
   Blanket orders/open orders
   Systems contracting
   Blank check system
   Group buying
   Materials requirements planning
   Long-term contracts
   Ethics
   Aggressive or passive
   Purchasing research
   Value analysis

9. Why?
   Objectives congruent
   Market reasons
   Internal reasons
   1. Outside supply
   2. Inside supply

Supplier Quality Assurance Programs. Many firms have concluded that a more consistent quality of end-product output is absolutely essential to the maintenance of, or growth in, market share. To achieve this, suppliers must deliver more consistent quality materials, parts, and components; this also will effect a marked reduction in production costs and in-house quality control administrative costs. Therefore, a strategy of developing suppliers' knowledge of quality requirements and assisting them in implementation of programs to achieve desired results may be needed. Three of the programs which might be used are (1) zero defect (ZD) plans, which are basically motivational training programs to convince the supplier and its employees that only the agreed-upon quality should be produced and shipped. "Do it right the first time" is far more cost-effective than making corrections after the fact. (2) Process quality control programs, which use statistical control charts to monitor various production processes to isolate developing problems and make needed adjustments (corrections) before bad product is produced. The buying firm may need to assist the supplier with the introduction of the needed statistical techniques. (3) Quality certification programs, in

Zero-Defects Plans

Process Quality Control Programs

Quality Certification Programs

which the supplier agrees to perform the agreed-upon quality tests and supply the test data, with the shipment, to the buying firm. If the seller does the requisite outgoing quality checks and can be depended on to do them correctly, the buying firm then can eliminate its incoming inspection procedures and attendant costs. This approach almost always is a key element in any just-in-time purchasing system, as discussed in the following section.

How Much?

Another major component of any supply strategy deals with the question of how much is to be acquired in total and per delivery. Chapter 6 discussed a number of trade-offs possible under quantity. Generally, the trend has been to go toward smaller quantities to be delivered as needed, as opposed to the former stance of buying large quantities at a time to ensure better prices. Ideally, the buyer and supplier try to identify and eliminate the causes of uncertainty in the system that drive the need for inventory, thus reducing the amount of inventory in the total system. One option available under the how much question may involve the shifting of inventory.

Supplier Managed Inventory

Shift Inventory to Supplier. The supplier may be able to manage finished goods inventory (which is the buyer's raw material inventory) more effectively than the buyer, due to the supplier's greater knowledge of inventory control procedures for a given line of product. Also, because the supplier may be supplying a common item to several customers, the safety stock required to service a group of customers may be much less than the combined total of the safety stocks if the several customers were to manage their own inventories separately. This concept is integral to the successful implementation of systems contracting (discussed in Chapter 3). From a strategic standpoint, supply may wish to analyze its inventory position on all of its major items, with a view to working out a partnership arrangement with key suppliers whereby they agree to maintain the inventory, physically and financially, with delivery as required by the production schedule. Ideally, of course, the intent of both buyer and supplier should be to take inventory out of the system. An area in the buyer's facility may even be placed under the supplier's control.

Inventory Elimination Key to Dell's Success

Dell is one example of a company that has successfully used its supply relationships to create a competitive advantage, beating out traditional industry powerhouses like IBM, Compaq, and Hewlett-Packard. One of the critical aspects of Dell's success is that it carries almost no inventories, either finished products or materials, and everything that Dell buys from its suppliers is immediately assembled into a computer and sold. Its supply relationships have allowed Dell to be the low-cost producer in the industry and become an industry leader.[13]

---

[13]Charles H. Fine, *Clock Speed* (Reading, MA: Perseus Books, 1998).

Other options are to switch to just-in-time purchasing, or to consignment buying.

Just-in-Time Purchasing. If a supplier can be depended on to deliver needed purchased items, of the agreed-upon quality, in small quantities, and at the specified time, the buying firm can substantially reduce its investment in purchased inventories, enjoy needed continuity of supply, and reduce its receiving and incoming inspection costs. To accomplish this requires a long-term plan and substantial cooperation and understanding between buyer and seller.

Advantages For Buyer and Seller

Consignment Buying. In some instances, a supplier may be induced to maintain an inventory bank in the buyer's facility, under the buyer's control. The buyer assumes responsibility for accounting for withdrawals of stock from that consignment inventory, payment for quantities used, and notification to the supplier of the need to replenish inventory. Verification of quantities remaining in inventory then would be done jointly, at periodic intervals. This strategy has advantages for both supplier (assured volume) and buyer (reduced inventory investment), and often is used in the distribution industry. It can be considered in other industries as well.

Who?

The whole question of who should do the buying has been addressed in Chapter 2 as part of the organizational issue. The key decisions are whether the supply function should be centralized or not, what the quality of staff should be, and to what extent top management will be involved in the total process. Other options include the choice of materials management, project management, and cross-functional sourcing teams.

When?

The question of when to buy is tied very closely to the one of how much. The obvious choices are now versus later. The key strategy issue really lies with the question of forward buying and inventory policy. In the area of commodities, the opportunity exists to go into the futures market and use hedging.

Futures Market (Hedging). The organized commodity exchanges present the opportunity to offset transactions in the spot and future markets to avoid the risk of substantial price fluctuation. Chapter 9 discusses this strategy, which is available to firms that are large buyers of the many basic commodities traded continually, or from time to time, on an organized market.

What Price?

It is possible for any organization to follow some specific price strategies. This topic already has been extensively discussed in Chapter 9. Key trade-

Key Trade-offs in Price Determination

offs may be whether the organization intends to pursue paying a premium price in return for exceptional service and other commitments from the supplier, a standard price target in line with the rest of the market, or a low price intended to give a cost advantage. Furthermore, the pursuit of a cost-based strategy as opposed to a market-based strategy may require extensive use of ideas like value analysis, cost analysis, and intensive negotiation.

Compare Function to Cost

Value Analysis/Value Engineering. The "function versus cost" comparison approach has been employed in an organized fashion for many years (since the 1950s). Chapter 13 discusses this approach. The possibilities of reducing costs through changes involving actions such as substitution and standardization are many, and the dollar results can be substantial. As a strategy, it requires a concentrated, organized approach, with a plan, timetable, and assignment of specific responsibility. The assumption that it is an understood part of every buyer's job often turns out to be something for which no one really accepts responsibility.

Another option may be transportation.

Transport Cost Reduction. Deregulation has opened up many new cost-reduction strategies, such as contract freight services, single-transport-supplier agreements, negotiated rates, intermodal systems, use of owned transport facilities and equipment, and third-party logistics. Only a long-term transport strategy will exploit the cost-saving possibilities. The elements to be considered in developing such a strategy are discussed in Chapter 10.

In another vein, lease or buy may offer opportunities.

Advantages to Leasing

Lease or Buy. An often overlooked cost-reduction strategy is the possibility of leasing equipment and/or facilities from a producer of those items or from a third party (perhaps a financial concern which has purchased equipment from a manufacturer with the intent of then leasing it to the user firm—many of the aircraft used by commercial airline operators are under such an arrangement). In some instances, a firm may decide to enter into the sale of a building or production equipment and then a lease-back arrangement. While the primary purpose of this strategy may be to free up capital for more productive uses (with a higher rate of return), there also may be significant tax benefits. This cost-reduction strategy often is an integral part of a firm's overall financial strategy. Article 2A of the most recent *Uniform Commercial Code* deals specifically with leases.

Where?

Several possibilities present themselves under the question of where to buy. Many of these were discussed in Chapter 7 under Source Selection. Obvious trade-offs include local, regional, domestic, or international sourcing; buying from small versus large suppliers; single versus multiple sourcing; and low versus high supplier turnover, as well as supplier certification and supplier ownership. Just a few of these will be discussed here.

Purchasing Takes the Initiative

Supplier Development. This implies an aggressive search, with the purchaser taking the initiative to create a supplier(s) where none currently exists. It may involve a broad look at technical, financial, and management processes; quality levels; costs; and requirements forecasting and planning. Aggressive supplier development was one of the key factors enabling the computer industry to bring adequate capacity online to permit output volume to meet customer demand.

Pros and Cons of Single Sourcing

Single Sourcing. Traditional wisdom says that in the case of the major materials and components (or critical purchased items regardless of the monies involved), two or more suppliers should be used to ensure continuity of supply. However, splitting the requirements may increase the per-unit price paid, because it denies the benefits of quantity pricing. The price-break benefit may be possible only if the entire quantity is purchased from one supplier. In addition, the single-sourcing strategy may reduce purchasing administrative costs by cutting down the number of individual transactions, and it may obtain faster and more reliable delivery service, because the larger quantity may cause the supplier to value the buyer's account more highly.

Global Sourcing. Over the past decade, the activity in international purchasing has increased substantially, due primarily to two considerations: the increased design, production, and distribution capabilities of international suppliers; and the pressures for cost reduction in the manufacturing process. Chapter 14, "Global Supply Management," presents the concepts and approaches of global sourcing.

Minimizing Time and Distance Factors

International Supplier Facilities in North America. Major problems in global sourcing, as pointed out in Chapter 14, are time and distance. As a means of minimizing those problems, the buying firm may structure arrangements with international suppliers whereby they provide for production in North America, along with warehousing and distribution, and/or repair, maintenance, and support of product. Because such arrangements are long-term in nature, working them out requires a conscious, strategic purchasing approach.

Needed Information for Forecasting

Long-Term Supplier Forecasting. The better the buyer understands the situation of the supplier and changes likely to occur over the next five or so years, the easier it will be to develop a partnership atmosphere. To develop this forecast and understanding will require a good deal of cooperation and supplier-furnished information. Some of the areas in which such forecast information is needed are (1) growth plans, in terms of product lines and output capacity; (2) research and development and design capabilities; (3) financial stability and capacity to support new product/application developmental efforts; (4) management strengths and potential; and (5) technological prowess. If the buying firm develops this long-term understanding with key suppliers, it then has a much better basis for formulating a long-term strategy that hopefully will ensure supply at cost-competitive prices.

Minority/Disadvantaged Supplier Development. Various government programs (see the section on "Social Issues and Trends" earlier in this chapter) have been established to encourage certain types of firms, for example, small businesses, to pursue economic development more vigorously. If the buying firm is committed to such economic development, it must develop a strategy to accomplish this. While the overall commitment must come from top management, it is purchasing's role to determine the actions needed to produce the desired results. Normally, a concentrated effort, over a relatively long time period, will be needed if the firm is to provide more than simply "window dressing" for their efforts.

How?

A very large array of options exists under the heading of how to buy. These include, but certainly are not limited to, such areas as systems and procedures, e-commerce applications, use of various types of teams, use of negotiations, competitive bids, blanket orders and open order systems, systems contracting, group buying, long-term contracts, the ethics of acquisition, aggressive or passive buying, the use of purchasing research and value analysis, quality assurance programs, and reduction of the supply base. Most of these have been discussed in the earlier chapters in this text. Several will be further highlighted here.

Strategic Advantages to Long-Term Contracting

Long-Term Contracting. Entering into a 5- to 15-year supply contract melds the supplier's and buyer's operation together in a mutual interdependence, where schedules and plans must be closely coordinated and monitored. The strategic advantages to the buyer are greater supply assurance and stability, supplier design support, and often a lower acquisition cost base. The supplier gains assured business and operating stability, which should result in a reduction in its long-term cost posture. This may be a sufficient incentive to persuade a supplier to develop and produce a product (supplier development). Before a decision can be made on such a strategic arrangement, long-term projections on costs, advantages, and downside risks must be made.

Commodity Forecasting. The uncertainty of supply, due to the growth of conglomerates through mergers and acquisitions, and the world geopolitical situation, make it critical for many firms to anticipate changes in the supply environment. If such developments can be anticipated through in-depth commodity-economic research, alternatives to ensure supply at a reasonable overall cost can be identified far enough in advance to allow the buyer to take timely action.

Supplier Risk Sharing. In the development of a major new product, such as a new-generation jet aircraft, major investment costs are required. The technological complexity of the product is so great that the risk to, and resources required by, the air-frame maker are so large that it can be done successfully only through a partnership arrangement between buyer and seller.

Supplier/Buyer Data Sharing. As part of developing a partnership philosophy with key suppliers, arrangements must be made to share planning and production information between both buyer and seller. The buyer needs access to the supplier's cost data, production schedules, pricing schedules, inventory availability, and lead times. The seller must have information about the buyer's production plans and schedules, material requirements, and future product and marketing plans.

Why?

Reasons For Developing a Supply Strategy

Every strategy needs to be examined not only for its various optional components, but also for the reason why it should be pursued. The normal reason for a strategy in supply is to make supply objectives congruent with overall organizational objectives and strategies. Other reasons may include market conditions, both current and future. Furthermore, there may be reasons internal to the organization, both outside of supply and inside supply, to pursue certain strategies. For example, a strong engineering department may afford an opportunity to pursue a strategy based on specially engineered requirements. The availability of excess funds may afford an opportunity to acquire a supplier through backward/vertical integration. The reasons inside supply may be related to the capability and availability of supply personnel. A highly trained and effective buying group can pursue much more aggressive strategies than one less qualified. Other reasons may include the environment. For example, government regulations and controls in product liability and environmental protection may require the pursuit of certain strategies.

Government Regulations and Controls. To meet perceived economic problems, the federal government may impose specific economic limitations on the firm's supply decision processes. For example, tariff and import regulations and schedules are being changed continually by various governments. Any purchasing strategy must be formulated within this overall structure if purchasing actions are to meet legal constraints and exploit the ever-changing economic possibilities.

Legal Exposure Part of Supply Strategy

Product Liability. As Chapter 12 discusses, product safety and product liability considerations have assumed more importance in the purchasing decision process over the past decade, as various court rulings have interpreted the existing law. The potential financial risk has increased, and the firm must factor this additional legal exposure into its long-term purchase strategy as it works with suppliers and its own engineering, manufacturing, and marketing functions. As a strategy, with the advice of legal counsel, the purchaser will want to transfer product liability to the supplier where possible, to minimize the risk of financial obligation from product liability lawsuits. Supply also must consider potential liability connected to the acquisition of any material and alert others in the firm.

The Environment. Concern has grown markedly about a firm's responsibility to protect the environment (air, water, ground) and has resulted in passage of various environmental protection laws and regulations. This has resulted in suppliers and purchasers having to make many changes in products and services and methods of doing business. For example, in the case of the castings industry, it has resulted in an overall reduction in the number of suppliers and changes in the product line mix of some suppliers.

Zero Emissions Programs

In the 1970s and 1980s manufacturers and environmental groups clashed over the concept of zero emissions. However, some current research on environmental management compares pollution prevention to total quality management.[14] Both build on the concept of continuous improvement and elimination of waste. Effective manufacturing processes incorporate clean operating systems that are designed to eliminate pollutants entirely, rather than filter or capture them downstream. Just as the zero defects movement calls for defect-free manufacture, a zero-emission program would be geared toward designing processes to eliminate effluents.

Sustainable Growth

The strategic question for the organization is how to achieve *sustainable* growth where future quality of life is not sacrificed for short-term economic gain. The 1999 *Harvard Business Review* article, "Bringing the Environment Down to Earth," argues that managers need to go beyond the question of "Does it pay to be green?" and suggests that, by incorporating environmental management into corporate strategy, firms can create competitive advantage.[15]

Environmental Effects Part of Life Cycle Costing

With a focus on sustainable growth, a company must then determine what products to develop, how they should be packaged, and what materials should be used in manufacturing. Life-cycle costing, or "cradle-to-grave"

---

[14]A.S. Powell, *TQM and Environmental Management,* (The Conference Board Inc., 1995); Sime Curkovic, Steven A. Melnyk, Robert B. Handfield and Roger Calantone, "Investigating the Linkage Between Total Quality Management and Environmentally Responsible Manufacturing," *IEEE Transactions on Engineering Management,* Vol. 47, No. 4, November 2000, pp. 444–463.

[15]Forest L. Reinhardt, "Bringing the Environment Down to Earth," *Harvard Business Review,* July-August 1999, pp. 149–157.

product accounting, should include the environmental effects of a product, such as landfill costs, potential legal penalties, and degradation in air or water quality.

Supply, in conjunction with other departments in the firm, must take these constraints into account in establishing its overall acquisition strategy. It may necessitate such things as a long-term strategy to (1) change the supplier base, (2) redesign product to permit substitution of certain materials, or (3) begin manufacture of certain components that previously were bought out.

Waste Disposal. Purchasing always has been responsible in most firms for the disposal of those residues of the manufacturing process (waste) that have no economic value (see Chapter 11). However, with the changes in materials and technology that have occurred in the post-nuclear era, many waste materials are hazardous in nature and require special disposal procedures. Many localities have enacted regulations to govern transport and disposal procedures, as has the federal government. If a firm generates waste, the purchasing department must factor into its overall disposal strategy the special requirements of environmental protection and hazardous materials.

Trends in Purchasing and Supply Management

While the evidence is not conclusive that all the following changes will take place over the coming years, it appears that they are under way now. Individual trends may be altered somewhat and some could be reversed (although that seems unlikely).

1. *Nontraditional people will be in many supply management positions.* As organizations continue to rightsize or downsize, many talented managers will be available to move out of their current, now-redundant positions into other managerial functions. Some will come to supply, where managerial skills may be more important than technical skills.

2. *Technical entry route into purchasing.* In highly technical firms, a requirement for employment in a professional purchasing capacity may be a technical educational background; for example, a pharmaceutical manufacturer may require its key purchasing professionals to have educational credentials in either pharmacy or chemistry.

3. *Emphasis on total quality management and customer satisfaction.* Purchasing will think strategically about its responsibility for, and involvement in, total quality management and satisfying the organization's customers. It will "buy into" responsibility for the quality of output of goods and/or services. One such example is Honda's BP

program that uses quality analysis and problem-solving techniques to develop excellent suppliers.[16]

4. *Emphasis on the process used in acquisition, rather than the transactions.* Purchasing must do the right things, as well as doing things right! Continuous process improvement will be a way of life in forward-thinking purchasing operations.

5. *Purchase of systems and services, as well as products.* To increase value added, more suppliers will offer ancillary services, like storage, accounting, and so on, in addition to production.

6. *Strategic cost management.* Cost management begins with early supply involvement in product design and represents ongoing efforts to analyze cost drivers and target opportunities to reduce total supply chain costs. Such efforts require cross-functional support, supplier involvement, and trained cost management specialists to lead the initiative. Cost management was one of three strategic initiatives at Deere and Company, supported by 70 cost management specialists.[17]

7. *Design engineering and purchasing capitalize on their potential synergy.* While these functions will not merge, they will recognize their interdependence and develop the communication and coordination to maximize the combined contribution of both.

8. *The supplier base will be reformulated.* The key to results in purchasing is the supplier(s) selected. The trend to single sourcing, greater use of buyer/supplier alliances and partnerships, and greater sharing of design information will continue.

9. *Longer term contracts.* Many of the agreements for supply of key items will be partnerships/alliances expected to have a life of 5,10, or 15 years, or even longer.

10. *E-Commerce.* To simplify and reduce transactions, and speed up communication, e-commerce transactions between firms and their major suppliers will continue to grow. Applications will be extended to Web-based fulfillment processes, planning and scheduling, and product development.

11. *Global Supply Management.* Supply managers will need to look globally to identify best possible suppliers. Further reductions and elimination of trade barriers will facilitate globalization of supply networks.

---

[16]Dave Nelson, Rick Mayo and Patricia Moody, *Powered By Honda* (New York, NY: John Wiley & Sons, 1998).
[17]Michiel R. Leenders, and P. Fraser Johnson, *Major Changes in Supply Chain Responsibilities* (Tempe, AZ: Center for Advanced Purchasing Studies, 2001).

12. *MRO items handled by a third-party contractor.* MRO buying involves many transactions, but low average dollars for each. It is difficult to add real value in MRO buying. If it were contracted out, it would free the time of key buying personnel to concentrate on the high-potential buys.

13. *Sourcing will include the complete end product or service and be done proactively.* Sourcing out of items manufactured previously was done as a matter of short-term survival. Due to its dollar potential, firms will become proactive in identifying and pursuing both products *and* services—for example, legal, training, internal auditing—that might provide a competitive advantage if successfully outsourced.

14. *Closer supplier relationships.* Sourcing out end products shifts technology from the buying firm to the supplying firm. The two firms will grow closer together (conceptually).

15. *Teaming.* The complexity of many procurements requires that the analysis and decision making be done by a cross-functional group of key professionals/managers, including a team member from, for example, purchasing, design, engineering, and manufacturing.

16. *Empowerment.* As the ability and skill levels of people in the purchasing activity increase, organizations will delegate increasing amounts of authority to their purchasing people to make decisions and to improve the supply process. If their creativity can be unleashed, the results could exceed expectations by a wide margin.

17. *End-product manufacturers will focus on design and assembly.* To capitalize on their core competency, some manufacturers will reduce their basic manufacturing processes and emphasize design and assembly. This will mean purchasing fewer raw materials and component parts, but more subassemblies and components, from suppliers. Purchases will become a greater percentage of cost of goods sold.

18. *Consortiums for purchasing.* Requirements of two or more separate organizations will be combined to gain price, design, and supply availability benefits of higher volume (see Chapter 2).

19. *Separation of strategic and tactical purchasing.* As purchasing processes, practices, and strategies change, the roles in purchasing will become differentiated between strategic and operational (tactical).

20. *Greater purchasing involvement in nontraditional purchases.* Opportunities will be recognized where supply expertise can be successfully applied to areas like insurance, travel, real estate, and health plans.

21. *Environmental purchasing.* Firms will become more proactive to ensure their suppliers not just conform to environmental regulations,

but have systems and strategies in place that support sustainable development, and compliance with ISO 14000 standards will become more commonplace.

22. *Value enhancement versus cost reductions.* Supply management's role in cost reductions will be replaced by a focus on value enhancement as senior management and chief purchasing officers recognized that enhancing the performance of the total enterprise provides lower total supply chain costs and competitive advantage.

The Future

In addition to the trends that now are under way, or those on which there is strong evidence that they are beginning (as discussed in the previous section), there are our additional trends on which the evidence of their beginning is embryonic. However, they are significant enough that they should be commented on briefly.

1. *Supply chain management.* Supply chain design will become a source of competitive advantage. Companies will need to consider the strategic implications of decisions associated with make or buy and the capabilities of their key suppliers and their suppliers' suppliers.[18]

2. *Cycle time reductions.* Total development and manufacturing cycle times are heavily impacted by procurement cycle times. With the continuing emphasis on time-to-market competition, and the need for early customer response, purchasing, through close cooperation with a limited number of suppliers, will be able to reduce overall cycle time by 50 or 60 percent from what it is today.

3. *Video communication with suppliers.* Buyers will have immediate video communications capability with their strategic suppliers' technical, application, design, and commercial support personnel. This will assist buyer and seller in resolving problems and developing new solutions in a downsized environment, and increasing productivity by decreasing travel time and reducing problem-resolution cycle time.

4. *Integration into business strategy.* What's possible in purchasing and supply may influence business strategy. Purchasing will differentiate its methods and practices based on overall business objectives.

5. *Outsource the procurement process.* The services of an organization's purchasing department could be bought, in part or in total, from a

---

[18]Charles H. Fine, *Clock Speed* (Reading, MA: Perseus Books, 1998).

third-party supplier, just as many firms now outsource their training department and training services. Some firms now outsource their entire MRO buy. This might obtain greater expertise, leverage volume, and/or reduce administrative costs.

6. *Functional lines blurred or even eliminated.* Experts in disciplines associated in the past with specific functions, such as design, quality assurance, production planning, manufacturing, and purchasing, will work together at each stage in the business process. More of the processes will work in parallel rather than in series. The functional walls will come down slowly.

7. *Design for procurability.* The options/alternatives available for the acquisition of materials/services may influence the design activity, just as some firms emphasize "design for producibility."

8. *"Pull systems" become common in manufacturing.* As cycle times come down, and as inventory turns increase, the concept of material and products being made available only as ordered by customers will replace long-term planned production. EDI and the Internet will be key tools assisting in the quick communication necessary to make this work.

9. *Reduction of third- and fourth-tier suppliers.* Because of the need for quick response, the processes of many third- and fourth-tier suppliers will be integrated into those of the second-tier suppliers.

10. *Networking of suppliers.* Suppliers will network among each other to gain the synergy of their collective design and application expertise, which will provide better products and services and result in further reduction in cycle time. At the center of the network will be the prime customer, the buying firm.

11. *Contract with two suppliers simultaneously to design and build.* Strategic alliance teams will be formed with multiple suppliers to ensure low-cost processes, incorporating leading edge technology with improved design reliability and guaranteed process output. These multiorganization teams will work with the business units on design of new or expansion projects and work toward improved reliability and continuous improvement of existing processes.

12. *Rationalization of B2B marketplace.* While Internet technologies will change the way business is conducted, this sector will move through a period of rationalization characterized by standardization of application software and the emergence of clear industry leaders. Inevitably the number of players will shrink as companies merge, become acquired, or exit the marketplace. Similarly, many companies will reevaluate their e-commerce strategies and focus efforts on initiatives that offer value-added savings (see Chapter 4.)

13. *Expert systems/artificial intelligence.* Expert systems are software applications that contain rules embedded in the program that can

make decisions, or can provide decisions/solutions for consideration of the user. To simplify the routine transactions in purchasing, firms will develop and use such systems (see Chapter 3).

The increasing interest in supply strategies and their potential contribution to organizational objectives and strategies is one of the exciting new developments in the whole field of supply. Fortunately, as this chapter indicates, the number of strategic options open to any supply manager is almost endless. A significant difficulty may exist in making these strategies congruent with those of the organization as a whole. The long-term perspective required for effective supply strategy development will force supply managers to concentrate more on the future. The coming decade should be a highly rewarding one for those supply managers willing to accept the challenge of realizing the full potential of supply's contribution to organizational success.

Questions for Review and Discussion

1. What factors have caused the current interest in, and attention to, strategic purchasing and supply planning?
2. What role can (should) purchasing play in determining a firm's strategy in the area of social issues and trends?
3. What can purchasing do to assist in minimizing a firm's risk of product liability lawsuits?
4. What type of data would purchasing need to contribute to an organization's strategic plans for merger, acquisition, or disinvestment? How might purchasing obtain such data?
5. Which of the five major categories of purchasing functional strategies can make the greatest contribution to overall purchasing effectiveness?
6. Give some examples of firms which might consider a backward vertical integration strategy. What would the difficulties be in formulating and implementing the strategy?
7. How can the purchasing manager determine which cost-reduction strategies to pursue?
8. Will a global purchasing strategy become more or less important in the future?
9. How can purchasing achieve the attitude changes necessary to introduce the several supply support strategies?
10. How can purchasing strategies be related to stages in the product life cycle?
11. What major changes will have occurred in the purchasing and supply management function by the year 2005? By the year 2010?

References

Arnold, Ulli, Andrew Cox, Marion Debruyne, Jacques de Rijcke, Thomas Hendrick, Paul Iyongun, Jacques Liouville and Gyongyi Vorosmarty. *A Multi-Country Study of Strategic Topics in Purchasing and Supply Management.* Tempe, AZ: Center for Advanced Purchasing Studies, June 1999.

Carter, Joseph R. and Ram Narasimhan. *Purchasing and Supply Management: Future Directions and Trends.* Tempe, AZ: Center for Advanced Purchasing Studies, 1995.

Carter, Phillip L., Joseph R. Carter, Robert M. Monczka, Thomas H. Slaight and Andrew J. Swan. *The Future of Purchasing and Supply: A Five- and Ten-Year Forecast.* Tempe, AZ: Center for Advanced Purchasing Studies, 1998.

Curkovic, Sime, Steven A. Melnyk, Robert B. Handfield and Roger Calantone. "Investigating the Linkage Between Total Quality Management and Environmentally Responsible Manufacturing." *IEEE Transactions on Engineering Management.* Vol. 47, No. 4, November 2000, pp. 444–463.

Delphi Automotive Systems, *www.delphiautomotive.com,* February 2001.

Drucker, Peter F. *Management: Tasks, Responsibilities, Practices.* New York, NY: Harper & Row, 1974.

Fearon, Harold E. *Purchasing Organizational Relationships.* Tempe, AZ: Center for Advanced Purchasing Studies, 1988.

Fearon, Harold E. and Michiel R. Leenders. *Purchasing's Organizational Roles and Responsibilities.* Tempe, AZ: Center for Advanced Purchasing Studies, 1995.

Fine, Charles H. *Clock Speed.* Reading, MA: Perseus Books, 1998.

Hendrick, Thomas E. *Purchasing's Contributions to Time-Based Strategies.* Tempe, AZ: Center for Advanced Purchasing Studies, 1994.

Leenders, Michiel R. and P. Fraser Johnson. *Major Changes in Supply Chain Responsibilities.* Tempe AZ: Center for Advanced Purchasing Studies, 2001.

Monczka, Robert M. and Robert J. Trent. *Purchasing and Sourcing Strategy: Trends and Implications.* Tempe, AZ: Center for Advanced Purchasing Studies, 1995.

Nelson, Dave, Rick Mayo and Patricia Moody. *Powered By Honda.* New York, NY: John Wiley & Sons, 1998.

Powell, A.S. *TQM and Environmental Management.* The Conference Board Inc., 1995.

Reinhardt, Forest L. "Bringing the Environment Down to Earth." *Harvard Business Review.* July–August 1999, pp. 149–157.

The Wall Street Journal. "Buy Suppliers, Not Just Supplies—That's the Strategy of More Manufacturers." January 4, 1996, p. A1.

Tully, Shawn. "Purchasing's New Muscle." *Fortune,* February 20, 1995, p. 83.

Wise, Richard and David Morrison. "Beyond the Exchange: The Future of B2B." *Harvard Business Review.* November–December 2000, pp. 86–96.

CASE 18-1
SAINT MARY'S HEALTH CENTER

In December, Mr. John Smith, vice president of Support Service at Saint Mary's Health Center, was faced with the decision of how to meet the Health Center's savings objective. The total purchases of the Health Center had to target 15 percent savings the following year because of significant funding restrictions.

The Saint Mary's Health Center Background. Saint Mary's Health Center was a 400-bed hospital affiliated with a local university with excellence in patient care, teaching, and research. There were two other medium-sized hospitals nearby in the regional area, which had a population of about half a million people.

The Health Center had just experienced the two most difficult years since its founding in 1965, with a $12 million estimated operating deficit. This sizable deficit was the result of declining revenues and increasing expenses. Therefore, balancing the budget would be a major challenge confronting the Health Center. The Health Center turned to staff for their input and support in attempting to reduce the projected $9 million shortfall for the coming year.

The Purchasing Area. Total annual purchasing activity consumed about 30 percent of the Health Center's total annual budget of approximately $150 million. Therefore, the savings from purchases were crucial to reducing the deficit. The new target for the following year was a saving of 15 percent in total purchases.

There were three purchasing divisions within the Health Center reporting to two different vice presidents (Exhibit 1). These were Nutrition Purchasing, Service Purchasing, and Pharmaceutical Purchasing. Each purchasing division bought what was required in its respective department independently in the traditional way—that is, item by item from suppliers at the lowest price per unit. There was normally no supplier switching provided suppliers' prices and quality remained competitive.

There was a very large variety of products purchased from about 2,000 suppliers. However, 50 large suppliers supplied approximately 60 percent of the total products. Sometimes different purchasing divisions bought different products from the same supplier or the same product from different suppliers.

In order to meet the new savings target, the purchasing process had to be refocused internally and externally to find different ways of reducing cost and increasing efficiency.

Mr. Smith was considering the following three alternatives:

1. The internal centralization of purchasing would eliminate duplicated buying, reduce staff and administrative costs, reintegrate related activities, and lower total inventory investment without lowering service levels. However, this would mean greater lead times and less flexibility in sourcing a particular product.

2. Eliminating suppliers from whom the Health Center bought less than $100,000 per year and reducing their number from 2,000 to about 350 would help the Health Center gain bargaining power. It would buy large volumes at discount and increase competition among suppliers. It could establish stable, long-term buyer-supplier relationships with the largest suppliers by guaranteeing business in exchange for price cuts of 15 percent in some way. For example, free products or

EXHIBIT 1   Decentralized Purchasing at Saint Mary's Health Center

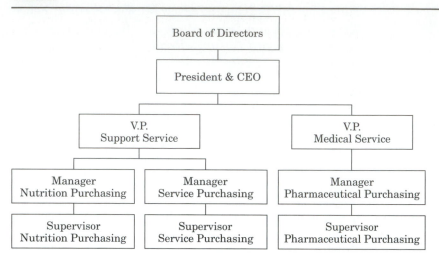

donations to medical research would be tax-deductible to suppliers. Flexibility was a large advantage of having at least two sources.

3. The installation of a computer system connecting the Health Center's inventory to that of suppliers would realize just-in-time delivery and reduced inventory costs. A warehouse shared with other nearby hospitals could also achieve the same effect.

It was only one week until Christmas and Mr. Smith had to present his proposal to the president on December 22 for his final approval. He wondered which alternative would best meet his target.

CASE 18-2
HEAT TRANSFER SYSTEMS INC.

Stan Durnford, the new purchasing manager at Heat Transfer Systems Inc. (HTS), had reviewed the firm's purchasing policies and practices for alu-

minum tubing, one of its prime raw materials. He wanted to formulate a purchasing strategy that would help improve the competitiveness of HTS.

Heat Transfer Systems Inc. HTS was a leading designer and custom manufacturer of heat transfer systems for industries such as steel, pulp and paper, power plants, and the Navy. Products included heating and cooling coils, hydroelectric coolers, and transformer oil coolers, among others. The company's mission was "to deliver innovative engineered solutions and quality equipment for industrial heat systems worldwide." Exports to Canada, Mexico, and overseas exceeded 40 percent of total sales.

Heat Transfer Equipment. Heat exchangers or transfer units were vital in maintaining the temperatures of operating environments at specified levels. Process fluids (water, oil, etc.) travelled through a set of tubes, during which time they were cooled. These fluids then travelled back to the generator or engine and the process began again. An air-cooled fluid cooler consisted of a cooling bundle (tubes), a fan cabinet arranged to create air flow and the proper draft, and a frame or support structure.

Each system was custom designed. The engineering department specified requirements, created a preliminary bill of materials, and in concert with costing and purchasing provided the sales department with the relevant information to quote on the contract. Once the contract was secured, a completed bill of materials was generated, and materials were ordered if needed. Most jobs had delivery requirements of four to six weeks. No finished inventory was stocked; all products were built to order.

The Manufacturing Process. Each job moved from work center to work center. The first process involved fitting a liner tube (in which the fluid to be cooled passed) into a base tube. This base tube, made of aluminum, was then pressure-bonded to the inner liner tube through a rotary extrusion process that formed spiral fins on the base tube. The depth of the fins, and the distance between them, determined the amount of air flow across the tubes, and thus the cooling efficiency and power of the unit. The length, diameter, wall thickness, and number of tubes needed were job dependent. The tubing was cut to length in-house and scrap lengths were disposed of by HTS.

The quality of the aluminum tube was a critical factor. Even a slight impurity or an oil inclusion could create a weakness on the fin which might not become apparent until after bonding to the base tube, creating expensive scrap situations and, possibly, delaying the order.

After the tubes were formed, cabinet and endplate fabrication began. The tubes were welded to the cabinet and end plates. Flanges were then welded to pairs of tubes on the other side of the end plates to create a looped system. The unit was then painted and fans and motors were installed. Finally, the unit was tested for leaks and performance, crated, and shipped to the job site for installation.

Purchasing at HTS. Material and component parts such as motors and fans were not stocked for future use (purchased as required). The company had multiple suppliers for major products. On sales of $16 million in the past year there was approximately $6 million in raw material and component inventory. Aluminum tubing was normally purchased in 15 different wall thickness and diameter combinations, of which 5 were the most common. Aluminum tubing accounted for about 35 percent of HTS' yearly material and component purchases. Because European prices were lower, the previous purchasing manager had purchased about 40 percent of aluminum tube requirements from a European producer and split the remainder between two North American manufacturers. Because of transportation costs, all European purchases were in container loads normally in 50-feet lengths. European deliveries were invariably one or two months late and occasionally a shipment would be three months late. The European price at $1.20/lb FOB origin, compared with the North American price of $1.50/lb, was attractive enough in the opinion of the previous purchasing manager to put up with the delivery costs and uncertainty. Normal lead time for Europe was about six to eight weeks. Normal North American lead time was two to three weeks. It was also possible to buy aluminum tubing from wholesalers who cut to length and could provide the exact gross weight required. Because the quality and cleanliness of the tubing were critical to fin performance, HTS could use only some specialized grades of aluminum. The previous purchasing manager believed that splitting the business between three suppliers ensured supply and kept them on their toes. None of the three suppliers were aware of HTS' total aluminum tube requirements of 2,500,000 pounds of aluminum per year.

The Inventory Situation. Because HTS required different lengths, wall thicknesses, and diameter tubes for every job, it was very difficult to predict what combinations would have to be available for inventory. Also, given the size of the European shipments and their inevitable delays, the amount of aluminum tubing in storage amounted to $3.0 million. Aluminum tubing was stored on three large racks in the plant, in open spaces in the plant, and even in the employees' parking lot. HTS had normal inventory carrying costs of 25 percent of the purchase price.

The Aluminum Tube Decision. Stan Durnford was given a mandate to eliminate inventories entirely, if possible, decrease the purchase price, and still meet the customer delivery commitments needed in an increasingly competitive marketplace.

Stan wondered what course of action to take in the face of these competing priorities. As he was new in his position, Stan also had to learn how engineering, purchasing, operations, and sales interacted at HTS, and what plans and strategies he could put in place to make himself effective within the organization.

CASE 18-3
CUSTOM WINDOWS INC.

It was early April, and Caroline Joseph, supply manager at Custom Windows in Canton, Ohio, needed to decide which glass supplier to choose for the coming year. She was not sure whether her past approach to buying glass would still be appropriate in the future.

Custom Windows. Custom Windows competed in the regional window market in the Midwest home remodelling industry. The plant initially manufactured low-cost products such as storm doors, storm windows, school bus windows, and low-end replacement aluminum windows. Over the years, storm door and replacement aluminum window production was eliminated, and in 1987 vinyl window production was initiated. The 43,000-square feet facility manufactured vinyl windows (150–400/day), storm windows (50/day) and school bus aluminum windows (25/day). A total of about 80,000 windows was produced last year.

Sales were approximately $11 million. Sales of vinyl windows were seasonal with primary demand in the warmer months, from May to October. The company sold its high-priced, high-quality vinyl windows through a number of branches located across the Midwest. The delivery goal to customers was 10 days from the date the order was received at the plant.

In order to remain competitive and increase returns to shareholders, Custom Windows was committed to becoming a world-class manufacturer. Programs were developed and implemented to meet goals of improved quality, delivery performance, customer responsiveness, and better-engineered products.

Vinyl Window Production. All production at Custom Windows was based on custom orders. Windows were usually manufactured and shipped on the same day, reducing the need for work-in-process inventory. Demand for vinyl windows had increased annually since their introduction in 1987. Due to cost and performance advantages over wood and aluminum windows, management projected that demand would continue to grow and production would increase by an estimated 104 percent over the next five years. All of this growth was expected to be in low-energy glass windows.

Vinyl windows could be made with either clear glass or low-energy glass; both types of glass were available in thicknesses of either 3 mm or 4 mm. Low-energy glass was a special glass with an invisible metal coating that reduced penetration of infrared rays and decreased heat loss. Currently, low-energy glass windows accounted for about 40 to 45 percent of the plant's vinyl window production. Low-energy glass window production, as a percentage of total vinyl window production, was increasing monthly.

Purchasing of Glass. Last year, Custom Windows purchased a total of $645,660 of clear and low-energy glass from four suppliers (Exhibit 1). Glass was purchased by the block, with each block consisting of 40 sheets for 4 mm glass and 50 sheets for 3 mm glass. Due to the nature of the glass-cutting equipment that the company used, 3 mm glass had to be ordered in sheets of 72 in × 96 in, and 4 mm glass in sheets of 60 in × 96 in.

Glass sheet order quantities were determined based on historical usage reports and sales forecasts. To take advantage of quantity discounts and obtain the best possible price, Caroline usually ordered by the truckload. Truckload size could vary between 8 to 18 blocks depending on the capacity of the truck, the packaging, and weight restrictions.

The amount of glass that could be held in inventory was constrained by a storage capacity of 32 blocks. During the past year, to maintain production during peak periods (May through October), 2.5 blocks of glass per day were required. Only 6 blocks of glass per week were needed for the November to

EXHIBIT 1   Custom Windows —Last Year's Glass Consumption

Supplier	3mm Clear	4mm Clear	3 mm Low Energy	4 mm Low Energy	Total
Ross Industries					
210 blks	270,545	0	0	0	$270,545
Clear View Distributors					
47 blks	38,906				
4 blks		2,809			
55 blks			155,428		
6 blks				14,448	$211,591
Travers Glass Ltd.					
52 blks	42,996				
21 blks		14,747			
18 blks			50,808	0	$108,551
West Bend Glass*					
18 blks	0	0	50,295		
2 blks				4,678	$54,973
433 blks Total	$352,447	$17,556	$256,531	$19,126	$645,660
Clear glass total		334 blocks	$370,003		
Low-energy glass total		99 blocks	$275,657		
Total			$645,660		

*As West Bend Glass was a Canadian manufacturer and unable to price their clear glass competitively in the United States, they were not asked to submit a quote for clear glass for the current year.

April period. Each week an inventory count was undertaken so that purchasing orders could be adjusted as necessary. Last year, raw-material glass inventory turned about 14 times.

Custom Windows occasionally manufactured products using obscure glass instead of clear or low-energy glass. Rather than stocking the obscure glass in inventory, it was only ordered as required.

Selecting Suppliers. Caroline wanted one or more suppliers to be able to meet forecasted needs. The company had set a goal of increasing raw-material inventory turns from 14 times a year to 30 to 35 times a year within two years. In addition to requiring less working capital, increased inventory turns would free up floor space that was needed for other production activities. A Vendor Certification Program was also being implemented to assist in the setup of long-term relationships with suppliers in a partnership mode to encourage delivery of on-time, zero-defect materials to the plant.

Steven Munro, the materials management manager, had asked Caroline Joseph to research the potential suppliers and recommend the arrangements the company should make for purchasing glass. Caroline had asked several suppliers to submit quotes, from which she had narrowed the alternatives to three of last year's suppliers and one former supplier, Jackson Glass Co. She summarized these quotes in her bid summary as shown in Exhibit 2.

Supplier Alternatives

Ross Industries. Ross Industries was a glass manufacturer that had provided Custom Windows with excellent service and good-quality glass for 20 years. Their low-energy glass did not meet Custom Windows testing standards and, therefore, mixed truckloads of clear and low-energy glass were not possible. To get the quoted 3 mm clear glass truckload price of $0.3278 /sq ft /blk delivered, a minimum of 12 blocks had to be ordered at one time. If quantities of less

EXHIBIT 2 Bid Summary and Past Year Prices Paid

	Clear			Low Energy	
	3mm (309 blocks 2400 ft^2/bl)		4 mm (25 blocks 1600 ft^2/bl)	3 mm (152 blocks 2400 ft^2/bl)	4 mm (13 blocks 1600 ft^2/bl)
Ross Ind.	0.3278 0.33 [0.3384][1]	12 min 1 min	0.4371 0.44		
Clear View	0.33 [0.3449]	8 min	0.44 [0.4389]	1.18 [1.1775]	1.51 [1.505]
Travers	0.3172 [0.3445]	12 min	0.4389 [0.4389]	1.17 [1.1761]	1.53
Jackson	0.33	6 min	0.44		
[West Bend]				[1.164]	[1.46]

[1]Brackets indicate last year's actual prices.

than 12 blocks were ordered, the delivered price was $0.33/sq ft/blk. The Ross plant was located 150 miles from Custom Windows and lead time was one week. They had access to an associated supplier in Illinois as an alternate source of glass if they were unable to meet Custom Windows' demands.

Clear View Distributors. Clear View Distributors was a small, local glass distributor that had supplied Custom Windows for three years. They had provided consistent, on-time delivery of low-energy glass. They had also built sealed units for Custom Windows, but there had been problems with some units. Both clear glass (made by Ross Industries) and low-energy glass (made by West Bend Glass) were available on a mixed 8-block truck. Delivery was available daily if requested and they were willing to stock inventory for Custom Windows.

Travers Glass Ltd. Travers Glass Ltd. was a glass distributor about twice the size of Clear View Distributors. They had provided Custom Windows with service for 15 years and had been an excellent backup service for Ross Industries. They offered clear glass (made by Jackson Glass Co.) at the lowest delivered price of $0.3172/sq ft/blk in a straight or mixed truckload of at least 12 blocks with low-energy glass (made by West Bend Glass). The quote for 4 mm clear glass was $0.4389/sq ft/blk. For low-

energy glass, their quote was $1.17/sq ft/blk for 3 mm and $1.53/sq ft/blk for 4 mm glass. Clear glass made by Ross Industries was also available at a higher price than the clear glass made by West Bend Glass. Their distribution center was located 135 miles from Custom Windows. Lead time was 2 to 3 days and they could deliver 3 to 4 times a week. They were willing to stock inventory for Custom Windows.

Jackson Glass Co. Jackson Glass Co. was a glass manufacturer which had been one of several suppliers to Custom Windows in the past. They were very interested in doing business with Custom Windows again. Their glass quality was good and they would supply 3 mm clear glass at a delivered price of $0.33/sq ft/blk for a minimum order of 6 blocks. Their quote for 4 mm clear glass was $0.44/sq ft/blk. Their low-energy glass would not be available for 2 to 3 months and then would require Custom Windows' approval. Their distribution center was located about 130 miles from Custom Windows and lead time was one week. They were aligned with a Canadian supplier that could provide an alternate source of glass if required.

Now that she had gathered the necessary information, Caroline needed to proceed with her analysis. With the start of the peak season approaching, she knew that she would have to make her recommendation soon.